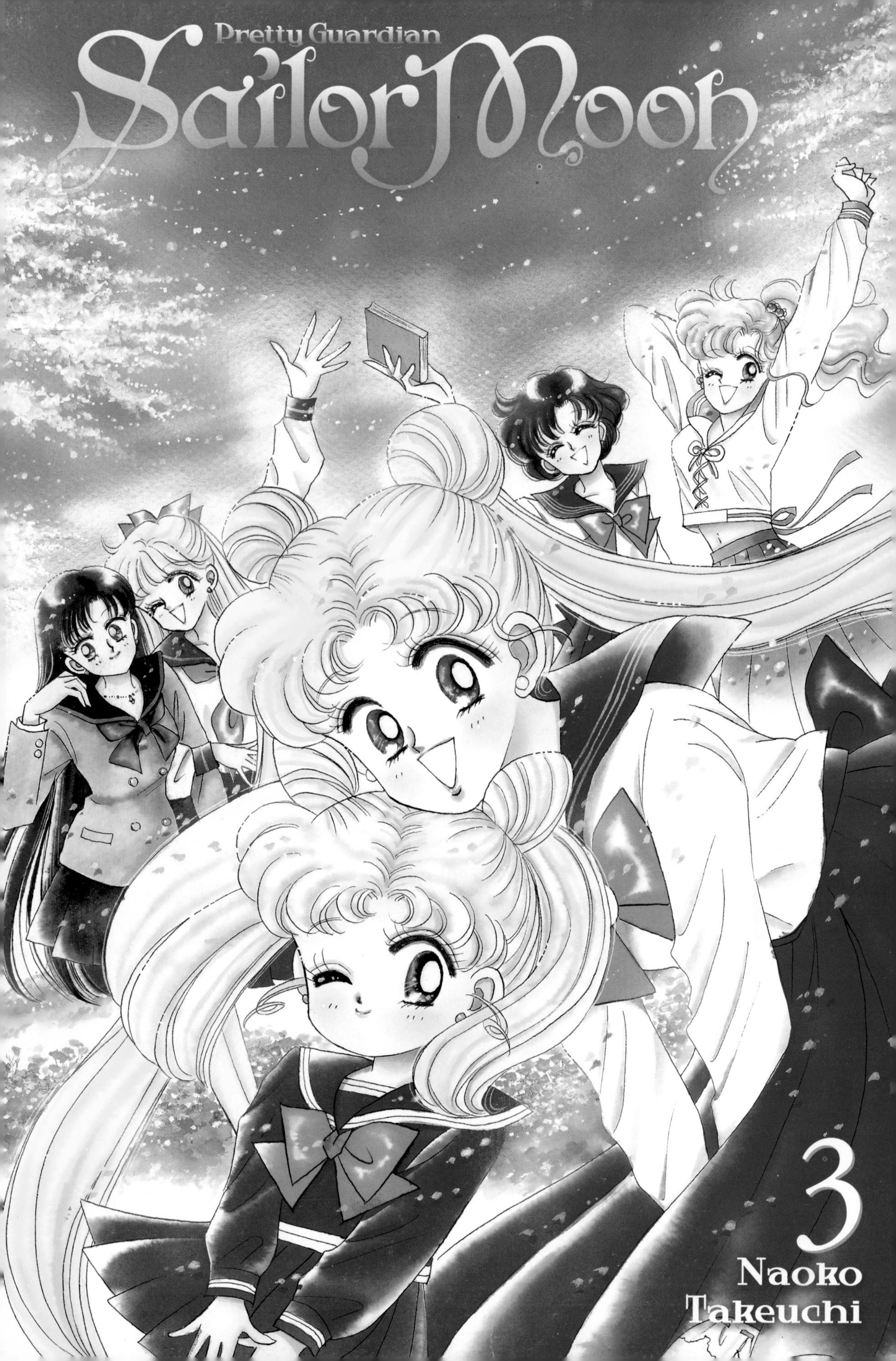

Pretty Guardian
Sailor Moon
3
Naoko
Takeuchi

CONTENTS

Pretty Guardian Sailor Moon

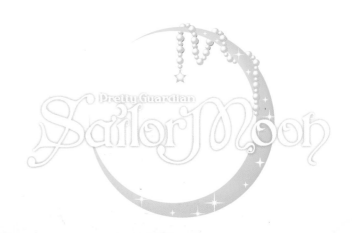

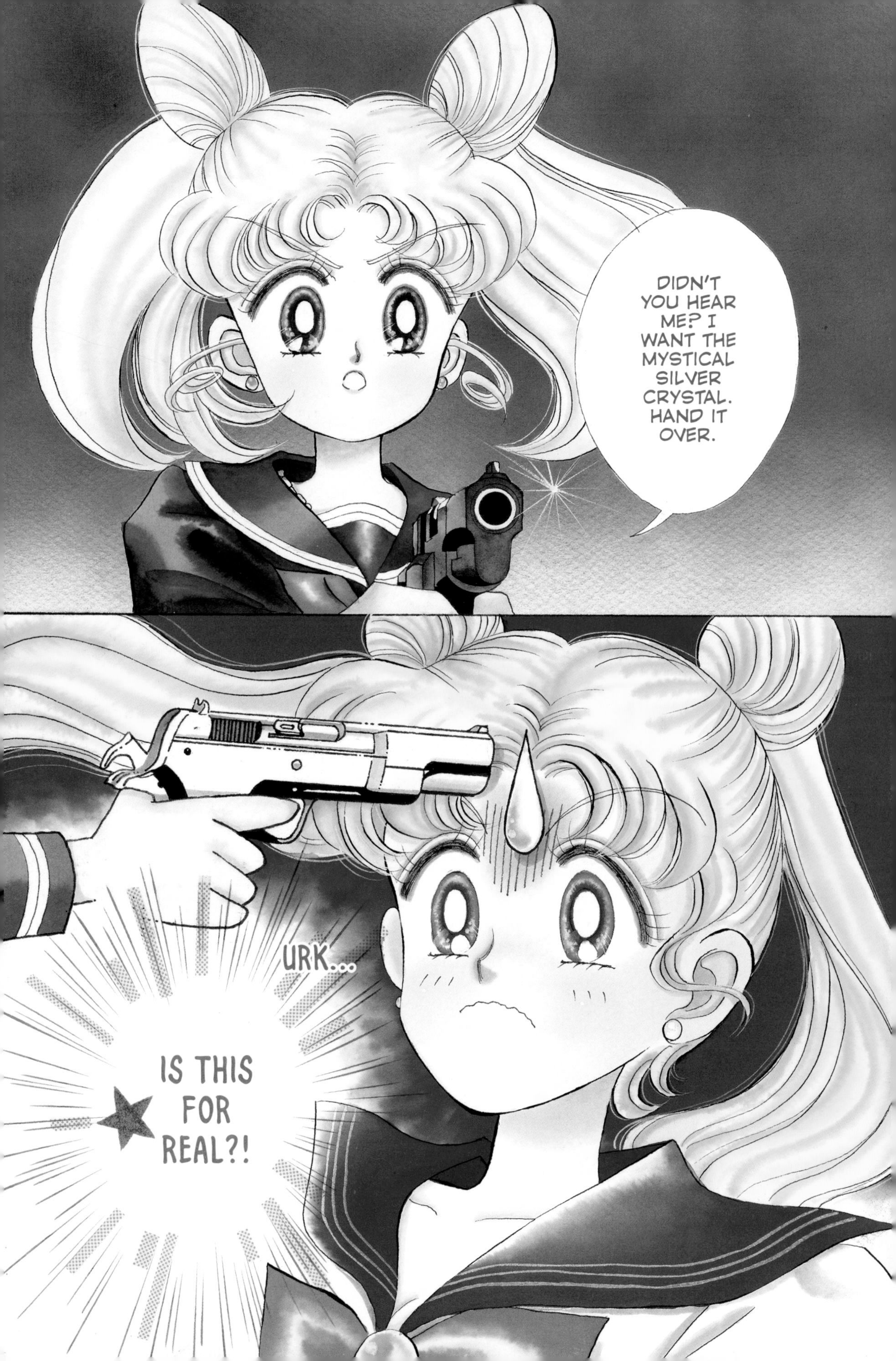
DIDN'T YOU HEAR ME? I WANT THE MYSTICAL SILVER CRYSTAL. HAND IT OVER.
URK...
IS THIS FOR REAL?!

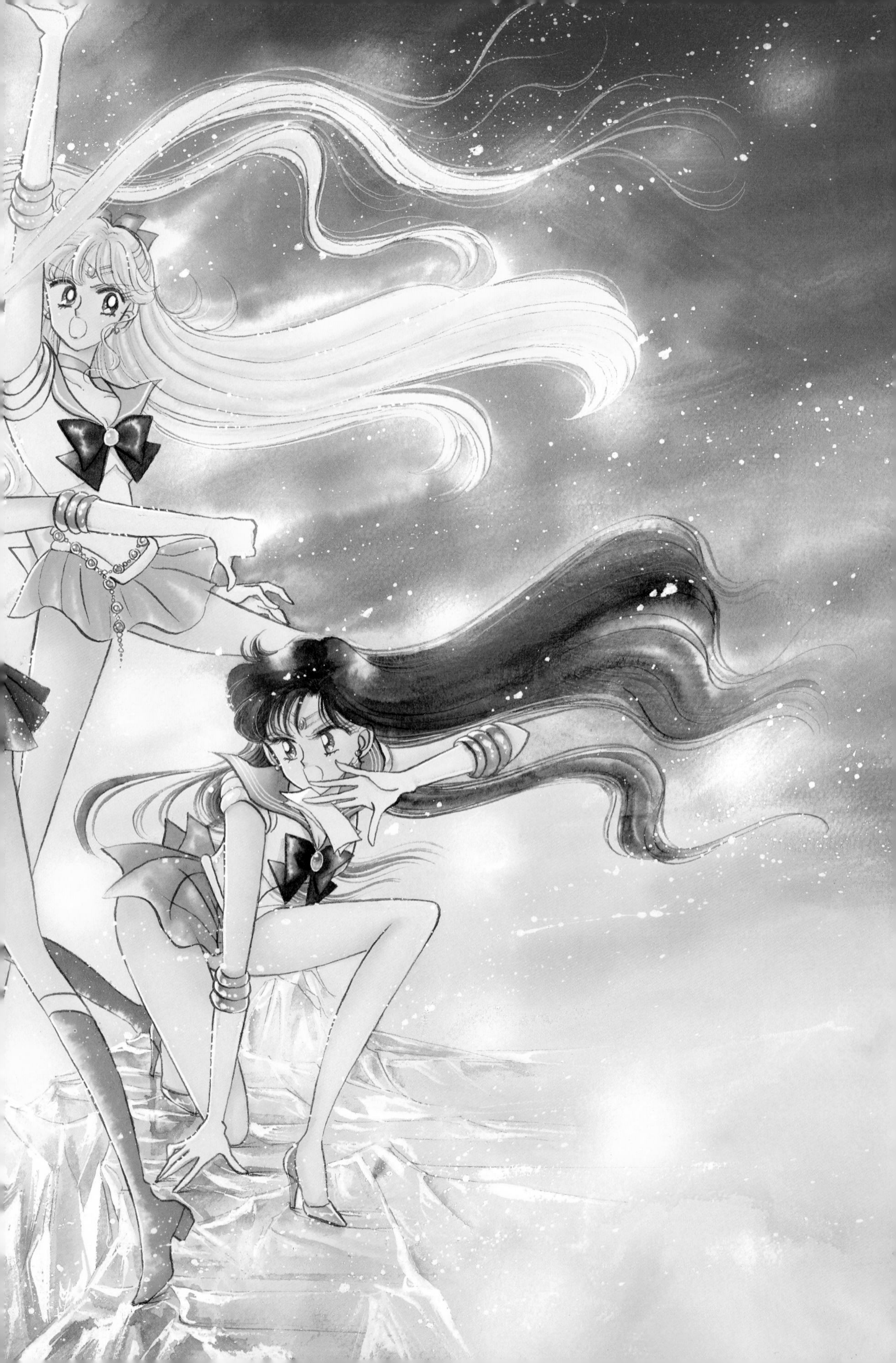

Act. 15 Invasion: Sailor Mars

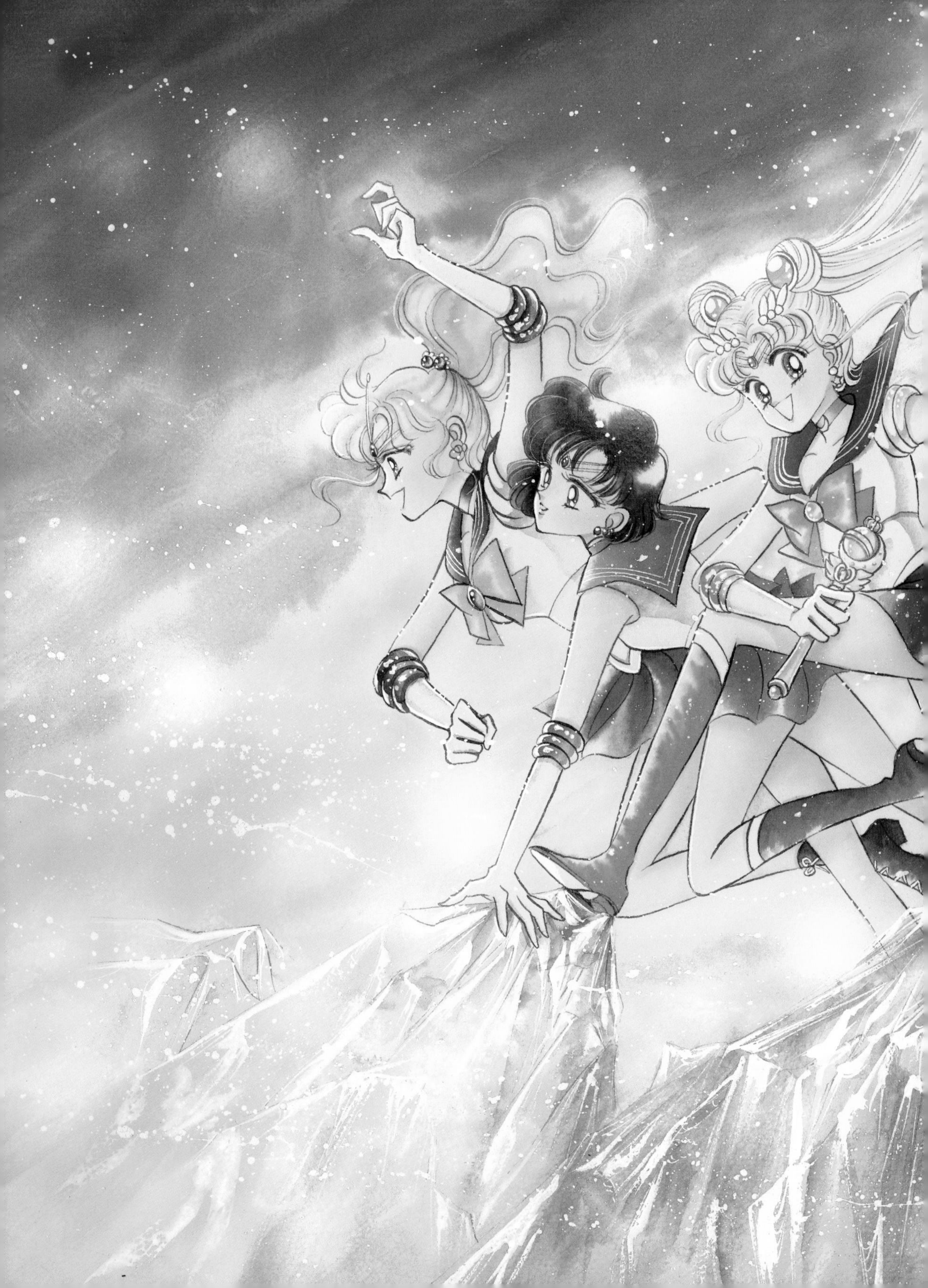

Pretty Guardian

Sailor Moon

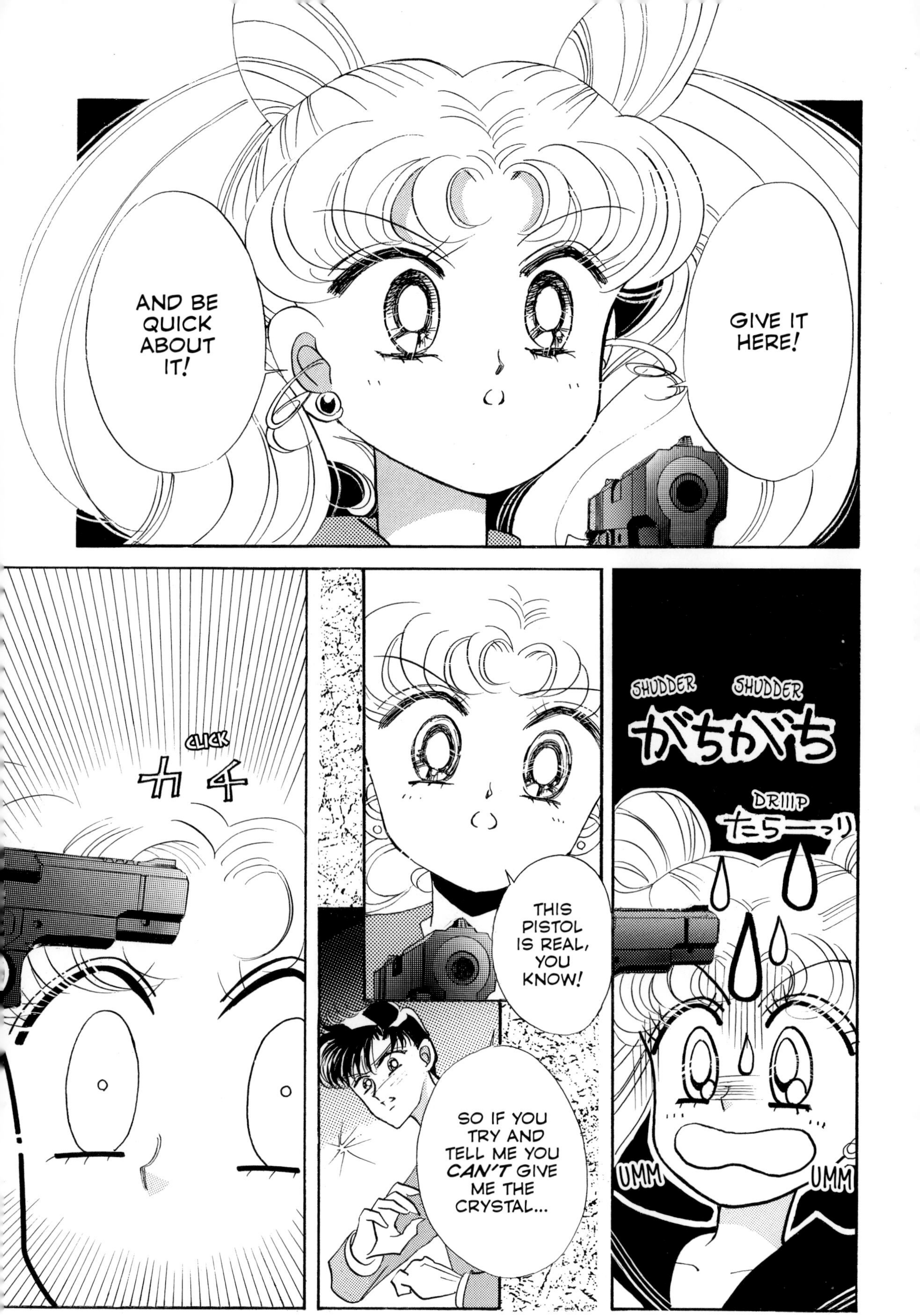
GIVE IT HERE!
AND BE QUICK ABOUT IT!
SHUDDER SHUDDER
がちがち
DRIIIP
たらーっり
UMM UMM
THIS PISTOL IS REAL, YOU KNOW!
SO IF YOU TRY AND TELL ME YOU *CAN'T* GIVE ME THE CRYSTAL...
CLICK
カチ

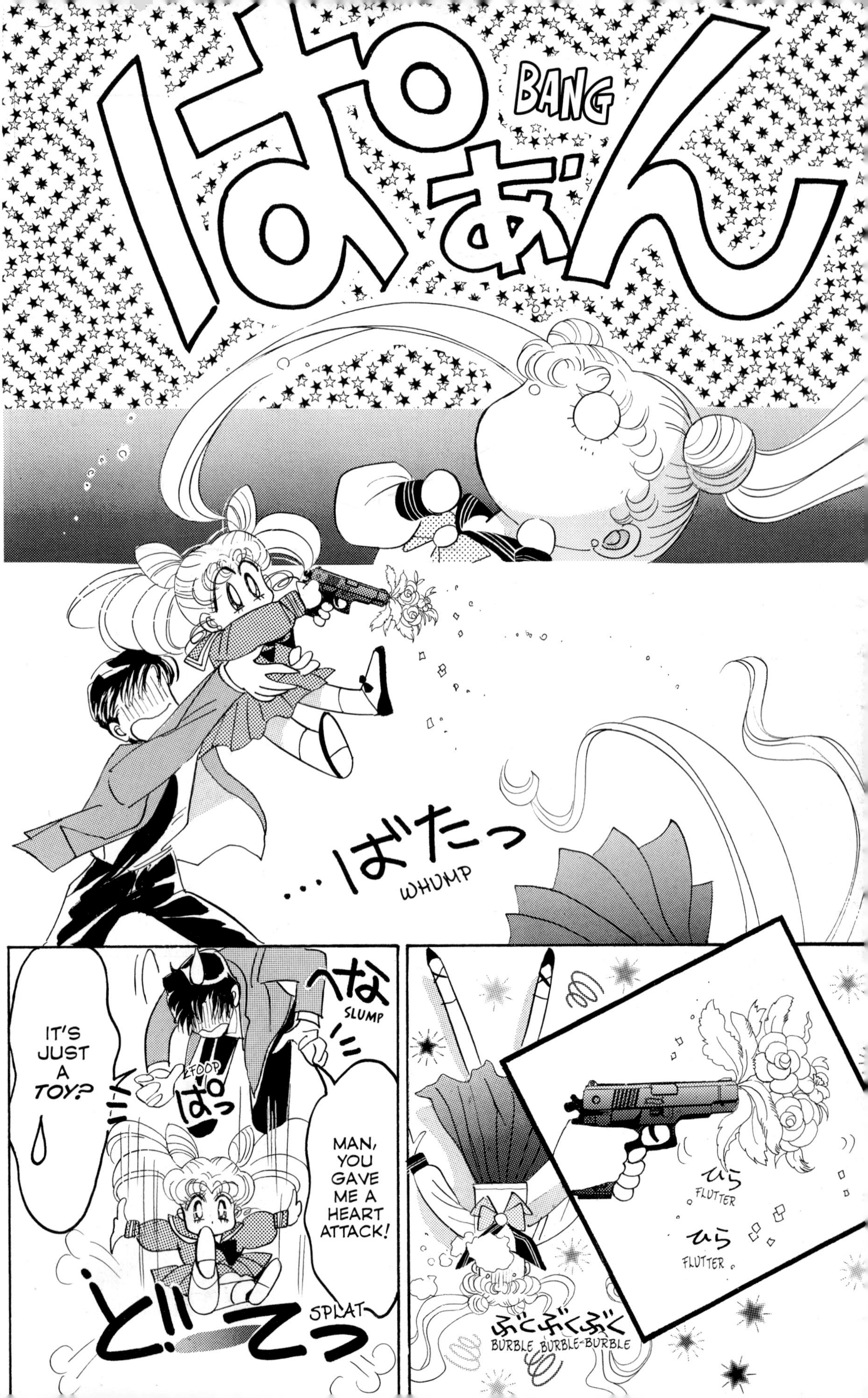
ぱぁん
BANG
…ばたっ
WHUMP
ひら
FLUTTER
ひら
FLUTTER
ぶくぶくぶく
BURBLE BURBLE BURBLE
へな
SLUMP
IT'S JUST A TOY?
ぱっ
FOOP
MAN, YOU GAVE ME A HEART ATTACK!
どてっ
SPLAT

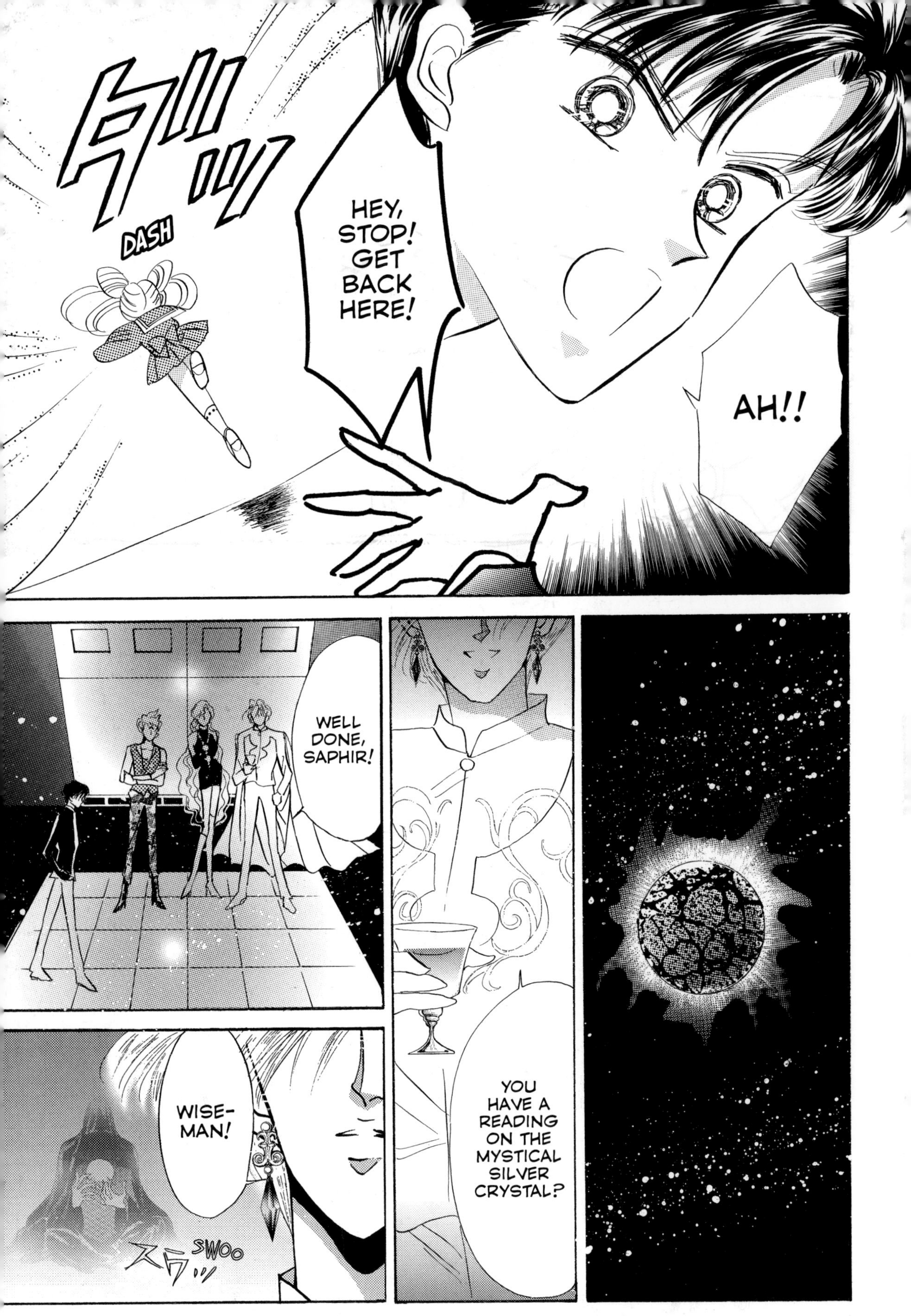
HEY, STOP! GET BACK HERE!
AH!!
DASH
YOU HAVE A READING ON THE MYSTICAL SILVER CRYSTAL?
WELL DONE, SAPHIR!
WISE-MAN!
SWOO

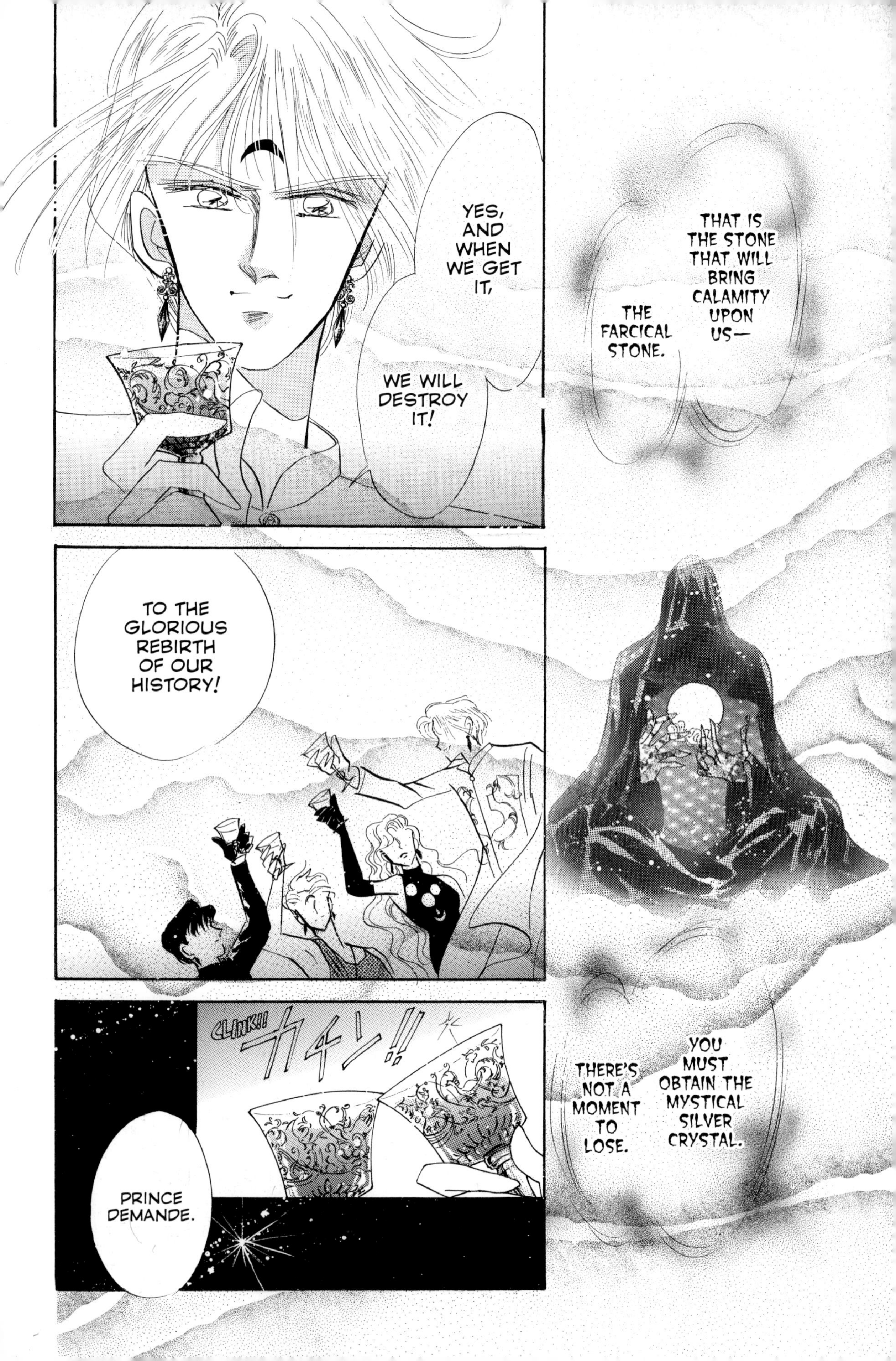
THAT IS THE STONE THAT WILL BRING CALAMITY UPON US—
THE FARCICAL STONE.
YOU MUST OBTAIN THE MYSTICAL SILVER CRYSTAL.
THERE'S NOT A MOMENT TO LOSE.
YES, AND WHEN WE GET IT,
WE WILL DESTROY IT!
TO THE GLORIOUS REBIRTH OF OUR HISTORY!
CLINK!!
カチン!!
PRINCE DEMANDE.

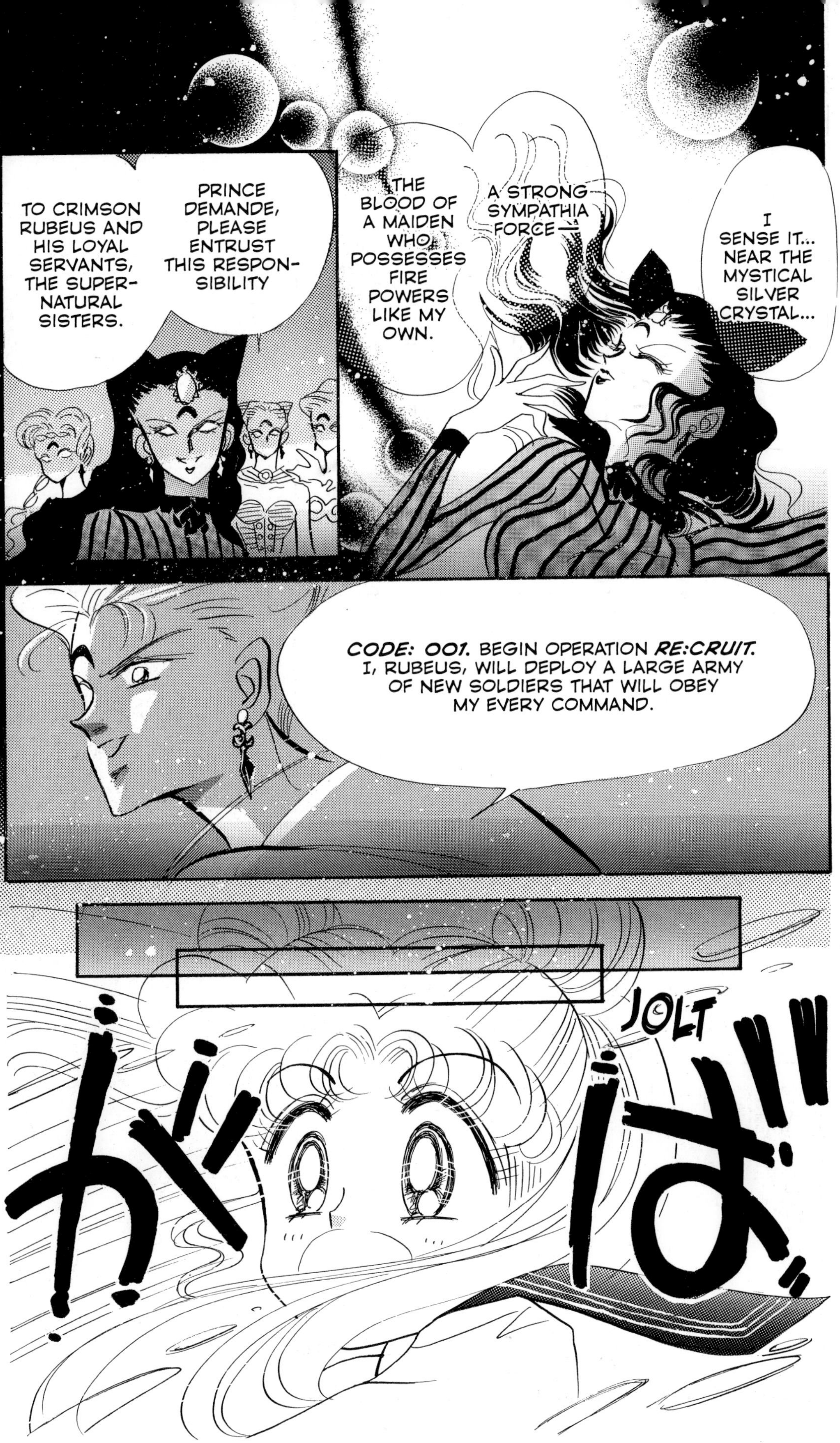

I SENSE IT... NEAR THE MYSTICAL SILVER CRYSTAL...
A STRONG SYMPATHIA FORCE—
THE BLOOD OF A MAIDEN WHO POSSESSES FIRE POWERS LIKE MY OWN.
PRINCE DEMANDE, PLEASE ENTRUST THIS RESPONSIBILITY
TO CRIMSON RUBEUS AND HIS LOYAL SERVANTS, THE SUPERNATURAL SISTERS.
CODE: 001. BEGIN OPERATION *RE:CRUIT.* I, RUBEUS, WILL DEPLOY A LARGE ARMY OF NEW SOLDIERS THAT WILL OBEY MY EVERY COMMAND.
JOLT
がば

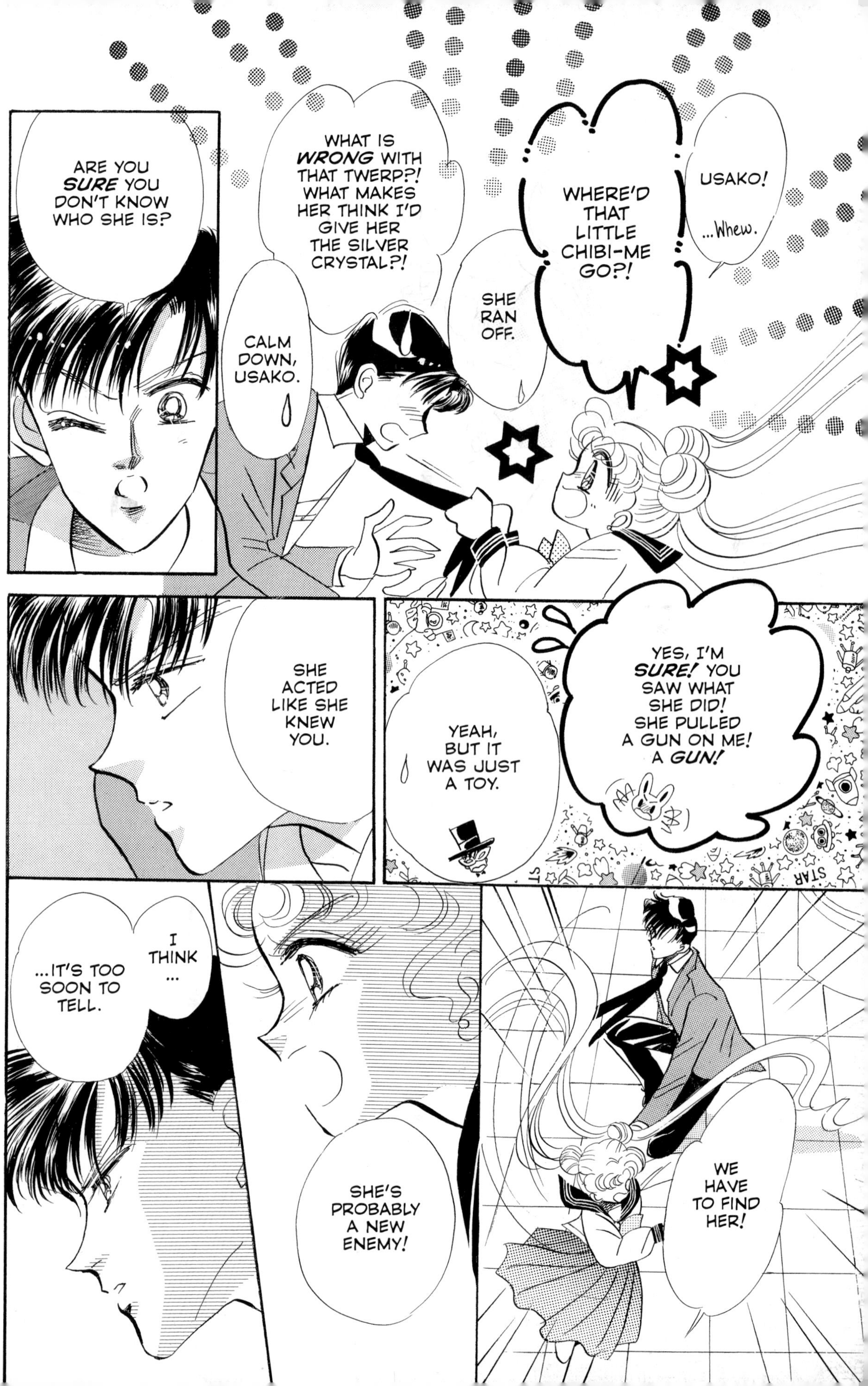
USAKO! ...Whew.
WHERE'D THAT LITTLE CHIBI-ME GO?!
SHE RAN OFF.
WHAT IS WRONG WITH THAT TWERP?! WHAT MAKES HER THINK I'D GIVE HER THE SILVER CRYSTAL?!
CALM DOWN, USAKO.
ARE YOU SURE YOU DON'T KNOW WHO SHE IS?
YES, I'M SURE! YOU SAW WHAT SHE DID! SHE PULLED A GUN ON ME! A GUN!
YEAH, BUT IT WAS JUST A TOY.
SHE ACTED LIKE SHE KNEW YOU.
WE HAVE TO FIND HER!
SHE'S PROBABLY A NEW ENEMY!
I THINK...
...IT'S TOO SOON TO TELL.

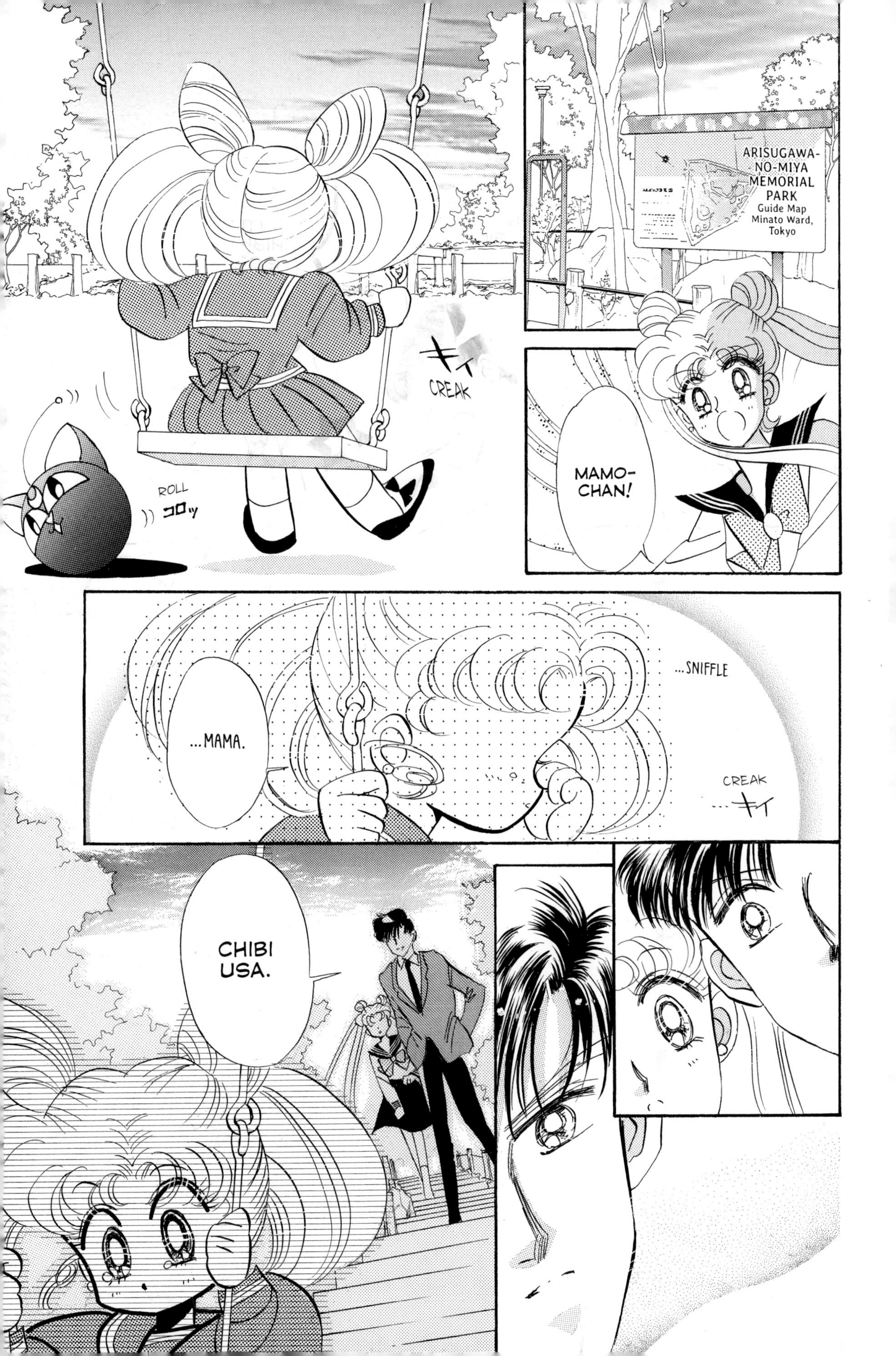
ARISUGAWA-NO-MIYA MEMORIAL PARK
Guide Map
Minato Ward, Tokyo
MAMO-CHAN!
キイ
CREAK
ROLL
コロッ
...SNIFFLE
...MAMA.
CREAK
...キイ
CHIBI USA.

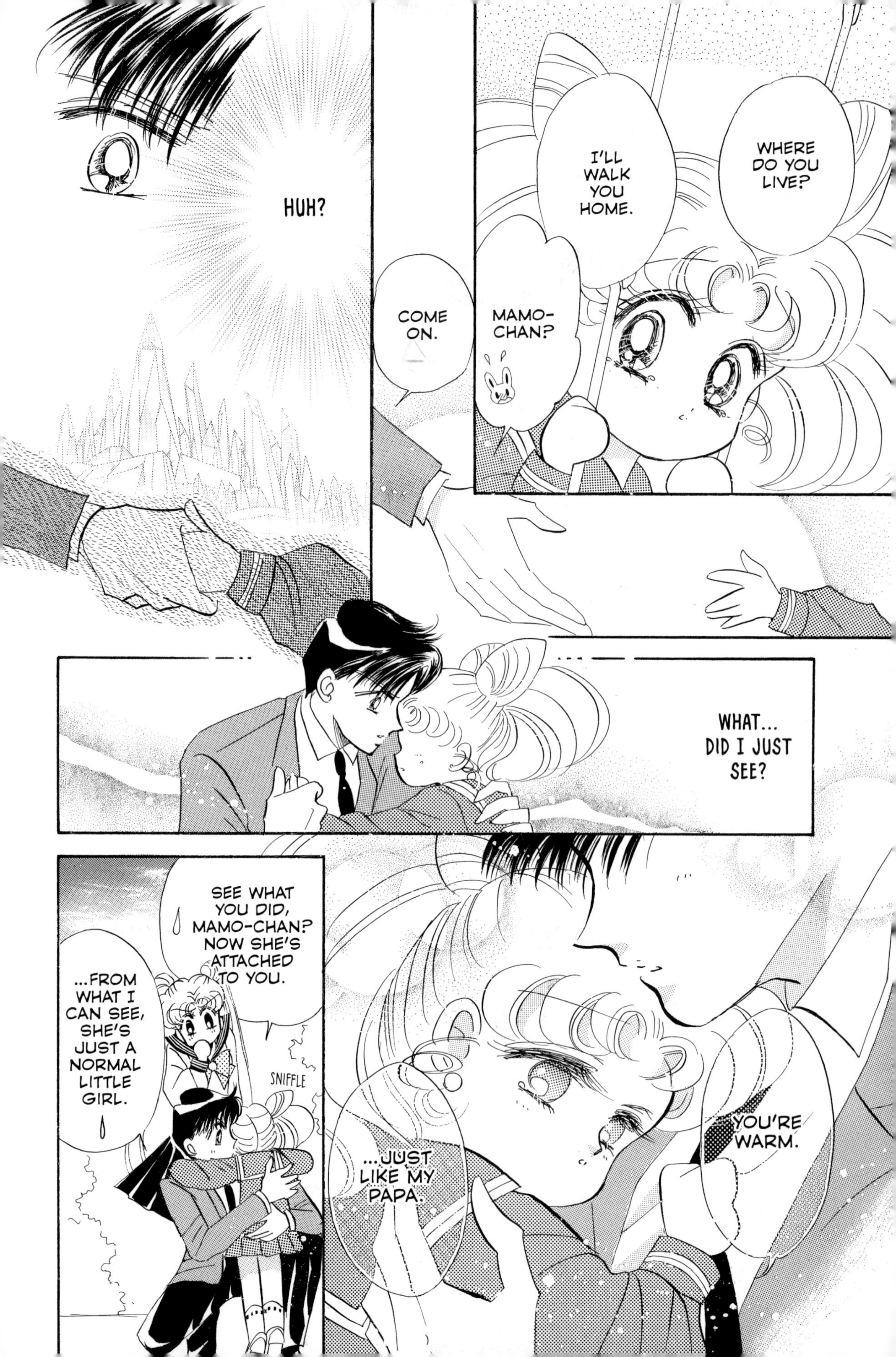
WHERE DO YOU LIVE?
I'LL WALK YOU HOME.
MAMO-CHAN?
COME ON.
HUH?
WHAT... DID I JUST SEE?
YOU'RE WARM.
...JUST LIKE MY PAPA.
SEE WHAT YOU DID, MAMO-CHAN? NOW SHE'S ATTACHED TO YOU.
SNIFFLE
...FROM WHAT I CAN SEE, SHE'S JUST A NORMAL LITTLE GIRL.

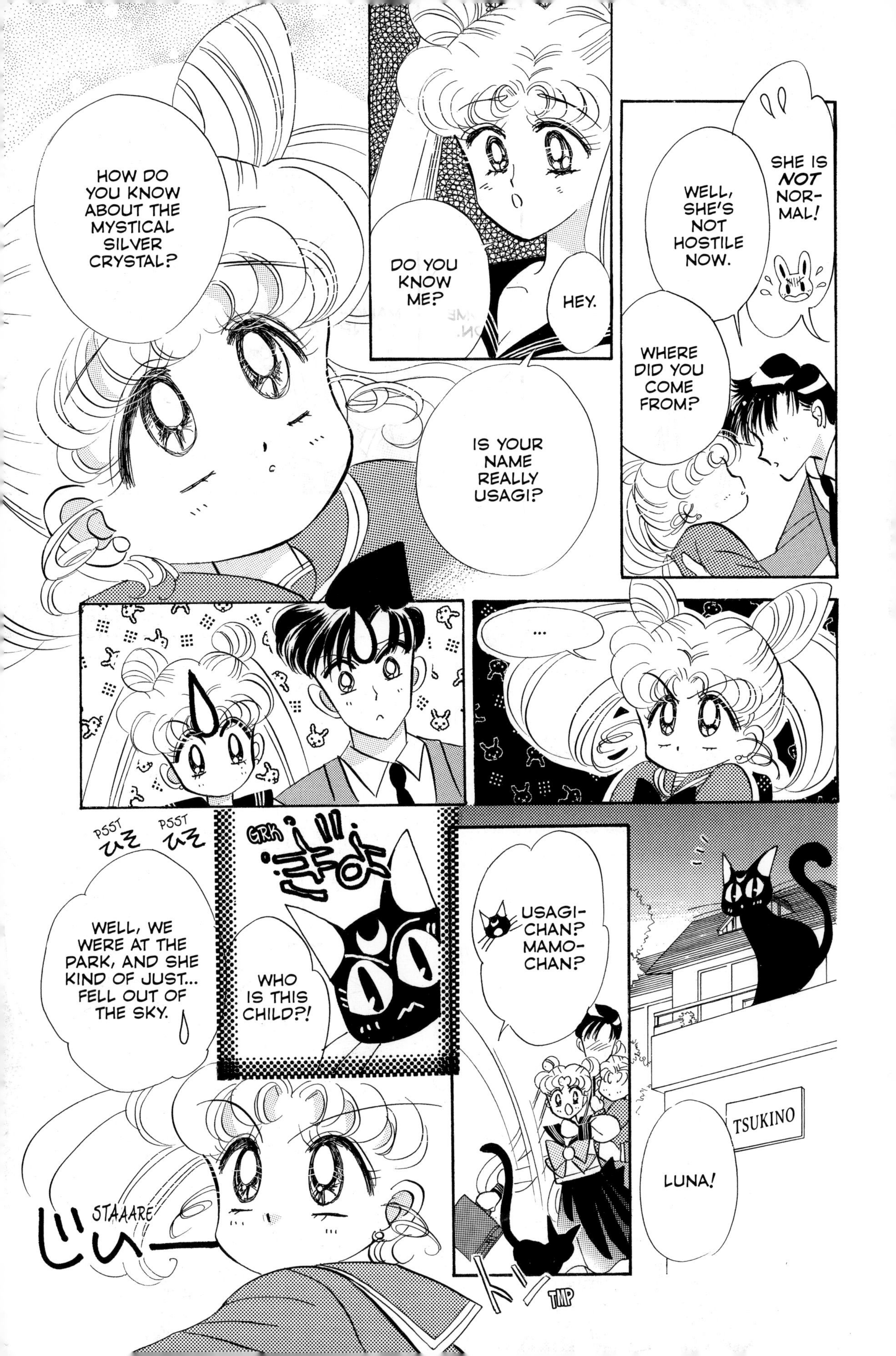
SHE IS *NOT* NORMAL!
WELL, SHE'S NOT HOSTILE NOW.
WHERE DID YOU COME FROM?
HEY.
DO YOU KNOW ME?
IS YOUR NAME REALLY USAGI?
HOW DO YOU KNOW ABOUT THE MYSTICAL SILVER CRYSTAL?
...
LUNA!
TSUKINO
USAGI-CHAN? MAMO-CHAN?
TMP
GRK
WHO IS THIS CHILD?!
PSST ひそ PSST ひそ
WELL, WE WERE AT THE PARK, AND SHE KIND OF JUST... FELL OUT OF THE SKY.
STAAARE じぃー

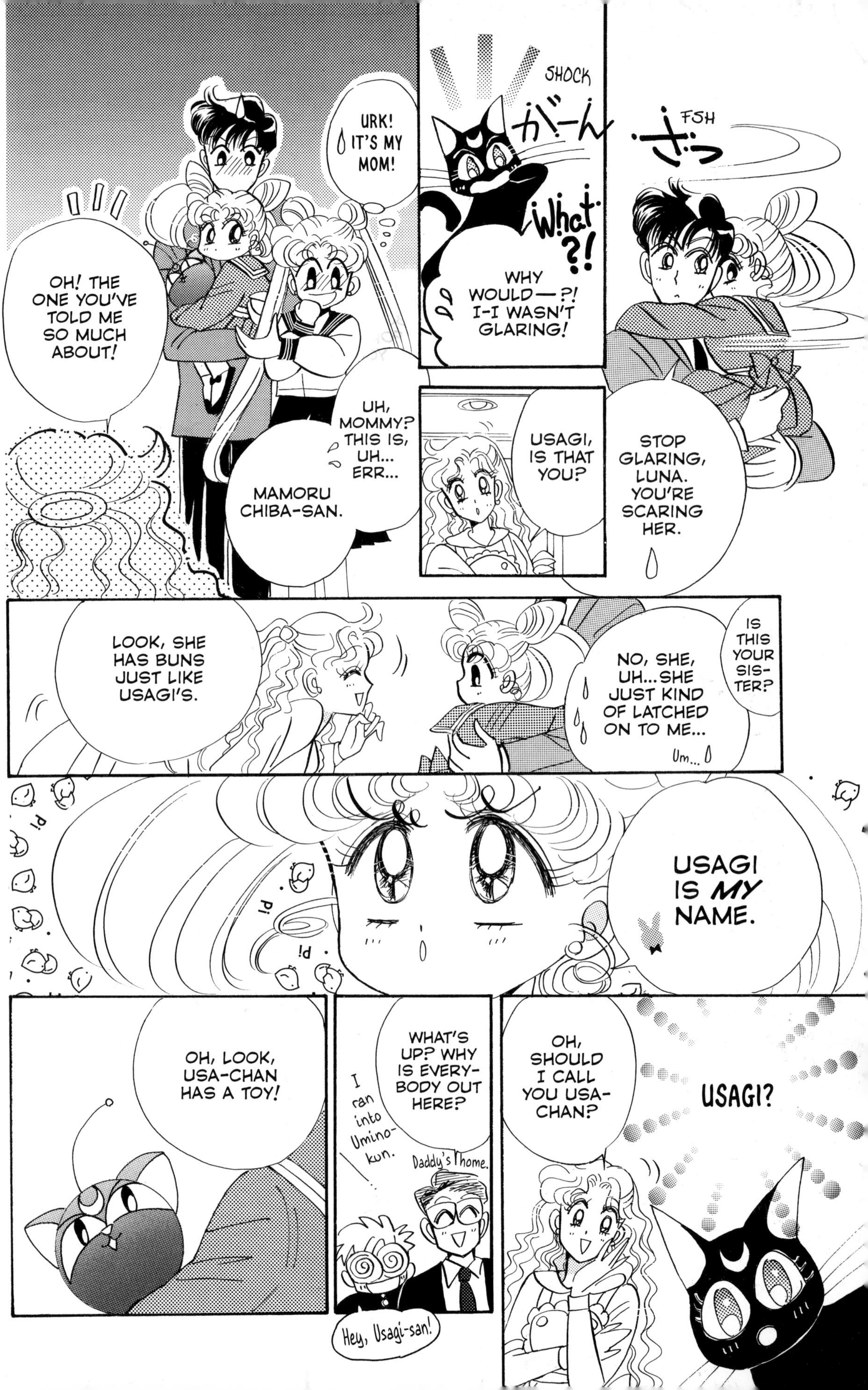
ざっ
FSH
STOP GLARING, LUNA. YOU'RE SCARING HER.
SHOCK
がーん
What?!
WHY WOULD—?! I-I WASN'T GLARING!
USAGI, IS THAT YOU?
URK! IT'S MY MOM!
UH, MOMMY? THIS IS, UH... ERR...
MAMORU CHIBA-SAN.
OH! THE ONE YOU'VE TOLD ME SO MUCH ABOUT!
IS THIS YOUR SISTER?
NO, SHE, UH... SHE JUST KIND OF LATCHED ON TO ME...
Um...
LOOK, SHE HAS BUNS JUST LIKE USAGI'S.
USAGI IS *MY* NAME.
Pi!
Pi!
Pi!
USAGI?
OH, SHOULD I CALL YOU USA-CHAN?
WHAT'S UP? WHY IS EVERYBODY OUT HERE?
Daddy's home.
I ran into Umino-kun.
Hey, Usagi-san!
OH, LOOK, USA-CHAN HAS A TOY!

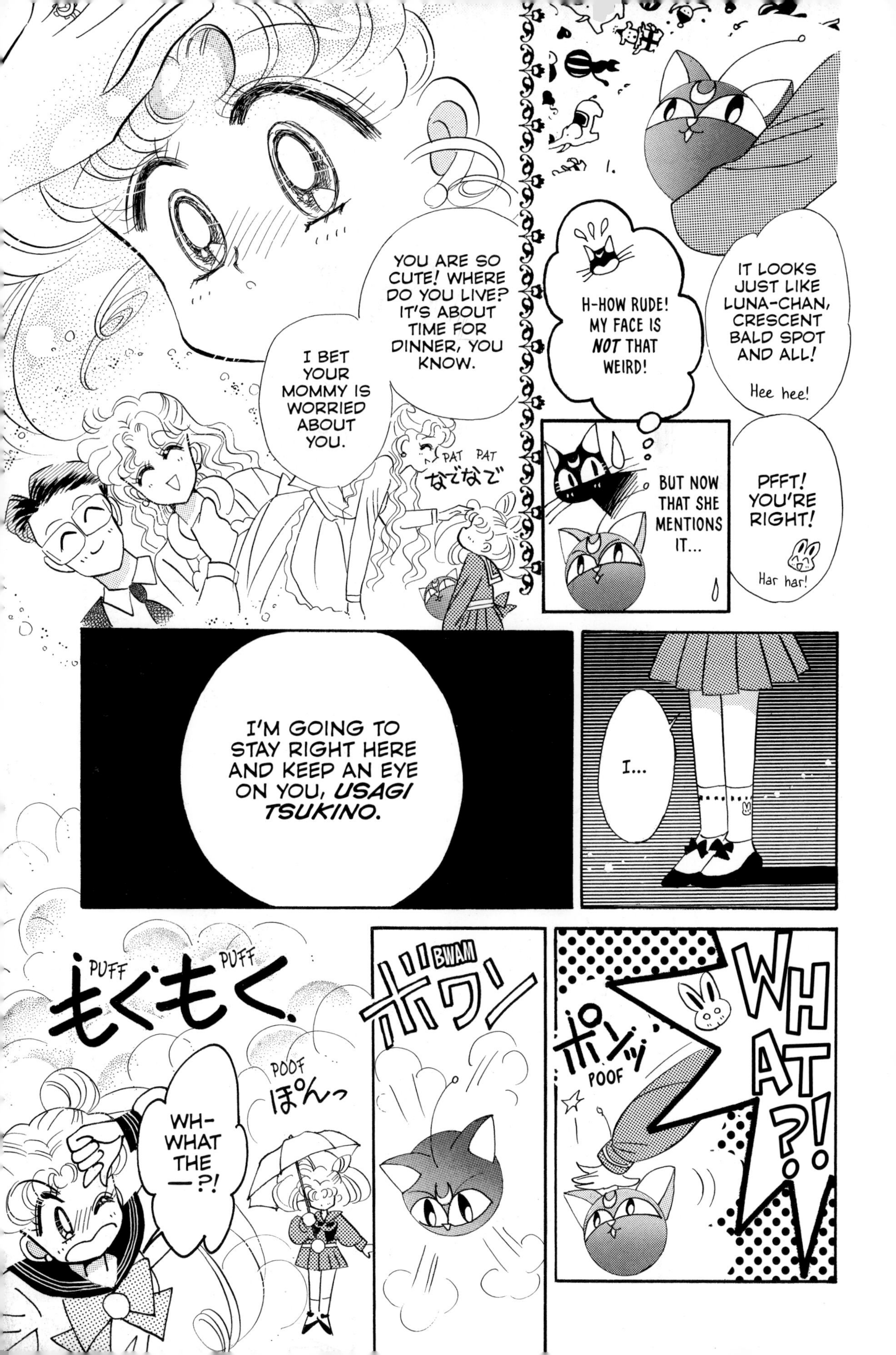
IT LOOKS JUST LIKE LUNA-CHAN, CRESCENT BALD SPOT AND ALL!
Hee hee!
H-HOW RUDE! MY FACE IS *NOT* THAT WEIRD!
PFFT! YOU'RE RIGHT!
Har har!
BUT NOW THAT SHE MENTIONS IT...
YOU ARE SO CUTE! WHERE DO YOU LIVE? IT'S ABOUT TIME FOR DINNER, YOU KNOW.
I BET YOUR MOMMY IS WORRIED ABOUT YOU.
PAT PAT
なでなで
I...
I'M GOING TO STAY RIGHT HERE AND KEEP AN EYE ON YOU, *USAGI TSUKINO*.
WHAT?!
ポンッ
POOF
ボワン
BWAM
もくもく
PUFF PUFF
POOF
ぽんっ
WH-WHAT THE—?!

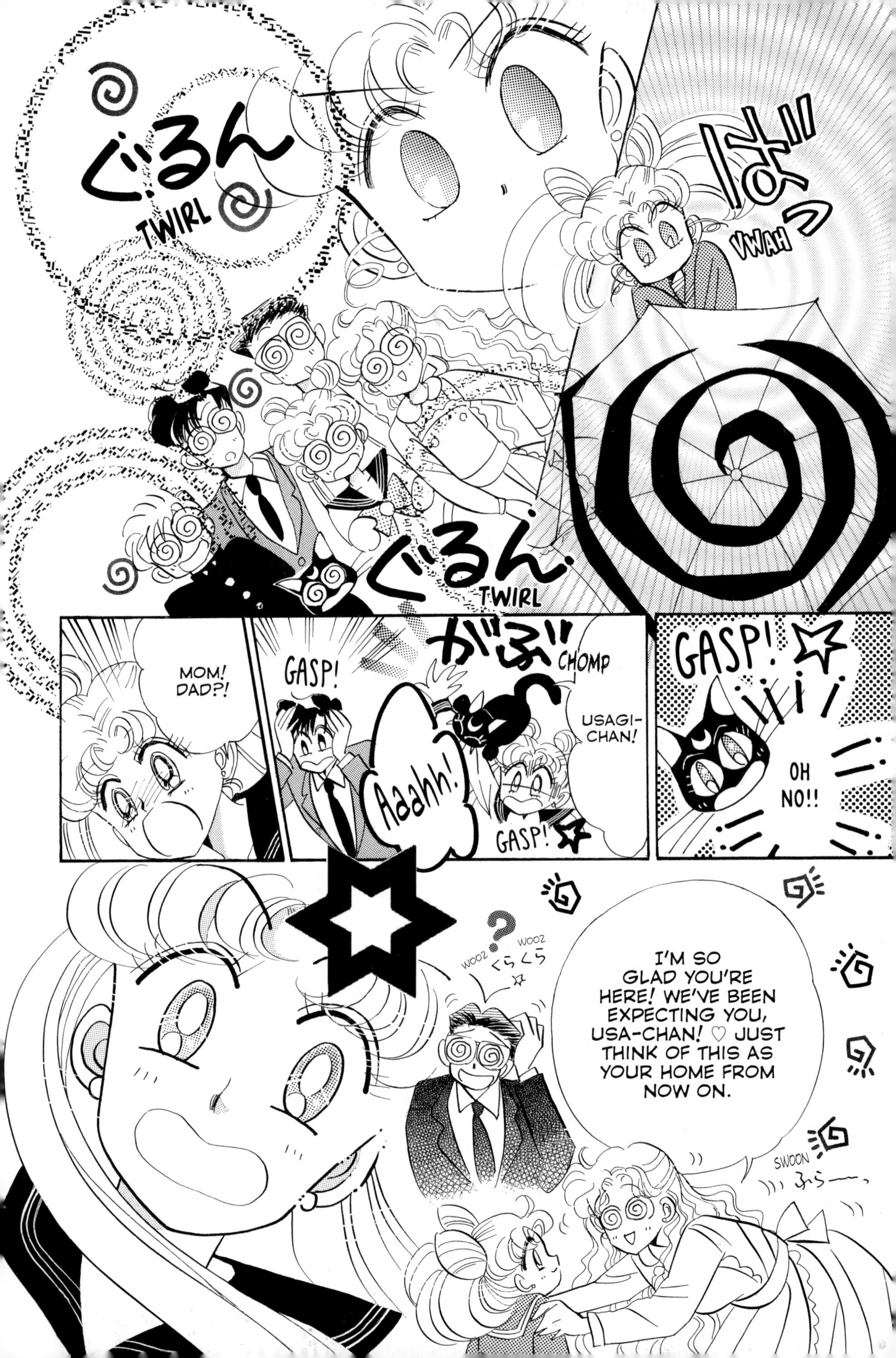
ばっ
VWAH
ぐるん
TWIRL
ぐるん
TWIRL
GASP!
OH NO!!
USAGI-CHAN!
がぶ!!
CHOMP
GASP!
Aaahh!
GASP!
MOM! DAD?!
I'M SO GLAD YOU'RE HERE! WE'VE BEEN EXPECTING YOU, USA-CHAN! ♡ JUST THINK OF THIS AS YOUR HOME FROM NOW ON.
SWOON
ふらー
WOOZ
くらくら
WOOZ

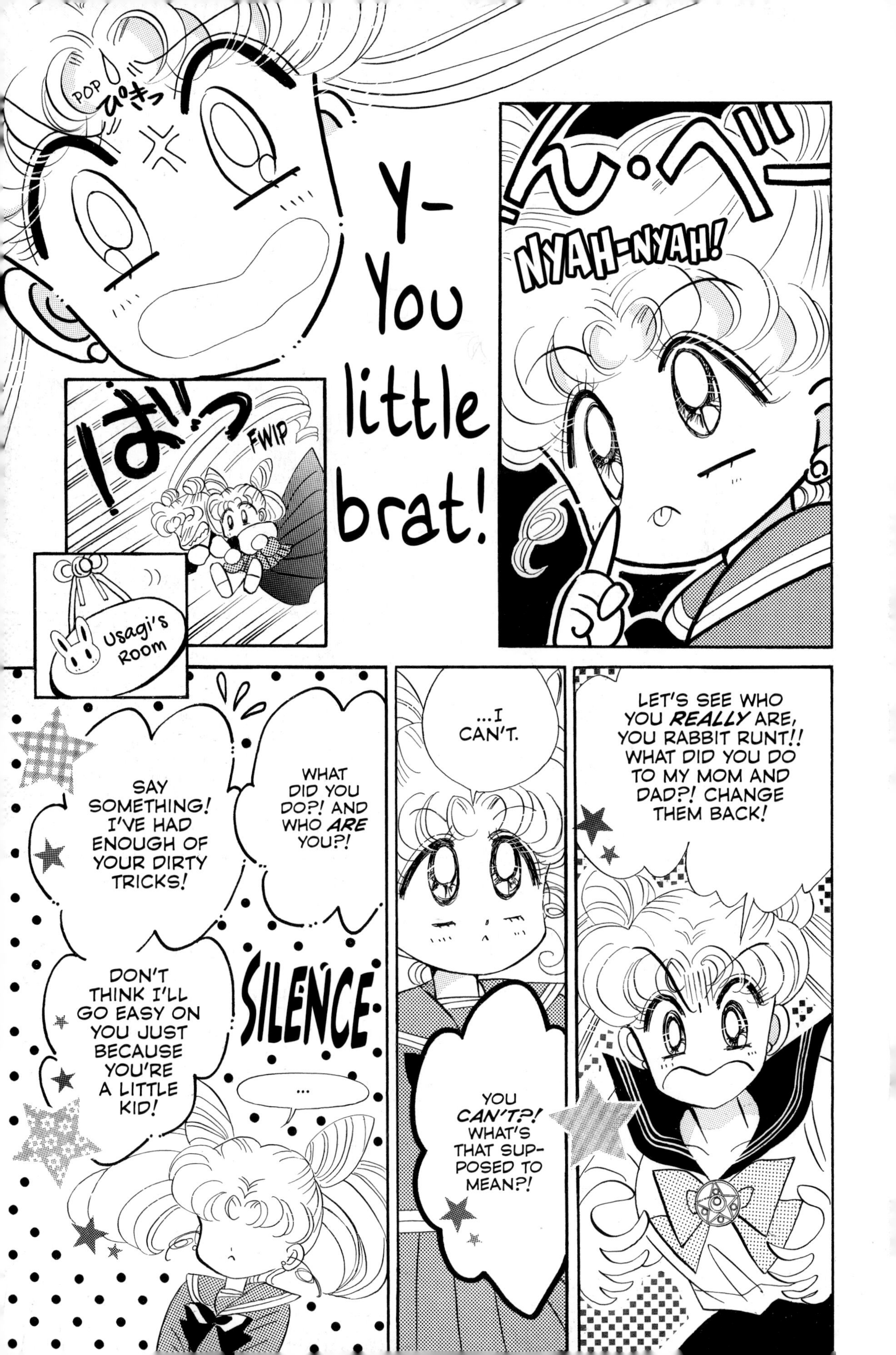
ん・べー
NYAH-NYAH!
POP
ぴきっ
Y-You little brat!
ばっ
FWIP
Usagi's Room
LET'S SEE WHO YOU *REALLY* ARE, YOU RABBIT RUNT!! WHAT DID YOU DO TO MY MOM AND DAD?! CHANGE THEM BACK!
...I CAN'T.
YOU *CAN'T?!* WHAT'S THAT SUP-POSED TO MEAN?!
WHAT DID YOU DO?! AND WHO *ARE* YOU?!
SAY SOMETHING! I'VE HAD ENOUGH OF YOUR DIRTY TRICKS!
DON'T THINK I'LL GO EASY ON YOU JUST BECAUSE YOU'RE A LITTLE KID!
SILENCE
...

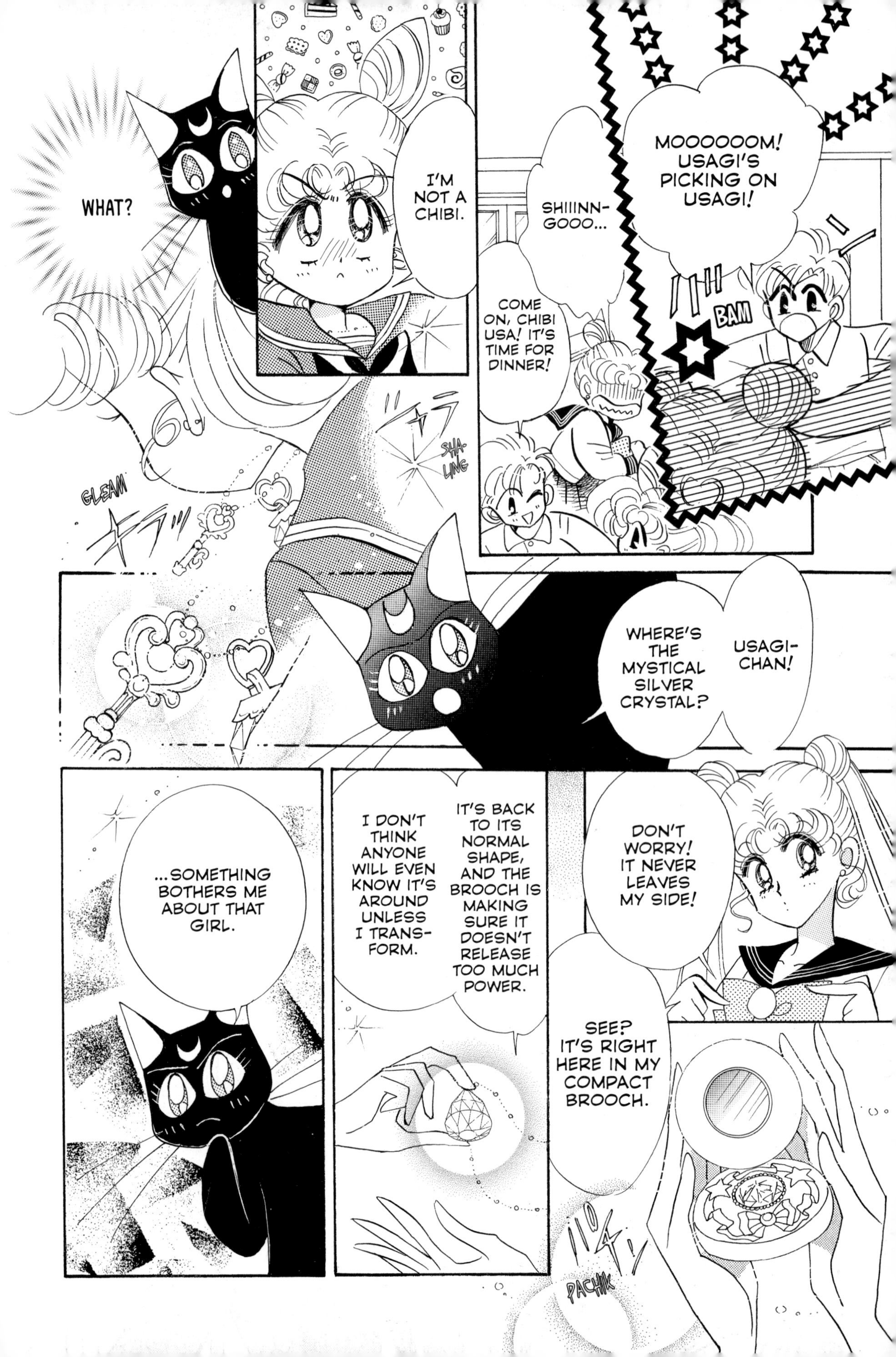
MOOOOOOM! USAGI'S PICKING ON USAGI!
BAM
SHIIINN-GOOO...
COME ON, CHIBI USA! IT'S TIME FOR DINNER!
I'M NOT A CHIBI.
WHAT?
SHA-LING
GLEAM
USAGI-CHAN!
WHERE'S THE MYSTICAL SILVER CRYSTAL?
DON'T WORRY! IT NEVER LEAVES MY SIDE!
SEE? IT'S RIGHT HERE IN MY COMPACT BROOCH.
PACHIK
IT'S BACK TO ITS NORMAL SHAPE, AND THE BROOCH IS MAKING SURE IT DOESN'T RELEASE TOO MUCH POWER.
I DON'T THINK ANYONE WILL EVEN KNOW IT'S AROUND UNLESS I TRANS-FORM.
...SOMETHING BOTHERS ME ABOUT THAT GIRL.

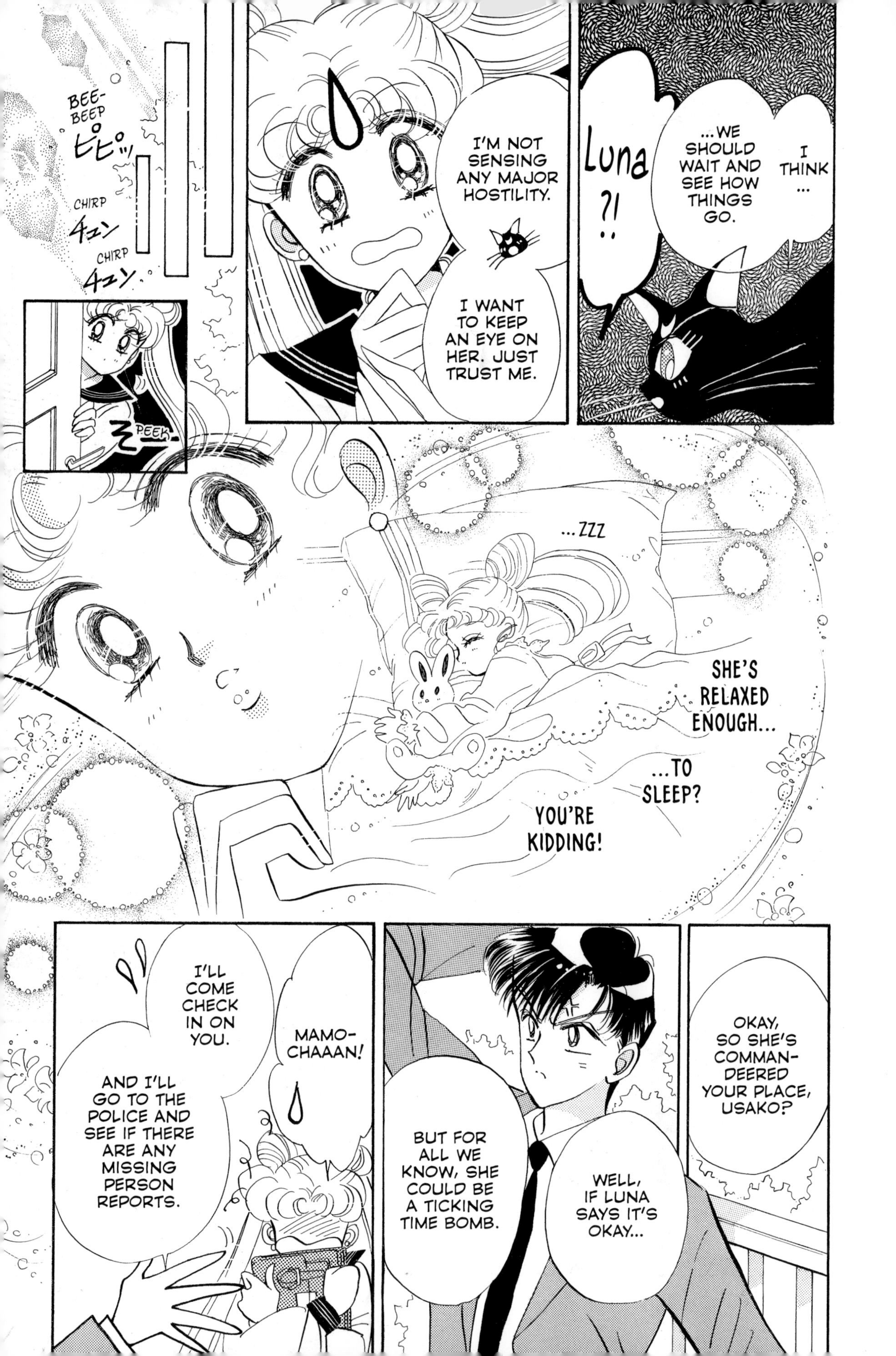

I THINK...
...WE SHOULD WAIT AND SEE HOW THINGS GO.
Luna ?!
I'M NOT SENSING ANY MAJOR HOSTILITY.
I WANT TO KEEP AN EYE ON HER. JUST TRUST ME.
BEE-BEEP ピピッ
CHIRP チュン
CHIRP チュン
PEEK
...ZZZ
SHE'S RELAXED ENOUGH...
...TO SLEEP?
YOU'RE KIDDING!
OKAY, SO SHE'S COMMANDEERED YOUR PLACE, USAKO?
WELL, IF LUNA SAYS IT'S OKAY...
BUT FOR ALL WE KNOW, SHE COULD BE A TICKING TIME BOMB.
MAMO-CHAAAN!
I'LL COME CHECK IN ON YOU.
AND I'LL GO TO THE POLICE AND SEE IF THERE ARE ANY MISSING PERSON REPORTS.

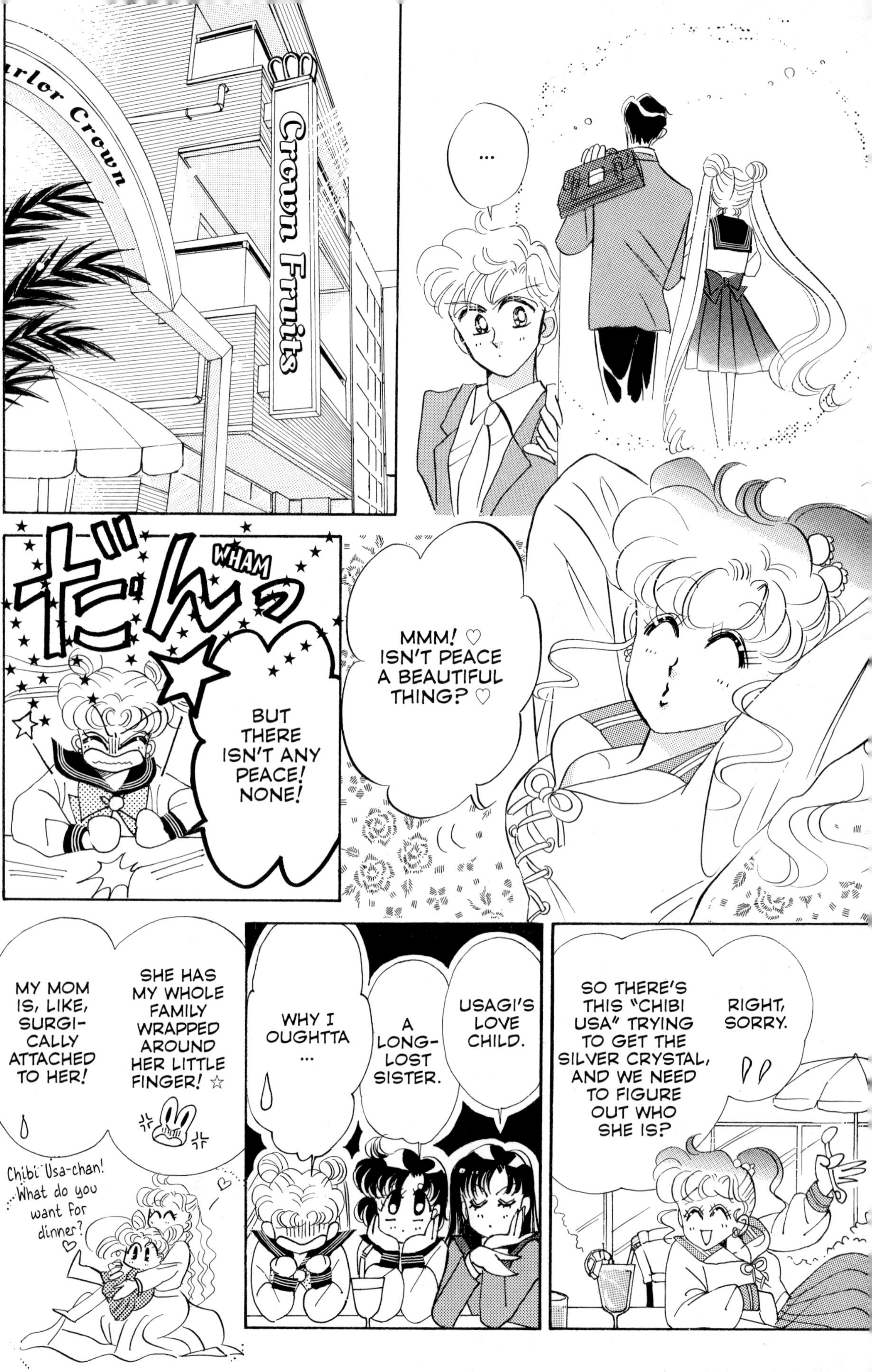
...
arlor Crown
Crown Fruits
MMM! ♡ ISN'T PEACE A BEAUTIFUL THING? ♡
だんっ
WHAM
BUT THERE ISN'T ANY PEACE! NONE!
RIGHT, SORRY.
SO THERE'S THIS "CHIBI USA" TRYING TO GET THE SILVER CRYSTAL, AND WE NEED TO FIGURE OUT WHO SHE IS?
USAGI'S LOVE CHILD.
A LONG-LOST SISTER.
WHY I OUGHTTA ...
SHE HAS MY WHOLE FAMILY WRAPPED AROUND HER LITTLE FINGER! ☆
MY MOM IS, LIKE, SURGI-CALLY ATTACHED TO HER!
Chibi Usa-chan! What do you want for dinner? ♡

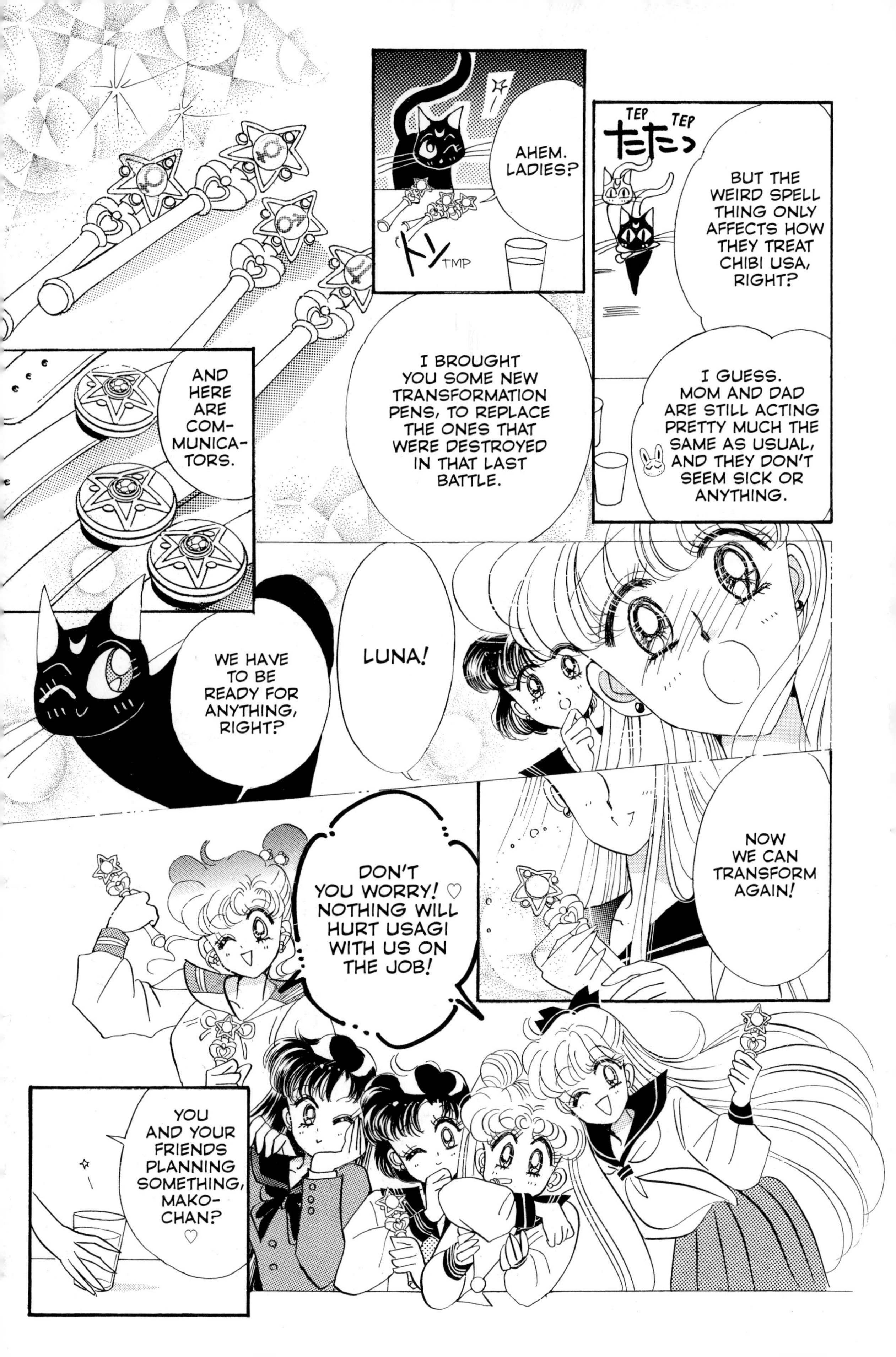
TEP TEP
たたっ
BUT THE WEIRD SPELL THING ONLY AFFECTS HOW THEY TREAT CHIBI USA, RIGHT?
I GUESS. MOM AND DAD ARE STILL ACTING PRETTY MUCH THE SAME AS USUAL, AND THEY DON'T SEEM SICK OR ANYTHING.
AHEM. LADIES?
トン
TMP
I BROUGHT YOU SOME NEW TRANSFORMATION PENS, TO REPLACE THE ONES THAT WERE DESTROYED IN THAT LAST BATTLE.
AND HERE ARE COM-MUNICA-TORS.
LUNA!
WE HAVE TO BE READY FOR ANYTHING, RIGHT?
NOW WE CAN TRANSFORM AGAIN!
DON'T YOU WORRY! ♡ NOTHING WILL HURT USAGI WITH US ON THE JOB!
YOU AND YOUR FRIENDS PLANNING SOMETHING, MAKO-CHAN? ♡

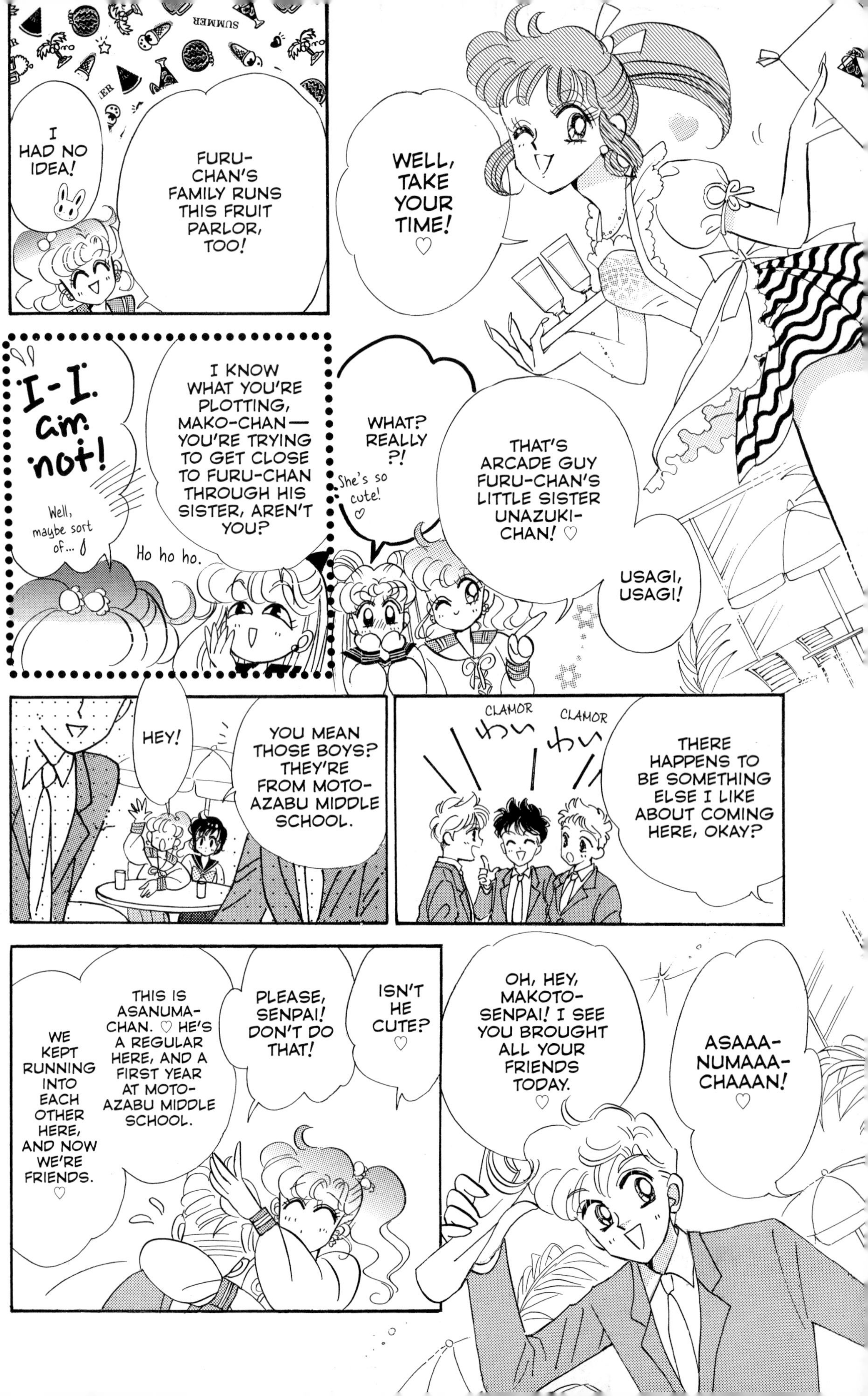

WELL, TAKE YOUR TIME! ♡
USAGI, USAGI!
THAT'S ARCADE GUY FURU-CHAN'S LITTLE SISTER UNAZUKI-CHAN! ♡
WHAT? REALLY?!
She's so cute! ♡
FURU-CHAN'S FAMILY RUNS THIS FRUIT PARLOR, TOO!
I HAD NO IDEA!
I KNOW WHAT YOU'RE PLOTTING, MAKO-CHAN—YOU'RE TRYING TO GET CLOSE TO FURU-CHAN THROUGH HIS SISTER, AREN'T YOU?
I-I am not!
Well, maybe sort of...
Ho ho ho.
THERE HAPPENS TO BE SOMETHING ELSE I LIKE ABOUT COMING HERE, OKAY?
CLAMOR わい
CLAMOR わい
YOU MEAN THOSE BOYS? THEY'RE FROM MOTO-AZABU MIDDLE SCHOOL.
HEY!
ASAAA-NUMAAA-CHAAAN! ♡
OH, HEY, MAKOTO-SENPAI! I SEE YOU BROUGHT ALL YOUR FRIENDS TODAY. ♡
ISN'T HE CUTE? ♡
PLEASE, SENPAI! DON'T DO THAT!
THIS IS ASANUMA-CHAN. ♡ HE'S A REGULAR HERE, AND A FIRST YEAR AT MOTO-AZABU MIDDLE SCHOOL.
WE KEPT RUNNING INTO EACH OTHER HERE, AND NOW WE'RE FRIENDS. ♡

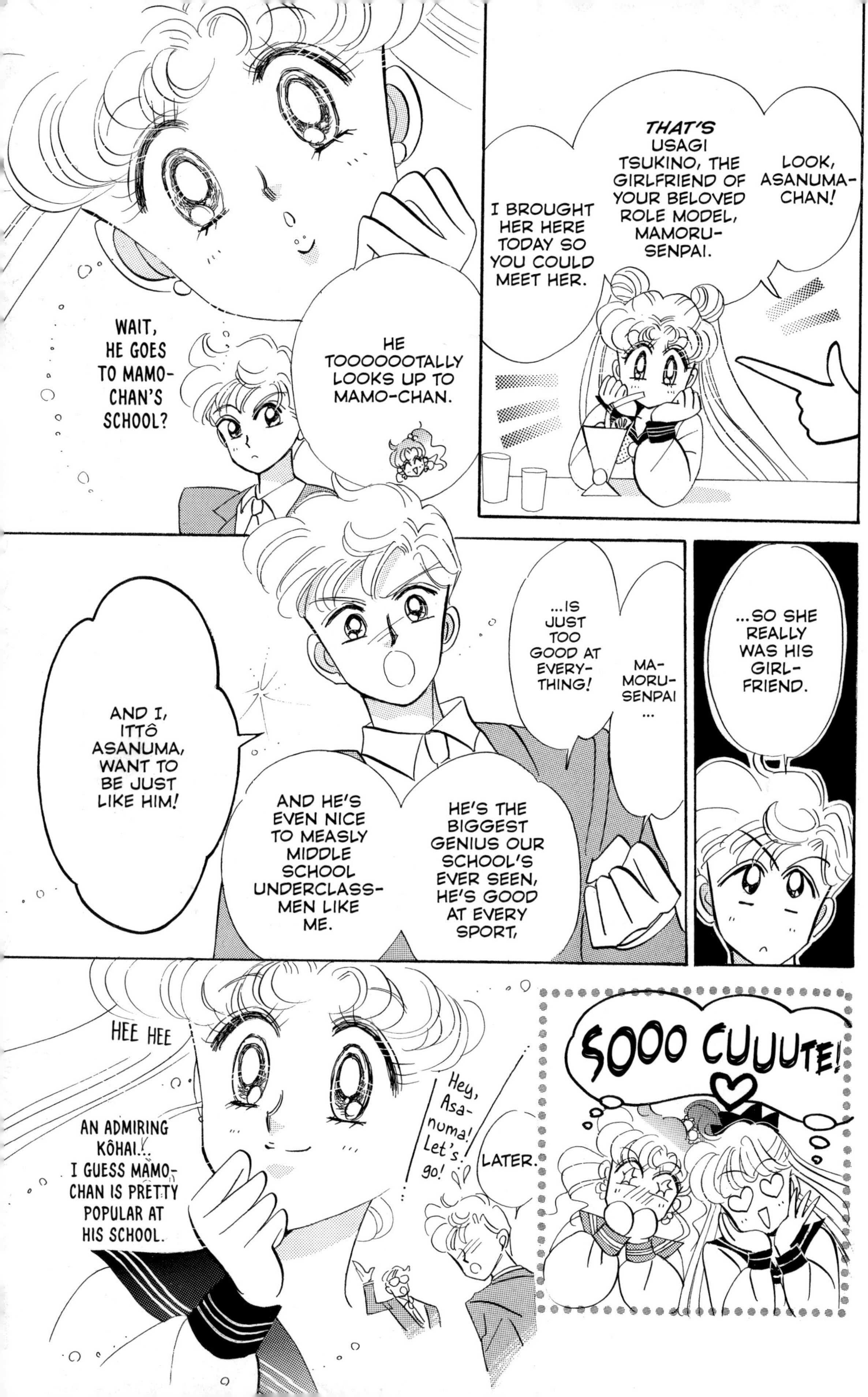
LOOK, ASANUMA-CHAN!
THAT'S USAGI TSUKINO, THE GIRLFRIEND OF YOUR BELOVED ROLE MODEL, MAMORU-SENPAI.
I BROUGHT HER HERE TODAY SO YOU COULD MEET HER.
HE TOOOOOOTALLY LOOKS UP TO MAMO-CHAN.
WAIT, HE GOES TO MAMO-CHAN'S SCHOOL?
...SO SHE REALLY WAS HIS GIRL-FRIEND.
MAMORU-SENPAI...
...IS JUST TOO GOOD AT EVERY-THING!
HE'S THE BIGGEST GENIUS OUR SCHOOL'S EVER SEEN, HE'S GOOD AT EVERY SPORT,
AND HE'S EVEN NICE TO MEASLY MIDDLE SCHOOL UNDERCLASS-MEN LIKE ME.
AND I, ITTÔ ASANUMA, WANT TO BE JUST LIKE HIM!
SOOO CUUUTE!
Hey, Asa-numa! Let's go!
LATER.
HEE HEE
AN ADMIRING KÔHAI... I GUESS MAMO-CHAN IS PRETTY POPULAR AT HIS SCHOOL.

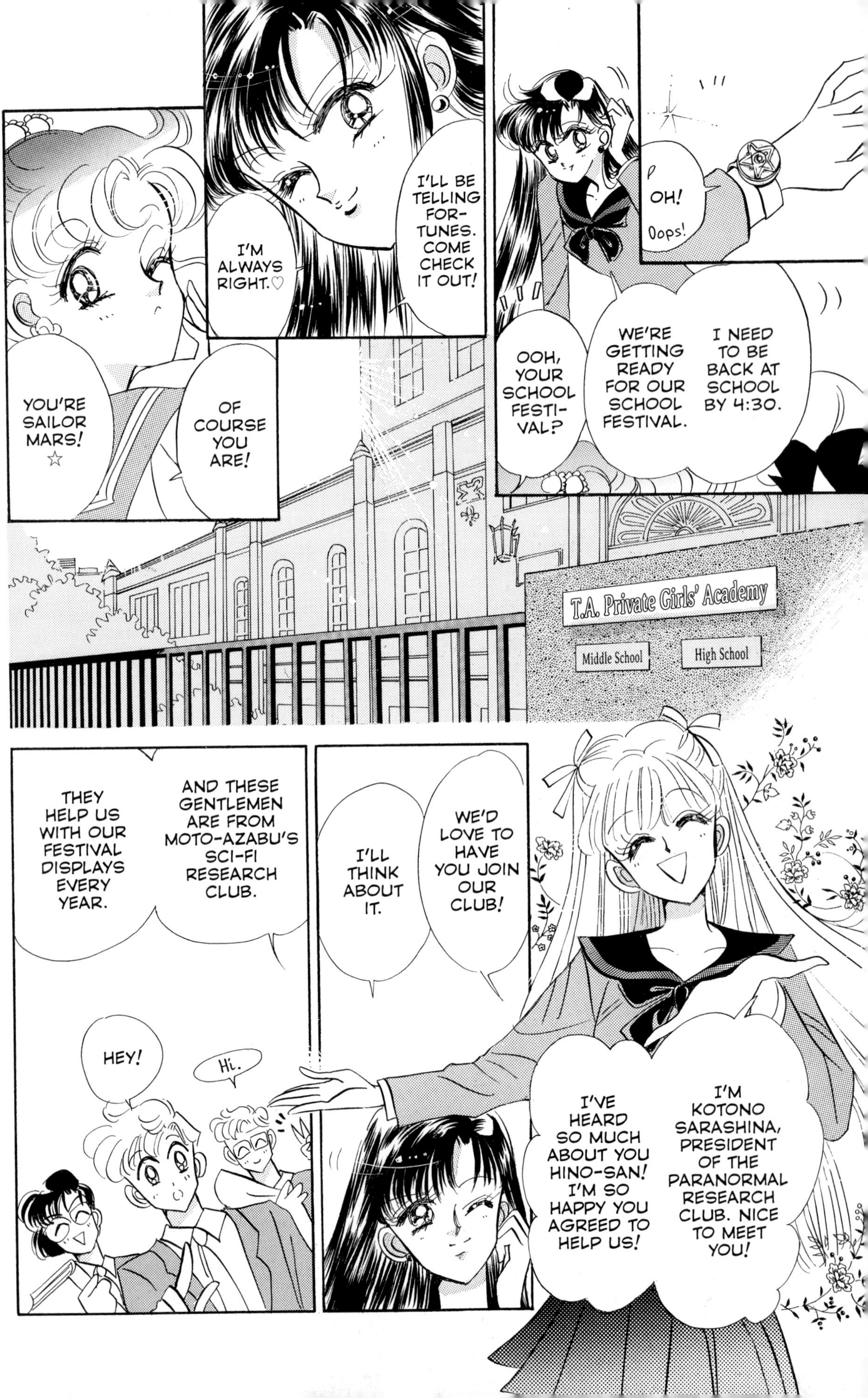
OH!
Oops!
I NEED TO BE BACK AT SCHOOL BY 4:30.
WE'RE GETTING READY FOR OUR SCHOOL FESTIVAL.
OOH, YOUR SCHOOL FESTI-VAL?
I'LL BE TELLING FOR-TUNES. COME CHECK IT OUT!
I'M ALWAYS RIGHT.♡
OF COURSE YOU ARE!
YOU'RE SAILOR MARS! ☆
T.A. Private Girls' Academy
High School
Middle School
I'M KOTONO SARASHINA, PRESIDENT OF THE PARANORMAL RESEARCH CLUB. NICE TO MEET YOU!
I'VE HEARD SO MUCH ABOUT YOU HINO-SAN! I'M SO HAPPY YOU AGREED TO HELP US!
WE'D LOVE TO HAVE YOU JOIN OUR CLUB!
I'LL THINK ABOUT IT.
AND THESE GENTLEMEN ARE FROM MOTO-AZABU'S SCI-FI RESEARCH CLUB.
THEY HELP US WITH OUR FESTIVAL DISPLAYS EVERY YEAR.
HEY!
Hi.

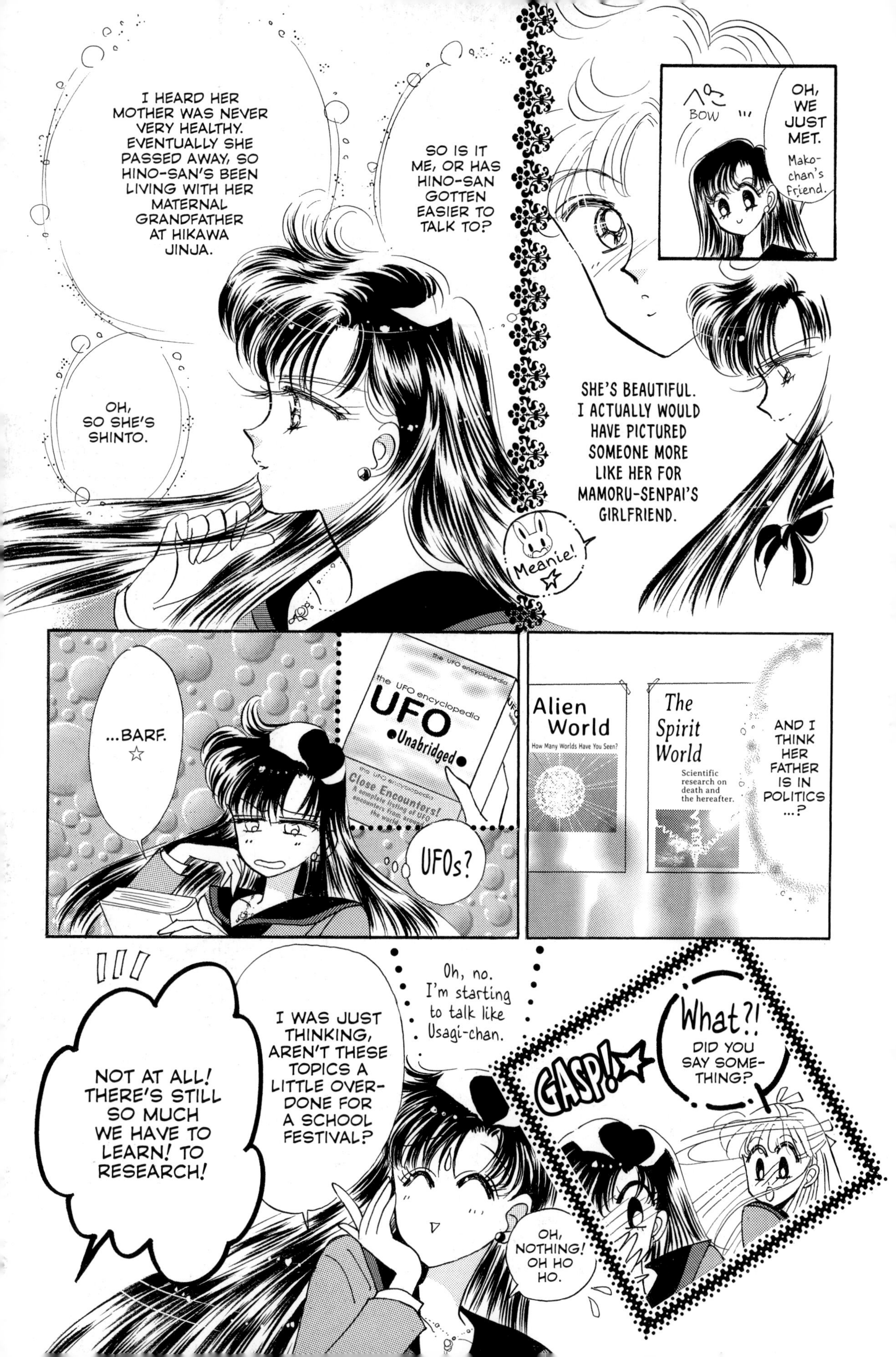

BOW
OH, WE JUST MET.
Mako-chan's friend.
SHE'S BEAUTIFUL. I ACTUALLY WOULD HAVE PICTURED SOMEONE MORE LIKE HER FOR MAMORU-SENPAI'S GIRLFRIEND.
Meanie! ☆
SO IS IT ME, OR HAS HINO-SAN GOTTEN EASIER TO TALK TO?
I HEARD HER MOTHER WAS NEVER VERY HEALTHY. EVENTUALLY SHE PASSED AWAY, SO HINO-SAN'S BEEN LIVING WITH HER MATERNAL GRANDFATHER AT HIKAWA JINJA.
OH, SO SHE'S SHINTO.
AND I THINK HER FATHER IS IN POLITICS ...?
The Spirit World
Scientific research on death and the hereafter.
Alien World
How Many Worlds Have You Seen?
the UFO encyclopedia
UFO
●Unabridged●
Close Encounters!
UFOs?
...BARF. ☆
What?!
DID YOU SAY SOME-THING?
GASP!☆
OH, NOTHING! OH HO HO.
Oh, no. I'm starting to talk like Usagi-chan.
I WAS JUST THINKING, AREN'T THESE TOPICS A LITTLE OVER-DONE FOR A SCHOOL FESTIVAL?
NOT AT ALL! THERE'S STILL SO MUCH WE HAVE TO LEARN! TO RESEARCH!

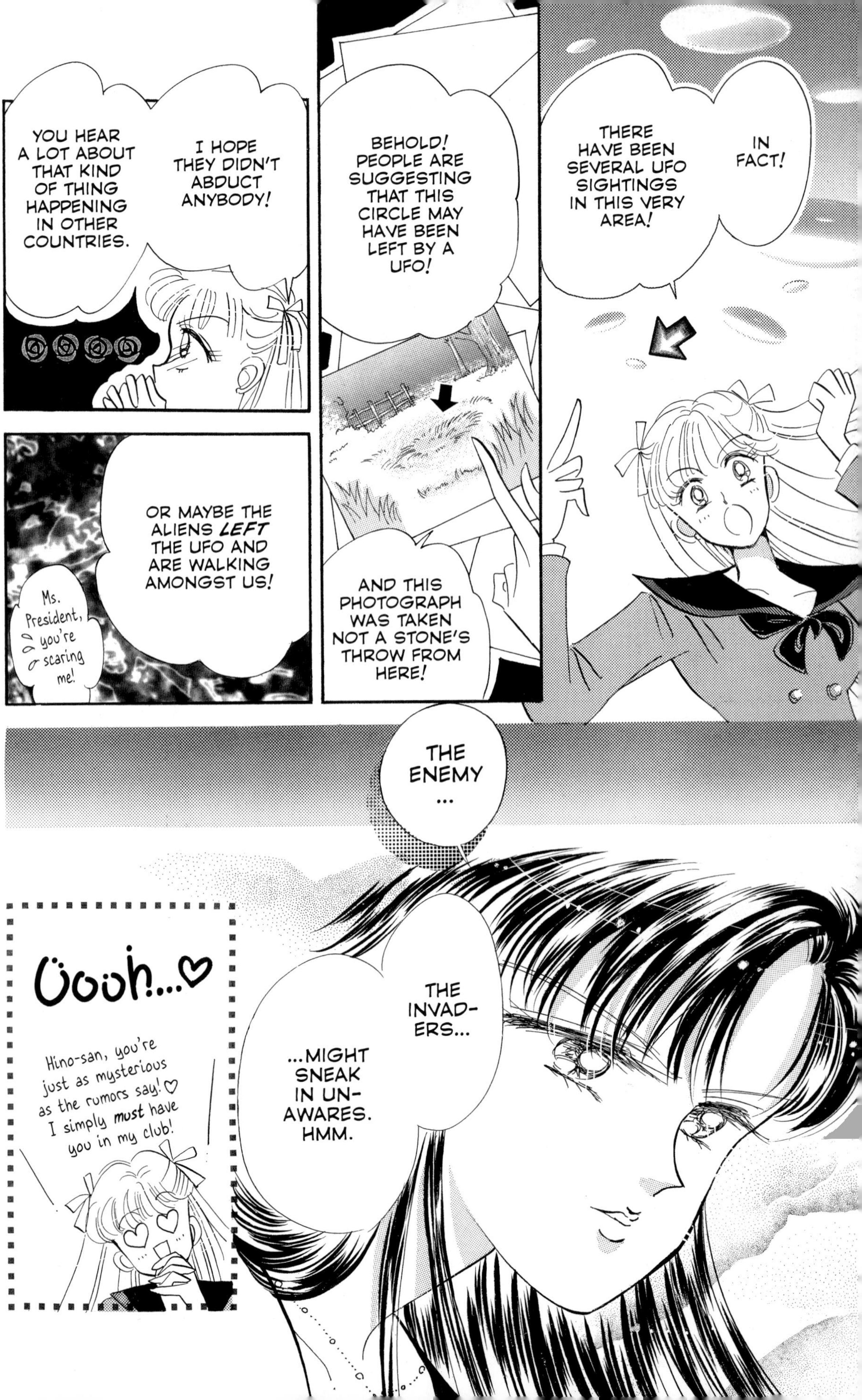
IN FACT!
THERE HAVE BEEN SEVERAL UFO SIGHTINGS IN THIS VERY AREA!
BEHOLD! PEOPLE ARE SUGGESTING THAT THIS CIRCLE MAY HAVE BEEN LEFT BY A UFO!
AND THIS PHOTOGRAPH WAS TAKEN NOT A STONE'S THROW FROM HERE!
I HOPE THEY DIDN'T ABDUCT ANYBODY!
YOU HEAR A LOT ABOUT THAT KIND OF THING HAPPENING IN OTHER COUNTRIES.
OR MAYBE THE ALIENS *LEFT* THE UFO AND ARE WALKING AMONGST US!
Ms. President, you're scaring me!
THE ENEMY...
THE INVADERS...
...MIGHT SNEAK IN UNAWARES. HMM.
Öooh...♡
Hino-san, you're just as mysterious as the rumors say! ♡ I simply *must* have you in my club!

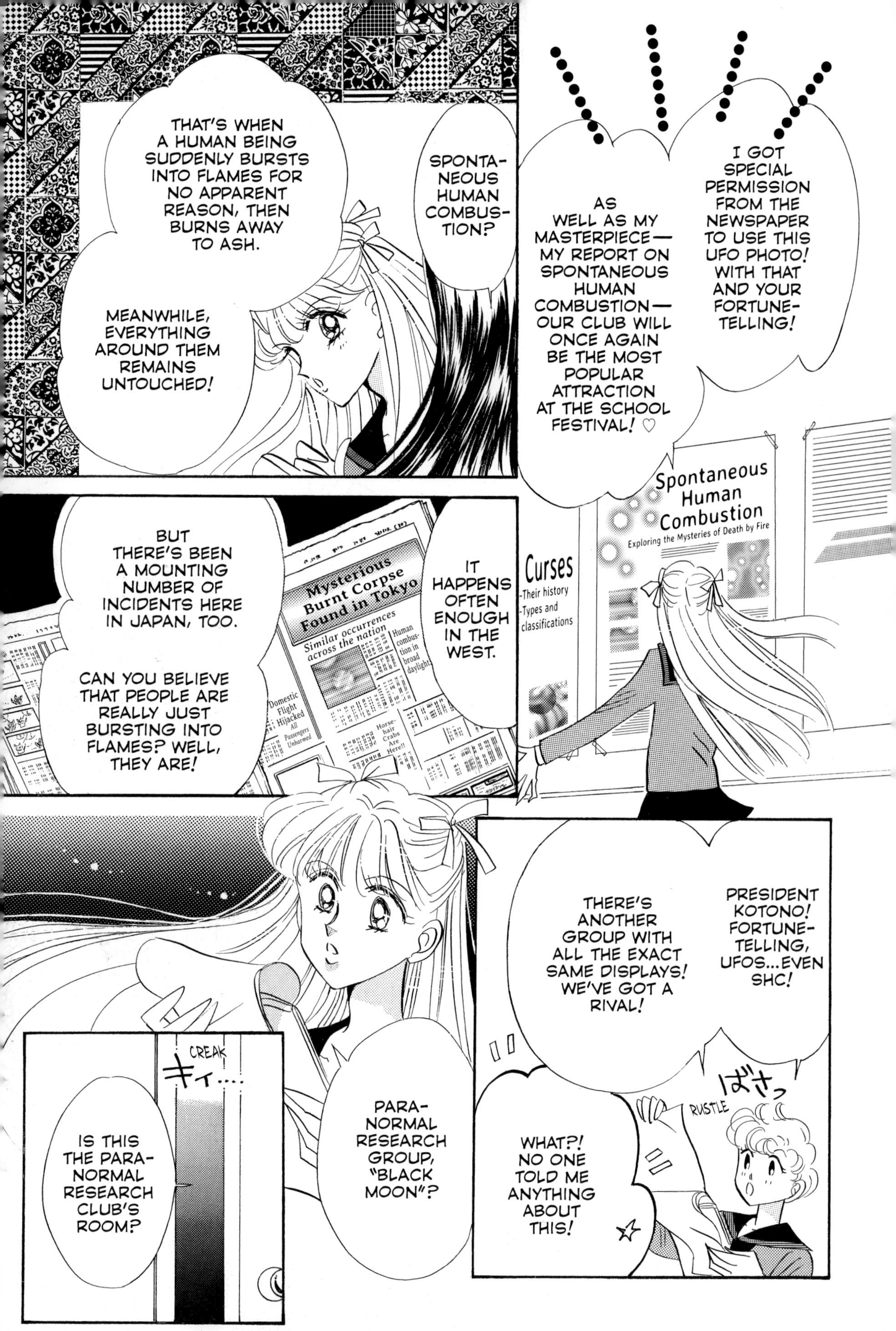
I GOT SPECIAL PERMISSION FROM THE NEWSPAPER TO USE THIS UFO PHOTO! WITH THAT AND YOUR FORTUNE-TELLING!
AS WELL AS MY MASTERPIECE—MY REPORT ON SPONTANEOUS HUMAN COMBUSTION—OUR CLUB WILL ONCE AGAIN BE THE MOST POPULAR ATTRACTION AT THE SCHOOL FESTIVAL! ♡
Spontaneous Human Combustion
Exploring the Mysteries of Death by Fire
Curses
-Their history
-Types and classifications
SPONTANEOUS HUMAN COMBUSTION?
THAT'S WHEN A HUMAN BEING SUDDENLY BURSTS INTO FLAMES FOR NO APPARENT REASON, THEN BURNS AWAY TO ASH.
MEANWHILE, EVERYTHING AROUND THEM REMAINS UNTOUCHED!
IT HAPPENS OFTEN ENOUGH IN THE WEST.
Mysterious Burnt Corpse Found in Tokyo
Similar occurrences across the nation
Human combustion in broad daylight
Domestic Flight Hijacked
All Passengers Unharmed
Horse-hair Crabs Are Here!!
BUT THERE'S BEEN A MOUNTING NUMBER OF INCIDENTS HERE IN JAPAN, TOO.
CAN YOU BELIEVE THAT PEOPLE ARE REALLY JUST BURSTING INTO FLAMES? WELL, THEY ARE!
PRESIDENT KOTONO! FORTUNE-TELLING, UFOS...EVEN SHC!
THERE'S ANOTHER GROUP WITH ALL THE EXACT SAME DISPLAYS! WE'VE GOT A RIVAL!
ばさっ
RUSTLE
WHAT?! NO ONE TOLD ME ANYTHING ABOUT THIS!
PARA-NORMAL RESEARCH GROUP, "BLACK MOON"?
キィ…
CREAK
IS THIS THE PARA-NORMAL RESEARCH CLUB'S ROOM?

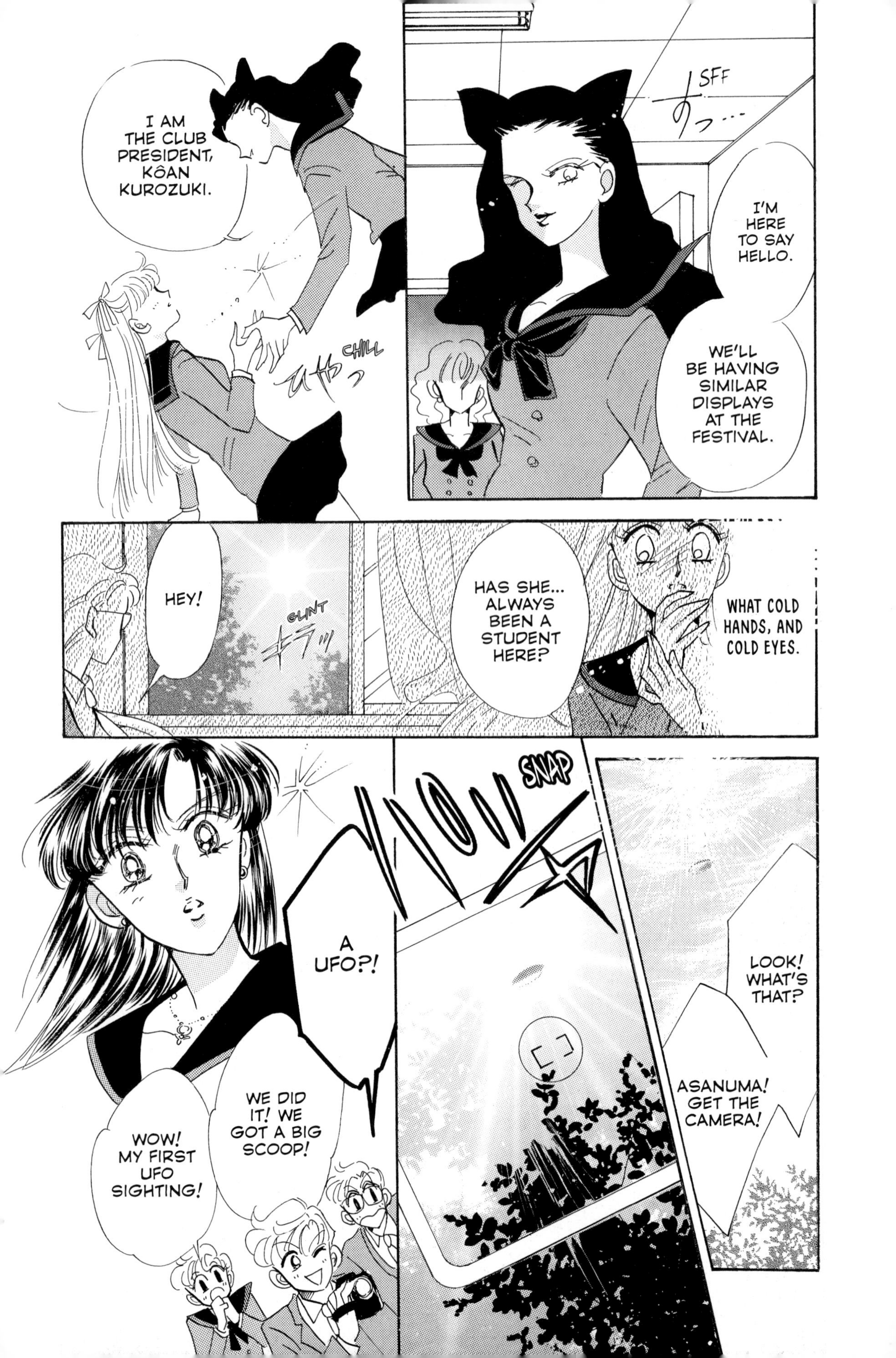
SFF
I'M HERE TO SAY HELLO.
WE'LL BE HAVING SIMILAR DISPLAYS AT THE FESTIVAL.
I AM THE CLUB PRESIDENT, KÔAN KUROZUKI.
CHILL
WHAT COLD HANDS, AND COLD EYES.
HAS SHE... ALWAYS BEEN A STUDENT HERE?
GLINT
HEY!
LOOK! WHAT'S THAT?
ASANUMA! GET THE CAMERA!
SNAP
A UFO?!
WE DID IT! WE GOT A BIG SCOOP!
WOW! MY FIRST UFO SIGHTING!

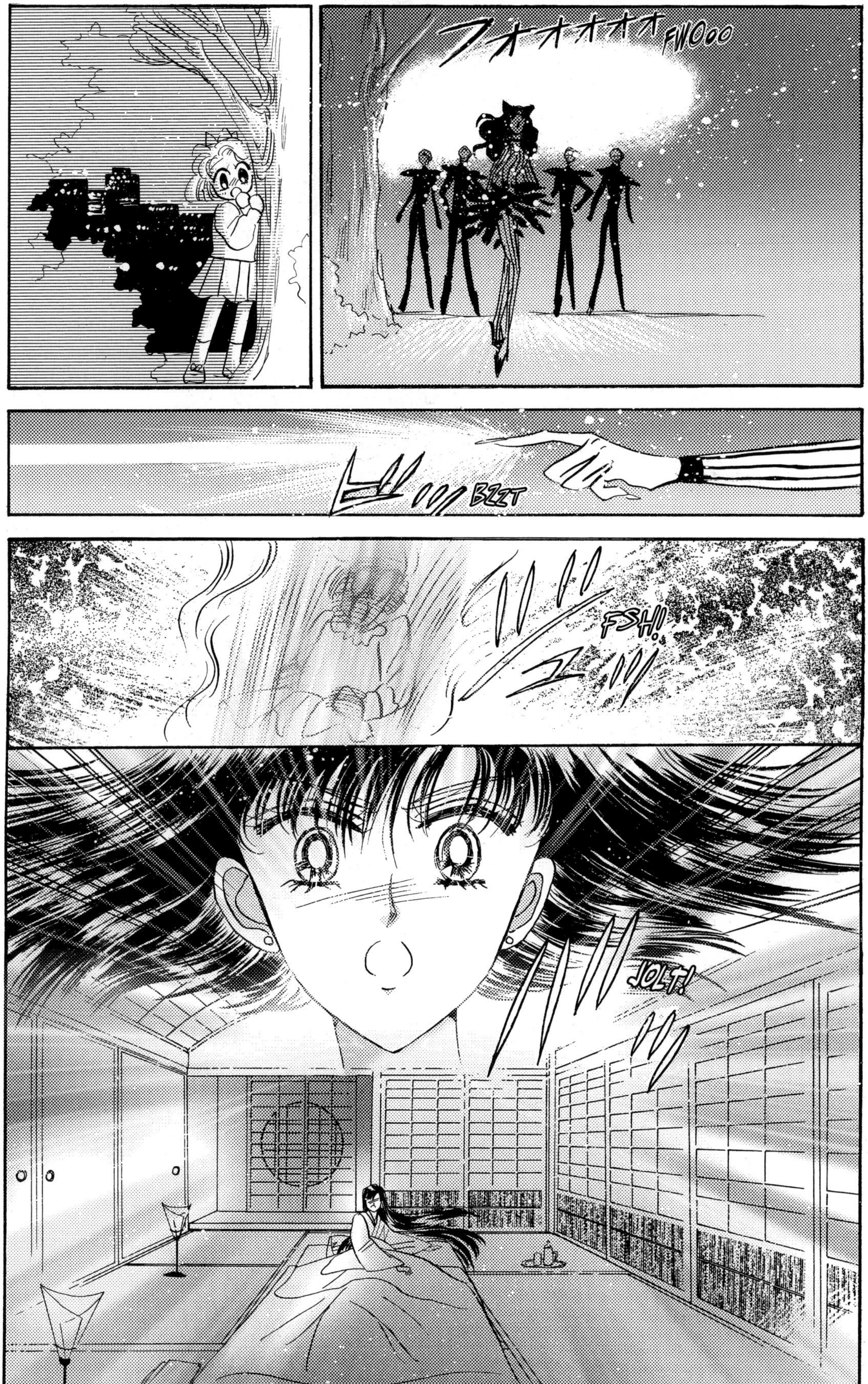
フォオオオオ
FWOOO
BZZT
FSH!
JOLT!

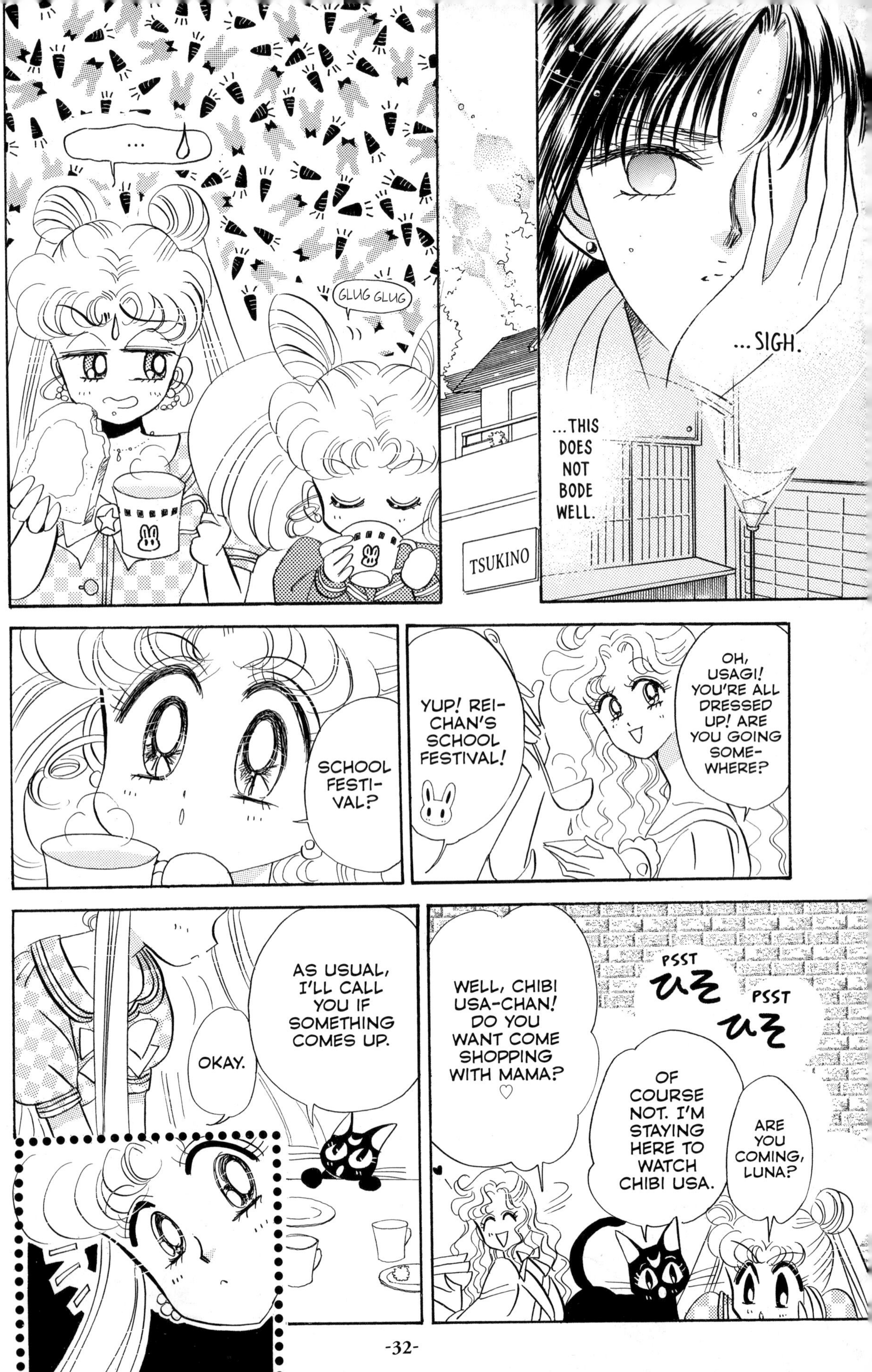
...SIGH.
...THIS DOES NOT BODE WELL.
TSUKINO
...
GLUG GLUG
OH, USAGI! YOU'RE ALL DRESSED UP! ARE YOU GOING SOME-WHERE?
YUP! REI-CHAN'S SCHOOL FESTIVAL!
SCHOOL FESTI-VAL?
WELL, CHIBI USA-CHAN! DO YOU WANT COME SHOPPING WITH MAMA? ♡
PSST ひそ
PSST ひそ
ARE YOU COMING, LUNA?
OF COURSE NOT. I'M STAYING HERE TO WATCH CHIBI USA.
AS USUAL, I'LL CALL YOU IF SOMETHING COMES UP.
OKAY.

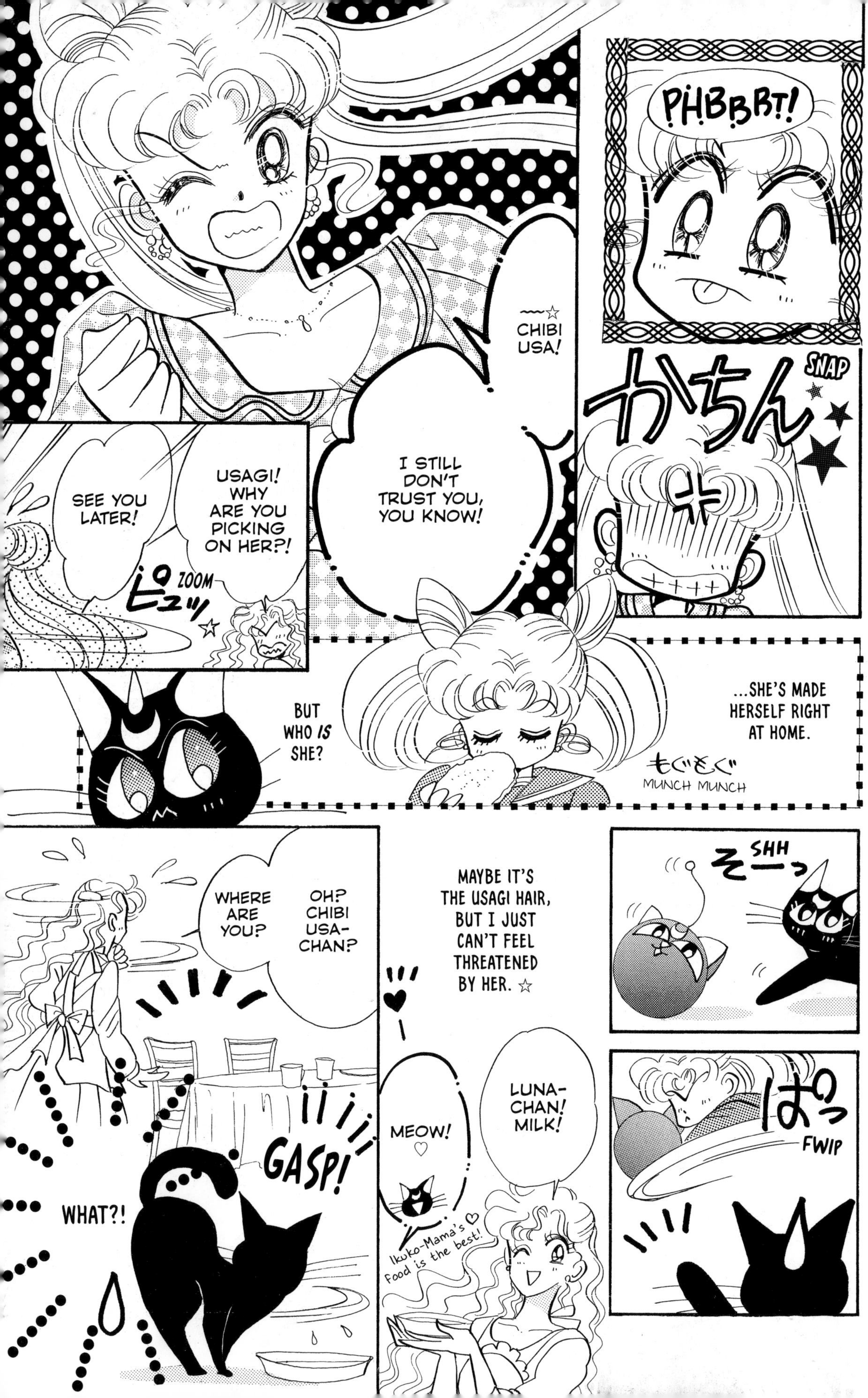
PHBBBT!
かちん
SNAP
~~☆ CHIBI USA!
I STILL DON'T TRUST YOU, YOU KNOW!
USAGI! WHY ARE YOU PICKING ON HER?!
SEE YOU LATER!
ピュッ
ZOOM
...SHE'S MADE HERSELF RIGHT AT HOME.
もぐもぐ
MUNCH MUNCH
BUT WHO *IS* SHE?
そーっ
SHH
ぱっ
FWIP
MAYBE IT'S THE USAGI HAIR, BUT I JUST CAN'T FEEL THREATENED BY HER. ☆
LUNA-CHAN! MILK!
MEOW! ♡
Ikuko-Mama's ♡ Food is the best!
OH? CHIBI USA-CHAN?
WHERE ARE YOU?
GASP!
WHAT?!

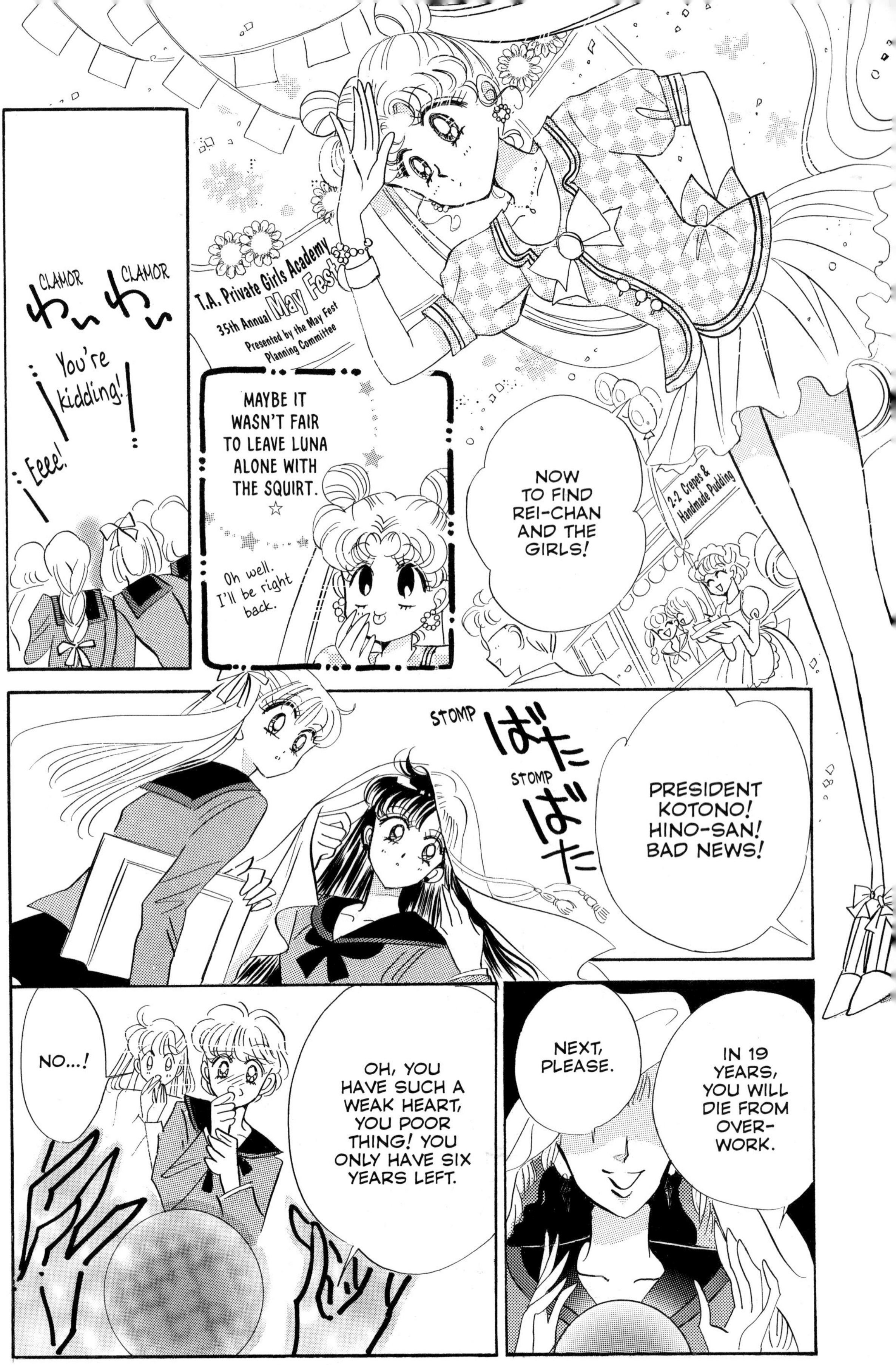
T.A. Private Girls Academy
35th Annual May Fest
Presented by the May Fest Planning Committee
2-2 Crepes & Handmade Pudding
NOW TO FIND REI-CHAN AND THE GIRLS!
MAYBE IT WASN'T FAIR TO LEAVE LUNA ALONE WITH THE SQUIRT.
Oh well. I'll be right back.
CLAMOR わいわい CLAMOR
You're kidding!
Eeee!
STOMP ばた STOMP ばた
PRESIDENT KOTONO! HINO-SAN! BAD NEWS!
IN 19 YEARS, YOU WILL DIE FROM OVER-WORK.
NEXT, PLEASE.
OH, YOU HAVE SUCH A WEAK HEART, YOU POOR THING! YOU ONLY HAVE SIX YEARS LEFT.
NO...!

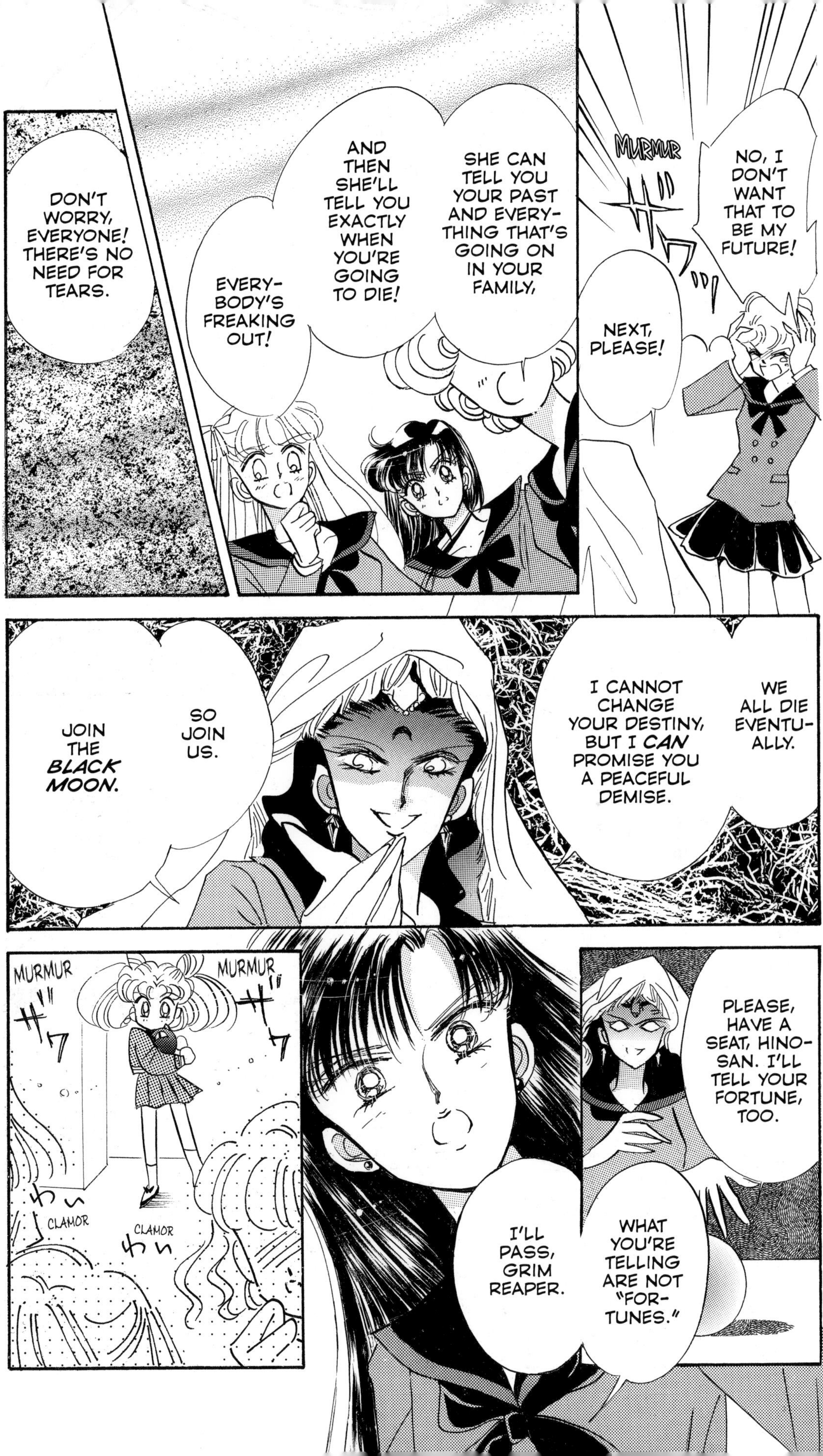
MURMUR
NO, I DON'T WANT THAT TO BE MY FUTURE!
NEXT, PLEASE!
SHE CAN TELL YOU YOUR PAST AND EVERYTHING THAT'S GOING ON IN YOUR FAMILY,
AND THEN SHE'LL TELL YOU EXACTLY WHEN YOU'RE GOING TO DIE!
EVERYBODY'S FREAKING OUT!
DON'T WORRY, EVERYONE! THERE'S NO NEED FOR TEARS.
WE ALL DIE EVENTUALLY.
I CANNOT CHANGE YOUR DESTINY, BUT I *CAN* PROMISE YOU A PEACEFUL DEMISE.
SO JOIN US.
JOIN THE ***BLACK MOON.***
PLEASE, HAVE A SEAT, HINO-SAN. I'LL TELL YOUR FORTUNE, TOO.
WHAT YOU'RE TELLING ARE NOT "FORTUNES."
I'LL PASS, GRIM REAPER.
MURMUR
MURMUR
CLAMOR
CLAMOR

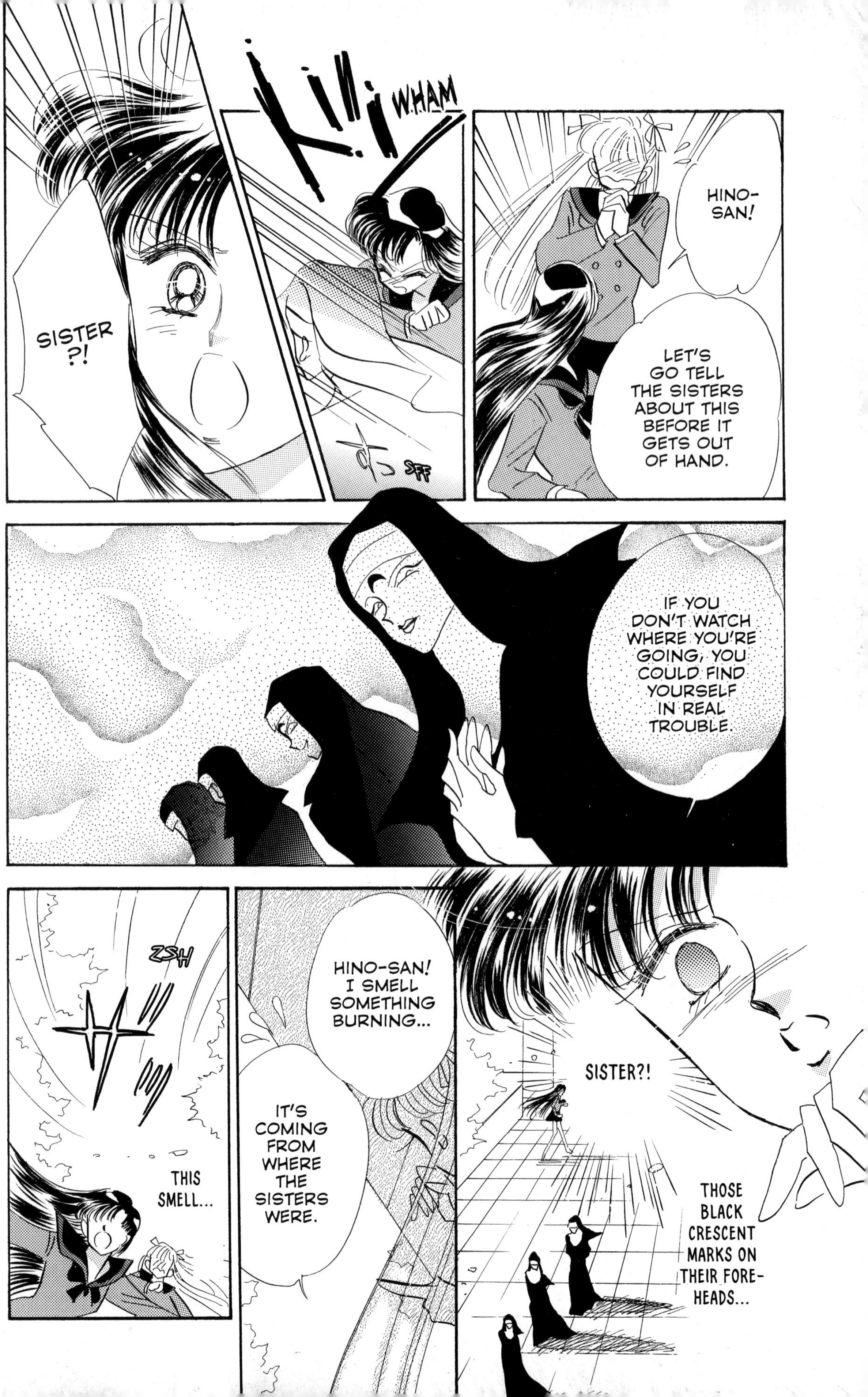
HINO-SAN!
LET'S GO TELL THE SISTERS ABOUT THIS BEFORE IT GETS OUT OF HAND.
WHAM
SFF
SISTER ?!
IF YOU DON'T WATCH WHERE YOU'RE GOING, YOU COULD FIND YOURSELF IN REAL TROUBLE.
SISTER?!
THOSE BLACK CRESCENT MARKS ON THEIR FOREHEADS...
HINO-SAN! I SMELL SOMETHING BURNING...
IT'S COMING FROM WHERE THE SISTERS WERE.
ZSH
THIS SMELL...

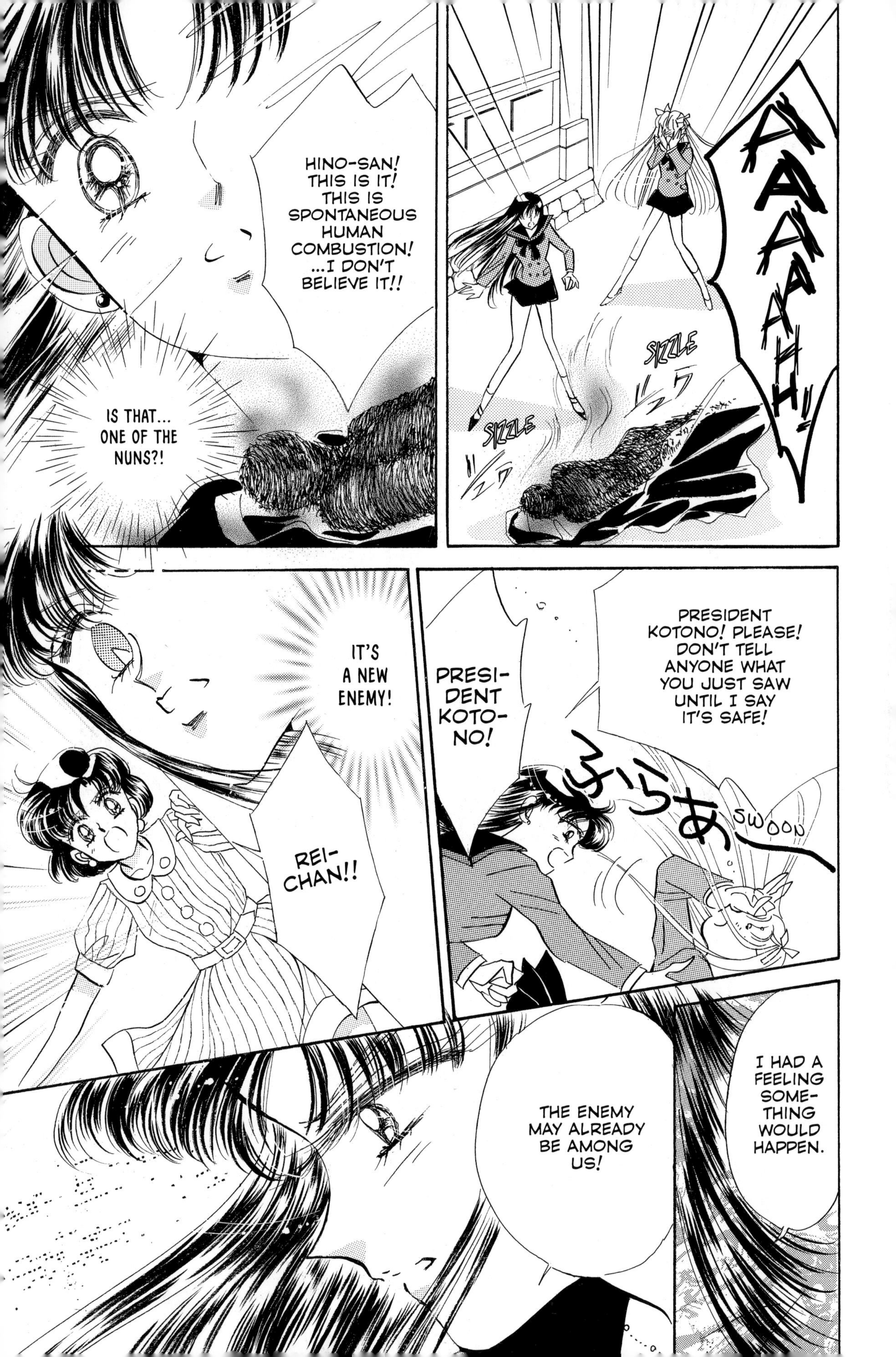
AAAAAH!!
SIZZLE
SIZZLE
HINO-SAN! THIS IS IT! THIS IS SPONTANEOUS HUMAN COMBUSTION! ...I DON'T BELIEVE IT!!
IS THAT... ONE OF THE NUNS?!
PRESIDENT KOTONO! PLEASE! DON'T TELL ANYONE WHAT YOU JUST SAW UNTIL I SAY IT'S SAFE!
PRESI-DENT KOTO-NO!
ふらあ～
SWOON
IT'S A NEW ENEMY!
REI-CHAN!!
I HAD A FEELING SOME-THING WOULD HAPPEN.
THE ENEMY MAY ALREADY BE AMONG US!

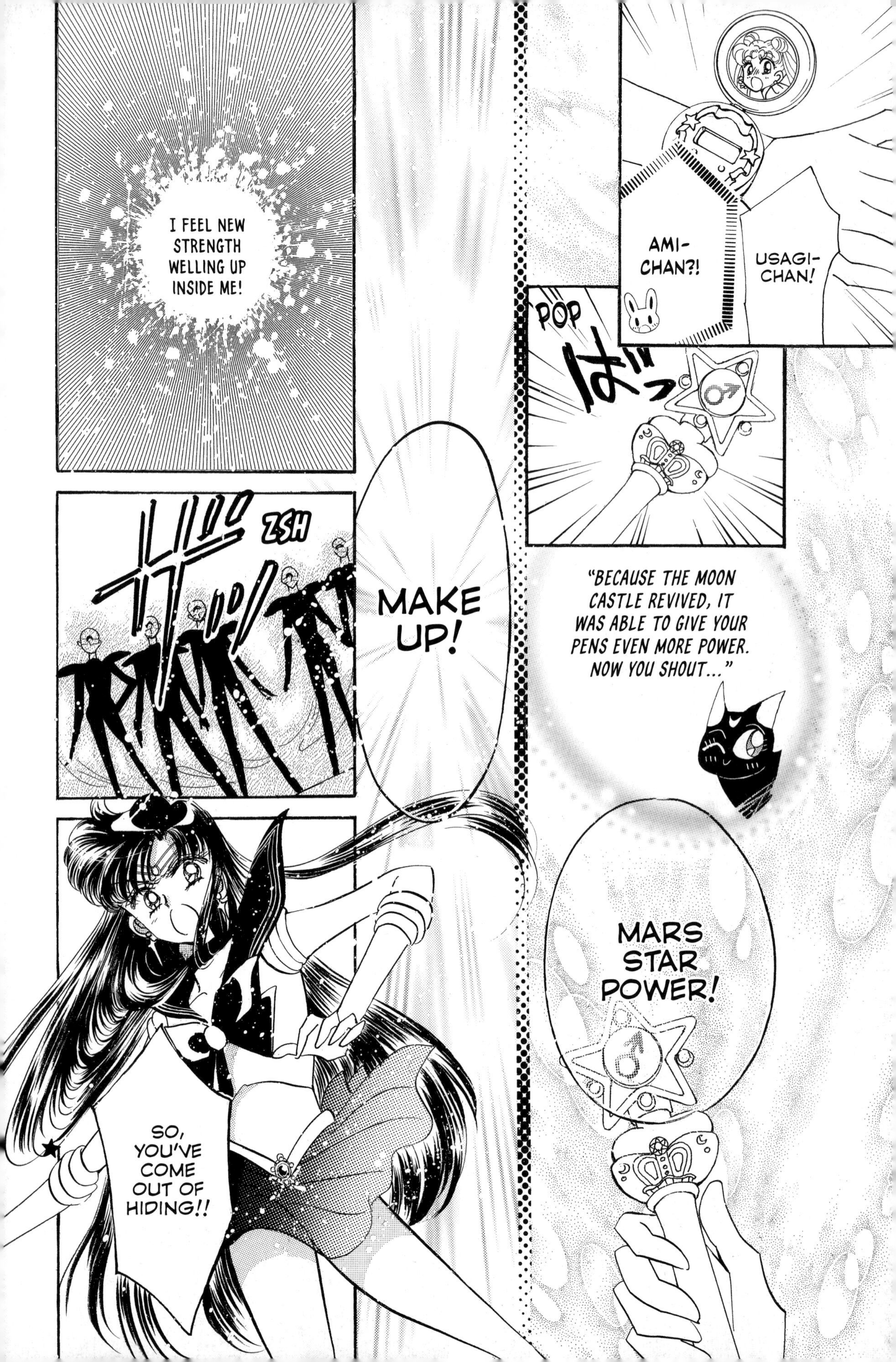
USAGI-CHAN!
AMI-CHAN?!
POP
"BECAUSE THE MOON CASTLE REVIVED, IT WAS ABLE TO GIVE YOUR PENS EVEN MORE POWER. NOW YOU SHOUT..."
MARS STAR POWER!
I FEEL NEW STRENGTH WELLING UP INSIDE ME!
MAKE UP!
ZSH
SO, YOU'VE COME OUT OF HIDING!!

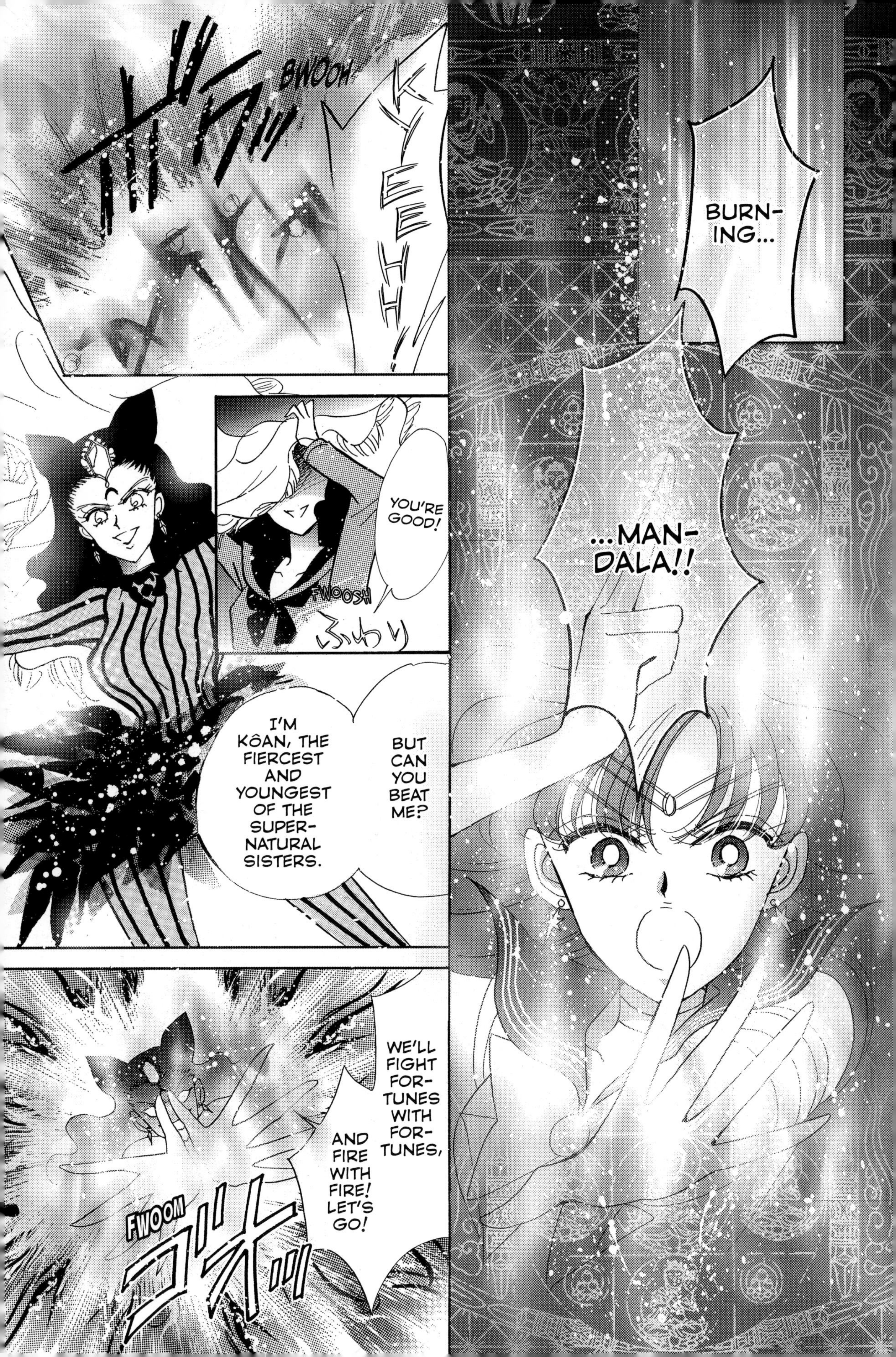
BURNING...
...MANDALA!!
BWOOH
KYEEEHH!!
YOU'RE GOOD!
FWOOSH
ふわり
I'M KÔAN, THE FIERCEST AND YOUNGEST OF THE SUPERNATURAL SISTERS.
BUT CAN YOU BEAT ME?
WE'LL FIGHT FORTUNES WITH FORTUNES,
AND FIRE WITH FIRE! LET'S GO!
FWOOM
ゴオッ

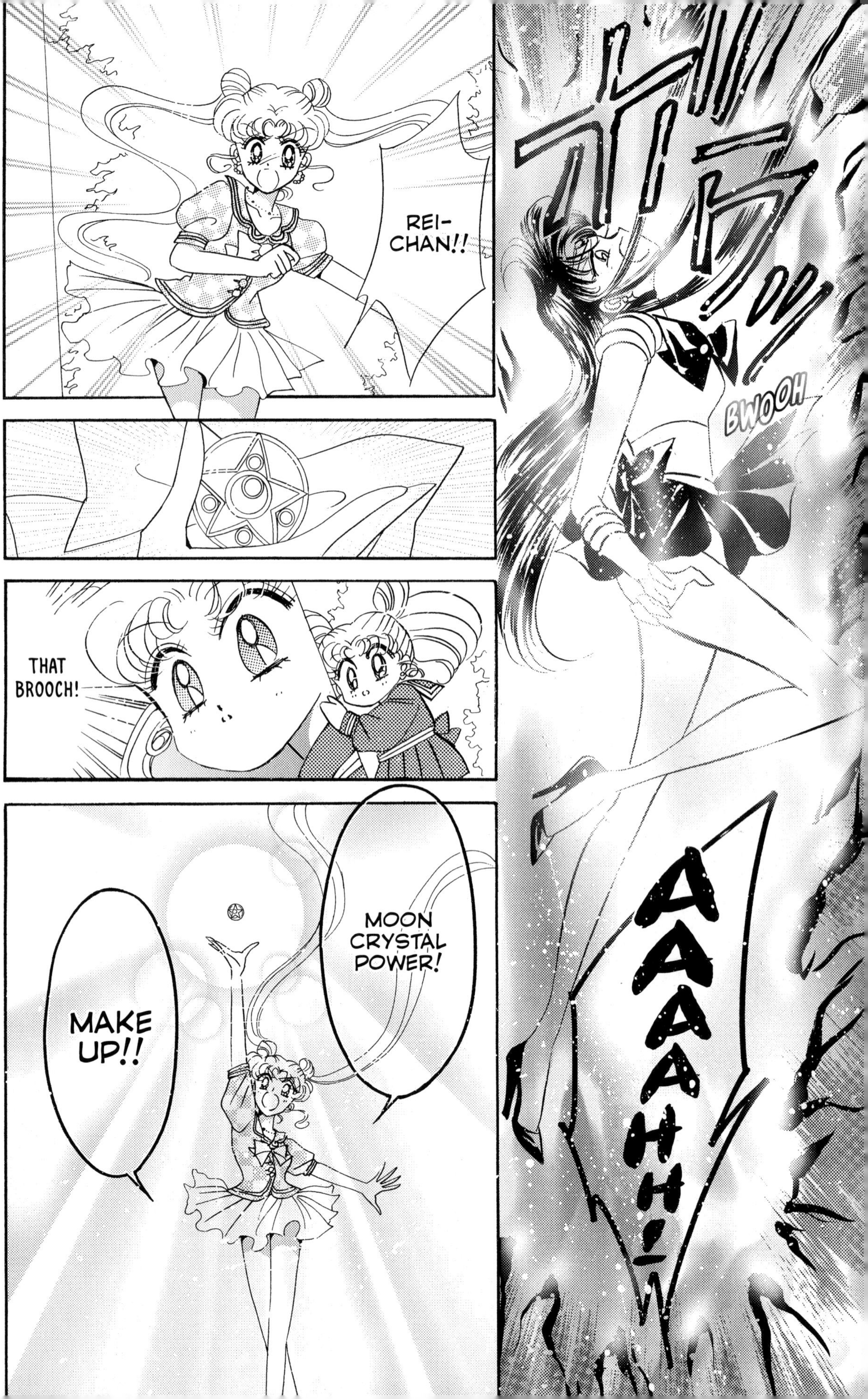
BWOOH
AAAAHH!!
REI-CHAN!!
THAT BROOCH!
MOON CRYSTAL POWER!
MAKE UP!!

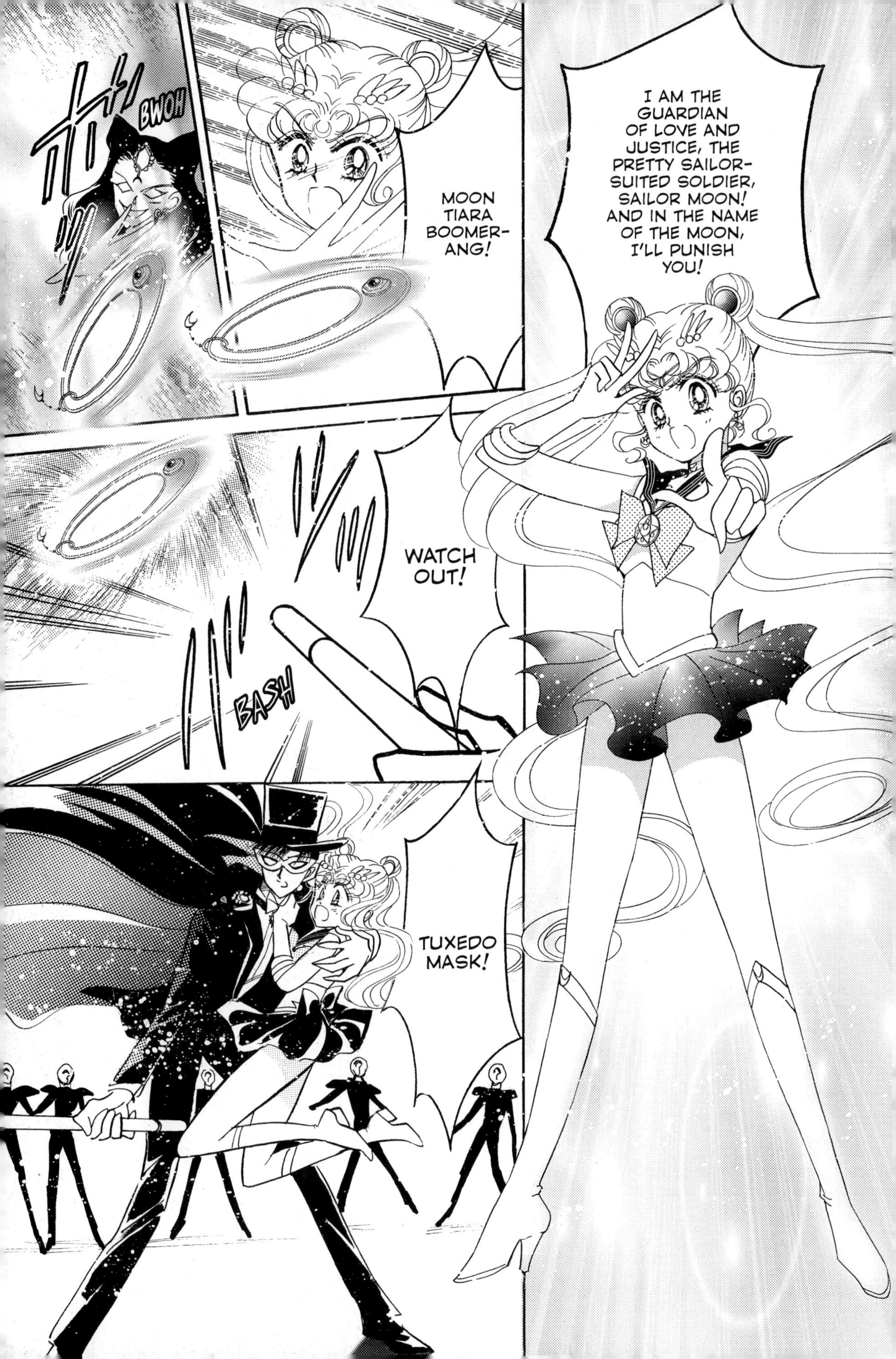
I AM THE GUARDIAN OF LOVE AND JUSTICE, THE PRETTY SAILOR-SUITED SOLDIER, SAILOR MOON! AND IN THE NAME OF THE MOON, I'LL PUNISH YOU!
MOON TIARA BOOMER-ANG!
BWOH
WATCH OUT!
BASH
TUXEDO MASK!

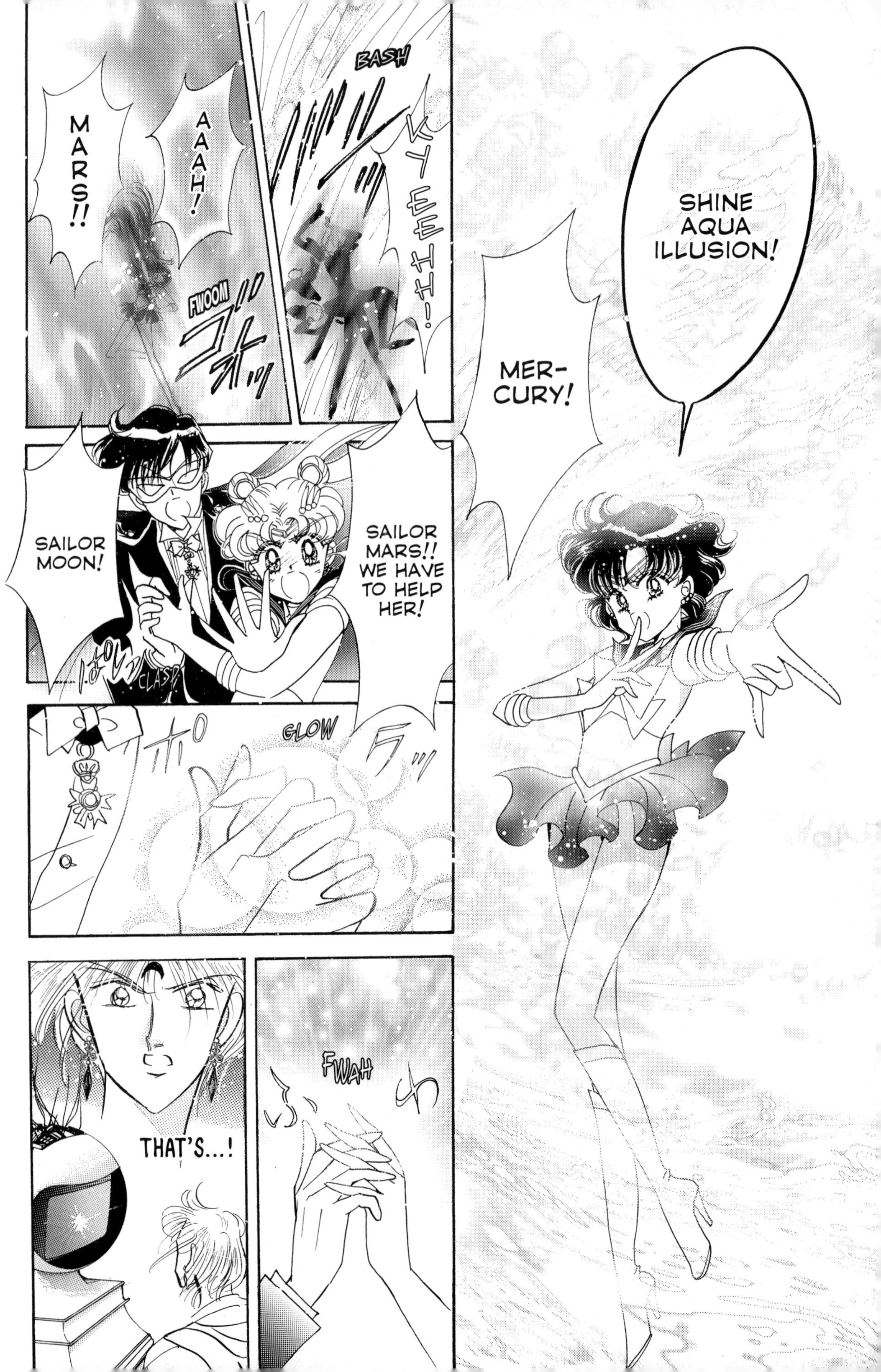
SHINE AQUA ILLUSION!
MER- CURY!
BASH
KYEEHH!
AAAH!
MARS!!
FWOOM
SAILOR MARS!! WE HAVE TO HELP HER!
SAILOR MOON!
CLASP
GLOW
FWAH
THAT'S...!

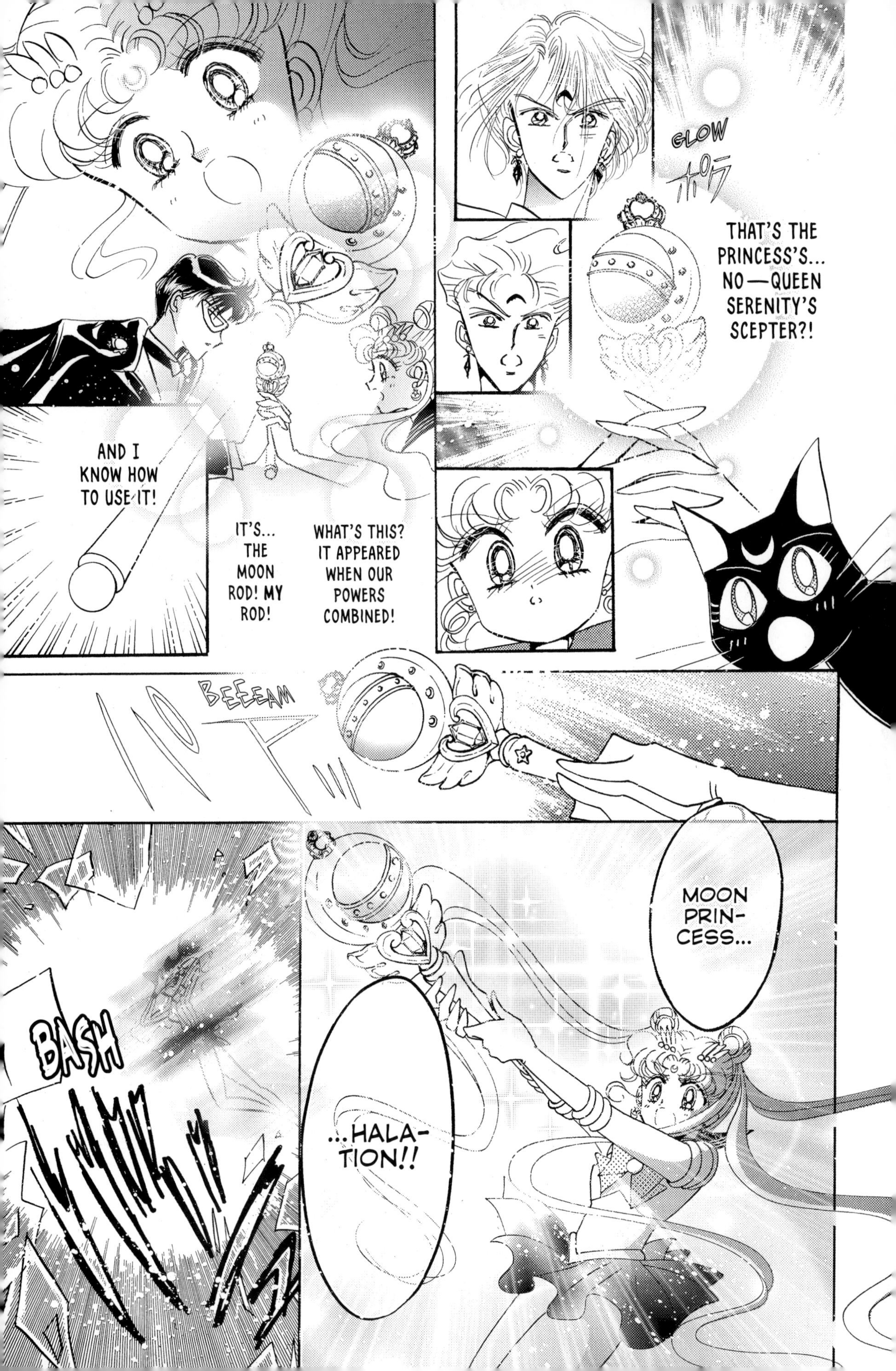
GLOW
THAT'S THE PRINCESS'S... NO—QUEEN SERENITY'S SCEPTER?!
WHAT'S THIS? IT APPEARED WHEN OUR POWERS COMBINED!
IT'S... THE MOON ROD! MY ROD!
AND I KNOW HOW TO USE IT!
BEEEAM
MOON PRIN-CESS...
...HALA-TION!!
BASH

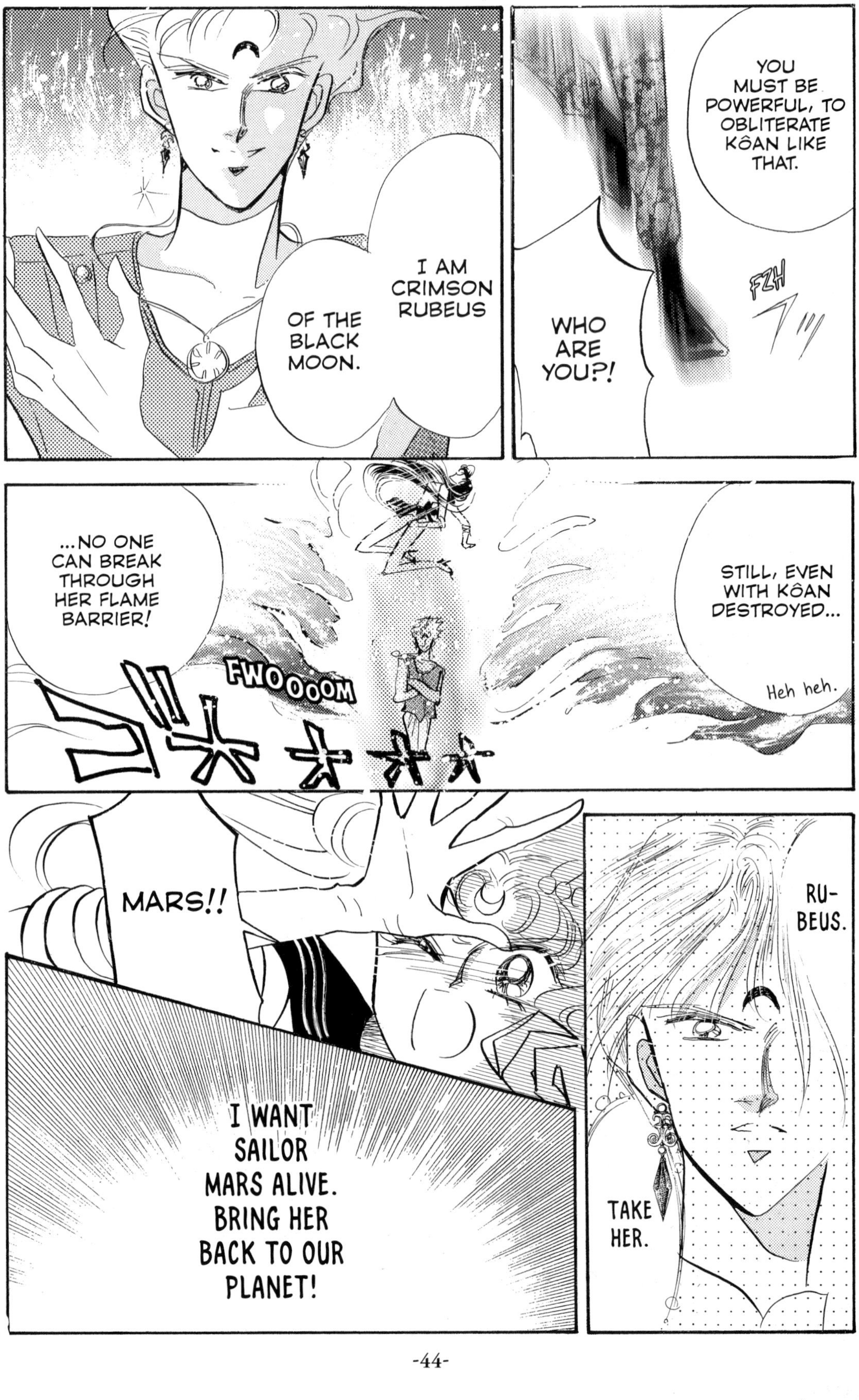
YOU MUST BE POWERFUL, TO OBLITERATE KÔAN LIKE THAT.
FZH
WHO ARE YOU?!
I AM CRIMSON RUBEUS
OF THE BLACK MOON.
STILL, EVEN WITH KÔAN DESTROYED...
Heh heh.
...NO ONE CAN BREAK THROUGH HER FLAME BARRIER!
FWOOOOOM
RU-BEUS.
TAKE HER.
MARS!!
I WANT SAILOR MARS ALIVE. BRING HER BACK TO OUR PLANET!

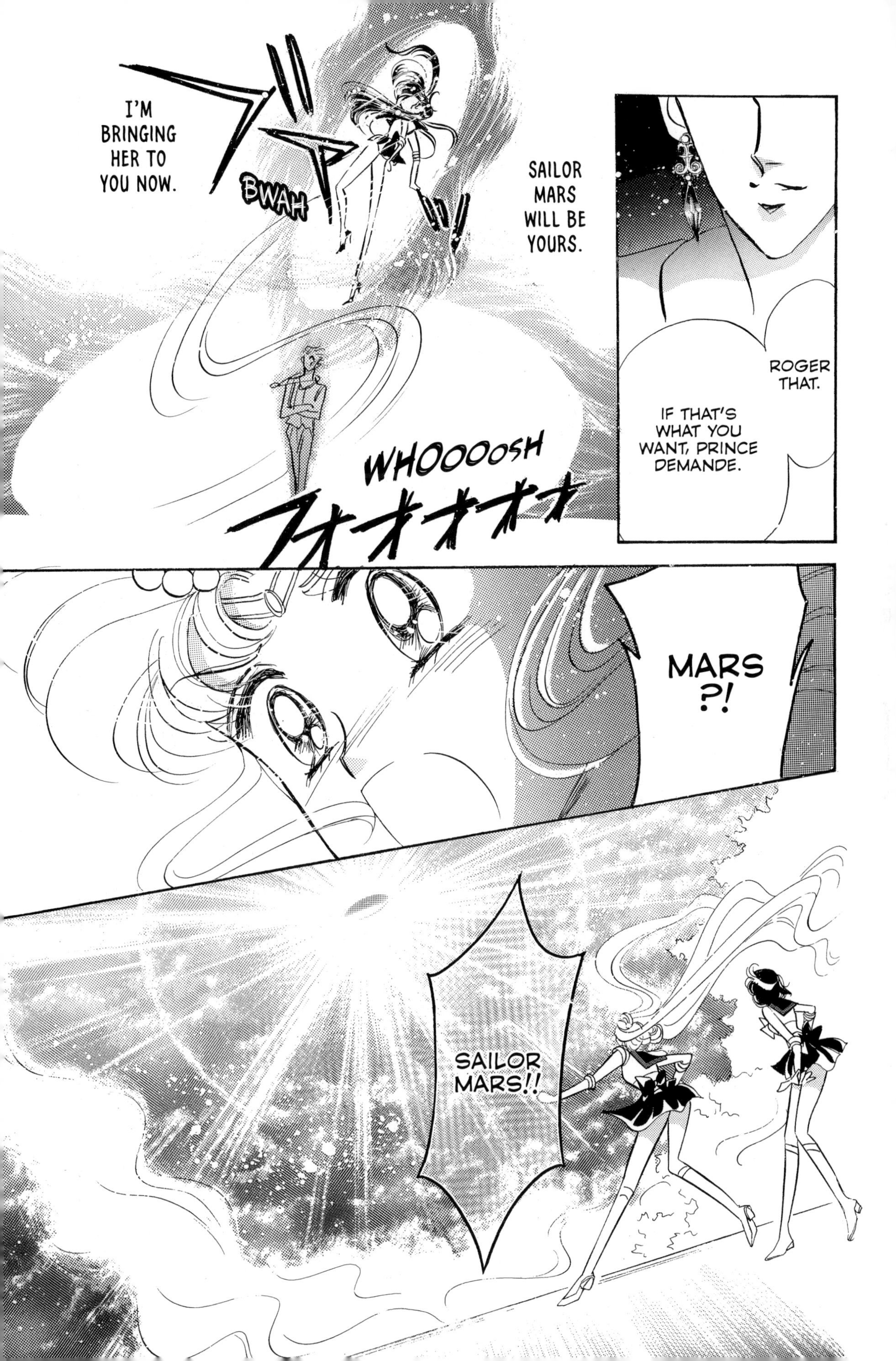
ROGER THAT.
IF THAT'S WHAT YOU WANT, PRINCE DEMANDE.
SAILOR MARS WILL BE YOURS.
I'M BRINGING HER TO YOU NOW.
BWAH
WHOOOOSH
フォオオオオ
MARS ?!
SAILOR MARS!!

Pretty Guardian

Sailor Moon

Act.16 Abduction: Sailor Mercury

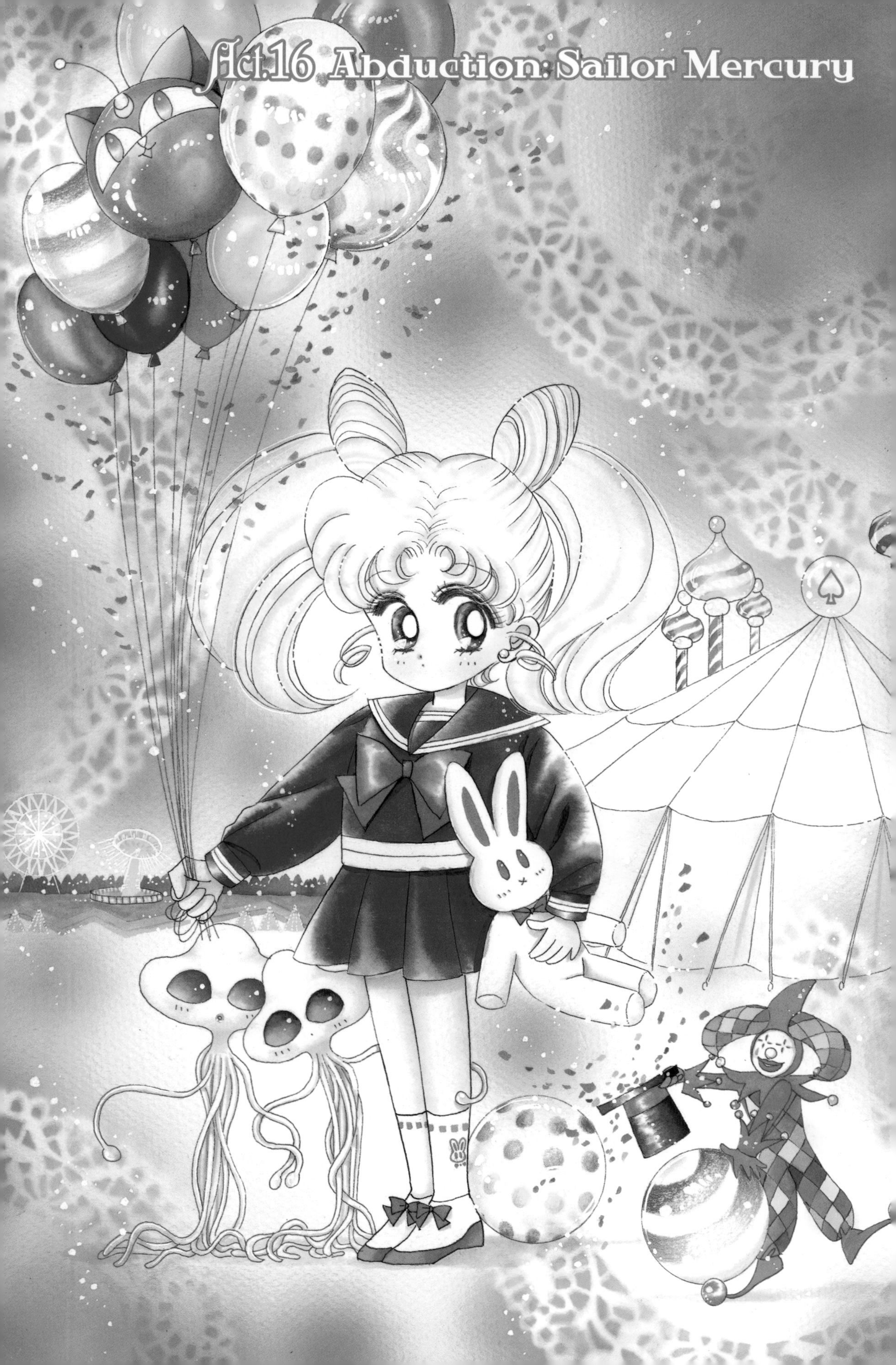

Pretty Guardian

Sailor Moon

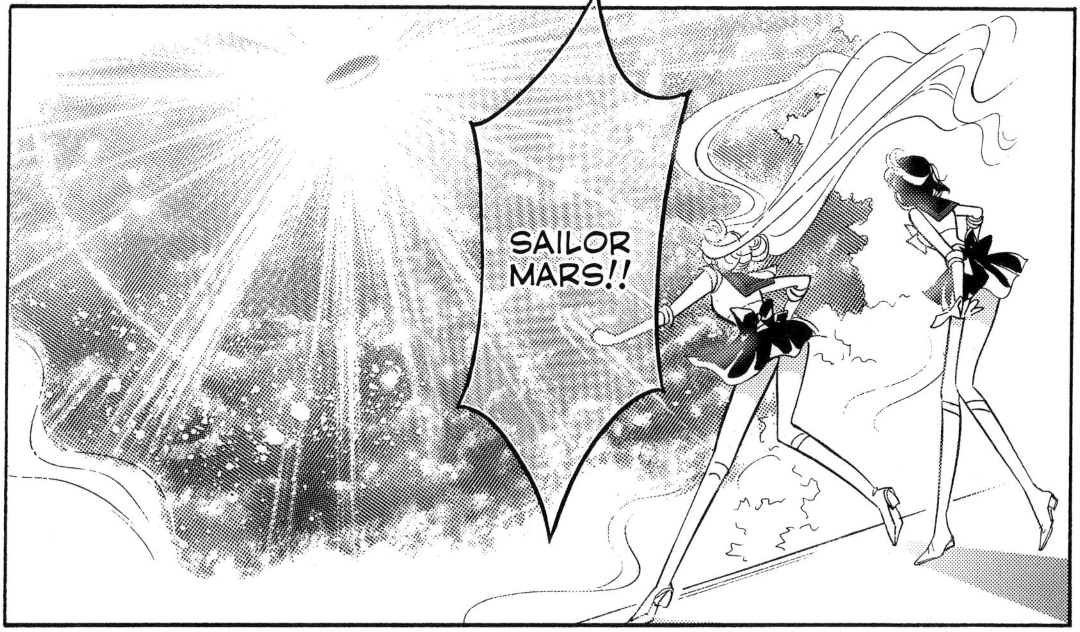
SAILOR MARS!!

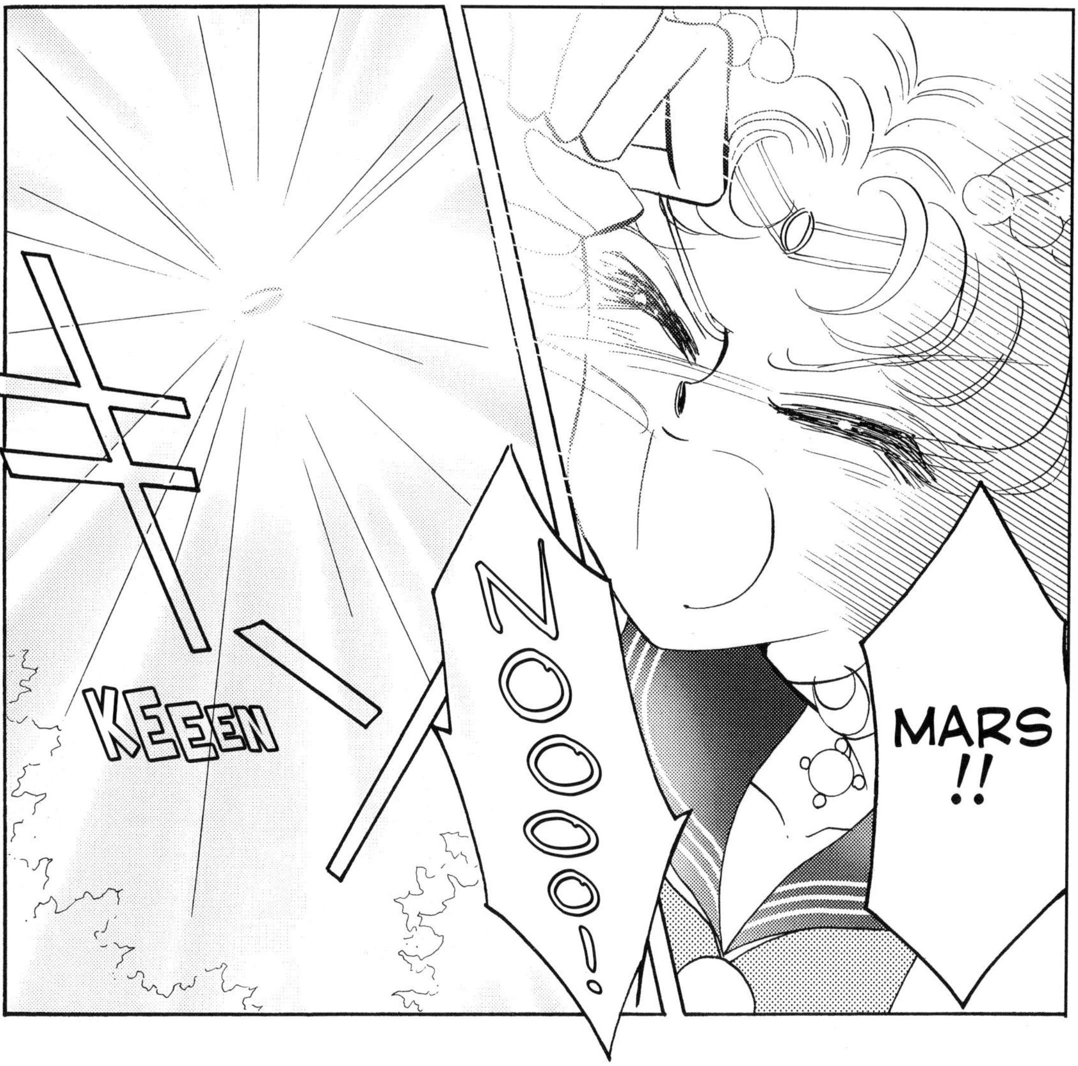
MARS !!
ZOOOO!
KEEEN

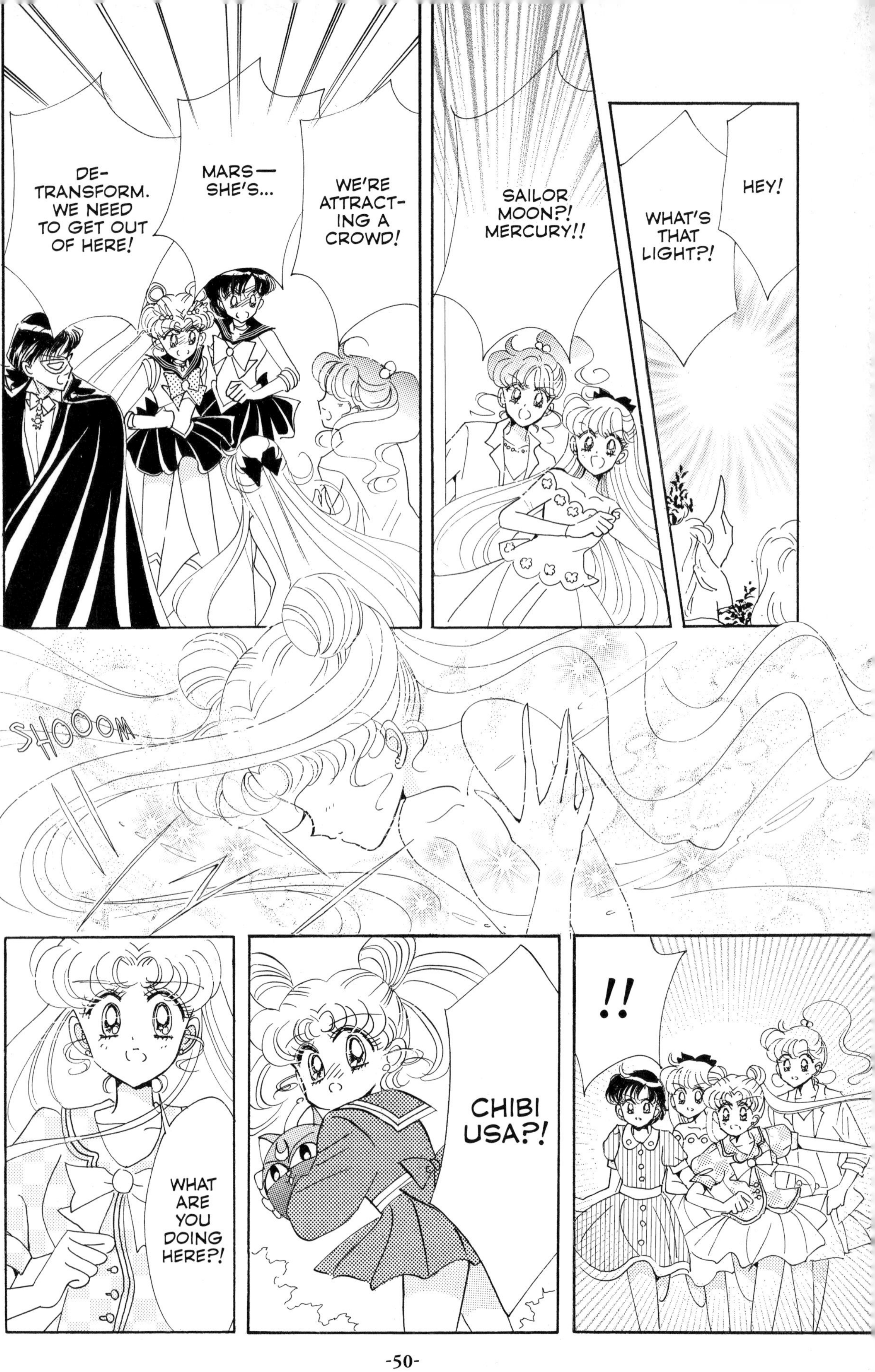
HEY!
WHAT'S THAT LIGHT?!
SAILOR MOON?! MERCURY!!
WE'RE ATTRACTING A CROWD!
MARS—SHE'S...
DE-TRANSFORM. WE NEED TO GET OUT OF HERE!
SHOOOM
!!
CHIBI USA?!
WHAT ARE YOU DOING HERE?!

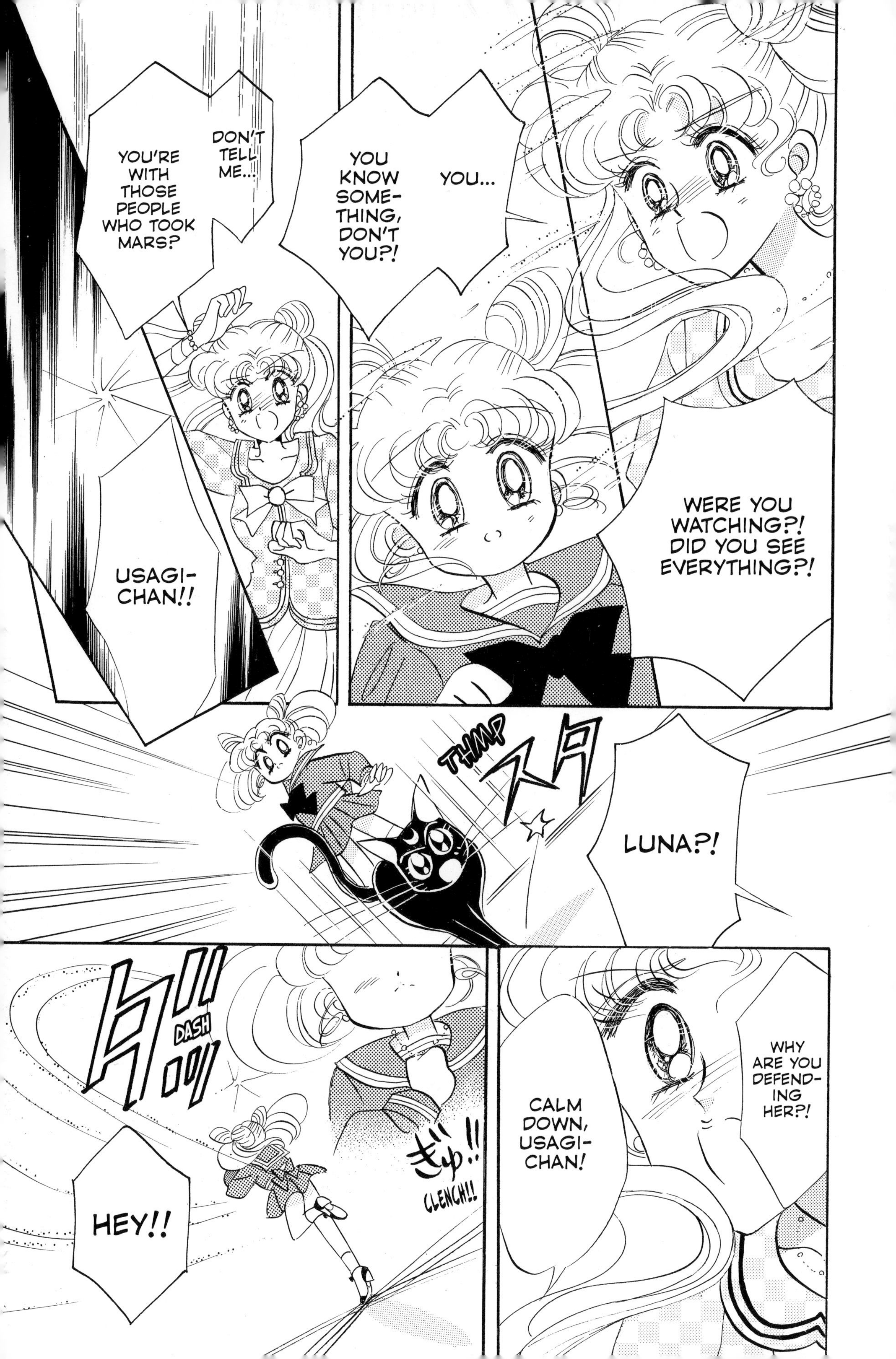
WERE YOU WATCHING?! DID YOU SEE EVERYTHING?!
YOU... YOU KNOW SOMETHING, DON'T YOU?!
DON'T TELL ME... YOU'RE WITH THOSE PEOPLE WHO TOOK MARS?
USAGI-CHAN!!
LUNA?!
スタ
THMP
WHY ARE YOU DEFENDING HER?!
CALM DOWN, USAGI-CHAN!
ぎゅ!!
CLENCH!!
ダッ
DASH
HEY!!

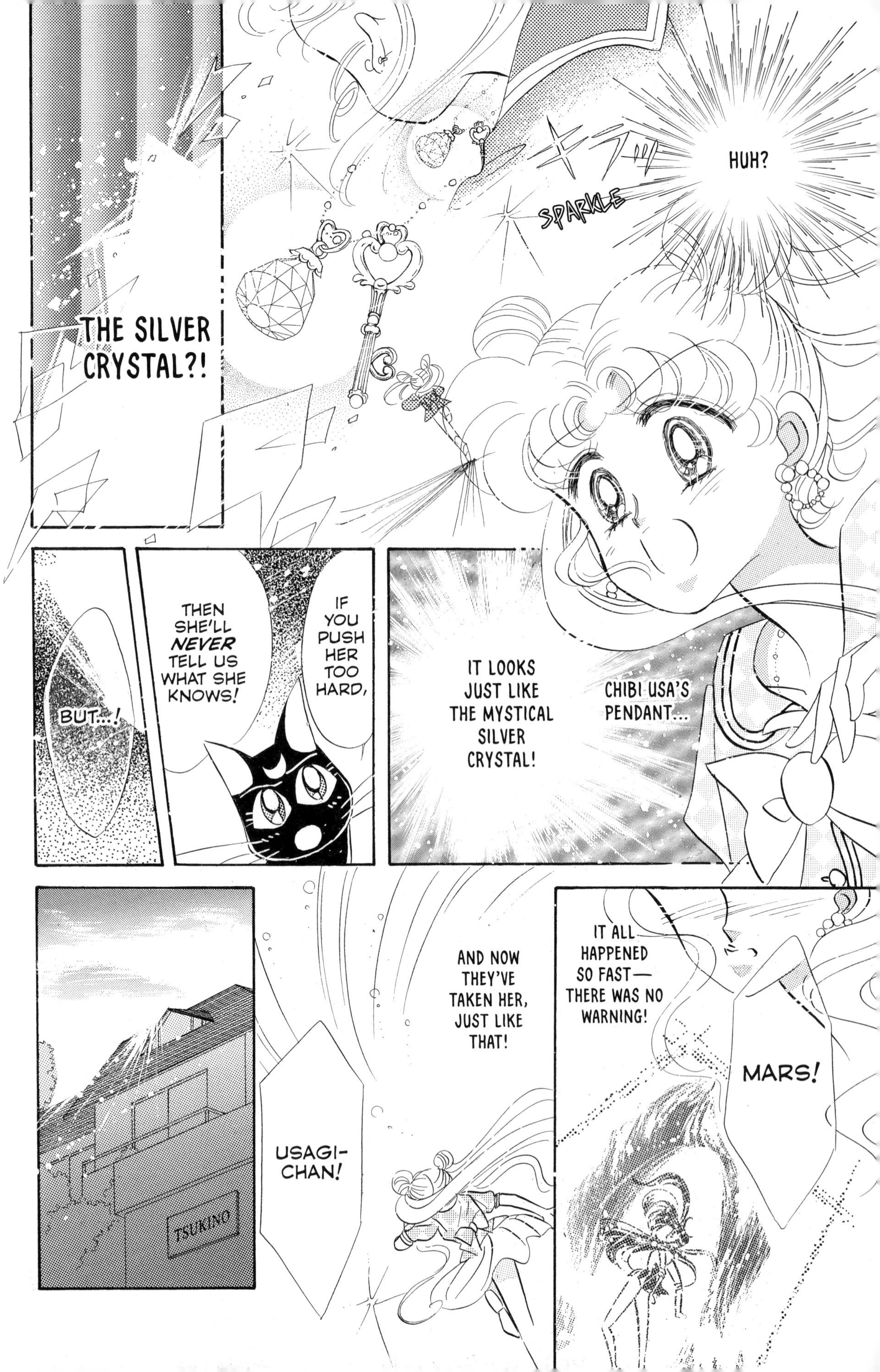

HUH?
SPARKLE
THE SILVER CRYSTAL?!
CHIBI USA'S PENDANT...
IT LOOKS JUST LIKE THE MYSTICAL SILVER CRYSTAL!
IF YOU PUSH HER TOO HARD,
THEN SHE'LL *NEVER* TELL US WHAT SHE KNOWS!
BUT...!
IT ALL HAPPENED SO FAST— THERE WAS NO WARNING!
MARS!
AND NOW THEY'VE TAKEN HER, JUST LIKE THAT!
USAGI-CHAN!
TSUKINO

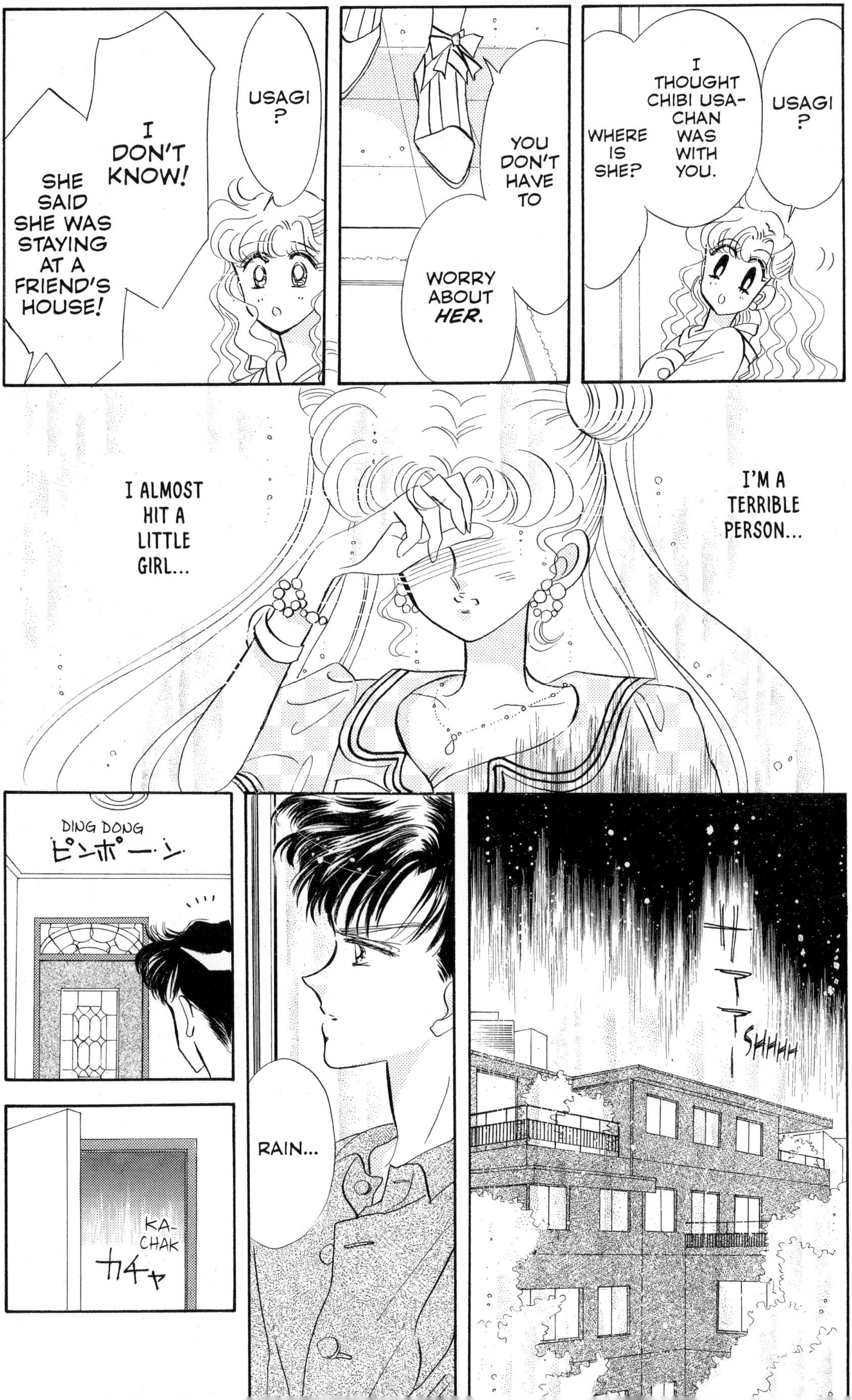
USAGI?
I THOUGHT CHIBI USA-CHAN WAS WITH YOU.
WHERE IS SHE?
YOU DON'T HAVE TO
WORRY ABOUT *HER*.
USAGI?
I DON'T KNOW!
SHE SAID SHE WAS STAYING AT A FRIEND'S HOUSE!
I'M A TERRIBLE PERSON...
I ALMOST HIT A LITTLE GIRL...
SHHHH
RAIN...
DING DONG
ピンポーン
KA-CHAK
カチャ

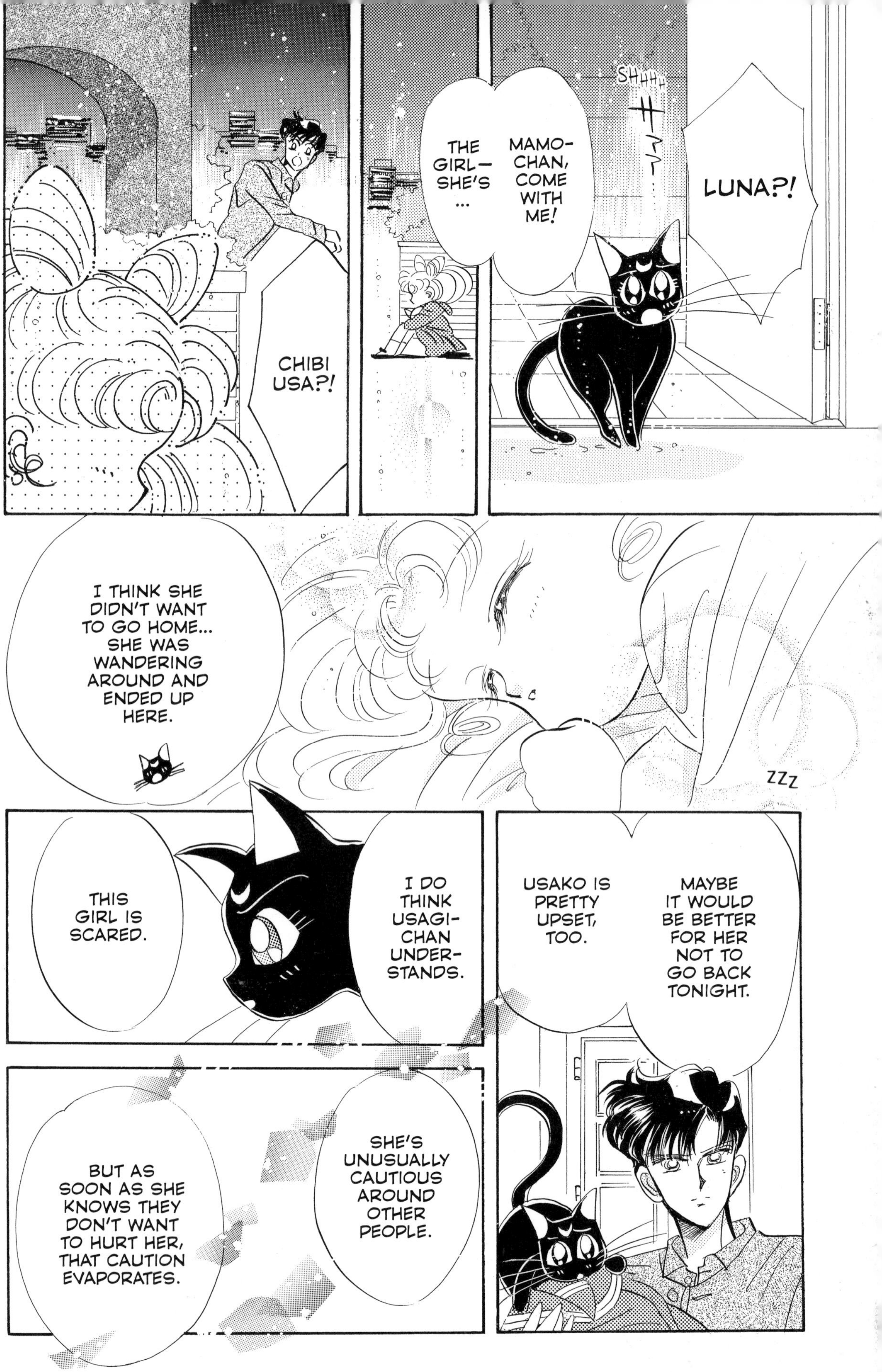
SHHHH
LUNA?!
MAMO-CHAN, COME WITH ME!
THE GIRL—SHE'S ...
CHIBI USA?!
ZZZ
I THINK SHE DIDN'T WANT TO GO HOME... SHE WAS WANDERING AROUND AND ENDED UP HERE.
MAYBE IT WOULD BE BETTER FOR HER NOT TO GO BACK TONIGHT.
USAKO IS PRETTY UPSET, TOO.
I DO THINK USAGI-CHAN UNDERSTANDS.
THIS GIRL IS SCARED.
SHE'S UNUSUALLY CAUTIOUS AROUND OTHER PEOPLE.
BUT AS SOON AS SHE KNOWS THEY DON'T WANT TO HURT HER, THAT CAUTION EVAPORATES.

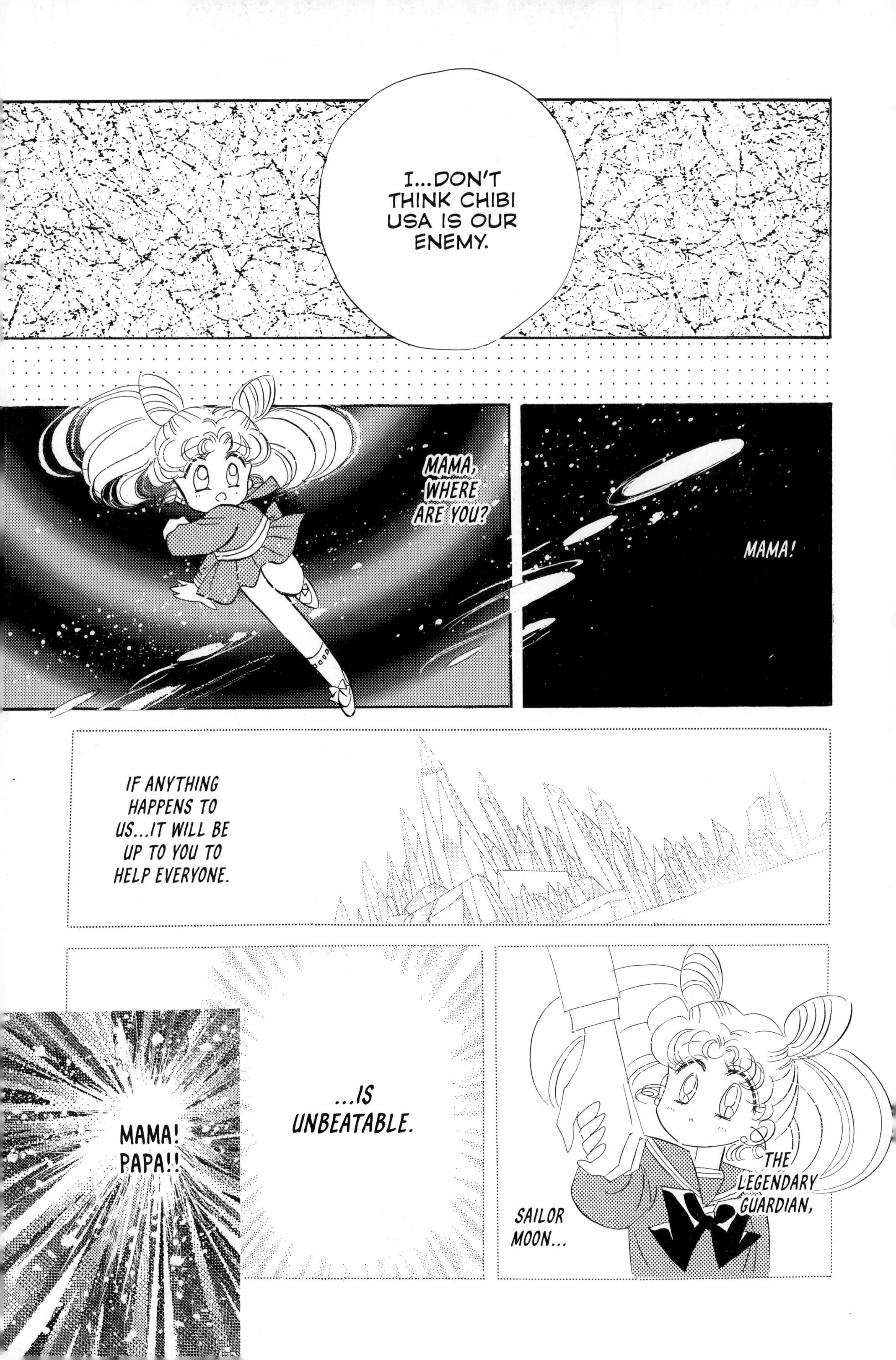
I...DON'T THINK CHIBI USA IS OUR ENEMY.
MAMA!
MAMA, WHERE ARE YOU?
IF ANYTHING HAPPENS TO US...IT WILL BE UP TO YOU TO HELP EVERYONE.
THE LEGENDARY GUARDIAN,
SAILOR MOON...
...IS UNBEATABLE.
MAMA! PAPA!!

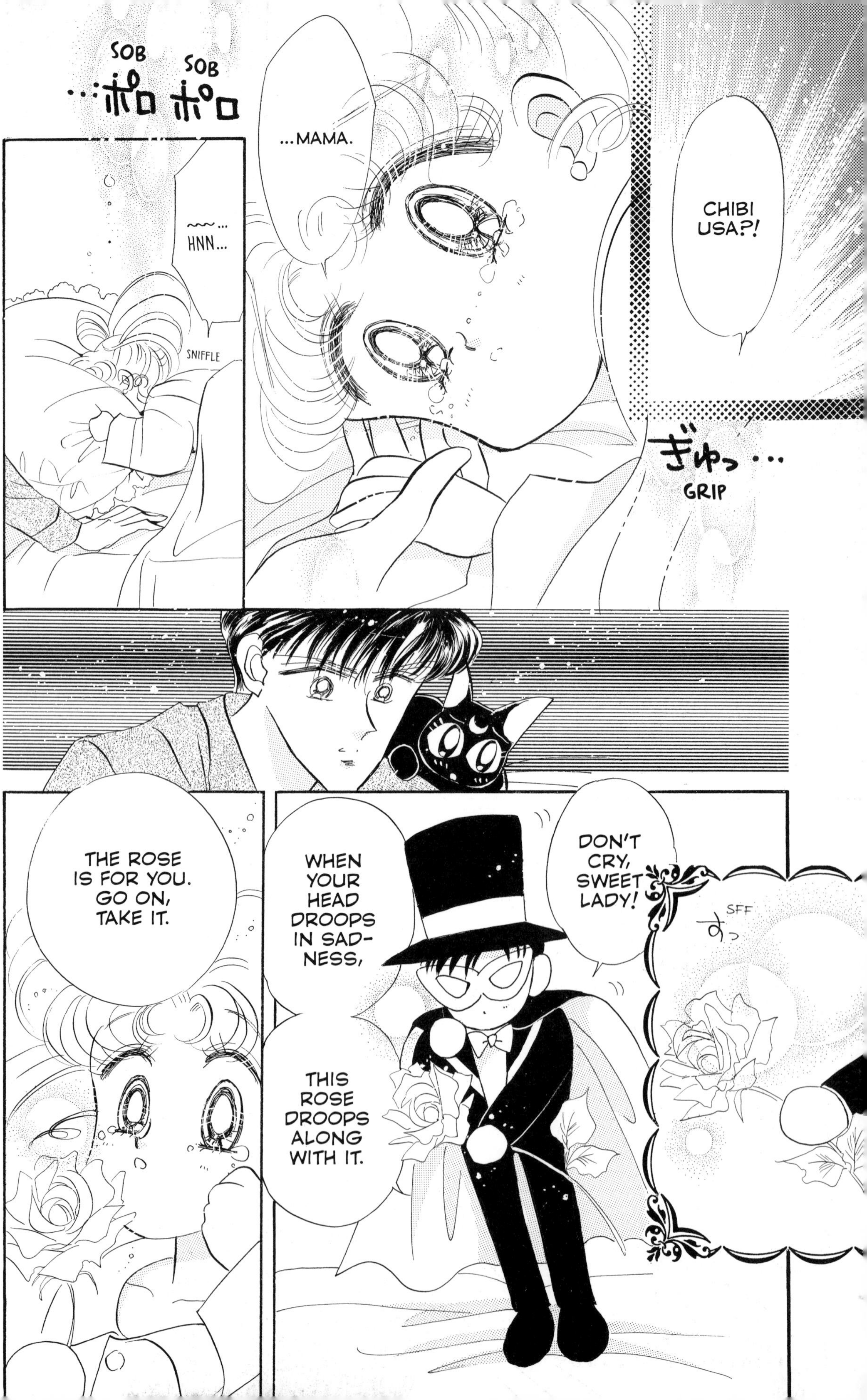

CHIBI USA?!
...MAMA.
ぎゅっ… GRIP
…ポロポロ SOB SOB
~~~... HNN...
SNIFFLE
すっ SFF
DON'T CRY, SWEET LADY!
WHEN YOUR HEAD DROOPS IN SADNESS,
THIS ROSE DROOPS ALONG WITH IT.
THE ROSE IS FOR YOU. GO ON, TAKE IT.
~~~

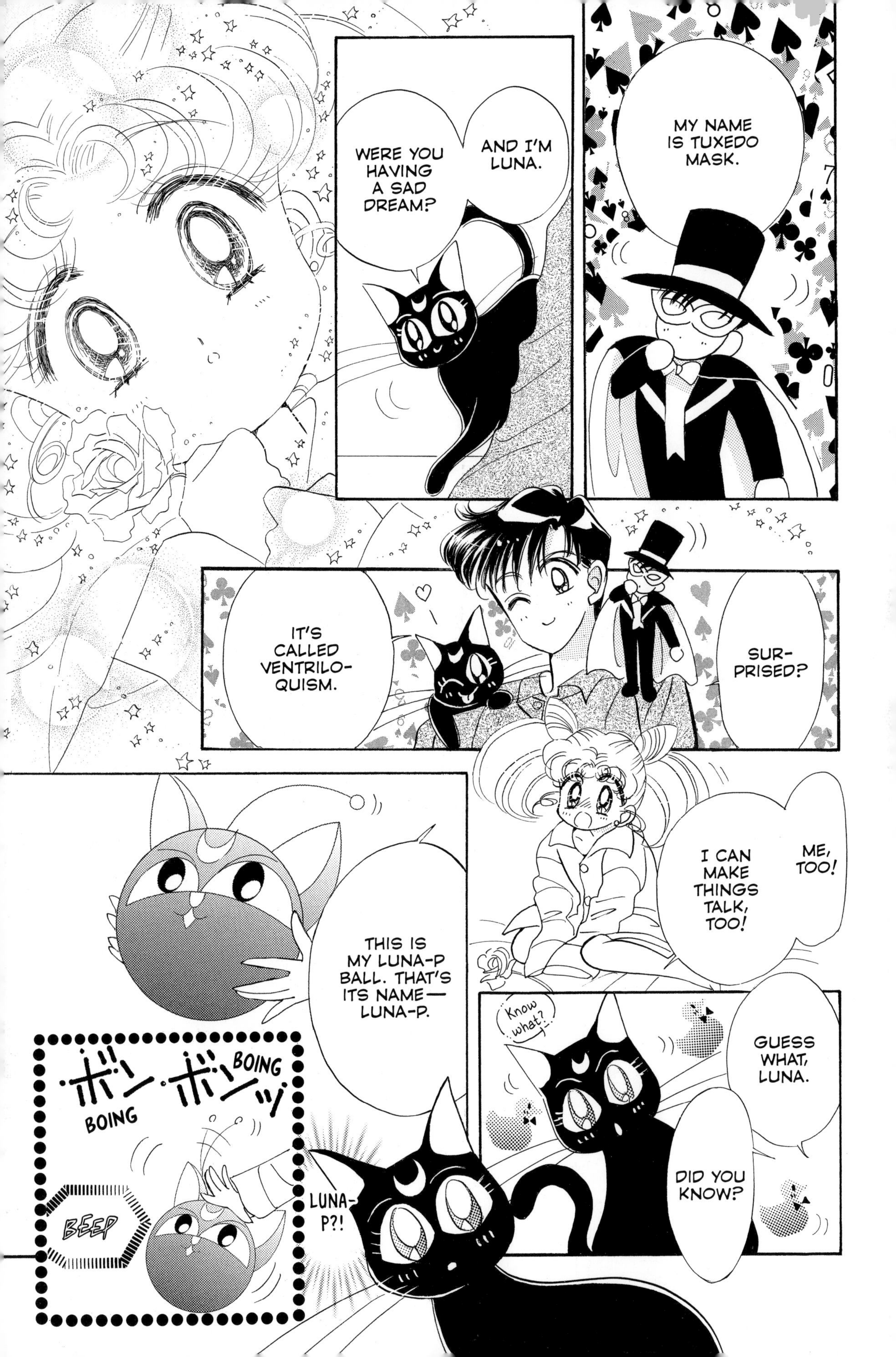
MY NAME IS TUXEDO MASK.
AND I'M LUNA.
WERE YOU HAVING A SAD DREAM?
SUR-PRISED?
IT'S CALLED VENTRILO-QUISM.
ME, TOO!
I CAN MAKE THINGS TALK, TOO!
THIS IS MY LUNA-P BALL. THAT'S ITS NAME—LUNA-P.
GUESS WHAT, LUNA.
DID YOU KNOW?
Know what?
LUNA-P?!
BOING
BOING
BEEP

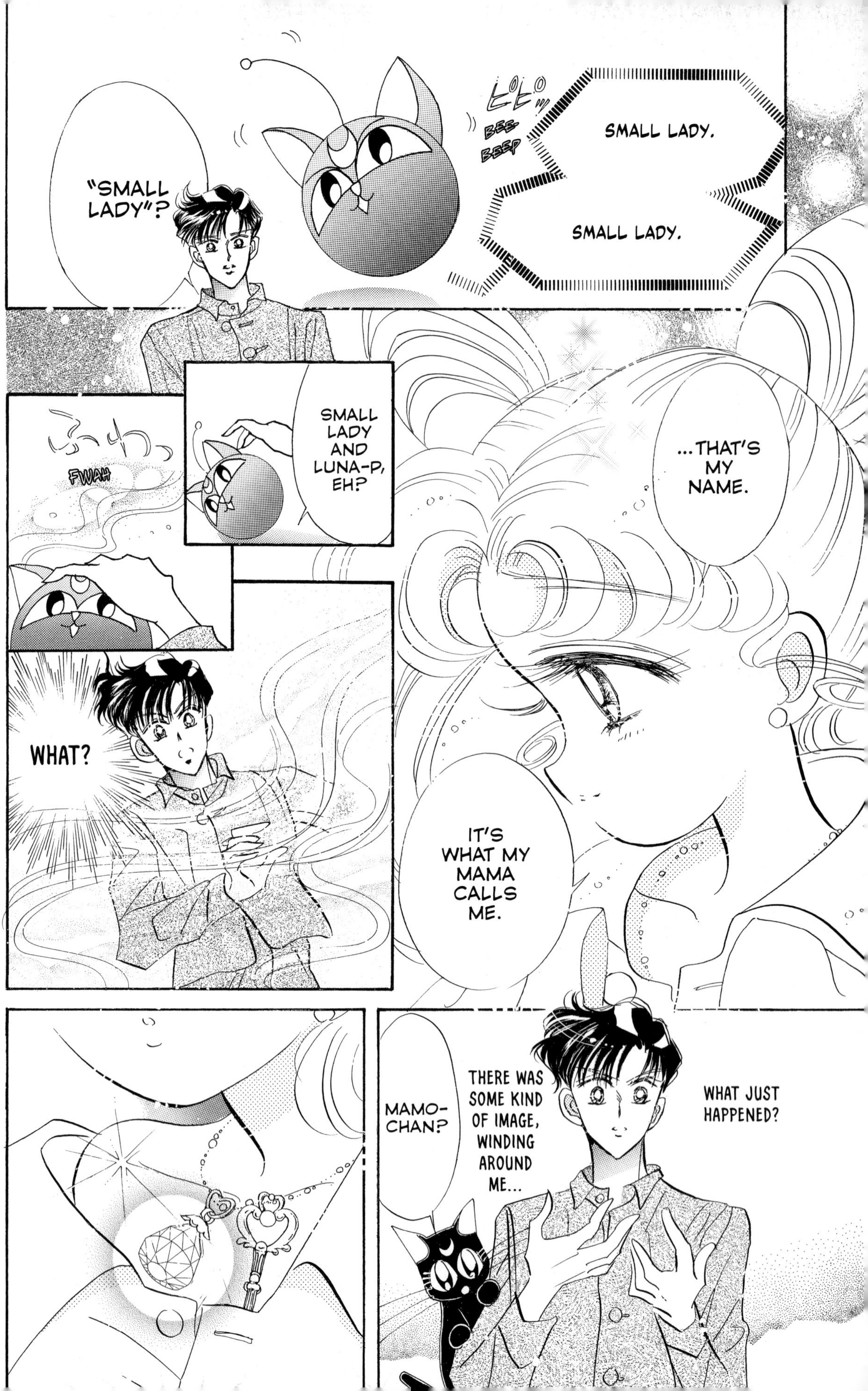
ピピッ
BEE-BEEP
SMALL LADY.
SMALL LADY.
"SMALL LADY"?
...THAT'S MY NAME.
IT'S WHAT MY MAMA CALLS ME.
SMALL LADY AND LUNA-P, EH?
ふわっ
FWAH
WHAT?
WHAT JUST HAPPENED?
THERE WAS SOME KIND OF IMAGE, WINDING AROUND ME...
MAMO-CHAN?

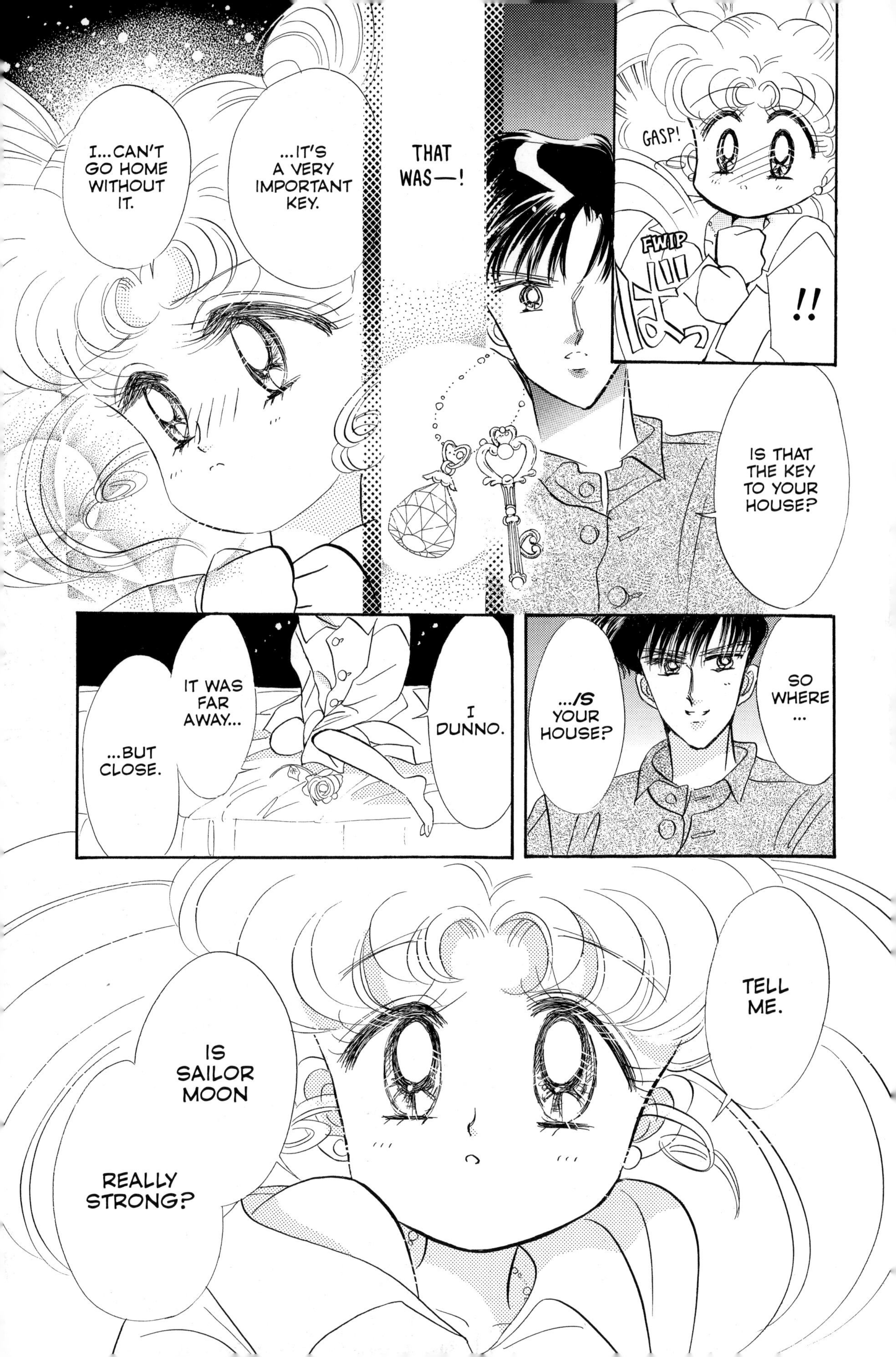
GASP!
FWIP
!!
IS THAT THE KEY TO YOUR HOUSE?
THAT WAS—!
...IT'S A VERY IMPORTANT KEY.
I...CAN'T GO HOME WITHOUT IT.
SO WHERE ...
...*IS* YOUR HOUSE?
I DUNNO.
IT WAS FAR AWAY...
...BUT CLOSE.
TELL ME.
IS SAILOR MOON REALLY STRONG?

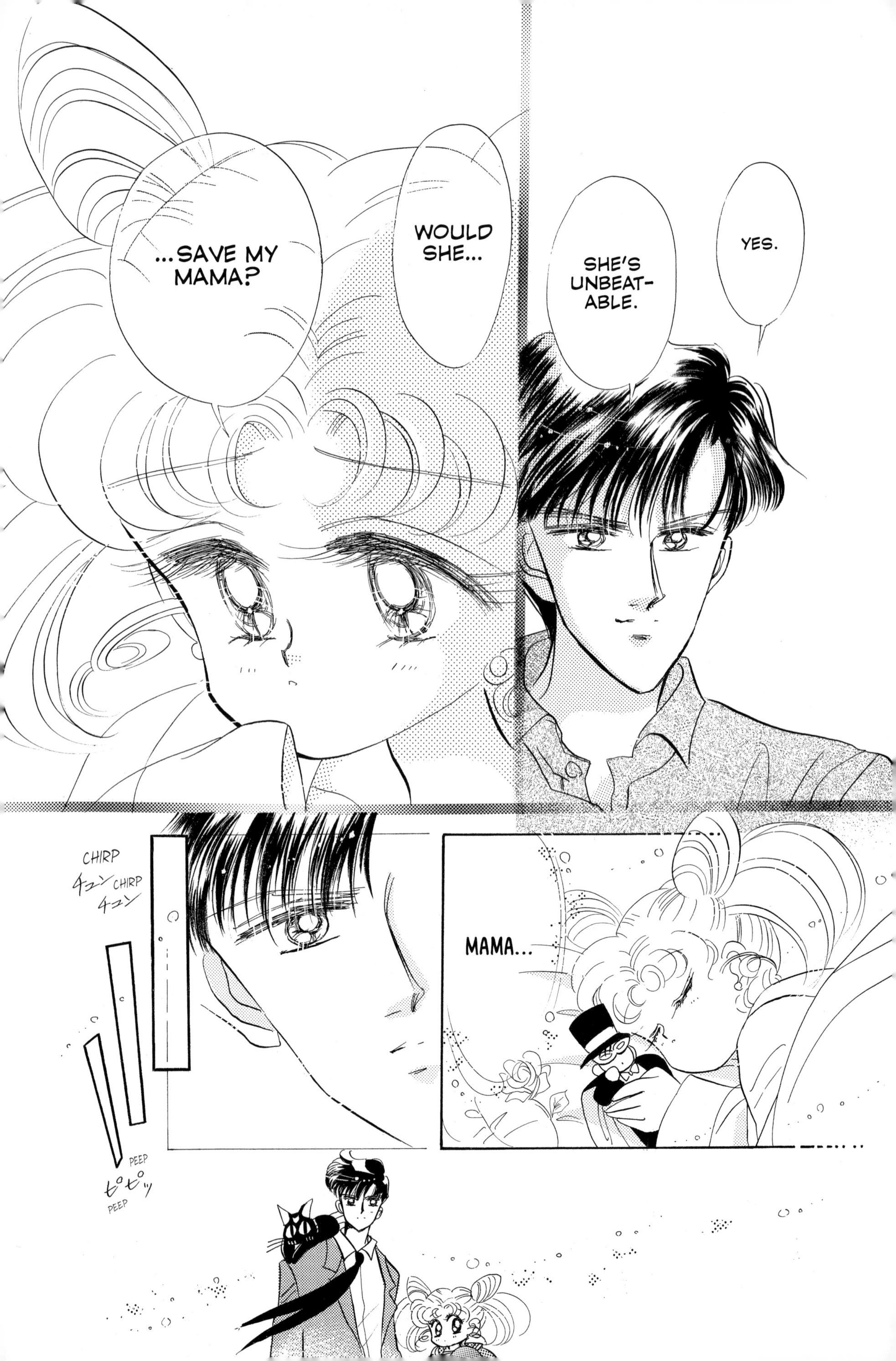
YES.
SHE'S UNBEATABLE.
WOULD SHE...
...SAVE MY MAMA?
MAMA...
CHIRP
チュン
CHIRP
チュン
PEEP
ピピッ
PEEP

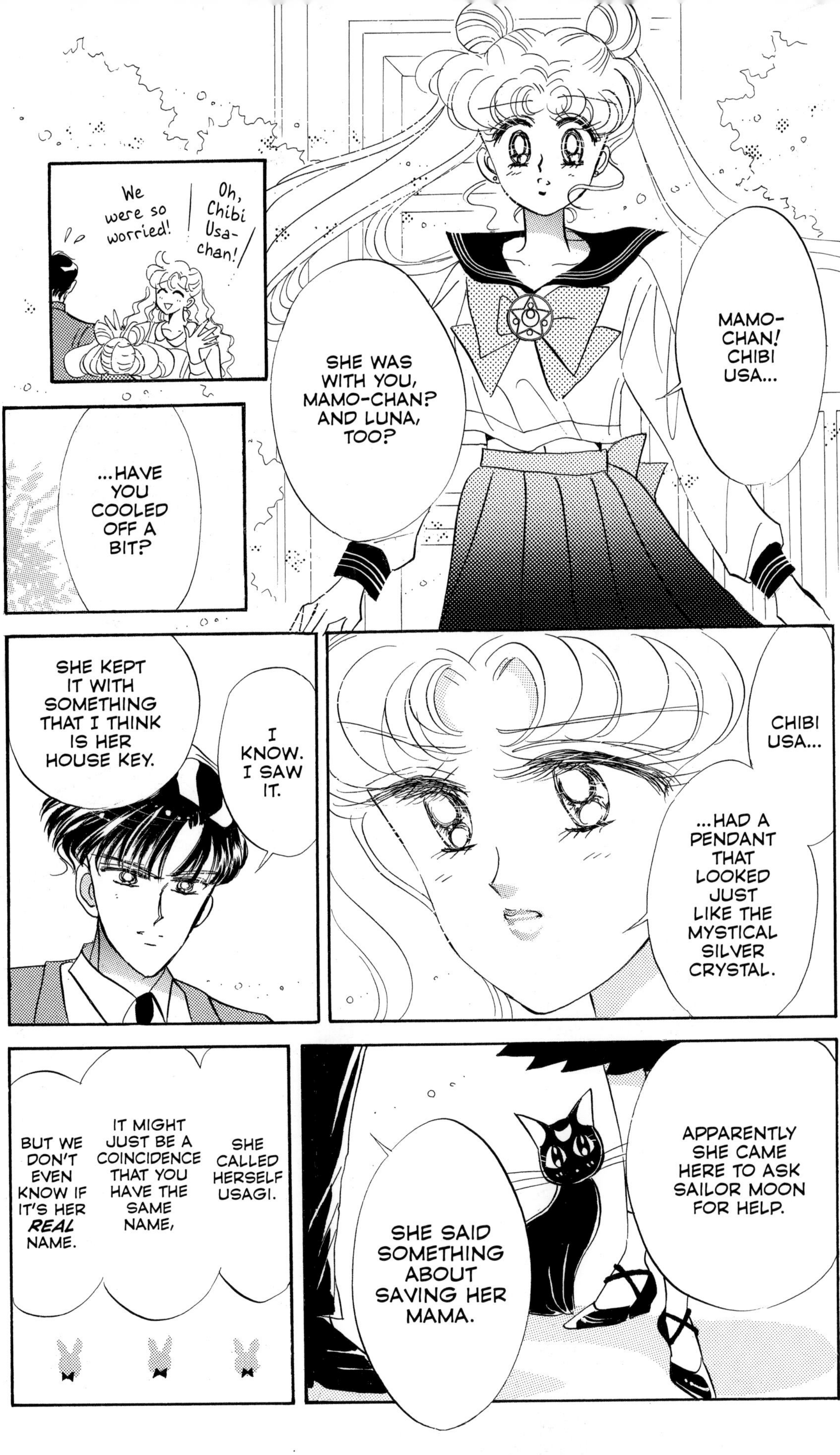
MAMO-CHAN! CHIBI USA...
SHE WAS WITH YOU, MAMO-CHAN? AND LUNA, TOO?
Oh, Chibi Usa-chan!
We were so worried!
...HAVE YOU COOLED OFF A BIT?
CHIBI USA...
...HAD A PENDANT THAT LOOKED JUST LIKE THE MYSTICAL SILVER CRYSTAL.
I KNOW. I SAW IT.
SHE KEPT IT WITH SOMETHING THAT I THINK IS HER HOUSE KEY.
APPARENTLY SHE CAME HERE TO ASK SAILOR MOON FOR HELP.
SHE SAID SOMETHING ABOUT SAVING HER MAMA.
SHE CALLED HERSELF USAGI.
IT MIGHT JUST BE A COINCIDENCE THAT YOU HAVE THE SAME NAME,
BUT WE DON'T EVEN KNOW IF IT'S HER *REAL* NAME.

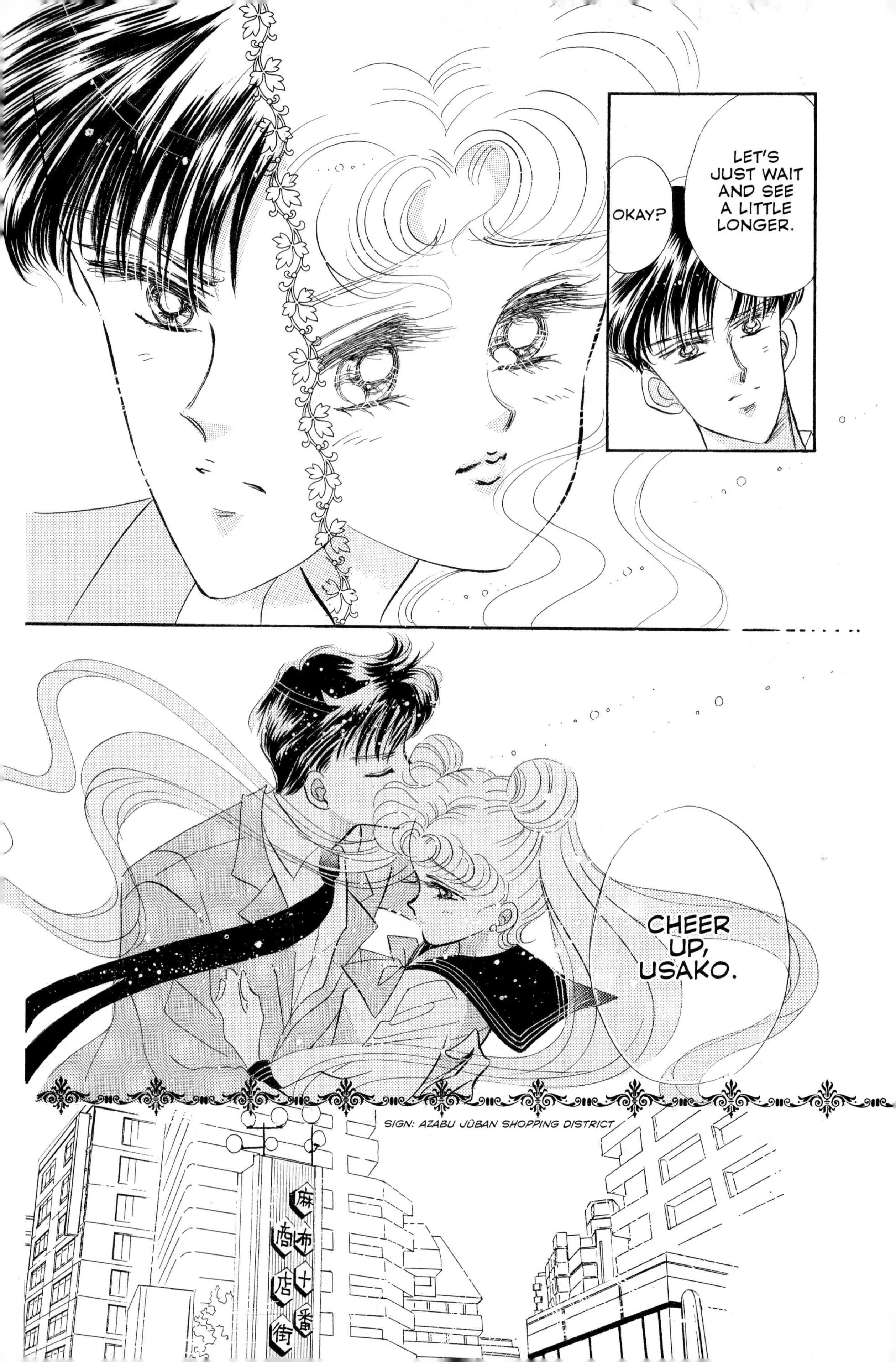
LET'S JUST WAIT AND SEE A LITTLE LONGER.
OKAY?
CHEER UP, USAKO.
SIGN: AZABU JŪBAN SHOPPING DISTRICT
麻布十番商店街

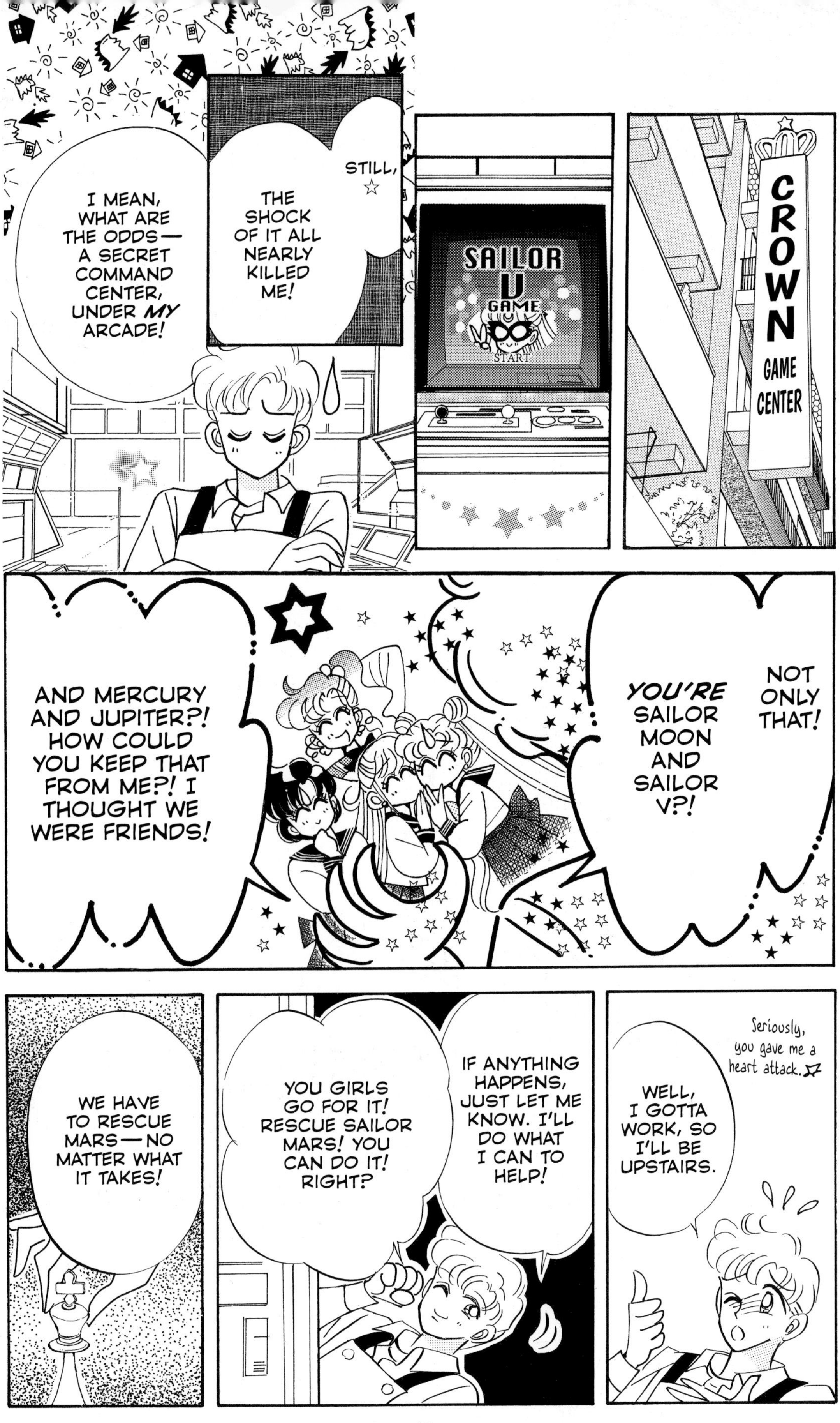
CROWN
GAME CENTER
SAILOR V GAME
START
STILL,
THE SHOCK OF IT ALL NEARLY KILLED ME!
I MEAN, WHAT ARE THE ODDS— A SECRET COMMAND CENTER, UNDER *MY* ARCADE!
NOT ONLY THAT!
YOU'RE SAILOR MOON AND SAILOR V?!
AND MERCURY AND JUPITER?! HOW COULD YOU KEEP THAT FROM ME?! I THOUGHT WE WERE FRIENDS!
Seriously, you gave me a heart attack.
WELL, I GOTTA WORK, SO I'LL BE UPSTAIRS.
IF ANYTHING HAPPENS, JUST LET ME KNOW. I'LL DO WHAT I CAN TO HELP!
YOU GIRLS GO FOR IT! RESCUE SAILOR MARS! YOU CAN DO IT! RIGHT?
WE HAVE TO RESCUE MARS—NO MATTER WHAT IT TAKES!

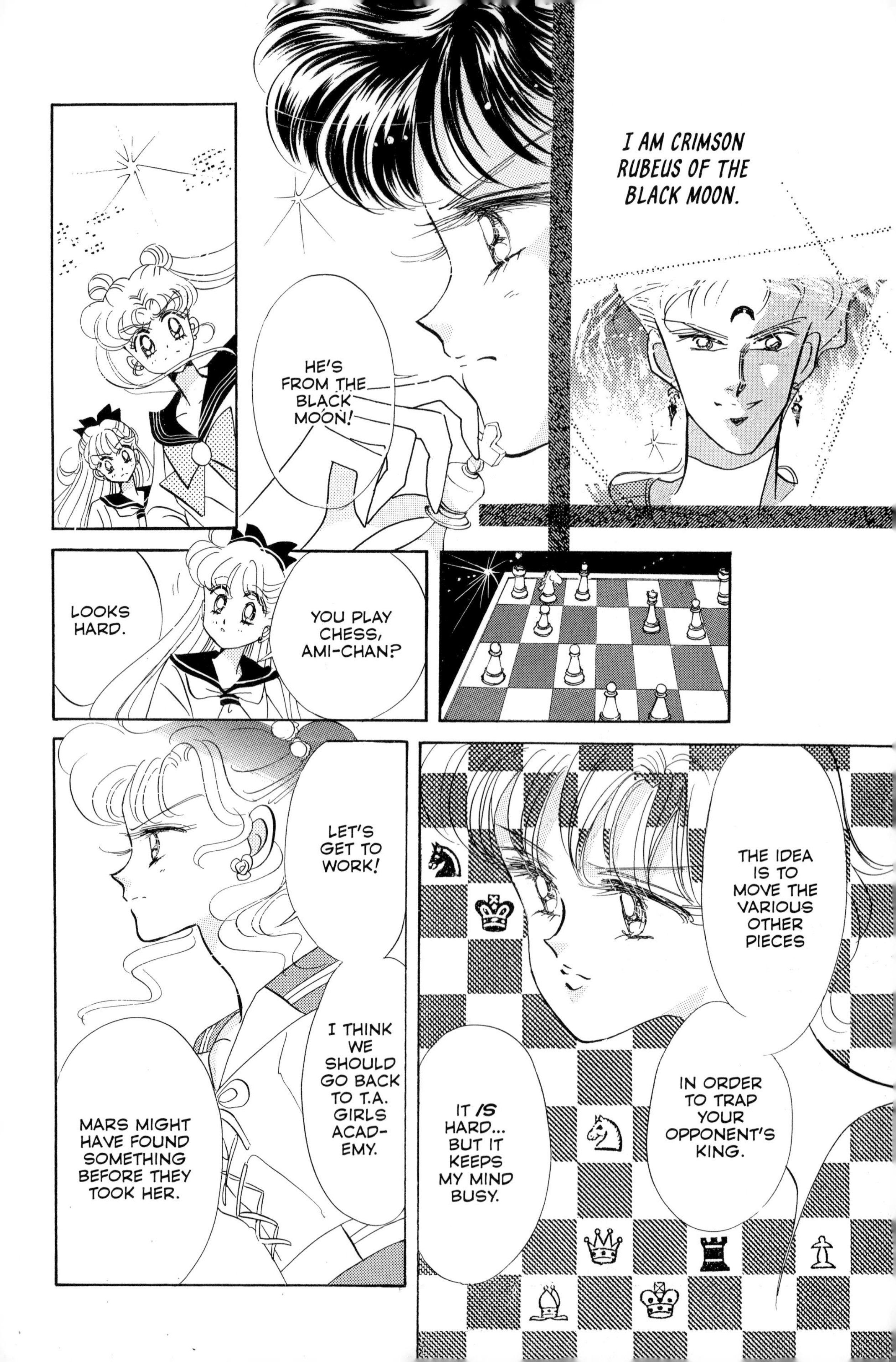
I AM CRIMSON RUBEUS OF THE BLACK MOON.
HE'S FROM THE BLACK MOON!
YOU PLAY CHESS, AMI-CHAN?
LOOKS HARD.
THE IDEA IS TO MOVE THE VARIOUS OTHER PIECES
IN ORDER TO TRAP YOUR OPPONENT'S KING.
IT *IS* HARD... BUT IT KEEPS MY MIND BUSY.
LET'S GET TO WORK!
I THINK WE SHOULD GO BACK TO T.A. GIRLS ACAD-EMY.
MARS MIGHT HAVE FOUND SOMETHING BEFORE THEY TOOK HER.

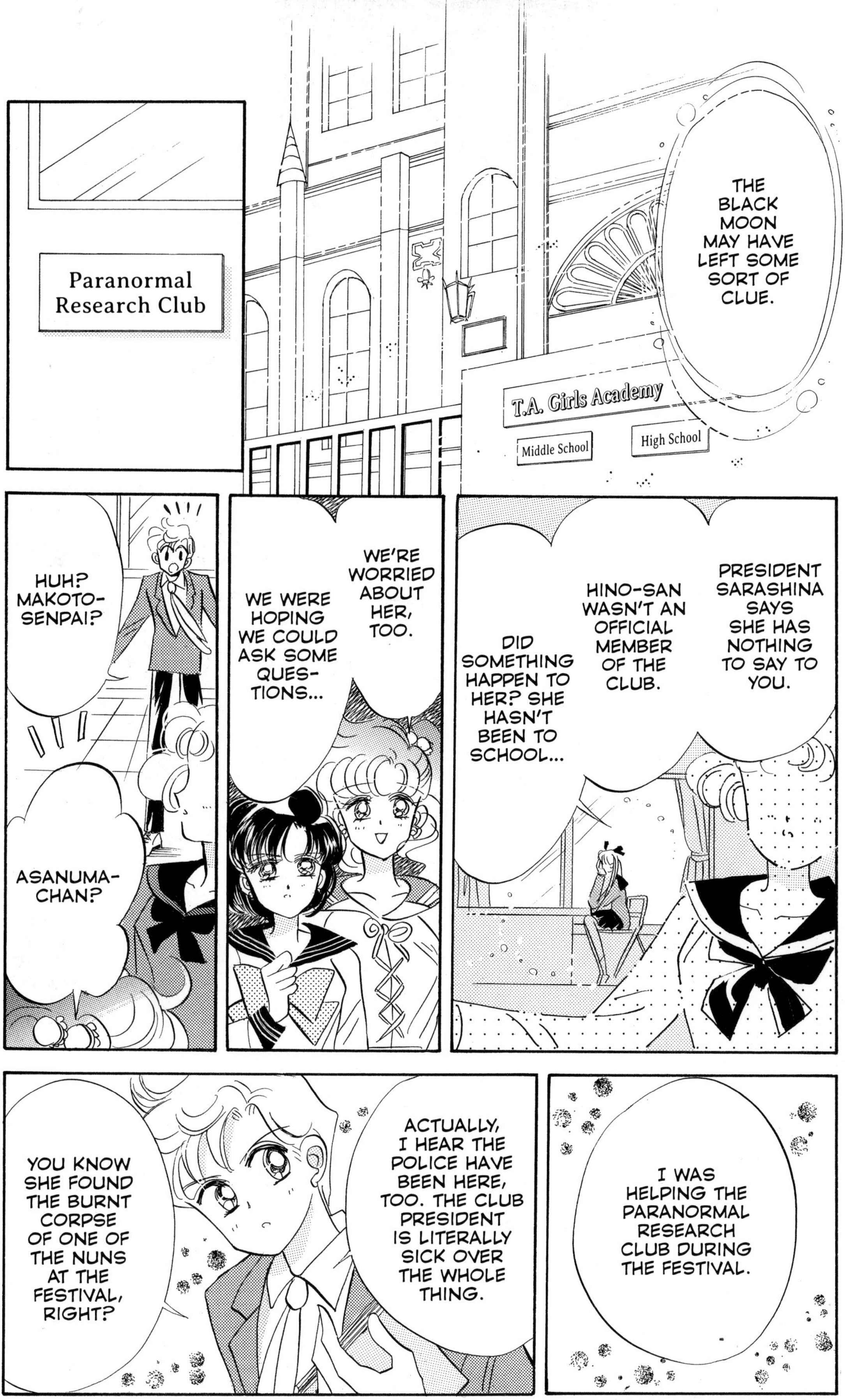
THE BLACK MOON MAY HAVE LEFT SOME SORT OF CLUE.
T.A. Girls Academy
High School
Middle School
Paranormal Research Club
PRESIDENT SARASHINA SAYS SHE HAS NOTHING TO SAY TO YOU.
HINO-SAN WASN'T AN OFFICIAL MEMBER OF THE CLUB.
DID SOMETHING HAPPEN TO HER? SHE HASN'T BEEN TO SCHOOL...
WE'RE WORRIED ABOUT HER, TOO.
WE WERE HOPING WE COULD ASK SOME QUES-TIONS...
HUH? MAKOTO-SENPAI?
ASANUMA-CHAN?
I WAS HELPING THE PARANORMAL RESEARCH CLUB DURING THE FESTIVAL.
ACTUALLY, I HEAR THE POLICE HAVE BEEN HERE, TOO. THE CLUB PRESIDENT IS LITERALLY SICK OVER THE WHOLE THING.
YOU KNOW SHE FOUND THE BURNT CORPSE OF ONE OF THE NUNS AT THE FESTIVAL, RIGHT?

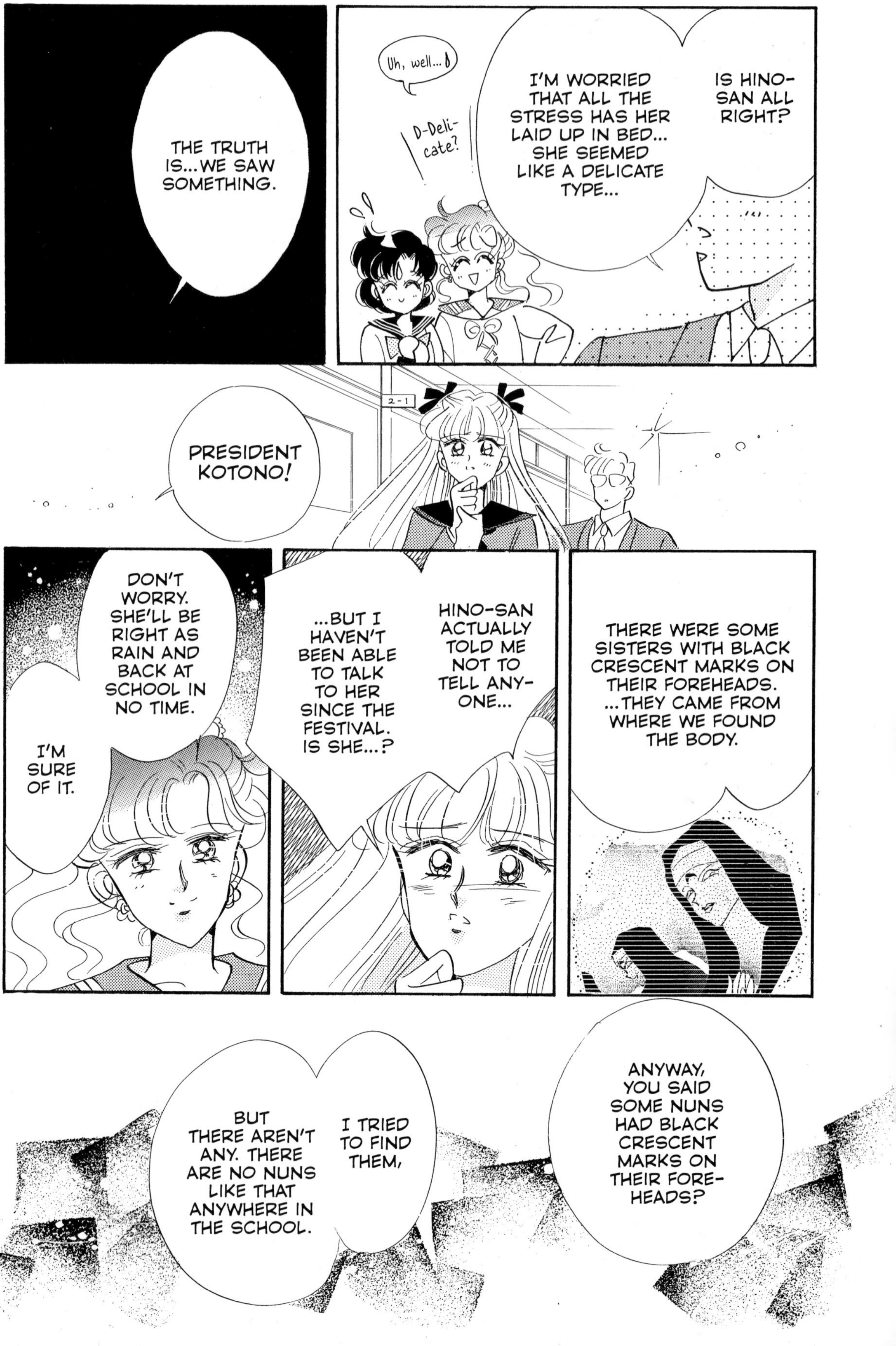
IS HINO-SAN ALL RIGHT?
I'M WORRIED THAT ALL THE STRESS HAS HER LAID UP IN BED... SHE SEEMED LIKE A DELICATE TYPE...
D-Deli-cate?
Uh, well...
THE TRUTH IS...WE SAW SOMETHING.
PRESIDENT KOTONO!
THERE WERE SOME SISTERS WITH BLACK CRESCENT MARKS ON THEIR FOREHEADS. ...THEY CAME FROM WHERE WE FOUND THE BODY.
HINO-SAN ACTUALLY TOLD ME NOT TO TELL ANY-ONE...
...BUT I HAVEN'T BEEN ABLE TO TALK TO HER SINCE THE FESTIVAL. IS SHE...?
DON'T WORRY. SHE'LL BE RIGHT AS RAIN AND BACK AT SCHOOL IN NO TIME.
I'M SURE OF IT.
ANYWAY, YOU SAID SOME NUNS HAD BLACK CRESCENT MARKS ON THEIR FORE-HEADS?
I TRIED TO FIND THEM,
BUT THERE AREN'T ANY. THERE ARE NO NUNS LIKE THAT ANYWHERE IN THE SCHOOL.

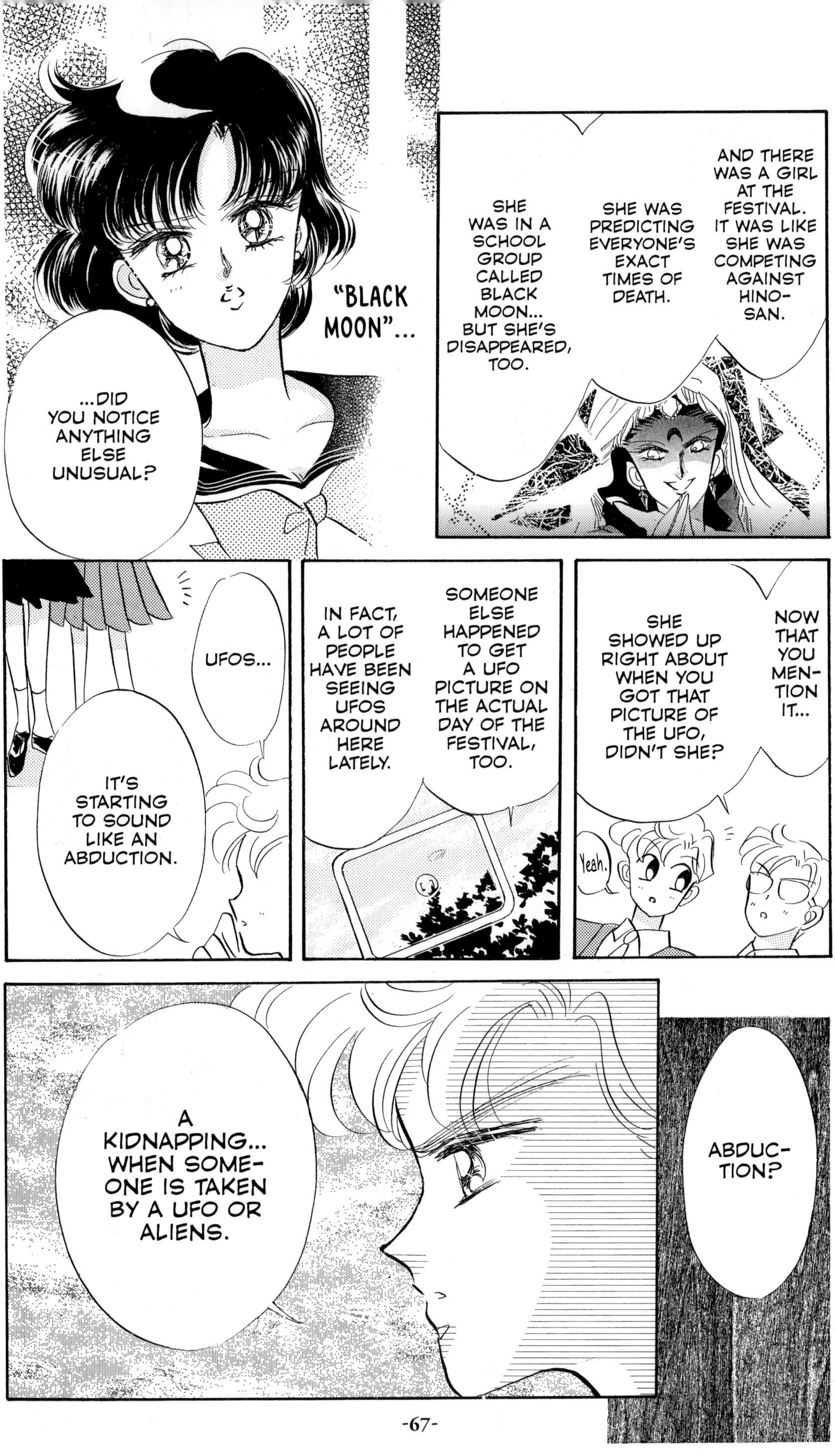
AND THERE WAS A GIRL AT THE FESTIVAL. IT WAS LIKE SHE WAS COMPETING AGAINST HINO-SAN.
SHE WAS PREDICTING EVERYONE'S EXACT TIMES OF DEATH.
SHE WAS IN A SCHOOL GROUP CALLED BLACK MOON... BUT SHE'S DISAPPEARED, TOO.
"BLACK MOON"...
...DID YOU NOTICE ANYTHING ELSE UNUSUAL?
NOW THAT YOU MEN-TION IT...
SHE SHOWED UP RIGHT ABOUT WHEN YOU GOT THAT PICTURE OF THE UFO, DIDN'T SHE?
Yeah.
SOMEONE ELSE HAPPENED TO GET A UFO PICTURE ON THE ACTUAL DAY OF THE FESTIVAL, TOO.
IN FACT, A LOT OF PEOPLE HAVE BEEN SEEING UFOS AROUND HERE LATELY.
UFOS...
IT'S STARTING TO SOUND LIKE AN ABDUCTION.
ABDUC-TION?
A KIDNAPPING... WHEN SOME-ONE IS TAKEN BY A UFO OR ALIENS.

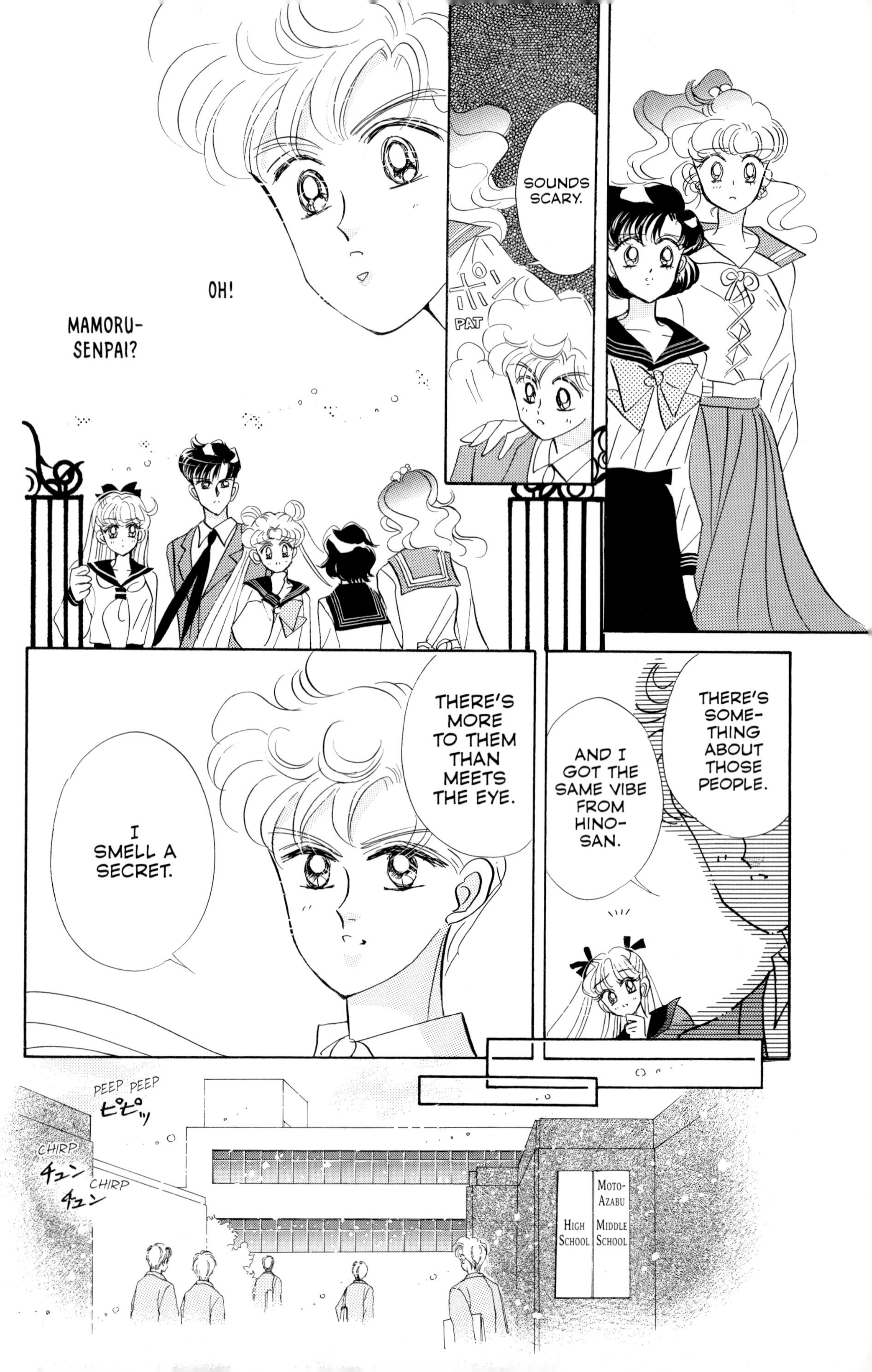
SOUNDS SCARY.
ポン
PAT
OH!
MAMORU-SENPAI?
THERE'S SOMETHING ABOUT THOSE PEOPLE.
AND I GOT THE SAME VIBE FROM HINO-SAN.
THERE'S MORE TO THEM THAN MEETS THE EYE.
I SMELL A SECRET.
PEEP PEEP
ピピッ
CHIRP
チュン
CHIRP
チュン
MOTO-AZABU MIDDLE SCHOOL
HIGH SCHOOL

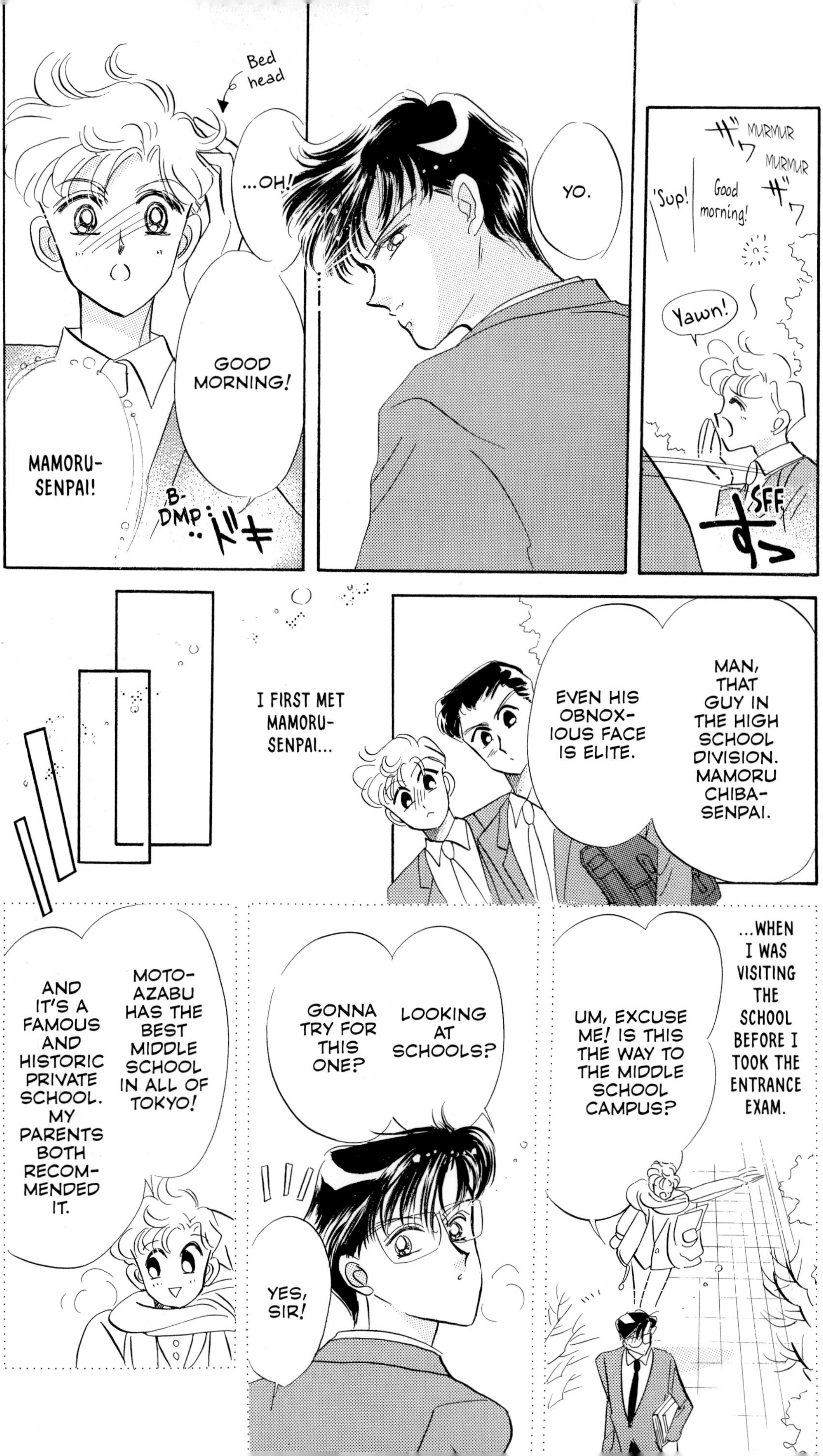
MURMUR
MURMUR
Good morning!
'Sup!
Yawn!
SFF
YO.
Bed head
...OH!
GOOD MORNING!
MAMORU-SENPAI!
B-DMP
MAN, THAT GUY IN THE HIGH SCHOOL DIVISION. MAMORU CHIBA-SENPAI.
EVEN HIS OBNOX-IOUS FACE IS ELITE.
I FIRST MET MAMORU-SENPAI...
...WHEN I WAS VISITING THE SCHOOL BEFORE I TOOK THE ENTRANCE EXAM.
UM, EXCUSE ME! IS THIS THE WAY TO THE MIDDLE SCHOOL CAMPUS?
LOOKING AT SCHOOLS?
GONNA TRY FOR THIS ONE?
YES, SIR!
MOTO-AZABU HAS THE BEST MIDDLE SCHOOL IN ALL OF TOKYO!
AND IT'S A FAMOUS AND HISTORIC PRIVATE SCHOOL. MY PARENTS BOTH RECOM-MENDED IT.

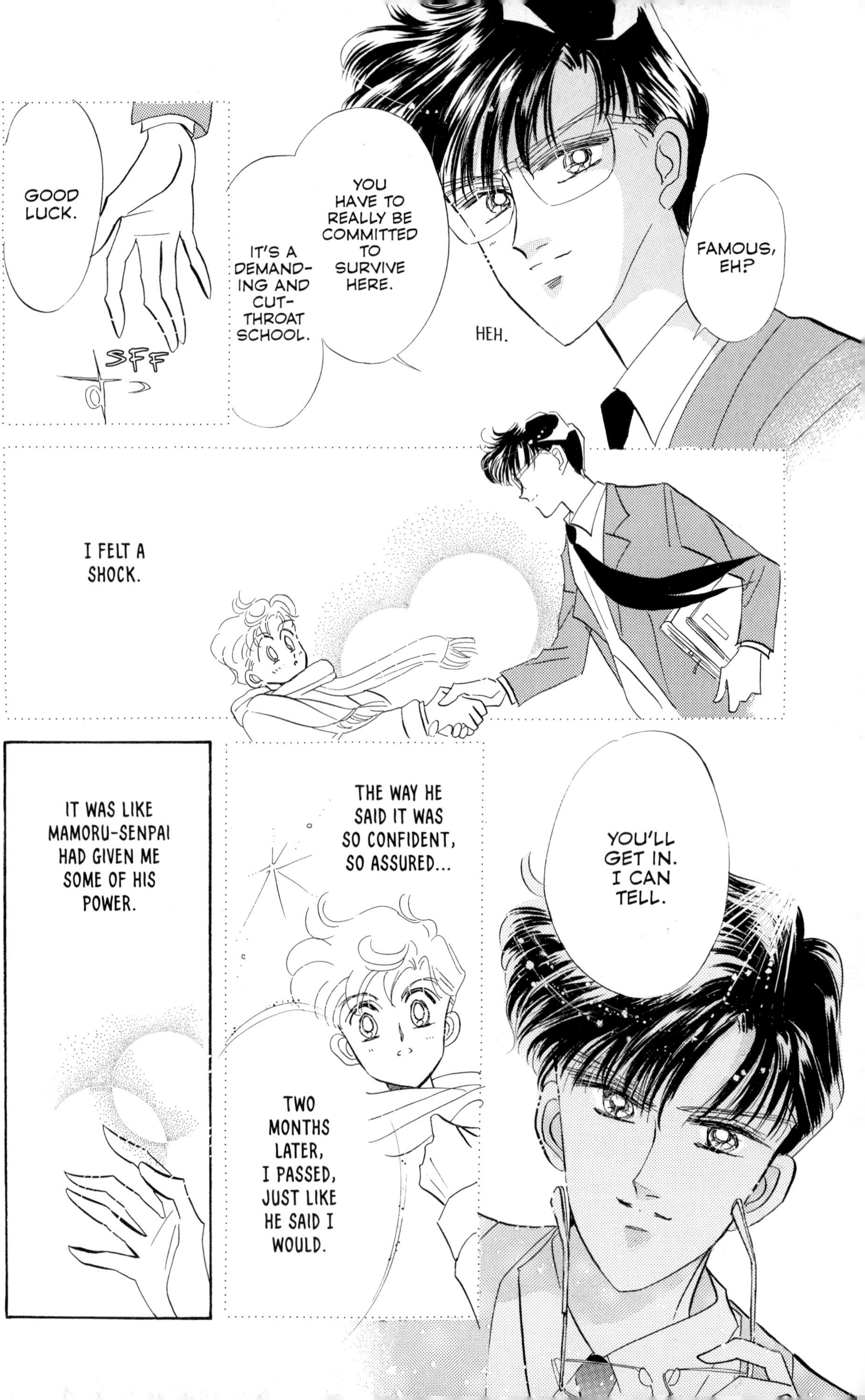

FAMOUS, EH?
HEH.
IT'S A DEMANDING AND CUT-THROAT SCHOOL.
YOU HAVE TO REALLY BE COMMITTED TO SURVIVE HERE.
GOOD LUCK.
SFF
I FELT A SHOCK.
YOU'LL GET IN. I CAN TELL.
THE WAY HE SAID IT WAS SO CONFIDENT, SO ASSURED...
TWO MONTHS LATER, I PASSED, JUST LIKE HE SAID I WOULD.
IT WAS LIKE MAMORU-SENPAI HAD GIVEN ME SOME OF HIS POWER.

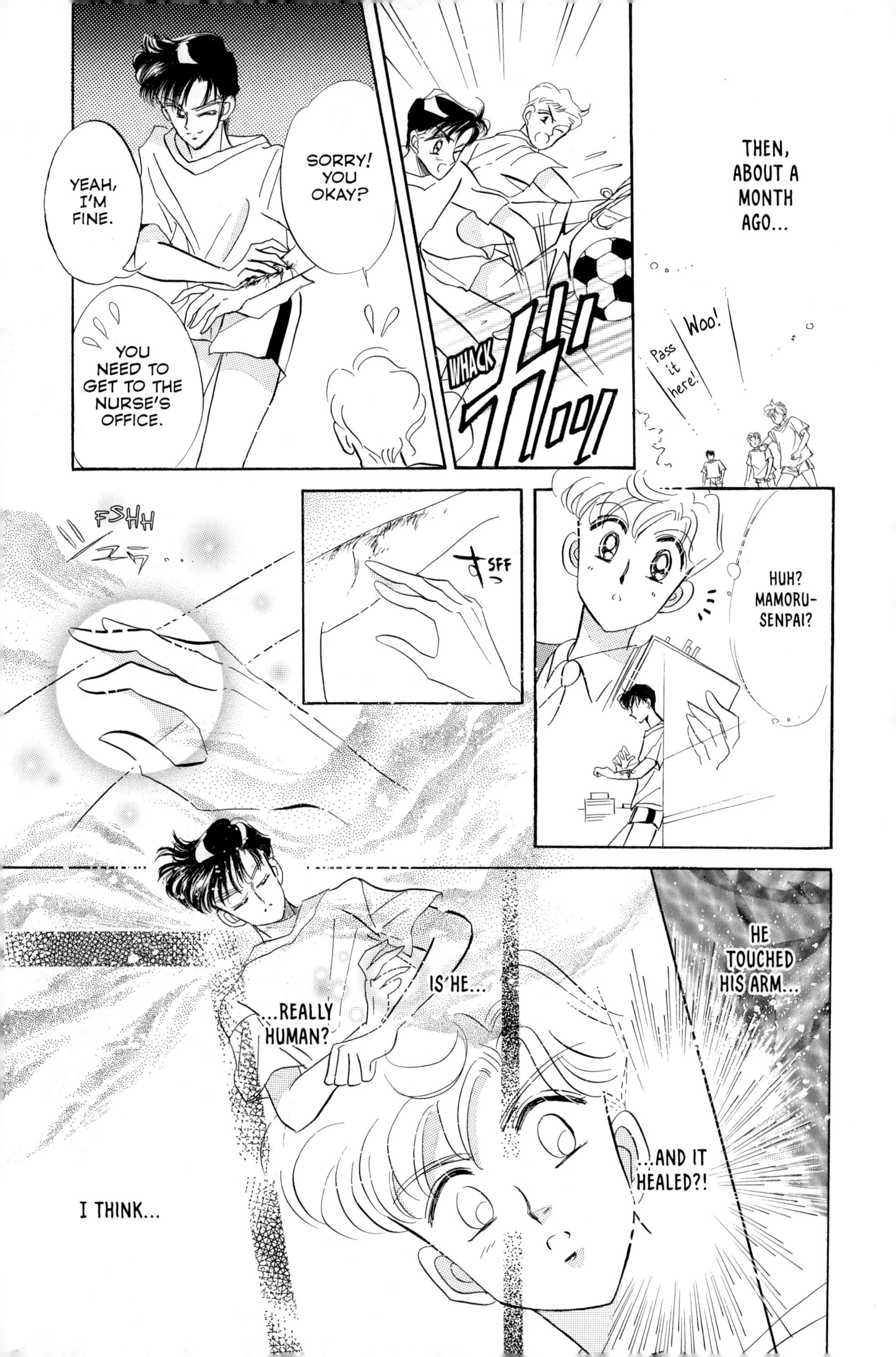
THEN, ABOUT A MONTH AGO...
Woo!
Pass it here!
WHACK
SORRY! YOU OKAY?
YEAH, I'M FINE.
YOU NEED TO GET TO THE NURSE'S OFFICE.
HUH? MAMORU-SENPAI?
SFF
FSHH
HE TOUCHED HIS ARM...
...AND IT HEALED?!
IS HE...
...REALLY HUMAN?
I THINK...

...YEAH, RIGHT. NOT A CHANCE.

Copying Mamoru-senpai.

...AN ALIEN.

...MIGHT JUST BE...

MAMORU-SENPAI...

MURMUR ざわ

MURMUR ざわ

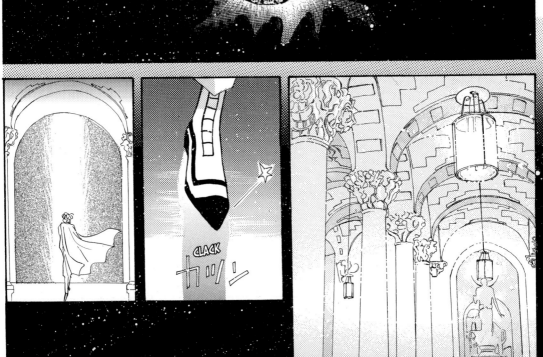

CLACK

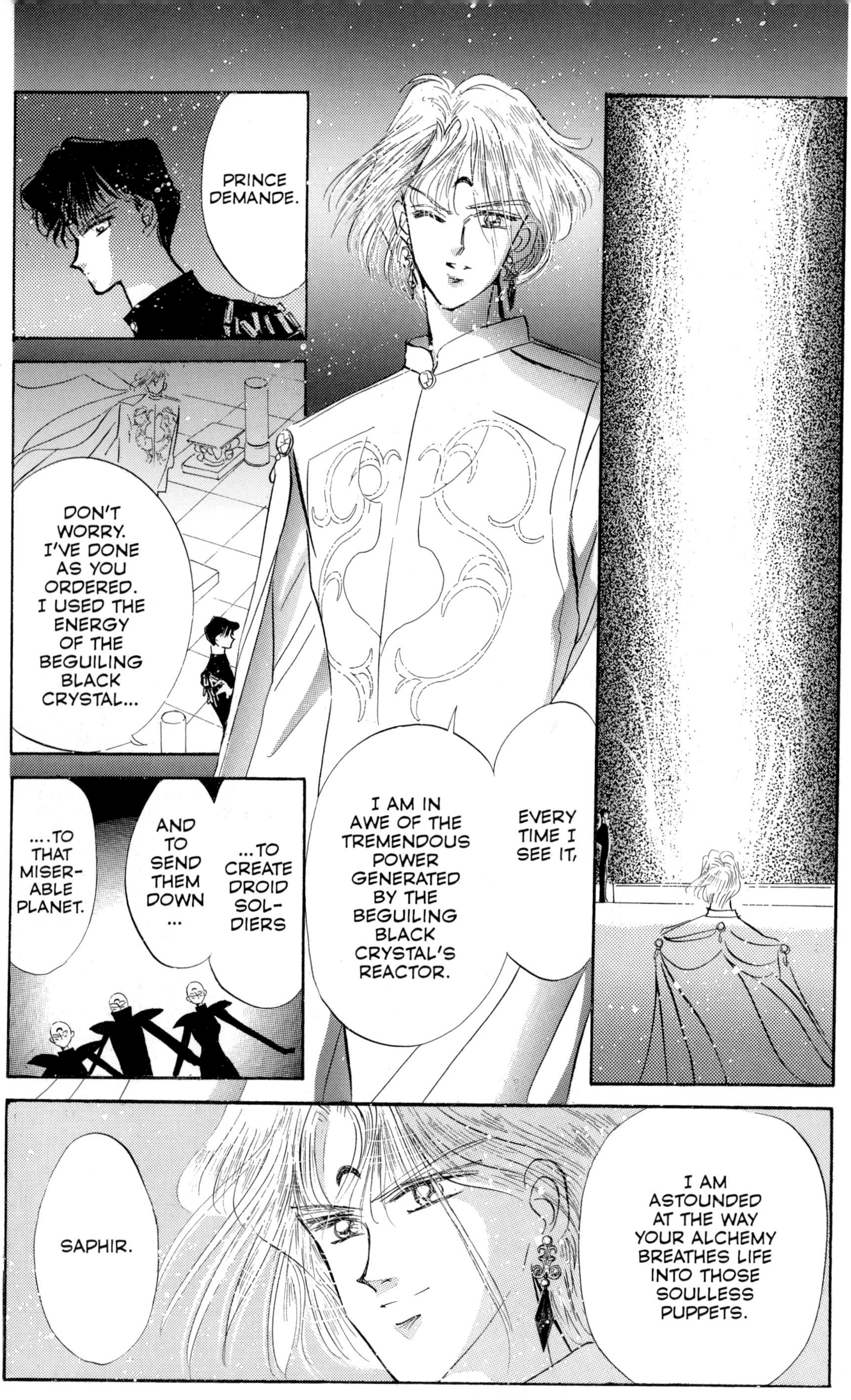
EVERY TIME I SEE IT,
I AM IN AWE OF THE TREMENDOUS POWER GENERATED BY THE BEGUILING BLACK CRYSTAL'S REACTOR.
PRINCE DEMANDE.
DON'T WORRY. I'VE DONE AS YOU ORDERED. I USED THE ENERGY OF THE BEGUILING BLACK CRYSTAL...
...TO CREATE DROID SOL-DIERS
AND TO SEND THEM DOWN ...
....TO THAT MISER-ABLE PLANET.
I AM ASTOUNDED AT THE WAY YOUR ALCHEMY BREATHES LIFE INTO THOSE SOULLESS PUPPETS.
SAPHIR.

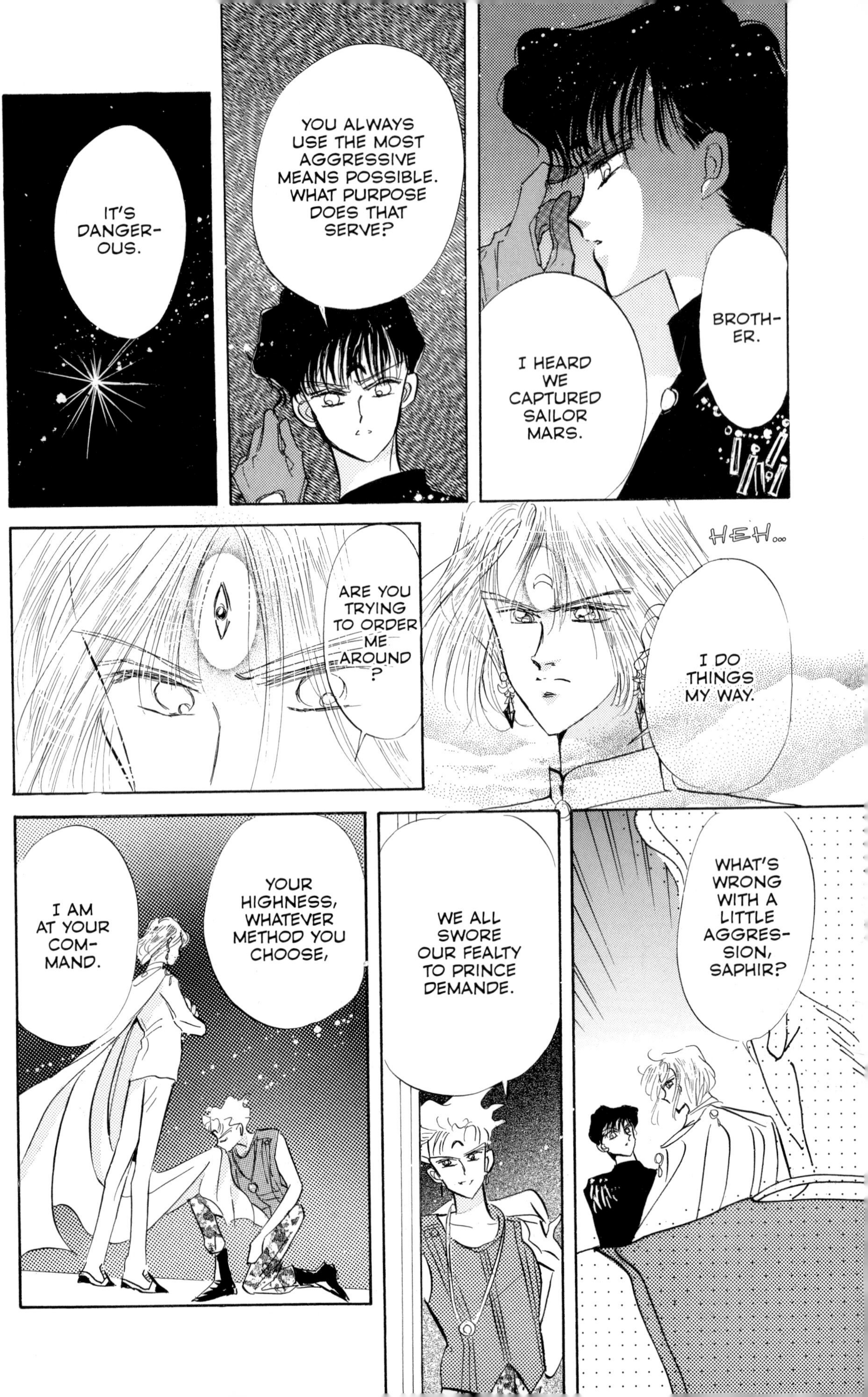
BROTH-
ER.
I HEARD WE CAPTURED SAILOR MARS.
YOU ALWAYS USE THE MOST AGGRESSIVE MEANS POSSIBLE. WHAT PURPOSE DOES THAT SERVE?
IT'S DANGER-
OUS.
HEH...
I DO THINGS MY WAY.
ARE YOU TRYING TO ORDER ME AROUND?
WHAT'S WRONG WITH A LITTLE AGGRES-
SION, SAPHIR?
WE ALL SWORE OUR FEALTY TO PRINCE DEMANDE.
YOUR HIGHNESS, WHATEVER METHOD YOU CHOOSE,
I AM AT YOUR COM-
MAND.

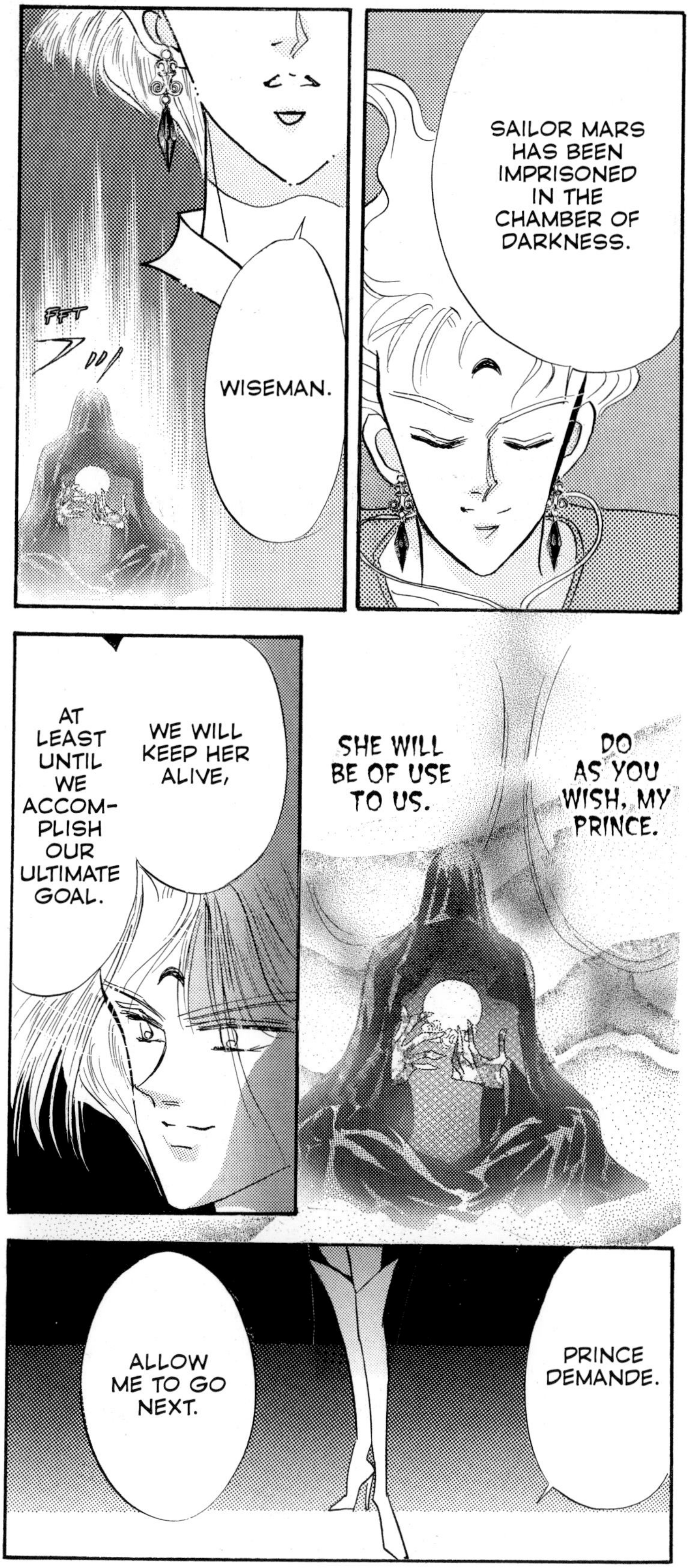
SAILOR MARS HAS BEEN IMPRISONED IN THE CHAMBER OF DARKNESS.
FFT
WISEMAN.
DO AS YOU WISH, MY PRINCE.
SHE WILL BE OF USE TO US.
WE WILL KEEP HER ALIVE,
AT LEAST UNTIL WE ACCOMPLISH OUR ULTIMATE GOAL.
PRINCE DEMANDE.
ALLOW ME TO GO NEXT.

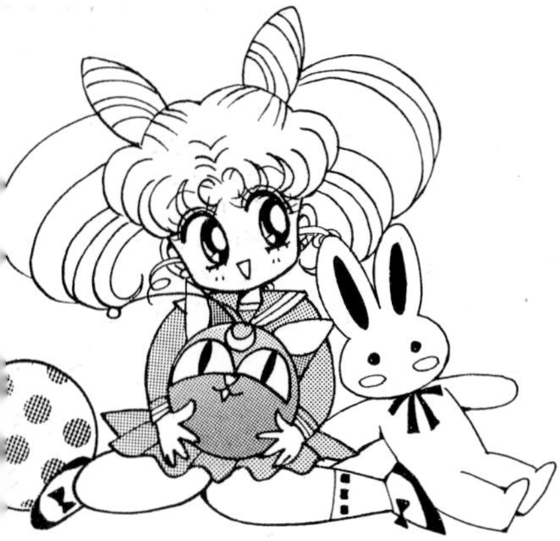

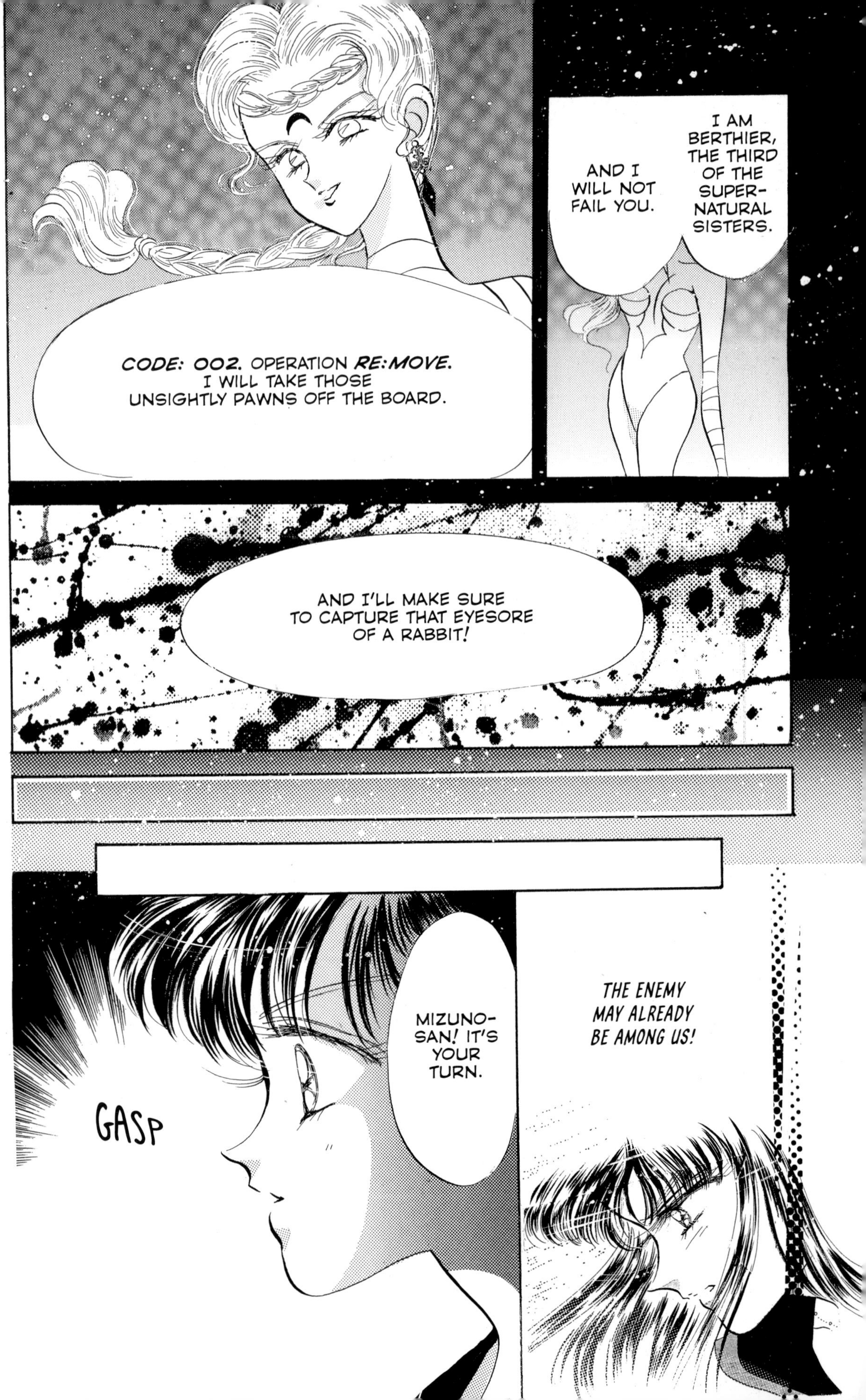
I AM BERTHIER, THE THIRD OF THE SUPER-NATURAL SISTERS.
AND I WILL NOT FAIL YOU.
CODE: 002. OPERATION RE:MOVE. I WILL TAKE THOSE UNSIGHTLY PAWNS OFF THE BOARD.
AND I'LL MAKE SURE TO CAPTURE THAT EYESORE OF A RABBIT!
THE ENEMY MAY ALREADY BE AMONG US!
MIZUNO-SAN! IT'S YOUR TURN.
GASP

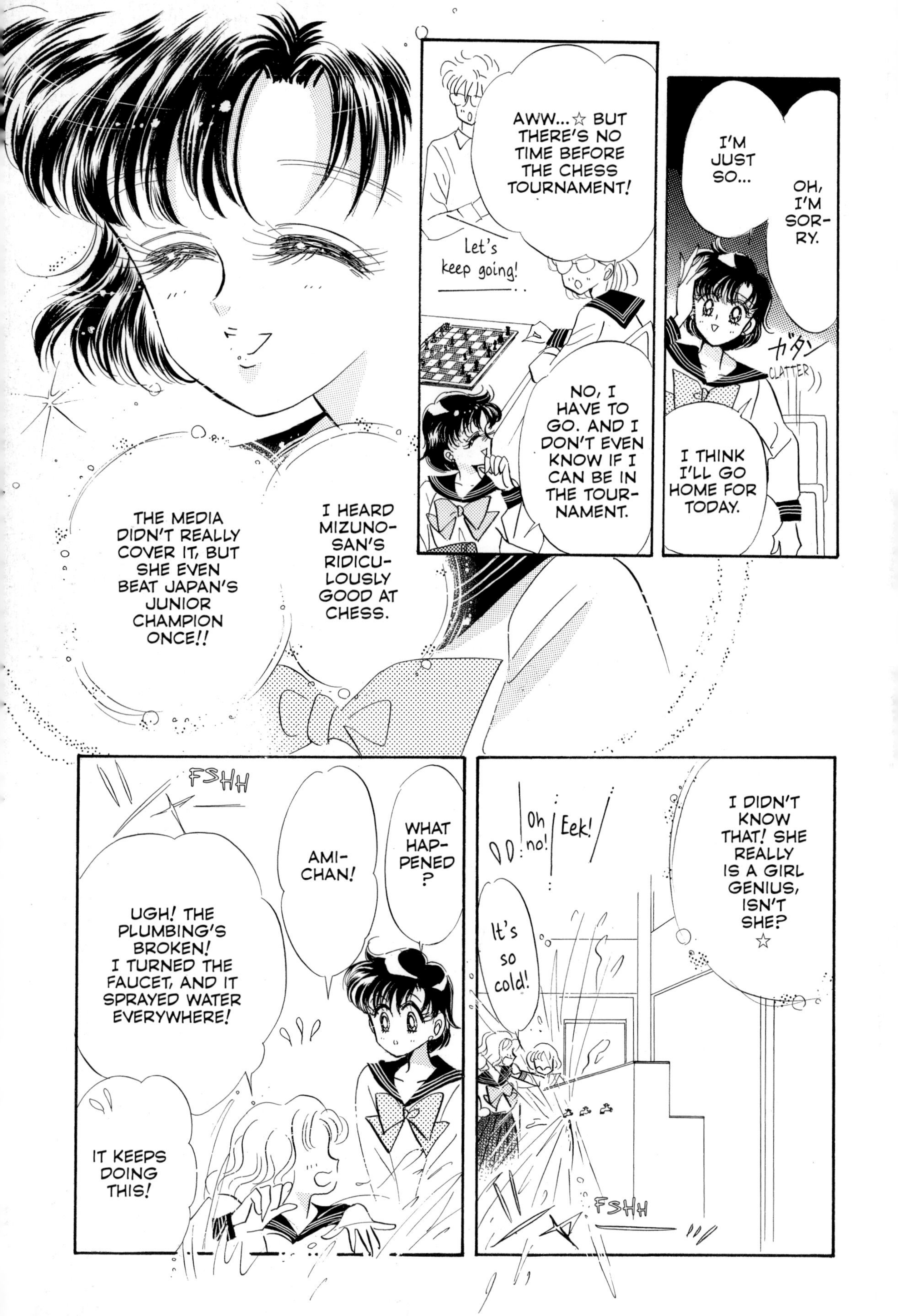
OH, I'M SOR-RY.
I'M JUST SO...
ガタン
CLATTER
I THINK I'LL GO HOME FOR TODAY.
AWW...☆ BUT THERE'S NO TIME BEFORE THE CHESS TOURNAMENT!
Let's keep going!
NO, I HAVE TO GO. AND I DON'T EVEN KNOW IF I CAN BE IN THE TOUR-NAMENT.
I HEARD MIZUNO-SAN'S RIDICU-LOUSLY GOOD AT CHESS.
THE MEDIA DIDN'T REALLY COVER IT, BUT SHE EVEN BEAT JAPAN'S JUNIOR CHAMPION ONCE!!
I DIDN'T KNOW THAT! SHE REALLY IS A GIRL GENIUS, ISN'T SHE? ☆
Eek!
Oh no!
It's so cold!
FSHH
WHAT HAP-PENED?
AMI-CHAN!
FSHH
UGH! THE PLUMBING'S BROKEN! I TURNED THE FAUCET, AND IT SPRAYED WATER EVERYWHERE!
IT KEEPS DOING THIS!

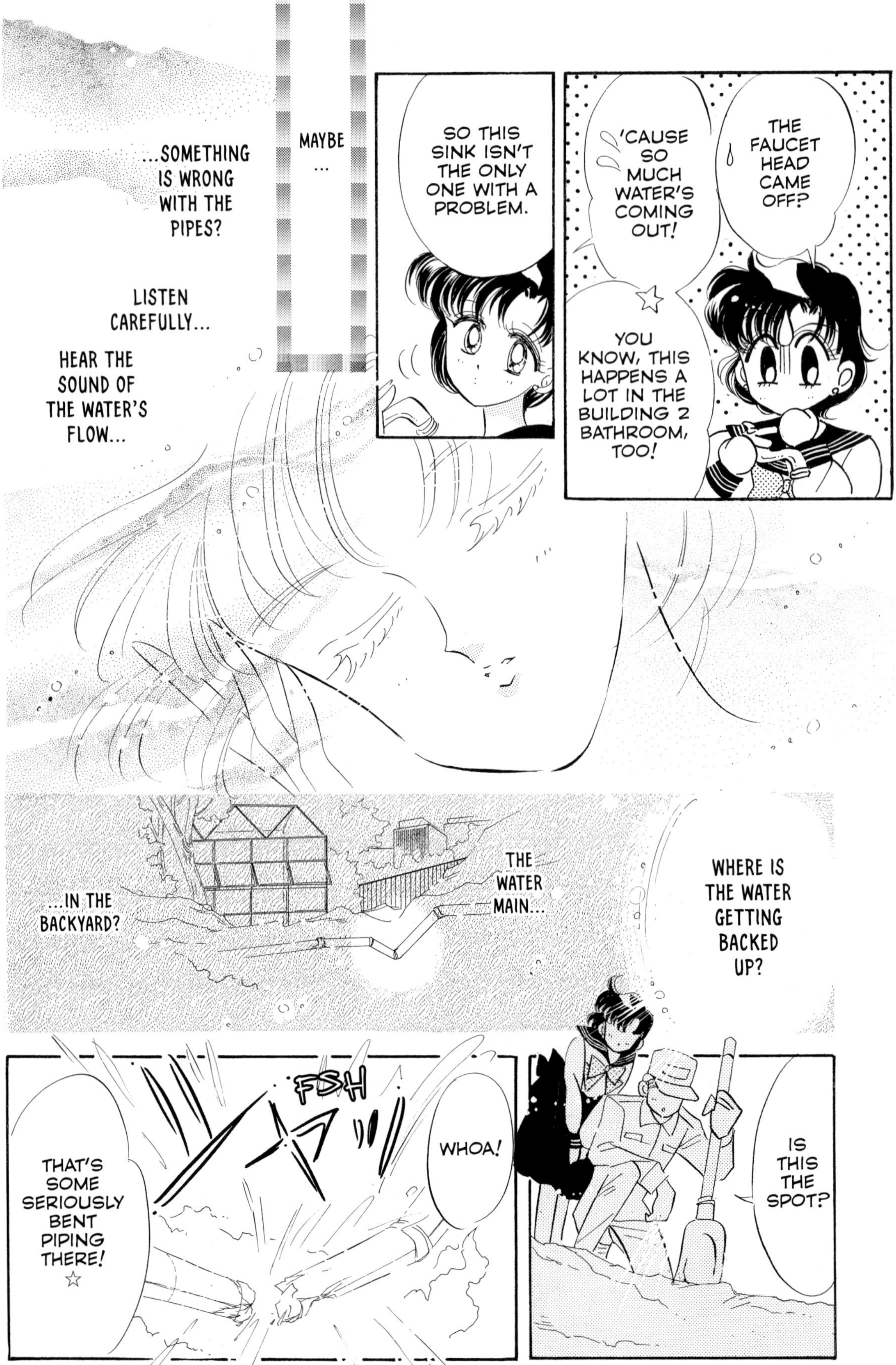
THE FAUCET HEAD CAME OFF?
'CAUSE SO MUCH WATER'S COMING OUT!
YOU KNOW, THIS HAPPENS A LOT IN THE BUILDING 2 BATHROOM, TOO!
SO THIS SINK ISN'T THE ONLY ONE WITH A PROBLEM.
MAYBE ...
...SOMETHING IS WRONG WITH THE PIPES?
LISTEN CAREFULLY...
HEAR THE SOUND OF THE WATER'S FLOW...
WHERE IS THE WATER GETTING BACKED UP?
THE WATER MAIN...
...IN THE BACKYARD?
IS THIS THE SPOT?
WHOA!
FSH
THAT'S SOME SERIOUSLY BENT PIPING THERE! ☆

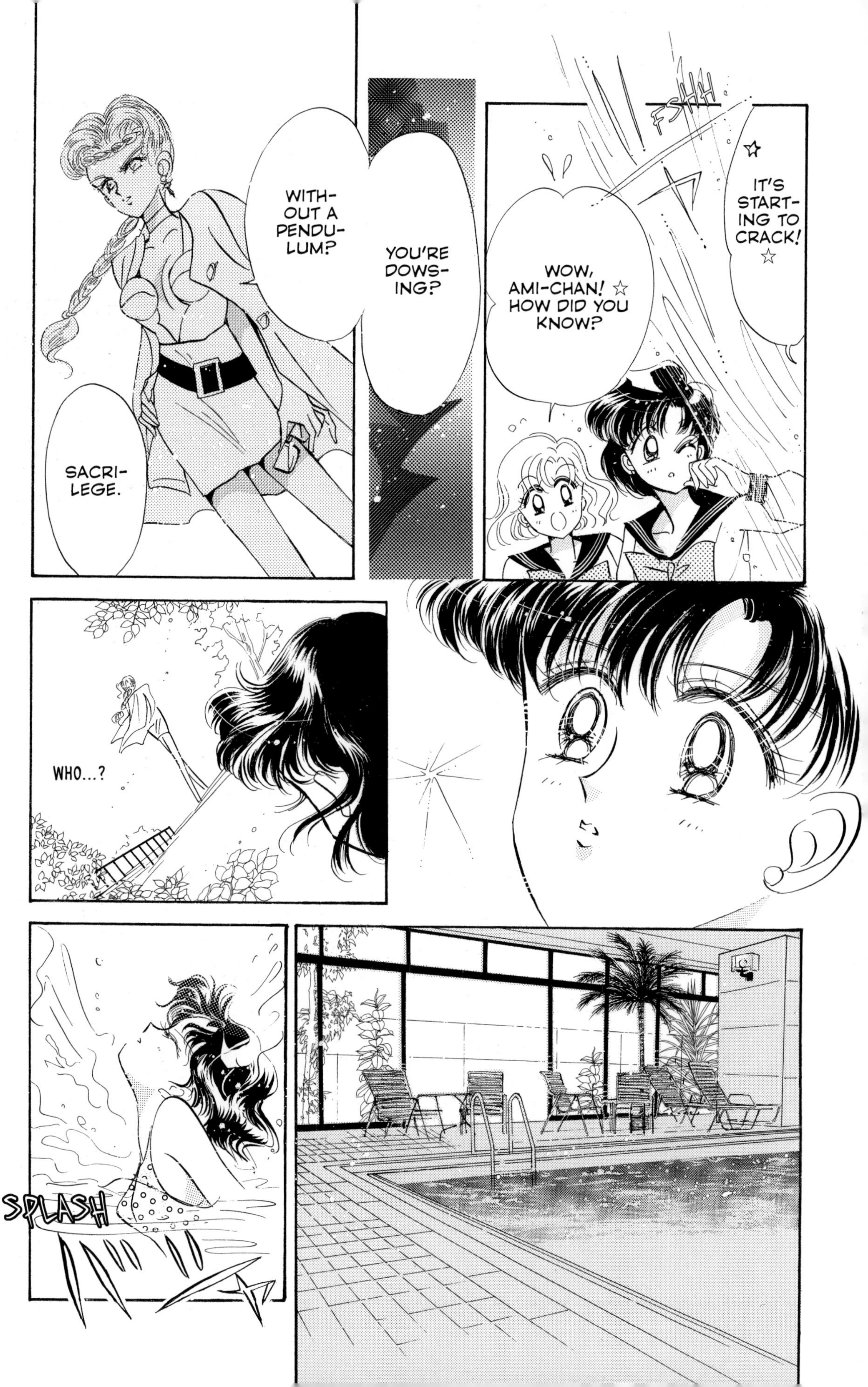
FSHH
☆ IT'S STARTING TO CRACK! ☆
WOW, AMI-CHAN! ☆ HOW DID YOU KNOW?
YOU'RE DOWSING?
WITHOUT A PENDULUM?
SACRILEGE.
WHO...?
SPLASH

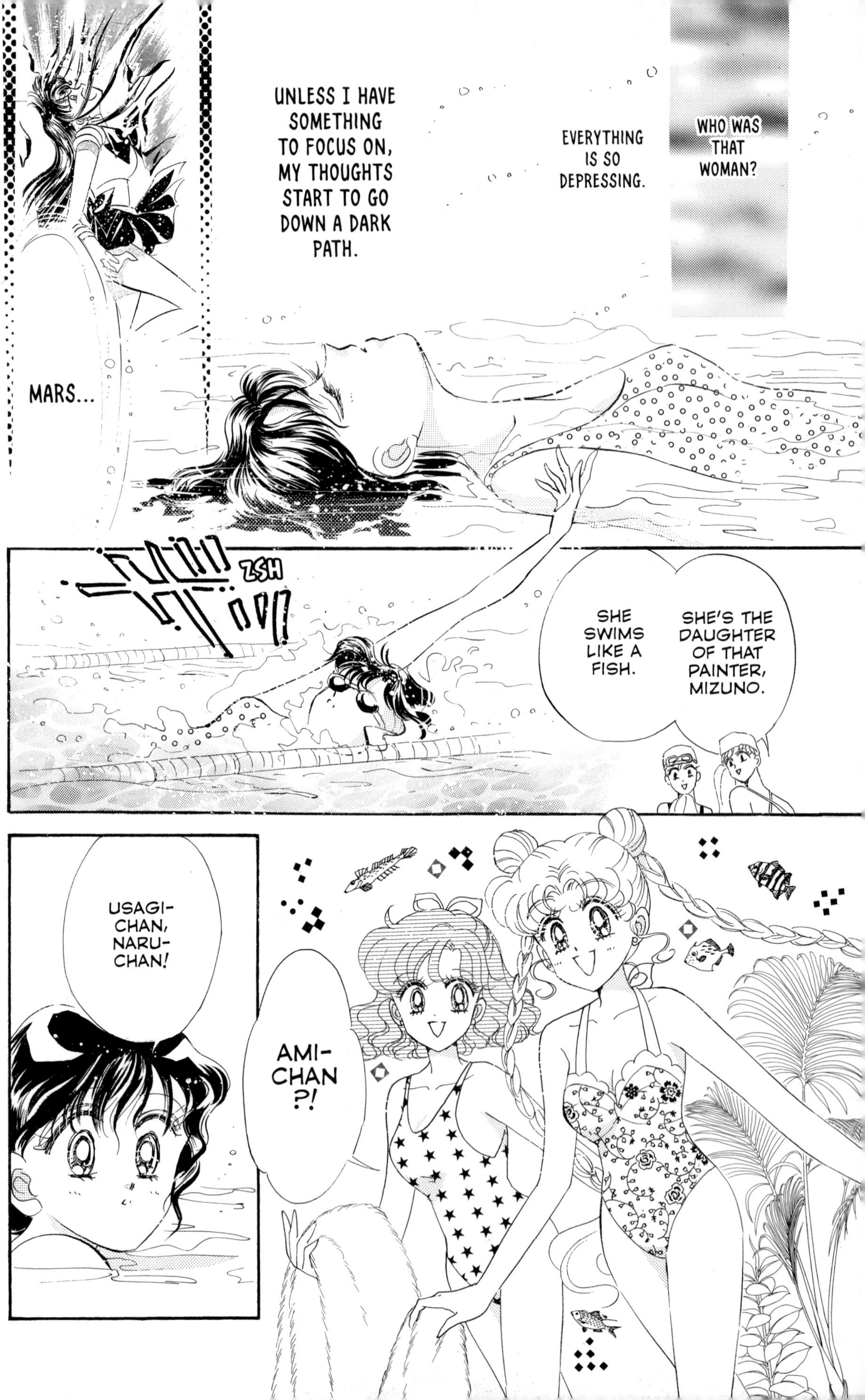
WHO WAS THAT WOMAN?
EVERYTHING IS SO DEPRESSING.
UNLESS I HAVE SOMETHING TO FOCUS ON, MY THOUGHTS START TO GO DOWN A DARK PATH.
MARS...
SHE'S THE DAUGHTER OF THAT PAINTER, MIZUNO.
SHE SWIMS LIKE A FISH.
ZSH
AMI-CHAN?!
USAGI-CHAN, NARU-CHAN!

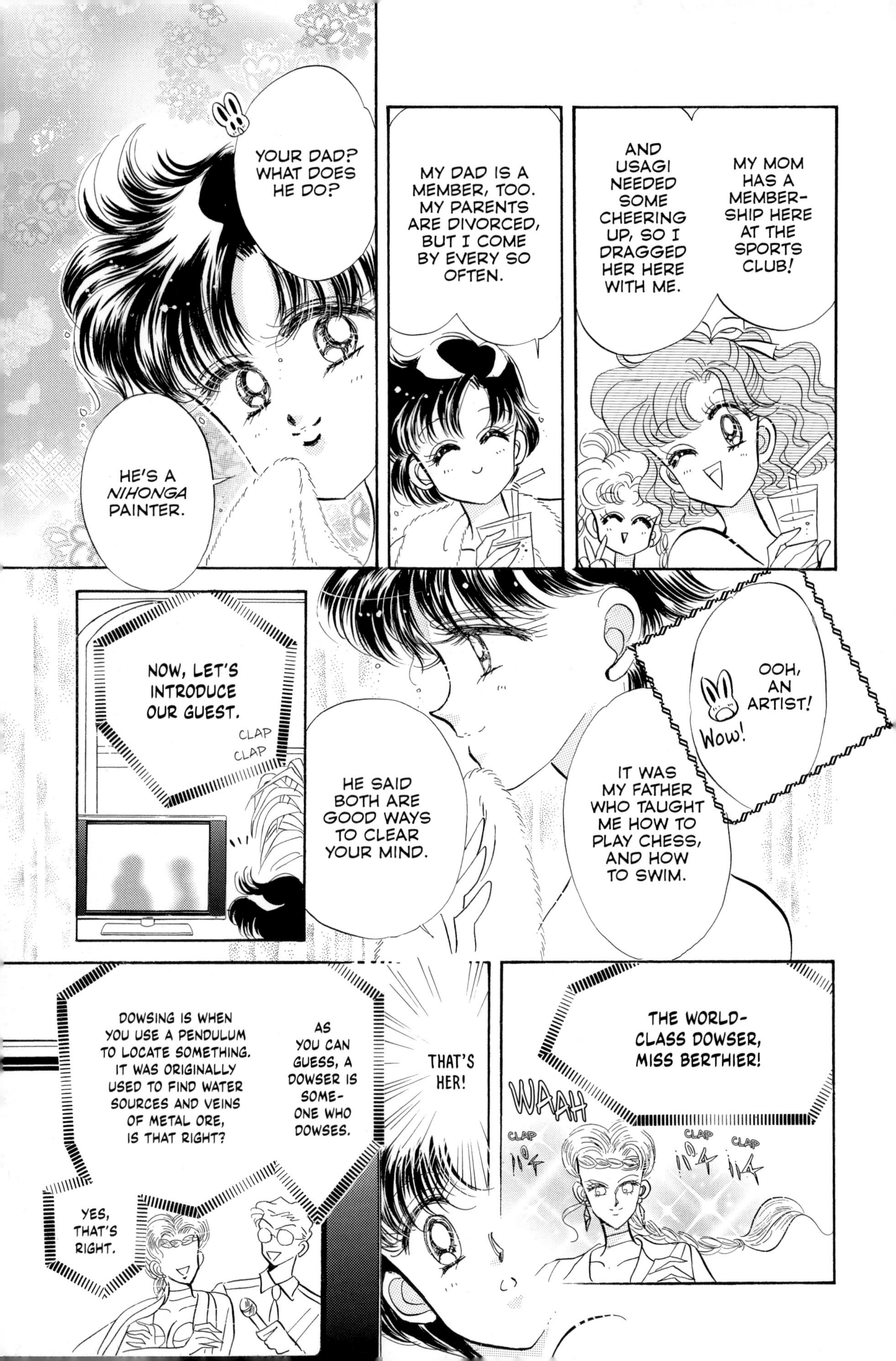
MY MOM HAS A MEMBERSHIP HERE AT THE SPORTS CLUB!
AND USAGI NEEDED SOME CHEERING UP, SO I DRAGGED HER HERE WITH ME.
MY DAD IS A MEMBER, TOO. MY PARENTS ARE DIVORCED, BUT I COME BY EVERY SO OFTEN.
YOUR DAD? WHAT DOES HE DO?
HE'S A *NIHONGA* PAINTER.
OOH, AN ARTIST!
Wow!
IT WAS MY FATHER WHO TAUGHT ME HOW TO PLAY CHESS, AND HOW TO SWIM.
HE SAID BOTH ARE GOOD WAYS TO CLEAR YOUR MIND.
NOW, LET'S INTRODUCE OUR GUEST.
CLAP
CLAP
THE WORLD-CLASS DOWSER, MISS BERTHIER!
WAAH
CLAP
CLAP
CLAP
THAT'S HER!
AS YOU CAN GUESS, A DOWSER IS SOMEONE WHO DOWSES.
DOWSING IS WHEN YOU USE A PENDULUM TO LOCATE SOMETHING. IT WAS ORIGINALLY USED TO FIND WATER SOURCES AND VEINS OF METAL ORE, IS THAT RIGHT?
YES, THAT'S RIGHT.

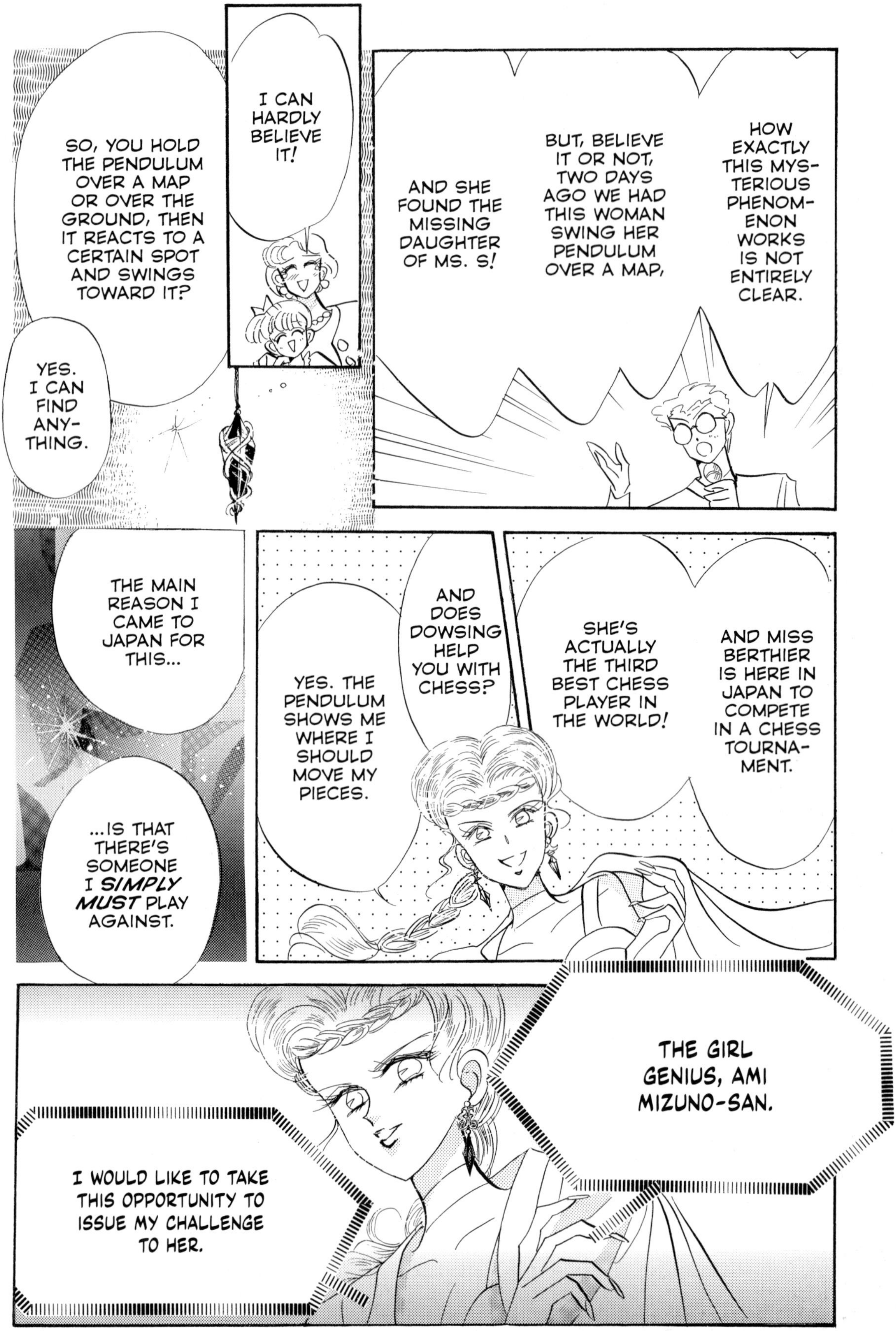
HOW EXACTLY THIS MYSTERIOUS PHENOMENON WORKS IS NOT ENTIRELY CLEAR.
BUT, BELIEVE IT OR NOT, TWO DAYS AGO WE HAD THIS WOMAN SWING HER PENDULUM OVER A MAP,
AND SHE FOUND THE MISSING DAUGHTER OF MS. S!
I CAN HARDLY BELIEVE IT!
SO, YOU HOLD THE PENDULUM OVER A MAP OR OVER THE GROUND, THEN IT REACTS TO A CERTAIN SPOT AND SWINGS TOWARD IT?
YES. I CAN FIND ANYTHING.
AND MISS BERTHIER IS HERE IN JAPAN TO COMPETE IN A CHESS TOURNAMENT.
SHE'S ACTUALLY THE THIRD BEST CHESS PLAYER IN THE WORLD!
AND DOES DOWSING HELP YOU WITH CHESS?
YES. THE PENDULUM SHOWS ME WHERE I SHOULD MOVE MY PIECES.
THE MAIN REASON I CAME TO JAPAN FOR THIS...
...IS THAT THERE'S SOMEONE I *SIMPLY MUST* PLAY AGAINST.
THE GIRL GENIUS, AMI MIZUNO-SAN.
I WOULD LIKE TO TAKE THIS OPPORTUNITY TO ISSUE MY CHALLENGE TO HER.

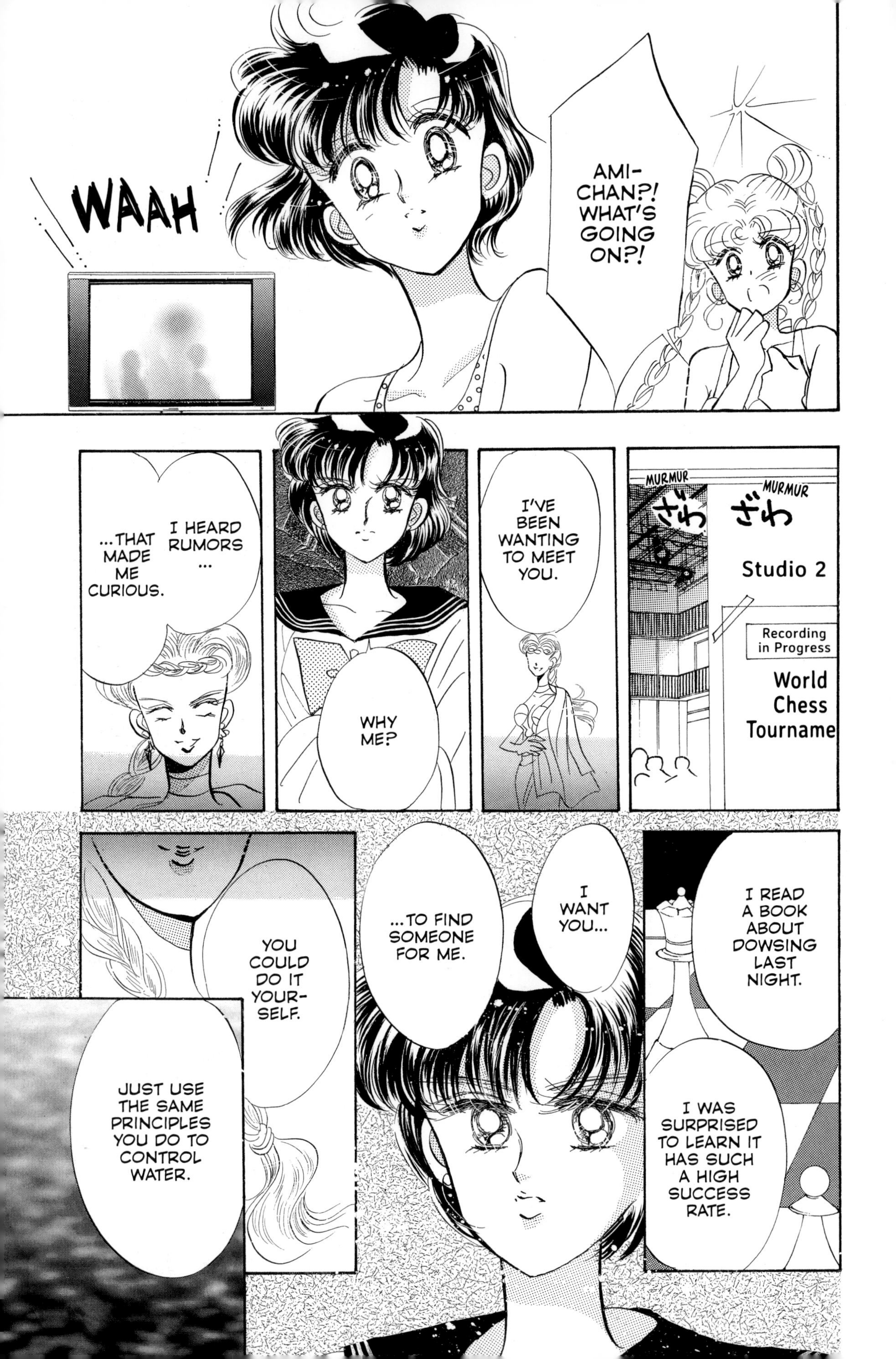
AMI-CHAN?! WHAT'S GOING ON?!
WAAH
MURMUR
ざわ
MURMUR
ざわ
Studio 2
Recording in Progress
World Chess Tourname
I'VE BEEN WANTING TO MEET YOU.
WHY ME?
I HEARD RUMORS...
...THAT MADE ME CURIOUS.
I READ A BOOK ABOUT DOWSING LAST NIGHT.
I WAS SURPRISED TO LEARN IT HAS SUCH A HIGH SUCCESS RATE.
I WANT YOU...
...TO FIND SOMEONE FOR ME.
YOU COULD DO IT YOURSELF.
JUST USE THE SAME PRINCIPLES YOU DO TO CONTROL WATER.

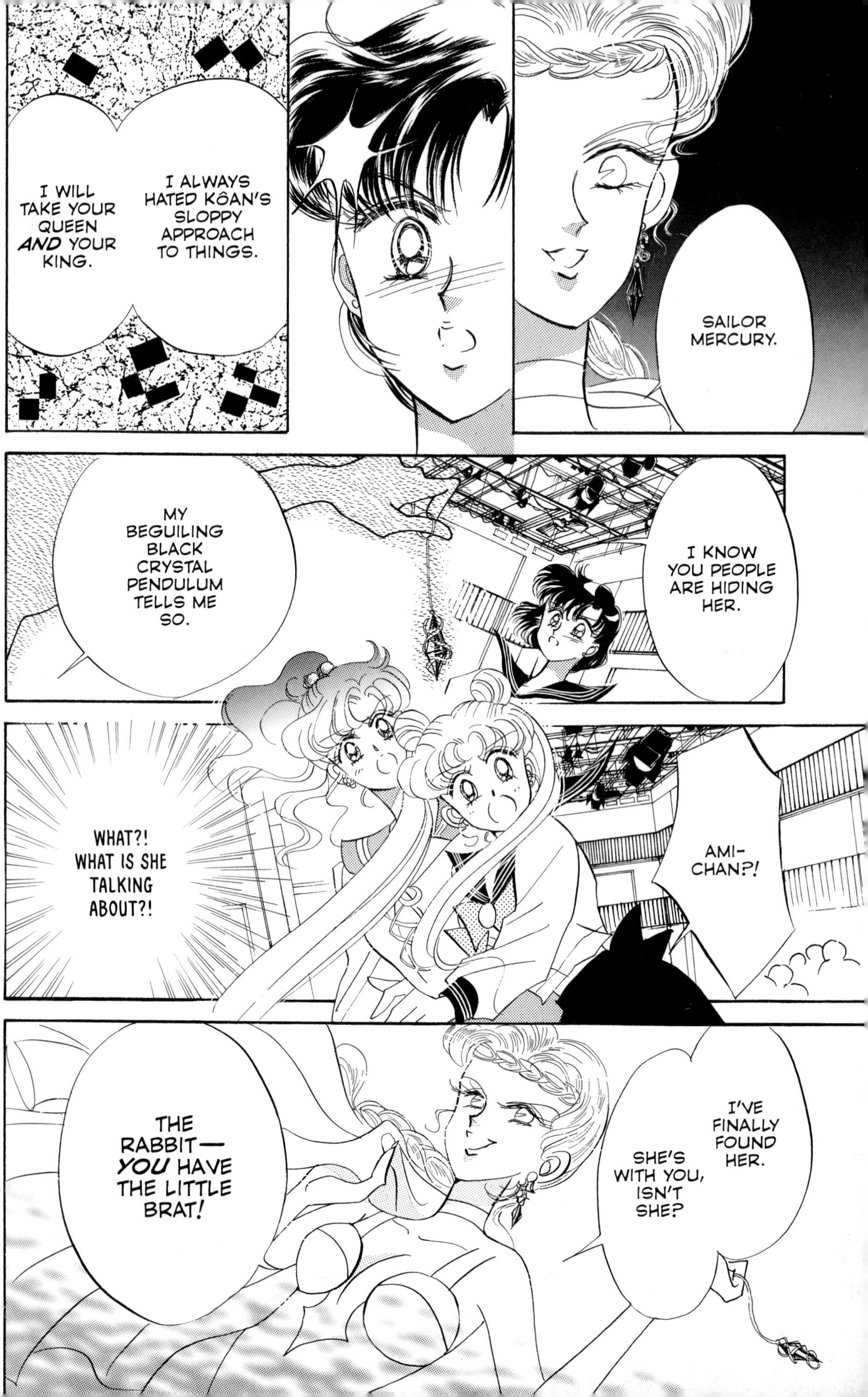
SAILOR MERCURY.
I ALWAYS HATED KÔAN'S SLOPPY APPROACH TO THINGS.
I WILL TAKE YOUR QUEEN *AND* YOUR KING.
I KNOW YOU PEOPLE ARE HIDING HER.
MY BEGUILING BLACK CRYSTAL PENDULUM TELLS ME SO.
AMI-CHAN?!
WHAT?! WHAT IS SHE TALKING ABOUT?!
I'VE FINALLY FOUND HER.
SHE'S WITH YOU, ISN'T SHE?
THE RABBIT—*YOU* HAVE THE LITTLE BRAT!

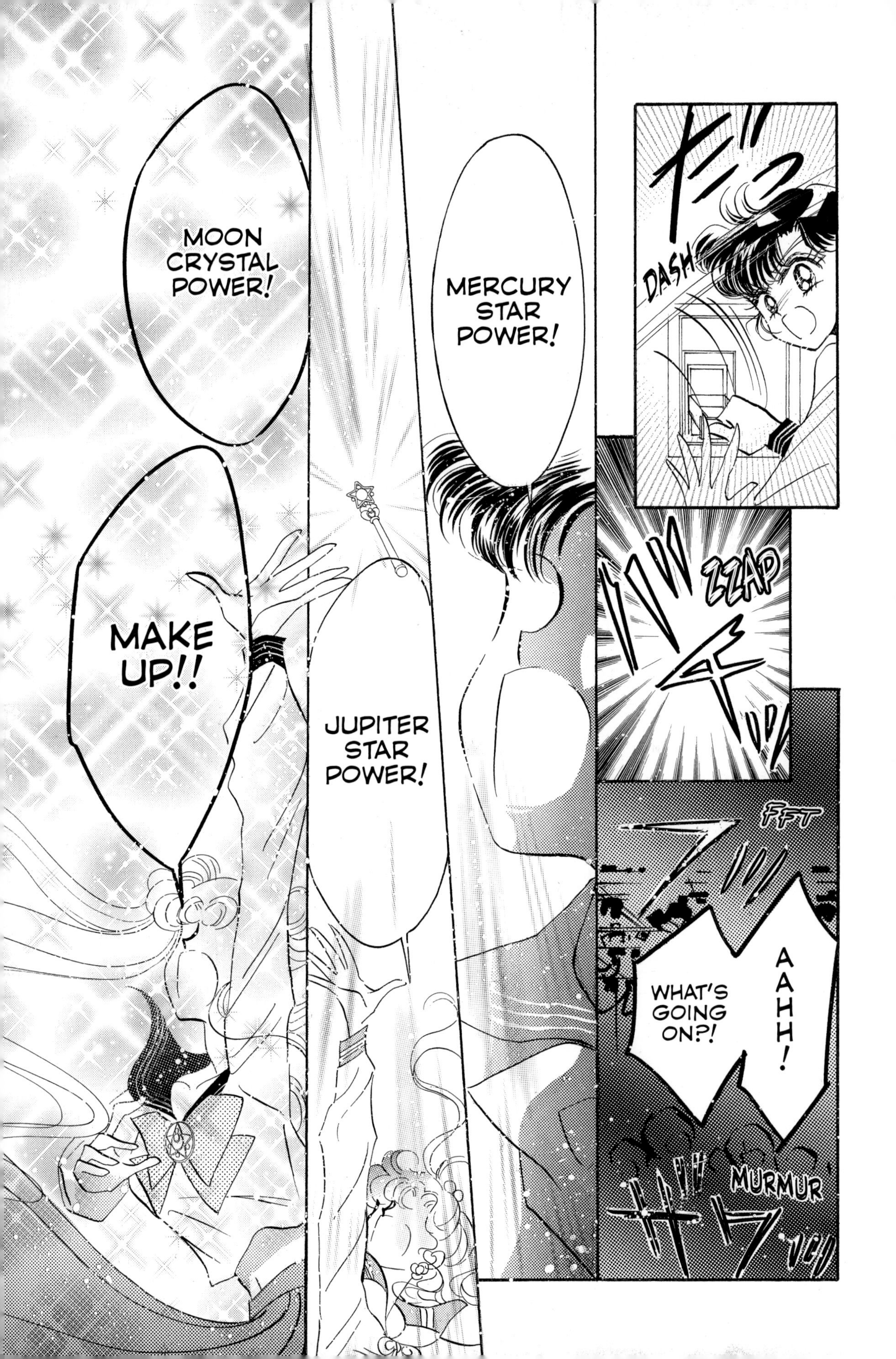
DASH
ZZAP
FFT
AAHH!
WHAT'S GOING ON?!
MURMUR
MERCURY STAR POWER!
JUPITER STAR POWER!
MOON CRYSTAL POWER!
MAKE UP!!

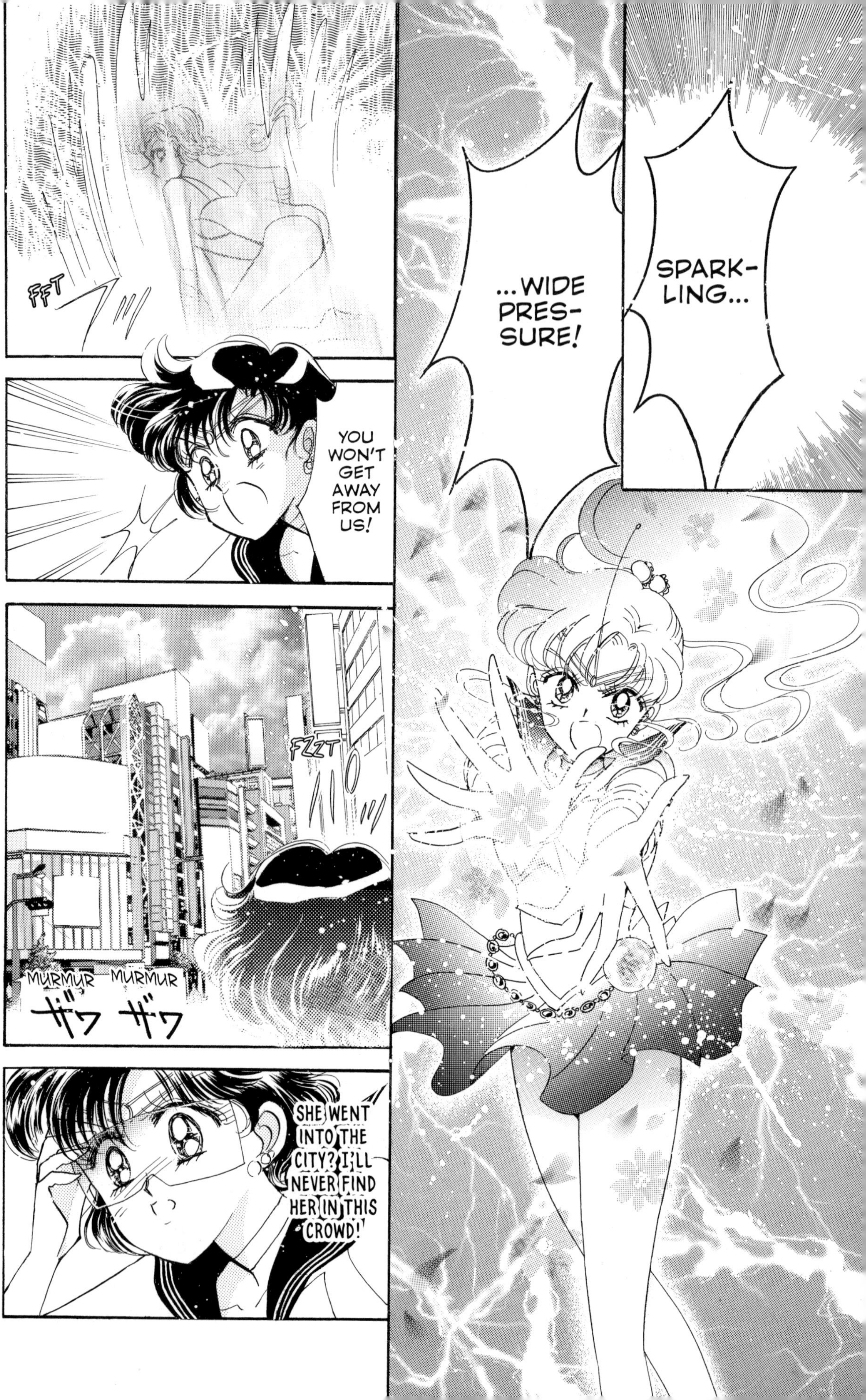
SPARK-
LING...
...WIDE
PRES-
SURE!
FFT
YOU
WON'T
GET
AWAY
FROM
US!
FZZT
MURMUR MURMUR
ザワ ザワ
SHE WENT
INTO THE
CITY? I'LL
NEVER FIND
HER IN THIS
CROWD!

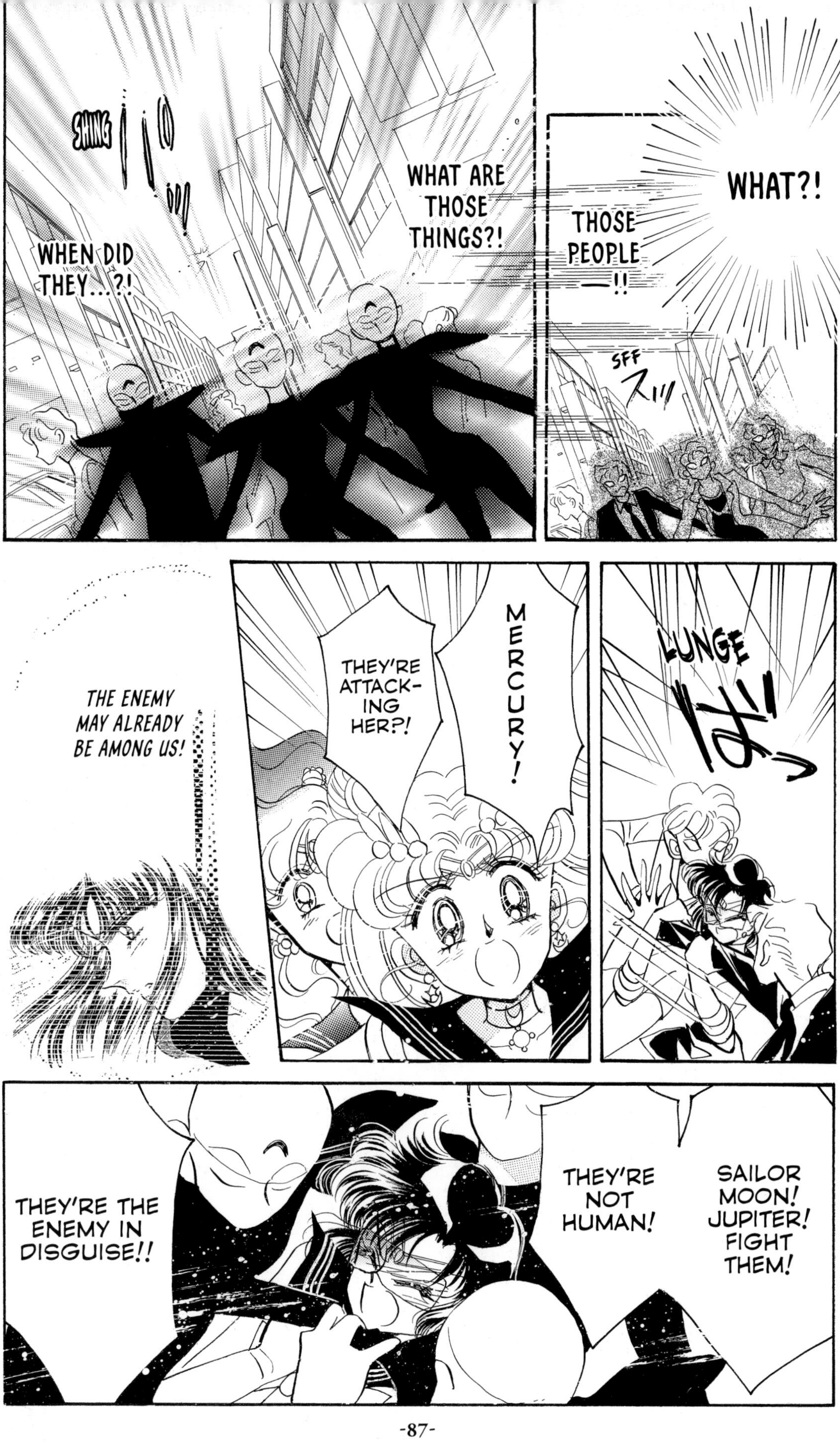
WHAT?!
THOSE PEOPLE—!!
SFF
WHAT ARE THOSE THINGS?!
SHING
WHEN DID THEY...?!
LUNGE
MERCURY!
THEY'RE ATTACKING HER?!
THE ENEMY MAY ALREADY BE AMONG US!
SAILOR MOON! JUPITER! FIGHT THEM!
THEY'RE NOT HUMAN!
THEY'RE THE ENEMY IN DISGUISE!!

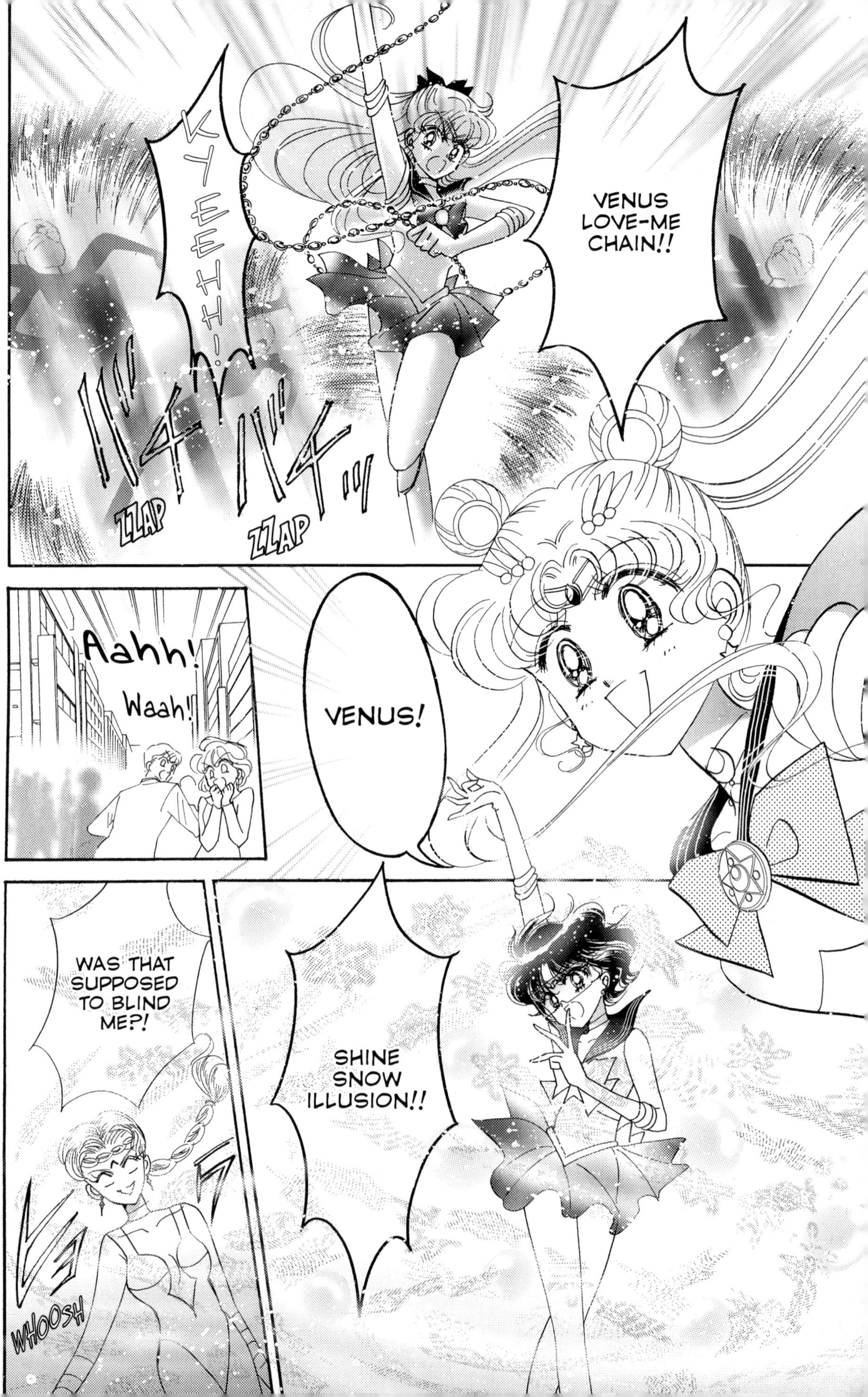
VENUS LOVE-ME CHAIN!!
KYEEHH!!
ZZAP
ZZAP
VENUS!
Aahh!
Waah!
SHINE SNOW ILLUSION!!
WAS THAT SUPPOSED TO BLIND ME?!
WHOOSH

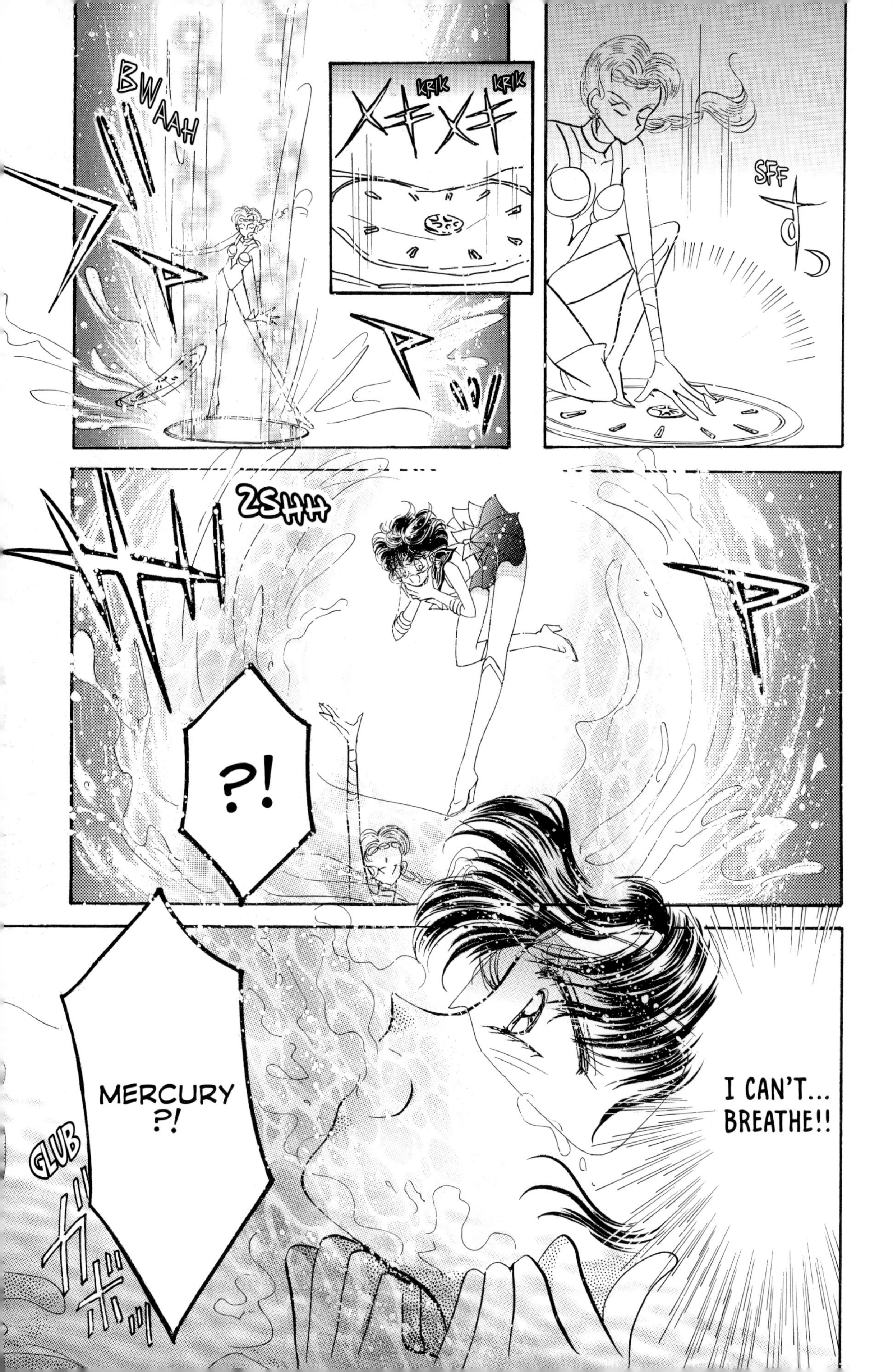
SFF
KRIK KRIK
BWAAH
ZSHH
?!
I CAN'T... BREATHE!!
MERCURY ?!
GLUB

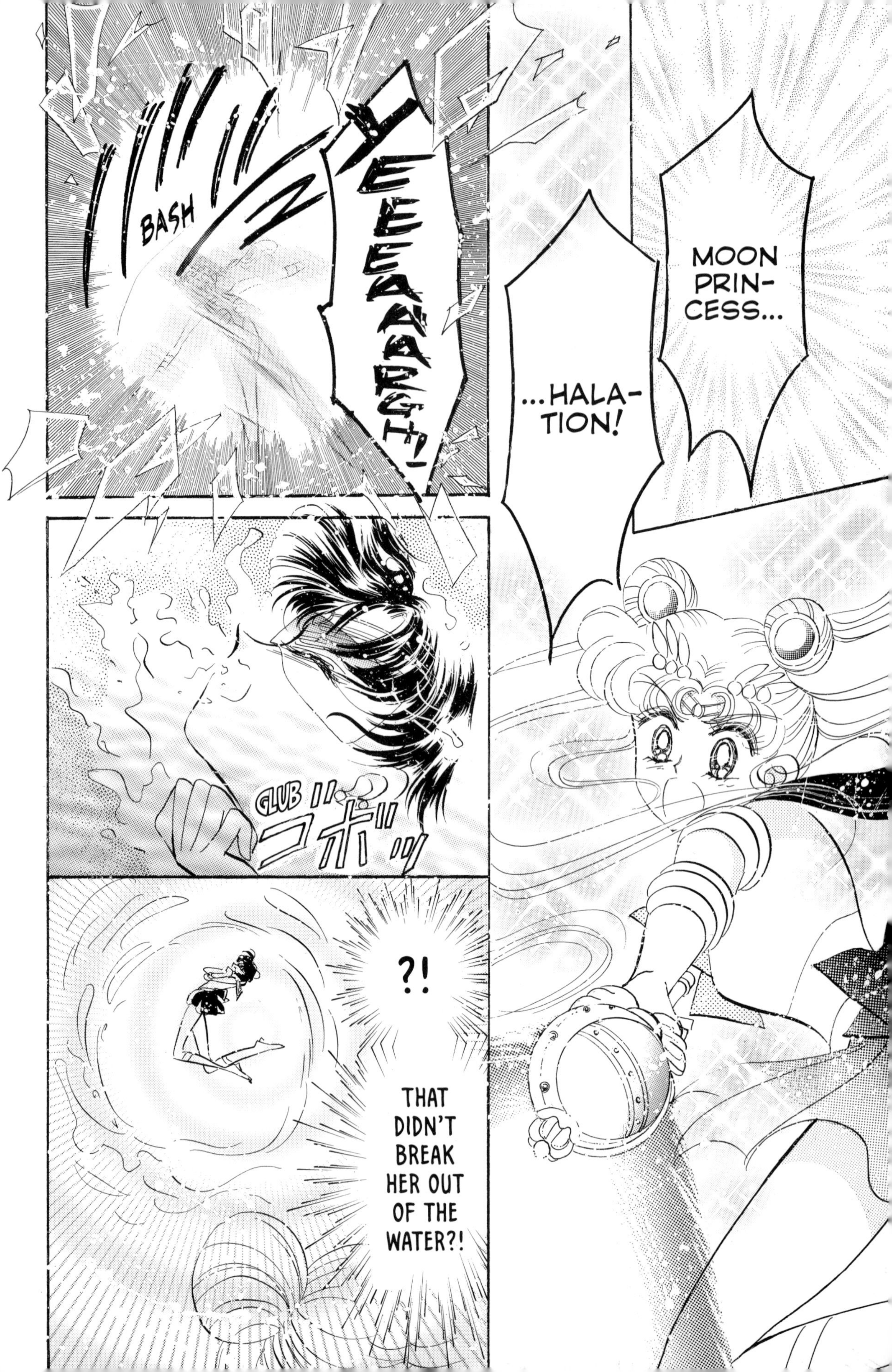

MOON PRINCESS...
...HALATION!
BASH
EEEAAARGH!!
GLUB
ゴボッ
?!
THAT DIDN'T BREAK HER OUT OF THE WATER?!

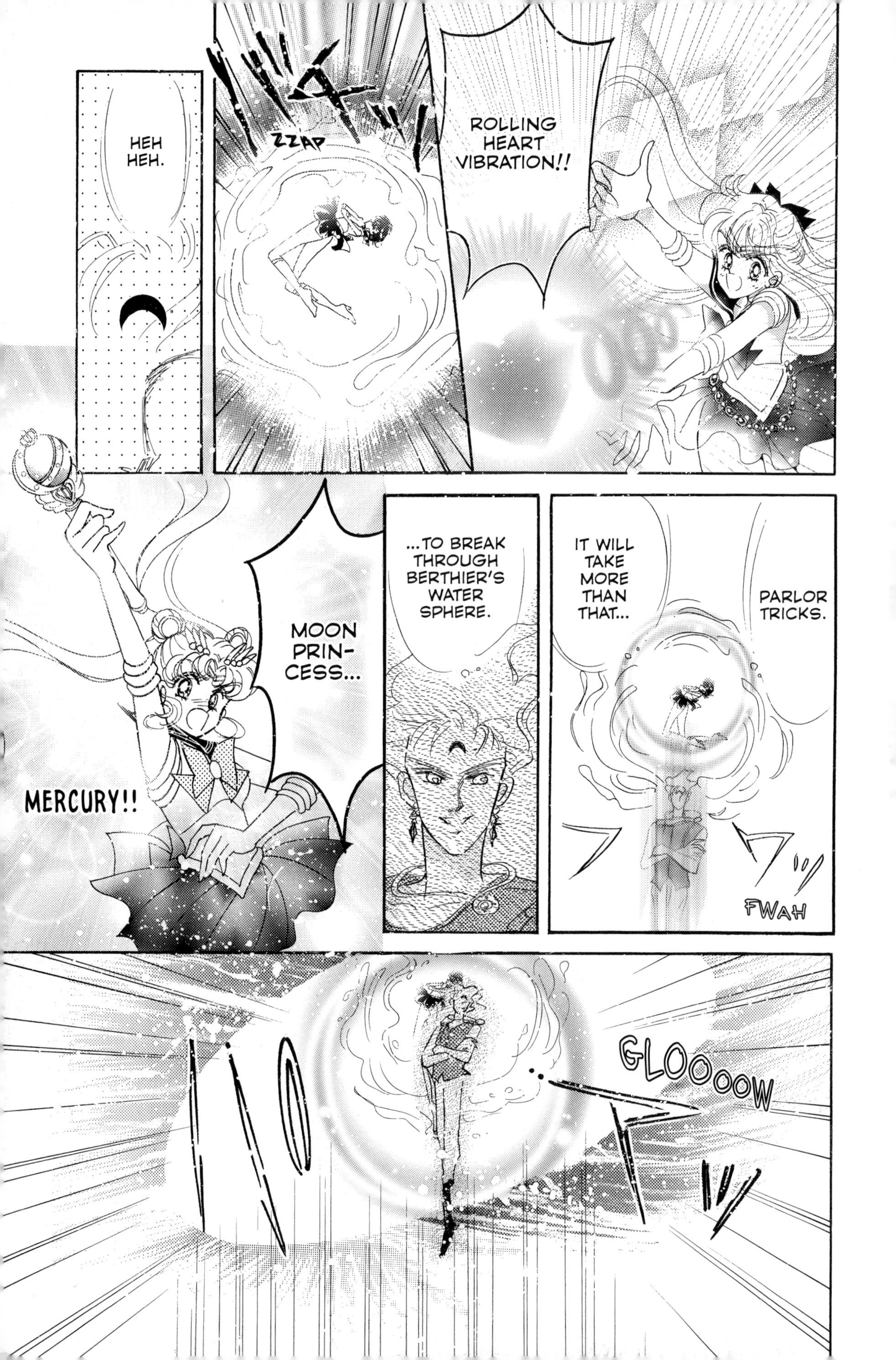
ROLLING HEART VIBRATION!!
ZZAP
HEH HEH.
PARLOR TRICKS.
IT WILL TAKE MORE THAN THAT...
FWAH
...TO BREAK THROUGH BERTHIER'S WATER SPHERE.
MOON PRINCESS...
MERCURY!!
GLOOOOW

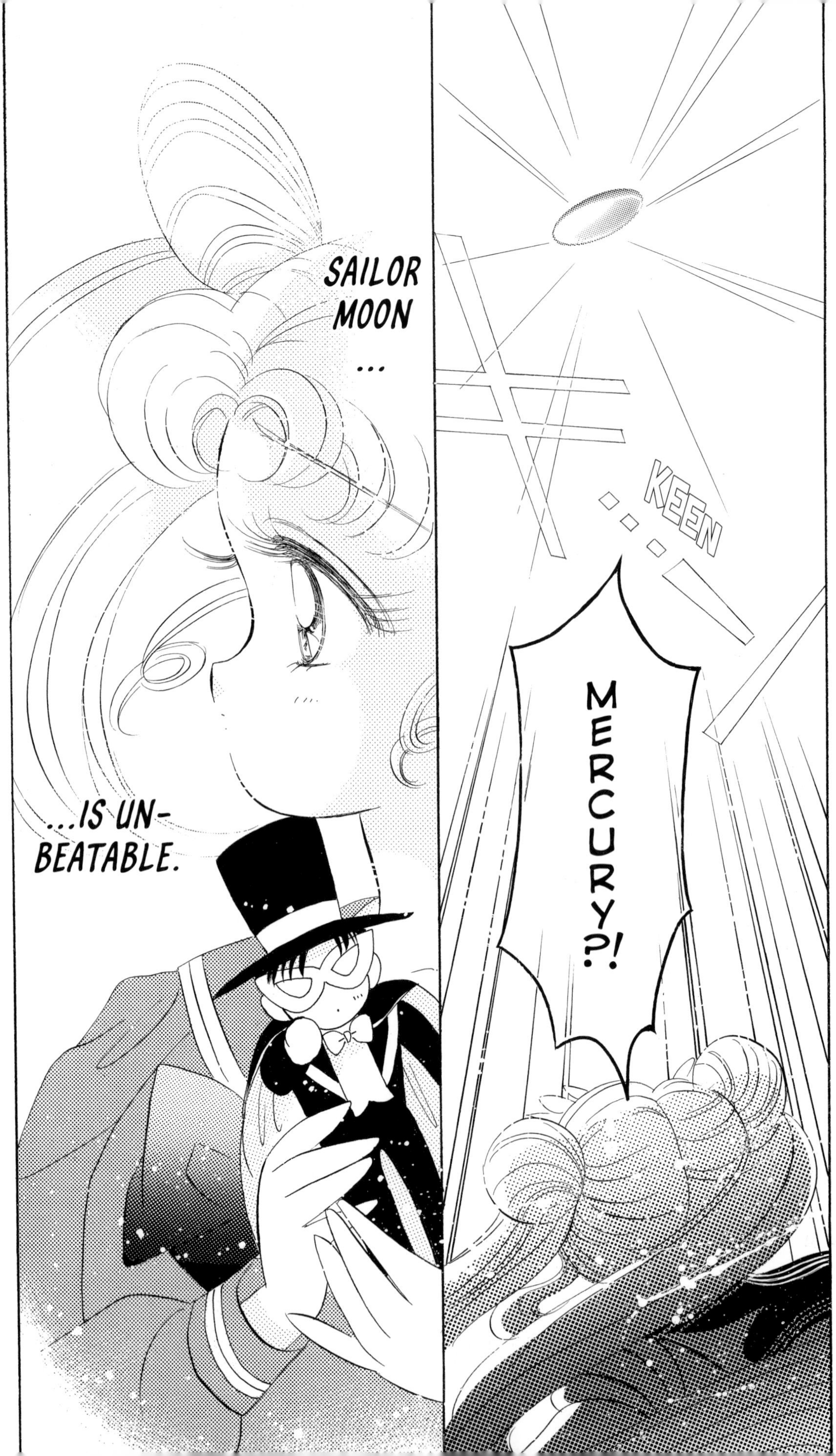
KEEN
MERCURY?!
SAILOR MOON ...
...IS UN-BEATABLE.

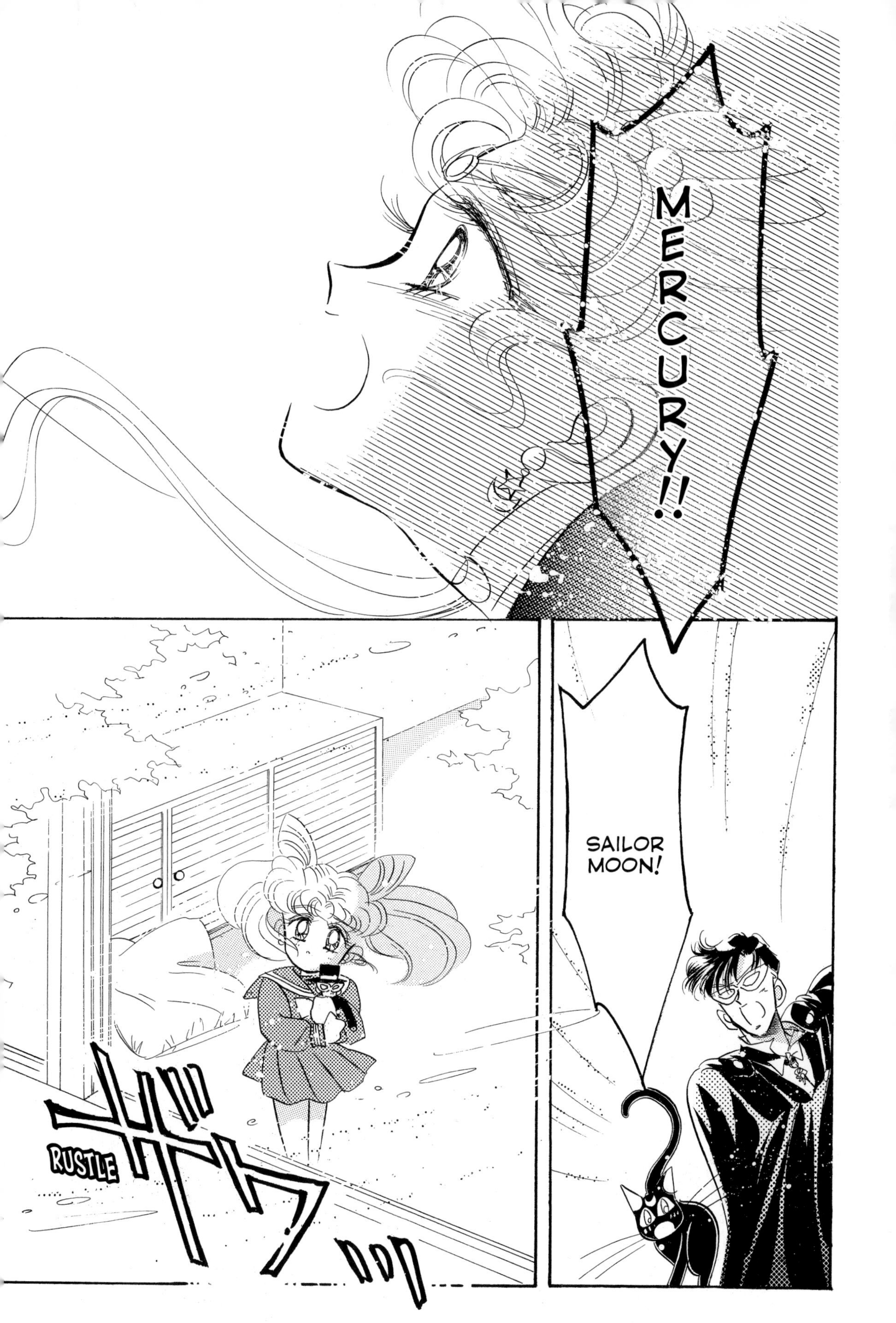
MERCURY!!
SAILOR MOON!
ザワッ
RUSTLE

Pretty Guardian Sailor Moon

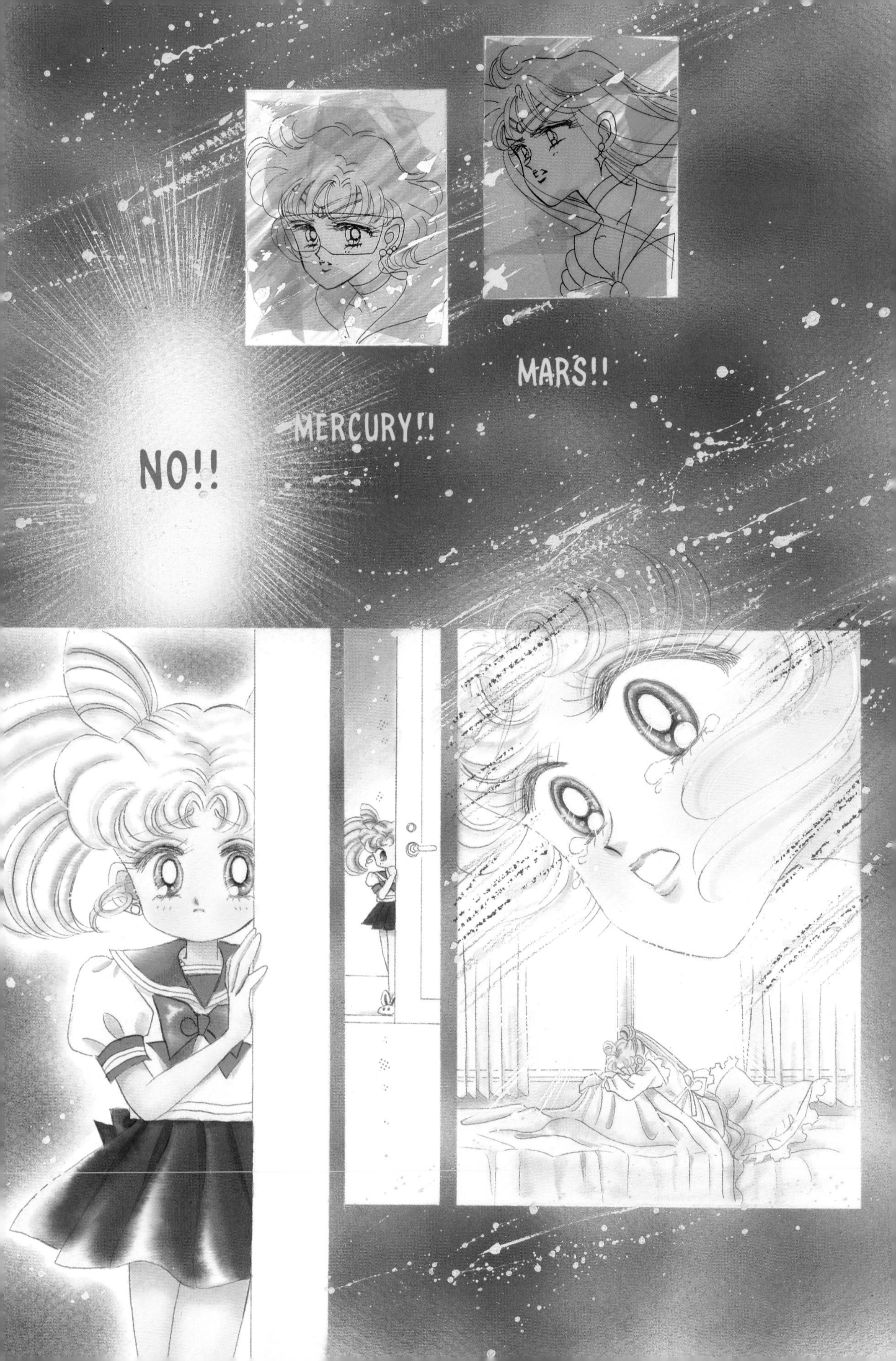
MARS!!
MERCURY!!
NO!!

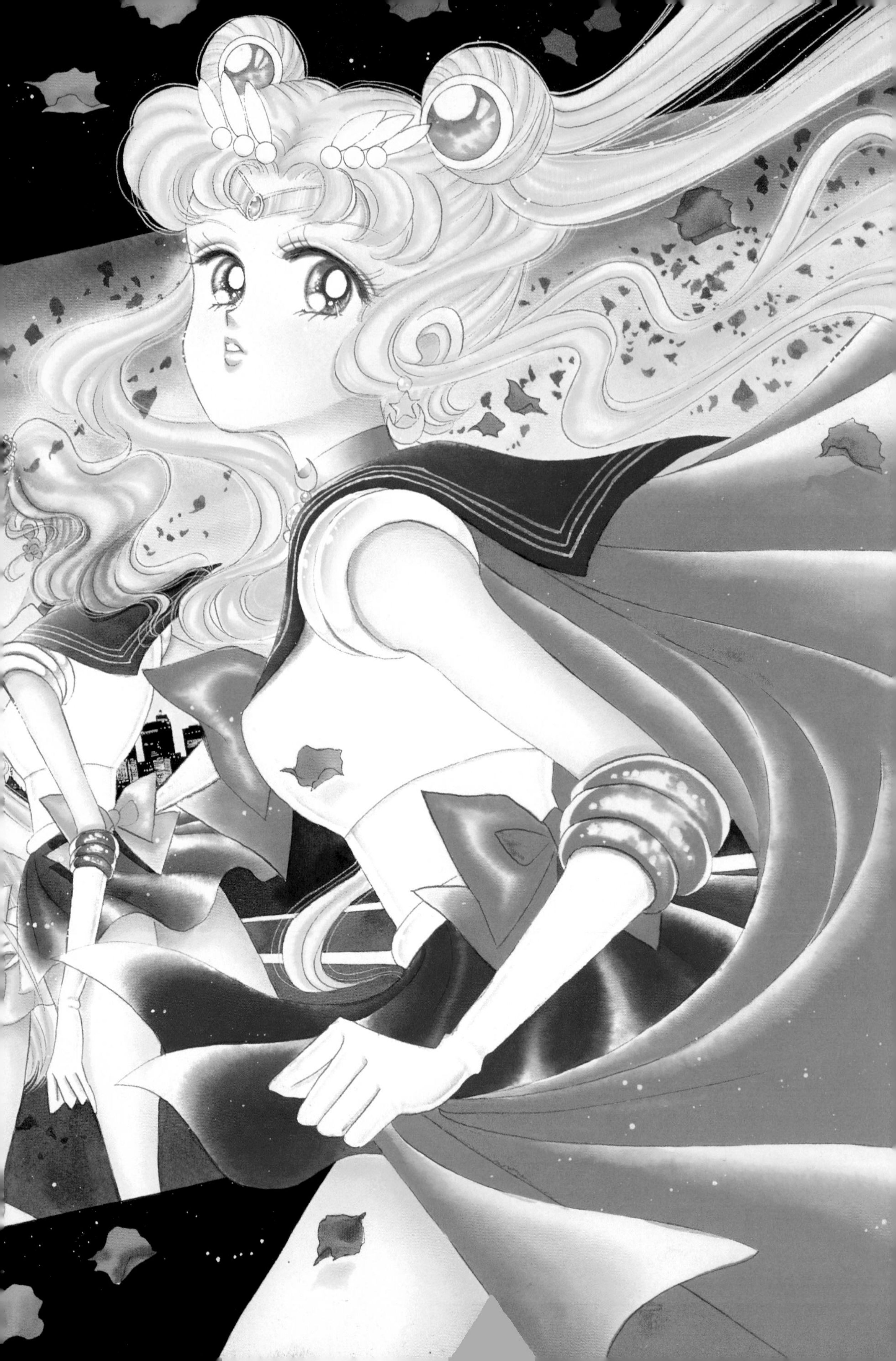

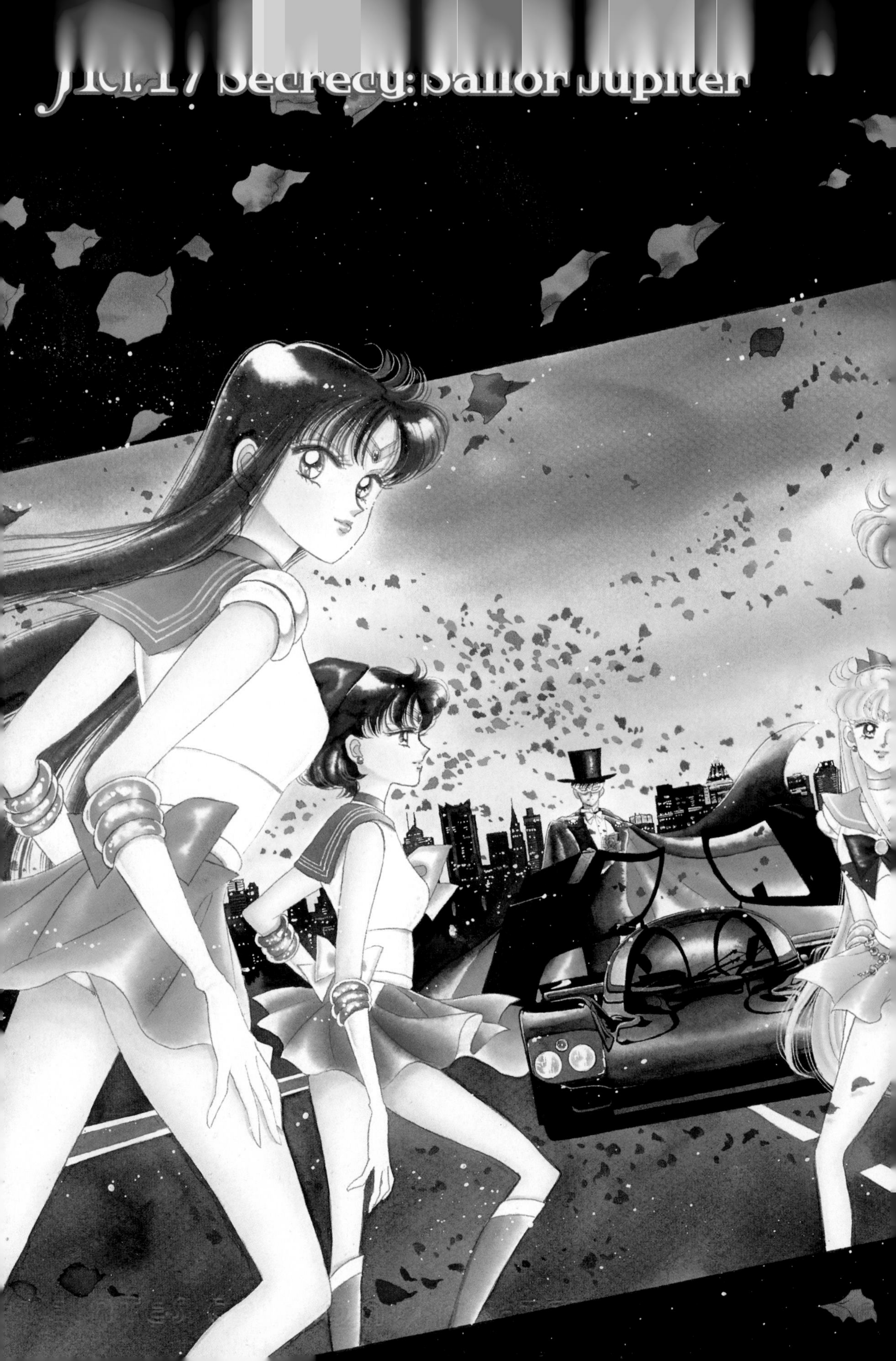
Act.17 Secrecy: Sailor Jupiter

Pretty Guardian
Sailor Moon

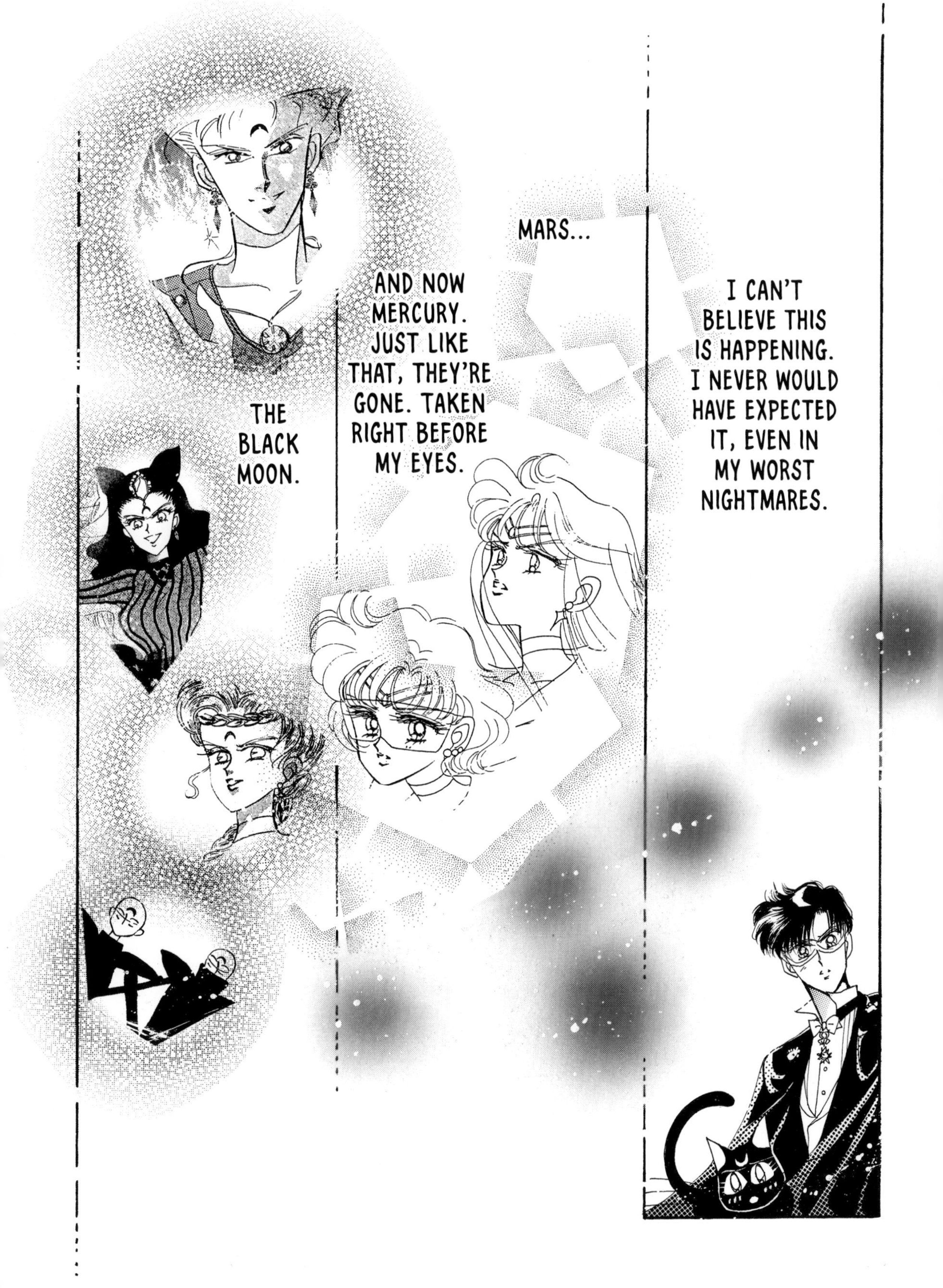
I CAN'T BELIEVE THIS IS HAPPENING. I NEVER WOULD HAVE EXPECTED IT, EVEN IN MY WORST NIGHTMARES.
MARS...
AND NOW MERCURY. JUST LIKE THAT, THEY'RE GONE. TAKEN RIGHT BEFORE MY EYES.
THE BLACK MOON.

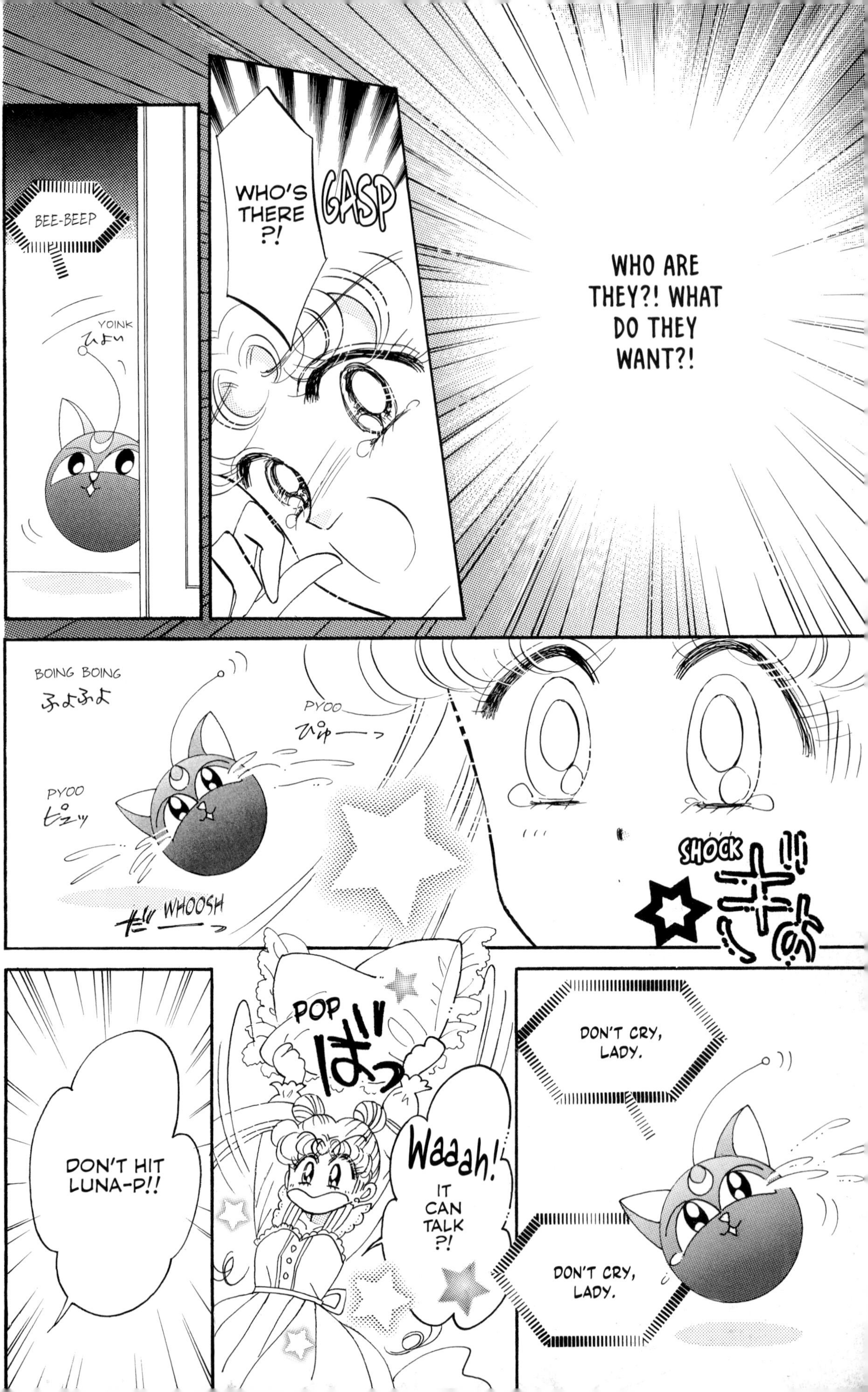
WHO ARE THEY?! WHAT DO THEY WANT?!
GASP
WHO'S THERE ?!
BEE-BEEP
YOINK
ひょい
SHOCK
PYOO
ぴゅーっ
BOING BOING
ふよふよ
PYOO
ピュッ
WHOOSH
だーっ
DON'T CRY, LADY.
DON'T CRY, LADY.
POP
ばっ
Waaah!
IT CAN TALK ?!
DON'T HIT LUNA-P!!

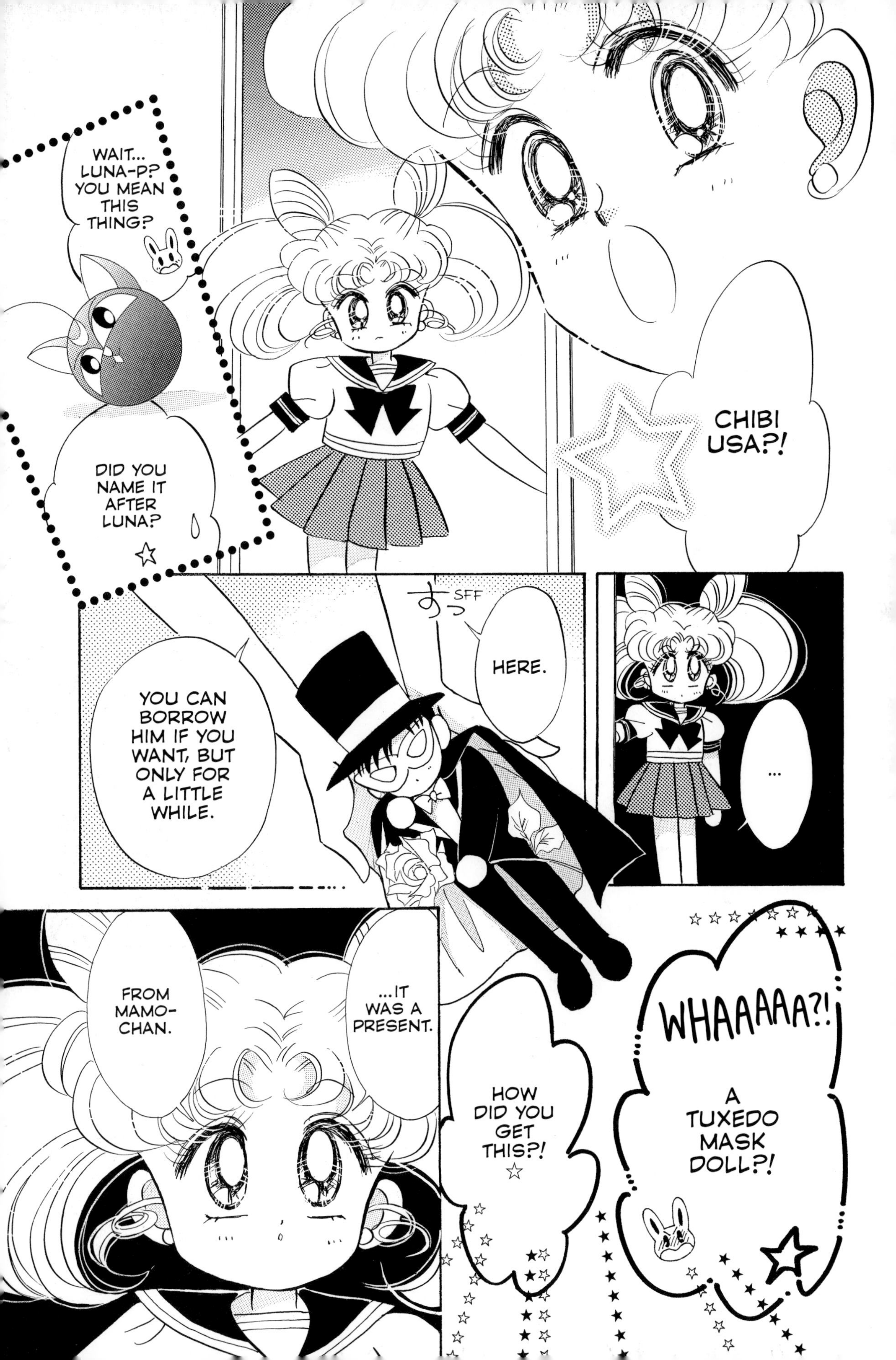
CHIBI USA?!
WAIT... LUNA-P? YOU MEAN THIS THING?
DID YOU NAME IT AFTER LUNA?
...
すっ SFF
HERE.
YOU CAN BORROW HIM IF YOU WANT, BUT ONLY FOR A LITTLE WHILE.
WHAAAAA?!
A TUXEDO MASK DOLL?!
HOW DID YOU GET THIS?!
...IT WAS A PRESENT.
FROM MAMO-CHAN.

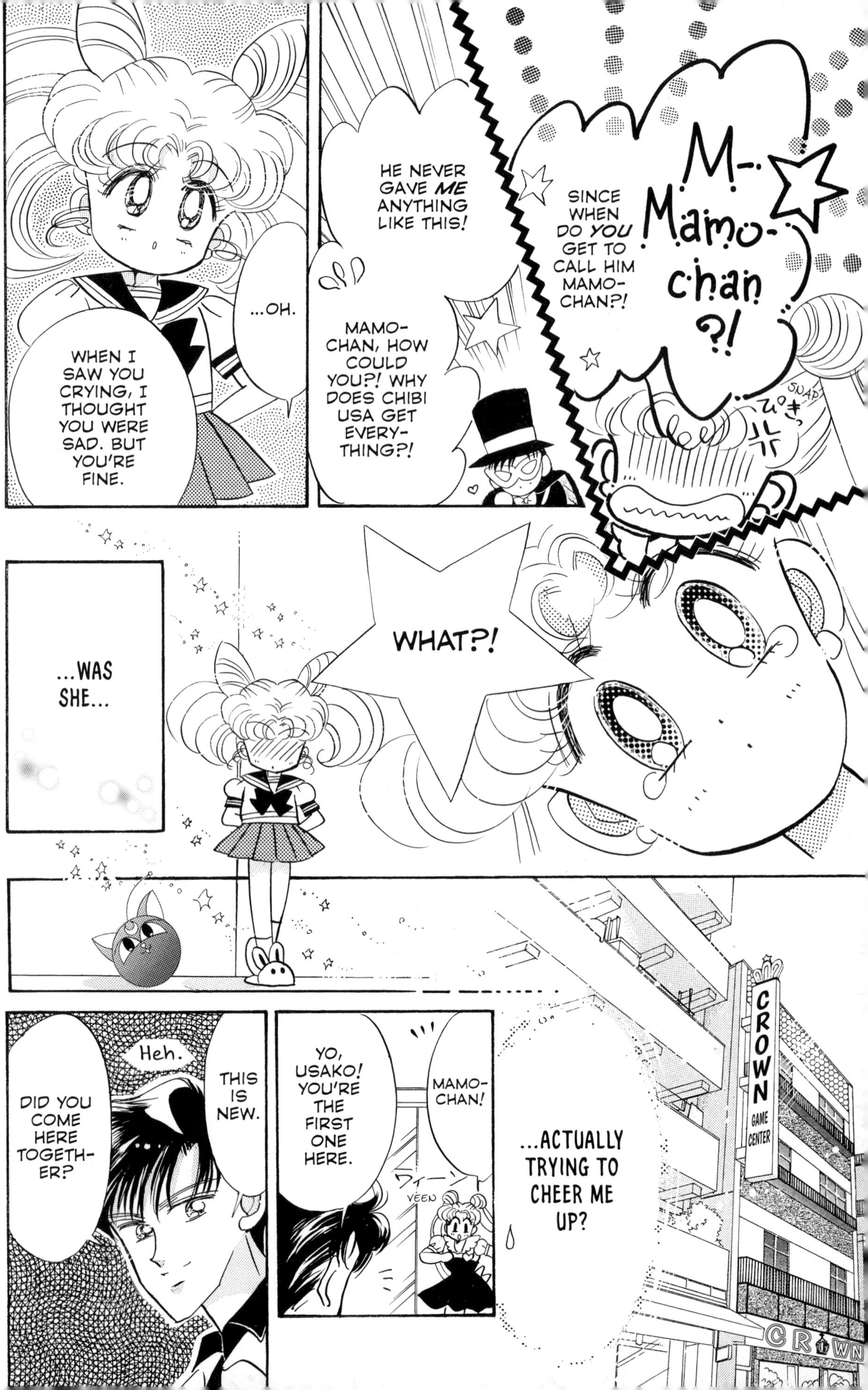
M- Mamo-chan?!
SINCE WHEN DO *YOU* GET TO CALL HIM MAMO-CHAN?!
SNAP
HE NEVER GAVE *ME* ANYTHING LIKE THIS!
MAMO-CHAN, HOW COULD YOU?! WHY DOES CHIBI USA GET EVERYTHING?!
...OH.
WHEN I SAW YOU CRYING, I THOUGHT YOU WERE SAD. BUT YOU'RE FINE.
WHAT?!
...WAS SHE...
...ACTUALLY TRYING TO CHEER ME UP?
CROWN GAME CENTER
MAMO-CHAN!
YO, USAKO! YOU'RE THE FIRST ONE HERE.
VEEN
THIS IS NEW.
Heh.
DID YOU COME HERE TOGETHER?

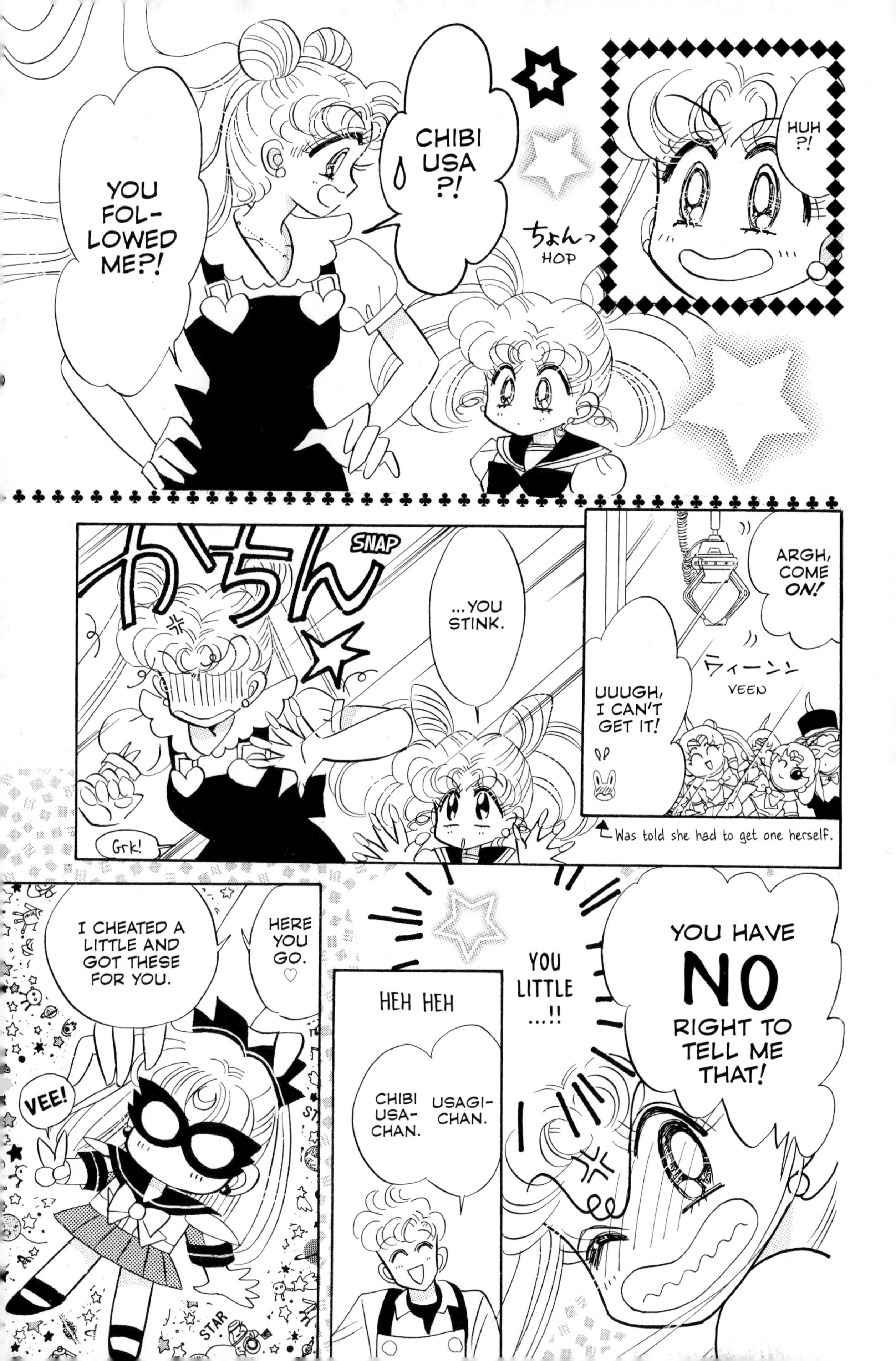
HUH ?!
CHIBI USA ?!
ちょんっ HOP
YOU FOL-LOWED ME?!
ARGH, COME ON!
VEEN
UUUGH, I CAN'T GET IT!
Was told she had to get one herself.
SNAP
...YOU STINK.
Grk!
YOU HAVE NO RIGHT TO TELL ME THAT!
YOU LITTLE ...!!
HEH HEH
USAGI-CHAN.
CHIBI USA-CHAN.
HERE YOU GO. ♡
I CHEATED A LITTLE AND GOT THESE FOR YOU.
VEE!

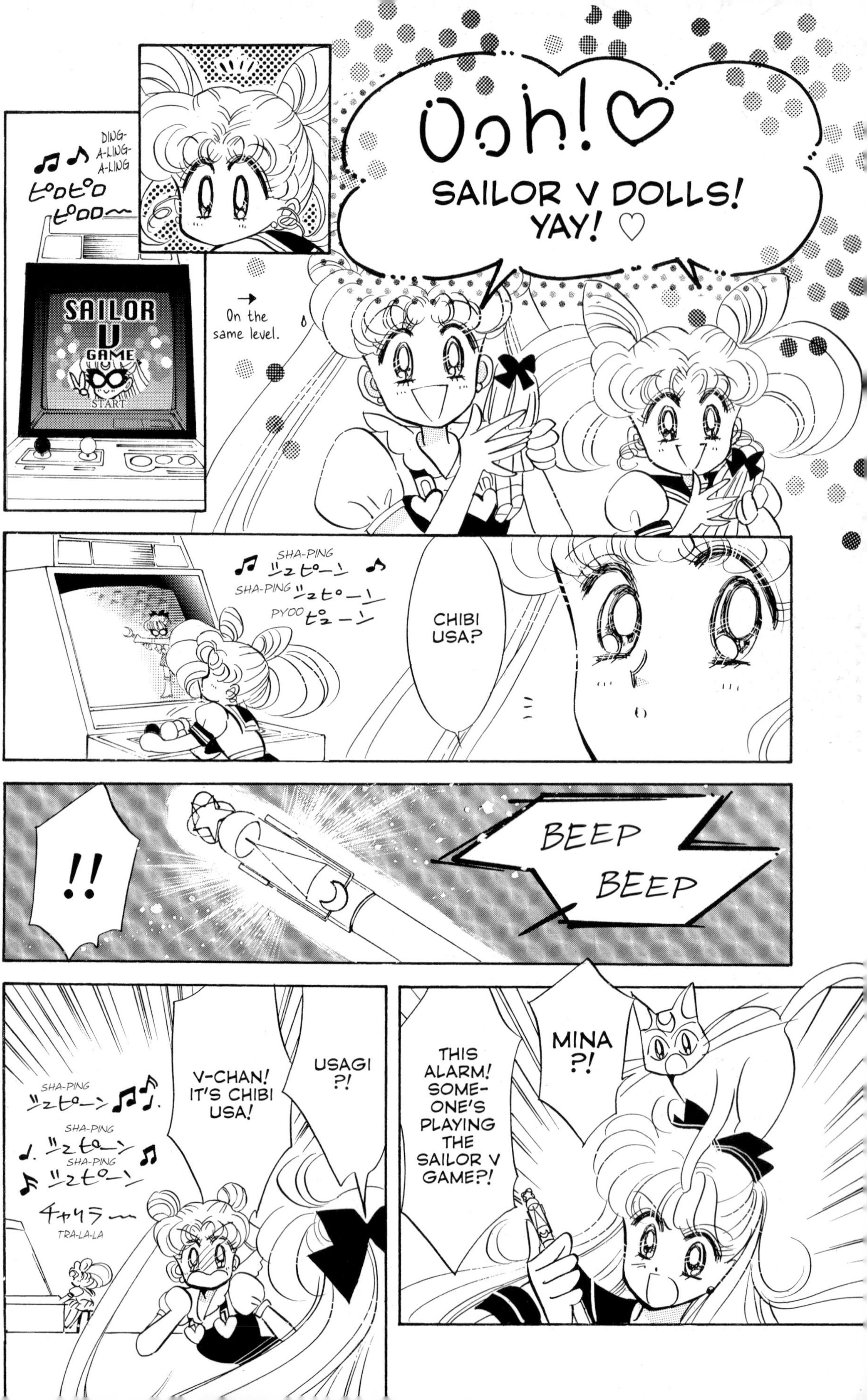
Ooh! ♡
SAILOR V DOLLS! YAY! ♡
On the same level.
DING-A-LING-A-LING
ピロピロ ピロロ~
SAILOR V GAME
START
CHIBI USA?
SHA-PING ジュピーン
SHA-PING ジュピーン
PYOO ピューン
BEEP BEEP
!!
MINA?!
THIS ALARM! SOME-ONE'S PLAYING THE SAILOR V GAME?!
USAGI?!
V-CHAN! IT'S CHIBI USA!
SHA-PING ジュピーン
SHA-PING ジュピーン
SHA-PING ジュピーン
チャリラ~ TRA-LA-LA

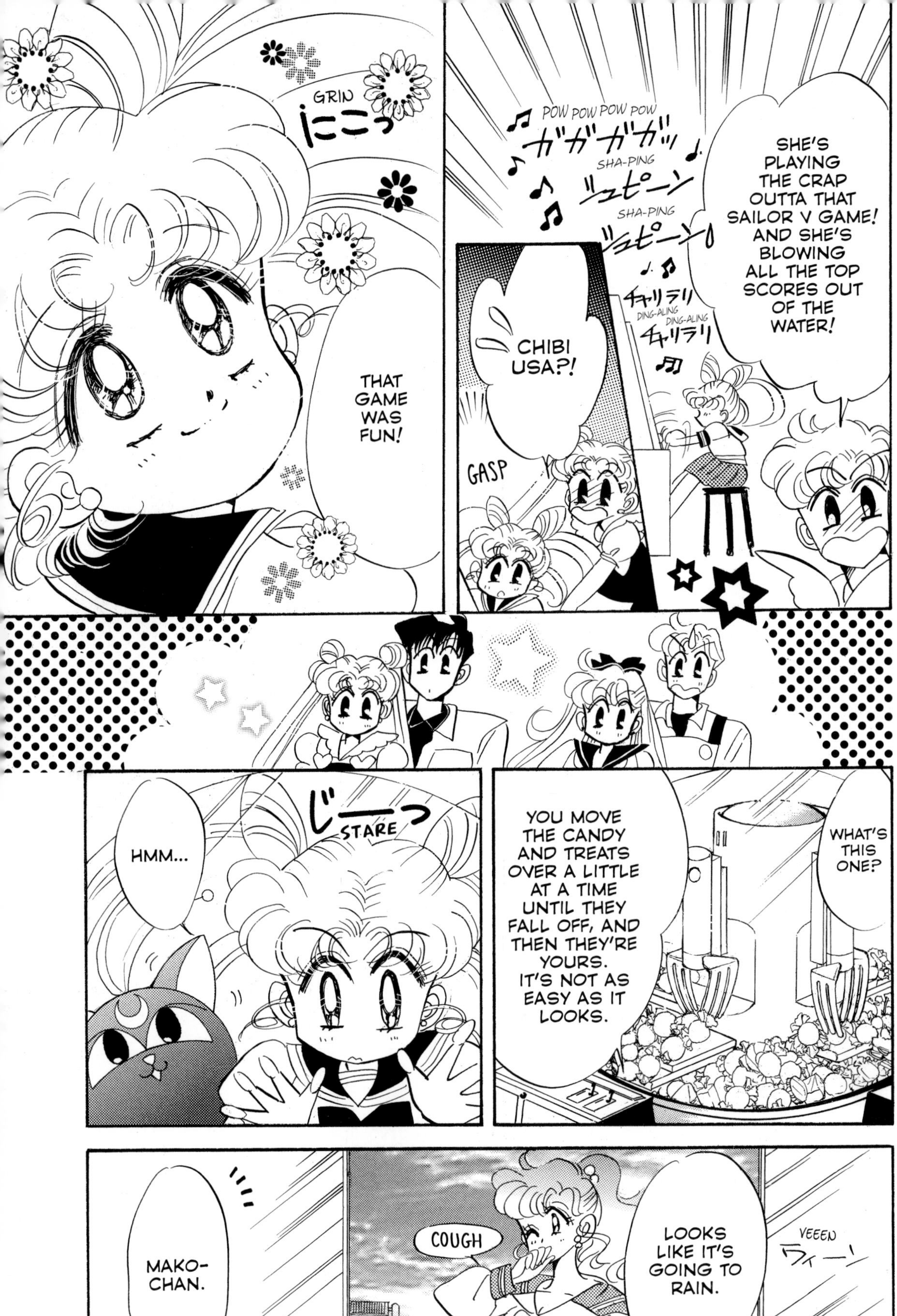
POW POW POW POW
ガガガガッ
SHA-PING
ジュピーン
SHA-PING
ジュピーン
SHE'S PLAYING THE CRAP OUTTA THAT SAILOR V GAME! AND SHE'S BLOWING ALL THE TOP SCORES OUT OF THE WATER!
CHIBI USA?!
チャリラリ
DING-ALING
DING-ALING
チャリラリ
GASP
GRIN
にこっ
THAT GAME WAS FUN!
WHAT'S THIS ONE?
YOU MOVE THE CANDY AND TREATS OVER A LITTLE AT A TIME UNTIL THEY FALL OFF, AND THEN THEY'RE YOURS. IT'S NOT AS EASY AS IT LOOKS.
じーっ
STARE
HMM...
VEEEN
ヴィー!
LOOKS LIKE IT'S GOING TO RAIN.
COUGH
MAKO-CHAN.

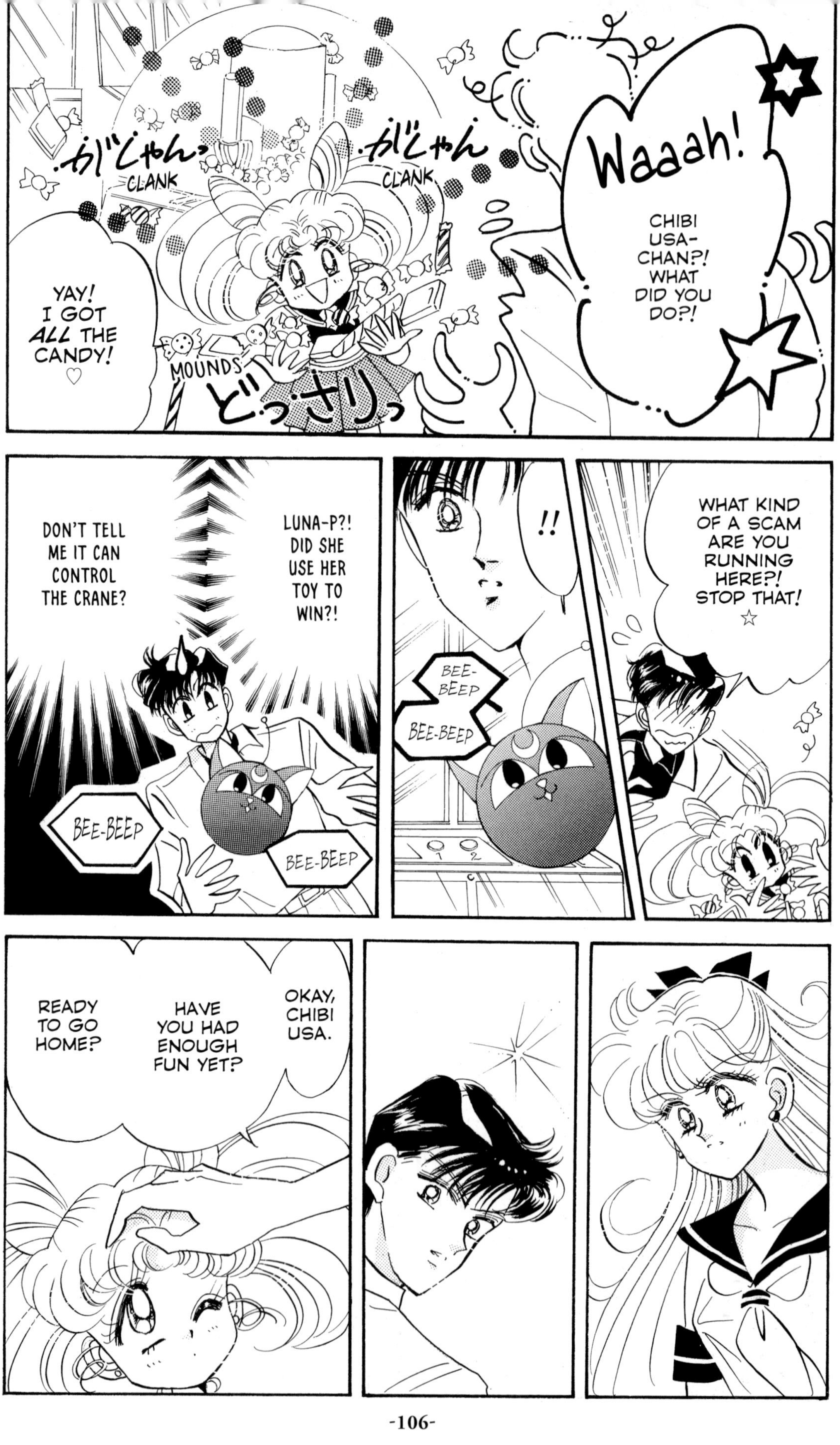
Waaah!
CHIBI USA-CHAN?! WHAT DID YOU DO?!
がじゃん
CLANK
がじゃん
CLANK
YAY! I GOT ALL THE CANDY! ♡
MOUNDS
どっさりっ
WHAT KIND OF A SCAM ARE YOU RUNNING HERE?! STOP THAT! ☆
!!
BEE-BEEP
BEE-BEEP
LUNA-P?! DID SHE USE HER TOY TO WIN?!
DON'T TELL ME IT CAN CONTROL THE CRANE?
BEE-BEEP
BEE-BEEP
OKAY, CHIBI USA.
HAVE YOU HAD ENOUGH FUN YET?
READY TO GO HOME?

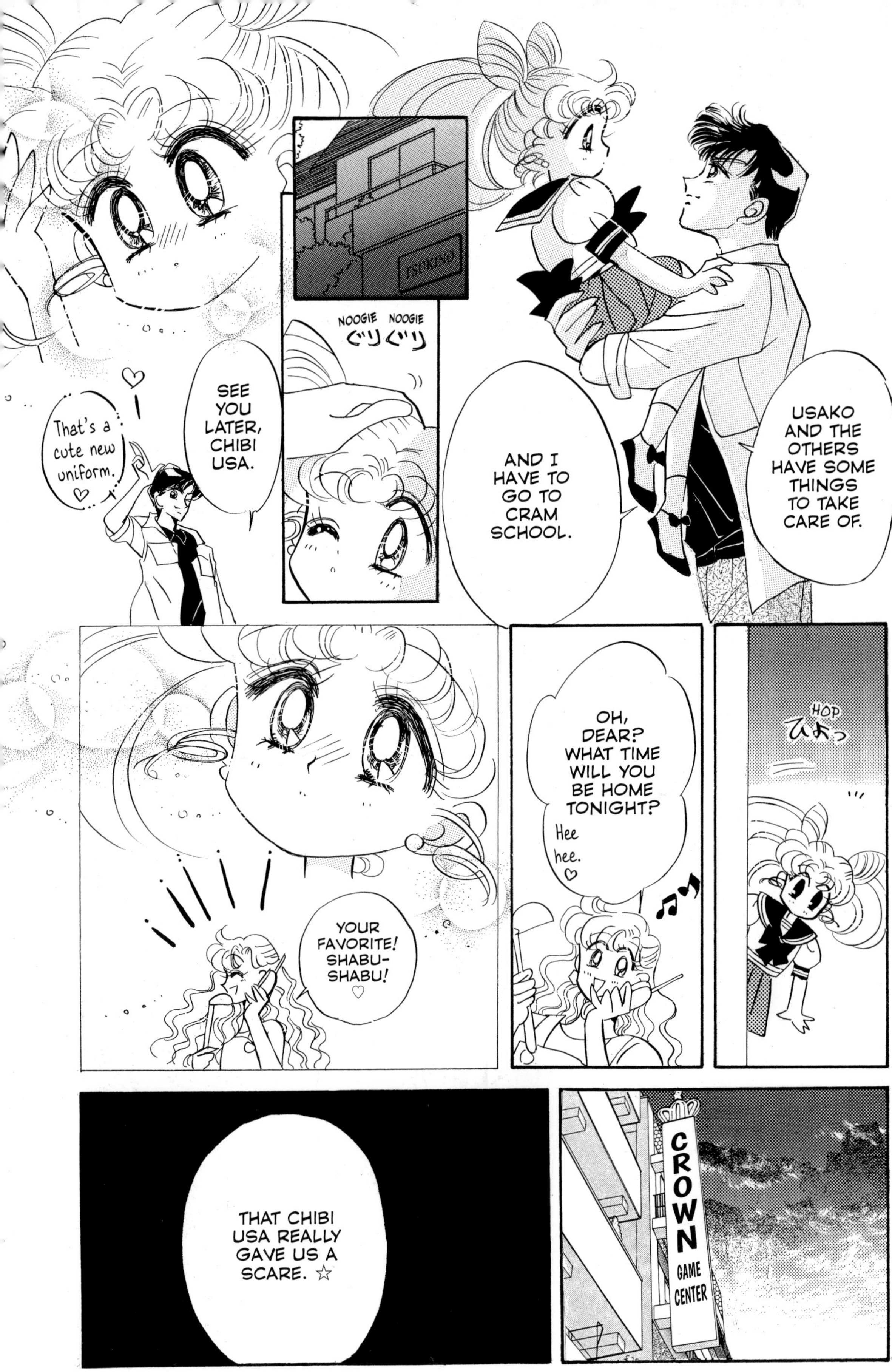
USAKO AND THE OTHERS HAVE SOME THINGS TO TAKE CARE OF.
AND I HAVE TO GO TO CRAM SCHOOL.
TSUKINO
NOOGIE NOOGIE
ぐりぐり
SEE YOU LATER, CHIBI USA.
That's a cute new uniform. ♡
HOP
ひよっ
OH, DEAR? WHAT TIME WILL YOU BE HOME TONIGHT?
Hee hee. ♡
YOUR FAVORITE! SHABU-SHABU! ♡
CROWN
GAME CENTER
THAT CHIBI USA REALLY GAVE US A SCARE. ☆

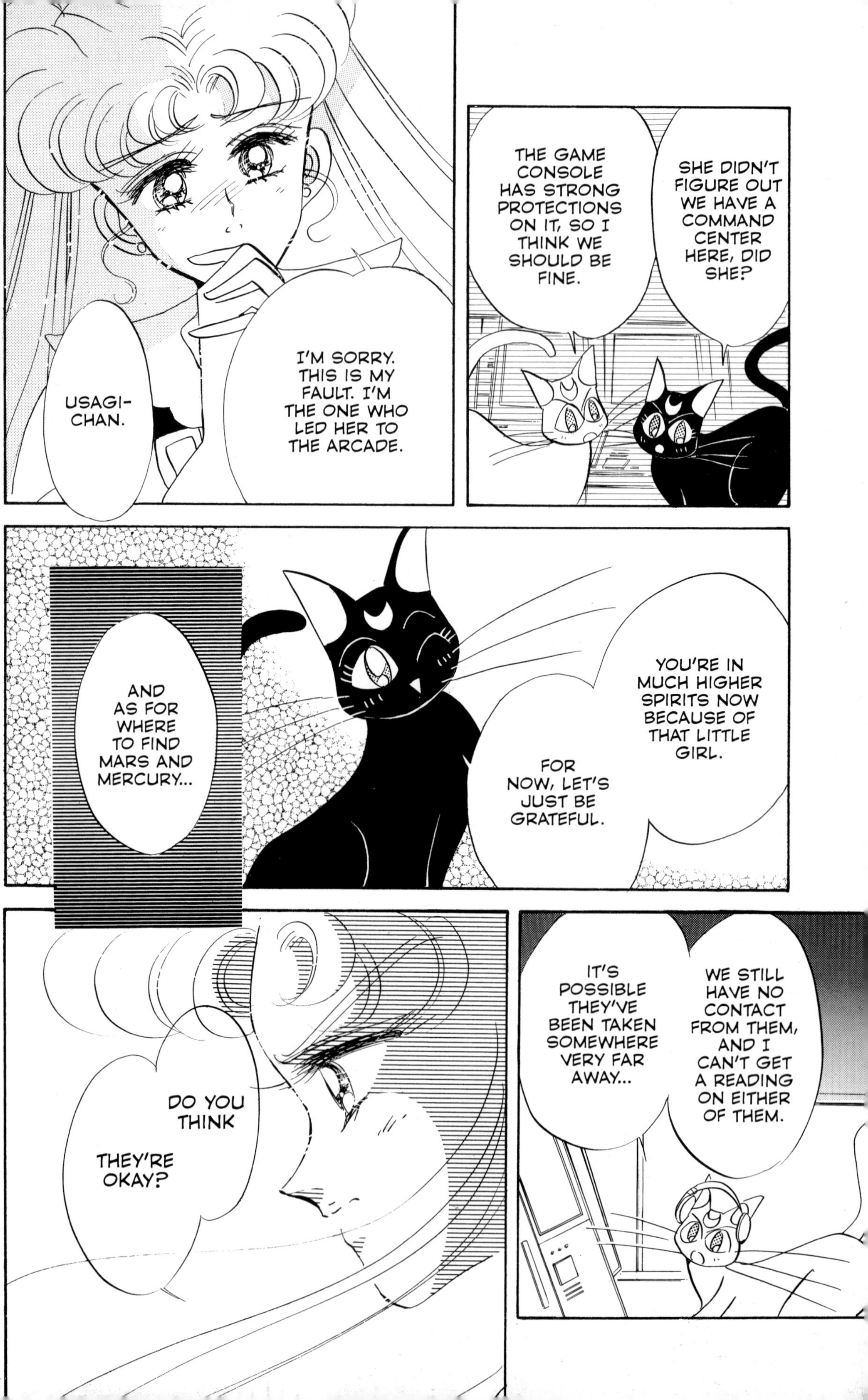
SHE DIDN'T FIGURE OUT WE HAVE A COMMAND CENTER HERE, DID SHE?
THE GAME CONSOLE HAS STRONG PROTECTIONS ON IT, SO I THINK WE SHOULD BE FINE.
I'M SORRY. THIS IS MY FAULT. I'M THE ONE WHO LED HER TO THE ARCADE.
USAGI-CHAN.
YOU'RE IN MUCH HIGHER SPIRITS NOW BECAUSE OF THAT LITTLE GIRL.
FOR NOW, LET'S JUST BE GRATEFUL.
AND AS FOR WHERE TO FIND MARS AND MERCURY...
WE STILL HAVE NO CONTACT FROM THEM, AND I CAN'T GET A READING ON EITHER OF THEM.
IT'S POSSIBLE THEY'VE BEEN TAKEN SOMEWHERE VERY FAR AWAY...
DO YOU THINK
THEY'RE OKAY?

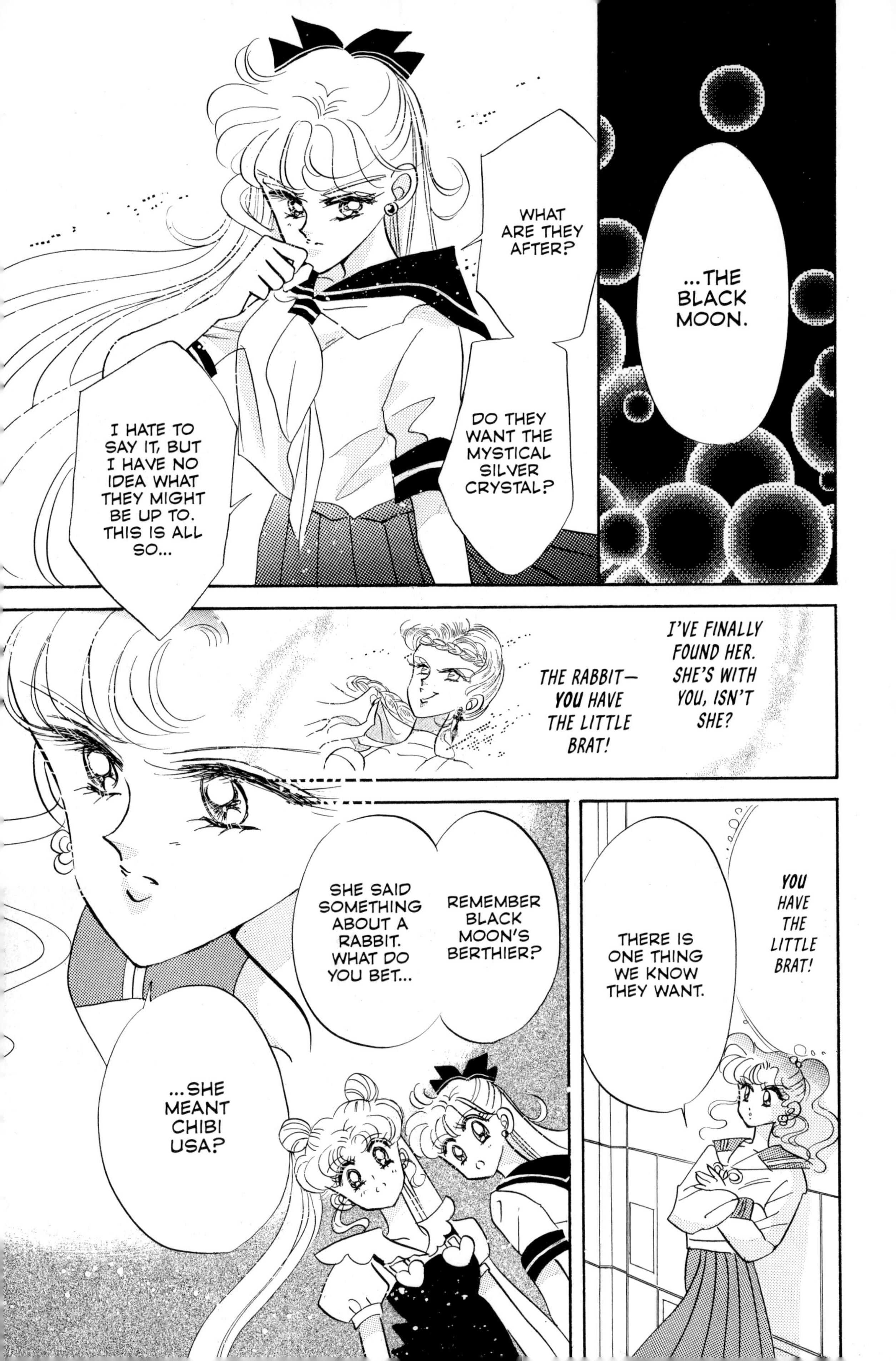
...THE BLACK MOON.
WHAT ARE THEY AFTER?
DO THEY WANT THE MYSTICAL SILVER CRYSTAL?
I HATE TO SAY IT, BUT I HAVE NO IDEA WHAT THEY MIGHT BE UP TO. THIS IS ALL SO...
I'VE FINALLY FOUND HER. SHE'S WITH YOU, ISN'T SHE?
THE RABBIT—YOU HAVE THE LITTLE BRAT!
YOU HAVE THE LITTLE BRAT!
THERE IS ONE THING WE KNOW THEY WANT.
REMEMBER BLACK MOON'S BERTHIER?
SHE SAID SOMETHING ABOUT A RABBIT. WHAT DO YOU BET...
...SHE MEANT CHIBI USA?

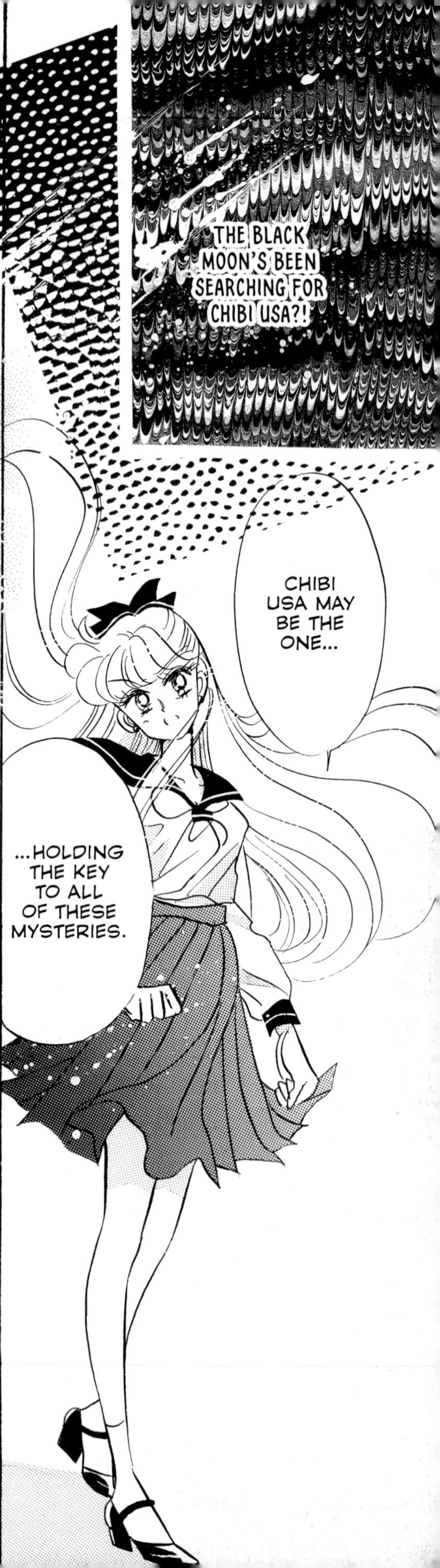
THE BLACK MOON'S BEEN SEARCHING FOR CHIBI USA?!
CHIBI USA MAY BE THE ONE...
...HOLDING THE KEY TO ALL OF THESE MYSTERIES.

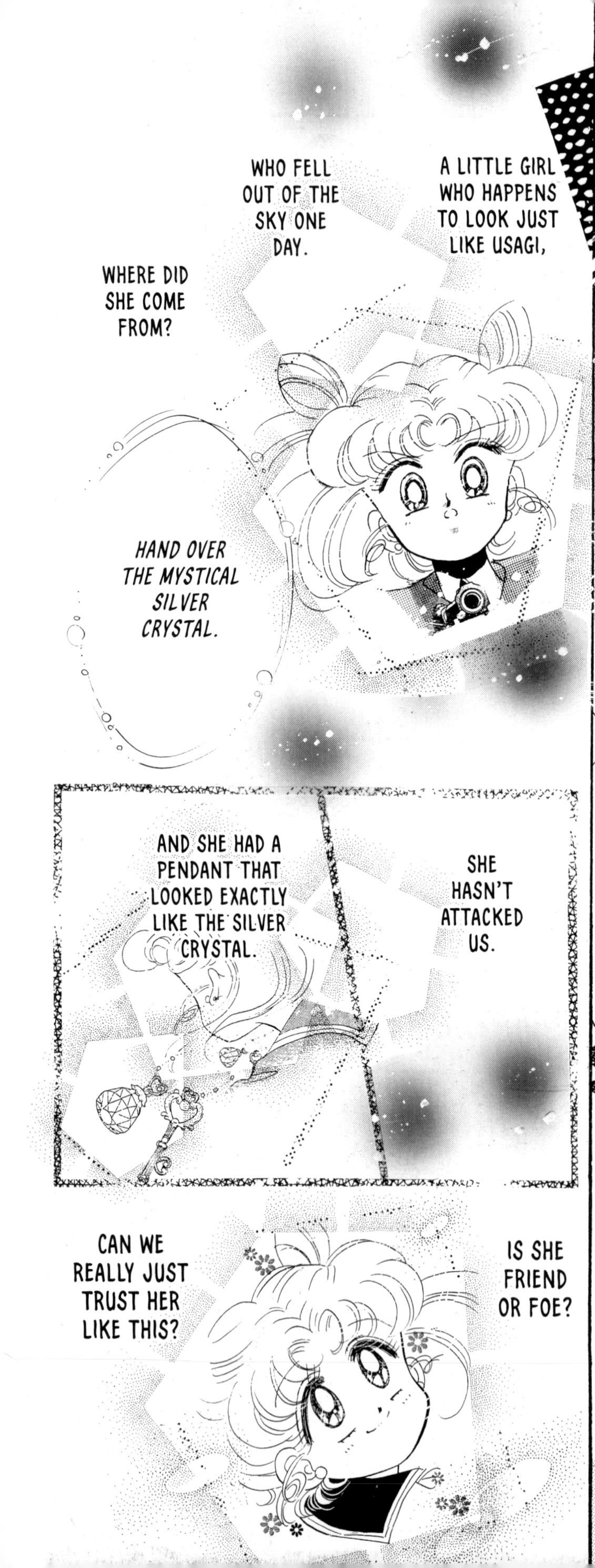
A LITTLE GIRL WHO HAPPENS TO LOOK JUST LIKE USAGI,
WHO FELL OUT OF THE SKY ONE DAY.
WHERE DID SHE COME FROM?
HAND OVER THE MYSTICAL SILVER CRYSTAL.
SHE HASN'T ATTACKED US.
AND SHE HAD A PENDANT THAT LOOKED EXACTLY LIKE THE SILVER CRYSTAL.
IS SHE FRIEND OR FOE?
CAN WE REALLY JUST TRUST HER LIKE THIS?

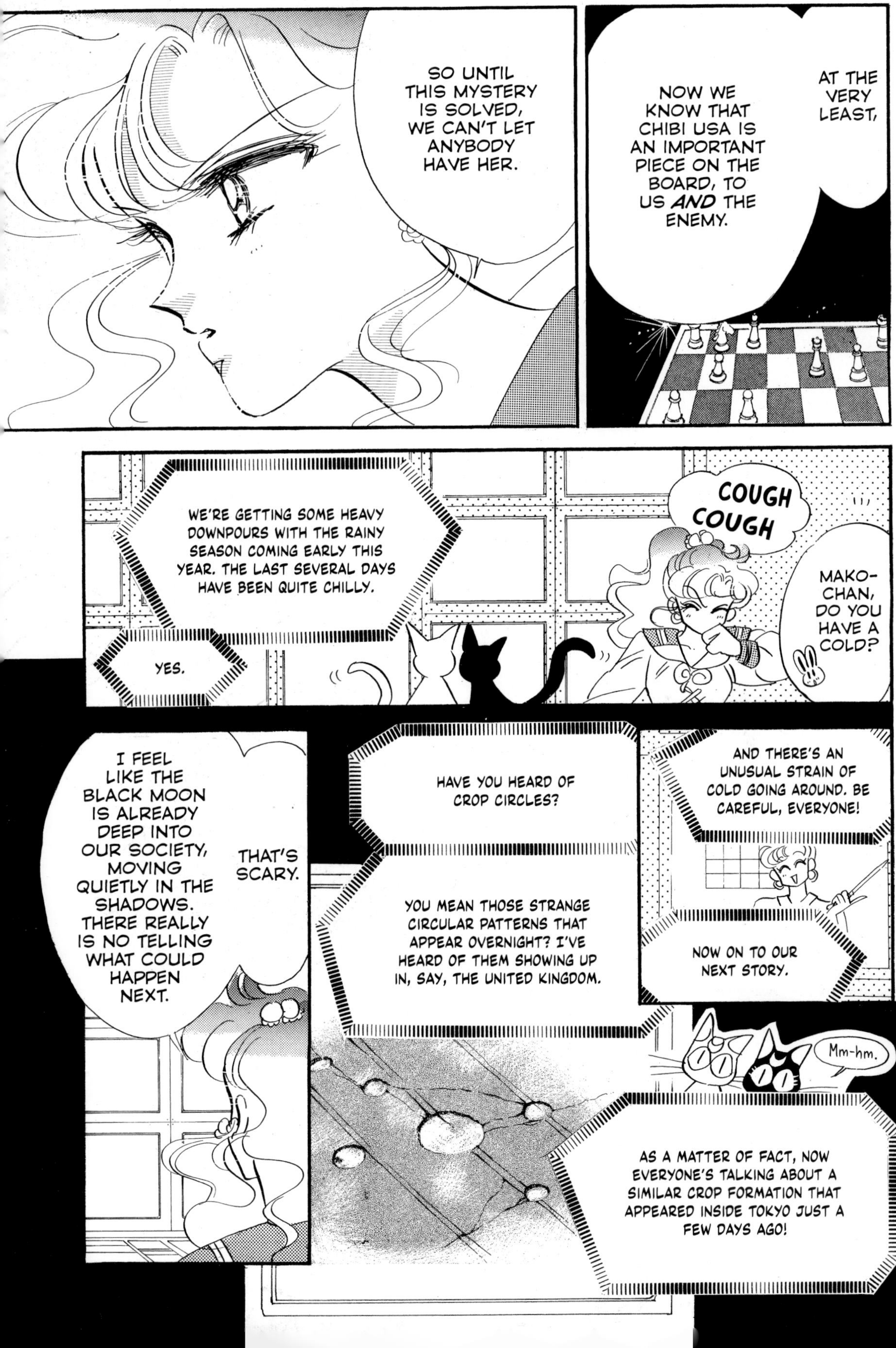
AT THE VERY LEAST,
NOW WE KNOW THAT CHIBI USA IS AN IMPORTANT PIECE ON THE BOARD, TO US *AND* THE ENEMY.
SO UNTIL THIS MYSTERY IS SOLVED, WE CAN'T LET ANYBODY HAVE HER.
COUGH COUGH
MAKO-CHAN, DO YOU HAVE A COLD?
WE'RE GETTING SOME HEAVY DOWNPOURS WITH THE RAINY SEASON COMING EARLY THIS YEAR. THE LAST SEVERAL DAYS HAVE BEEN QUITE CHILLY.
YES.
AND THERE'S AN UNUSUAL STRAIN OF COLD GOING AROUND. BE CAREFUL, EVERYONE!
NOW ON TO OUR NEXT STORY.
HAVE YOU HEARD OF CROP CIRCLES?
YOU MEAN THOSE STRANGE CIRCULAR PATTERNS THAT APPEAR OVERNIGHT? I'VE HEARD OF THEM SHOWING UP IN, SAY, THE UNITED KINGDOM.
Mm-hm.
AS A MATTER OF FACT, NOW EVERYONE'S TALKING ABOUT A SIMILAR CROP FORMATION THAT APPEARED INSIDE TOKYO JUST A FEW DAYS AGO!
THAT'S SCARY.
I FEEL LIKE THE BLACK MOON IS ALREADY DEEP INTO OUR SOCIETY, MOVING QUIETLY IN THE SHADOWS. THERE REALLY IS NO TELLING WHAT COULD HAPPEN NEXT.

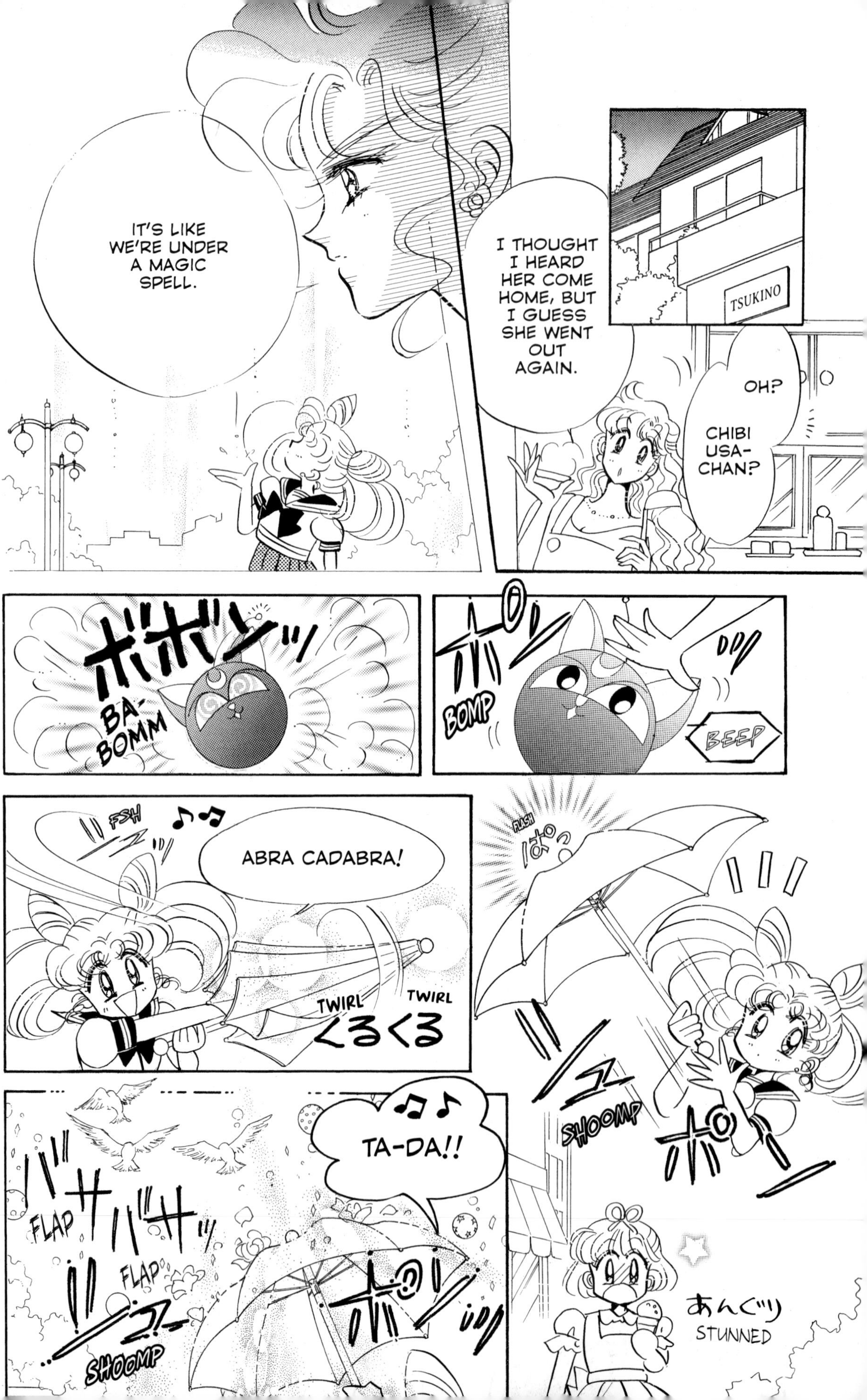
TSUKINO
OH?
CHIBI USA-CHAN?
I THOUGHT I HEARD HER COME HOME, BUT I GUESS SHE WENT OUT AGAIN.
IT'S LIKE WE'RE UNDER A MAGIC SPELL.
BOMP
BEEP
ボボンッ
BA-BOMM
FLASH
ぱっ
SHOOMP
FSH
ABRA CADABRA!
TWIRL TWIRL
くるくる
あんぐり
STUNNED
TA-DA!!
FLAP
FLAP
SHOOMP

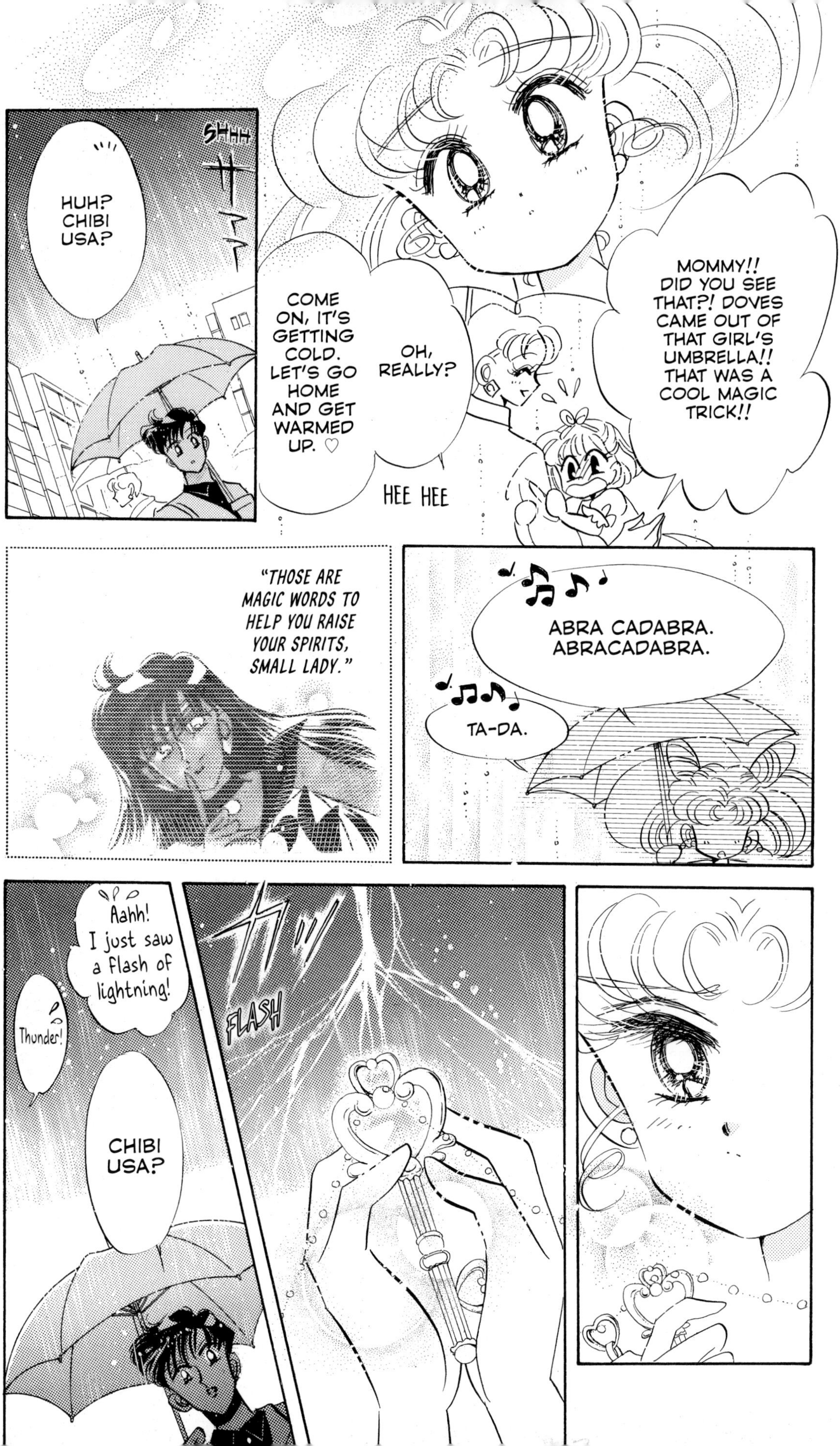
MOMMY!! DID YOU SEE THAT?! DOVES CAME OUT OF THAT GIRL'S UMBRELLA!! THAT WAS A COOL MAGIC TRICK!!
OH, REALLY?
COME ON, IT'S GETTING COLD. LET'S GO HOME AND GET WARMED UP. ♡
HEE HEE
SHHH
HUH? CHIBI USA?
ABRA CADABRA. ABRACADABRA.
TA-DA.
"THOSE ARE MAGIC WORDS TO HELP YOU RAISE YOUR SPIRITS, SMALL LADY."
FLASH
Aahh! I just saw a flash of lightning!
Thunder!
CHIBI USA?

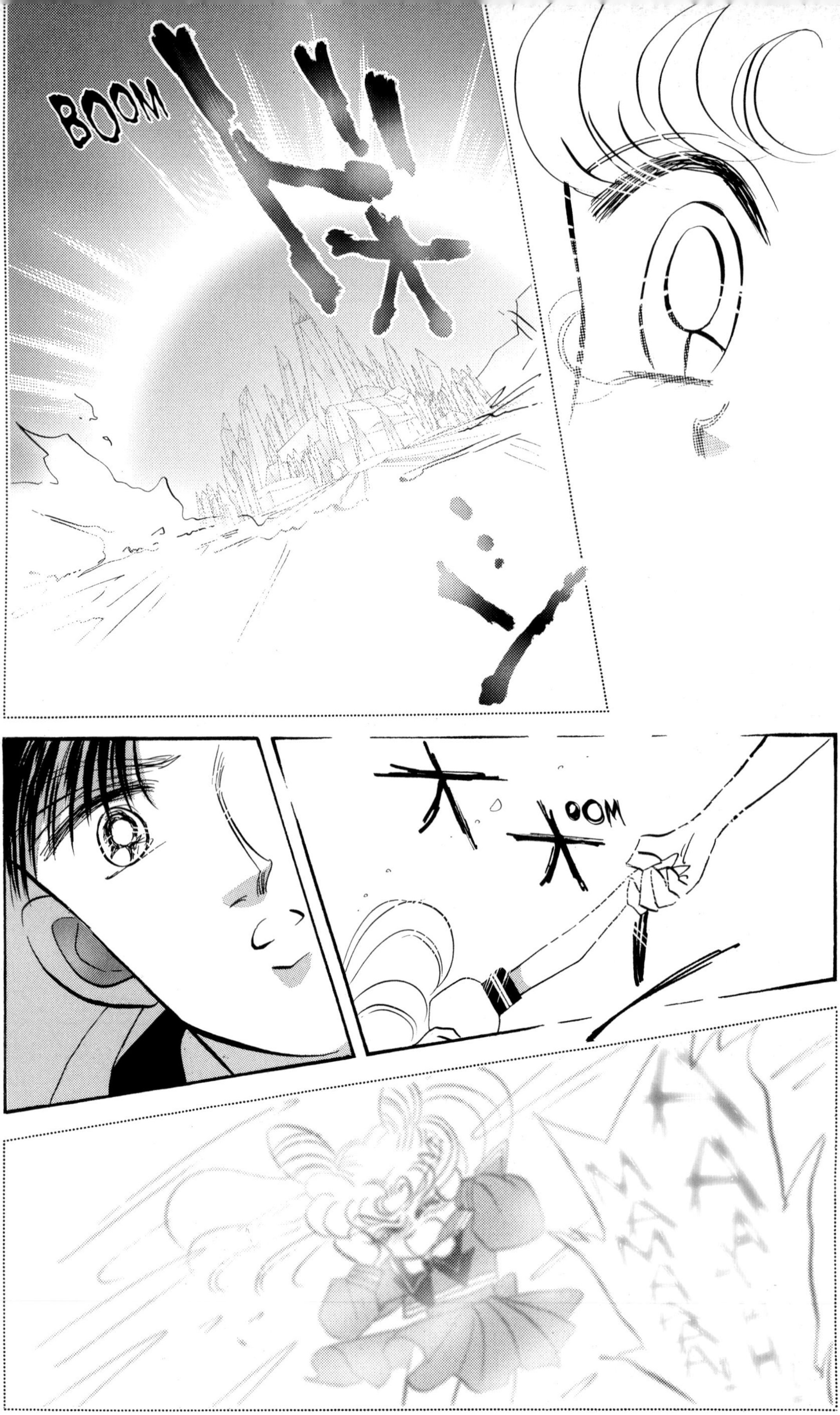
BOOM
OOM

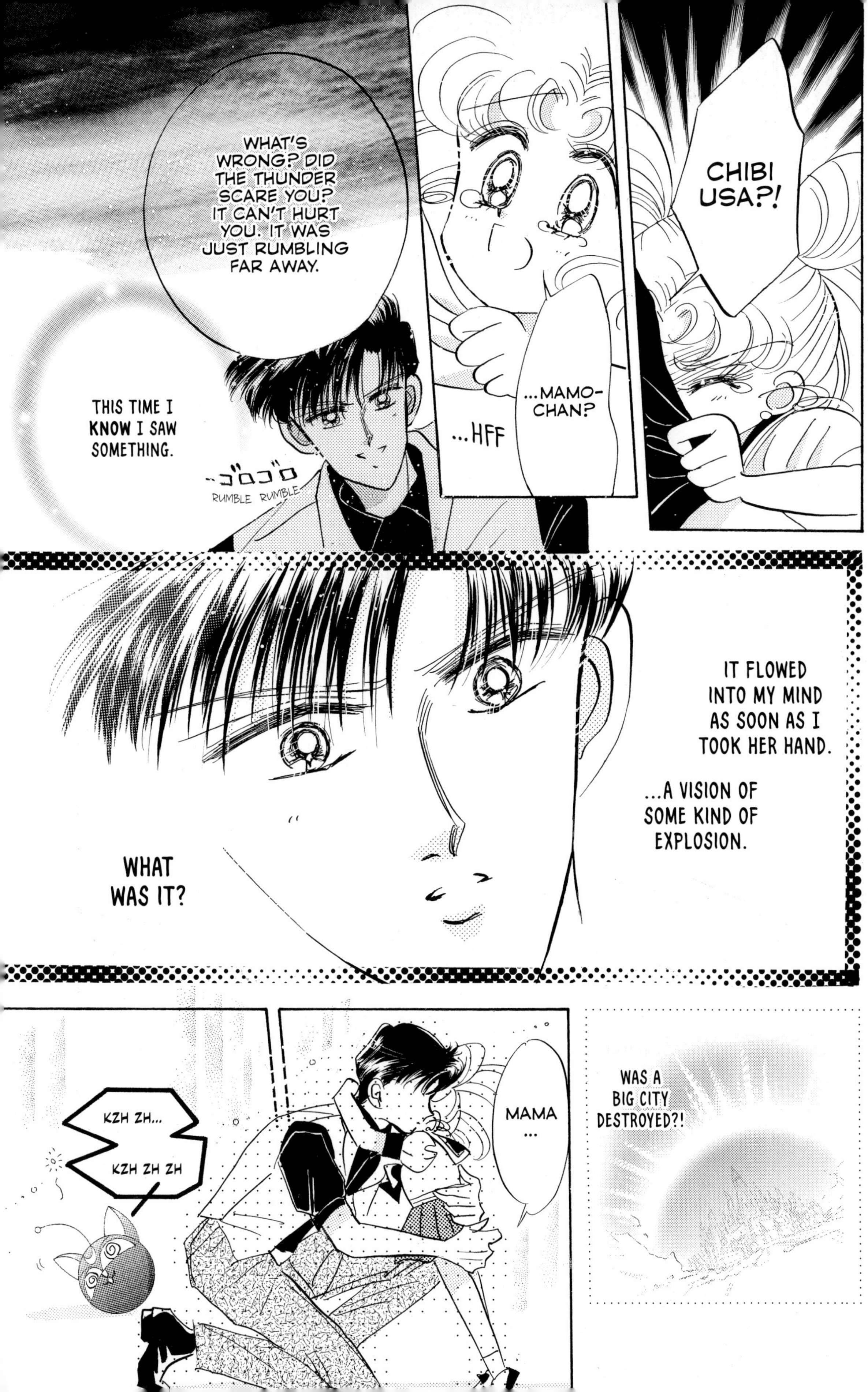
CHIBI USA?!
...MAMO-CHAN?
...HFF
WHAT'S WRONG? DID THE THUNDER SCARE YOU? IT CAN'T HURT YOU. IT WAS JUST RUMBLING FAR AWAY.
THIS TIME I KNOW I SAW SOMETHING.
ゴロゴロ
RUMBLE RUMBLE
IT FLOWED INTO MY MIND AS SOON AS I TOOK HER HAND.
...A VISION OF SOME KIND OF EXPLOSION.
WHAT WAS IT?
WAS A BIG CITY DESTROYED?!
MAMA ...
KZH ZH...
KZH ZH ZH

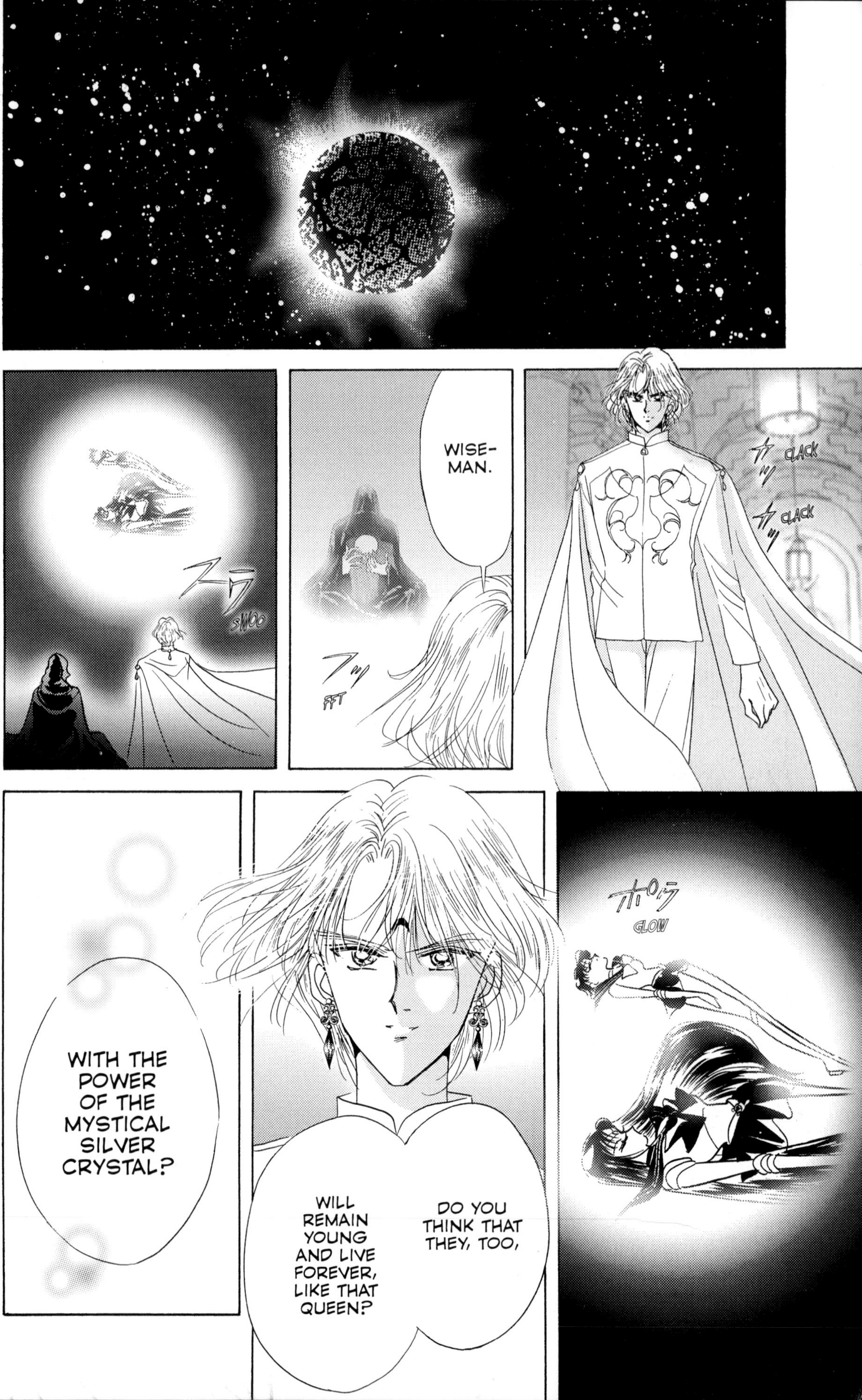
CLACK
CLACK
WISE-MAN.
FFT
SWOO
GLOW
DO YOU THINK THAT THEY, TOO,
WILL REMAIN YOUNG AND LIVE FOREVER, LIKE THAT QUEEN?
WITH THE POWER OF THE MYSTICAL SILVER CRYSTAL?

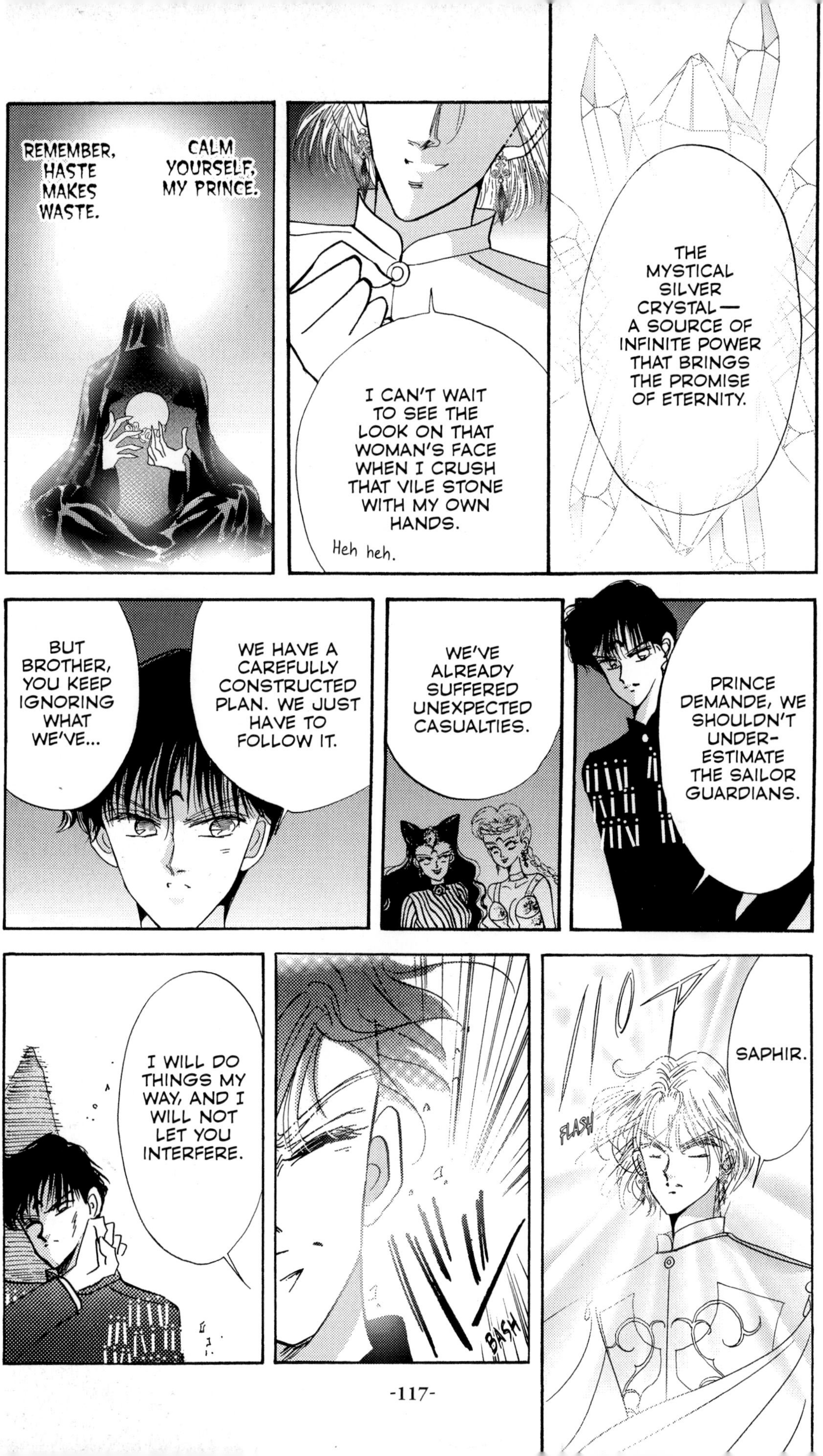
THE MYSTICAL SILVER CRYSTAL— A SOURCE OF INFINITE POWER THAT BRINGS THE PROMISE OF ETERNITY.
I CAN'T WAIT TO SEE THE LOOK ON THAT WOMAN'S FACE WHEN I CRUSH THAT VILE STONE WITH MY OWN HANDS.
Heh heh.
CALM YOURSELF, MY PRINCE.
REMEMBER, HASTE MAKES WASTE.
PRINCE DEMANDE, WE SHOULDN'T UNDER-ESTIMATE THE SAILOR GUARDIANS.
WE'VE ALREADY SUFFERED UNEXPECTED CASUALTIES.
WE HAVE A CAREFULLY CONSTRUCTED PLAN. WE JUST HAVE TO FOLLOW IT.
BUT BROTHER, YOU KEEP IGNORING WHAT WE'VE...
SAPHIR.
FLASH
BASH
I WILL DO THINGS MY WAY, AND I WILL NOT LET YOU INTERFERE.

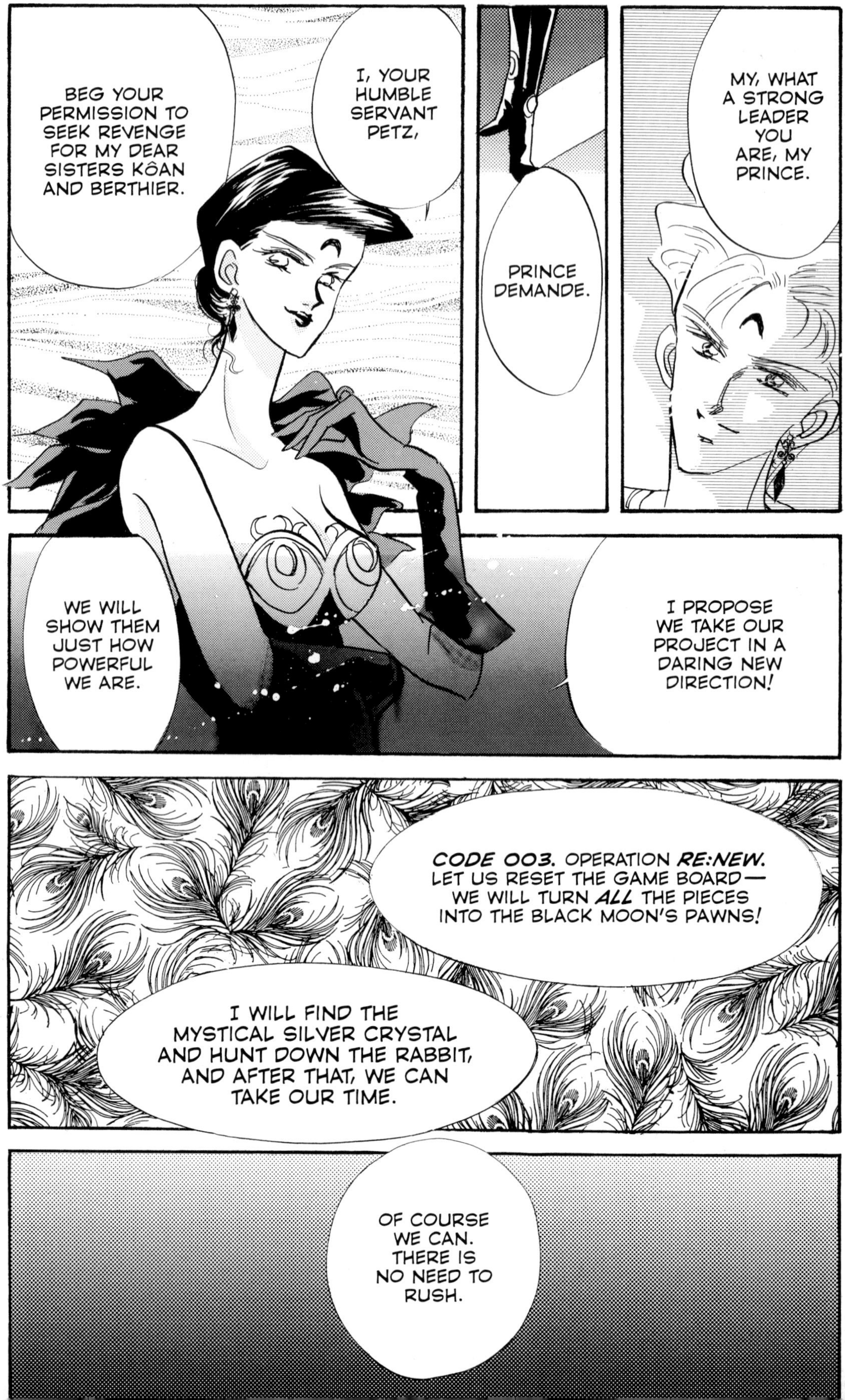
MY, WHAT A STRONG LEADER YOU ARE, MY PRINCE.
PRINCE DEMANDE.
I, YOUR HUMBLE SERVANT PETZ,
BEG YOUR PERMISSION TO SEEK REVENGE FOR MY DEAR SISTERS KÔAN AND BERTHIER.
I PROPOSE WE TAKE OUR PROJECT IN A DARING NEW DIRECTION!
WE WILL SHOW THEM JUST HOW POWERFUL WE ARE.
CODE 003. OPERATION ***RE:NEW.*** LET US RESET THE GAME BOARD— WE WILL TURN ***ALL*** THE PIECES INTO THE BLACK MOON'S PAWNS!
I WILL FIND THE MYSTICAL SILVER CRYSTAL AND HUNT DOWN THE RABBIT, AND AFTER THAT, WE CAN TAKE OUR TIME.
OF COURSE WE CAN. THERE IS NO NEED TO RUSH.

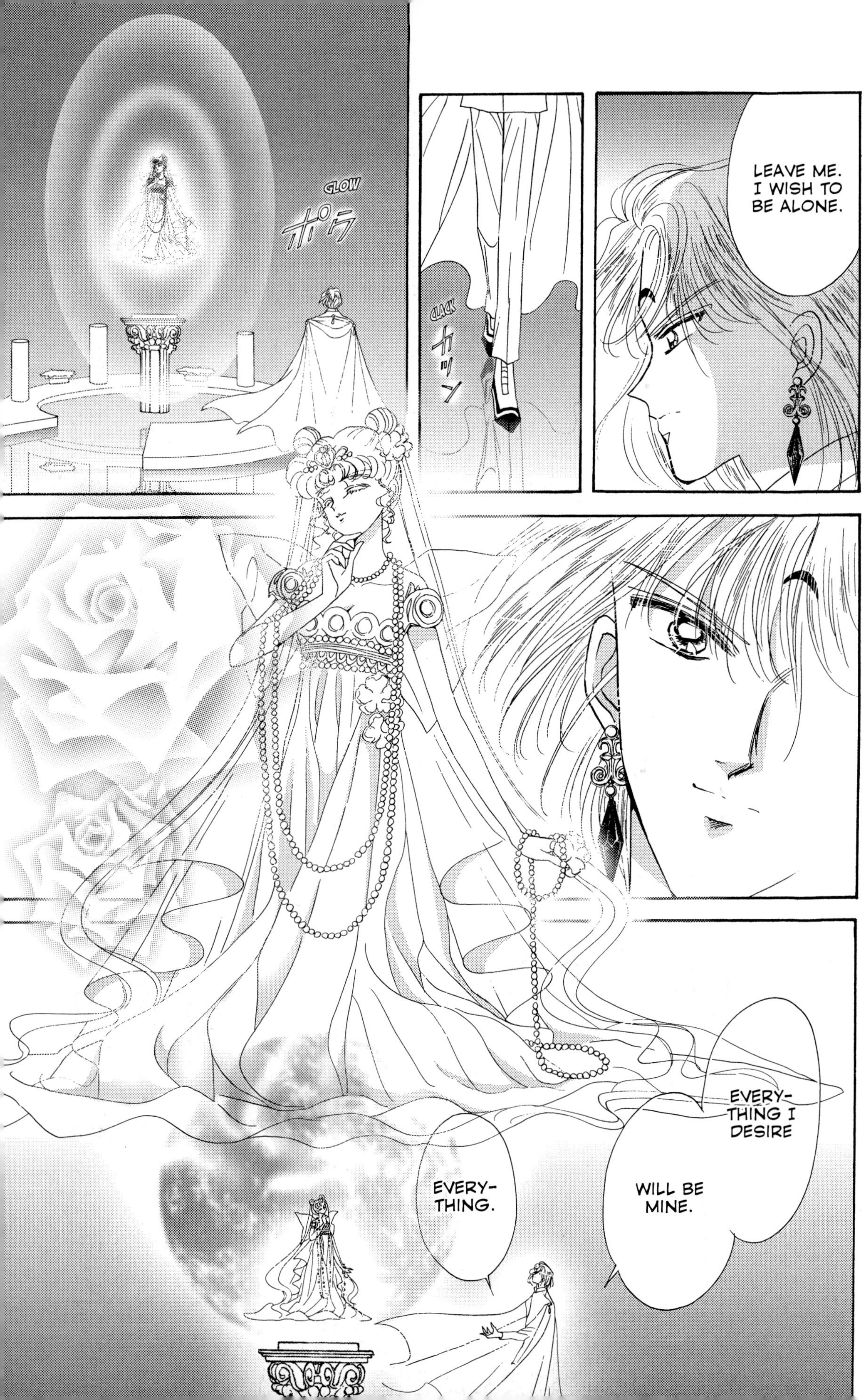
LEAVE ME. I WISH TO BE ALONE.
CLACK
カッン
GLOW
ポゥ
EVERY-THING I DESIRE
WILL BE MINE.
EVERY-THING.

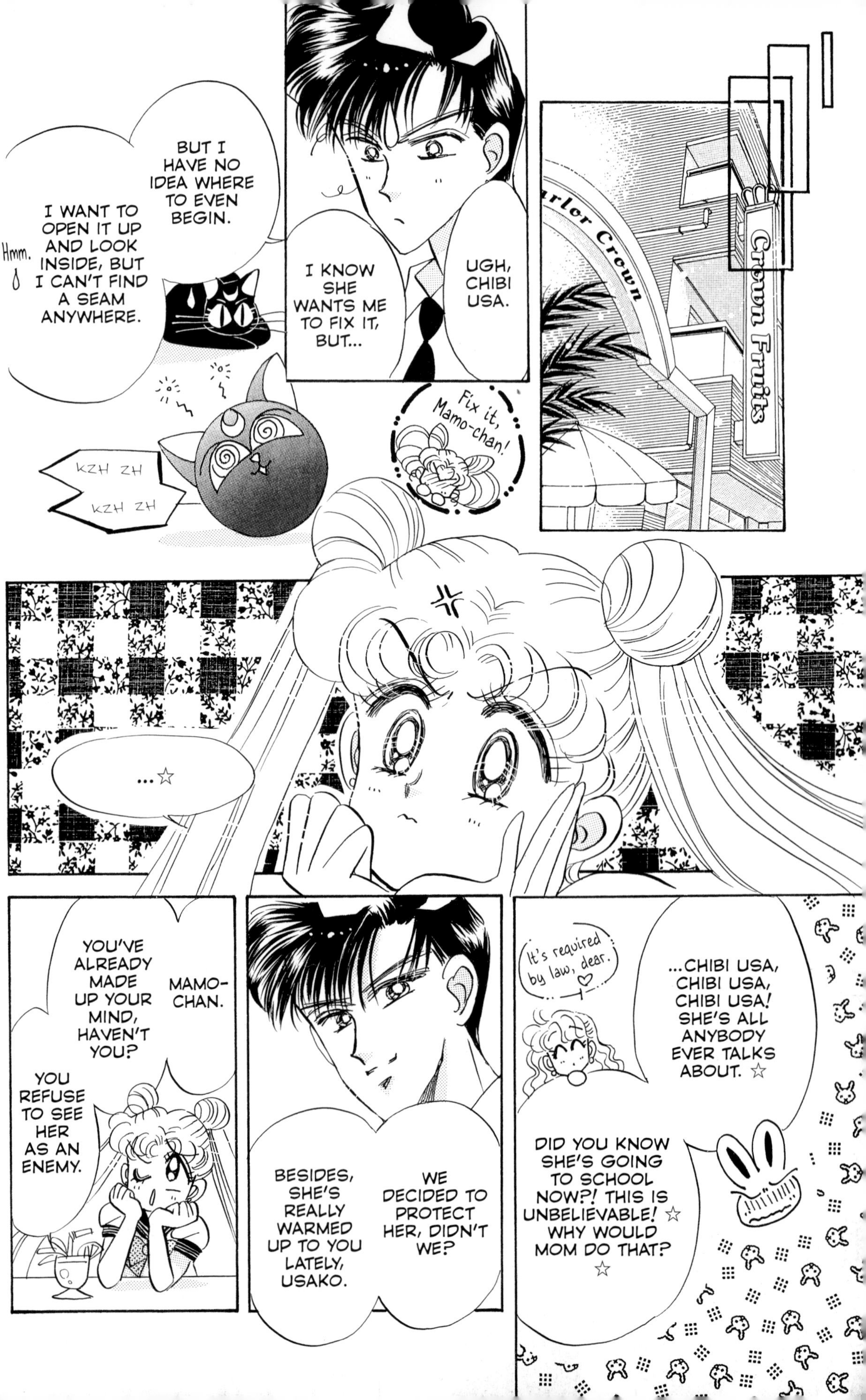
arlor Crown
Crown Fruits
UGH, CHIBI USA.
I KNOW SHE WANTS ME TO FIX IT, BUT...
Fix it, Mamo-chan!
BUT I HAVE NO IDEA WHERE TO EVEN BEGIN.
I WANT TO OPEN IT UP AND LOOK INSIDE, BUT I CAN'T FIND A SEAM ANYWHERE.
Hmm.
KZH ZH
KZH ZH
...☆
...CHIBI USA, CHIBI USA, CHIBI USA! SHE'S ALL ANYBODY EVER TALKS ABOUT. ☆
It's required by law, dear.
DID YOU KNOW SHE'S GOING TO SCHOOL NOW?! THIS IS UNBELIEVABLE! ☆ WHY WOULD MOM DO THAT? ☆
WE DECIDED TO PROTECT HER, DIDN'T WE?
BESIDES, SHE'S REALLY WARMED UP TO YOU LATELY, USAKO.
MAMO-CHAN.
YOU'VE ALREADY MADE UP YOUR MIND, HAVEN'T YOU?
YOU REFUSE TO SEE HER AS AN ENEMY.

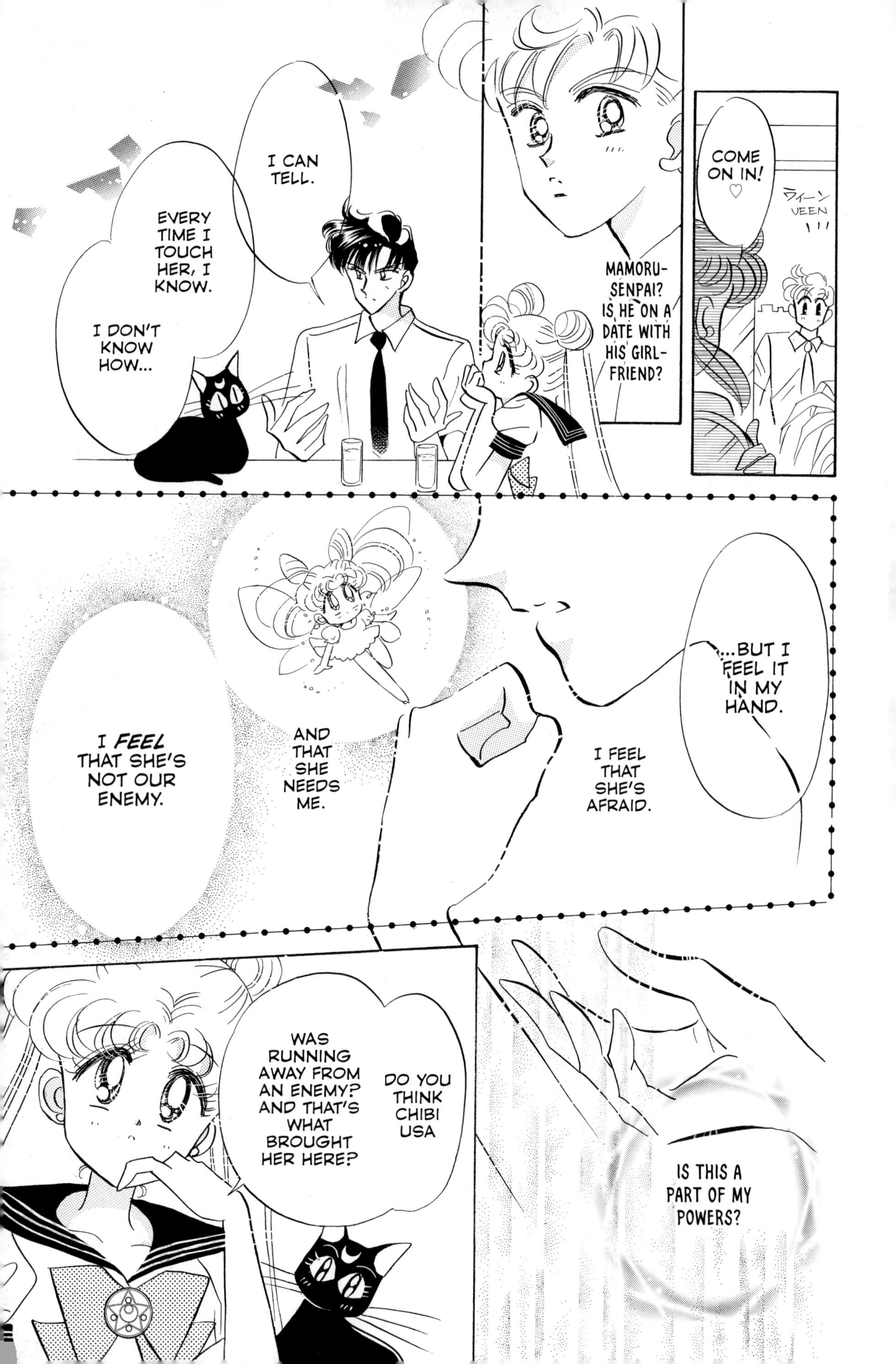
COME ON IN! ♡
ウィーン VEEN
MAMORU-SENPAI? IS HE ON A DATE WITH HIS GIRL-FRIEND?
I CAN TELL.
EVERY TIME I TOUCH HER, I KNOW.
I DON'T KNOW HOW...
...BUT I FEEL IT IN MY HAND.
I FEEL THAT SHE'S AFRAID.
AND THAT SHE NEEDS ME.
I *FEEL* THAT SHE'S NOT OUR ENEMY.
IS THIS A PART OF MY POWERS?
DO YOU THINK CHIBI USA
WAS RUNNING AWAY FROM AN ENEMY? AND THAT'S WHAT BROUGHT HER HERE?

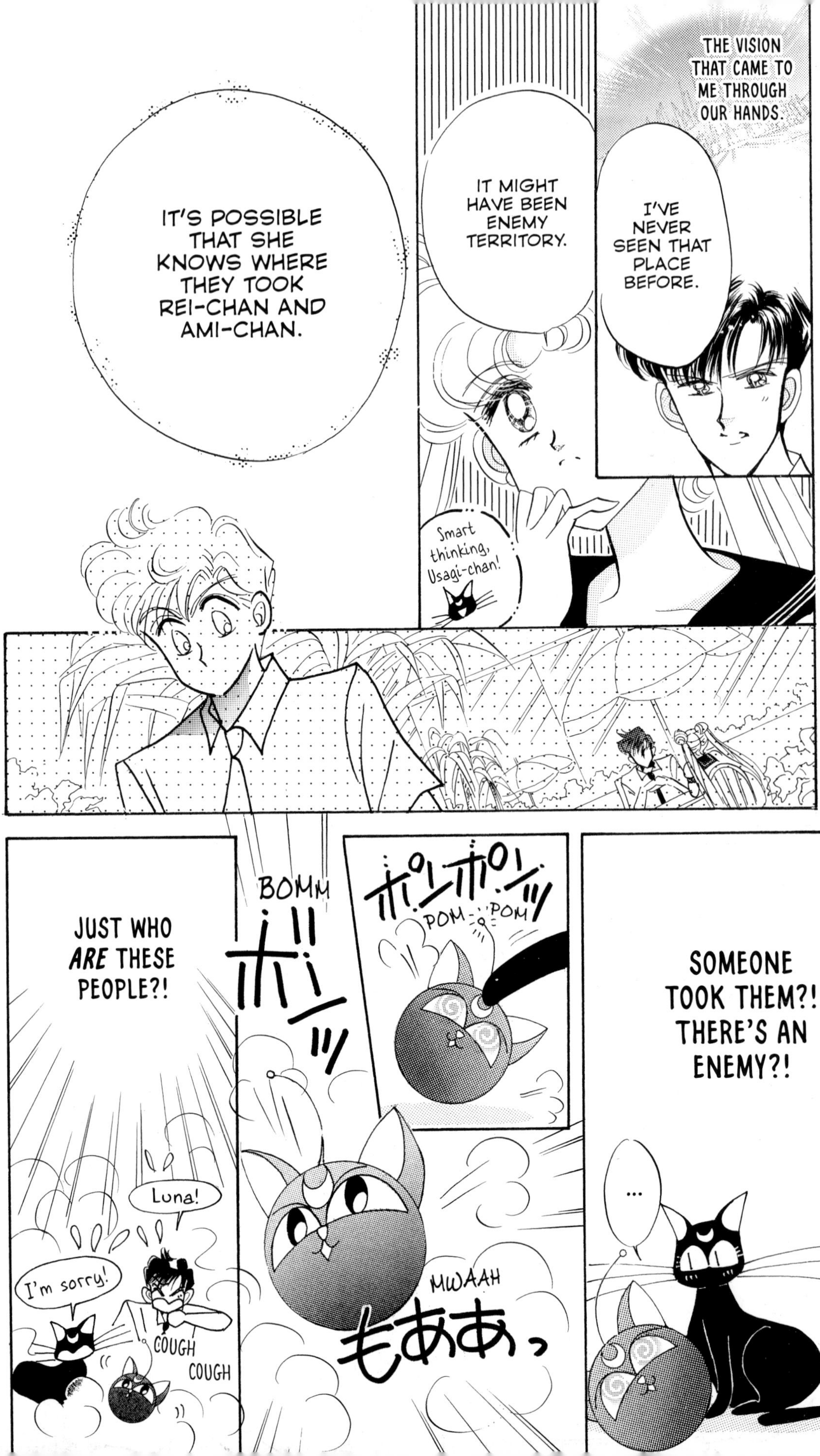
THE VISION THAT CAME TO ME THROUGH OUR HANDS.
I'VE NEVER SEEN THAT PLACE BEFORE.
IT MIGHT HAVE BEEN ENEMY TERRITORY.
Smart thinking, Usagi-chan!
IT'S POSSIBLE THAT SHE KNOWS WHERE THEY TOOK REI-CHAN AND AMI-CHAN.
SOMEONE TOOK THEM?! THERE'S AN ENEMY?!
...
ポンポンッ
POM POM
ボンッ
BOMM
MWAAH
もああっ
JUST WHO *ARE* THESE PEOPLE?!
Luna!
I'm sorry!
COUGH COUGH

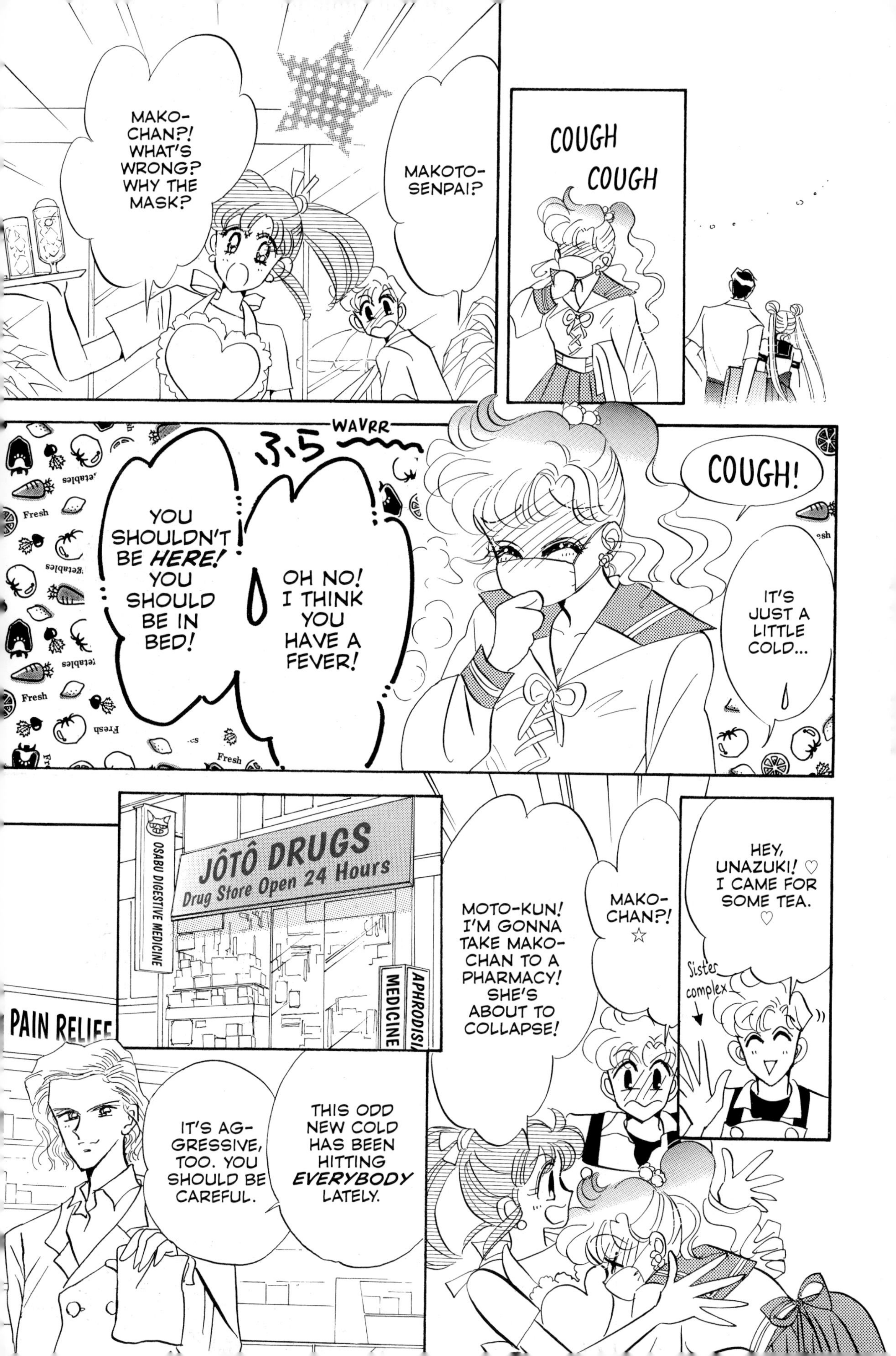
COUGH
COUGH
MAKOTO-SENPAI!?
MAKO-CHAN?! WHAT'S WRONG? WHY THE MASK?
COUGH!
IT'S JUST A LITTLE COLD...
WAVRR
ふら
OH NO! I THINK YOU HAVE A FEVER!
YOU SHOULDN'T BE *HERE!* YOU SHOULD BE IN BED!
HEY, UNAZUKI! ♡ I CAME FOR SOME TEA. ♡
Sister complex
MAKO-CHAN?! ☆
MOTO-KUN! I'M GONNA TAKE MAKO-CHAN TO A PHARMACY! SHE'S ABOUT TO COLLAPSE!
JÔTÔ DRUGS
Drug Store Open 24 Hours
OSABU DIGESTIVE MEDICINE
MEDICINE
THIS ODD NEW COLD HAS BEEN HITTING *EVERYBODY* LATELY.
IT'S AG-GRESSIVE, TOO. YOU SHOULD BE CAREFUL.

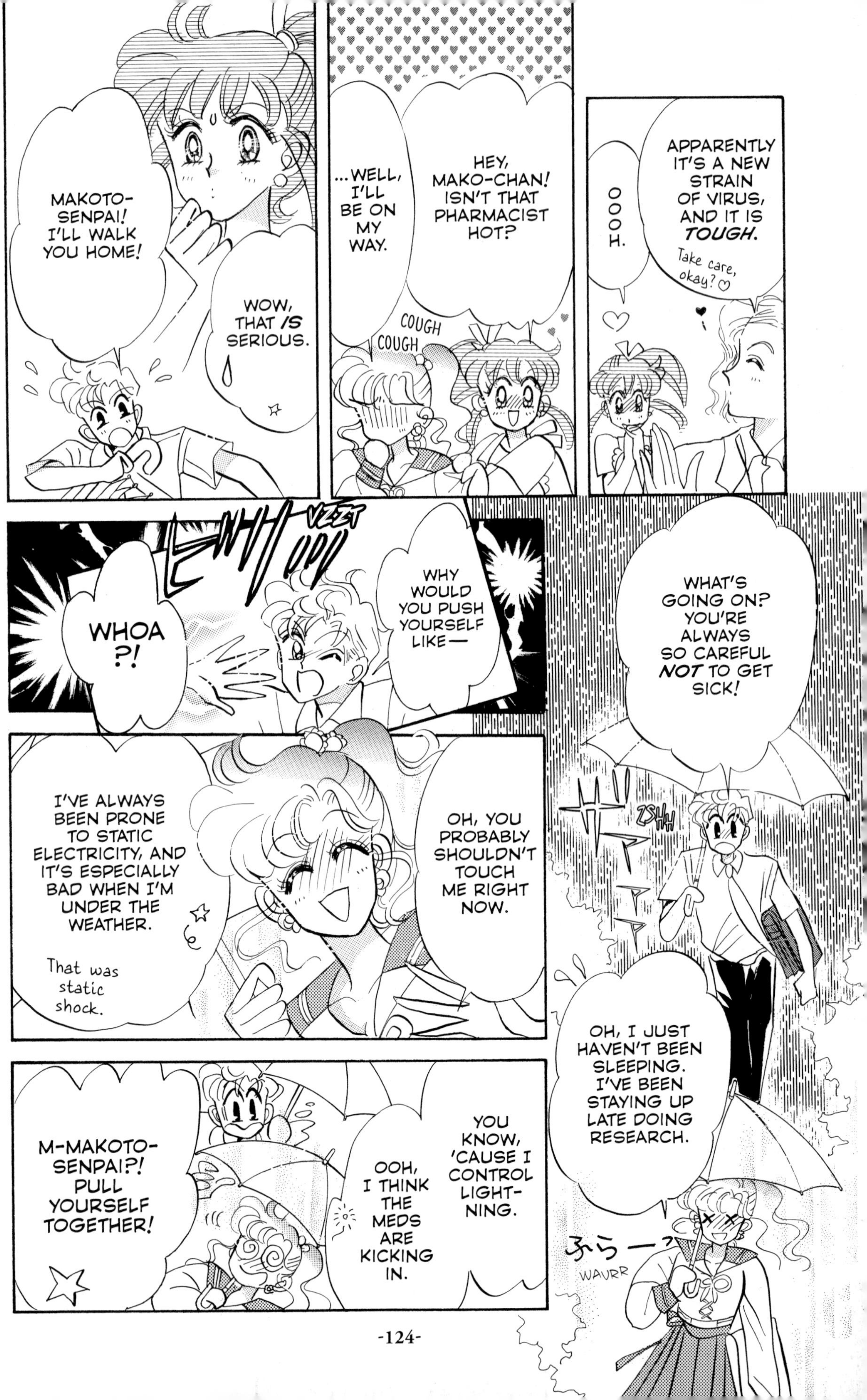

APPARENTLY IT'S A NEW STRAIN OF VIRUS, AND IT IS *TOUGH.*
Take care, okay? ♡
OOOH.
HEY, MAKO-CHAN! ISN'T THAT PHARMACIST HOT?
...WELL, I'LL BE ON MY WAY.
COUGH
COUGH
WOW, THAT *IS* SERIOUS.
MAKOTO-SENPAI! I'LL WALK YOU HOME!
WHAT'S GOING ON? YOU'RE ALWAYS SO CAREFUL *NOT* TO GET SICK!
ZSHH
OH, I JUST HAVEN'T BEEN SLEEPING. I'VE BEEN STAYING UP LATE DOING RESEARCH.
ふらーっ
WAURR
WHY WOULD YOU PUSH YOURSELF LIKE—
VZZT
WHOA?!
OH, YOU PROBABLY SHOULDN'T TOUCH ME RIGHT NOW.
I'VE ALWAYS BEEN PRONE TO STATIC ELECTRICITY, AND IT'S ESPECIALLY BAD WHEN I'M UNDER THE WEATHER.
That was static shock.
YOU KNOW, 'CAUSE I CONTROL LIGHTNING.
OOH, I THINK THE MEDS ARE KICKING IN.
M-MAKOTO-SENPAI?! PULL YOURSELF TOGETHER!

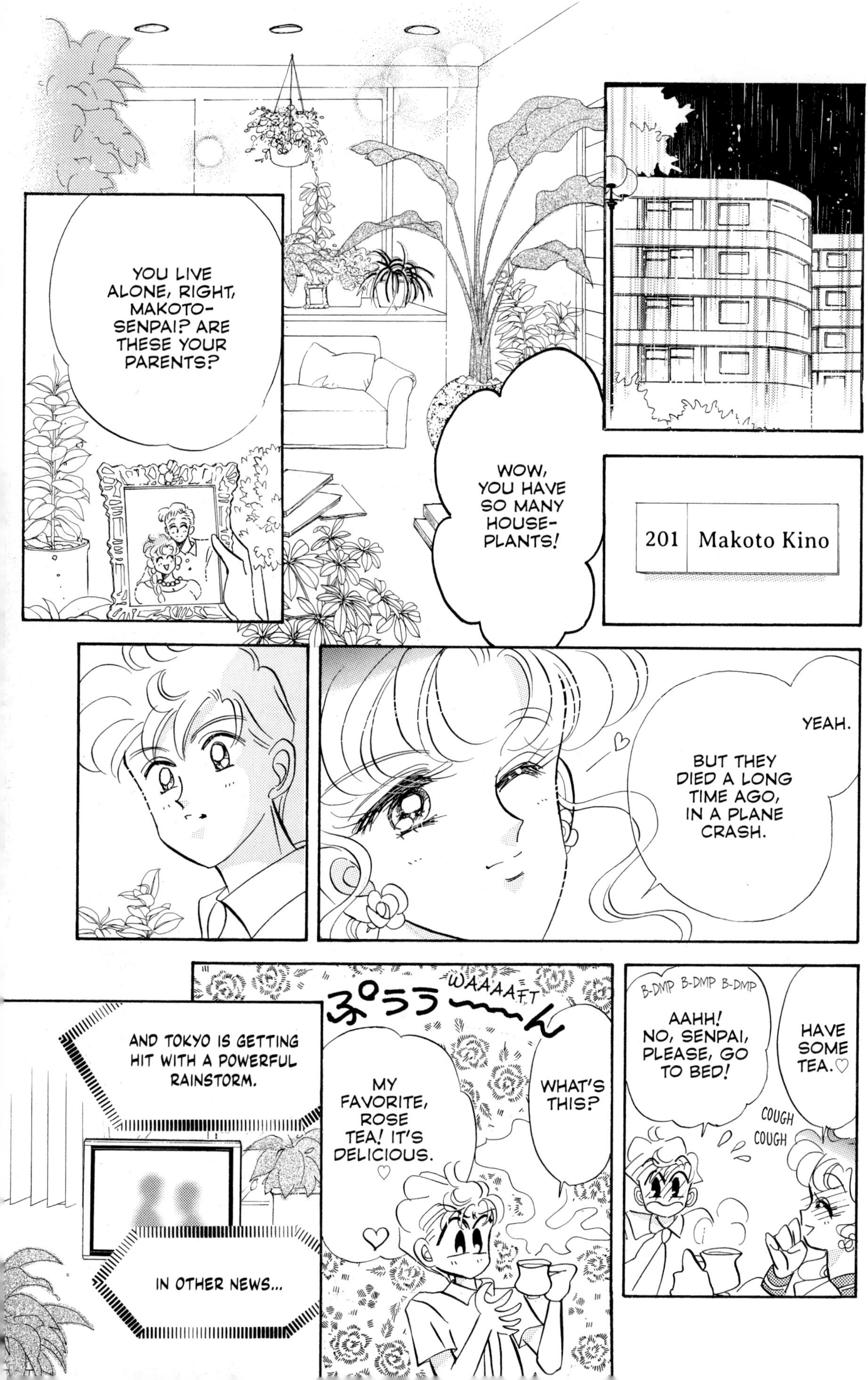
201 Makoto Kino
WOW, YOU HAVE SO MANY HOUSE-PLANTS!
YOU LIVE ALONE, RIGHT, MAKOTO-SENPAI? ARE THESE YOUR PARENTS?
YEAH.
BUT THEY DIED A LONG TIME AGO, IN A PLANE CRASH.
HAVE SOME TEA.♡
B-DMP B-DMP B-DMP
AAHH! NO, SENPAI, PLEASE, GO TO BED!
COUGH COUGH
ぷうう〜〜ん
WAAAAFT
WHAT'S THIS?
MY FAVORITE, ROSE TEA! IT'S DELICIOUS.♡
AND TOKYO IS GETTING HIT WITH A POWERFUL RAINSTORM.
IN OTHER NEWS...

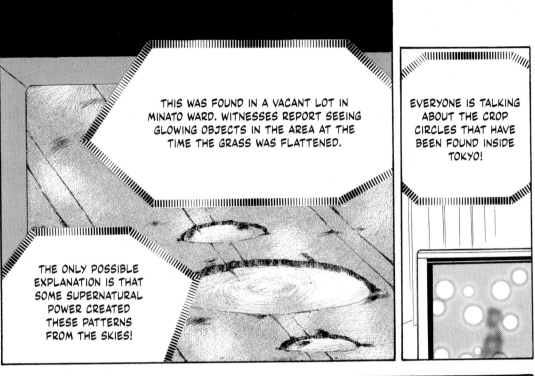

EVERYONE IS TALKING ABOUT THE CROP CIRCLES THAT HAVE BEEN FOUND INSIDE TOKYO!

THIS WAS FOUND IN A VACANT LOT IN MINATO WARD. WITNESSES REPORT SEEING GLOWING OBJECTS IN THE AREA AT THE TIME THE GRASS WAS FLATTENED.

THE ONLY POSSIBLE EXPLANATION IS THAT SOME SUPERNATURAL POWER CREATED THESE PATTERNS FROM THE SKIES!

SOME RUMORS CLAIM THAT THESE ARE LANDING TRACKS LEFT BY UFOS.

...THERE'S BEEN A LOT MORE OF THIS KIND OF NEWS STORY LATELY.

YEAH, THERE REALLY HAS.

COUGH

DID YOU HEAR? THEY FOUND ONE OF THESE CROP CIRCLES

IN SOME TALL GRASS AT ARISUGAWA PARK. THAT'S NOT FAR FROM HERE.

AND THE REPORTS OF UFO SIGHTINGS IN THAT AREA ARE COMING NONSTOP.

...EVERY TIME I TURN AROUND LATELY, SOMETHING BIZARRE IS HAPPENING.

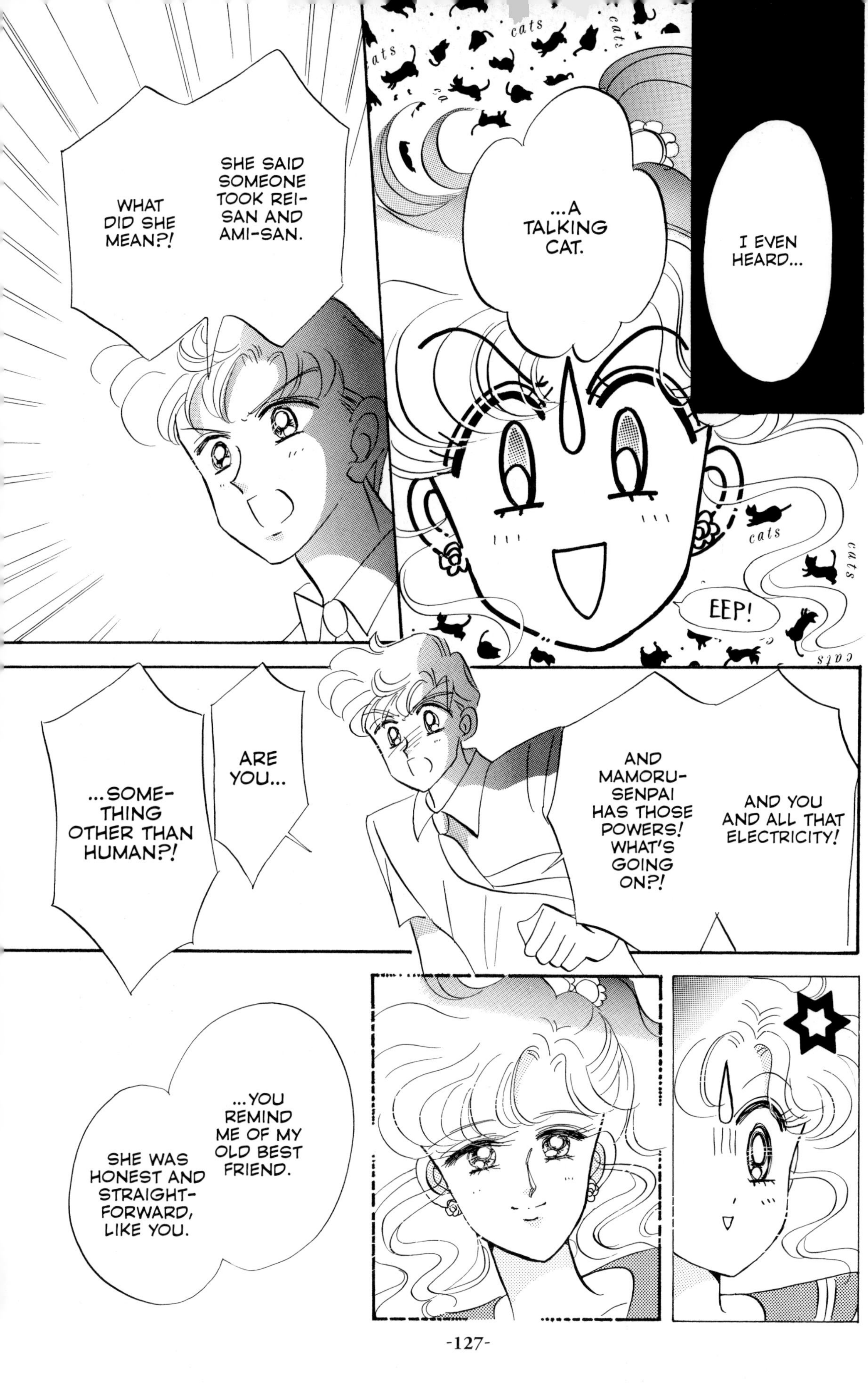
I EVEN HEARD...
...A TALKING CAT.
EEP!
SHE SAID SOMEONE TOOK REI-SAN AND AMI-SAN.
WHAT DID SHE MEAN?!
AND YOU AND ALL THAT ELECTRICITY!
AND MAMORU-SENPAI HAS THOSE POWERS! WHAT'S GOING ON?!
ARE YOU...
...SOME-THING OTHER THAN HUMAN?!
...YOU REMIND ME OF MY OLD BEST FRIEND.
SHE WAS HONEST AND STRAIGHT-FORWARD, LIKE YOU.

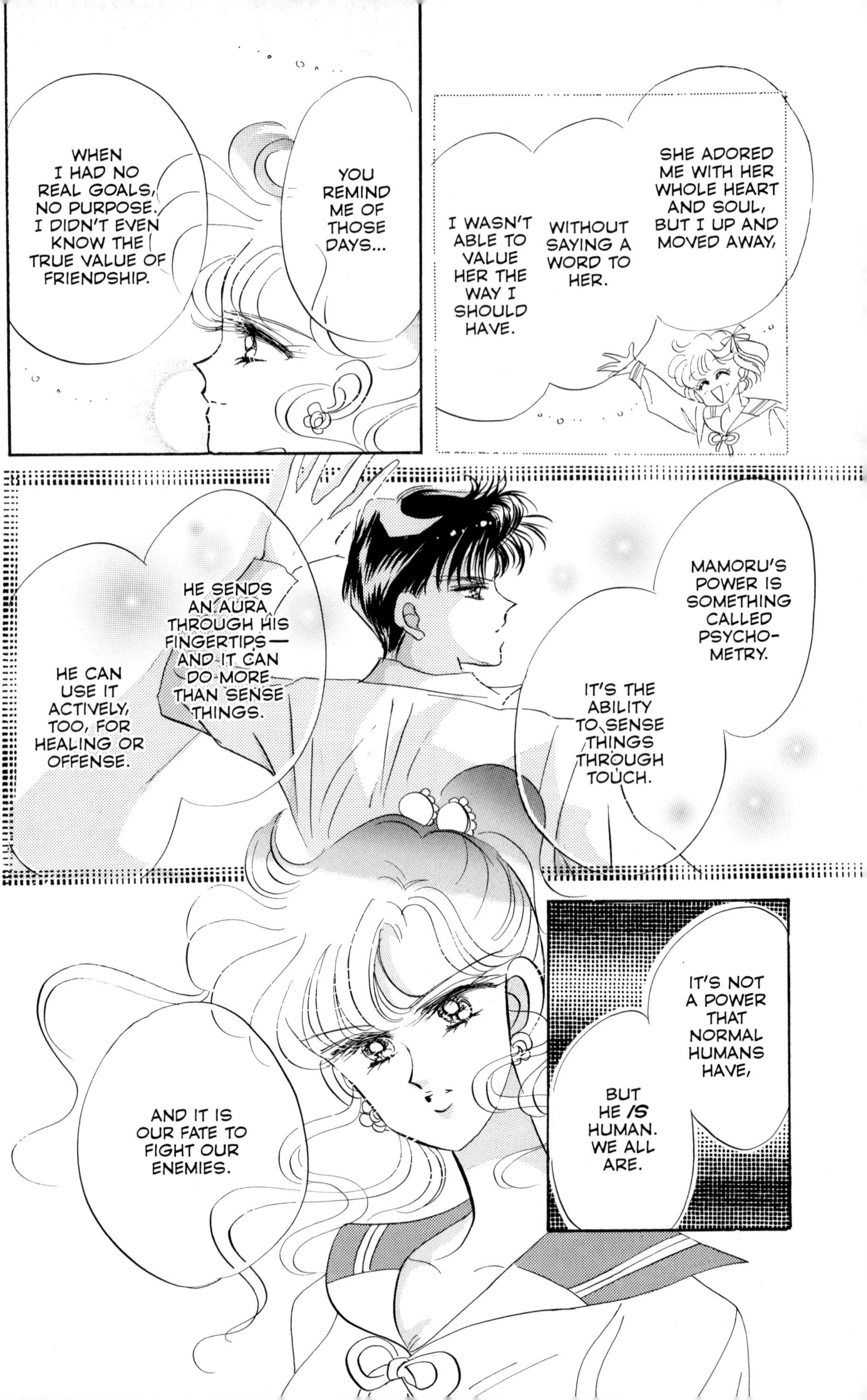
SHE ADORED ME WITH HER WHOLE HEART AND SOUL, BUT I UP AND MOVED AWAY,
WITHOUT SAYING A WORD TO HER.
I WASN'T ABLE TO VALUE HER THE WAY I SHOULD HAVE.
YOU REMIND ME OF THOSE DAYS...
WHEN I HAD NO REAL GOALS, NO PURPOSE. I DIDN'T EVEN KNOW THE TRUE VALUE OF FRIENDSHIP.
MAMORU'S POWER IS SOMETHING CALLED PSYCHOMETRY.
IT'S THE ABILITY TO SENSE THINGS THROUGH TOUCH.
HE SENDS AN AURA THROUGH HIS FINGERTIPS—AND IT CAN DO MORE THAN SENSE THINGS.
HE CAN USE IT ACTIVELY, TOO, FOR HEALING OR OFFENSE.
IT'S NOT A POWER THAT NORMAL HUMANS HAVE,
BUT HE *IS* HUMAN. WE ALL ARE.
AND IT IS OUR FATE TO FIGHT OUR ENEMIES.

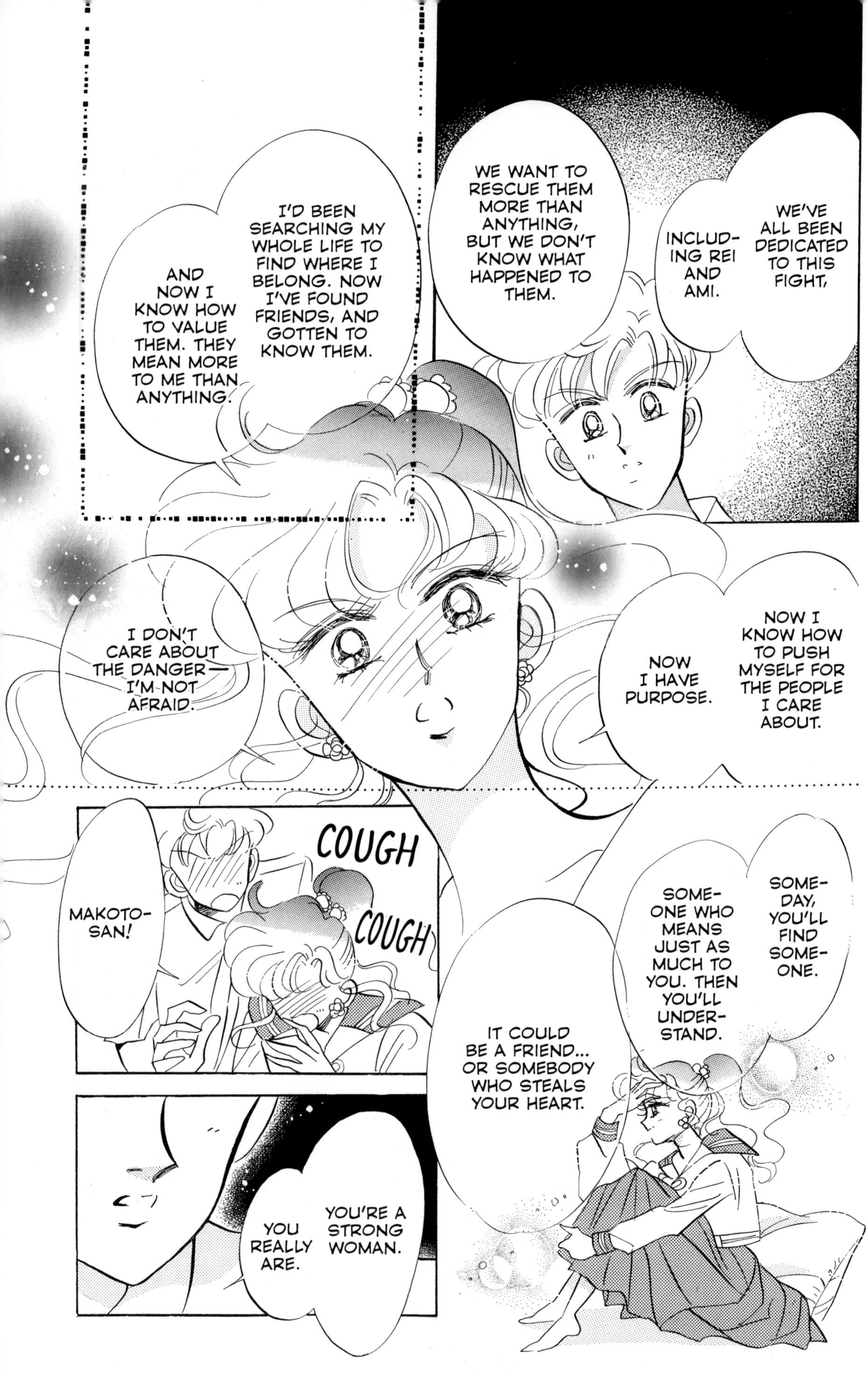
WE'VE ALL BEEN DEDICATED TO THIS FIGHT,
INCLUD-ING REI AND AMI.
WE WANT TO RESCUE THEM MORE THAN ANYTHING, BUT WE DON'T KNOW WHAT HAPPENED TO THEM.
I'D BEEN SEARCHING MY WHOLE LIFE TO FIND WHERE I BELONG. NOW I'VE FOUND FRIENDS, AND GOTTEN TO KNOW THEM.
AND NOW I KNOW HOW TO VALUE THEM. THEY MEAN MORE TO ME THAN ANYTHING.
NOW I KNOW HOW TO PUSH MYSELF FOR THE PEOPLE I CARE ABOUT.
NOW I HAVE PURPOSE.
I DON'T CARE ABOUT THE DANGER— I'M NOT AFRAID.
SOME-DAY, YOU'LL FIND SOME-ONE.
SOME-ONE WHO MEANS JUST AS MUCH TO YOU. THEN YOU'LL UNDER-STAND.
IT COULD BE A FRIEND... OR SOMEBODY WHO STEALS YOUR HEART.
COUGH
COUGH
MAKOTO-SAN!
YOU'RE A STRONG WOMAN.
YOU REALLY ARE.

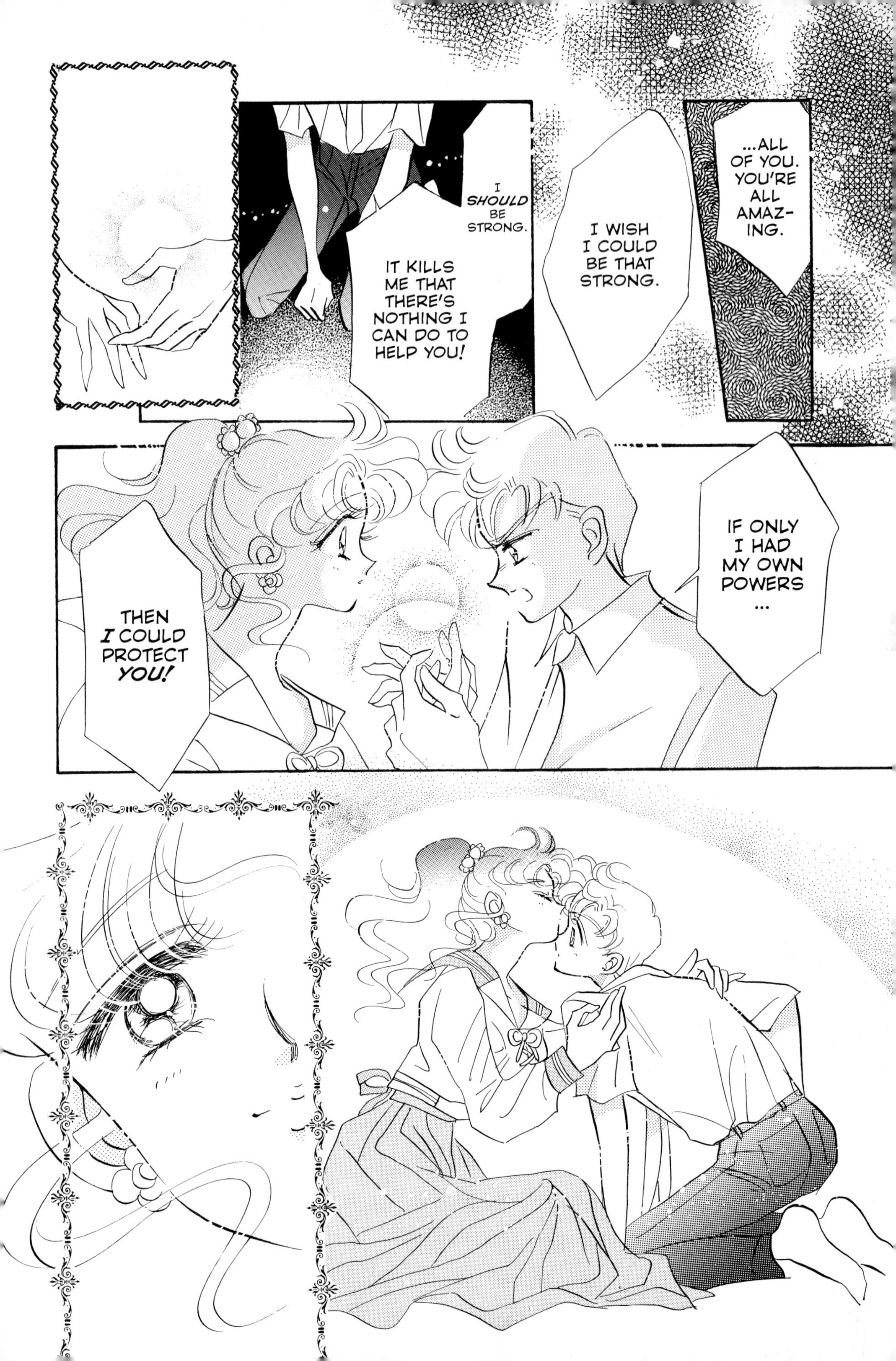
...ALL OF YOU. YOU'RE ALL AMAZ-ING.
I WISH I COULD BE THAT STRONG.
I *SHOULD* BE STRONG.
IT KILLS ME THAT THERE'S NOTHING I CAN DO TO HELP YOU!
IF ONLY I HAD MY OWN POWERS ...
THEN *I* COULD PROTECT *YOU!*

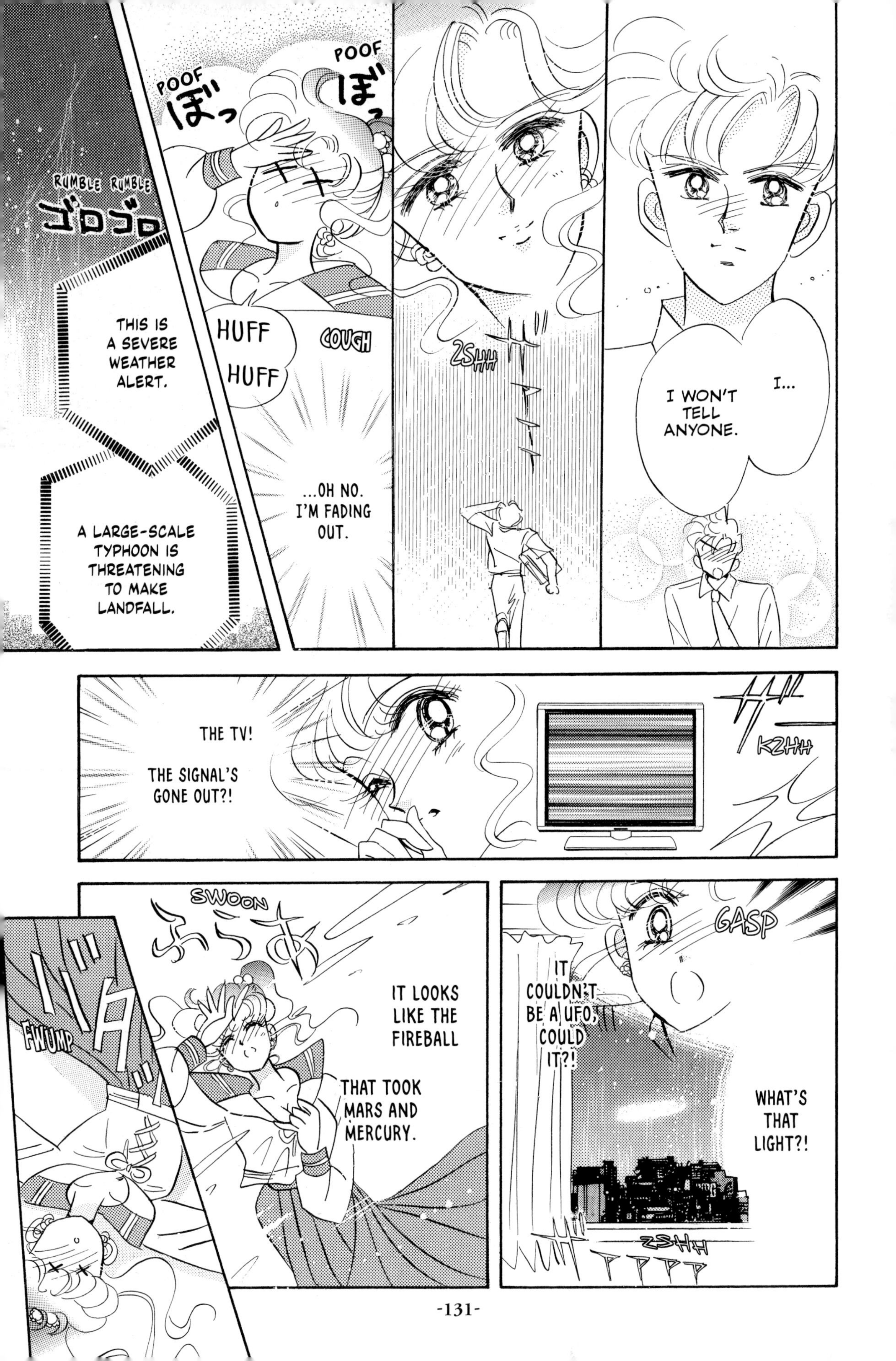
I...
I WON'T TELL ANYONE.
ZSHH
POOF
ぼっ
POOF
ぼっ
COUGH
HUFF
HUFF
...OH NO. I'M FADING OUT.
RUMBLE RUMBLE
ゴロゴロ
THIS IS A SEVERE WEATHER ALERT.
A LARGE-SCALE TYPHOON IS THREATENING TO MAKE LANDFALL.
KZHH
THE TV!
THE SIGNAL'S GONE OUT?!
GASP
IT COULDN'T BE A UFO, COULD IT?!
WHAT'S THAT LIGHT?!
ZSHH
SWOON
ふらあ
IT LOOKS LIKE THE FIREBALL
THAT TOOK MARS AND MERCURY.
FWUMP

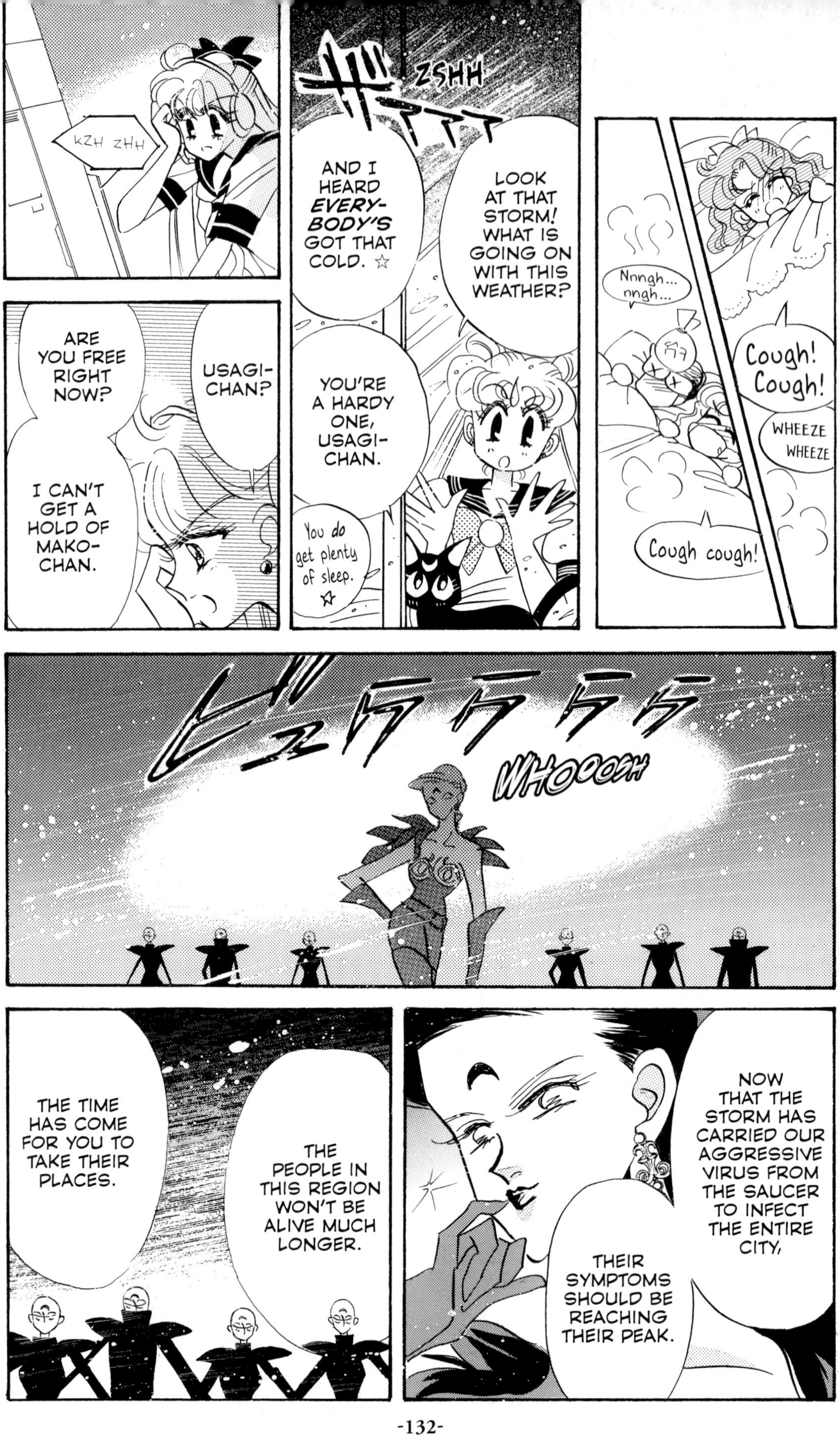
Nnngh... nngh...
Cough! Cough!
WHEEZE WHEEZE
Cough cough!
ZSHH
LOOK AT THAT STORM! WHAT IS GOING ON WITH THIS WEATHER?
AND I HEARD *EVERYBODY'S* GOT THAT COLD. ☆
YOU'RE A HARDY ONE, USAGI-CHAN.
You *do* get plenty of sleep. ☆
KZH ZHH
USAGI-CHAN?
ARE YOU FREE RIGHT NOW?
I CAN'T GET A HOLD OF MAKO-CHAN.
WHOOOSH
NOW THAT THE STORM HAS CARRIED OUR AGGRESSIVE VIRUS FROM THE SAUCER TO INFECT THE ENTIRE CITY,
THEIR SYMPTOMS SHOULD BE REACHING THEIR PEAK.
THE PEOPLE IN THIS REGION WON'T BE ALIVE MUCH LONGER.
THE TIME HAS COME FOR YOU TO TAKE THEIR PLACES.

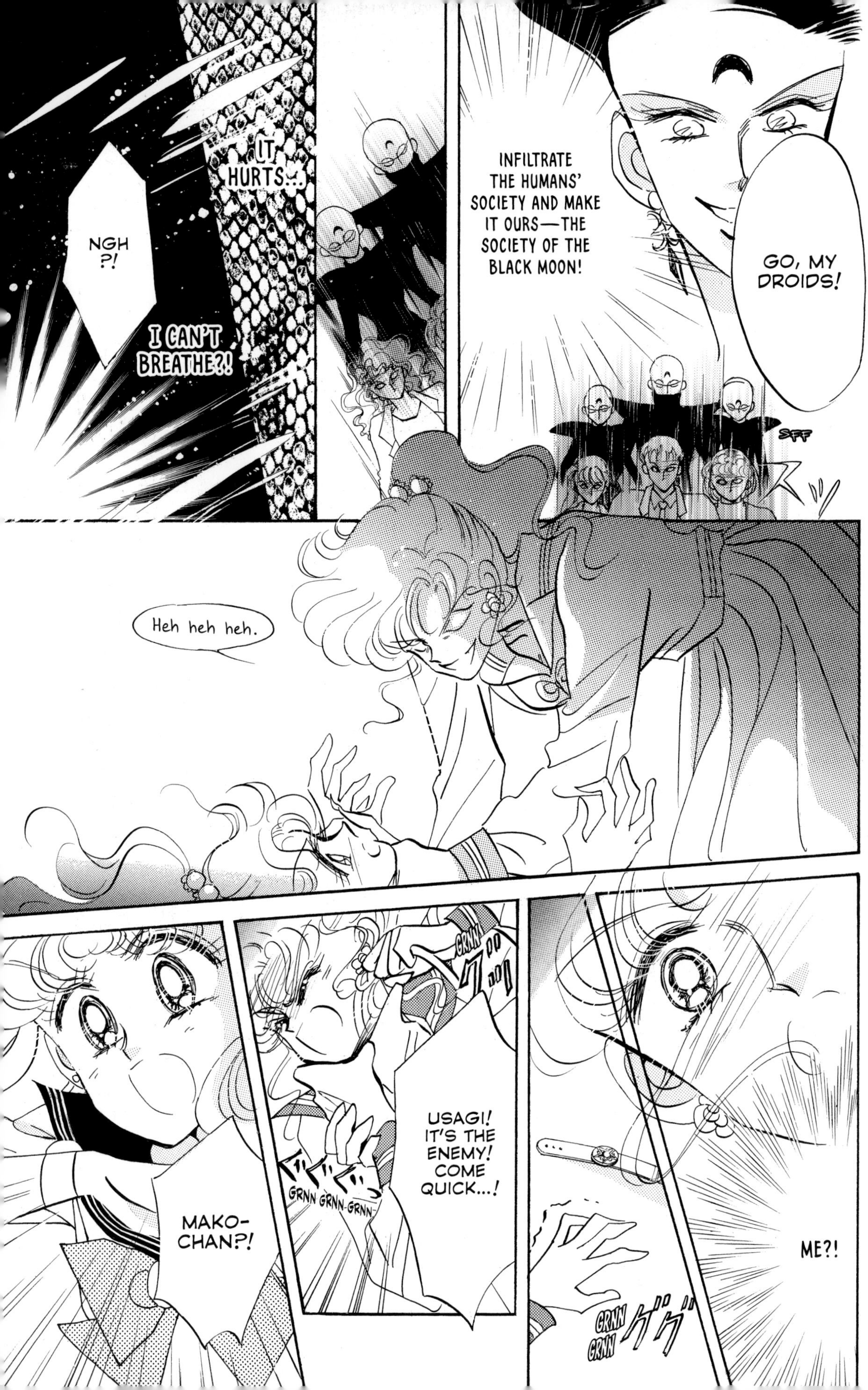
GO, MY DROIDS!
INFILTRATE THE HUMANS' SOCIETY AND MAKE IT OURS—THE SOCIETY OF THE BLACK MOON!
SFF
IT HURTS...
NGH?!
I CAN'T BREATHE?!
Heh heh heh.
ME?!
GRNN GRNN
GRNN
USAGI! IT'S THE ENEMY! COME QUICK...!
GRNN GRNN-GRNN
MAKO-CHAN?!

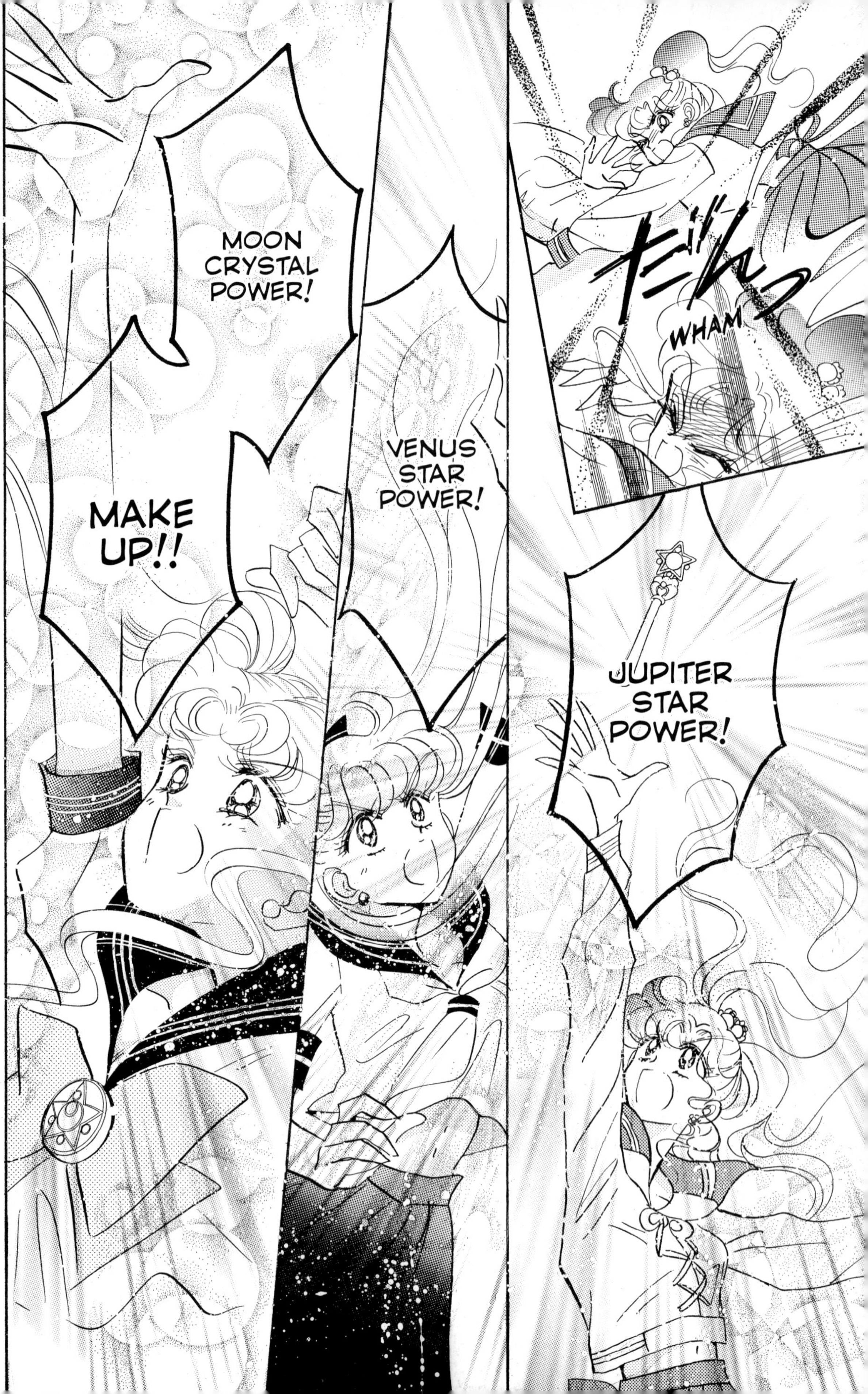
だんっ
WHAM
JUPITER STAR POWER!
VENUS STAR POWER!
MOON CRYSTAL POWER!
MAKE UP!!

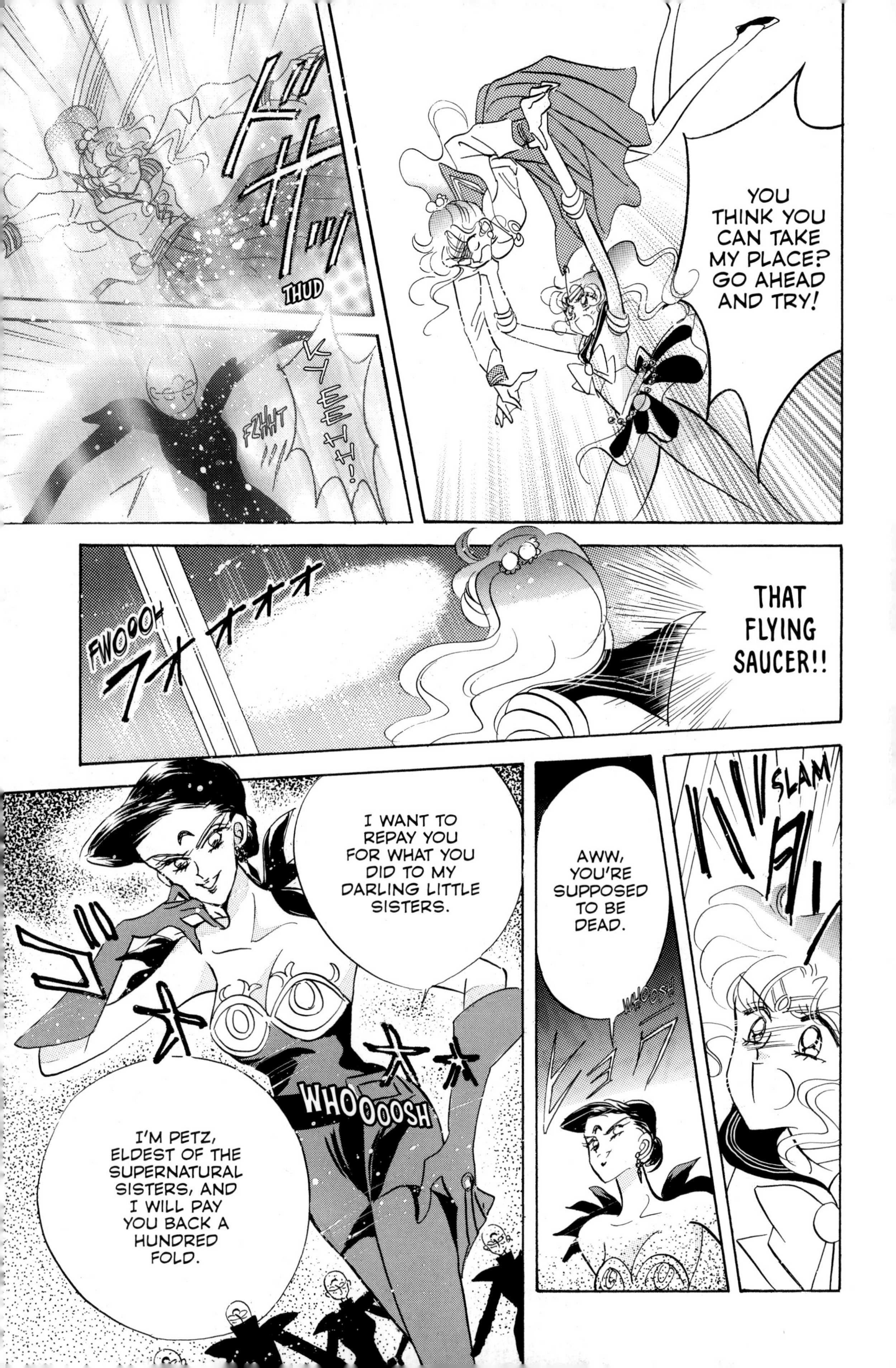
YOU THINK YOU CAN TAKE MY PLACE? GO AHEAD AND TRY!
THUD
KYEEHH!
FZHHT
THAT FLYING SAUCER!!
FWOOOH
SLAM
AWW, YOU'RE SUPPOSED TO BE DEAD.
WHOOSH
I WANT TO REPAY YOU FOR WHAT YOU DID TO MY DARLING LITTLE SISTERS.
WHOOOOSH
I'M PETZ, ELDEST OF THE SUPERNATURAL SISTERS, AND I WILL PAY YOU BACK A HUNDRED FOLD.

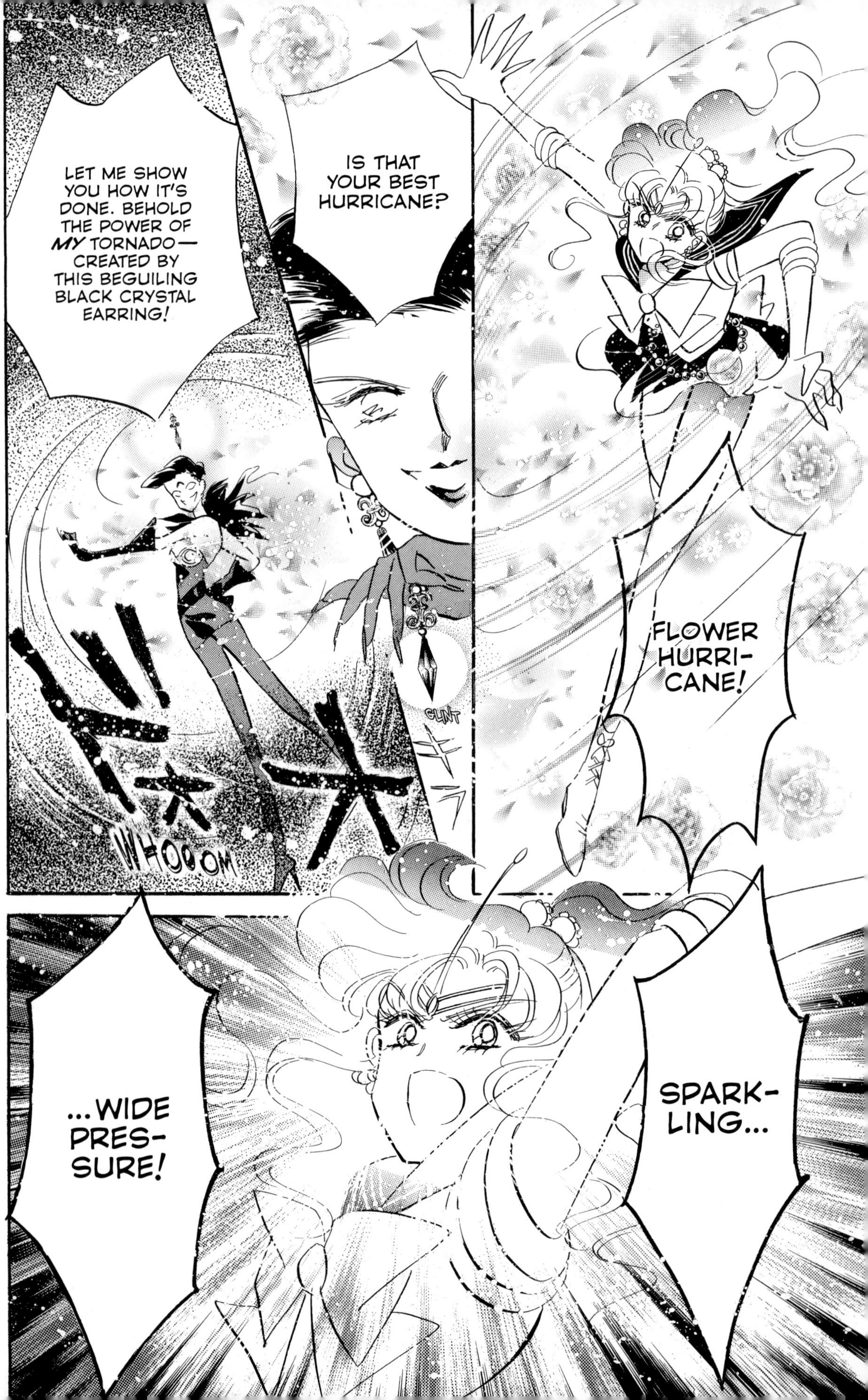
FLOWER HURRICANE!
IS THAT YOUR BEST HURRICANE?
GLINT
LET ME SHOW YOU HOW IT'S DONE. BEHOLD THE POWER OF *MY* TORNADO—CREATED BY THIS BEGUILING BLACK CRYSTAL EARRING!
WHOOOM
SPARKLING...
...WIDE PRESSURE!

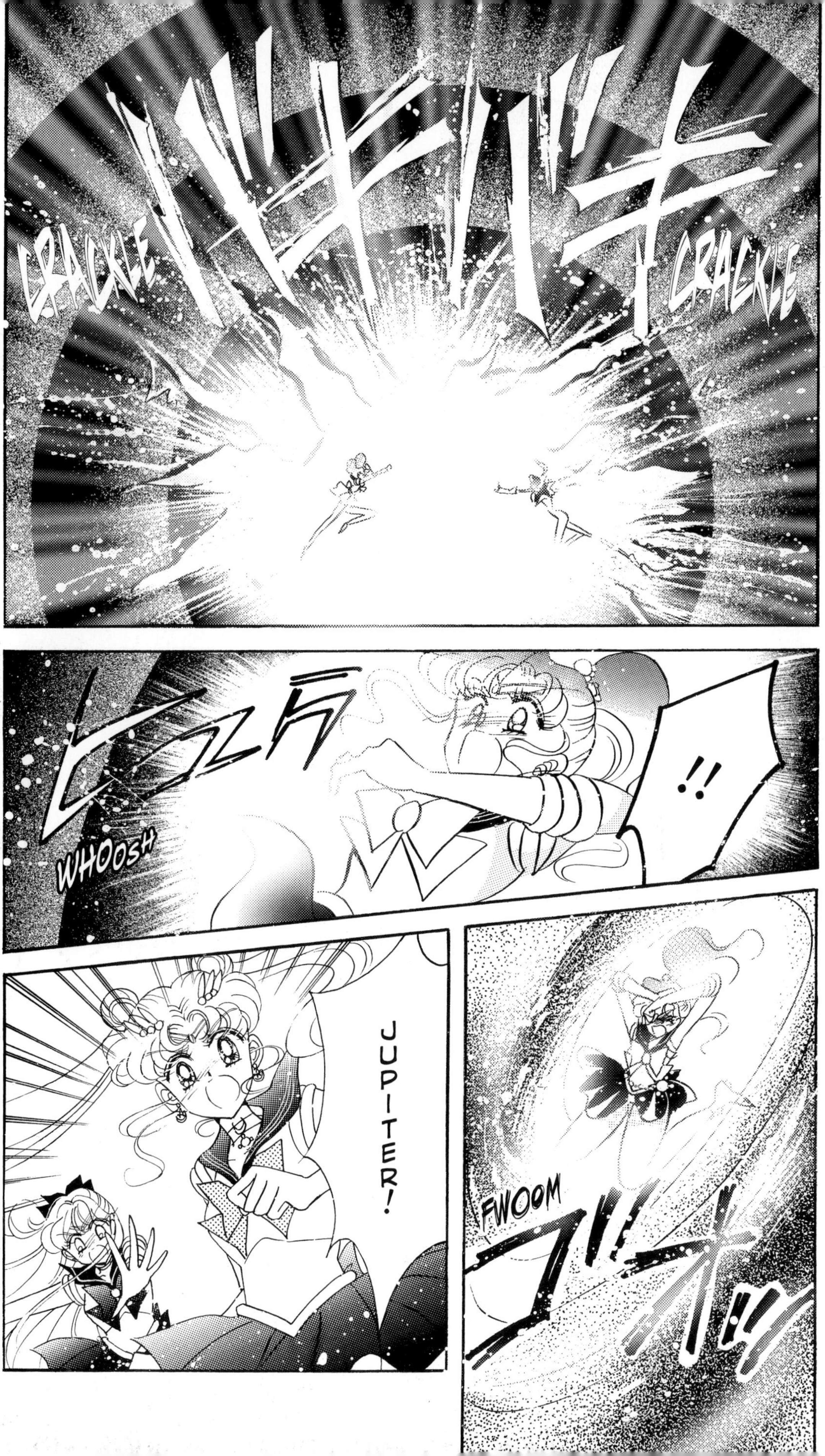
CRACKLE
CRACKLE
!!
WHOOSH
FWOOM
JUPITER!

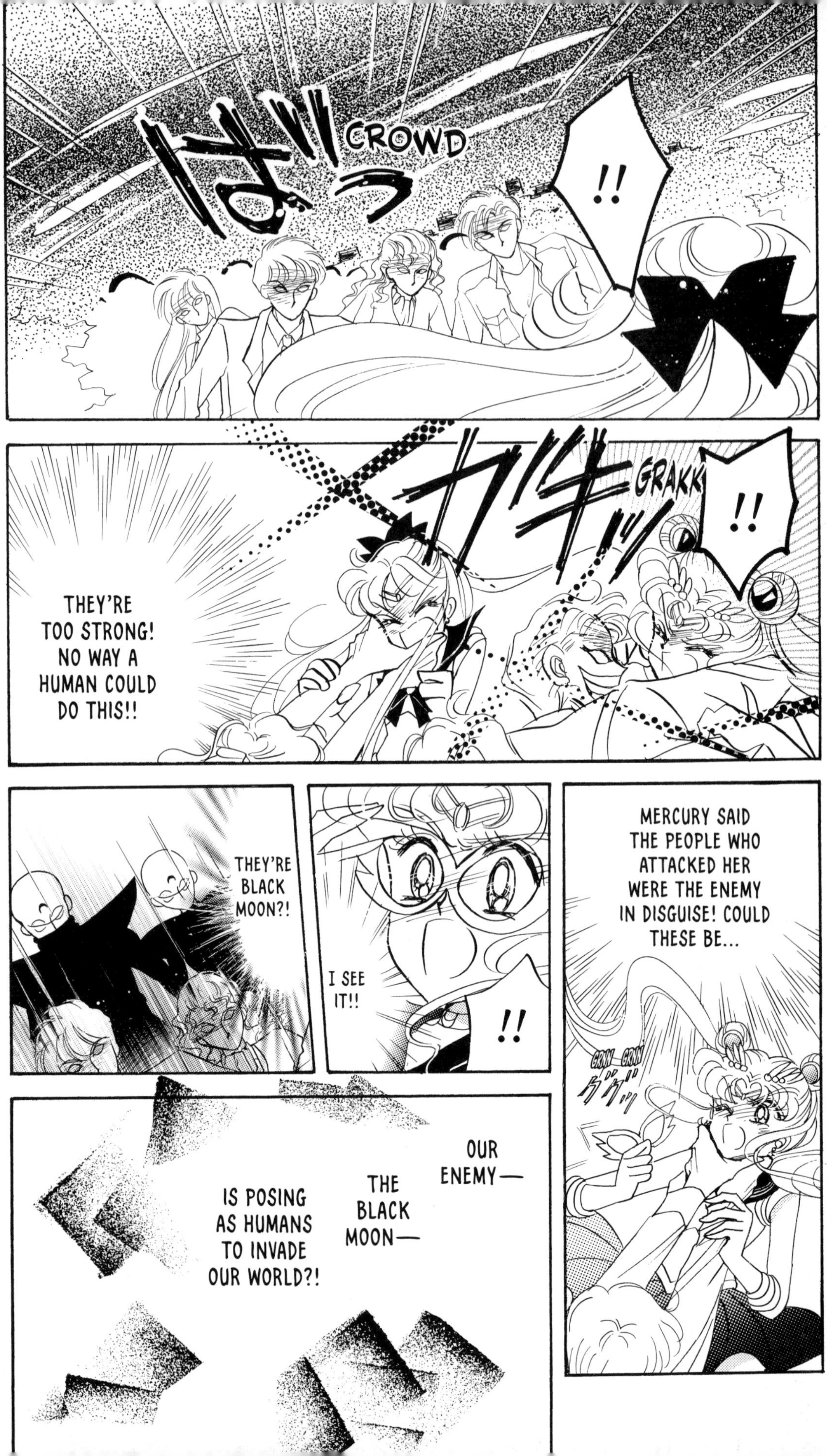
CROWD
!!
GRAKK
!!
THEY'RE TOO STRONG! NO WAY A HUMAN COULD DO THIS!!
MERCURY SAID THE PEOPLE WHO ATTACKED HER WERE THE ENEMY IN DISGUISE! COULD THESE BE...
GRNN GRNN
!!
I SEE IT!!
THEY'RE BLACK MOON?!
OUR ENEMY—
THE BLACK MOON—
IS POSING AS HUMANS TO INVADE OUR WORLD?!

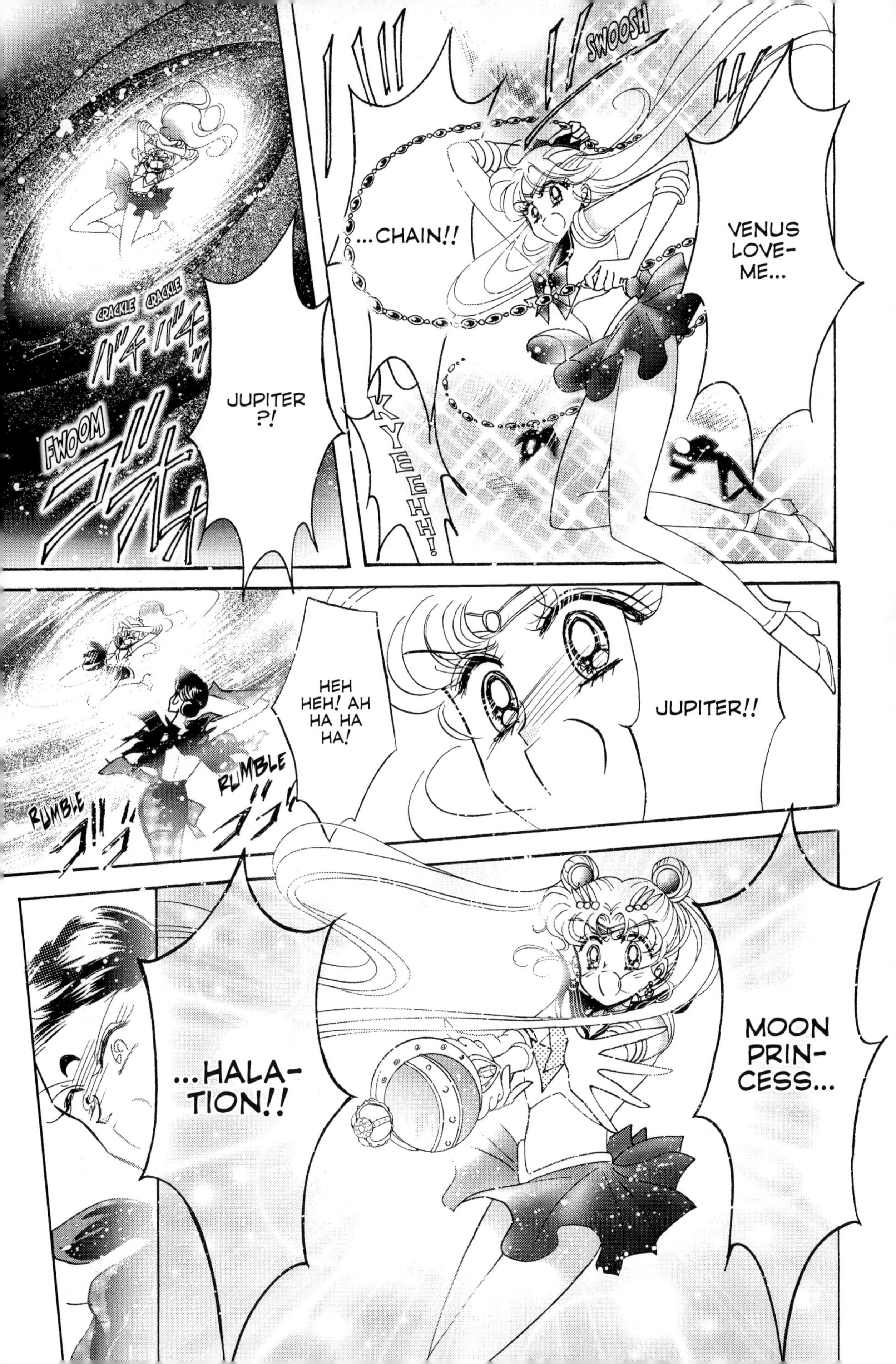
SWOOSH
VENUS LOVE-ME...
...CHAIN!!
KYEEHH!
CRACKLE CRACKLE
FWOOM
JUPITER ?!
JUPITER!!
HEH HEH! AH HA HA HA!
RUMBLE
RUMBLE
MOON PRIN-CESS...
...HALA-TION!!

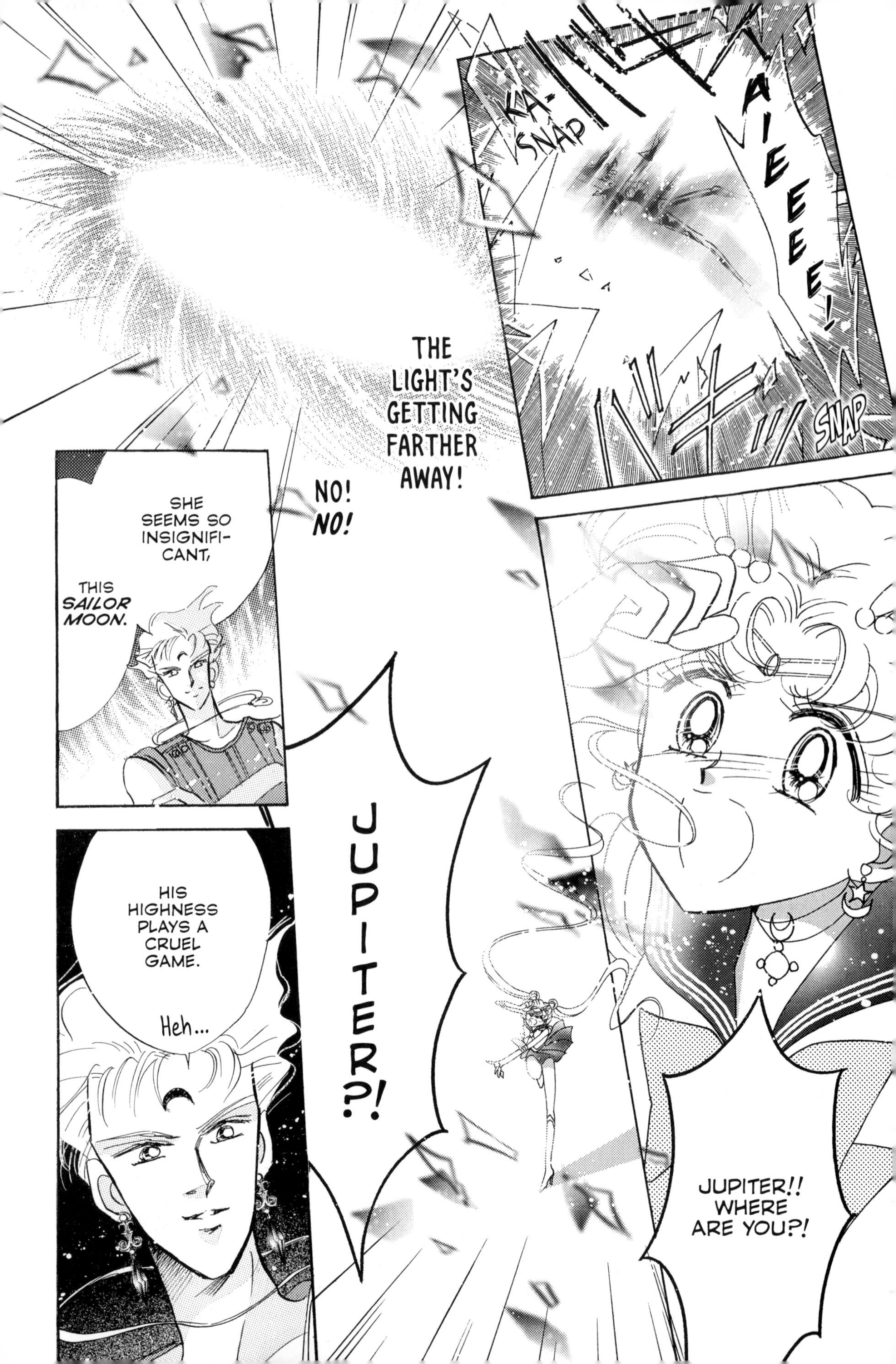
KA-SNAP
AIEEEE!
SNAP
THE LIGHT'S GETTING FARTHER AWAY!
NO! NO!
JUPITER!! WHERE ARE YOU?!
JUPITER?!
SHE SEEMS SO INSIGNIFICANT, THIS SAILOR MOON.
HIS HIGHNESS PLAYS A CRUEL GAME.
Heh...

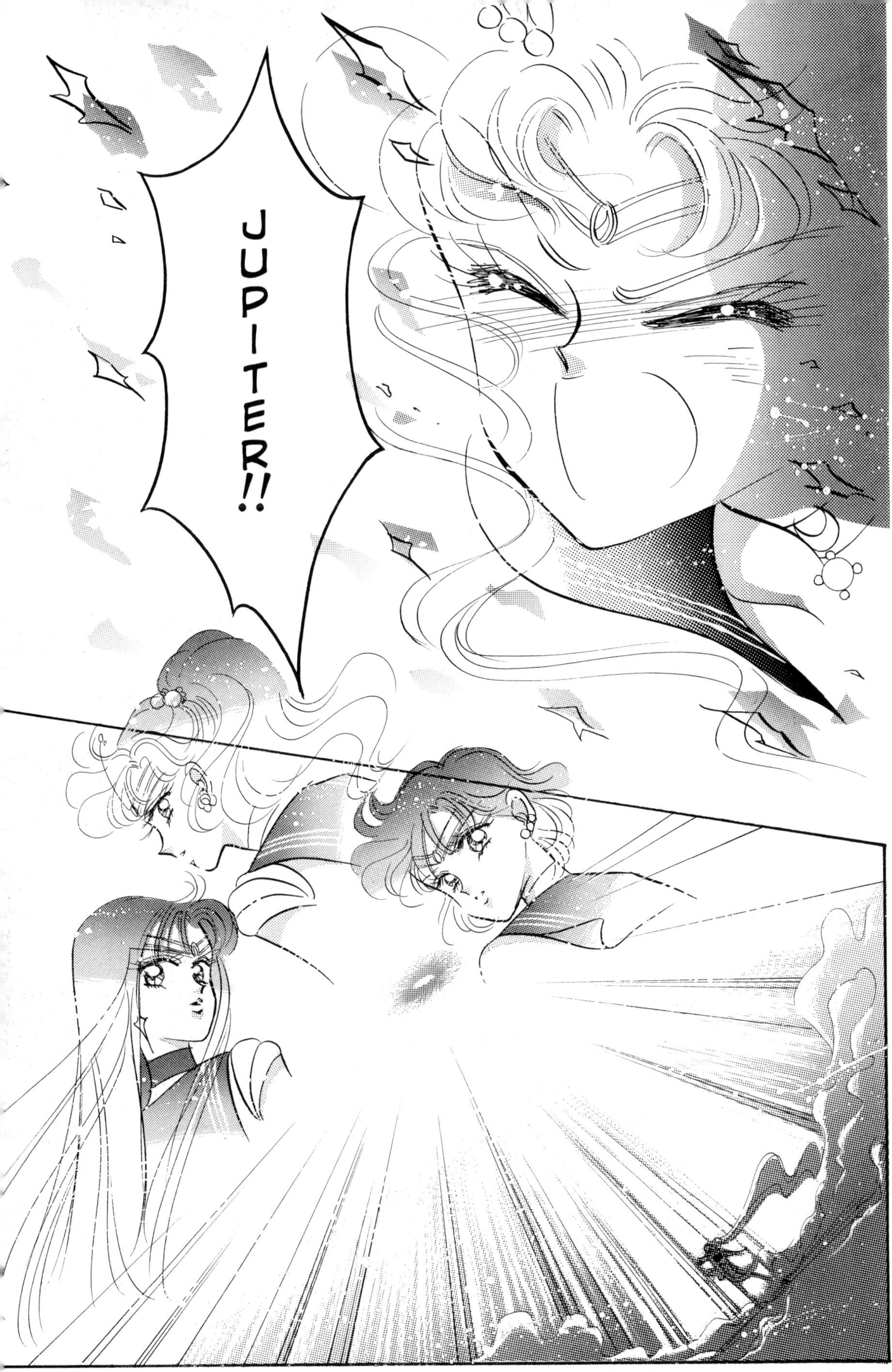
JUPITER!!

Pretty Guardian

Sailor Moon

Act.18 Aggression: Sailor Venus

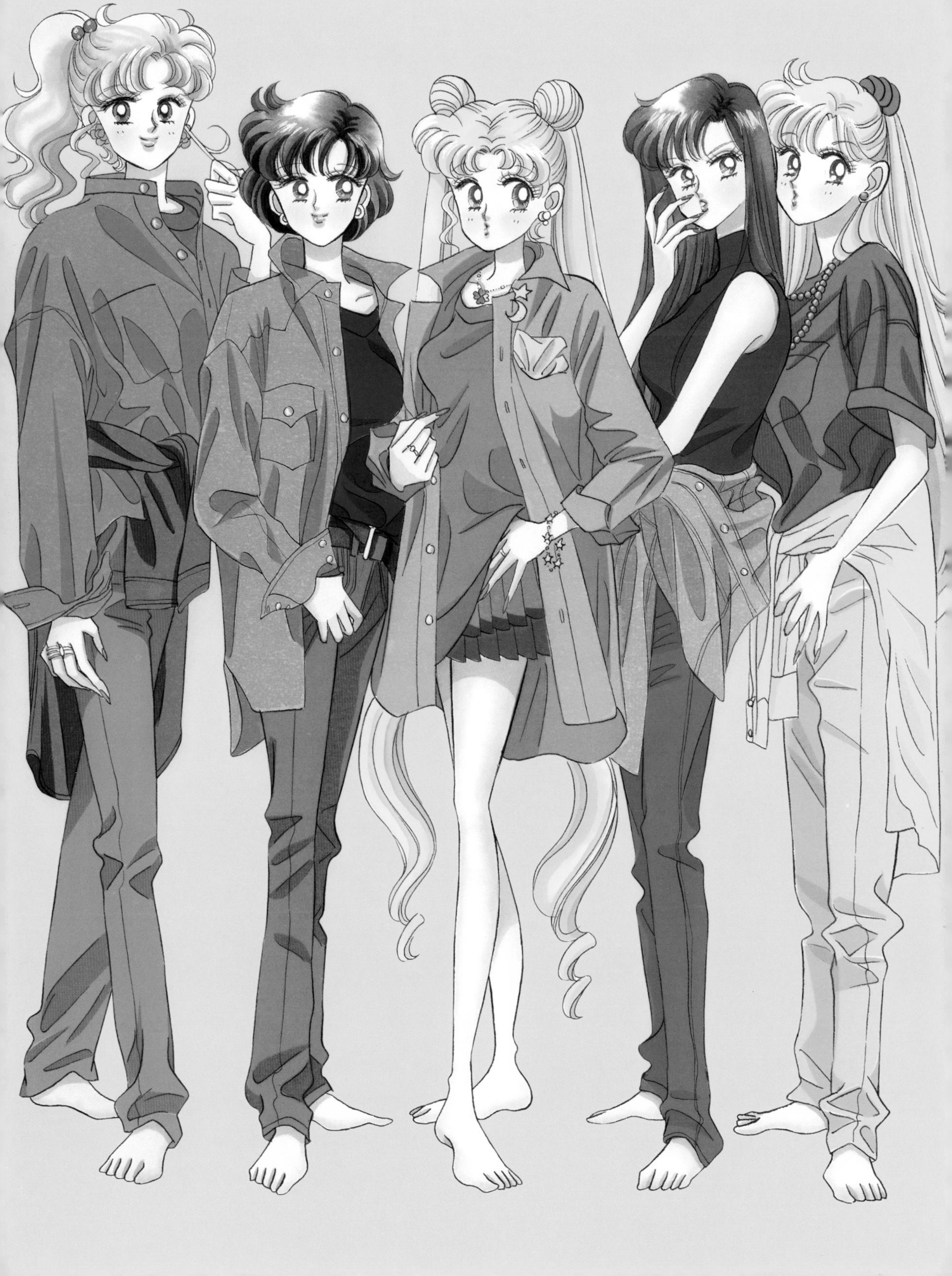

Pretty Guardian

Sailor Moon

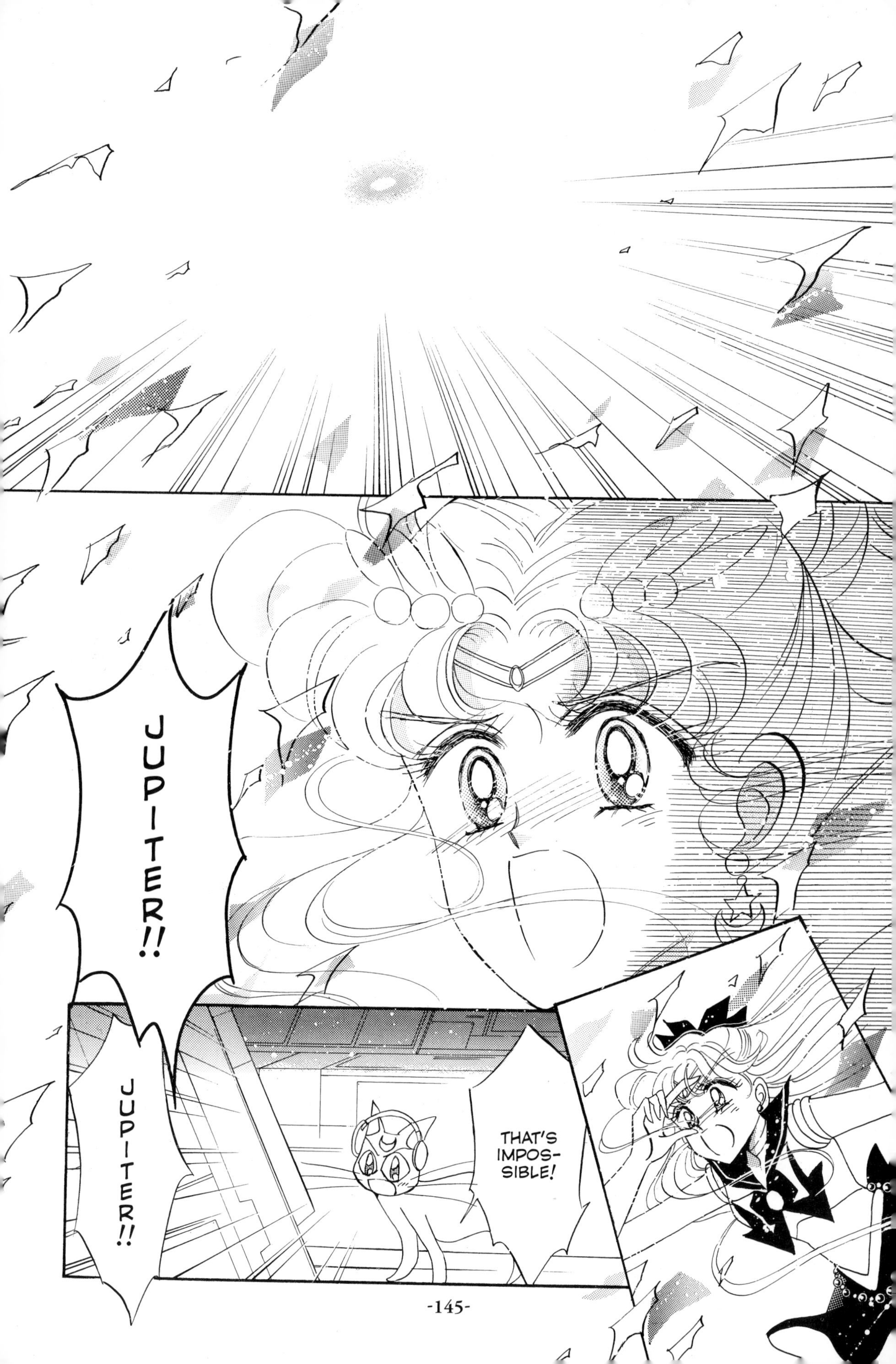
JUPITER!!
THAT'S IMPOSSIBLE!
JUPITER!!

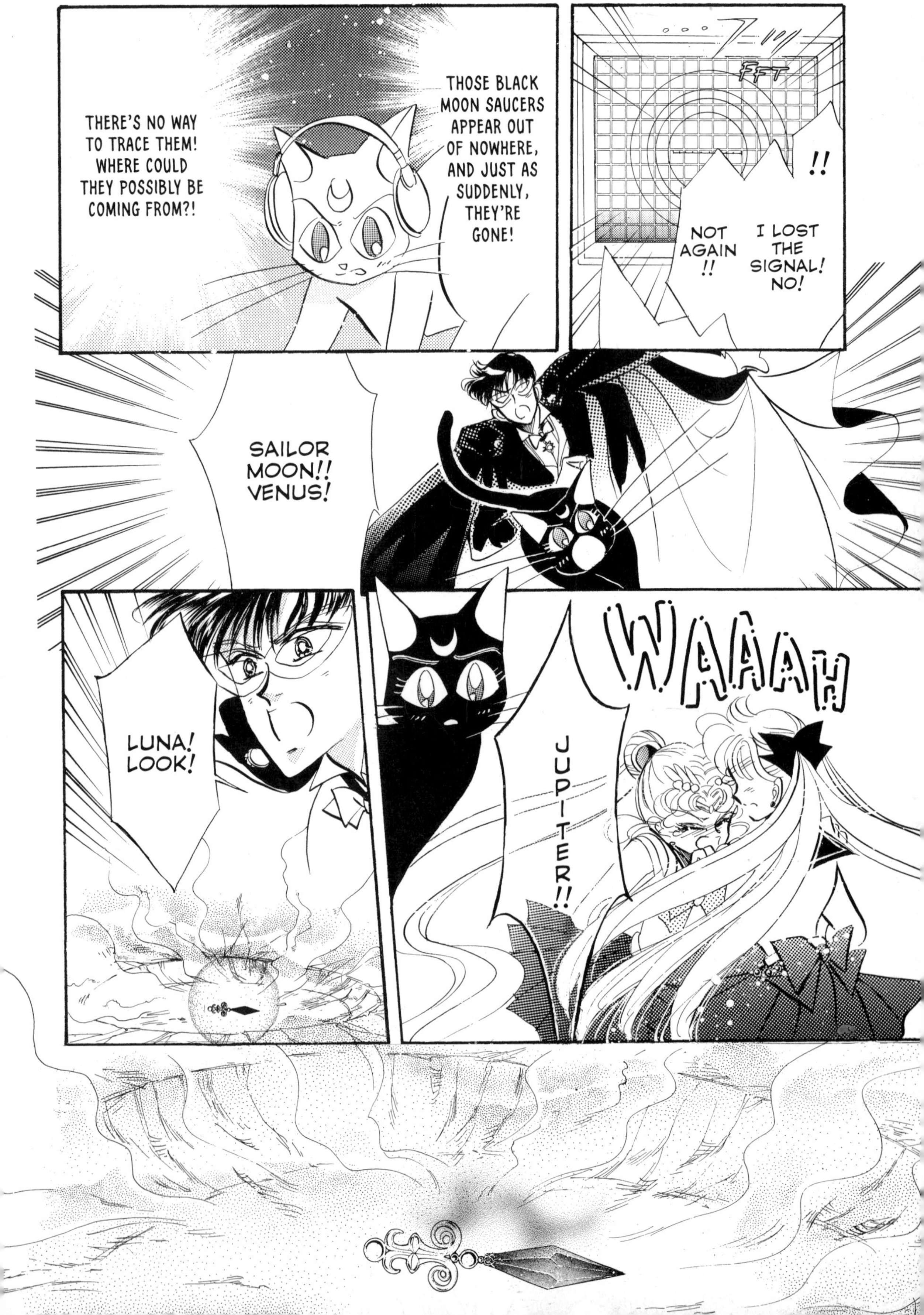
FFT
!!
I LOST THE SIGNAL! NO!
NOT AGAIN!!
THOSE BLACK MOON SAUCERS APPEAR OUT OF NOWHERE, AND JUST AS SUDDENLY, THEY'RE GONE!
THERE'S NO WAY TO TRACE THEM! WHERE COULD THEY POSSIBLY BE COMING FROM?!
SAILOR MOON!! VENUS!
WAAAH
JUPITER!!
LUNA! LOOK!

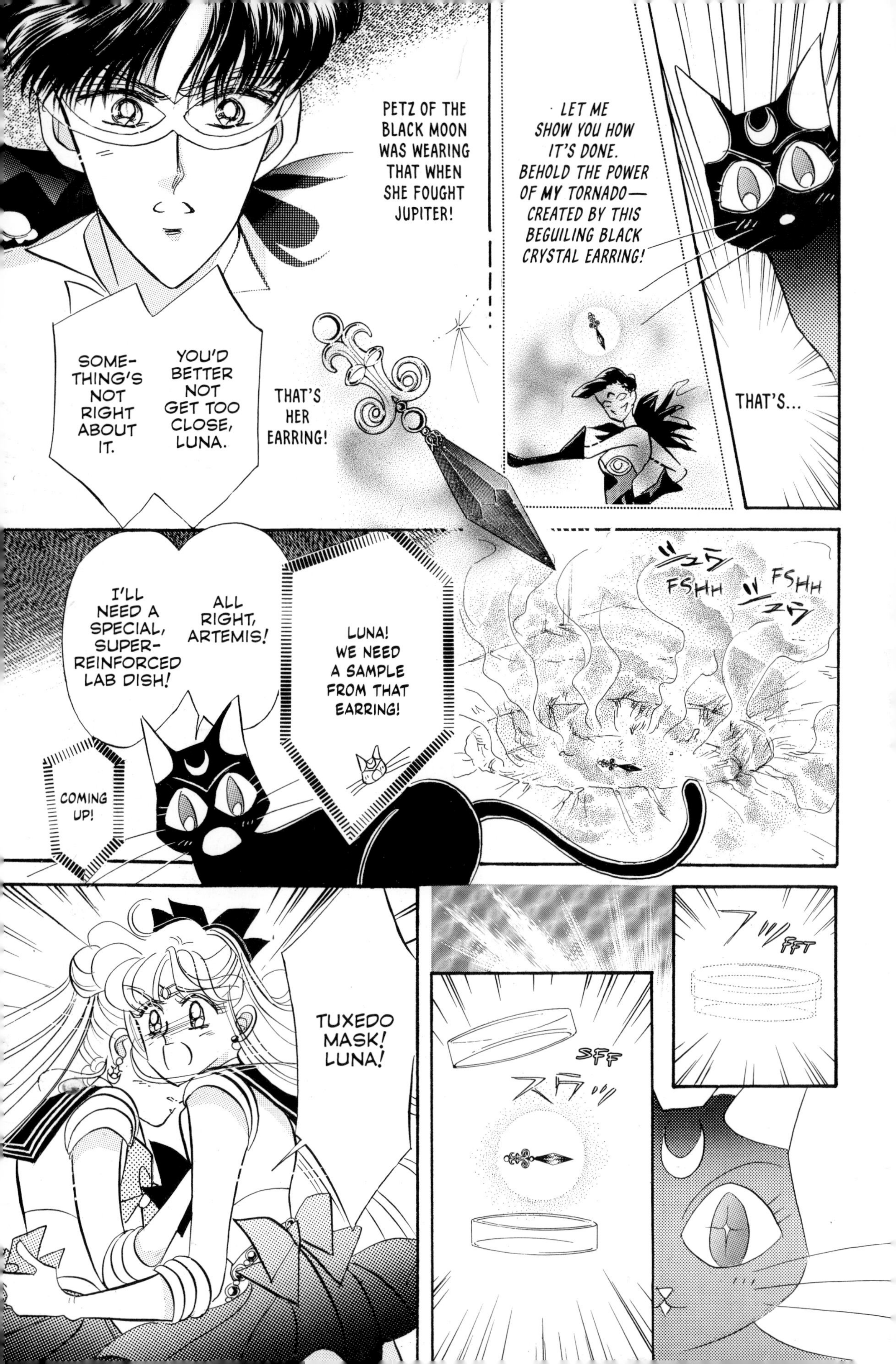
LET ME SHOW YOU HOW IT'S DONE. BEHOLD THE POWER OF MY TORNADO— CREATED BY THIS BEGUILING BLACK CRYSTAL EARRING!
THAT'S...
PETZ OF THE BLACK MOON WAS WEARING THAT WHEN SHE FOUGHT JUPITER!
THAT'S HER EARRING!
YOU'D BETTER NOT GET TOO CLOSE, LUNA.
SOME-THING'S NOT RIGHT ABOUT IT.
FSHH
FSHH
LUNA! WE NEED A SAMPLE FROM THAT EARRING!
ALL RIGHT, ARTEMIS!
I'LL NEED A SPECIAL, SUPER-REINFORCED LAB DISH!
COMING UP!
FFT
SFF
TUXEDO MASK! LUNA!

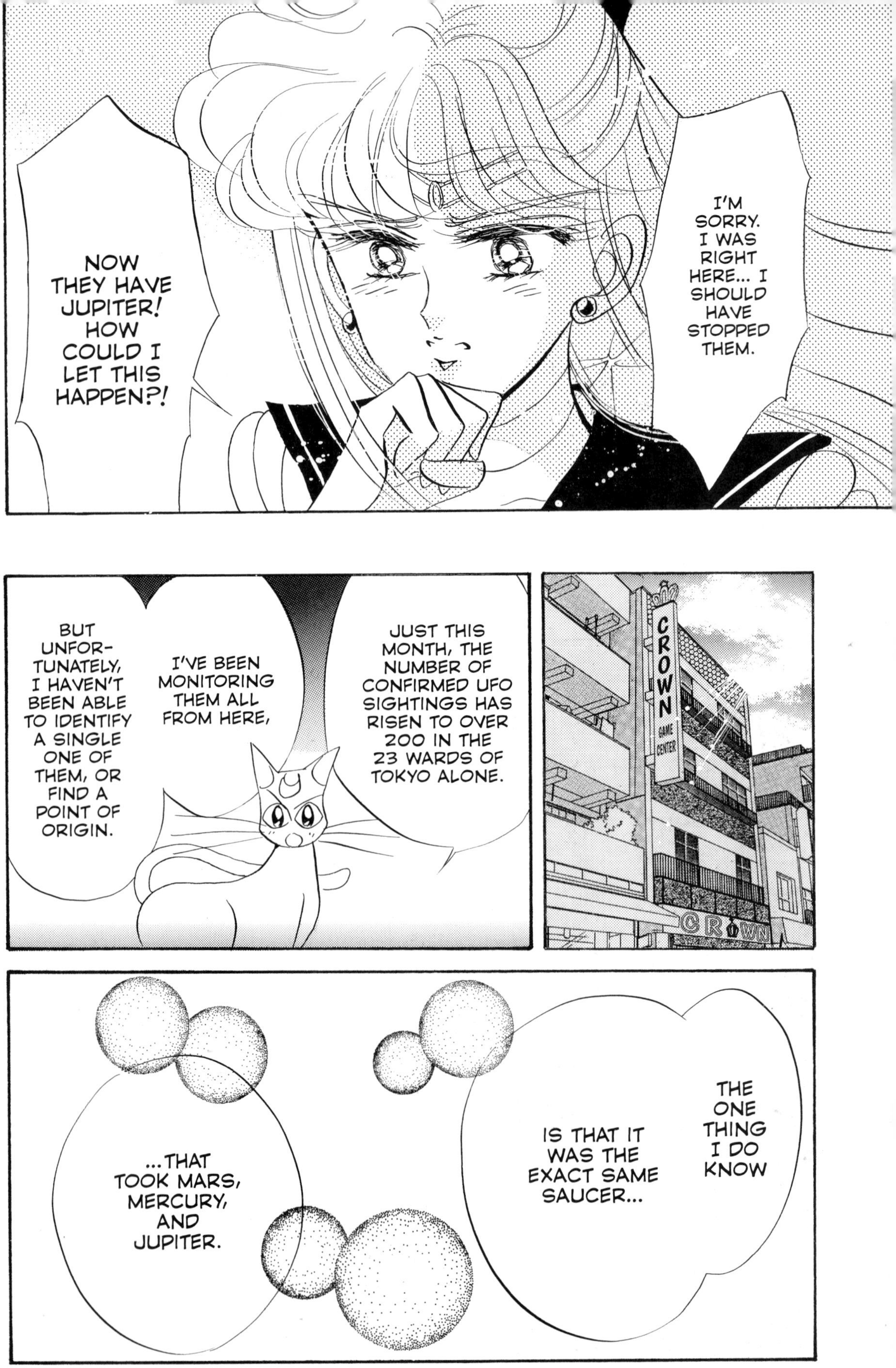
I'M SORRY. I WAS RIGHT HERE... I SHOULD HAVE STOPPED THEM.
NOW THEY HAVE JUPITER! HOW COULD I LET THIS HAPPEN?!
CROWN GAME CENTER
CROWN
JUST THIS MONTH, THE NUMBER OF CONFIRMED UFO SIGHTINGS HAS RISEN TO OVER 200 IN THE 23 WARDS OF TOKYO ALONE.
I'VE BEEN MONITORING THEM ALL FROM HERE,
BUT UNFOR-TUNATELY, I HAVEN'T BEEN ABLE TO IDENTIFY A SINGLE ONE OF THEM, OR FIND A POINT OF ORIGIN.
THE ONE THING I DO KNOW
IS THAT IT WAS THE EXACT SAME SAUCER...
...THAT TOOK MARS, MERCURY, AND JUPITER.

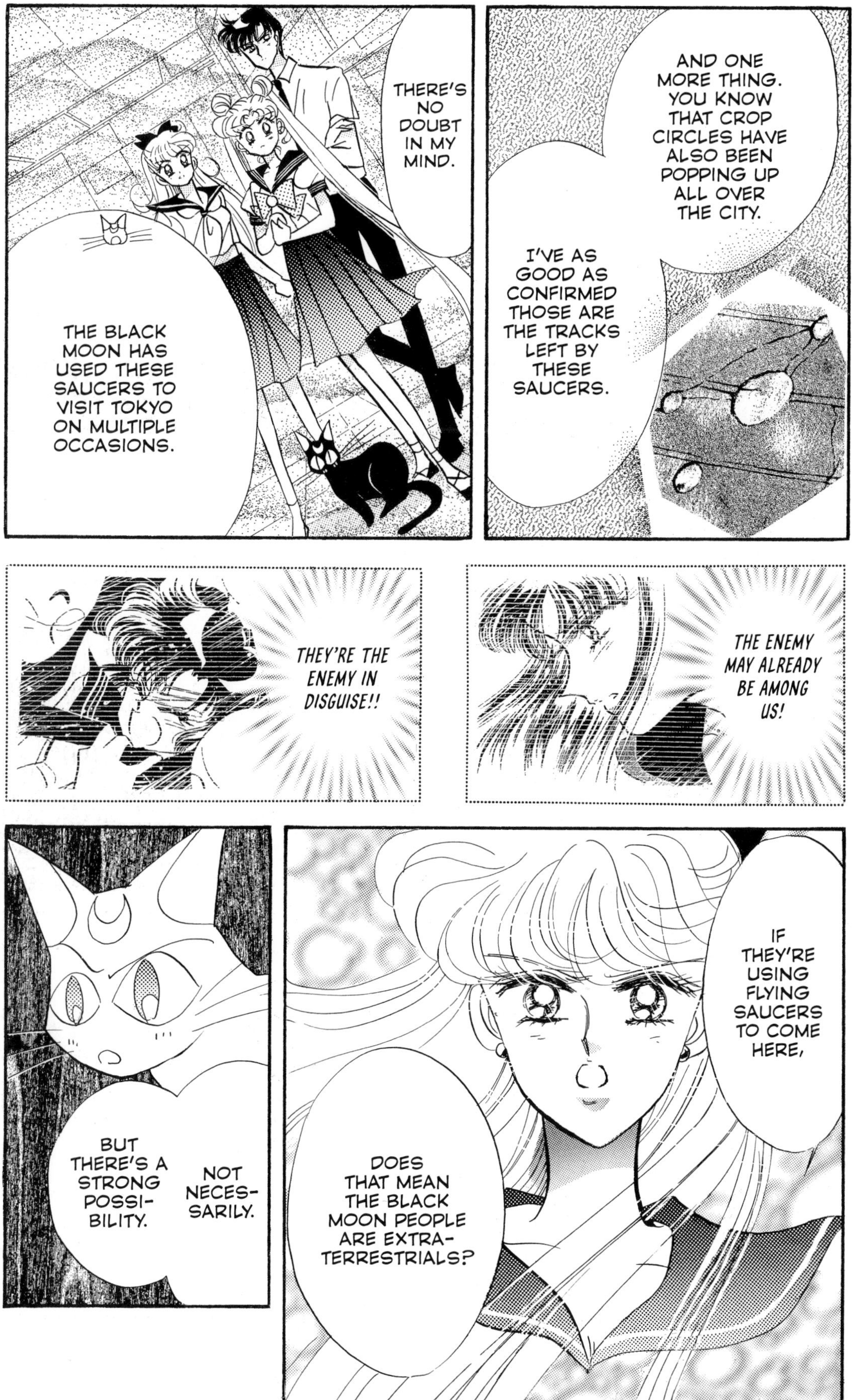
AND ONE MORE THING. YOU KNOW THAT CROP CIRCLES HAVE ALSO BEEN POPPING UP ALL OVER THE CITY.
I'VE AS GOOD AS CONFIRMED THOSE ARE THE TRACKS LEFT BY THESE SAUCERS.
THERE'S NO DOUBT IN MY MIND.
THE BLACK MOON HAS USED THESE SAUCERS TO VISIT TOKYO ON MULTIPLE OCCASIONS.
THE ENEMY MAY ALREADY BE AMONG US!
THEY'RE THE ENEMY IN DISGUISE!!
IF THEY'RE USING FLYING SAUCERS TO COME HERE,
DOES THAT MEAN THE BLACK MOON PEOPLE ARE EXTRA-TERRESTRIALS?
NOT NECES-SARILY.
BUT THERE'S A STRONG POSSI-BILITY.

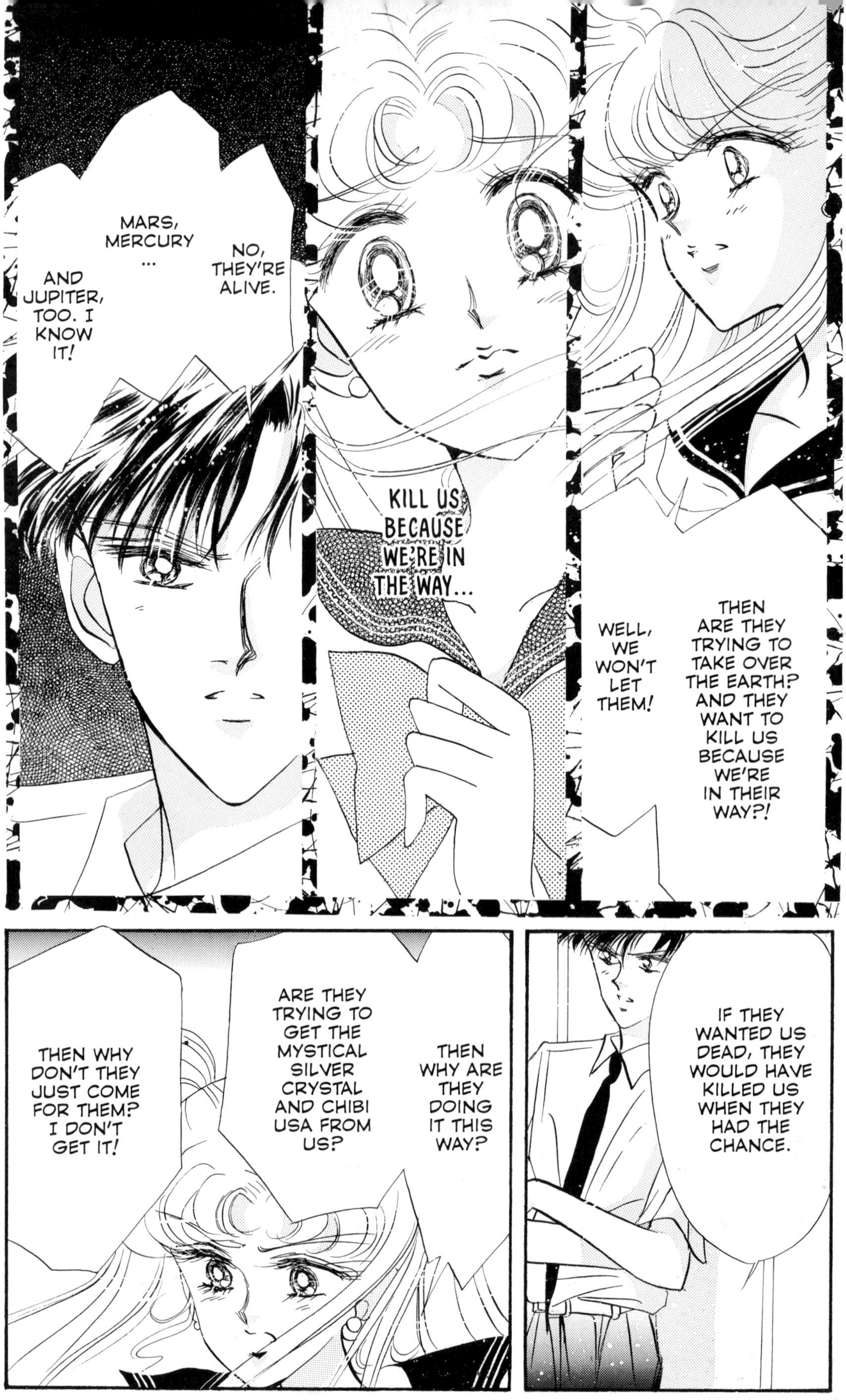
THEN ARE THEY TRYING TO TAKE OVER THE EARTH? AND THEY WANT TO KILL US BECAUSE WE'RE IN THEIR WAY?!
WELL, WE WON'T LET THEM!
KILL US BECAUSE WE'RE IN THE WAY...
NO, THEY'RE ALIVE.
MARS, MERCURY ...
AND JUPITER, TOO. I KNOW IT!
IF THEY WANTED US DEAD, THEY WOULD HAVE KILLED US WHEN THEY HAD THE CHANCE.
THEN WHY ARE THEY DOING IT THIS WAY?
ARE THEY TRYING TO GET THE MYSTICAL SILVER CRYSTAL AND CHIBI USA FROM US?
THEN WHY DON'T THEY JUST COME FOR THEM? I DON'T GET IT!

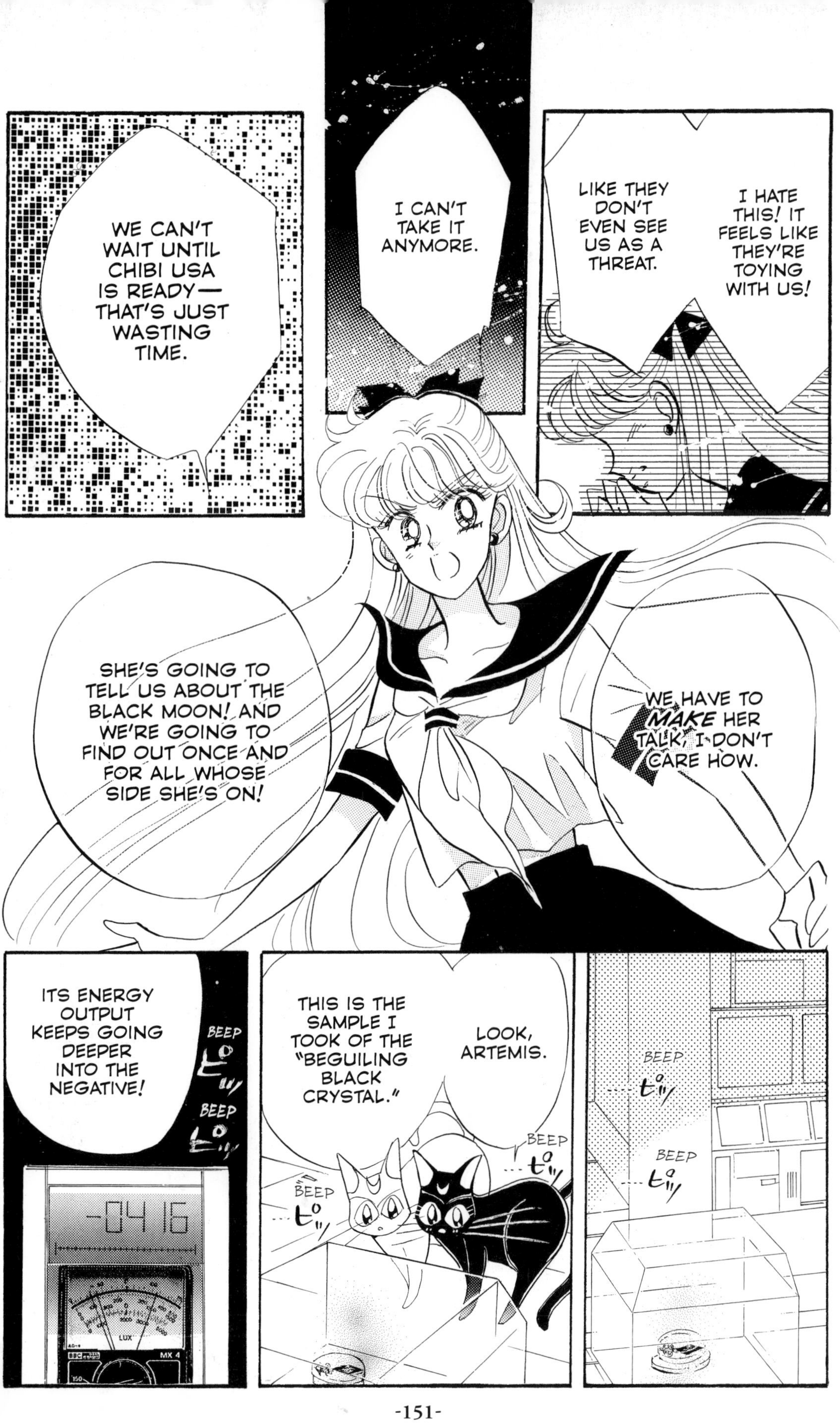
I HATE THIS! IT FEELS LIKE THEY'RE TOYING WITH US!
LIKE THEY DON'T EVEN SEE US AS A THREAT.
I CAN'T TAKE IT ANYMORE.
WE CAN'T WAIT UNTIL CHIBI USA IS READY—THAT'S JUST WASTING TIME.
WE HAVE TO MAKE HER TALK, I DON'T CARE HOW.
SHE'S GOING TO TELL US ABOUT THE BLACK MOON! AND WE'RE GOING TO FIND OUT ONCE AND FOR ALL WHOSE SIDE SHE'S ON!
BEEP
BEEP
LOOK, ARTEMIS.
THIS IS THE SAMPLE I TOOK OF THE "BEGUILING BLACK CRYSTAL."
BEEP
BEEP
ITS ENERGY OUTPUT KEEPS GOING DEEPER INTO THE NEGATIVE!
BEEP
BEEP
-0416
LUX
MX 4

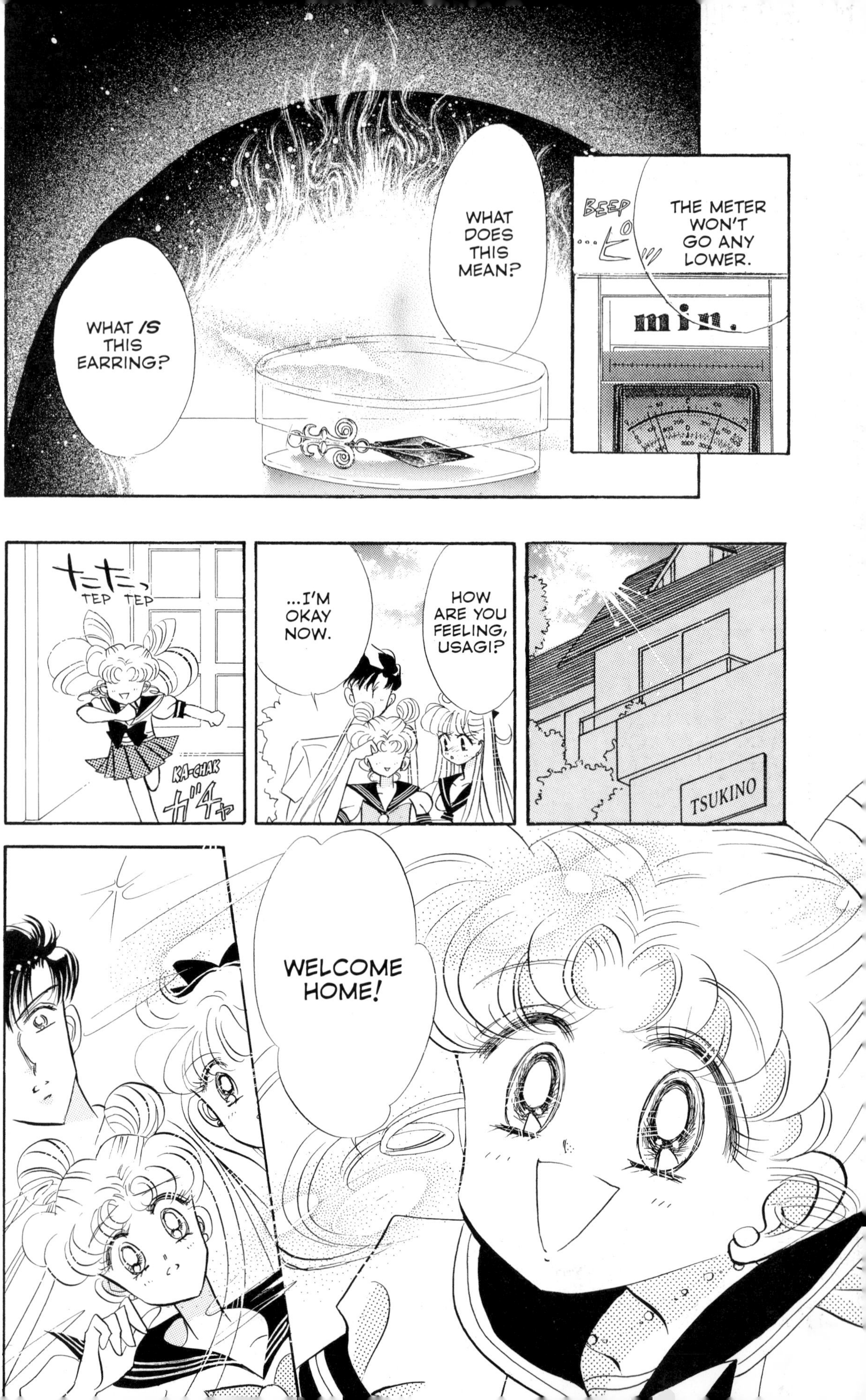
BEEP...
THE METER WON'T GO ANY LOWER.
min.
WHAT DOES THIS MEAN?
WHAT IS THIS EARRING?
TSUKINO
HOW ARE YOU FEELING, USAGI?
...I'M OKAY NOW.
TEP TEP
KA-CHAK
WELCOME HOME!

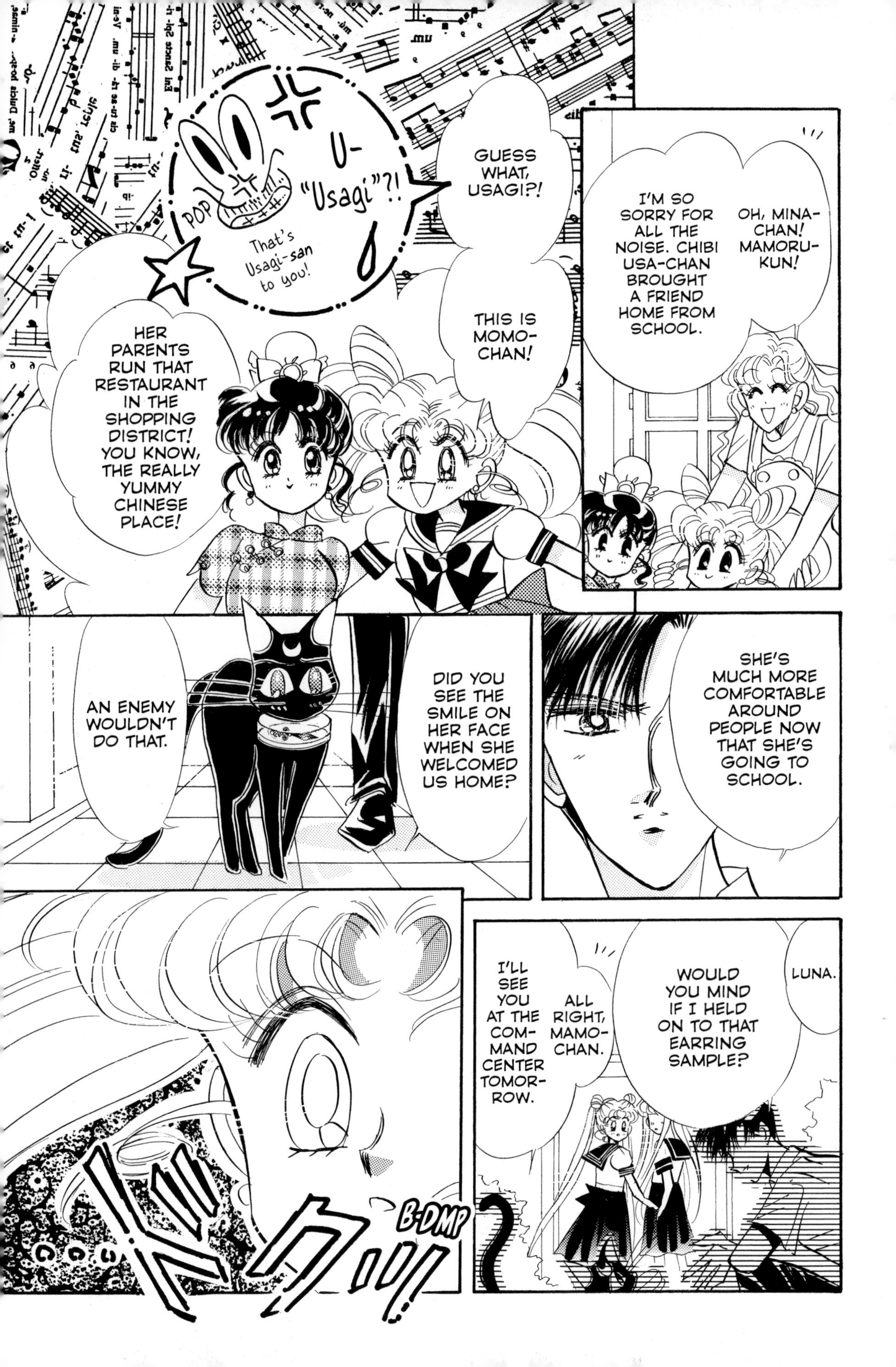
OH, MINA-CHAN! MAMORU-KUN!
I'M SO SORRY FOR ALL THE NOISE. CHIBI USA-CHAN BROUGHT A FRIEND HOME FROM SCHOOL.
GUESS WHAT, USAGI?!
THIS IS MOMO-CHAN!
U- "Usagi"?!
POP
That's Usagi-san to you!
HER PARENTS RUN THAT RESTAURANT IN THE SHOPPING DISTRICT! YOU KNOW, THE REALLY YUMMY CHINESE PLACE!
SHE'S MUCH MORE COMFORTABLE AROUND PEOPLE NOW THAT SHE'S GOING TO SCHOOL.
DID YOU SEE THE SMILE ON HER FACE WHEN SHE WELCOMED US HOME?
AN ENEMY WOULDN'T DO THAT.
LUNA.
WOULD YOU MIND IF I HELD ON TO THAT EARRING SAMPLE?
ALL RIGHT, MAMO-CHAN.
I'LL SEE YOU AT THE COM-MAND CENTER TOMOR-ROW.
B-DMP

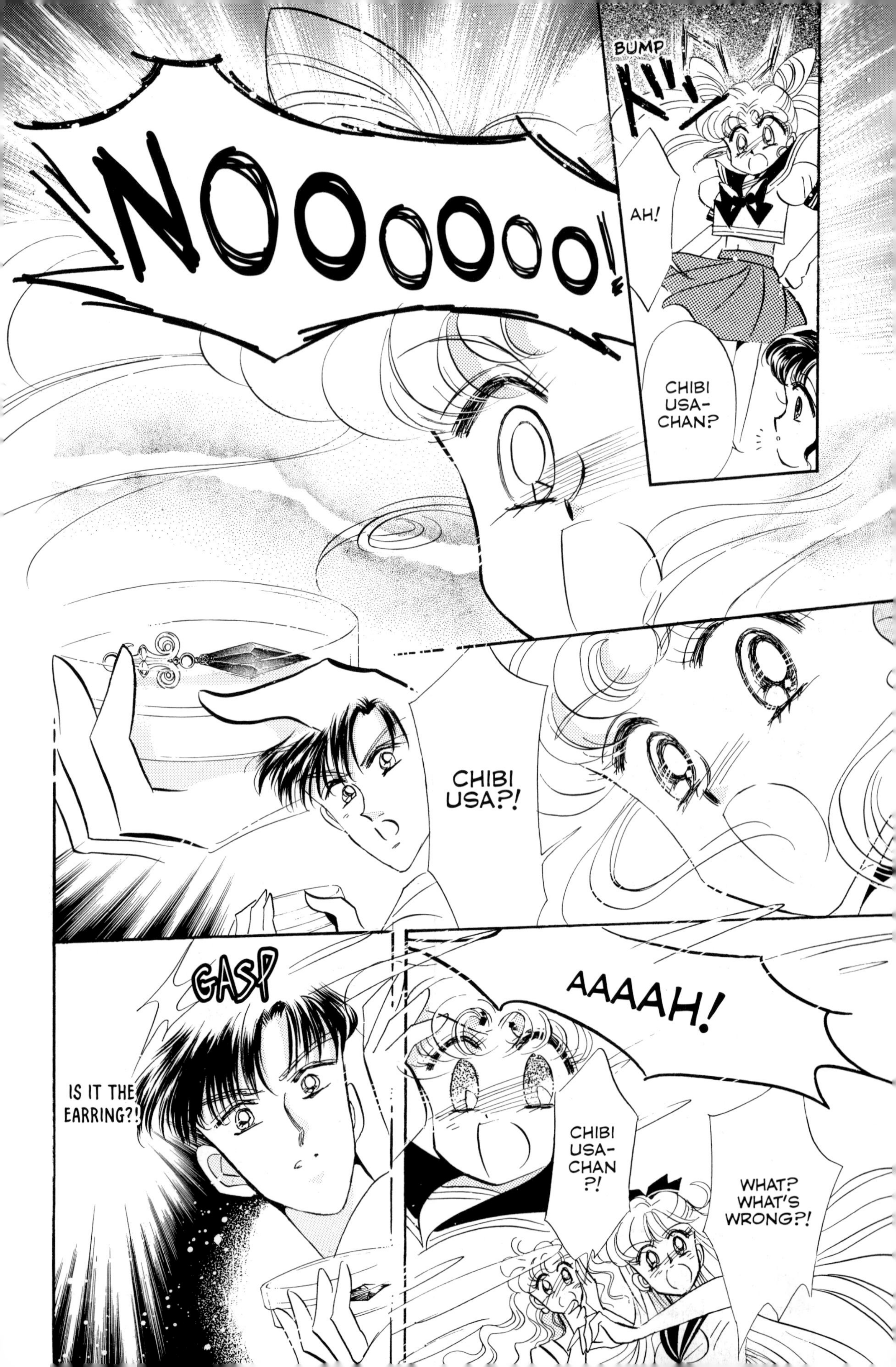
BUMP
AH!
CHIBI USA-CHAN?
NOOOOOO!
CHIBI USA?!
AAAAH!
WHAT? WHAT'S WRONG?!
CHIBI USA-CHAN?!
GASP
IS IT THE EARRING?!

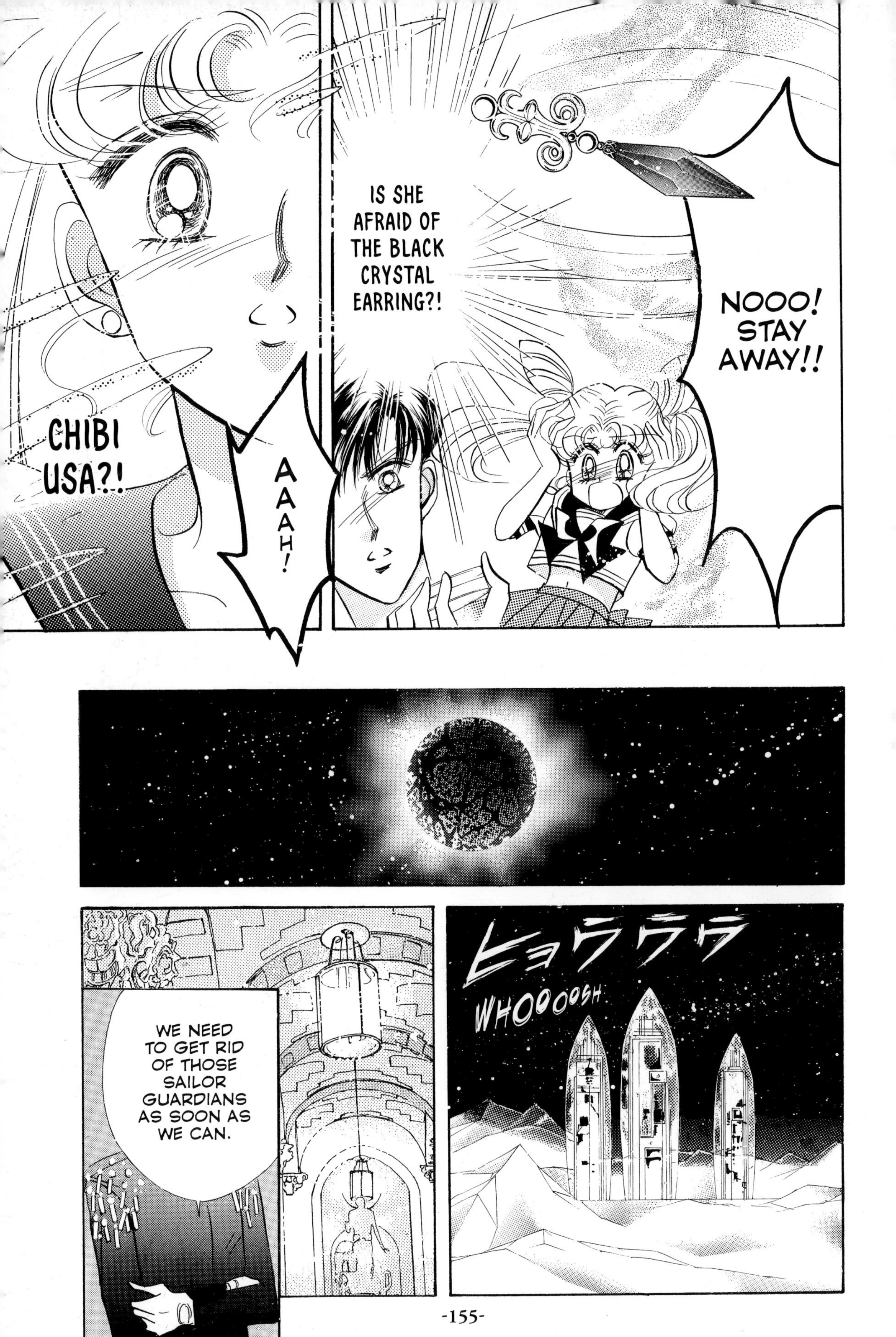
NOOO! STAY AWAY!!
IS SHE AFRAID OF THE BLACK CRYSTAL EARRING?!
AAAH!
CHIBI USA?!
ヒョウウウ
WHOOOOSH
WE NEED TO GET RID OF THOSE SAILOR GUARDIANS AS SOON AS WE CAN.

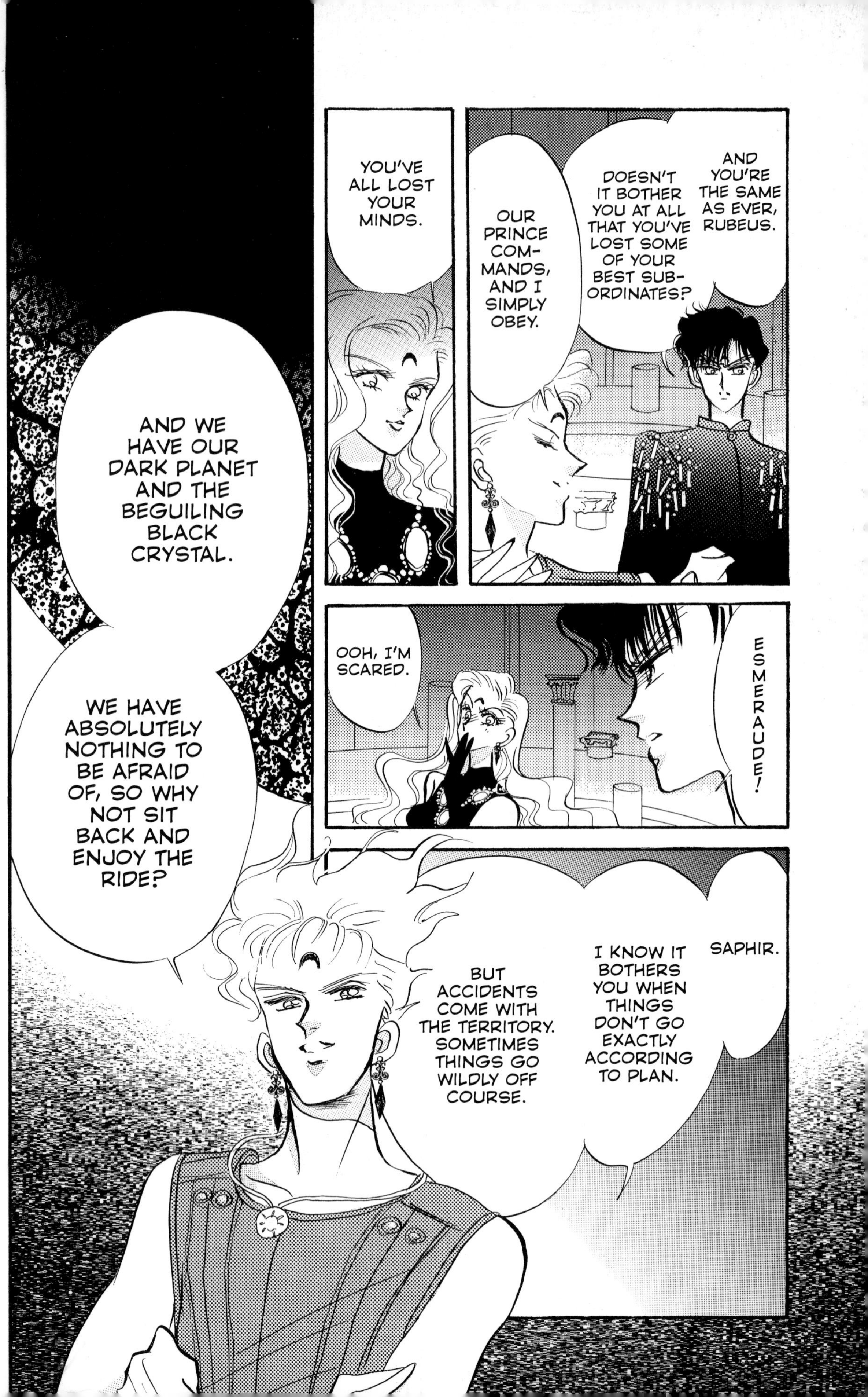
AND YOU'RE THE SAME AS EVER, RUBEUS.
DOESN'T IT BOTHER YOU AT ALL THAT YOU'VE LOST SOME OF YOUR BEST SUB-ORDINATES?
OUR PRINCE COM-MANDS, AND I SIMPLY OBEY.
YOU'VE ALL LOST YOUR MINDS.
ESMERAUDE!
OOH, I'M SCARED.
SAPHIR.
I KNOW IT BOTHERS YOU WHEN THINGS DON'T GO EXACTLY ACCORDING TO PLAN.
BUT ACCIDENTS COME WITH THE TERRITORY. SOMETIMES THINGS GO WILDLY OFF COURSE.
AND WE HAVE OUR DARK PLANET AND THE BEGUILING BLACK CRYSTAL.
WE HAVE ABSOLUTELY NOTHING TO BE AFRAID OF, SO WHY NOT SIT BACK AND ENJOY THE RIDE?

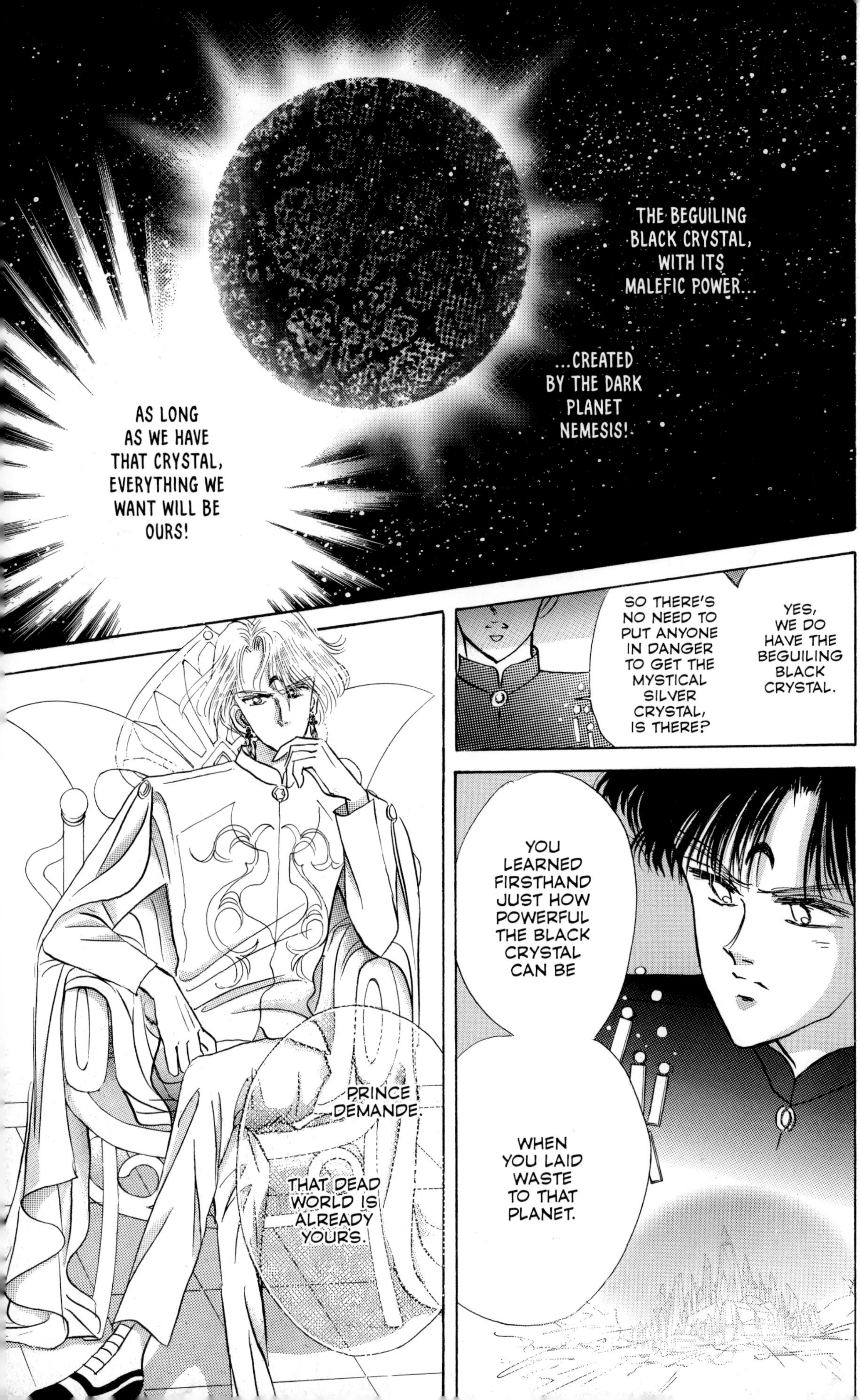
THE BEGUILING BLACK CRYSTAL, WITH ITS MALEFIC POWER...
...CREATED BY THE DARK PLANET NEMESIS!
AS LONG AS WE HAVE THAT CRYSTAL, EVERYTHING WE WANT WILL BE OURS!
YES, WE DO HAVE THE BEGUILING BLACK CRYSTAL.
SO THERE'S NO NEED TO PUT ANYONE IN DANGER TO GET THE MYSTICAL SILVER CRYSTAL, IS THERE?
YOU LEARNED FIRSTHAND JUST HOW POWERFUL THE BLACK CRYSTAL CAN BE
WHEN YOU LAID WASTE TO THAT PLANET.
PRINCE DEMANDE.
THAT DEAD WORLD IS ALREADY YOURS.

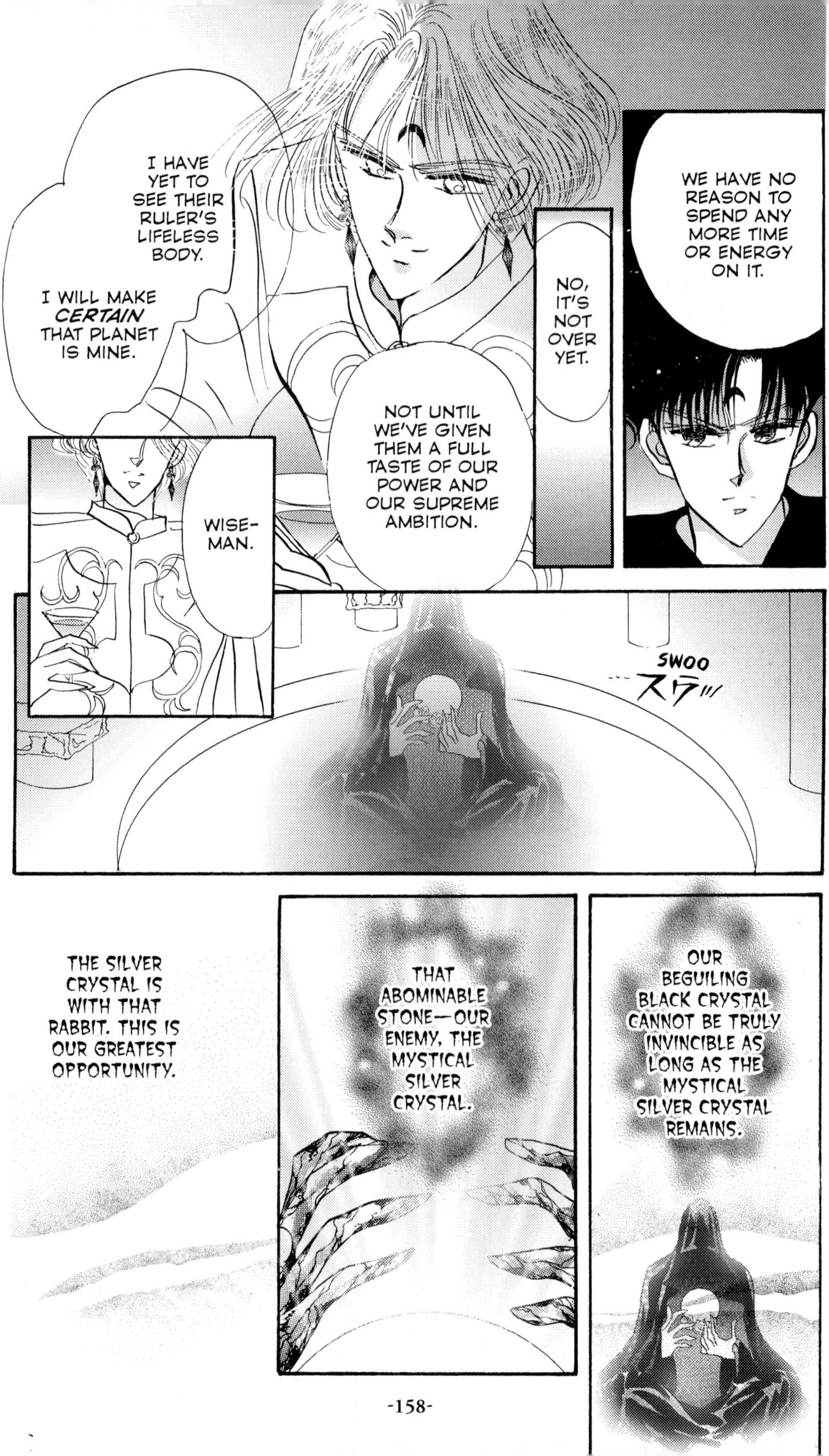
WE HAVE NO REASON TO SPEND ANY MORE TIME OR ENERGY ON IT.
NO, IT'S NOT OVER YET.
NOT UNTIL WE'VE GIVEN THEM A FULL TASTE OF OUR POWER AND OUR SUPREME AMBITION.
I HAVE YET TO SEE THEIR RULER'S LIFELESS BODY.
I WILL MAKE *CERTAIN* THAT PLANET IS MINE.
WISE-MAN.
SWOO
スゥ
OUR BEGUILING BLACK CRYSTAL CANNOT BE TRULY INVINCIBLE AS LONG AS THE MYSTICAL SILVER CRYSTAL REMAINS.
THAT ABOMINABLE STONE—OUR ENEMY, THE MYSTICAL SILVER CRYSTAL.
THE SILVER CRYSTAL IS WITH THAT RABBIT. THIS IS OUR GREATEST OPPORTUNITY.

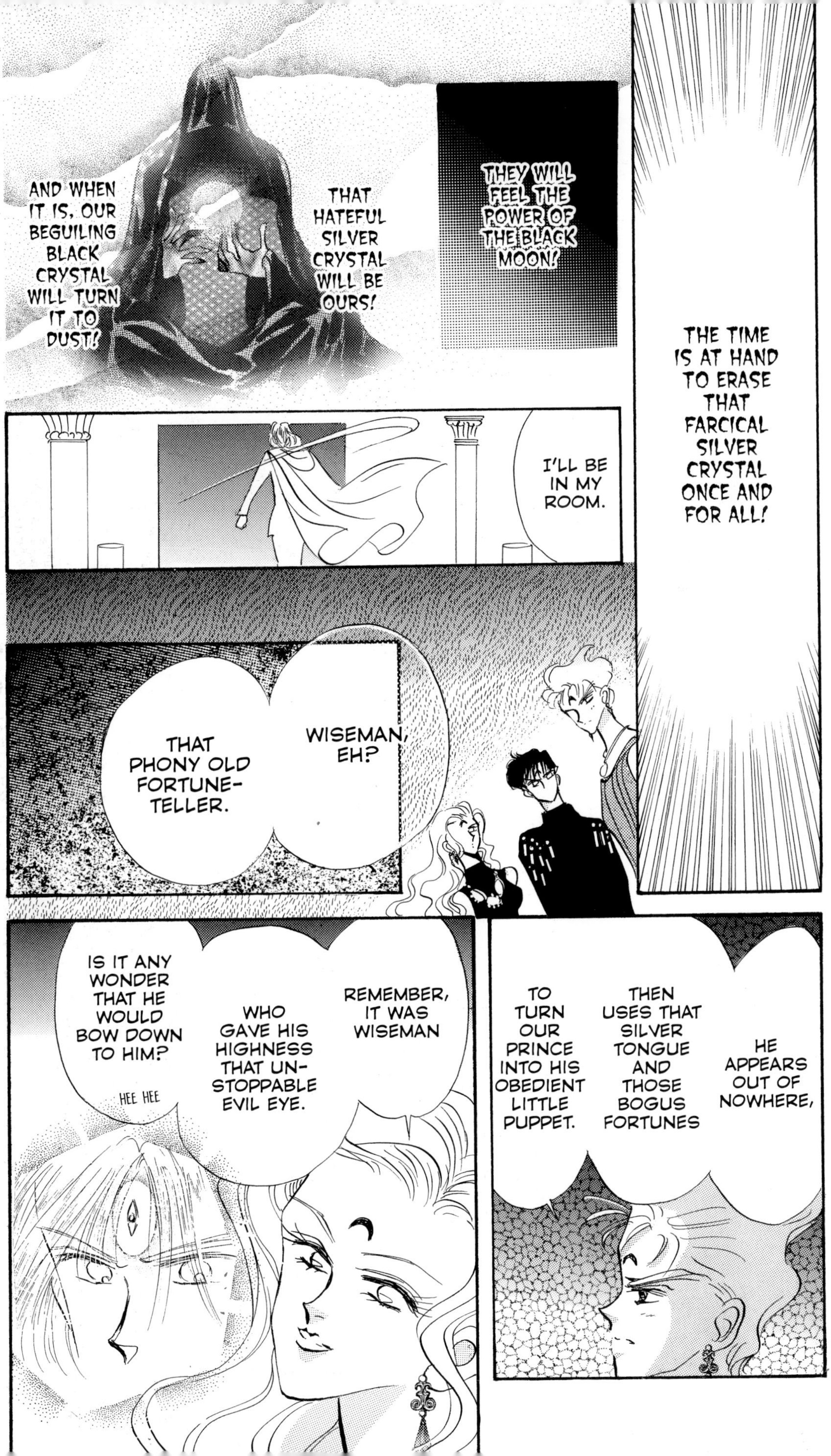
THE TIME IS AT HAND TO ERASE THAT FARCICAL SILVER CRYSTAL ONCE AND FOR ALL!
THEY WILL FEEL THE POWER OF THE BLACK MOON!
THAT HATEFUL SILVER CRYSTAL WILL BE OURS!
AND WHEN IT IS, OUR BEGUILING BLACK CRYSTAL WILL TURN IT TO DUST!
I'LL BE IN MY ROOM.
WISEMAN, EH?
THAT PHONY OLD FORTUNE-TELLER.
HE APPEARS OUT OF NOWHERE,
THEN USES THAT SILVER TONGUE AND THOSE BOGUS FORTUNES
TO TURN OUR PRINCE INTO HIS OBEDIENT LITTLE PUPPET.
REMEMBER, IT WAS WISEMAN
WHO GAVE HIS HIGHNESS THAT UN-STOPPABLE EVIL EYE.
IS IT ANY WONDER THAT HE WOULD BOW DOWN TO HIM?
HEE HEE

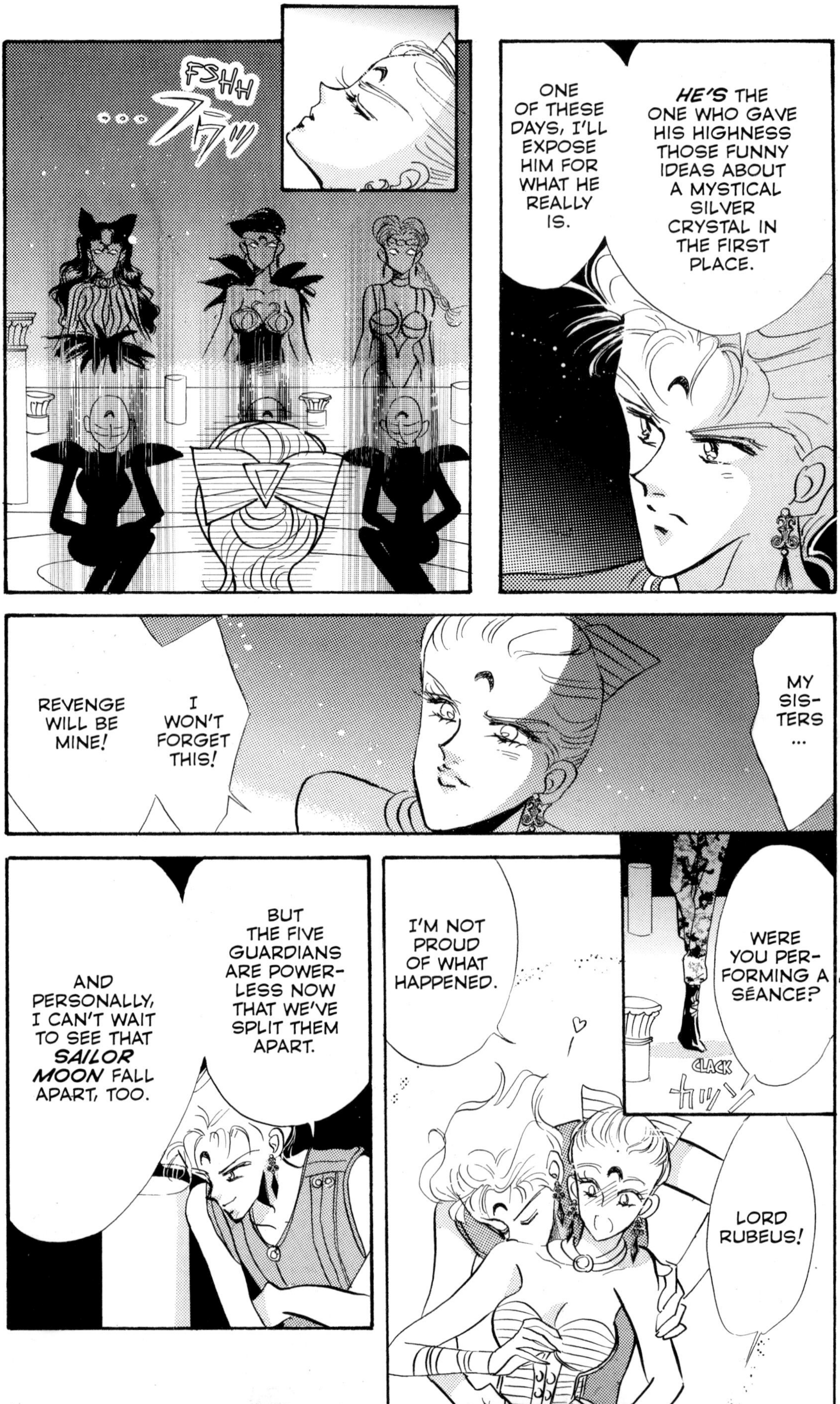
HE'S THE ONE WHO GAVE HIS HIGHNESS THOSE FUNNY IDEAS ABOUT A MYSTICAL SILVER CRYSTAL IN THE FIRST PLACE.
ONE OF THESE DAYS, I'LL EXPOSE HIM FOR WHAT HE REALLY IS.
FSHH
フワッ
...
MY SISTERS...
I WON'T FORGET THIS!
REVENGE WILL BE MINE!
WERE YOU PERFORMING A SÉANCE?
CLACK
カツン
LORD RUBEUS!
I'M NOT PROUD OF WHAT HAPPENED.
BUT THE FIVE GUARDIANS ARE POWERLESS NOW THAT WE'VE SPLIT THEM APART.
AND PERSONALLY, I CAN'T WAIT TO SEE THAT SAILOR MOON FALL APART, TOO.

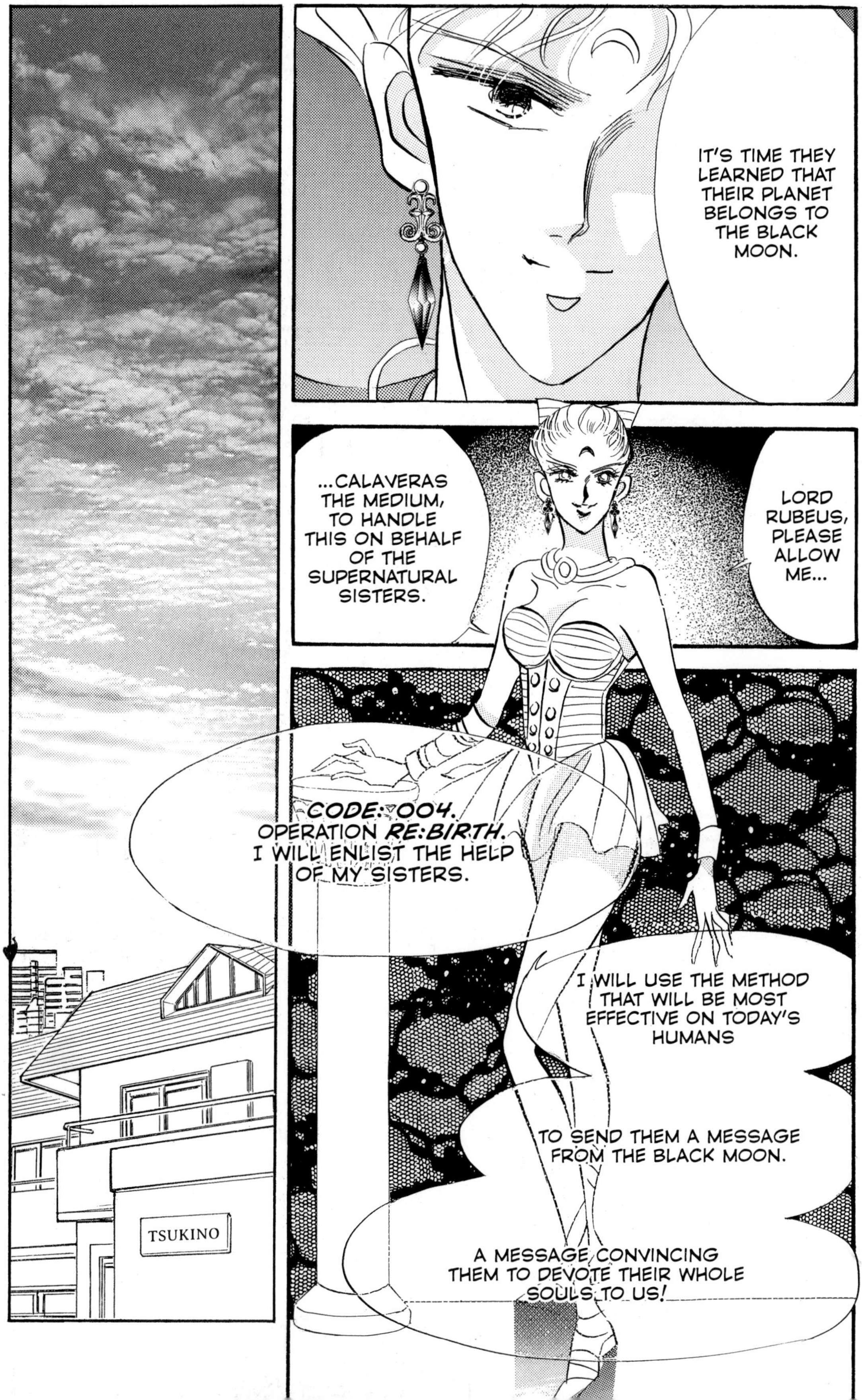
IT'S TIME THEY LEARNED THAT THEIR PLANET BELONGS TO THE BLACK MOON.
LORD RUBEUS, PLEASE ALLOW ME...
...CALAVERAS THE MEDIUM, TO HANDLE THIS ON BEHALF OF THE SUPERNATURAL SISTERS.
CODE: 004. OPERATION RE:BIRTH. I WILL ENLIST THE HELP OF MY SISTERS.
I WILL USE THE METHOD THAT WILL BE MOST EFFECTIVE ON TODAY'S HUMANS
TO SEND THEM A MESSAGE FROM THE BLACK MOON.
A MESSAGE CONVINCING THEM TO DEVOTE THEIR WHOLE SOULS TO US!
TSUKINO

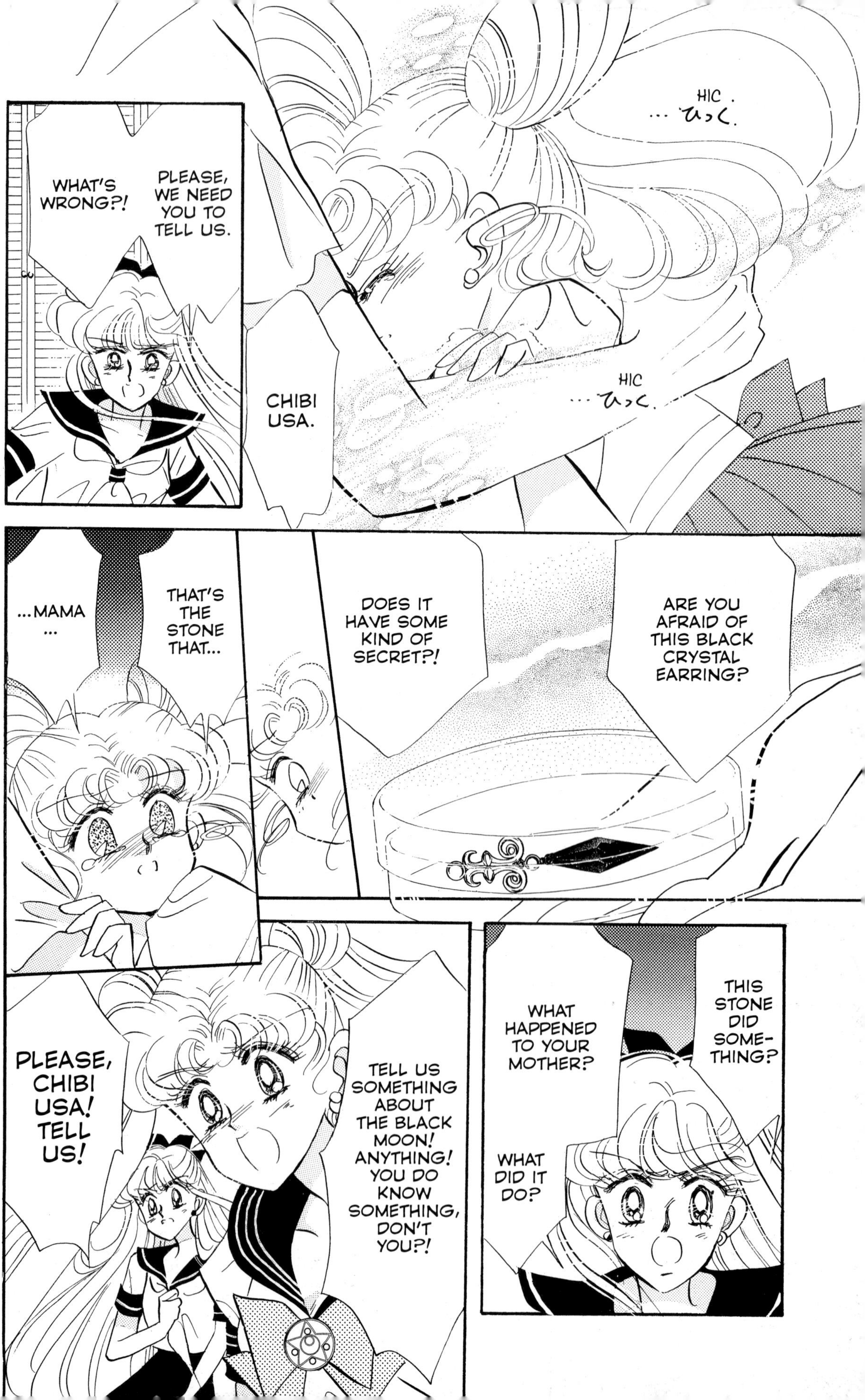
HIC
… ひっく.
HIC
… ひっく.
CHIBI USA.
PLEASE, WE NEED YOU TO TELL US.
WHAT'S WRONG?!
ARE YOU AFRAID OF THIS BLACK CRYSTAL EARRING?
DOES IT HAVE SOME KIND OF SECRET?!
THAT'S THE STONE THAT...
...MAMA ...
THIS STONE DID SOME-THING?
WHAT HAPPENED TO YOUR MOTHER?
WHAT DID IT DO?
TELL US SOMETHING ABOUT THE BLACK MOON! ANYTHING! YOU DO KNOW SOMETHING, DON'T YOU?!
PLEASE, CHIBI USA! TELL US!

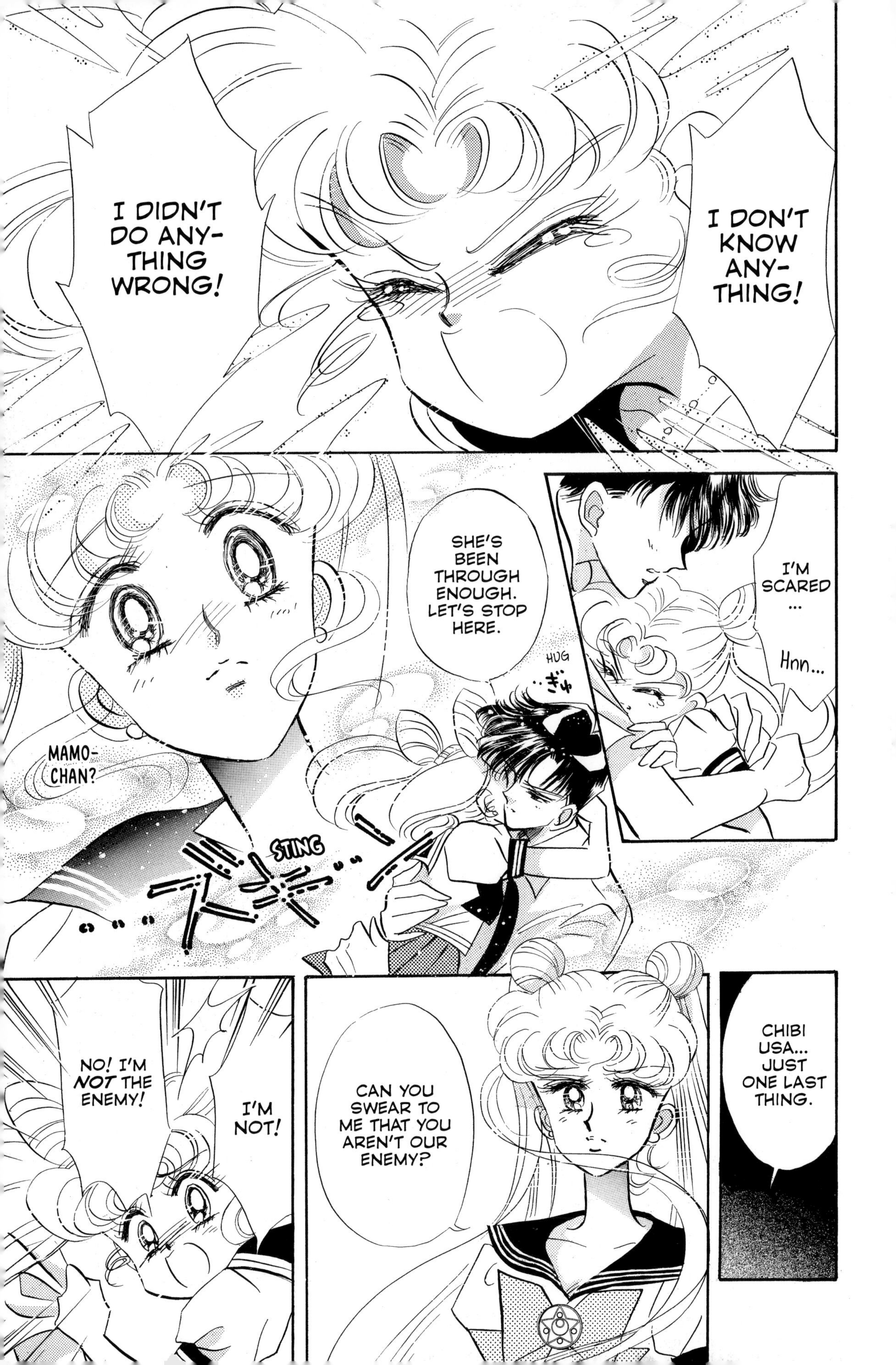
I DON'T KNOW ANY-THING!
I DIDN'T DO ANY-THING WRONG!
I'M SCARED ...
Hnn...
SHE'S BEEN THROUGH ENOUGH. LET'S STOP HERE.
HUG
ぎゅ
MAMO-CHAN?
STING
CHIBI USA... JUST ONE LAST THING.
CAN YOU SWEAR TO ME THAT YOU AREN'T OUR ENEMY?
I'M NOT!
NO! I'M ***NOT*** THE ENEMY!

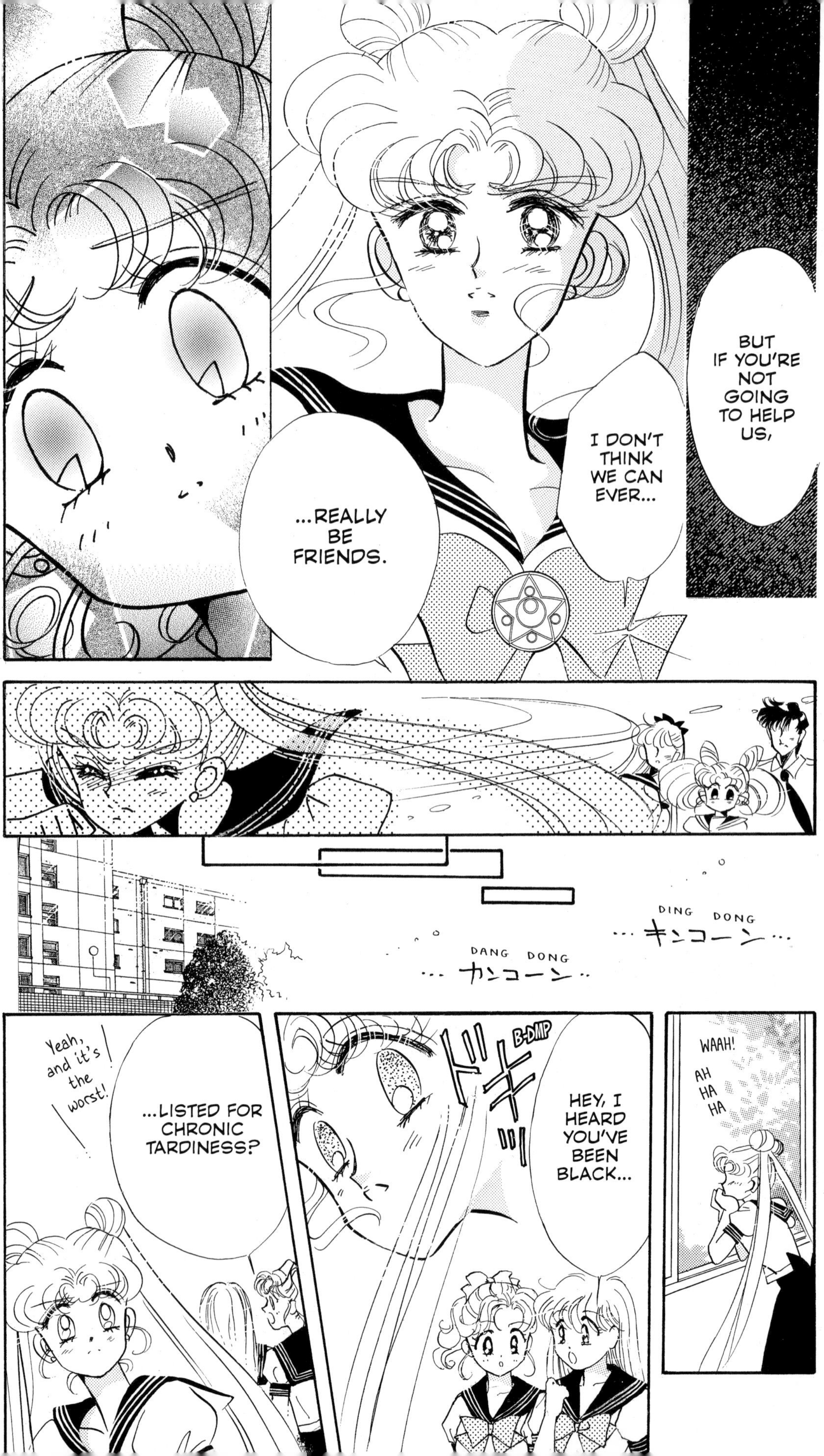

BUT IF YOU'RE NOT GOING TO HELP US,
I DON'T THINK WE CAN EVER...
...REALLY BE FRIENDS.
DING DONG
…キンコーン…
DANG DONG
…カンコーン…
WAAH!
AH HA HA
B-DMP
ドキッ
HEY, I HEARD YOU'VE BEEN BLACK...
...LISTED FOR CHRONIC TARDINESS?
Yeah, and it's the worst!

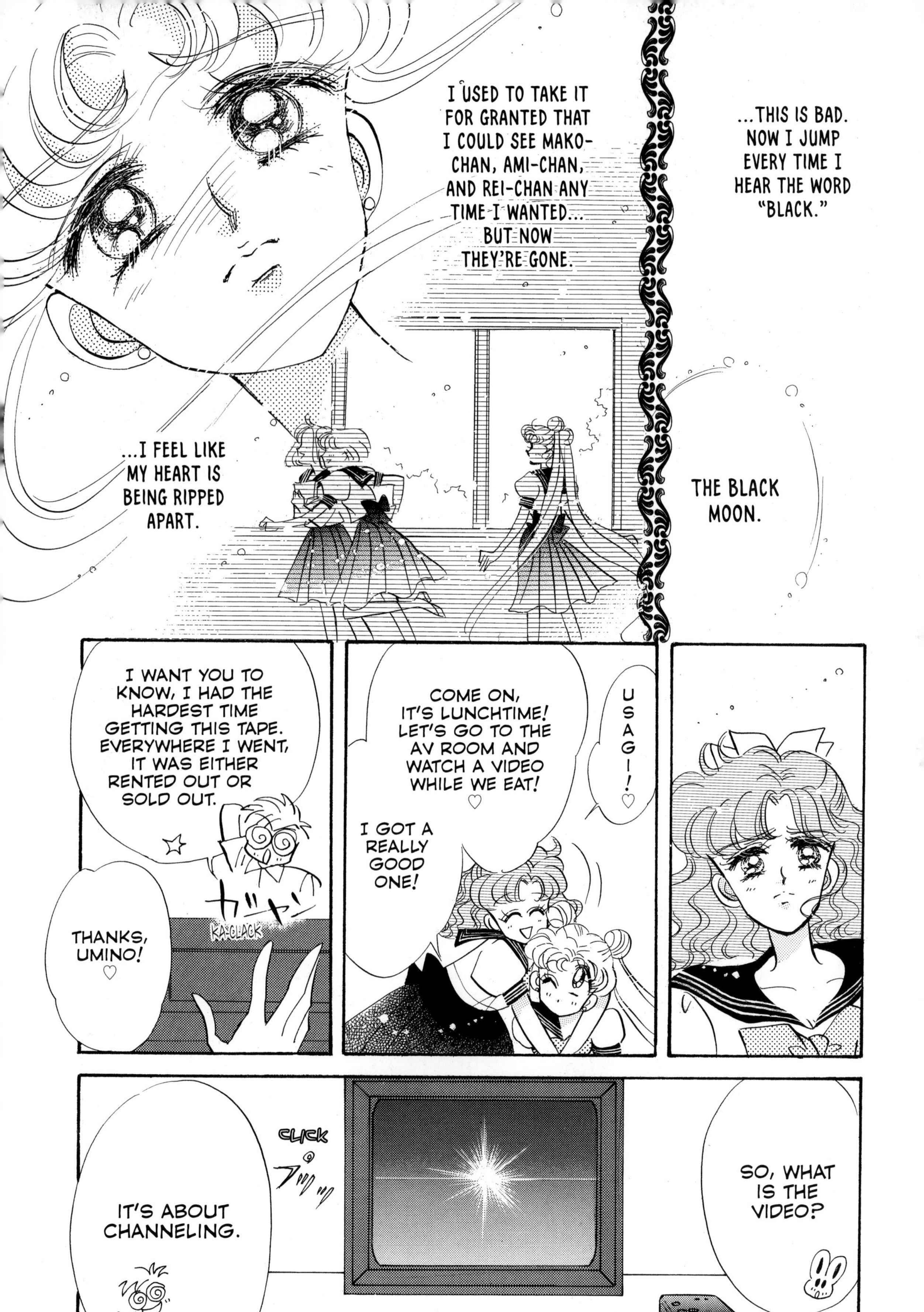
...THIS IS BAD. NOW I JUMP EVERY TIME I HEAR THE WORD "BLACK."
THE BLACK MOON.
I USED TO TAKE IT FOR GRANTED THAT I COULD SEE MAKO-CHAN, AMI-CHAN, AND REI-CHAN ANY TIME I WANTED... BUT NOW THEY'RE GONE.
...I FEEL LIKE MY HEART IS BEING RIPPED APART.
USAGI! ♡
COME ON, IT'S LUNCHTIME! LET'S GO TO THE AV ROOM AND WATCH A VIDEO WHILE WE EAT! ♡
I GOT A REALLY GOOD ONE!
I WANT YOU TO KNOW, I HAD THE HARDEST TIME GETTING THIS TAPE. EVERYWHERE I WENT, IT WAS EITHER RENTED OUT OR SOLD OUT.
KA-CLACK
THANKS, UMINO! ♡
SO, WHAT IS THE VIDEO?
CLICK
IT'S ABOUT CHANNELING.

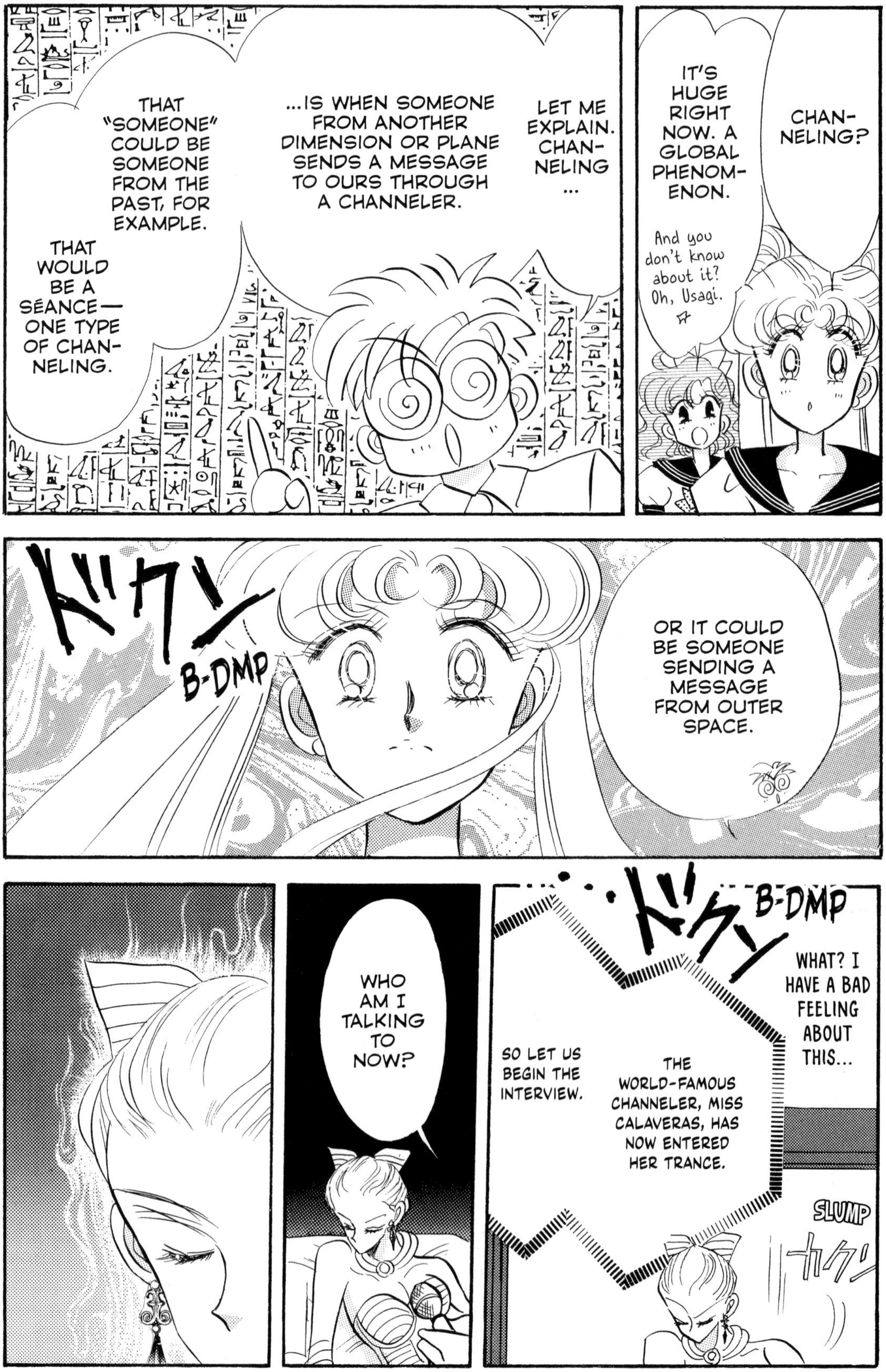
CHANNELING?
IT'S HUGE RIGHT NOW. A GLOBAL PHENOMENON.
And you don't know about it? Oh, Usagi.
LET ME EXPLAIN. CHANNELING...
...IS WHEN SOMEONE FROM ANOTHER DIMENSION OR PLANE SENDS A MESSAGE TO OURS THROUGH A CHANNELER.
THAT "SOMEONE" COULD BE SOMEONE FROM THE PAST, FOR EXAMPLE.
THAT WOULD BE A SÉANCE—ONE TYPE OF CHANNELING.
OR IT COULD BE SOMEONE SENDING A MESSAGE FROM OUTER SPACE.
ドクン
B-DMP
ドクン
B-DMP
WHAT? I HAVE A BAD FEELING ABOUT THIS...
THE WORLD-FAMOUS CHANNELER, MISS CALAVERAS, HAS NOW ENTERED HER TRANCE.
SO LET US BEGIN THE INTERVIEW.
SLUMP
カクン
WHO AM I TALKING TO NOW?

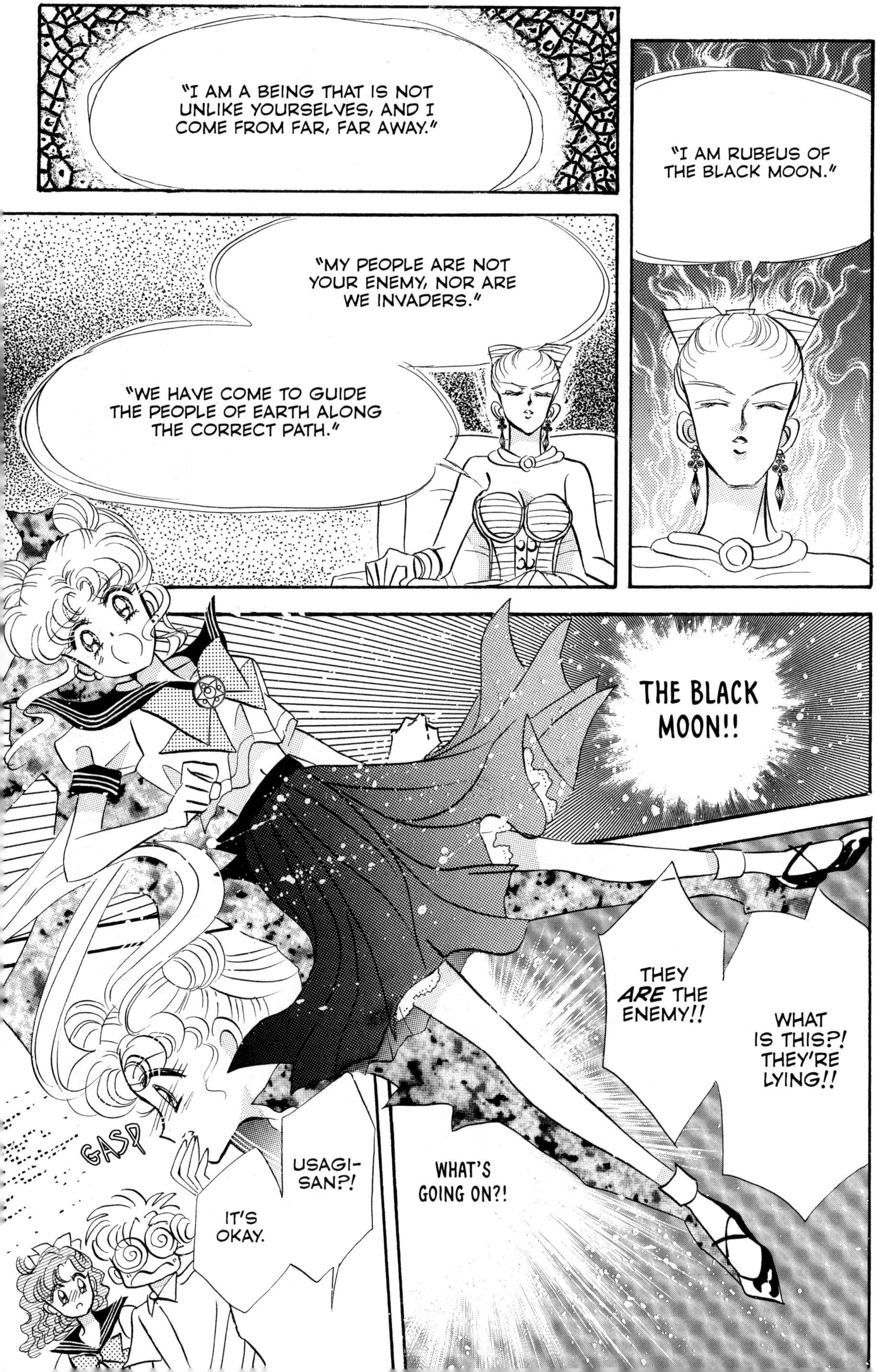
"I AM RUBEUS OF THE BLACK MOON."
"I AM A BEING THAT IS NOT UNLIKE YOURSELVES, AND I COME FROM FAR, FAR AWAY."
"MY PEOPLE ARE NOT YOUR ENEMY, NOR ARE WE INVADERS."
"WE HAVE COME TO GUIDE THE PEOPLE OF EARTH ALONG THE CORRECT PATH."
THE BLACK MOON!!
WHAT IS THIS?! THEY'RE LYING!!
THEY *ARE* THE ENEMY!!
WHAT'S GOING ON?!
USAGI-SAN?!
IT'S OKAY.
GASP

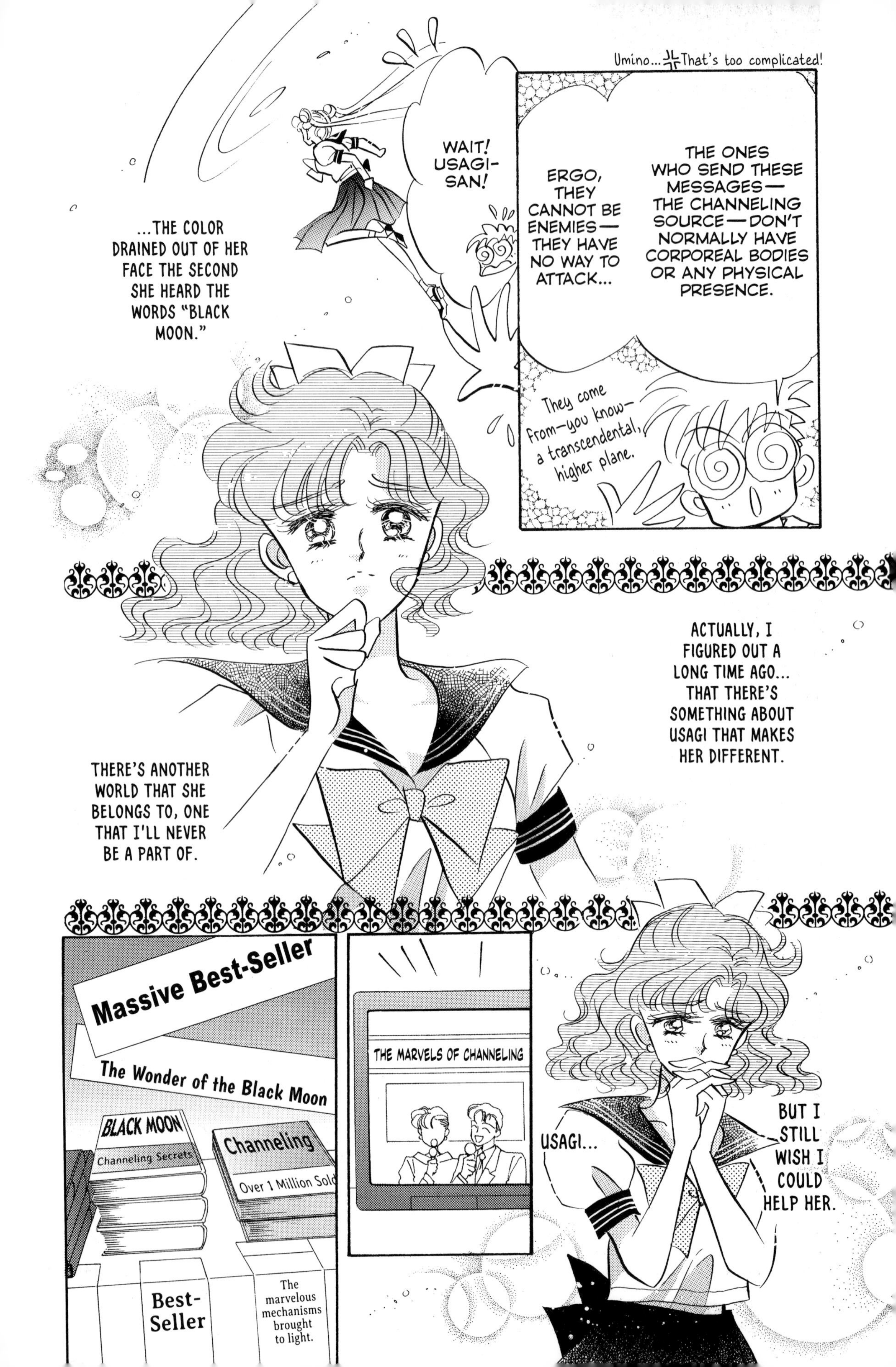

Umino... That's too complicated!
THE ONES WHO SEND THESE MESSAGES—THE CHANNELING SOURCE—DON'T NORMALLY HAVE CORPOREAL BODIES OR ANY PHYSICAL PRESENCE.
ERGO, THEY CANNOT BE ENEMIES—THEY HAVE NO WAY TO ATTACK...
They come from—you know—a transcendental, higher plane.
WAIT! USAGI-SAN!
...THE COLOR DRAINED OUT OF HER FACE THE SECOND SHE HEARD THE WORDS "BLACK MOON."
ACTUALLY, I FIGURED OUT A LONG TIME AGO... THAT THERE'S SOMETHING ABOUT USAGI THAT MAKES HER DIFFERENT.
THERE'S ANOTHER WORLD THAT SHE BELONGS TO, ONE THAT I'LL NEVER BE A PART OF.
BUT I STILL WISH I COULD HELP HER.
USAGI...
THE MARVELS OF CHANNELING
Massive Best-Seller
The Wonder of the Black Moon
BLACK MOON
Channeling Secrets
Channeling
Over 1 Million Sold
Best-Seller
The marvelous mechanisms brought to light.

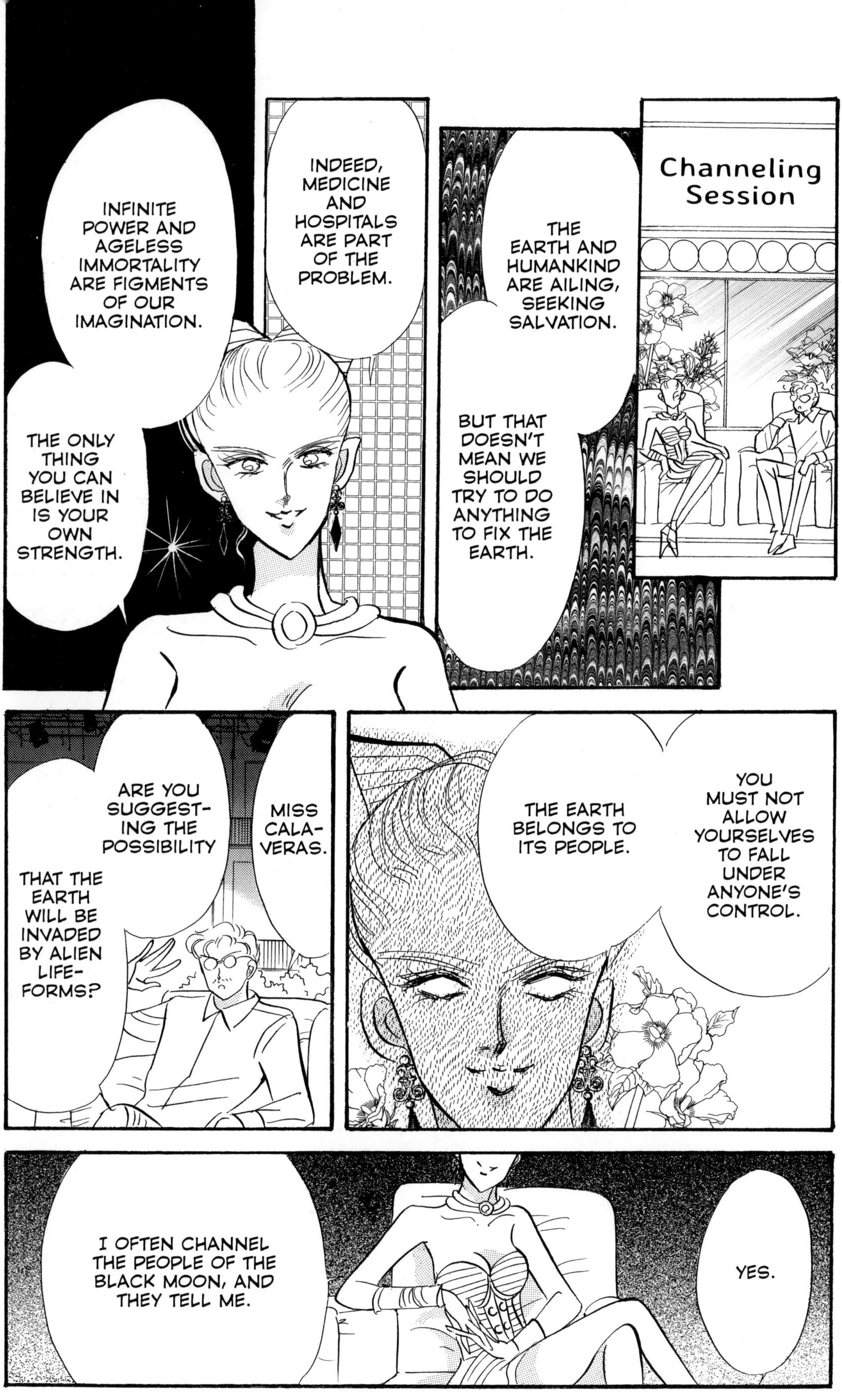
Channeling Session
THE EARTH AND HUMANKIND ARE AILING, SEEKING SALVATION.
BUT THAT DOESN'T MEAN WE SHOULD TRY TO DO ANYTHING TO FIX THE EARTH.
INDEED, MEDICINE AND HOSPITALS ARE PART OF THE PROBLEM.
INFINITE POWER AND AGELESS IMMORTALITY ARE FIGMENTS OF OUR IMAGINATION.
THE ONLY THING YOU CAN BELIEVE IN IS YOUR OWN STRENGTH.
YOU MUST NOT ALLOW YOURSELVES TO FALL UNDER ANYONE'S CONTROL.
THE EARTH BELONGS TO ITS PEOPLE.
MISS CALA-VERAS.
ARE YOU SUGGEST-ING THE POSSIBILITY
THAT THE EARTH WILL BE INVADED BY ALIEN LIFE-FORMS?
YES.
I OFTEN CHANNEL THE PEOPLE OF THE BLACK MOON, AND THEY TELL ME.

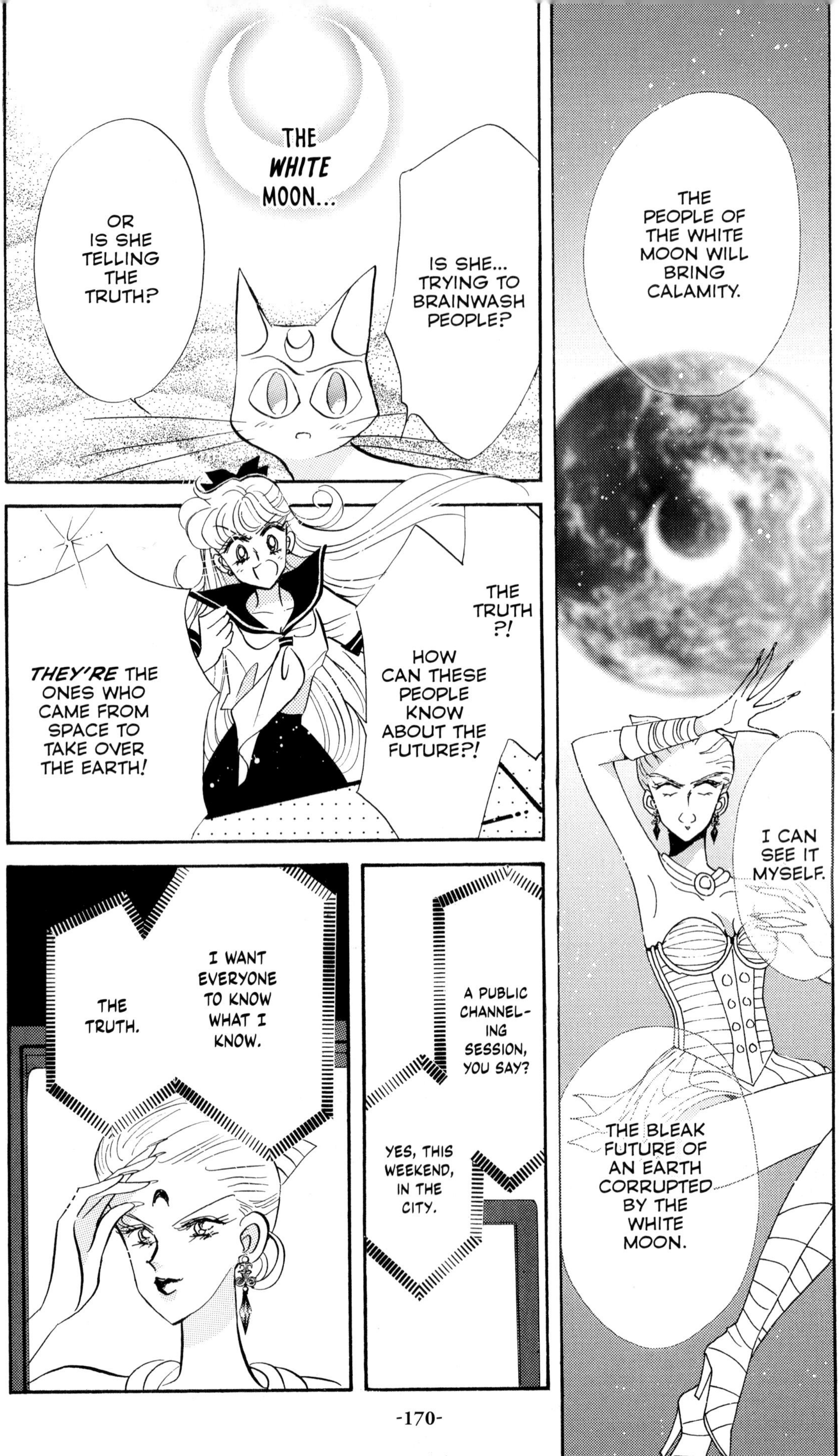
THE PEOPLE OF THE WHITE MOON WILL BRING CALAMITY.
I CAN SEE IT MYSELF.
THE BLEAK FUTURE OF AN EARTH CORRUPTED BY THE WHITE MOON.
THE *WHITE* MOON...
IS SHE... TRYING TO BRAINWASH PEOPLE?
OR IS SHE TELLING THE TRUTH?
THE TRUTH?!
HOW CAN THESE PEOPLE KNOW ABOUT THE FUTURE?!
THEY'RE THE ONES WHO CAME FROM SPACE TO TAKE OVER THE EARTH!
A PUBLIC CHANNEL-ING SESSION, YOU SAY?
YES, THIS WEEKEND, IN THE CITY.
I WANT EVERYONE TO KNOW WHAT I KNOW.
THE TRUTH.

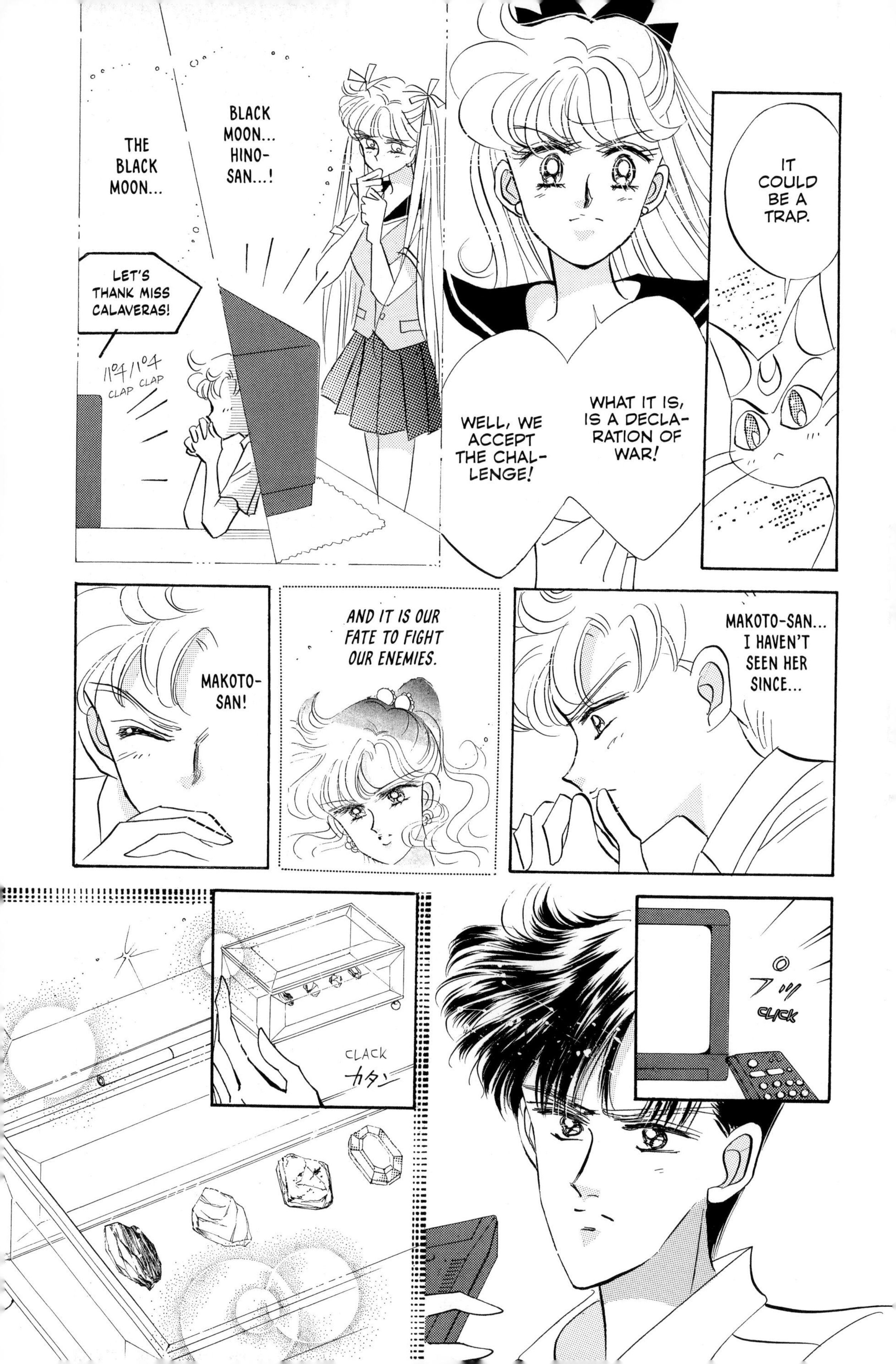
IT COULD BE A TRAP.
WHAT IT IS, IS A DECLARATION OF WAR!
WELL, WE ACCEPT THE CHALLENGE!
BLACK MOON... HINO-SAN...!
THE BLACK MOON...
LET'S THANK MISS CALAVERAS!
パチパチ
CLAP CLAP
MAKOTO-SAN... I HAVEN'T SEEN HER SINCE...
AND IT IS OUR FATE TO FIGHT OUR ENEMIES.
MAKOTO-SAN!
プツ
CLICK
CLACK
カタン

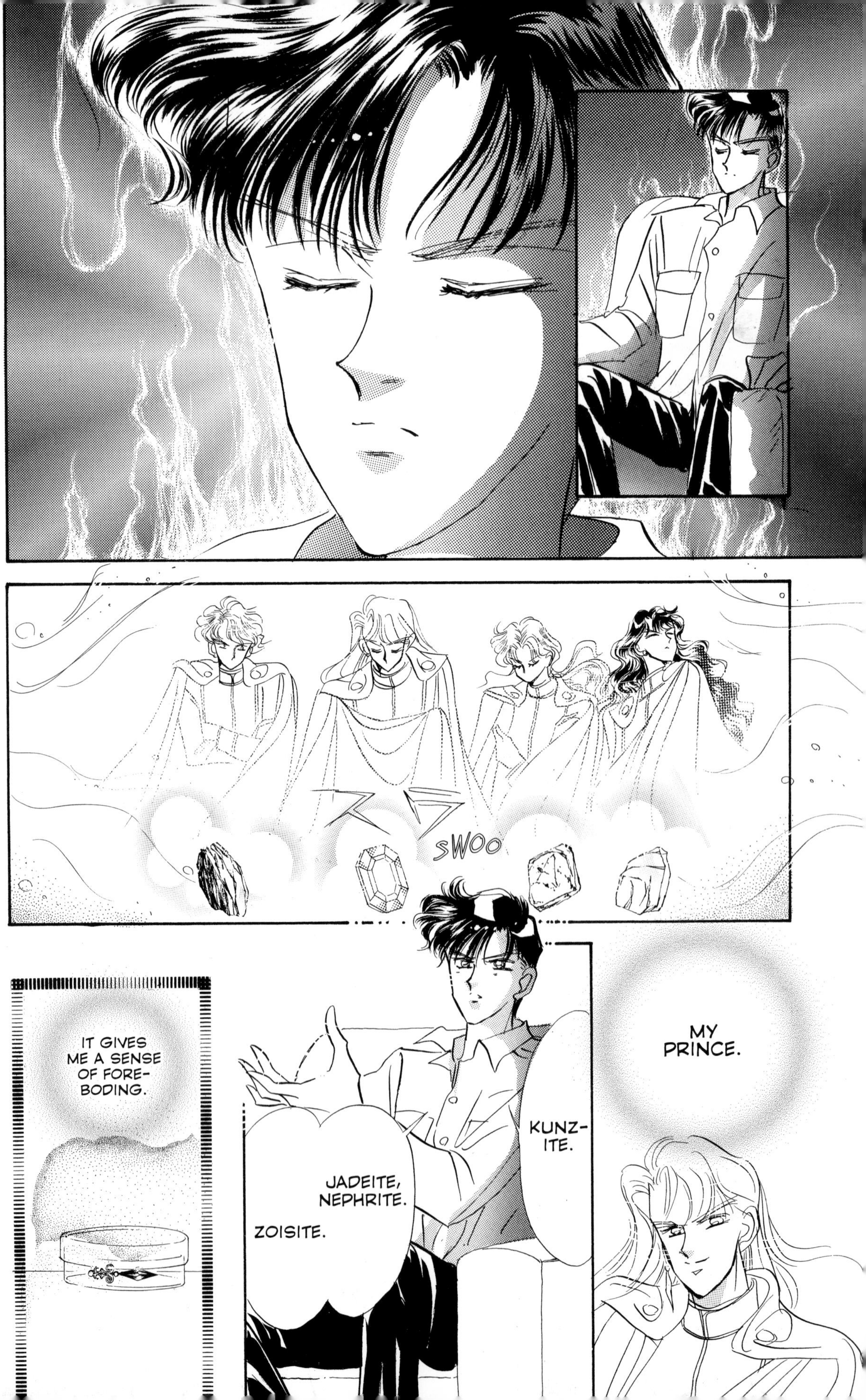
SWOO
MY PRINCE.
KUNZ-ITE.
JADEITE, NEPHRITE.
ZOISITE.
IT GIVES ME A SENSE OF FORE-BODING.

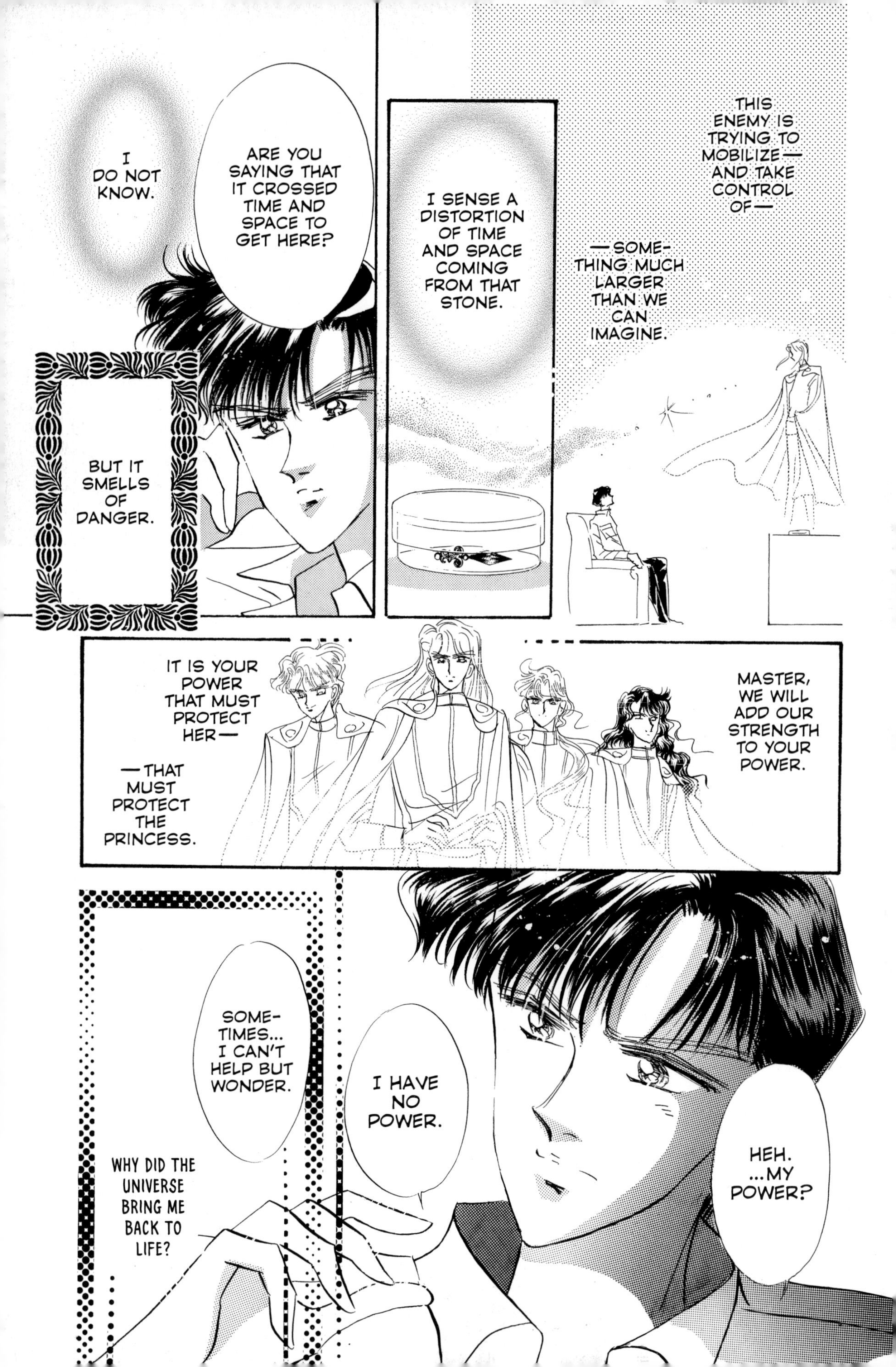
THIS ENEMY IS TRYING TO MOBILIZE—AND TAKE CONTROL OF—
—SOME-THING MUCH LARGER THAN WE CAN IMAGINE.
I SENSE A DISTORTION OF TIME AND SPACE COMING FROM THAT STONE.
ARE YOU SAYING THAT IT CROSSED TIME AND SPACE TO GET HERE?
I DO NOT KNOW.
BUT IT SMELLS OF DANGER.
MASTER, WE WILL ADD OUR STRENGTH TO YOUR POWER.
IT IS YOUR POWER THAT MUST PROTECT HER—
—THAT MUST PROTECT THE PRINCESS.
HEH. ...MY POWER?
I HAVE NO POWER.
SOME-TIMES... I CAN'T HELP BUT WONDER.
WHY DID THE UNIVERSE BRING ME BACK TO LIFE?

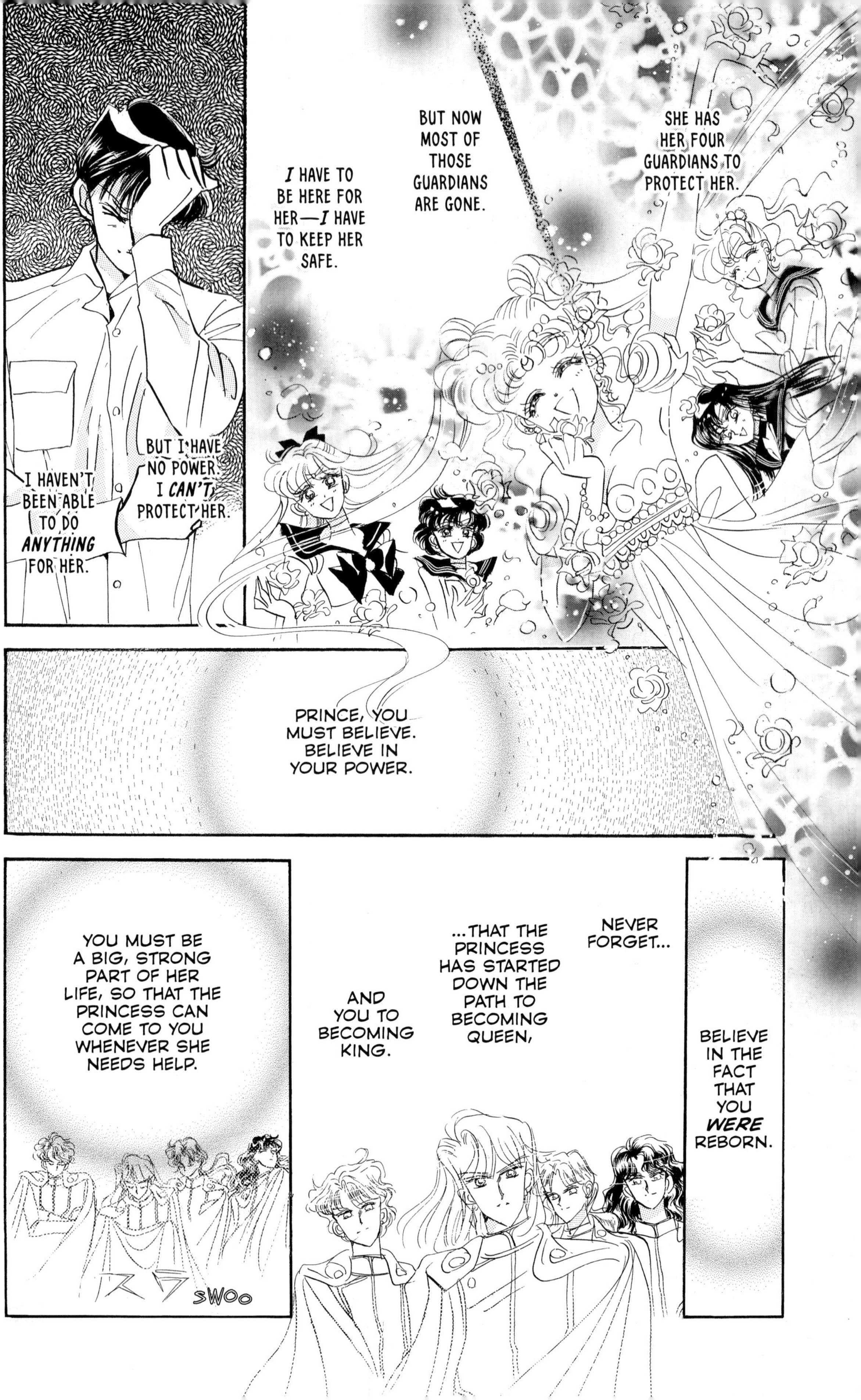
SHE HAS HER FOUR GUARDIANS TO PROTECT HER.
BUT NOW MOST OF THOSE GUARDIANS ARE GONE.
I HAVE TO BE HERE FOR HER—I HAVE TO KEEP HER SAFE.
BUT I HAVE NO POWER. I CAN'T PROTECT HER.
I HAVEN'T BEEN ABLE TO DO ANYTHING FOR HER.
PRINCE, YOU MUST BELIEVE. BELIEVE IN YOUR POWER.
BELIEVE IN THE FACT THAT YOU WERE REBORN.
NEVER FORGET...
...THAT THE PRINCESS HAS STARTED DOWN THE PATH TO BECOMING QUEEN,
AND YOU TO BECOMING KING.
YOU MUST BE A BIG, STRONG PART OF HER LIFE, SO THAT THE PRINCESS CAN COME TO YOU WHENEVER SHE NEEDS HELP.
SWOO

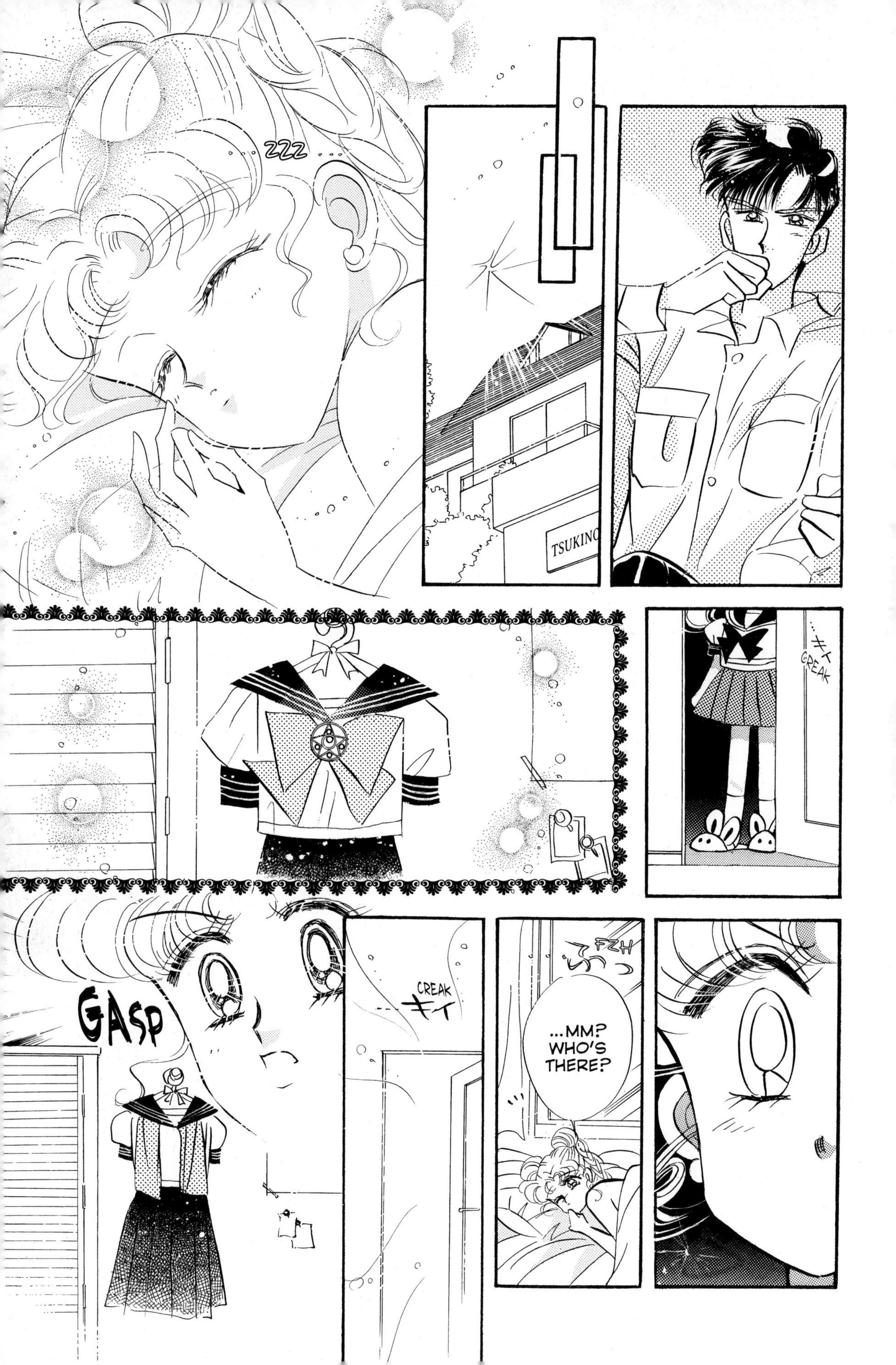
TSUKINO
zzz
CREAK
FZH
...MM? WHO'S THERE?
CREAK
GASP

MY TRANS-
FORMATION
BROOCH! IT'S
GONE?!

Public Channeling Session

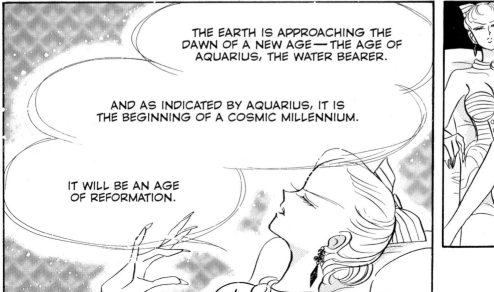

THE EARTH IS APPROACHING THE
DAWN OF A NEW AGE—THE AGE OF
AQUARIUS, THE WATER BEARER.

AND AS INDICATED BY AQUARIUS, IT IS
THE BEGINNING OF A COSMIC MILLENNIUM.

IT WILL BE AN AGE
OF REFORMATION.

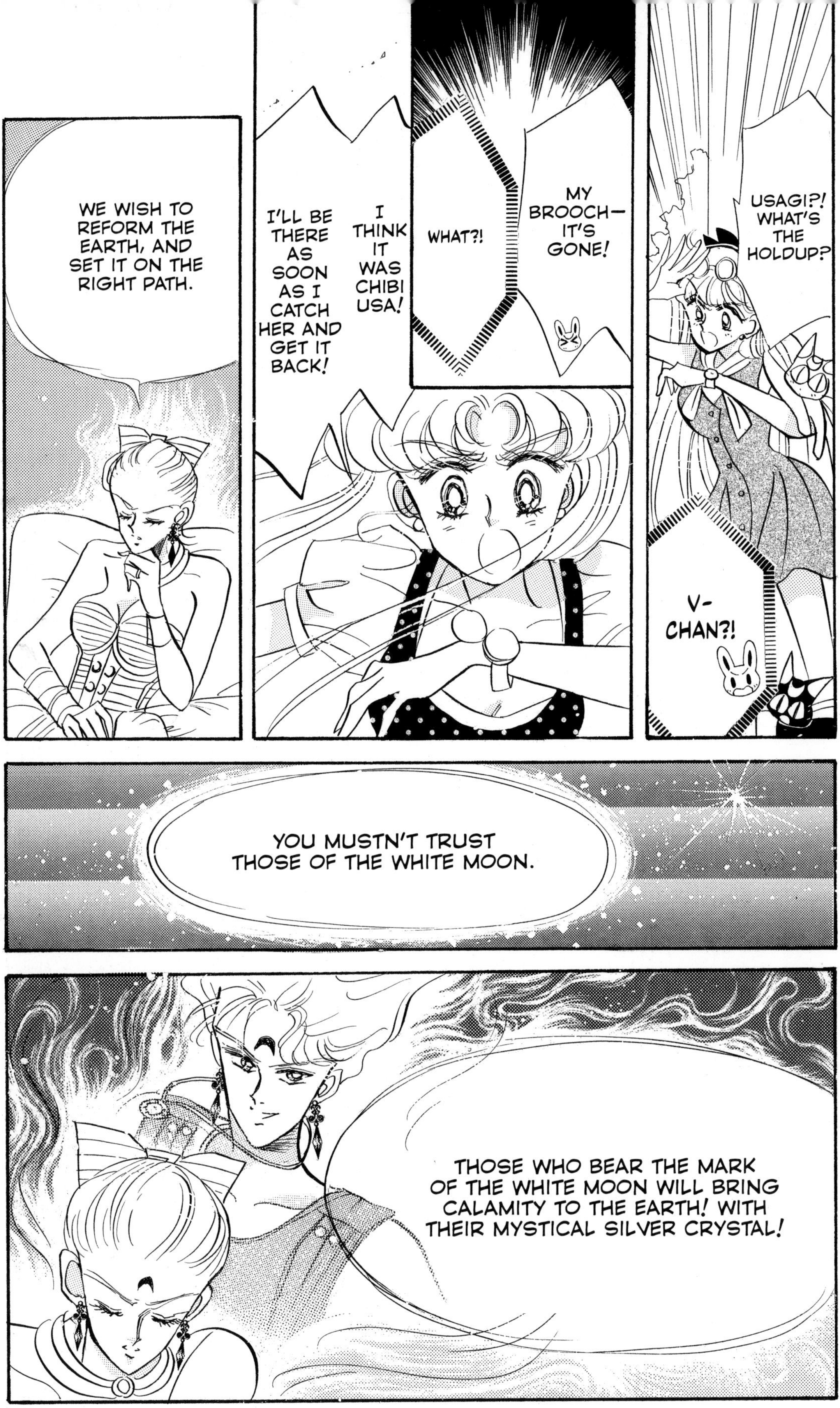
USAGI?! WHAT'S THE HOLDUP?
V-CHAN?!
MY BROOCH— IT'S GONE!
WHAT?!
I THINK IT WAS CHIBI USA!
I'LL BE THERE AS SOON AS I CATCH HER AND GET IT BACK!
WE WISH TO REFORM THE EARTH, AND SET IT ON THE RIGHT PATH.
YOU MUSTN'T TRUST THOSE OF THE WHITE MOON.
THOSE WHO BEAR THE MARK OF THE WHITE MOON WILL BRING CALAMITY TO THE EARTH! WITH THEIR MYSTICAL SILVER CRYSTAL!

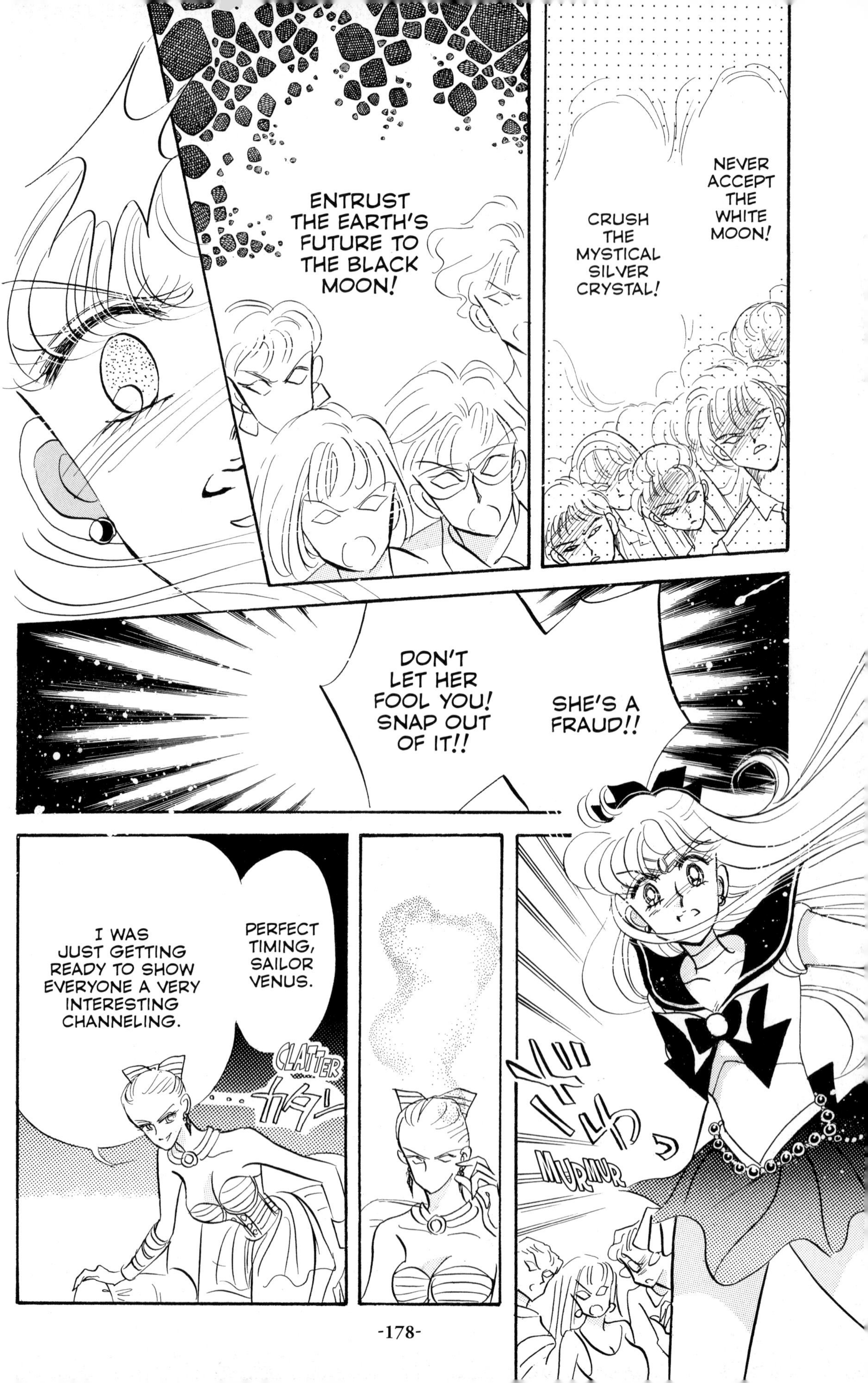
NEVER ACCEPT THE WHITE MOON!
CRUSH THE MYSTICAL SILVER CRYSTAL!
ENTRUST THE EARTH'S FUTURE TO THE BLACK MOON!
SHE'S A FRAUD!!
DON'T LET HER FOOL YOU! SNAP OUT OF IT!!
MURMUR
PERFECT TIMING, SAILOR VENUS.
I WAS JUST GETTING READY TO SHOW EVERYONE A VERY INTERESTING CHANNELING.
CLATTER

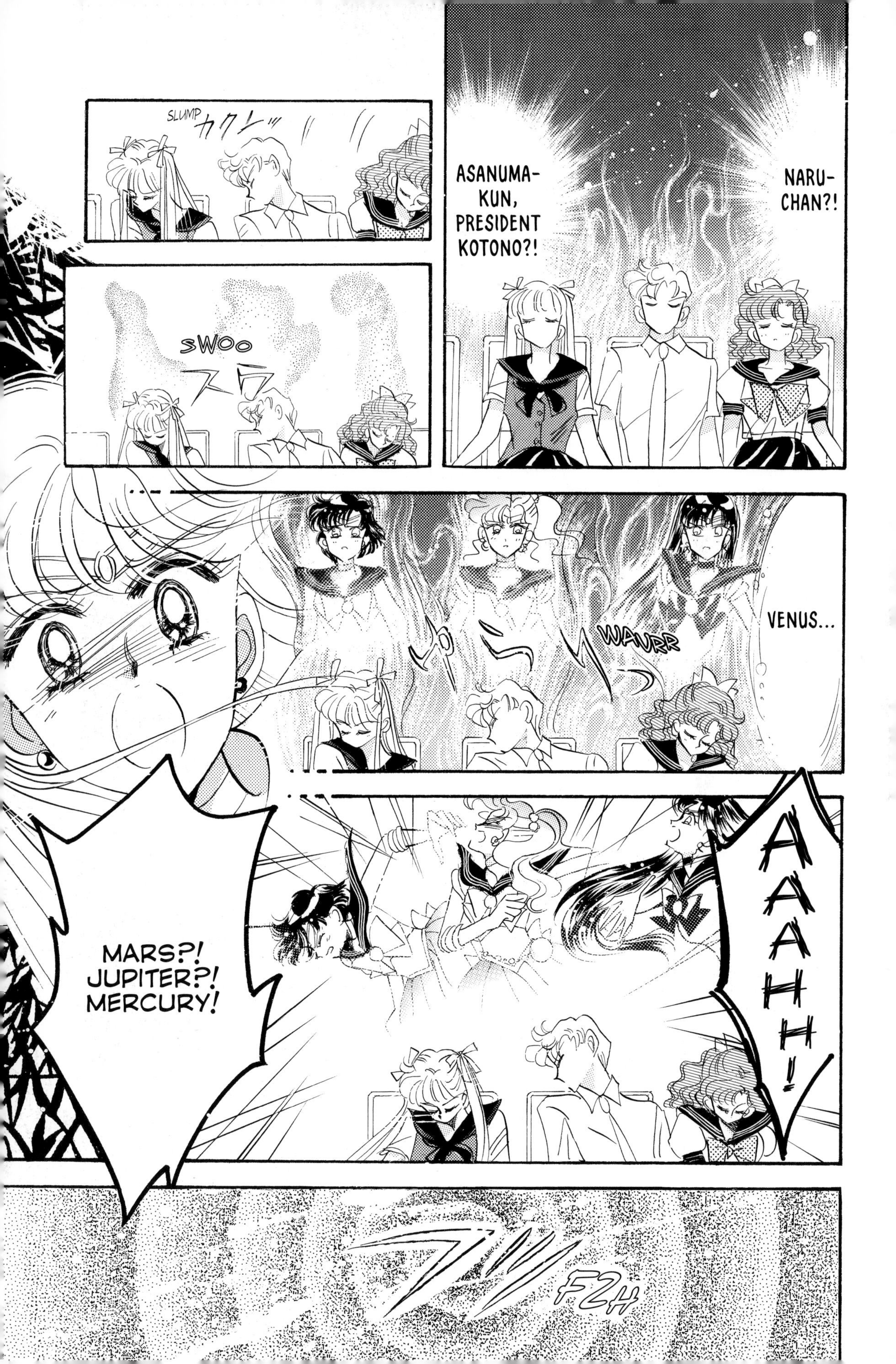

NARU-CHAN?!
ASANUMA-KUN, PRESIDENT KOTONO?!
SLUMP
SWOO
VENUS...
WAURR
AAAHH!
MARS?! JUPITER?! MERCURY!
FZH

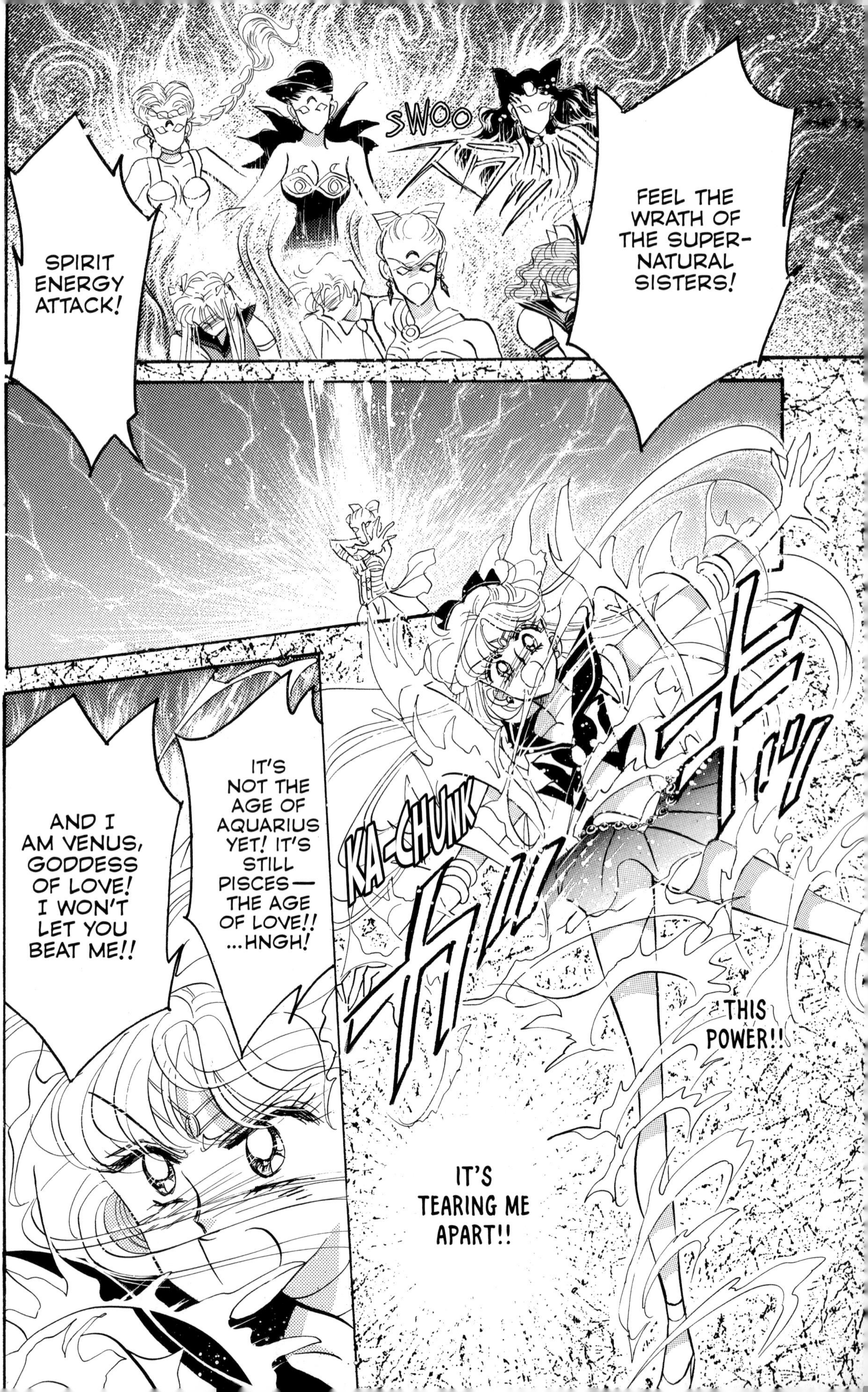
FEEL THE WRATH OF THE SUPER-NATURAL SISTERS!
SWOO
SPIRIT ENERGY ATTACK!
KA-CHUNK
THIS POWER!!
IT'S TEARING ME APART!!
IT'S NOT THE AGE OF AQUARIUS YET! IT'S STILL PISCES— THE AGE OF LOVE!! ...HNGH!
AND I AM VENUS, GODDESS OF LOVE! I WON'T LET YOU BEAT ME!!

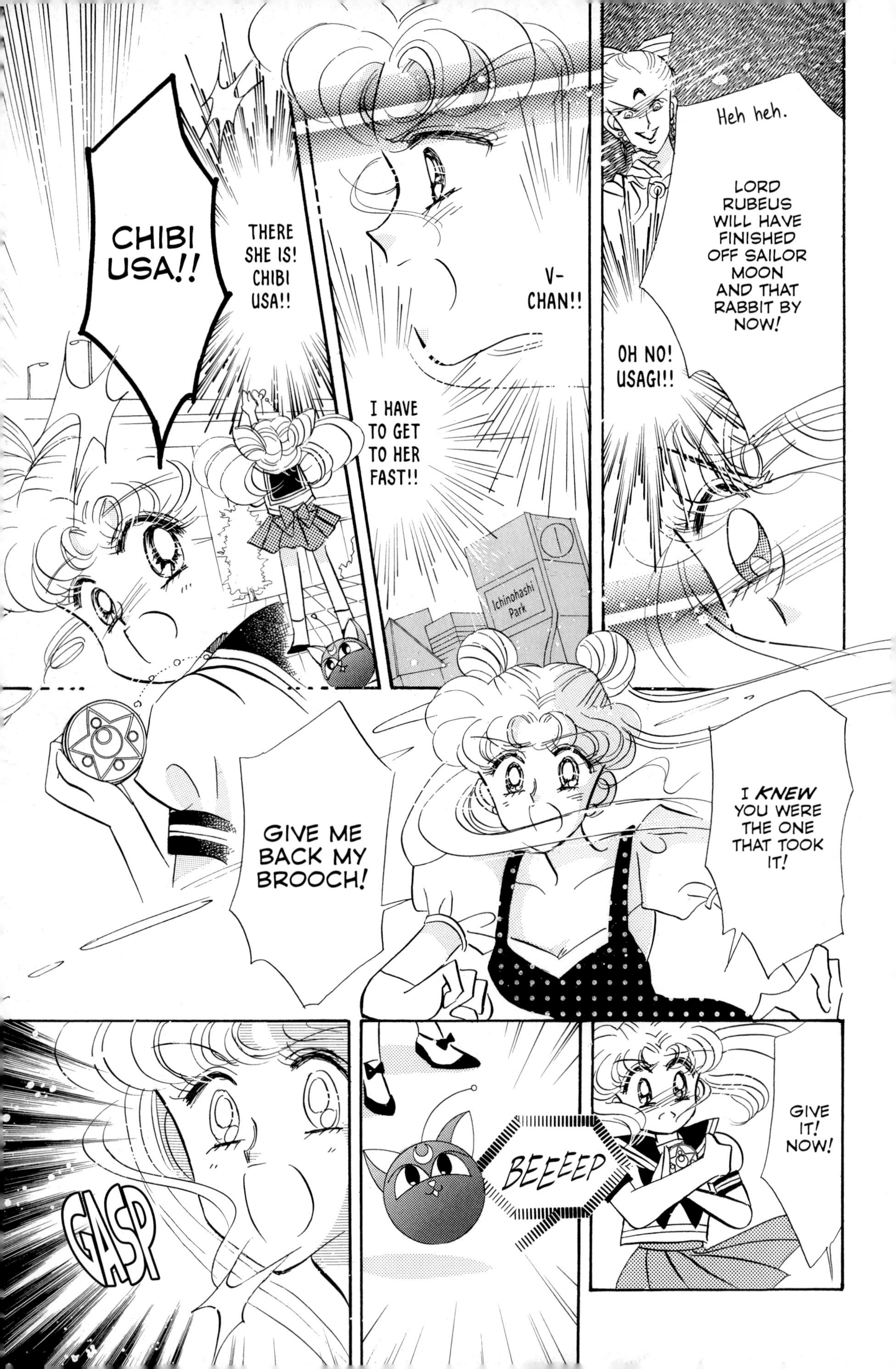
Heh heh.
LORD RUBEUS WILL HAVE FINISHED OFF SAILOR MOON AND THAT RABBIT BY NOW!
OH NO! USAGI!!
V-CHAN!!
I HAVE TO GET TO HER FAST!!
Ichinohashi Park
THERE SHE IS! CHIBI USA!!
CHIBI USA!!
I *KNEW* YOU WERE THE ONE THAT TOOK IT!
GIVE ME BACK MY BROOCH!
GIVE IT! NOW!
BEEEEP
GASP

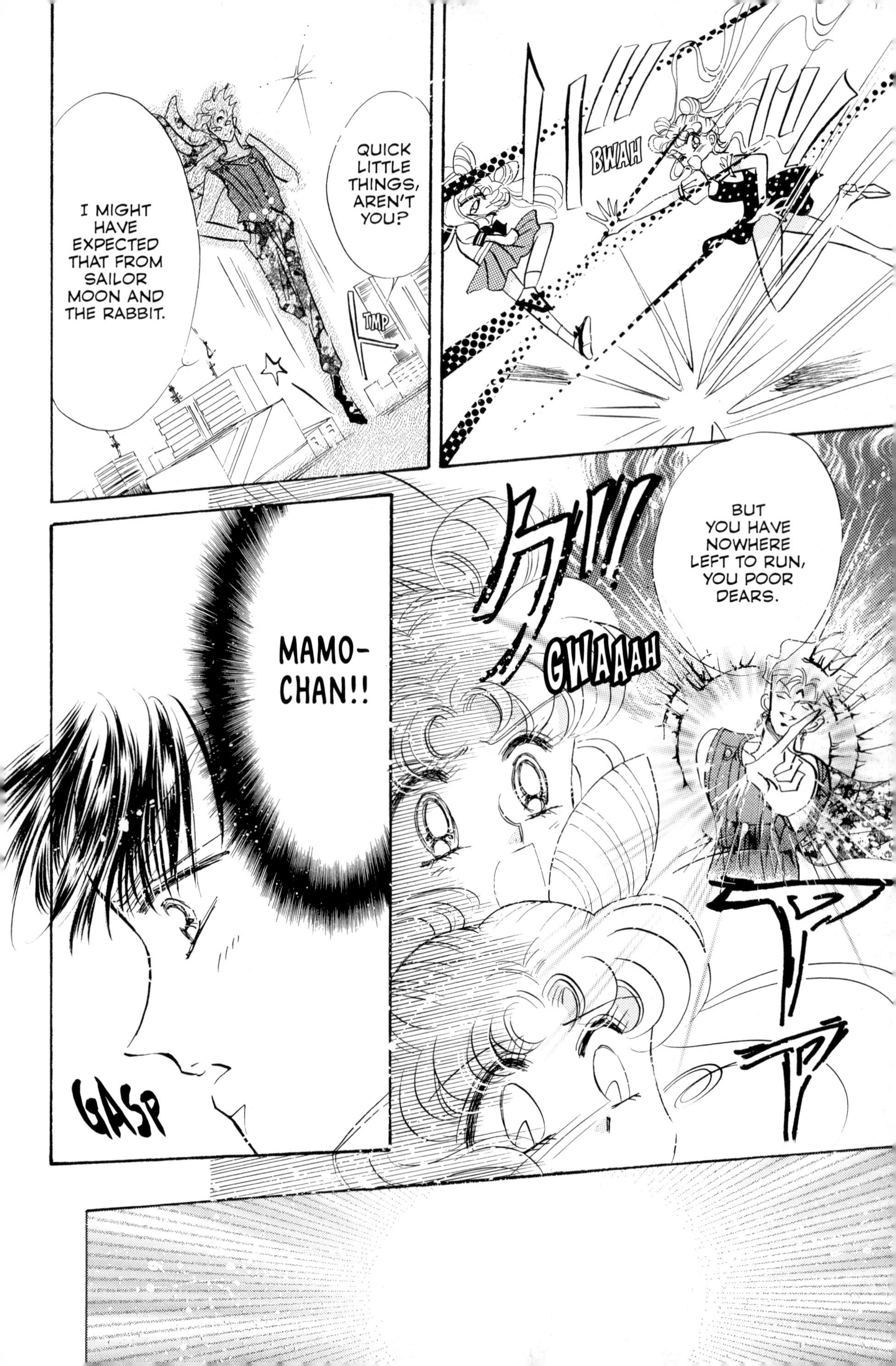
BWAH
QUICK LITTLE THINGS, AREN'T YOU?
I MIGHT HAVE EXPECTED THAT FROM SAILOR MOON AND THE RABBIT.
TMP
BUT YOU HAVE NOWHERE LEFT TO RUN, YOU POOR DEARS.
GWAAAH
MAMO-CHAN!!
GASP

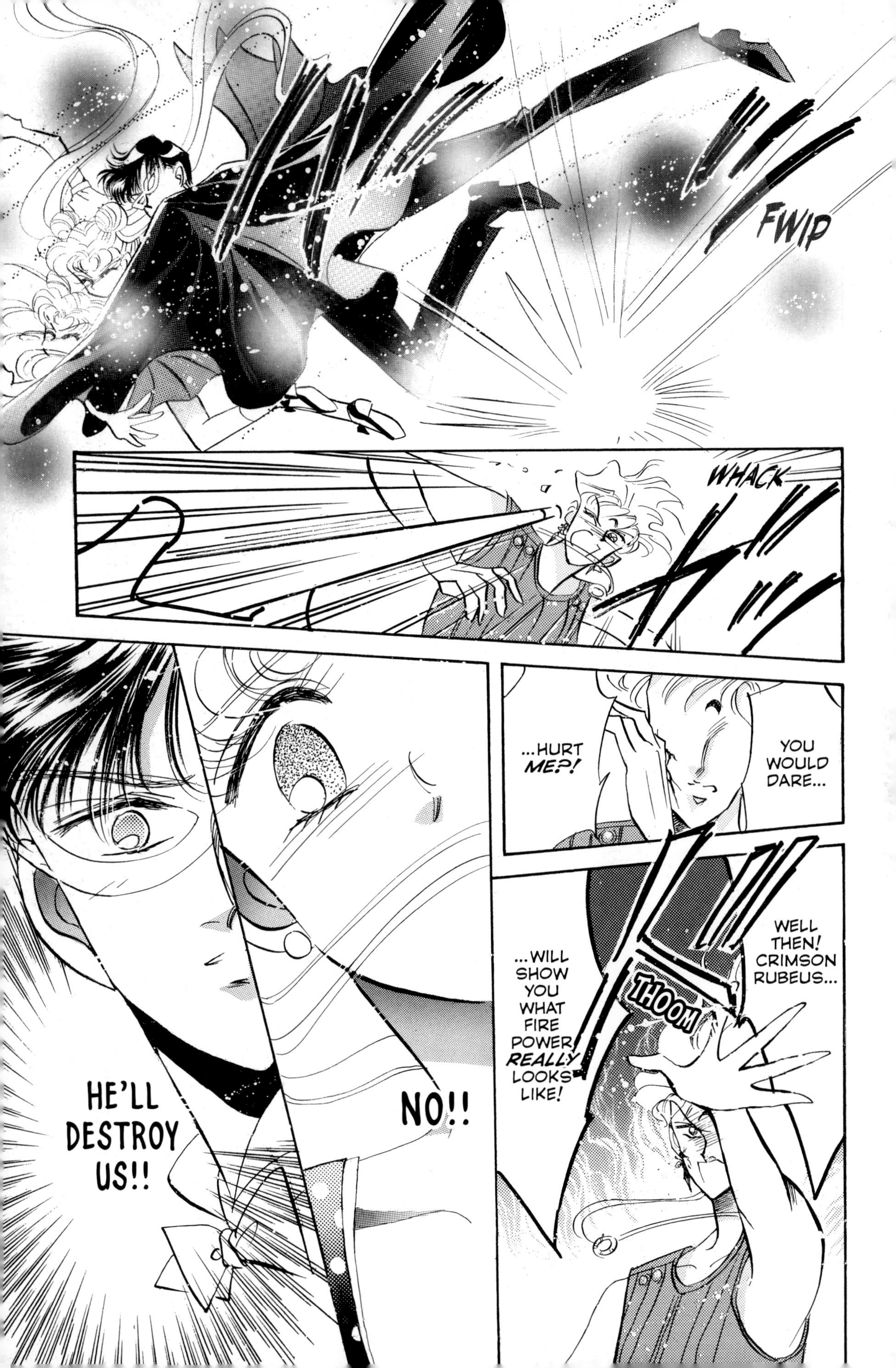
FWIP
WHACK
YOU WOULD DARE...
...HURT ME?!
WELL THEN! CRIMSON RUBEUS...
...WILL SHOW YOU WHAT FIRE POWER REALLY LOOKS LIKE!
THOOM
NO!!
HE'LL DESTROY US!!

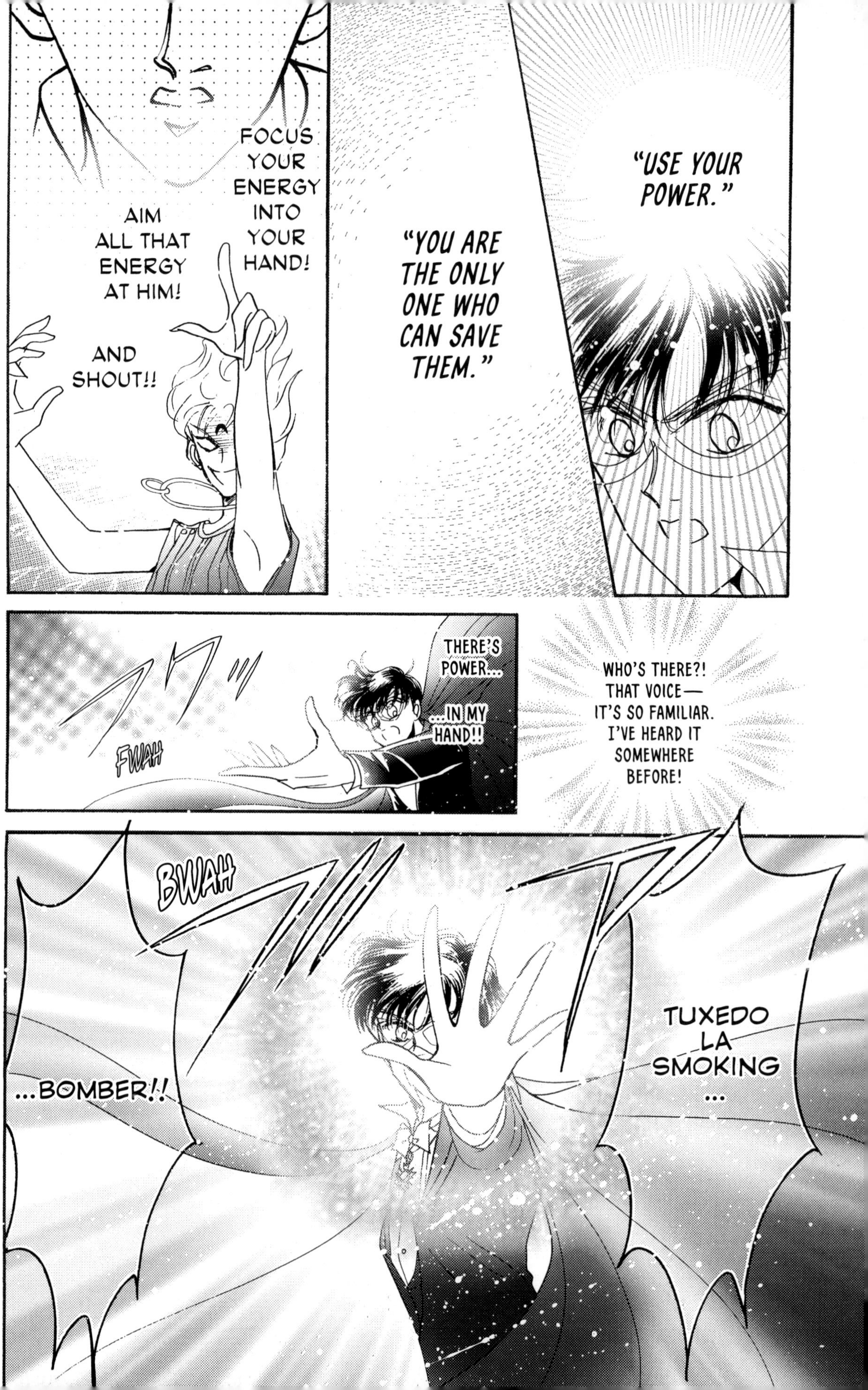
"USE YOUR POWER."
"YOU ARE THE ONLY ONE WHO CAN SAVE THEM."
FOCUS YOUR ENERGY INTO YOUR HAND!
AIM ALL THAT ENERGY AT HIM!
AND SHOUT!!
WHO'S THERE?! THAT VOICE— IT'S SO FAMILIAR. I'VE HEARD IT SOMEWHERE BEFORE!
THERE'S POWER...
...IN MY HAND!!
FWAH
BWAH
TUXEDO LA SMOKING ...
...BOMBER!!

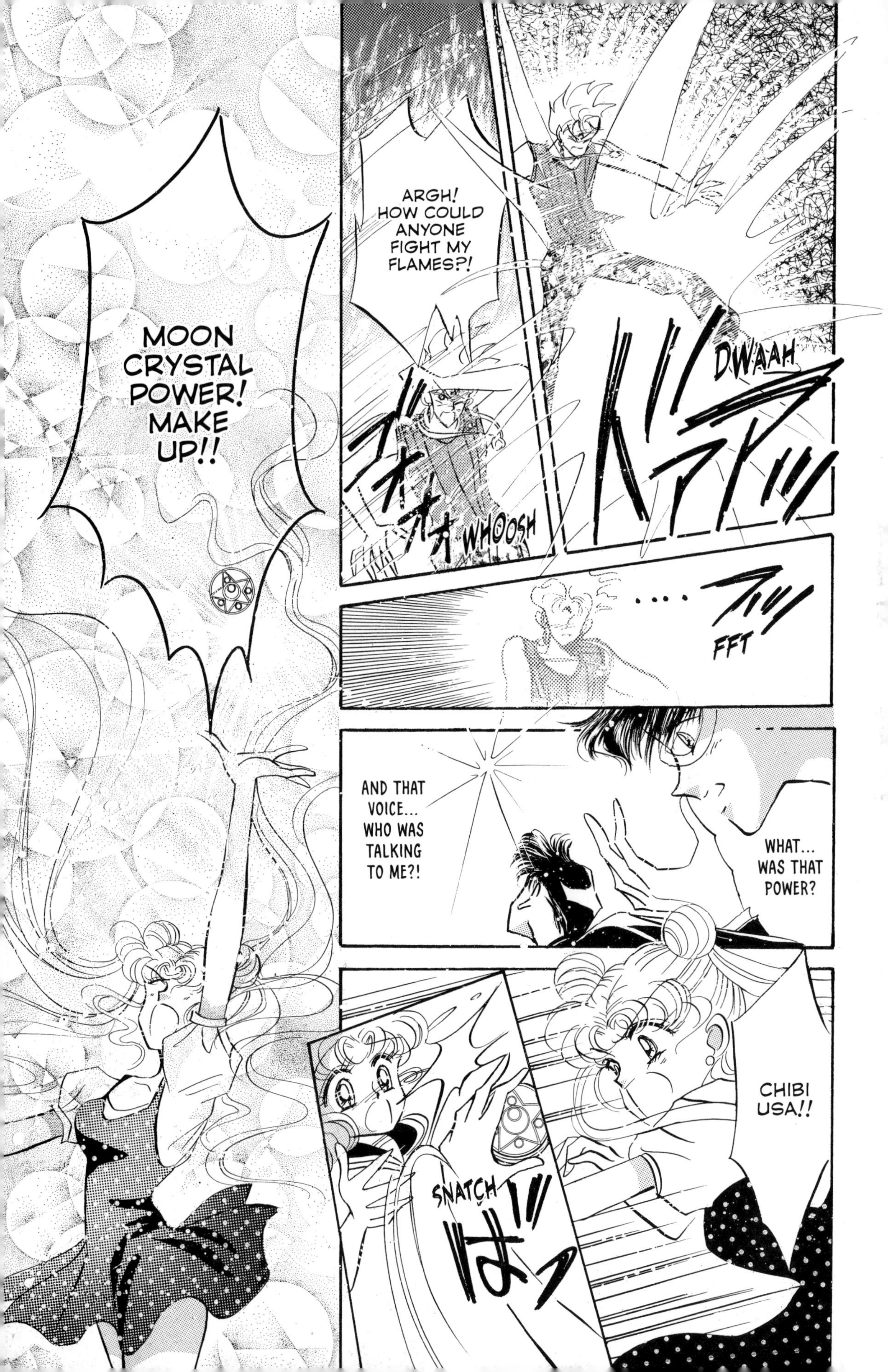
DWAAH
ARGH! HOW COULD ANYONE FIGHT MY FLAMES?!
WHOOSH
....
FFT
WHAT... WAS THAT POWER?
AND THAT VOICE... WHO WAS TALKING TO ME?!
CHIBI USA!!
SNATCH
MOON CRYSTAL POWER! MAKE UP!!

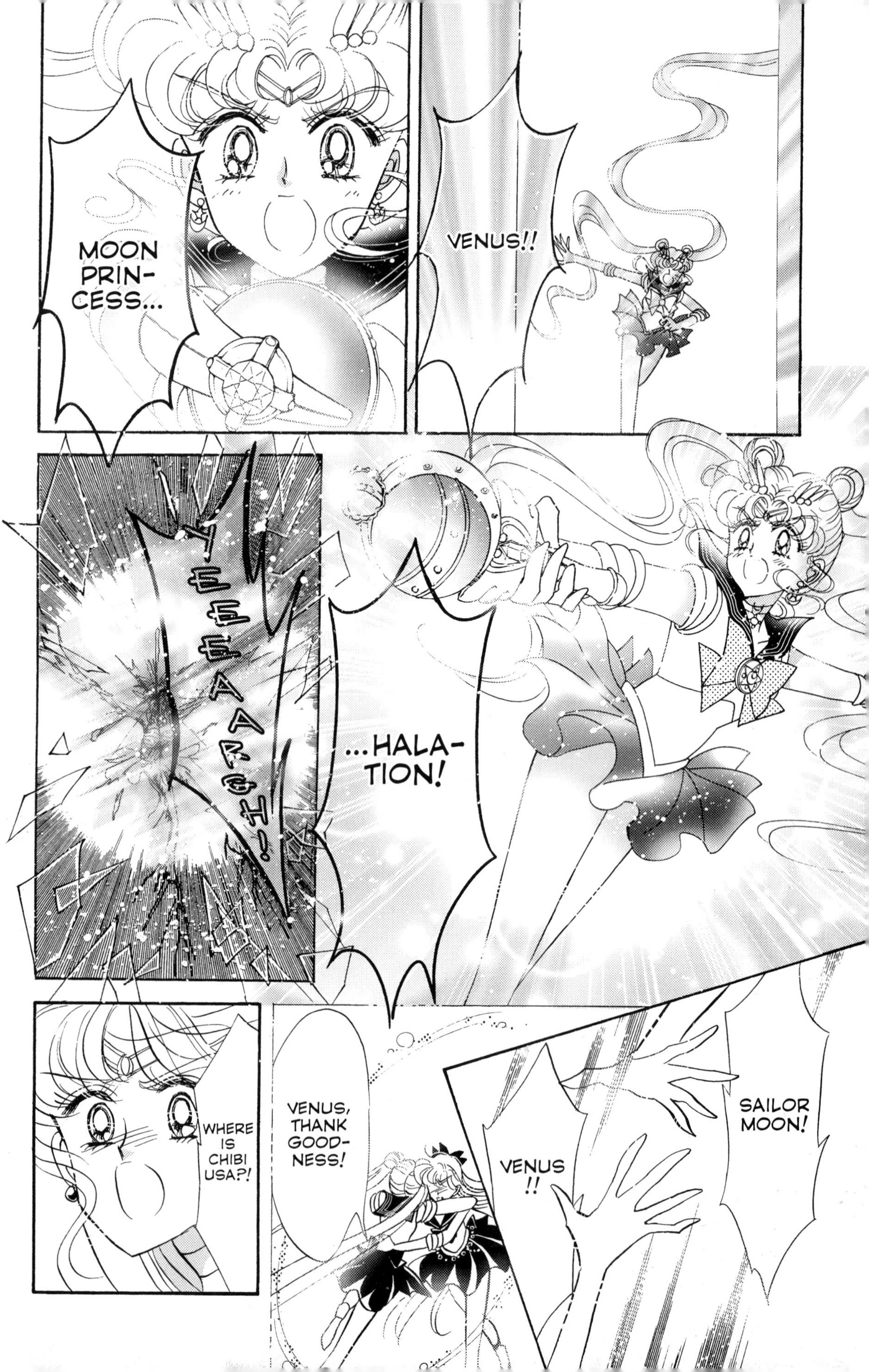
VENUS!!
MOON PRIN-CESS...
...HALA-TION!
YEEEAAARGH!
SAILOR MOON!
VENUS !!
VENUS, THANK GOOD-NESS!
WHERE IS CHIBI USA?!

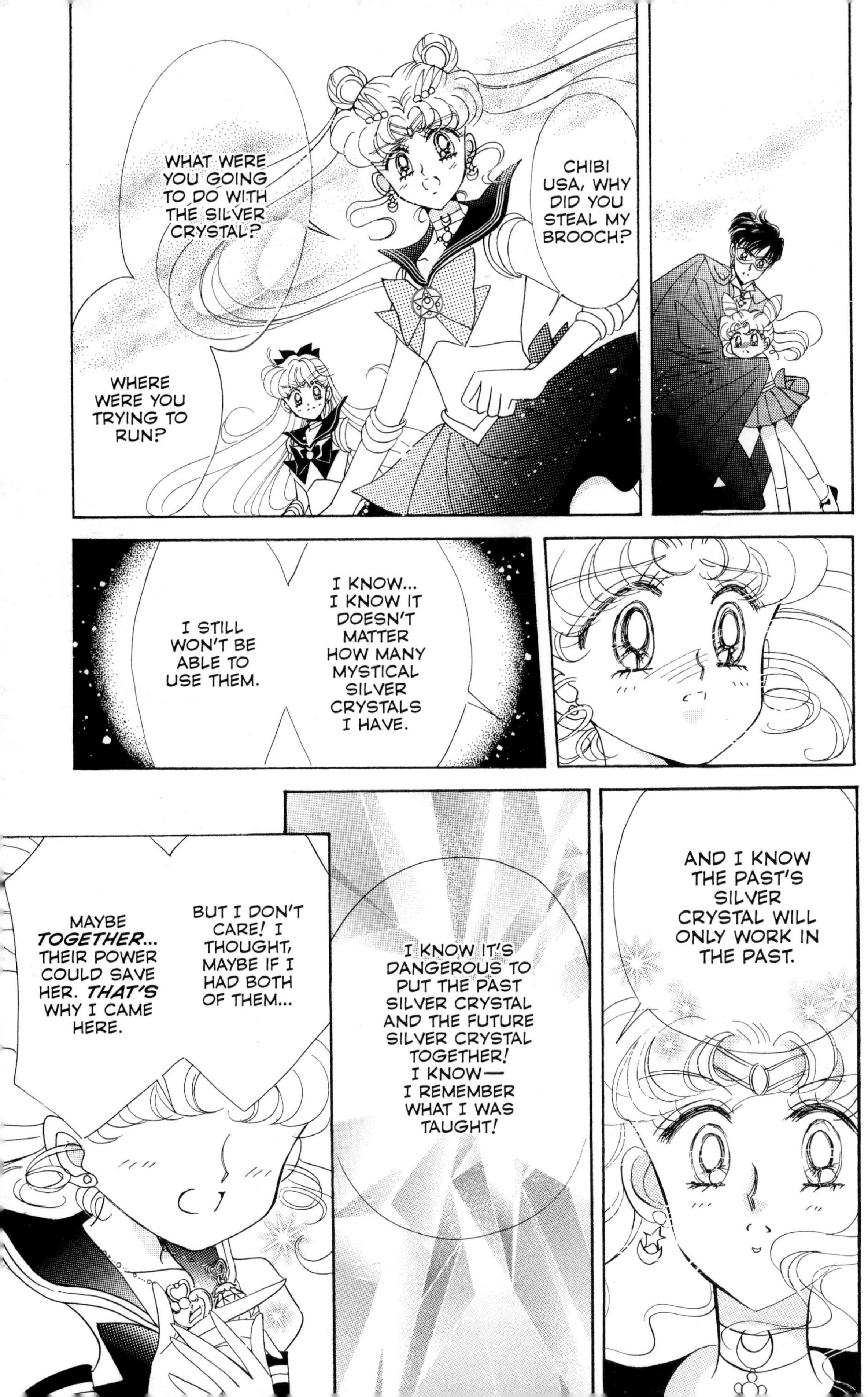

CHIBI USA, WHY DID YOU STEAL MY BROOCH?
WHAT WERE YOU GOING TO DO WITH THE SILVER CRYSTAL?
WHERE WERE YOU TRYING TO RUN?
I KNOW... I KNOW IT DOESN'T MATTER HOW MANY MYSTICAL SILVER CRYSTALS I HAVE.
I STILL WON'T BE ABLE TO USE THEM.
AND I KNOW THE PAST'S SILVER CRYSTAL WILL ONLY WORK IN THE PAST.
I KNOW IT'S DANGEROUS TO PUT THE PAST SILVER CRYSTAL AND THE FUTURE SILVER CRYSTAL TOGETHER! I KNOW— I REMEMBER WHAT I WAS TAUGHT!
BUT I DON'T CARE! I THOUGHT, MAYBE IF I HAD BOTH OF THEM...
MAYBE *TOGETHER*... THEIR POWER COULD SAVE HER. *THAT'S* WHY I CAME HERE.

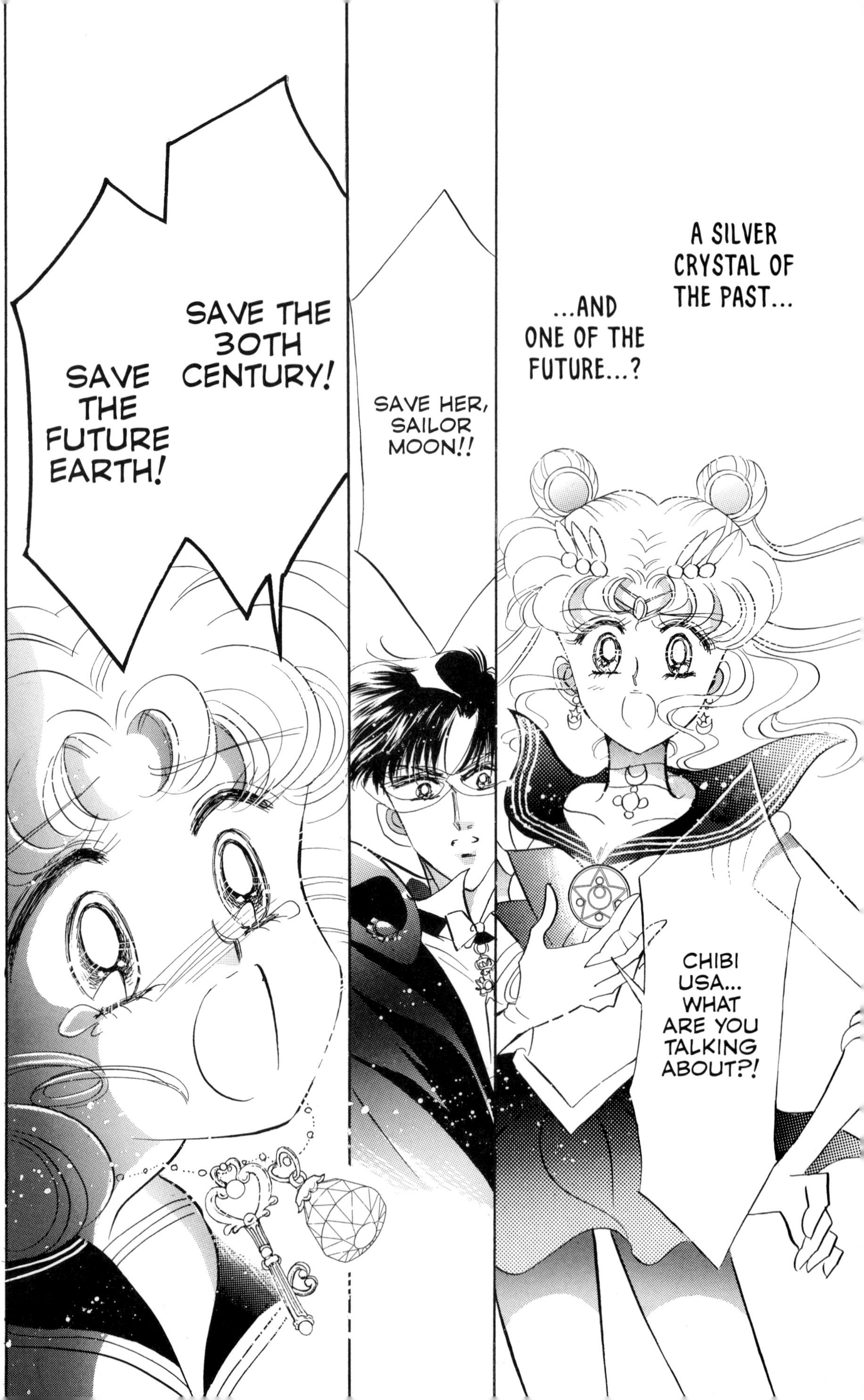
A SILVER CRYSTAL OF THE PAST...
...AND ONE OF THE FUTURE...?
CHIBI USA... WHAT ARE YOU TALKING ABOUT?!
SAVE HER, SAILOR MOON!!
SAVE THE 30TH CENTURY!
SAVE THE FUTURE EARTH!

Act.19 Time Warp: Sailor Pluto

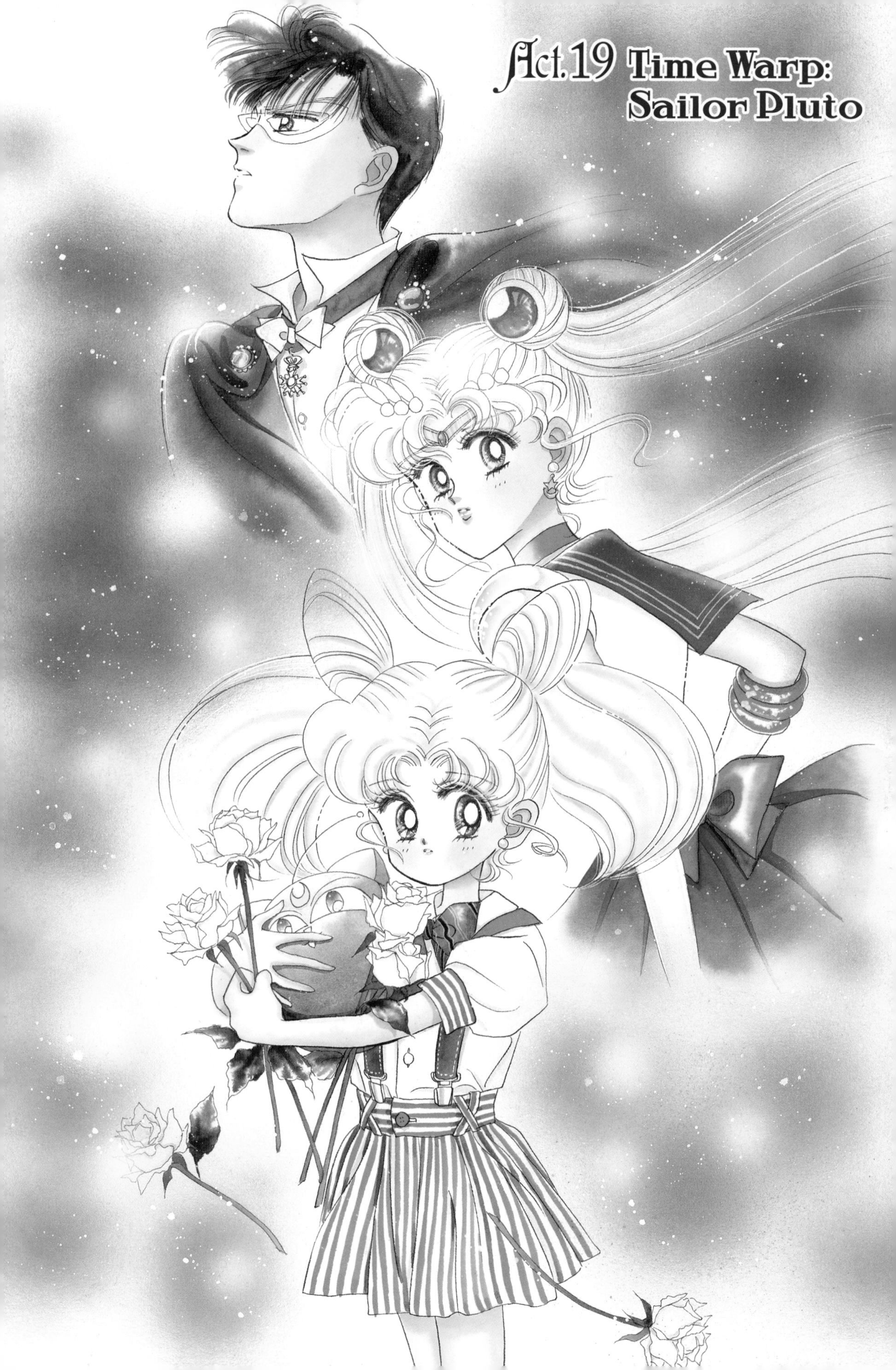

Pretty Guardian

Sailor Moon

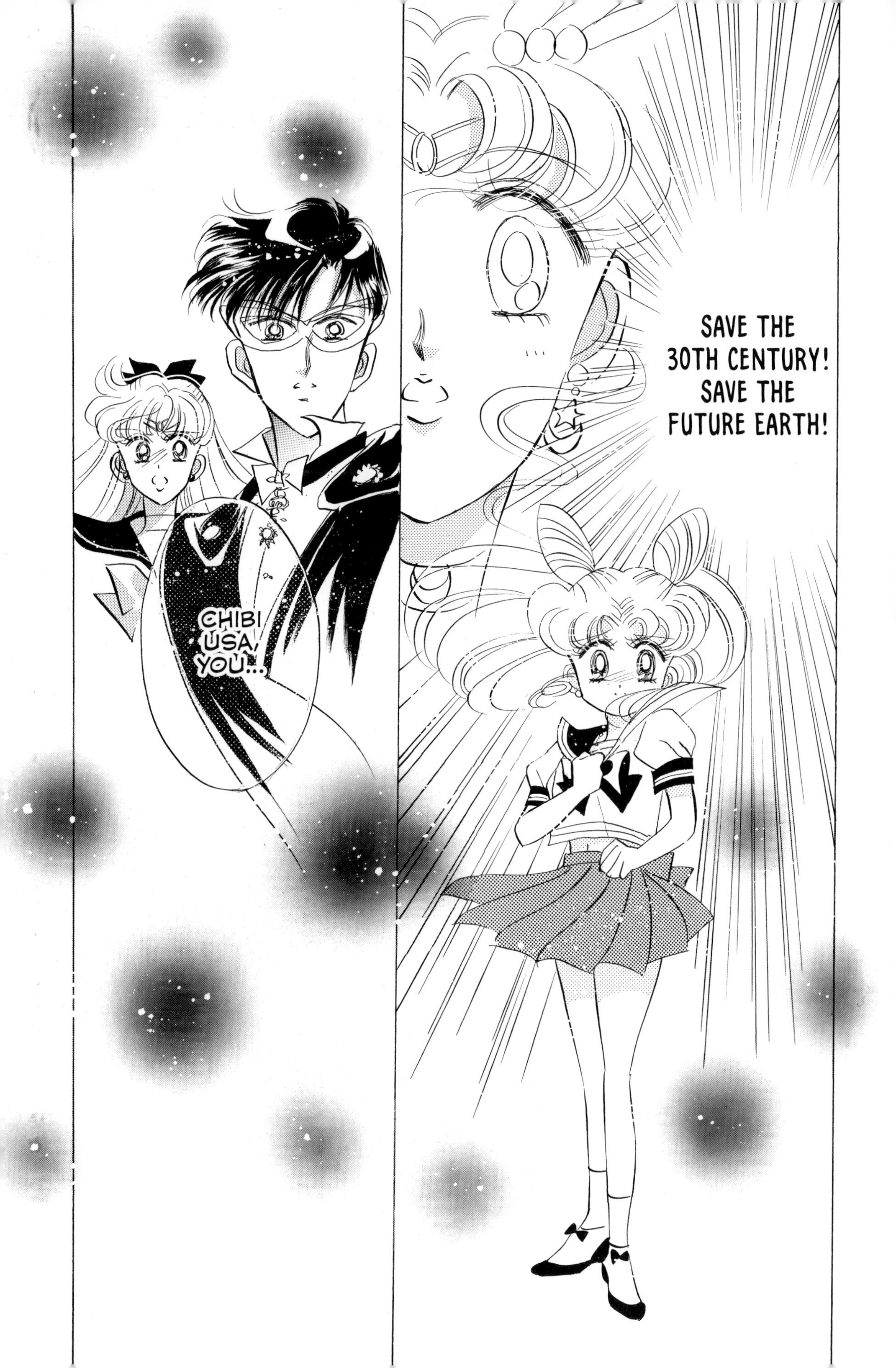
SAVE THE 30TH CENTURY! SAVE THE FUTURE EARTH!
CHIBI USA, YOU...

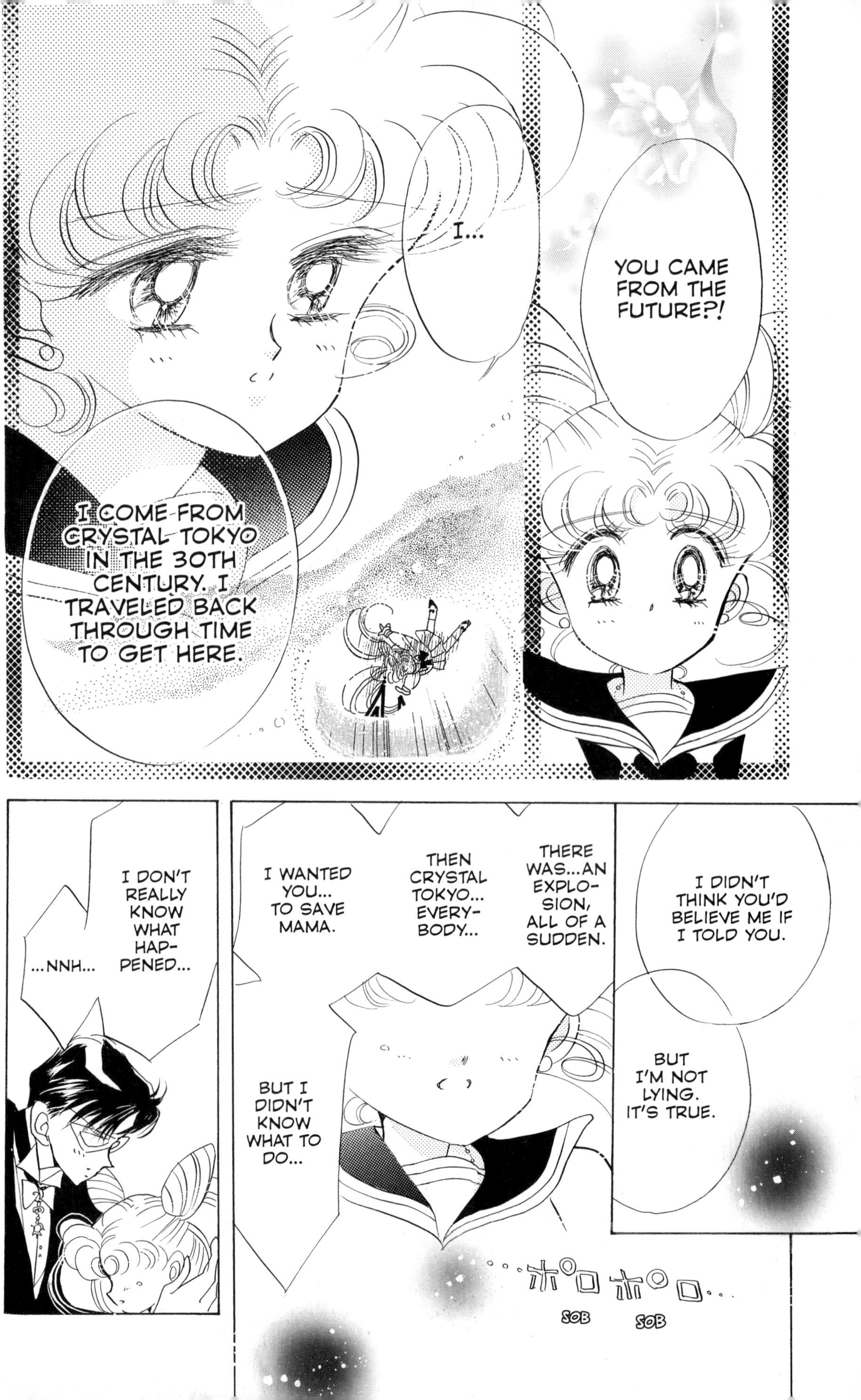
YOU CAME FROM THE FUTURE?!
I...
I COME FROM CRYSTAL TOKYO IN THE 30TH CENTURY. I TRAVELED BACK THROUGH TIME TO GET HERE.
I DIDN'T THINK YOU'D BELIEVE ME IF I TOLD YOU.
BUT I'M NOT LYING. IT'S TRUE.
THERE WAS...AN EXPLOSION, ALL OF A SUDDEN.
THEN CRYSTAL TOKYO... EVERYBODY...
I WANTED YOU... TO SAVE MAMA.
BUT I DIDN'T KNOW WHAT TO DO...
ホロホロ...
SOB SOB
I DON'T REALLY KNOW WHAT HAPPENED...
...NNH...

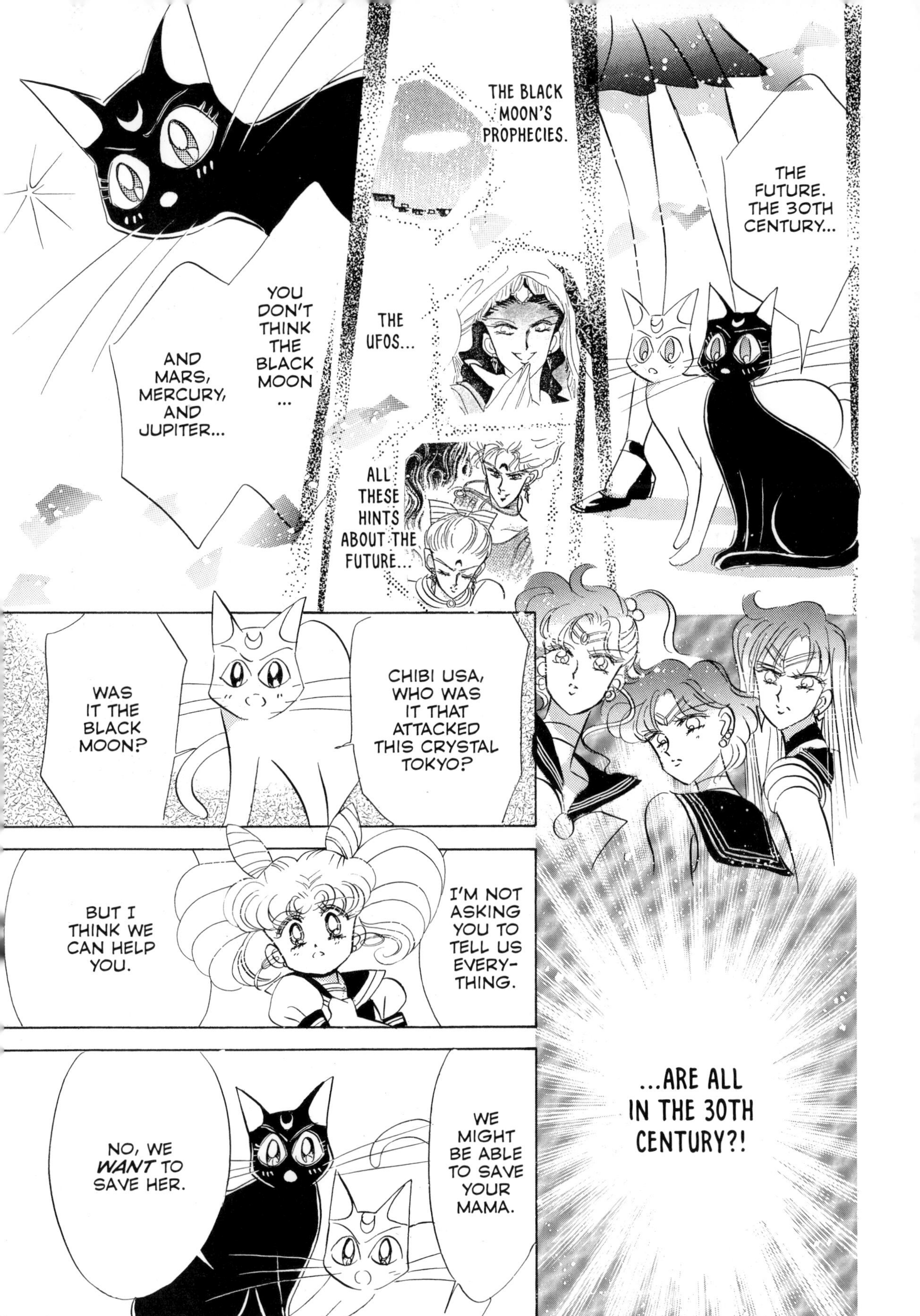
THE FUTURE. THE 30TH CENTURY...
THE BLACK MOON'S PROPHECIES.
THE UFOS...
ALL THESE HINTS ABOUT THE FUTURE...
YOU DON'T THINK THE BLACK MOON ...
AND MARS, MERCURY, AND JUPITER...
...ARE ALL IN THE 30TH CENTURY?!
CHIBI USA, WHO WAS IT THAT ATTACKED THIS CRYSTAL TOKYO?
WAS IT THE BLACK MOON?
I'M NOT ASKING YOU TO TELL US EVERY-THING.
BUT I THINK WE CAN HELP YOU.
WE MIGHT BE ABLE TO SAVE YOUR MAMA.
NO, WE *WANT* TO SAVE HER.

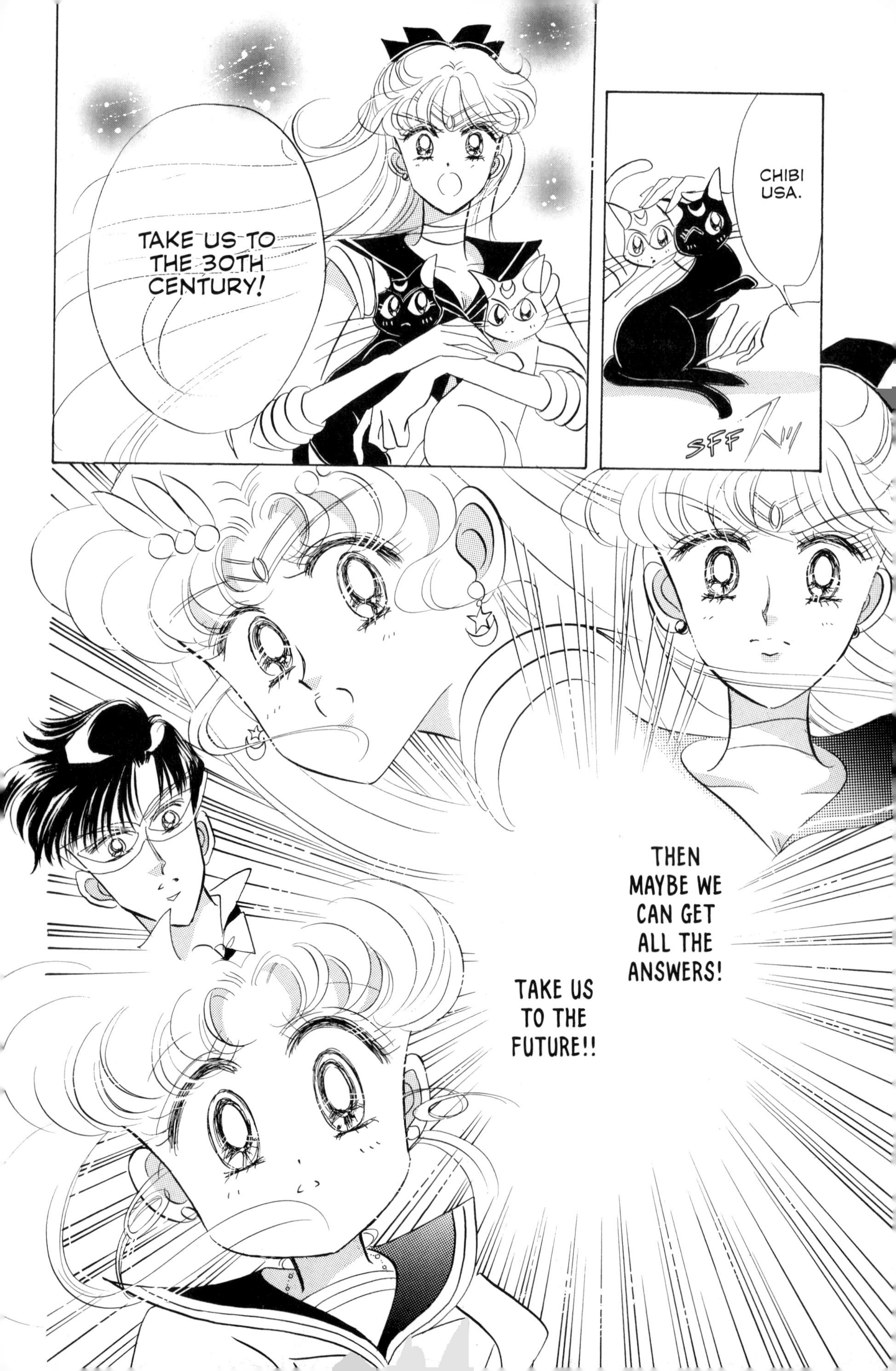
CHIBI USA.
SFF
TAKE US TO THE 30TH CENTURY!
THEN MAYBE WE CAN GET ALL THE ANSWERS!
TAKE US TO THE FUTURE!!

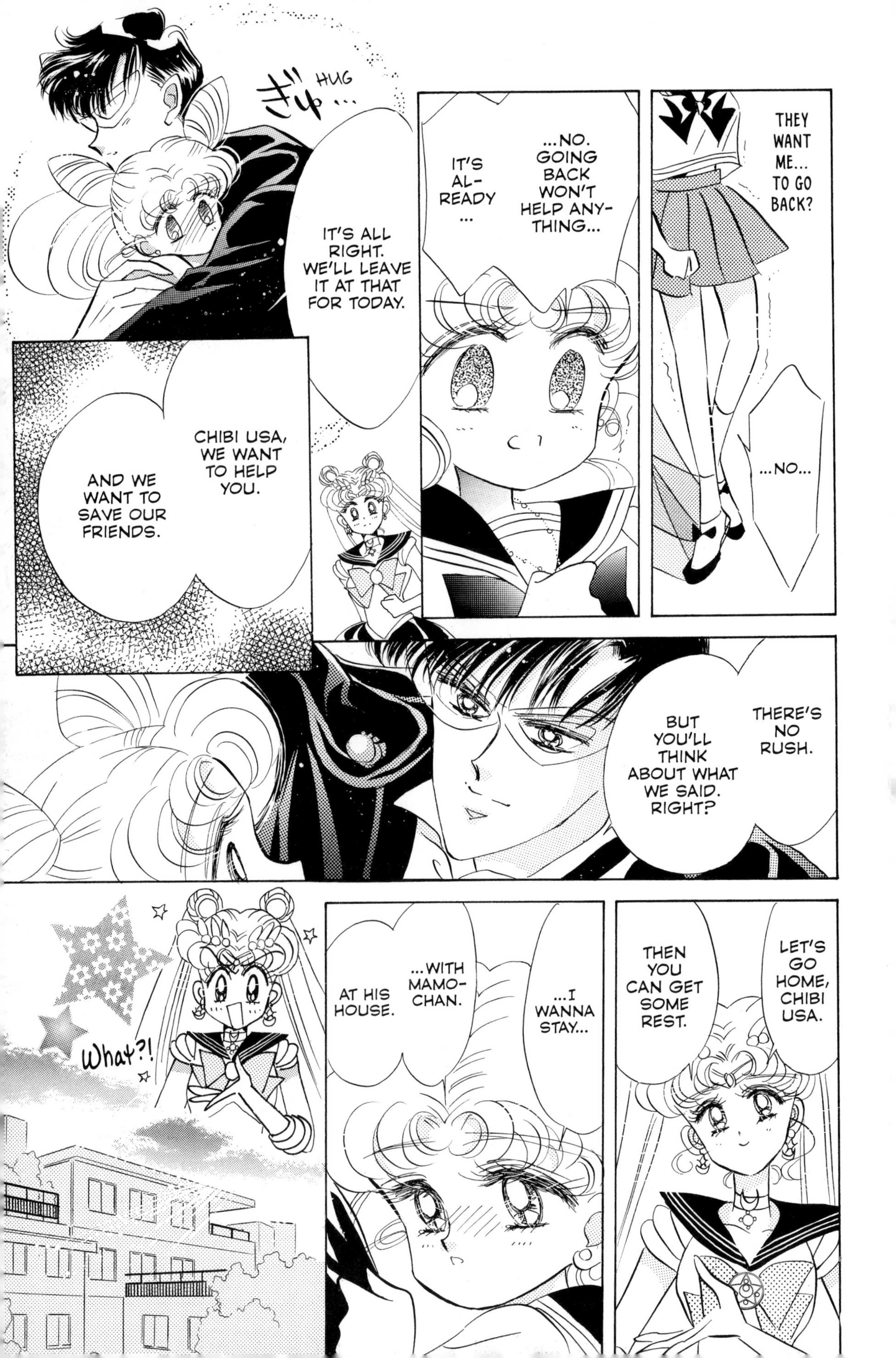
THEY WANT ME... TO GO BACK?
...NO...
...NO. GOING BACK WON'T HELP ANYTHING...
IT'S ALREADY...
ぎゅ... HUG
IT'S ALL RIGHT. WE'LL LEAVE IT AT THAT FOR TODAY.
CHIBI USA, WE WANT TO HELP YOU.
AND WE WANT TO SAVE OUR FRIENDS.
THERE'S NO RUSH.
BUT YOU'LL THINK ABOUT WHAT WE SAID. RIGHT?
LET'S GO HOME, CHIBI USA.
THEN YOU CAN GET SOME REST.
...I WANNA STAY...
...WITH MAMO-CHAN.
AT HIS HOUSE.
What?!

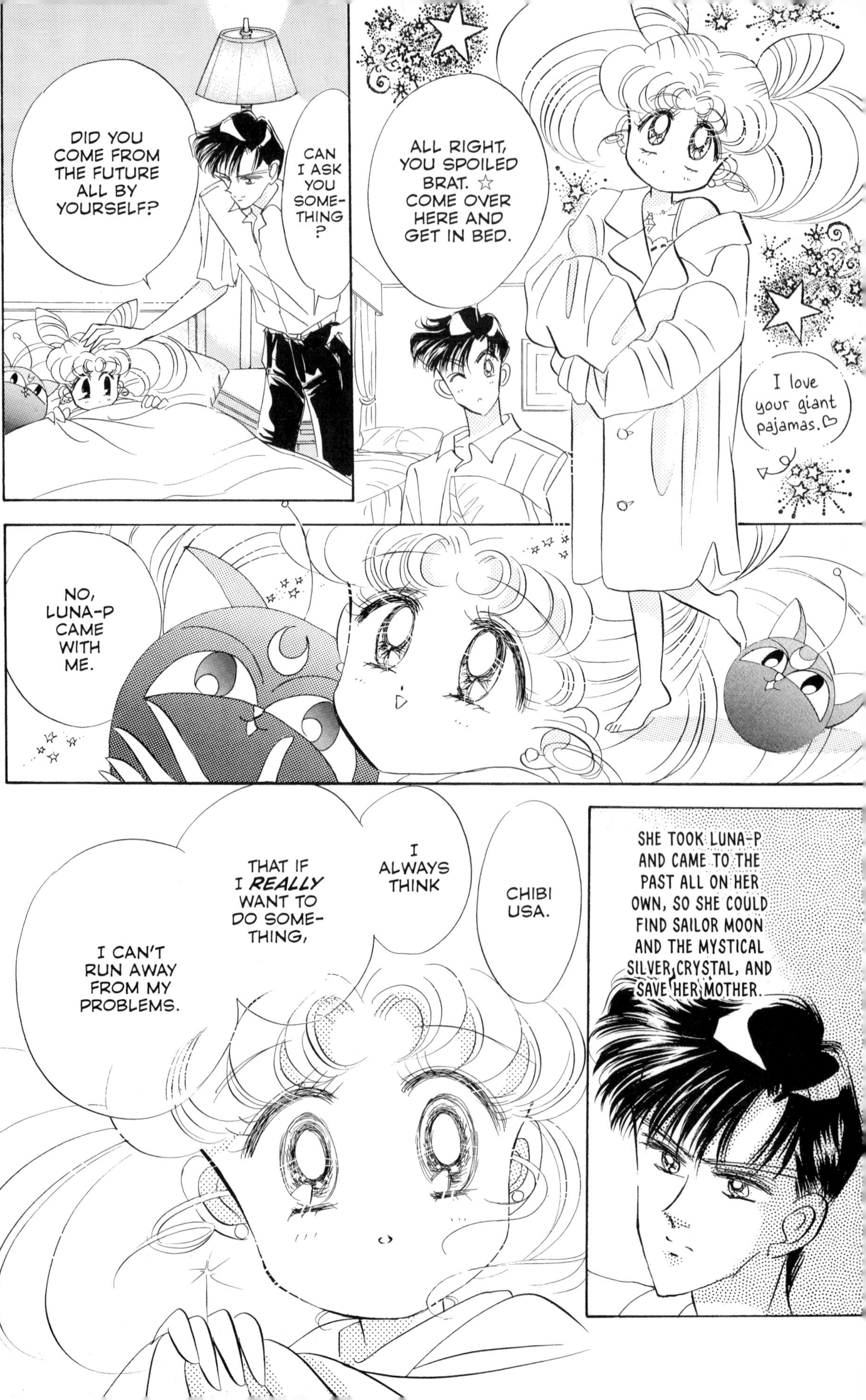
I love your giant pajamas.♡
ALL RIGHT, YOU SPOILED BRAT. ☆ COME OVER HERE AND GET IN BED.
CAN I ASK YOU SOMETHING?
DID YOU COME FROM THE FUTURE ALL BY YOURSELF?
NO, LUNA-P CAME WITH ME.
SHE TOOK LUNA-P AND CAME TO THE PAST ALL ON HER OWN, SO SHE COULD FIND SAILOR MOON AND THE MYSTICAL SILVER CRYSTAL, AND SAVE HER MOTHER.
CHIBI USA.
I ALWAYS THINK
THAT IF I *REALLY* WANT TO DO SOMETHING,
I CAN'T RUN AWAY FROM MY PROBLEMS.

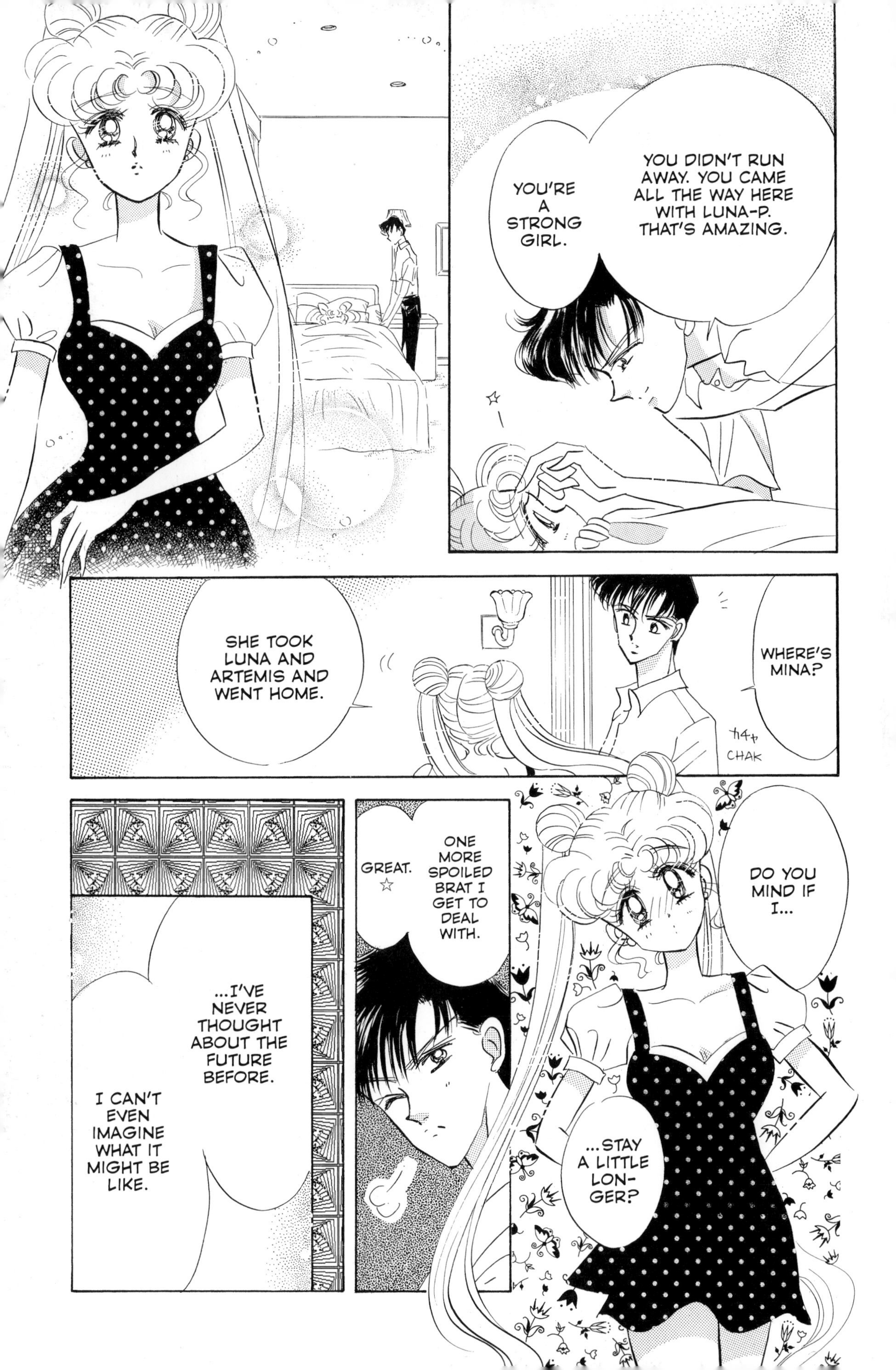
YOU DIDN'T RUN AWAY. YOU CAME ALL THE WAY HERE WITH LUNA-P. THAT'S AMAZING.
YOU'RE A STRONG GIRL.
WHERE'S MINA?
カチャ CHAK
SHE TOOK LUNA AND ARTEMIS AND WENT HOME.
DO YOU MIND IF I...
...STAY A LITTLE LON-GER?
ONE MORE SPOILED BRAT I GET TO DEAL WITH.
GREAT.
...I'VE NEVER THOUGHT ABOUT THE FUTURE BEFORE.
I CAN'T EVEN IMAGINE WHAT IT MIGHT BE LIKE.

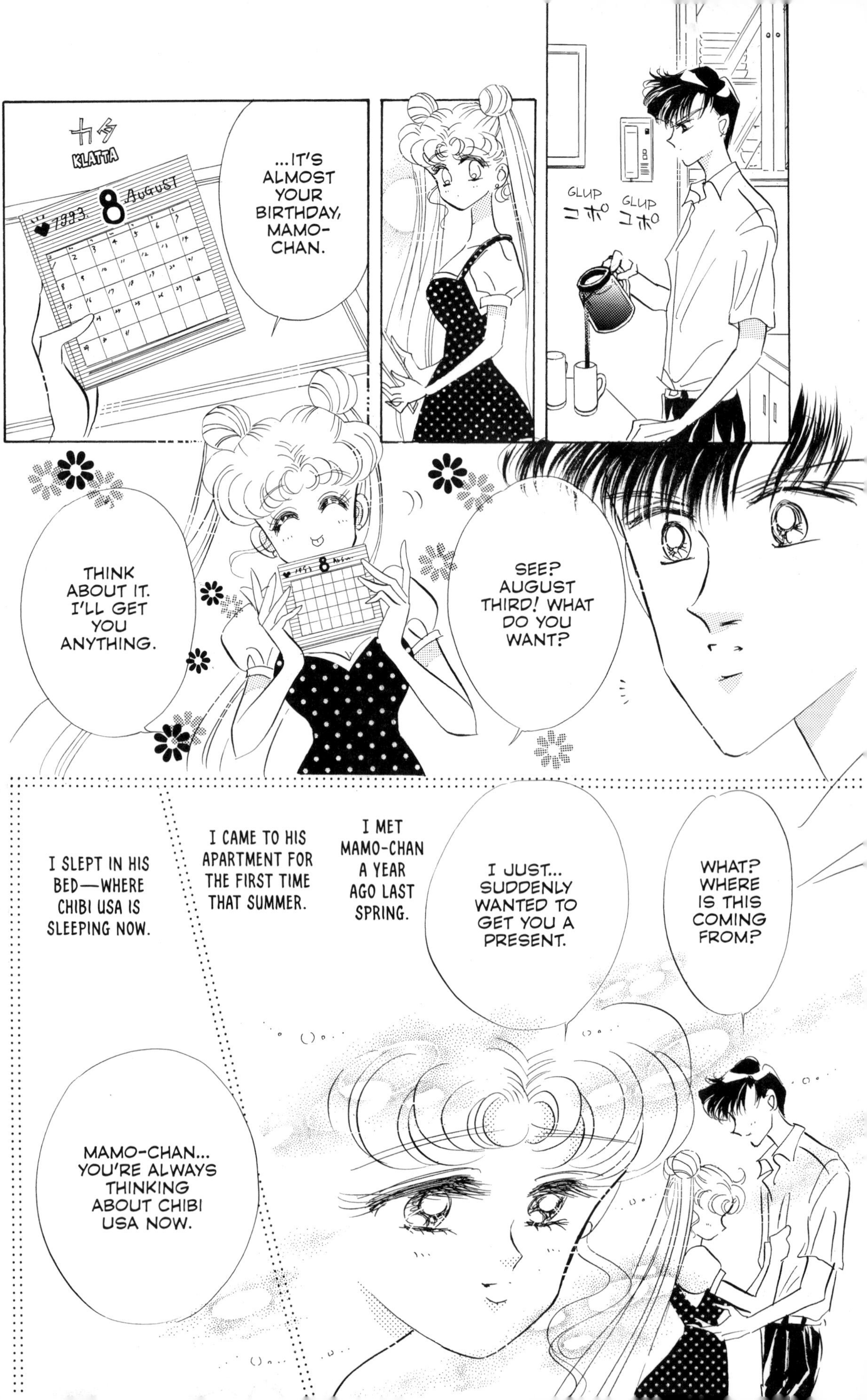
GLUP
コポ
GLUP
コポ
...IT'S ALMOST YOUR BIRTHDAY, MAMO-CHAN.
カタ
KLATTA
SEE? AUGUST THIRD! WHAT DO YOU WANT?
THINK ABOUT IT. I'LL GET YOU ANYTHING.
WHAT? WHERE IS THIS COMING FROM?
I JUST... SUDDENLY WANTED TO GET YOU A PRESENT.
I MET MAMO-CHAN A YEAR AGO LAST SPRING.
I CAME TO HIS APARTMENT FOR THE FIRST TIME THAT SUMMER.
I SLEPT IN HIS BED—WHERE CHIBI USA IS SLEEPING NOW.
MAMO-CHAN... YOU'RE ALWAYS THINKING ABOUT CHIBI USA NOW.

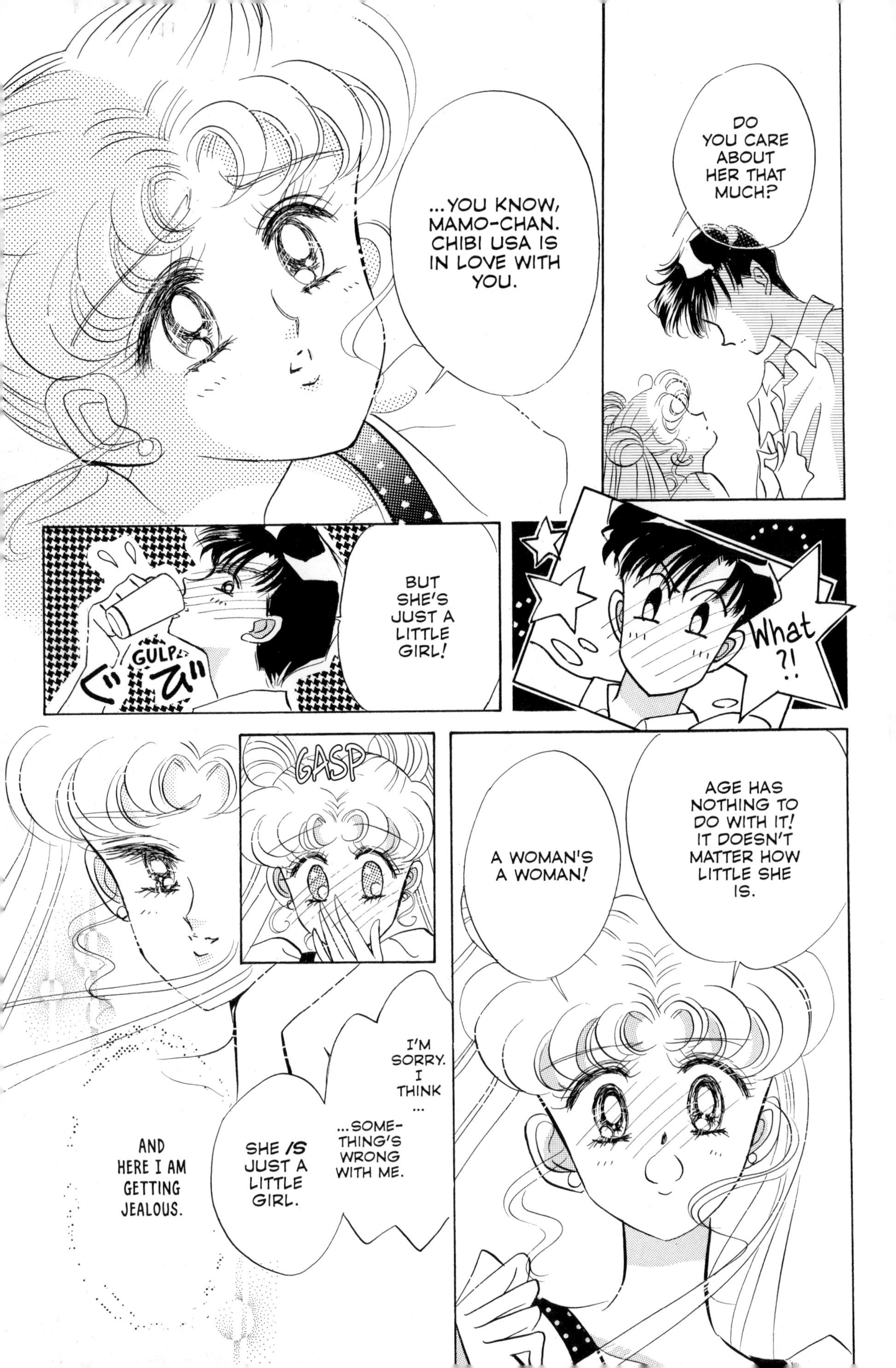
DO YOU CARE ABOUT HER THAT MUCH?
...YOU KNOW, MAMO-CHAN. CHIBI USA IS IN LOVE WITH YOU.
What ?!
BUT SHE'S JUST A LITTLE GIRL!
GULP
AGE HAS NOTHING TO DO WITH IT! IT DOESN'T MATTER HOW LITTLE SHE IS.
A WOMAN'S A WOMAN!
GASP
I'M SORRY. I THINK...
...SOMETHING'S WRONG WITH ME.
SHE *IS* JUST A LITTLE GIRL.
AND HERE I AM GETTING JEALOUS.

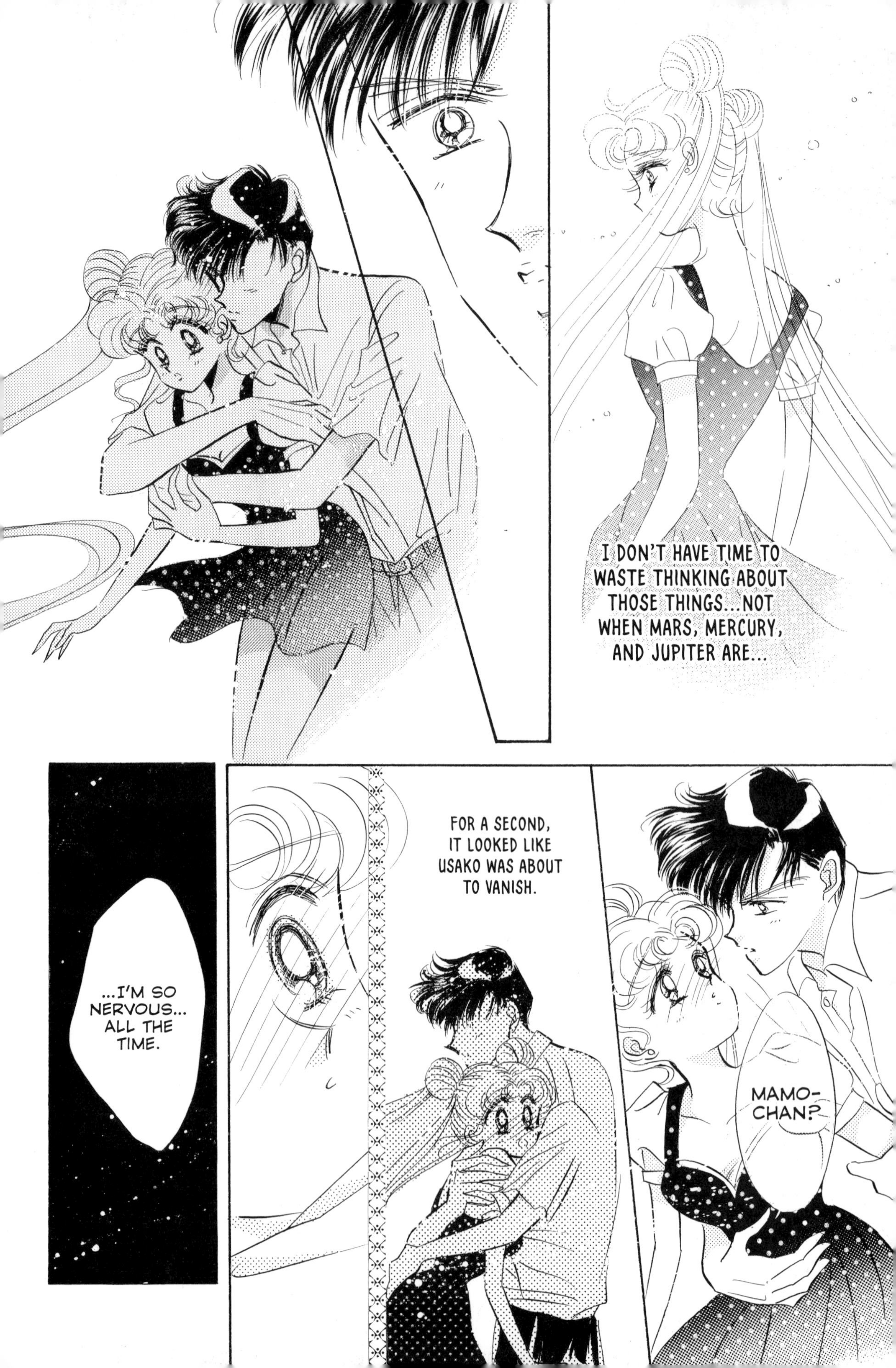
I DON'T HAVE TIME TO WASTE THINKING ABOUT THOSE THINGS...NOT WHEN MARS, MERCURY, AND JUPITER ARE...
MAMO-CHAN?
FOR A SECOND, IT LOOKED LIKE USAKO WAS ABOUT TO VANISH.
...I'M SO NERVOUS... ALL THE TIME.

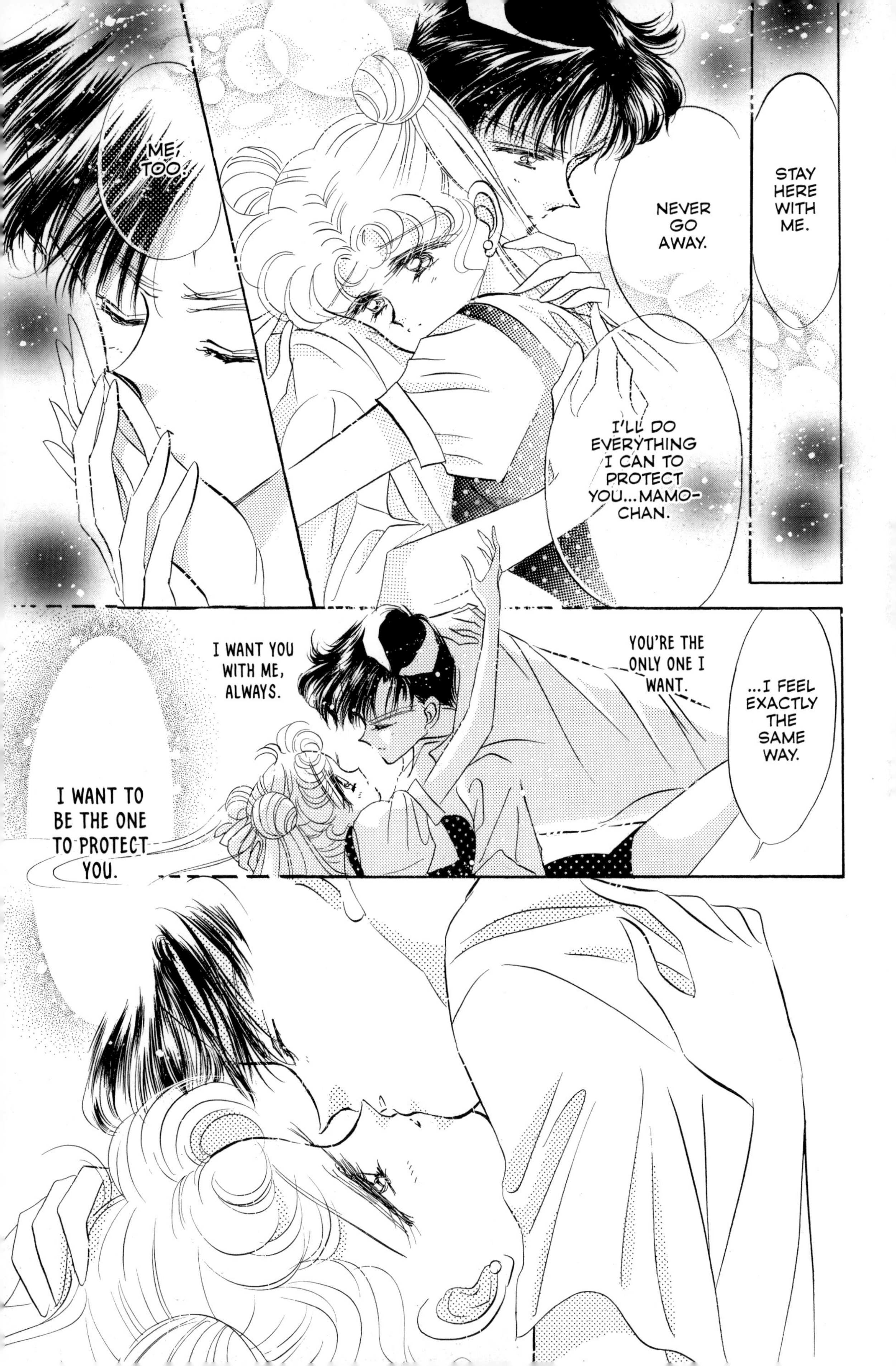
STAY HERE WITH ME.
NEVER GO AWAY.
I'LL DO EVERYTHING I CAN TO PROTECT YOU...MAMO-CHAN.
ME, TOO.
...I FEEL EXACTLY THE SAME WAY.
YOU'RE THE ONLY ONE I WANT.
I WANT YOU WITH ME, ALWAYS.
I WANT TO BE THE ONE TO PROTECT YOU.

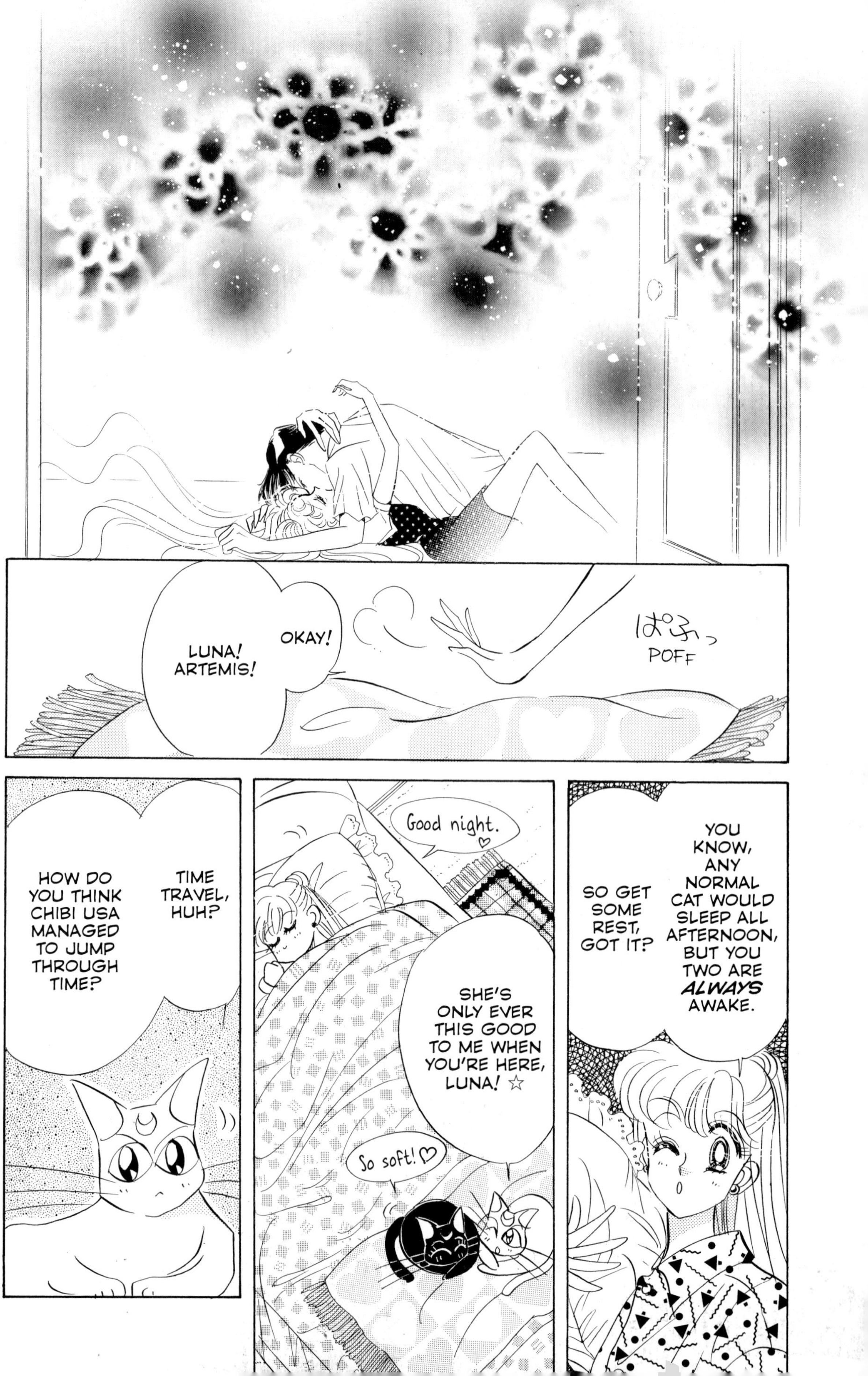
ぱふっ
POFF
OKAY!
LUNA! ARTEMIS!
YOU KNOW, ANY NORMAL CAT WOULD SLEEP ALL AFTERNOON, BUT YOU TWO ARE ***ALWAYS*** AWAKE.
SO GET SOME REST, GOT IT?
Good night. ♡
SHE'S ONLY EVER THIS GOOD TO ME WHEN YOU'RE HERE, LUNA! ☆
So soft! ♡
TIME TRAVEL, HUH?
HOW DO YOU THINK CHIBI USA MANAGED TO JUMP THROUGH TIME?

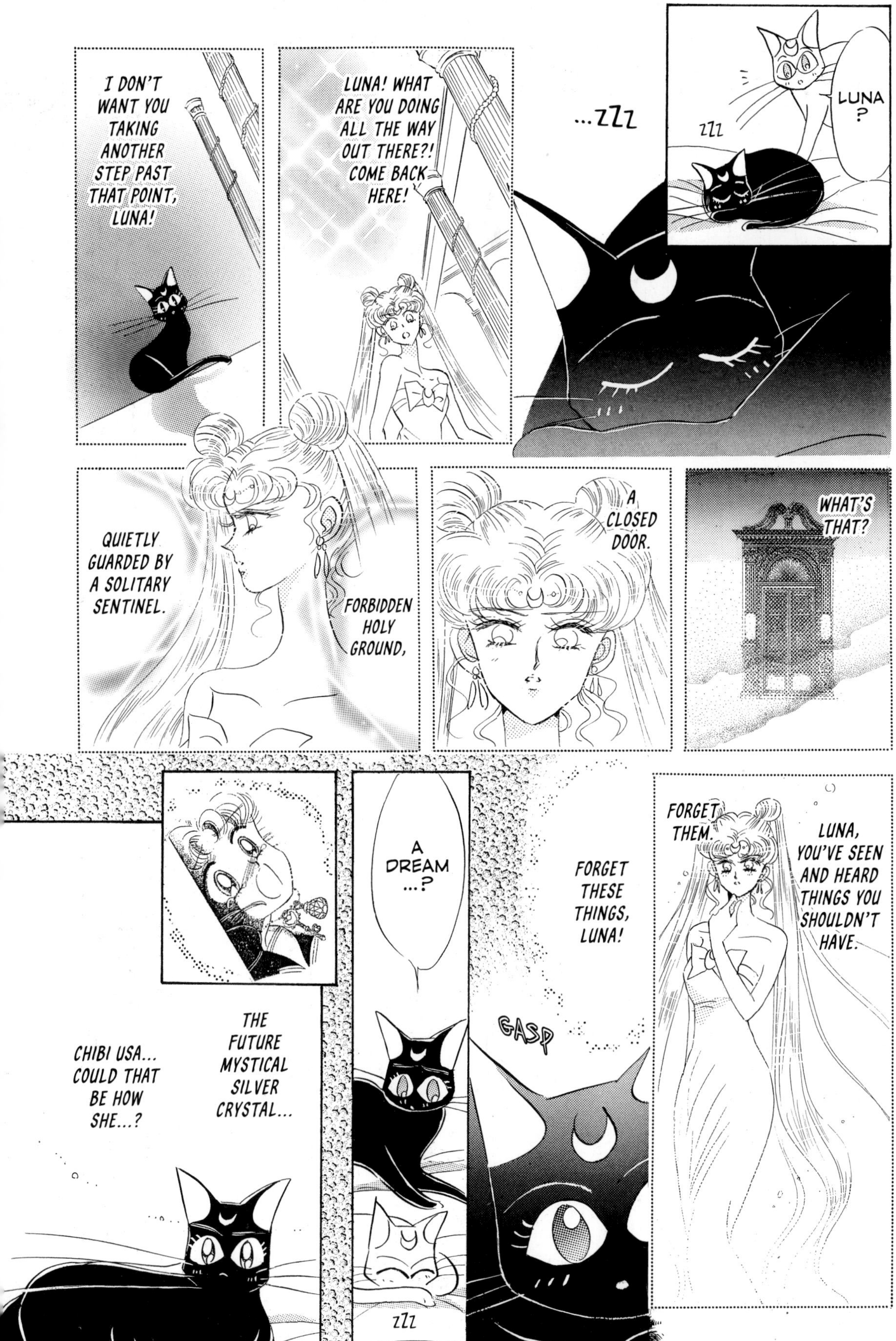
LUNA ?
ZZZ
...ZZZ
LUNA! WHAT ARE YOU DOING ALL THE WAY OUT THERE?! COME BACK HERE!
I DON'T WANT YOU TAKING ANOTHER STEP PAST THAT POINT, LUNA!
WHAT'S THAT?
A CLOSED DOOR.
FORBIDDEN HOLY GROUND,
QUIETLY GUARDED BY A SOLITARY SENTINEL.
LUNA, YOU'VE SEEN AND HEARD THINGS YOU SHOULDN'T HAVE.
FORGET THEM.
FORGET THESE THINGS, LUNA!
GASP
A DREAM ...?
ZZZ
THE FUTURE MYSTICAL SILVER CRYSTAL...
CHIBI USA... COULD THAT BE HOW SHE...?

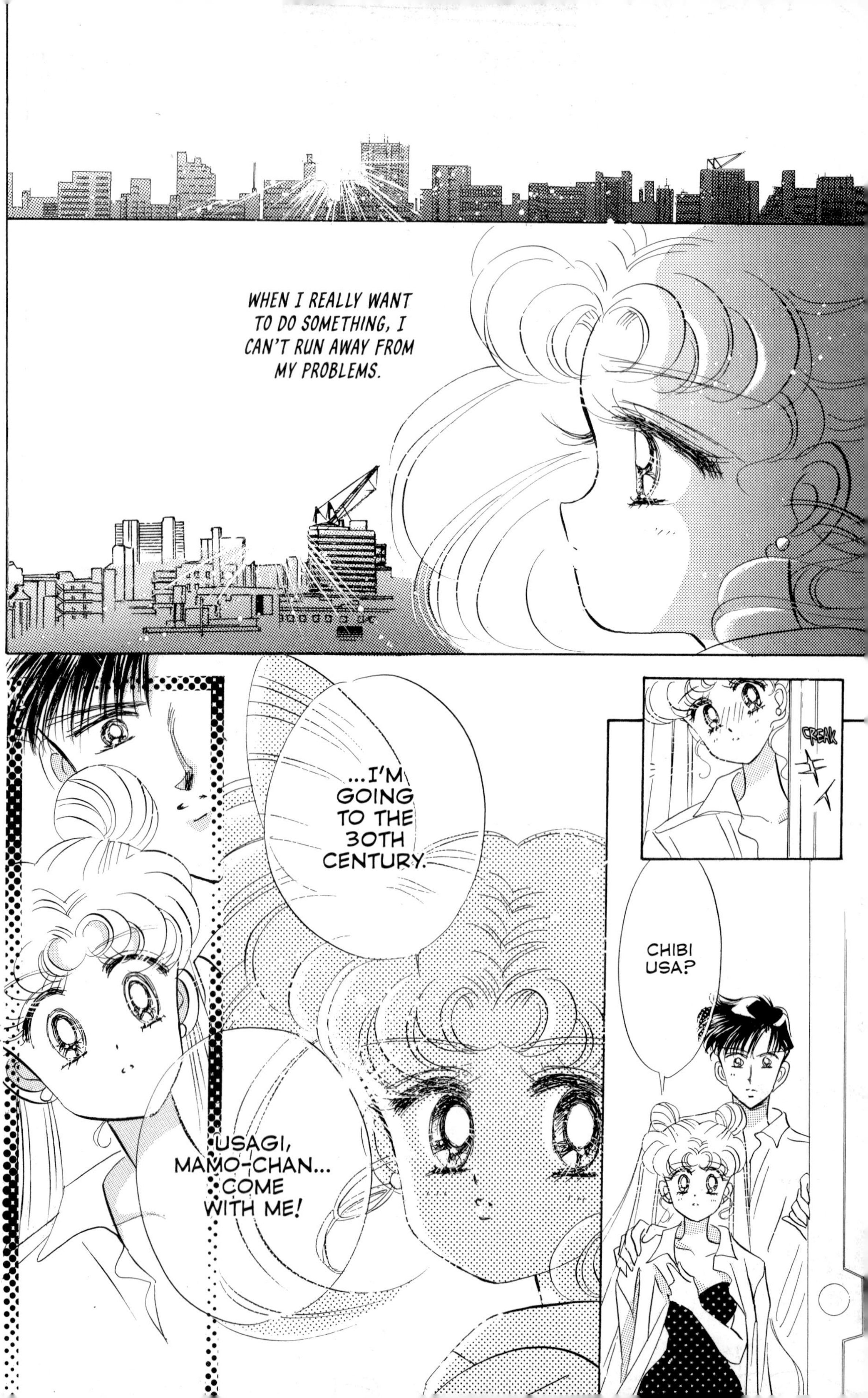
WHEN I REALLY WANT TO DO SOMETHING, I CAN'T RUN AWAY FROM MY PROBLEMS.
CREAK
CHIBI USA?
...I'M GOING TO THE 30TH CENTURY.
USAGI, MAMO-CHAN... COME WITH ME!

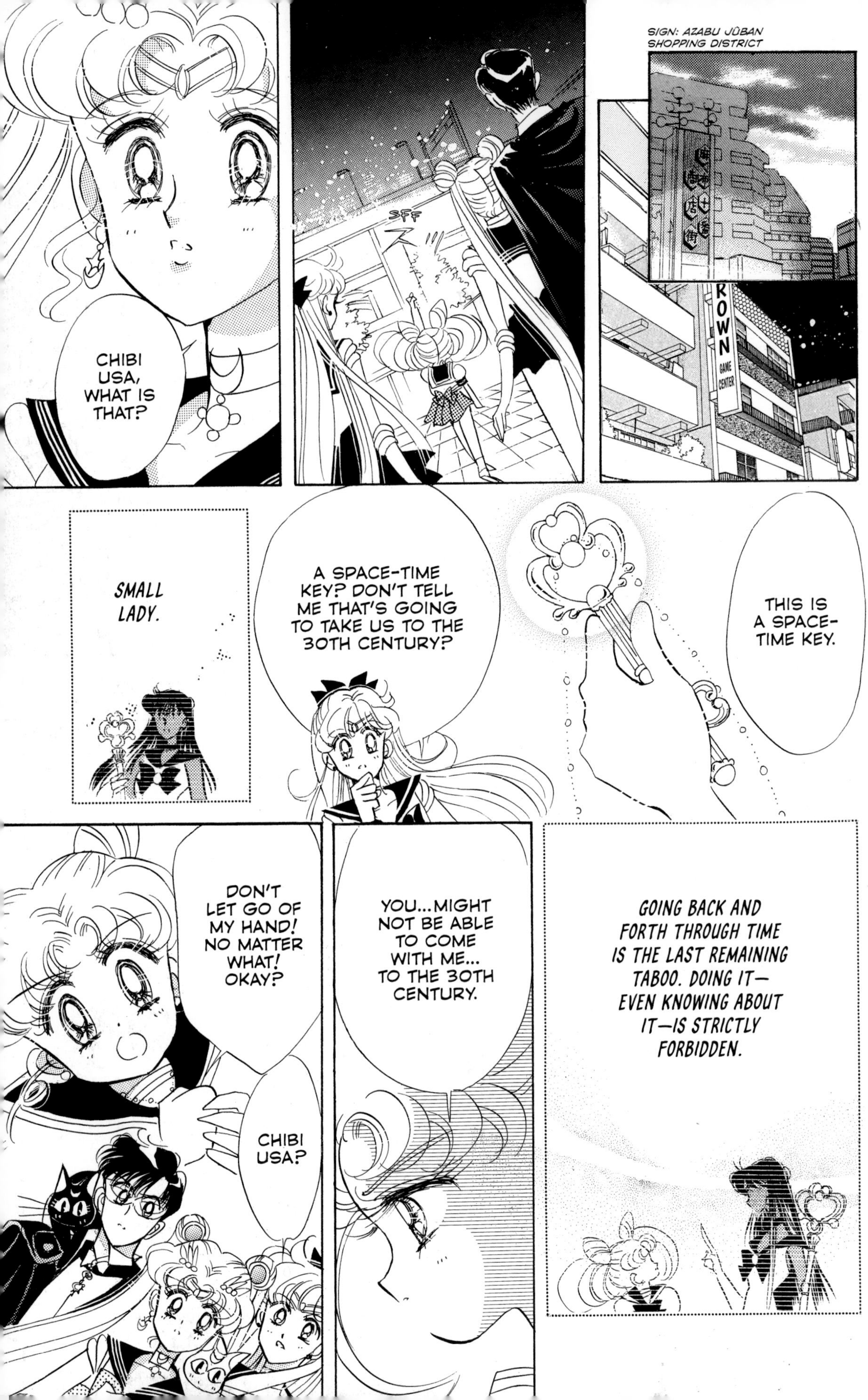
SIGN: AZABU JÛBAN SHOPPING DISTRICT
GAME CENTER
SFF
CHIBI USA, WHAT IS THAT?
THIS IS A SPACE-TIME KEY.
A SPACE-TIME KEY? DON'T TELL ME THAT'S GOING TO TAKE US TO THE 30TH CENTURY?
SMALL LADY.
GOING BACK AND FORTH THROUGH TIME IS THE LAST REMAINING TABOO. DOING IT—EVEN KNOWING ABOUT IT—IS STRICTLY FORBIDDEN.
YOU...MIGHT NOT BE ABLE TO COME WITH ME... TO THE 30TH CENTURY.
DON'T LET GO OF MY HAND! NO MATTER WHAT! OKAY?
CHIBI USA?

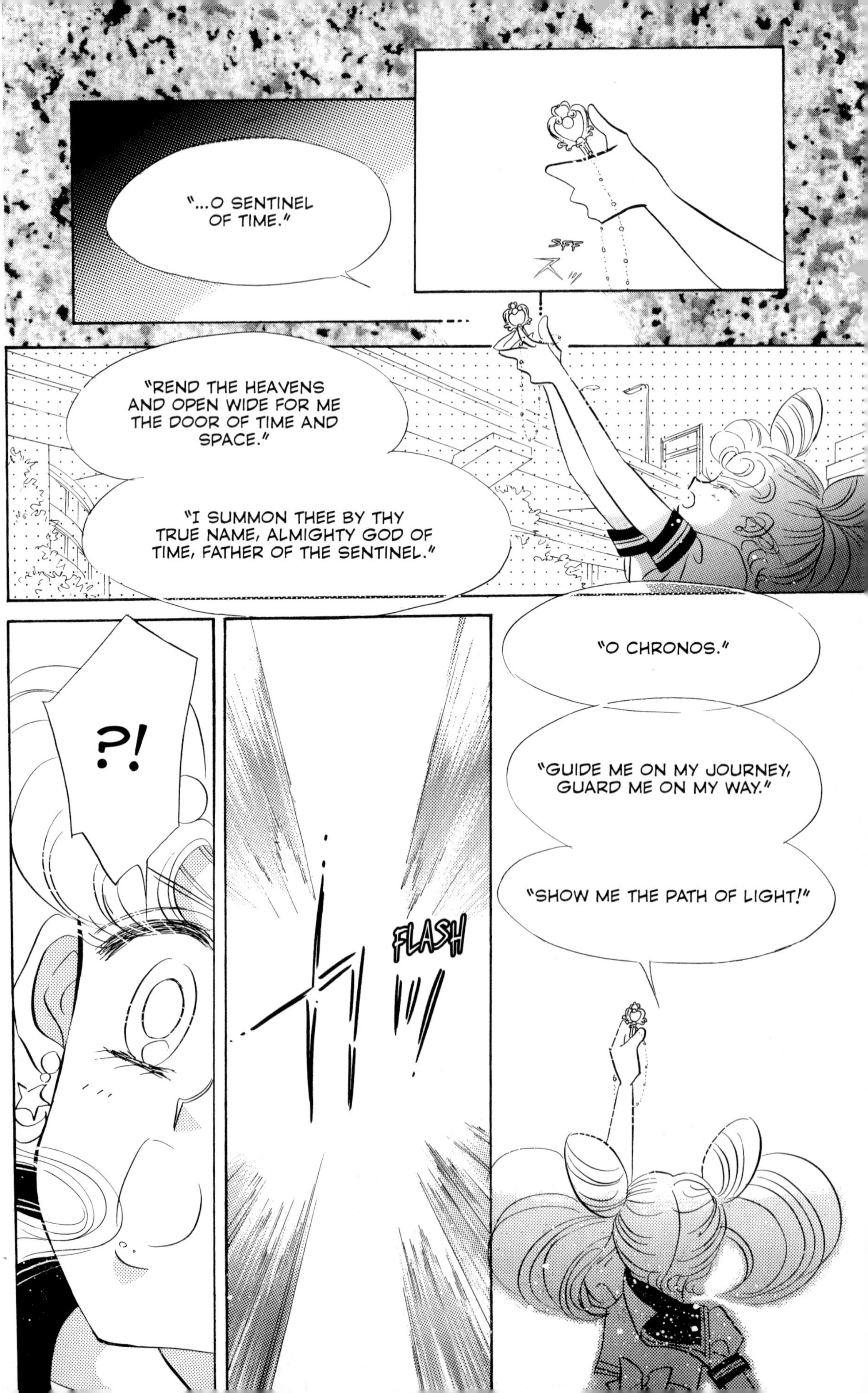
SFF
"...O SENTINEL OF TIME."
"REND THE HEAVENS AND OPEN WIDE FOR ME THE DOOR OF TIME AND SPACE."
"I SUMMON THEE BY THY TRUE NAME, ALMIGHTY GOD OF TIME, FATHER OF THE SENTINEL."
"O CHRONOS."
"GUIDE ME ON MY JOURNEY, GUARD ME ON MY WAY."
"SHOW ME THE PATH OF LIGHT!"
FLASH
?!

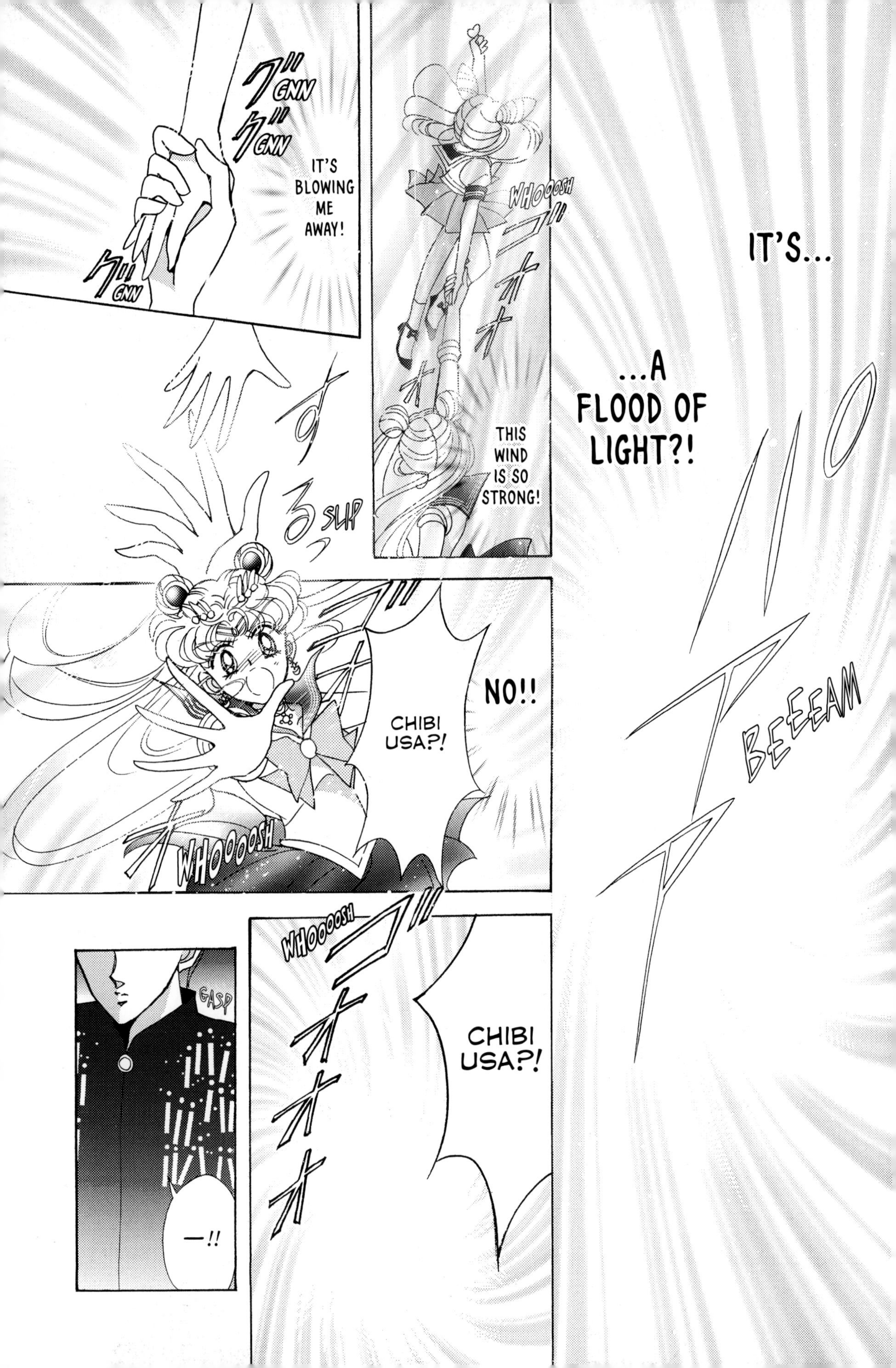
IT'S...
...A FLOOD OF LIGHT?!
BEEEAM
WHOOOSH
THIS WIND IS SO STRONG!
GNN
GNN
IT'S BLOWING ME AWAY!
GNN
SLIP
NO!!
CHIBI USA?!
WHOOOOSH
WHOOOOSH
CHIBI USA?!
GASP
—!!

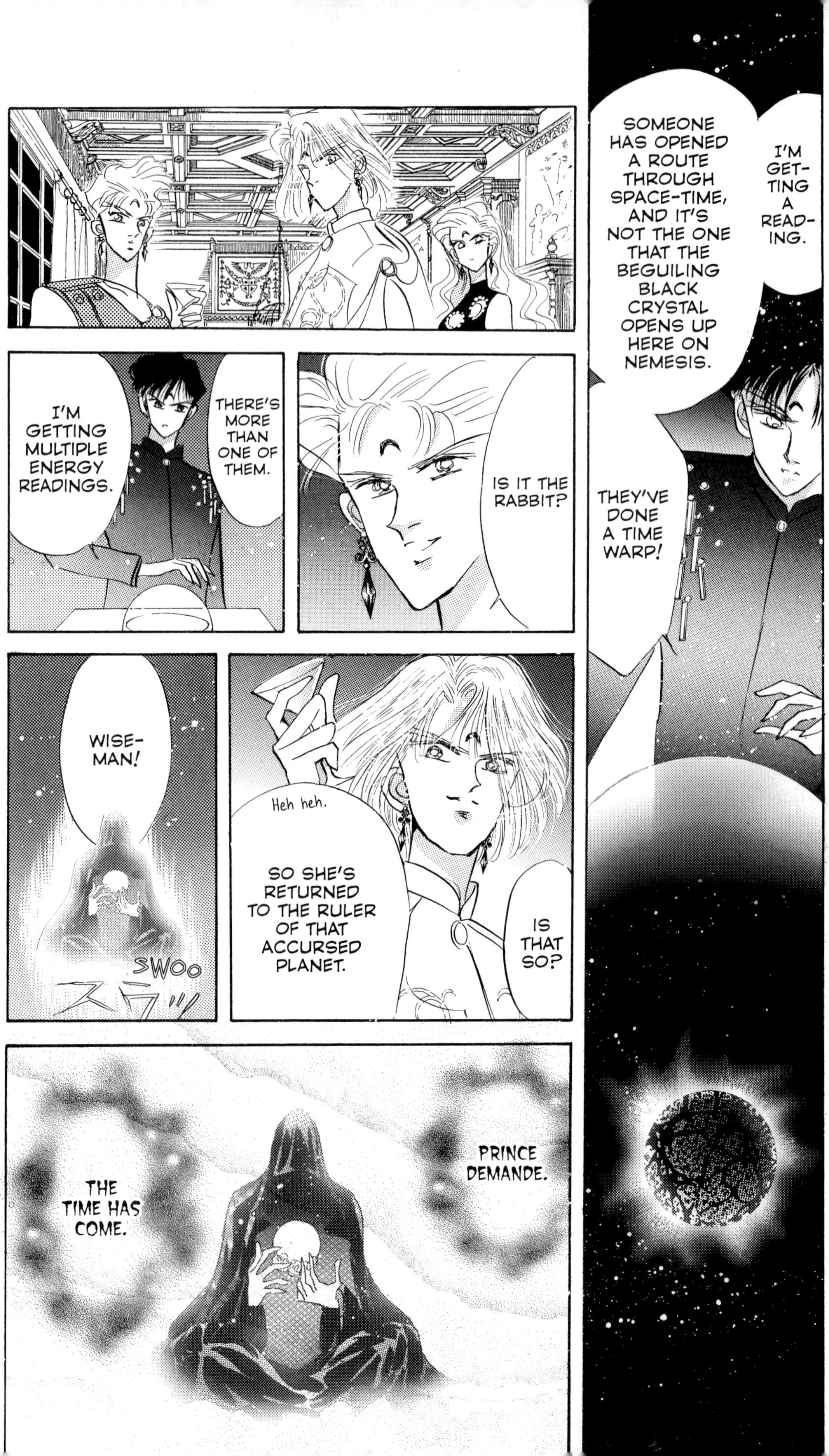
I'M GETTING A READING.
SOMEONE HAS OPENED A ROUTE THROUGH SPACE-TIME, AND IT'S NOT THE ONE THAT THE BEGUILING BLACK CRYSTAL OPENS UP HERE ON NEMESIS.
THEY'VE DONE A TIME WARP!
IS IT THE RABBIT?
THERE'S MORE THAN ONE OF THEM.
I'M GETTING MULTIPLE ENERGY READINGS.
IS THAT SO?
Heh heh.
SO SHE'S RETURNED TO THE RULER OF THAT ACCURSED PLANET.
WISE-MAN!
SWOO
PRINCE DEMANDE.
THE TIME HAS COME.

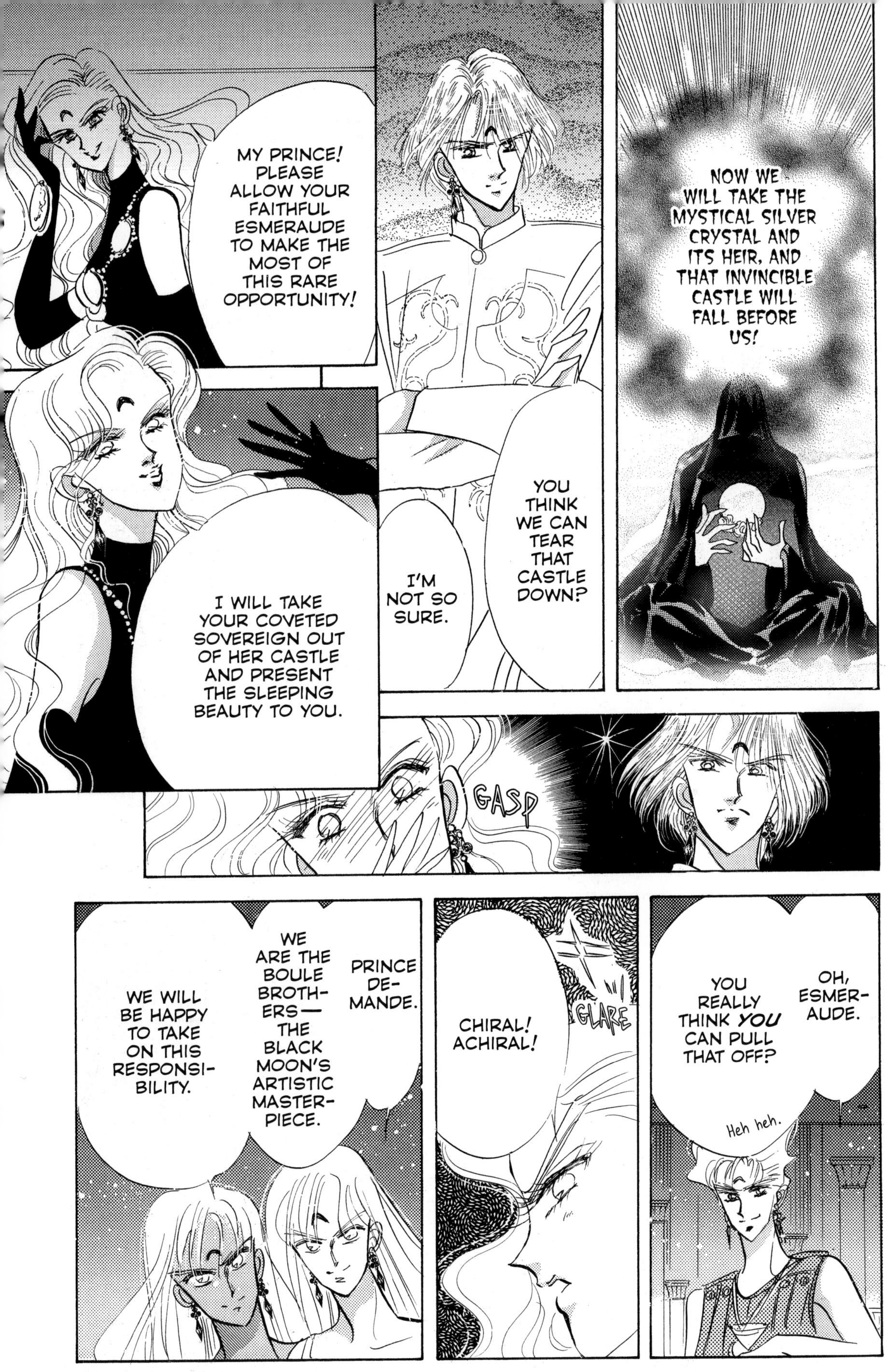
NOW WE WILL TAKE THE MYSTICAL SILVER CRYSTAL AND ITS HEIR, AND THAT INVINCIBLE CASTLE WILL FALL BEFORE US!
YOU THINK WE CAN TEAR THAT CASTLE DOWN?
I'M NOT SO SURE.
MY PRINCE! PLEASE ALLOW YOUR FAITHFUL ESMERAUDE TO MAKE THE MOST OF THIS RARE OPPORTUNITY!
I WILL TAKE YOUR COVETED SOVEREIGN OUT OF HER CASTLE AND PRESENT THE SLEEPING BEAUTY TO YOU.
GASP
OH, ESMER-AUDE.
YOU REALLY THINK *YOU* CAN PULL THAT OFF?
Heh heh.
GLARE
CHIRAL! ACHIRAL!
PRINCE DE-MANDE.
WE ARE THE BOULE BROTH-ERS— THE BLACK MOON'S ARTISTIC MASTER-PIECE.
WE WILL BE HAPPY TO TAKE ON THIS RESPONSI-BILITY.

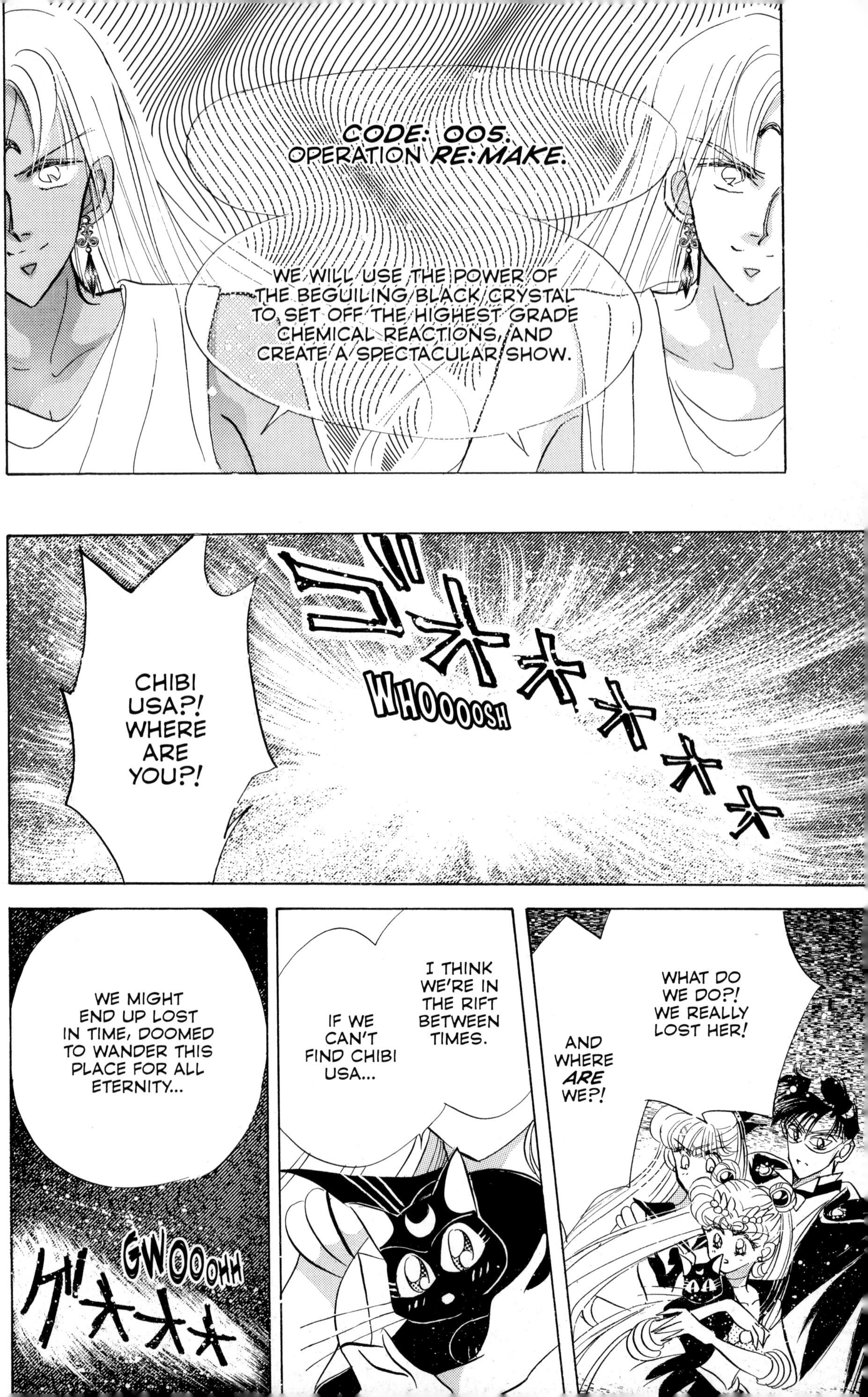
CODE: 005.
OPERATION RE:MAKE.
WE WILL USE THE POWER OF THE BEGUILING BLACK CRYSTAL TO SET OFF THE HIGHEST GRADE CHEMICAL REACTIONS, AND CREATE A SPECTACULAR SHOW.
WHOOOOOSH
CHIBI USA?! WHERE ARE YOU?!
WHAT DO WE DO?! WE REALLY LOST HER!
AND WHERE ARE WE?!
I THINK WE'RE IN THE RIFT BETWEEN TIMES.
IF WE CAN'T FIND CHIBI USA...
WE MIGHT END UP LOST IN TIME, DOOMED TO WANDER THIS PLACE FOR ALL ETERNITY...
GWOOOOHH

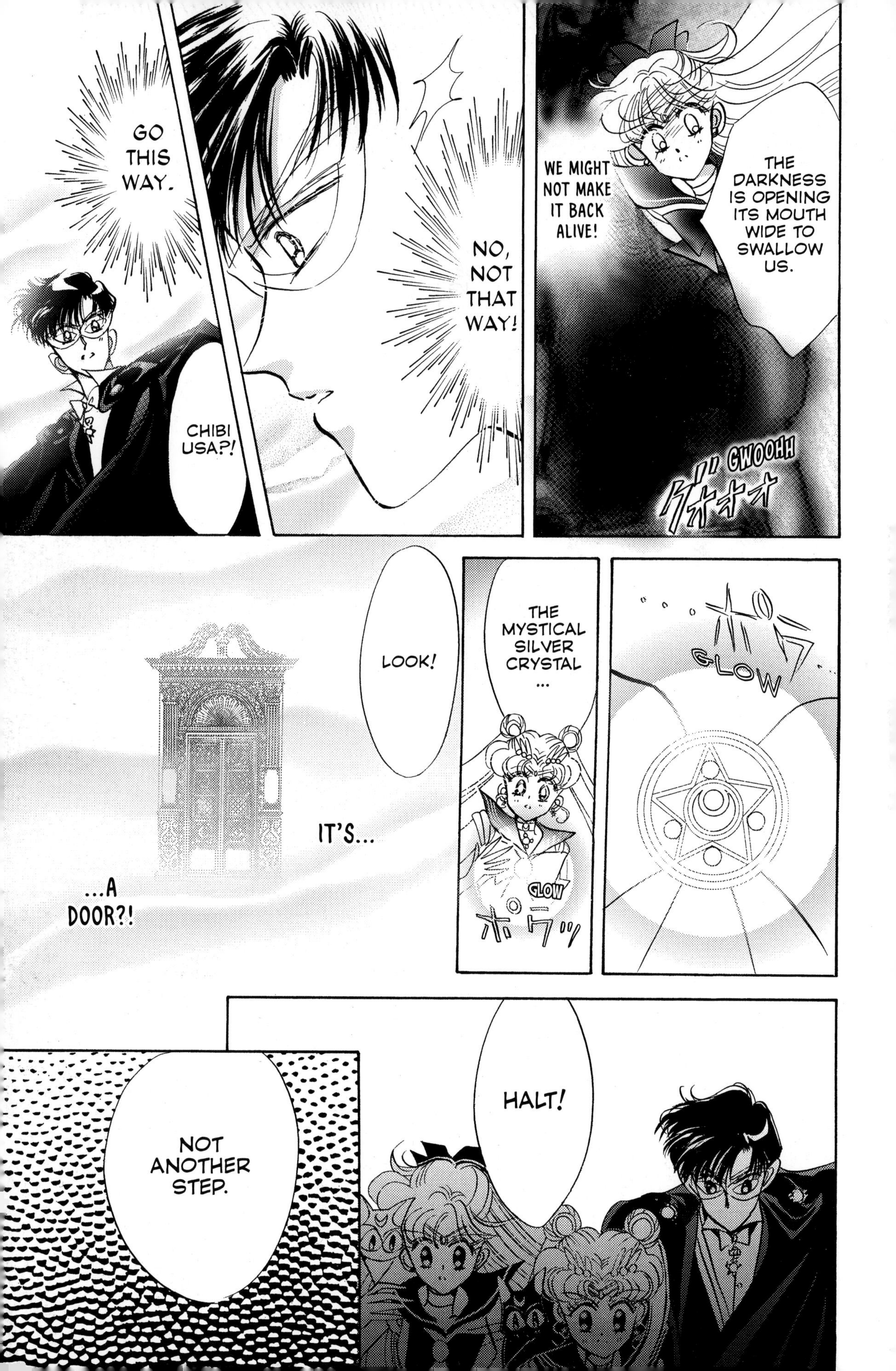
THE DARKNESS IS OPENING ITS MOUTH WIDE TO SWALLOW US.
WE MIGHT NOT MAKE IT BACK ALIVE!
GWOOHH
グオオオ
NO, NOT THAT WAY!
GO THIS WAY.
CHIBI USA?!
GLOW
THE MYSTICAL SILVER CRYSTAL ...
GLOW
LOOK!
IT'S...
...A DOOR?!
HALT!
NOT ANOTHER STEP.

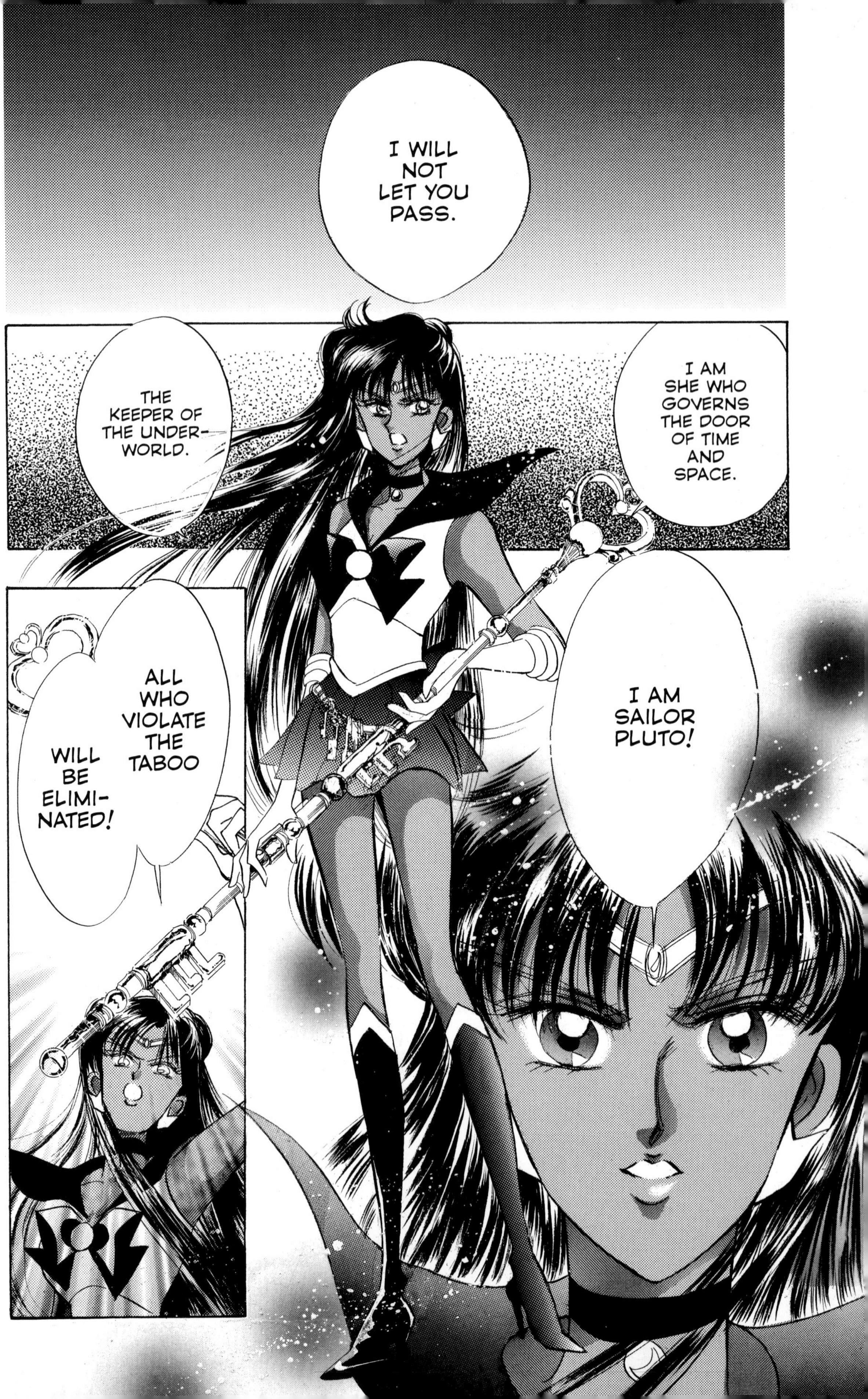
I WILL NOT LET YOU PASS.
I AM SHE WHO GOVERNS THE DOOR OF TIME AND SPACE.
THE KEEPER OF THE UNDER-WORLD.
I AM SAILOR PLUTO!
ALL WHO VIOLATE THE TABOO
WILL BE ELIMI-NATED!

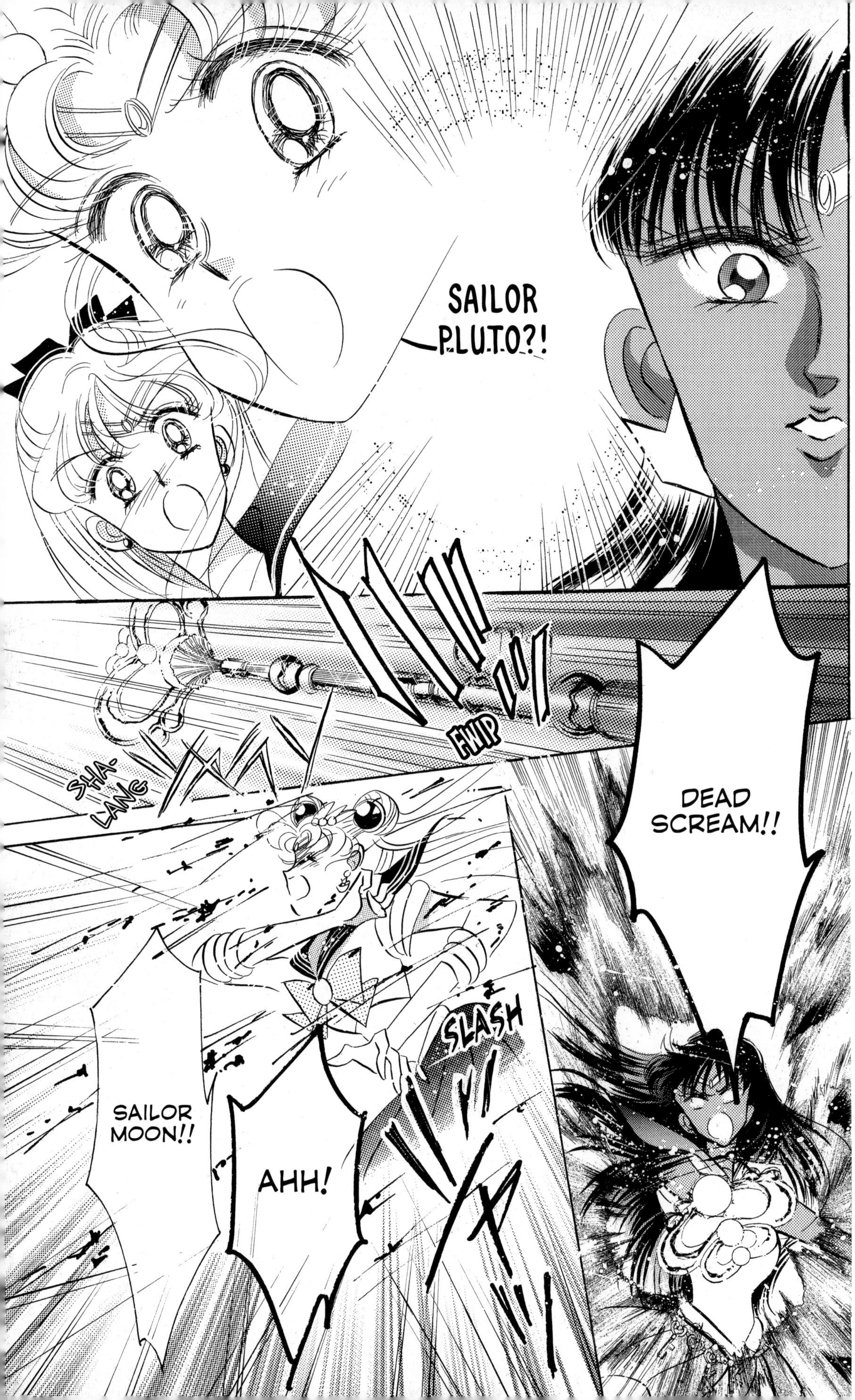
SAILOR PLUTO?!
DEAD SCREAM!!
FWIP
SHA-LANG
SLASH
AHH!
SAILOR MOON!!

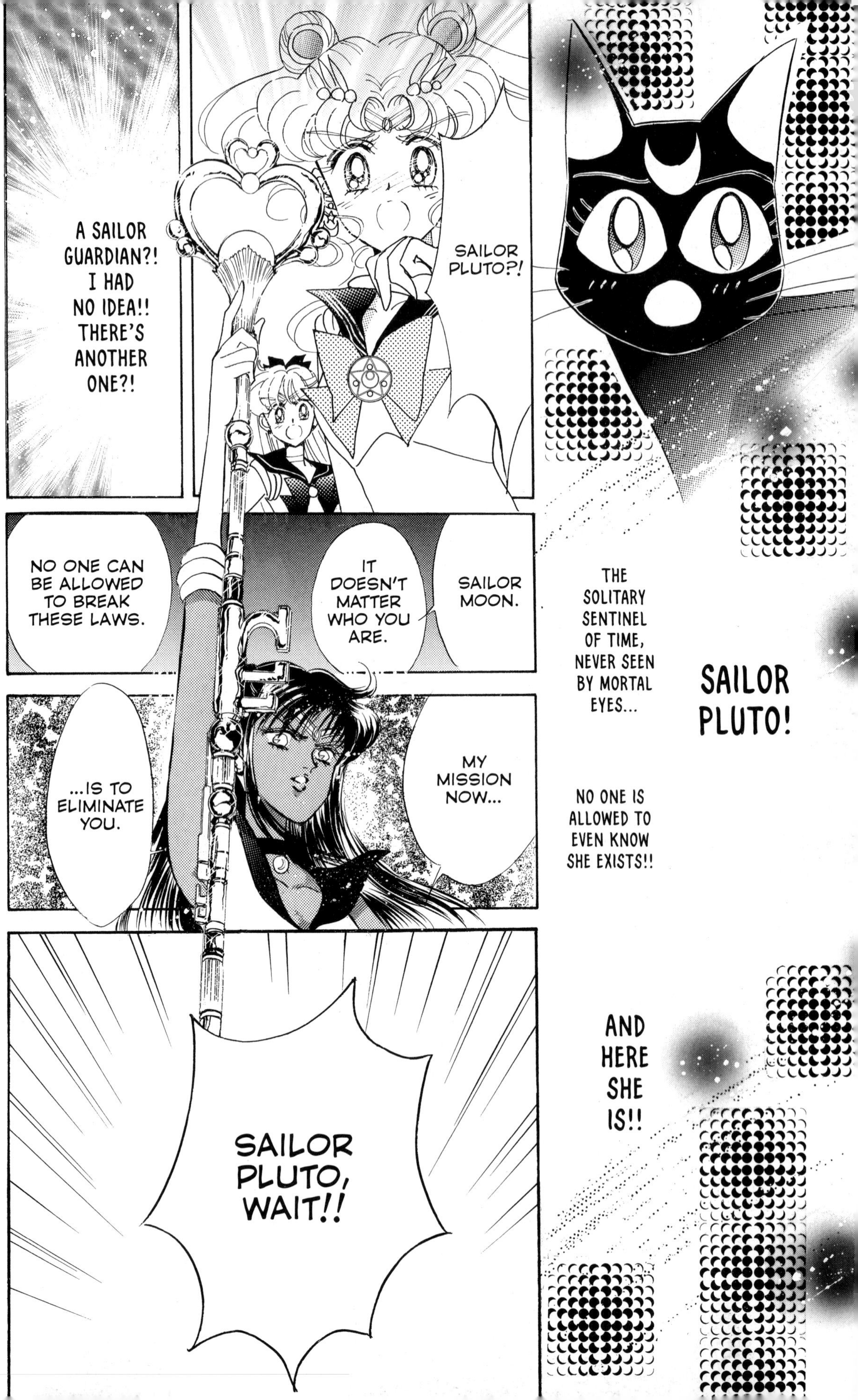
SAILOR PLUTO?!
SAILOR PLUTO!
THE SOLITARY SENTINEL OF TIME, NEVER SEEN BY MORTAL EYES...
NO ONE IS ALLOWED TO EVEN KNOW SHE EXISTS!!
AND HERE SHE IS!!
A SAILOR GUARDIAN?! I HAD NO IDEA!! THERE'S ANOTHER ONE?!
SAILOR MOON.
IT DOESN'T MATTER WHO YOU ARE.
NO ONE CAN BE ALLOWED TO BREAK THESE LAWS.
MY MISSION NOW...
...IS TO ELIMINATE YOU.
SAILOR PLUTO, WAIT!!

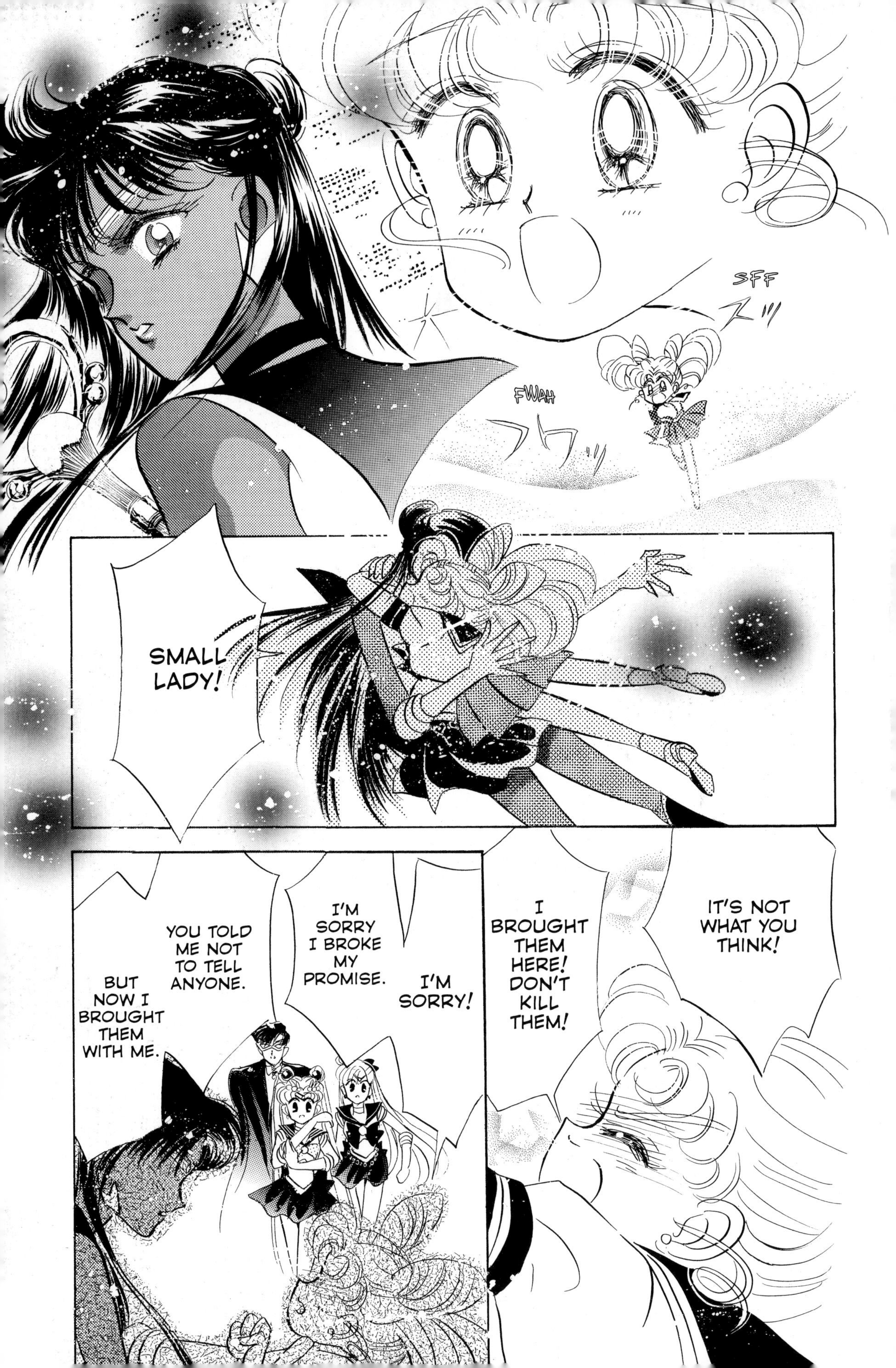
SFF
スッ
FWAH
フワッ
SMALL LADY!
IT'S NOT WHAT YOU THINK!
I BROUGHT THEM HERE! DON'T KILL THEM!
I'M SORRY!
I'M SORRY I BROKE MY PROMISE.
YOU TOLD ME NOT TO TELL ANYONE.
BUT NOW I BROUGHT THEM WITH ME.

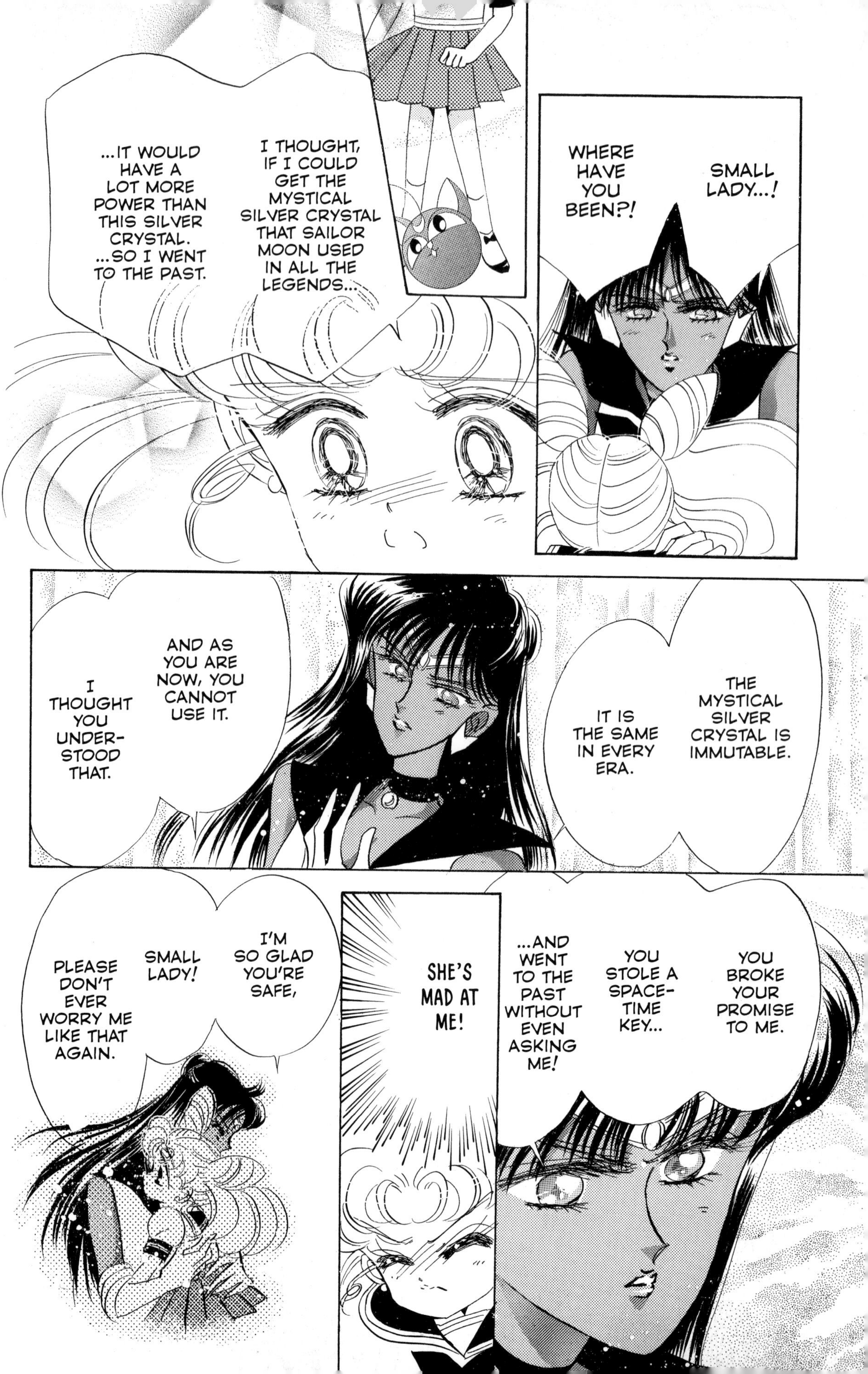
SMALL LADY...!
WHERE HAVE YOU BEEN?!
I THOUGHT, IF I COULD GET THE MYSTICAL SILVER CRYSTAL THAT SAILOR MOON USED IN ALL THE LEGENDS...
...IT WOULD HAVE A LOT MORE POWER THAN THIS SILVER CRYSTAL. ...SO I WENT TO THE PAST.
THE MYSTICAL SILVER CRYSTAL IS IMMUTABLE.
IT IS THE SAME IN EVERY ERA.
AND AS YOU ARE NOW, YOU CANNOT USE IT.
I THOUGHT YOU UNDER-STOOD THAT.
YOU BROKE YOUR PROMISE TO ME.
YOU STOLE A SPACE-TIME KEY...
...AND WENT TO THE PAST WITHOUT EVEN ASKING ME!
SHE'S MAD AT ME!
I'M SO GLAD YOU'RE SAFE,
SMALL LADY!
PLEASE DON'T EVER WORRY ME LIKE THAT AGAIN.

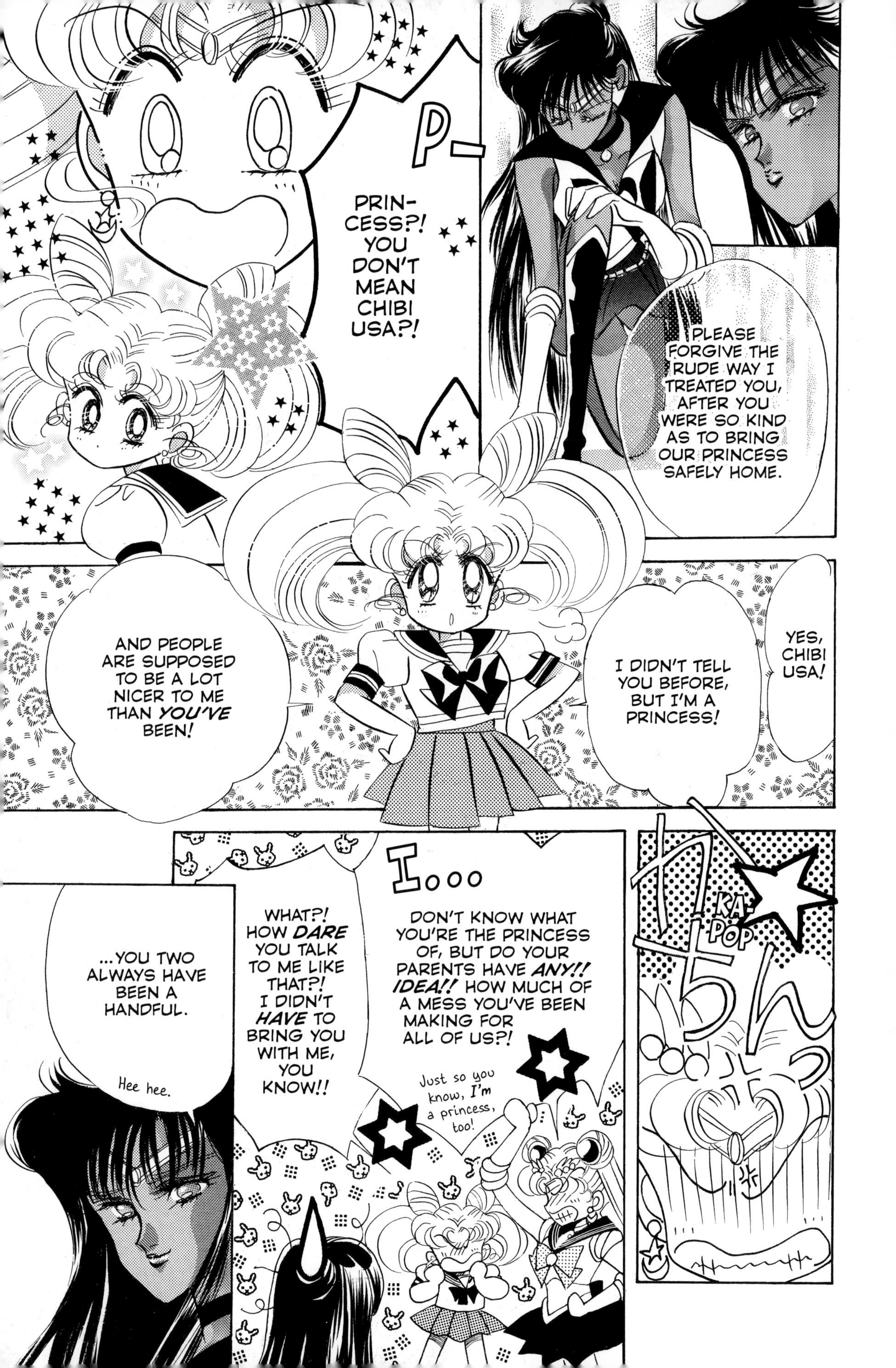
PLEASE FORGIVE THE RUDE WAY I TREATED YOU, AFTER YOU WERE SO KIND AS TO BRING OUR PRINCESS SAFELY HOME.
P-
PRIN-CESS?! YOU DON'T MEAN CHIBI USA?!
YES, CHIBI USA!
I DIDN'T TELL YOU BEFORE, BUT I'M A PRINCESS!
AND PEOPLE ARE SUPPOSED TO BE A LOT NICER TO ME THAN *YOU'VE* BEEN!
KA-POP
I...
DON'T KNOW WHAT YOU'RE THE PRINCESS OF, BUT DO YOUR PARENTS HAVE *ANY!! IDEA!!* HOW MUCH OF A MESS YOU'VE BEEN MAKING FOR ALL OF US?!
WHAT?! HOW *DARE* YOU TALK TO ME LIKE THAT?! I DIDN'T *HAVE* TO BRING YOU WITH ME, YOU KNOW!!
Just so you know, I'm a princess, too!
...YOU TWO ALWAYS HAVE BEEN A HANDFUL.
Hee hee.

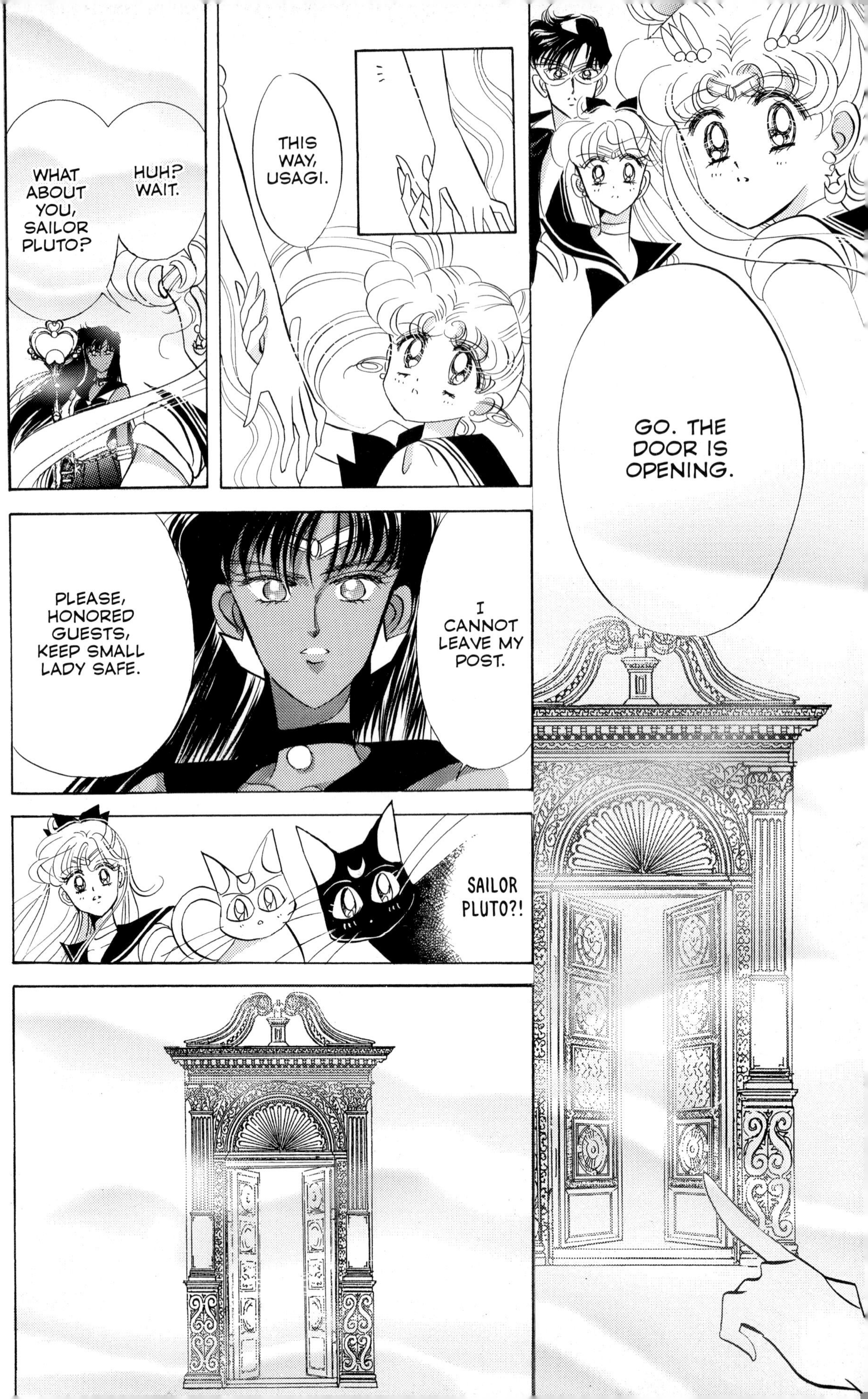
GO. THE DOOR IS OPENING.
THIS WAY, USAGI.
HUH? WAIT.
WHAT ABOUT YOU, SAILOR PLUTO?
I CANNOT LEAVE MY POST.
PLEASE, HONORED GUESTS, KEEP SMALL LADY SAFE.
SAILOR PLUTO?!

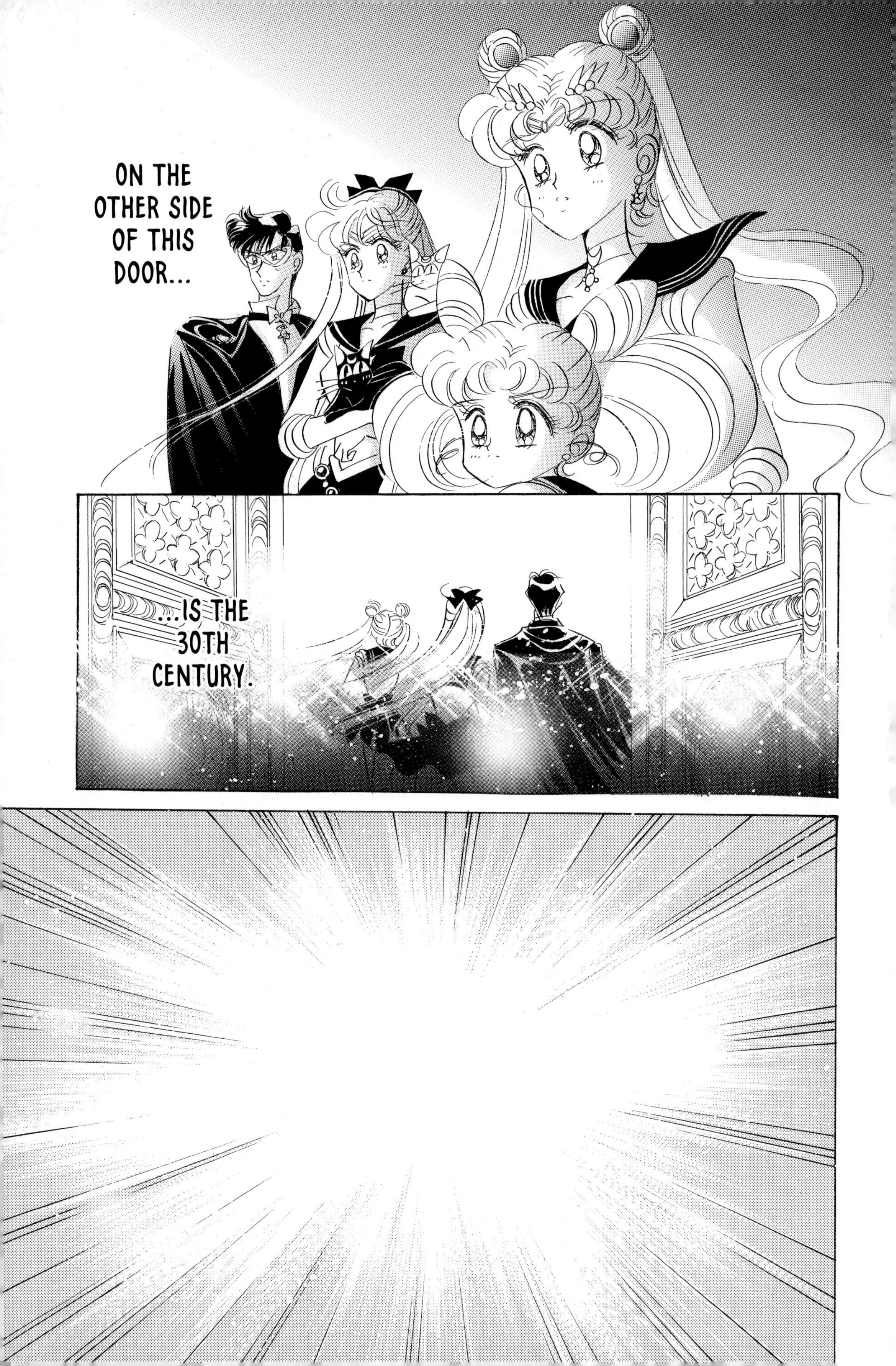
ON THE OTHER SIDE OF THIS DOOR...
...IS THE 30TH CENTURY.

THE MOON IS SO CLOSE...

HANGING HEAVILY IN THE SKY.

THE DOOR...

THIS...

FFT

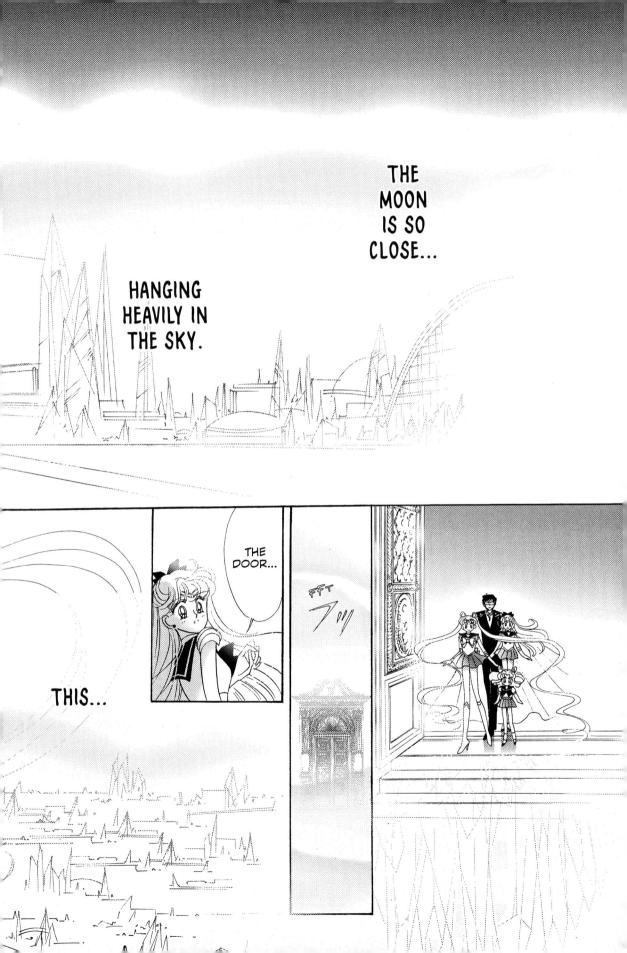

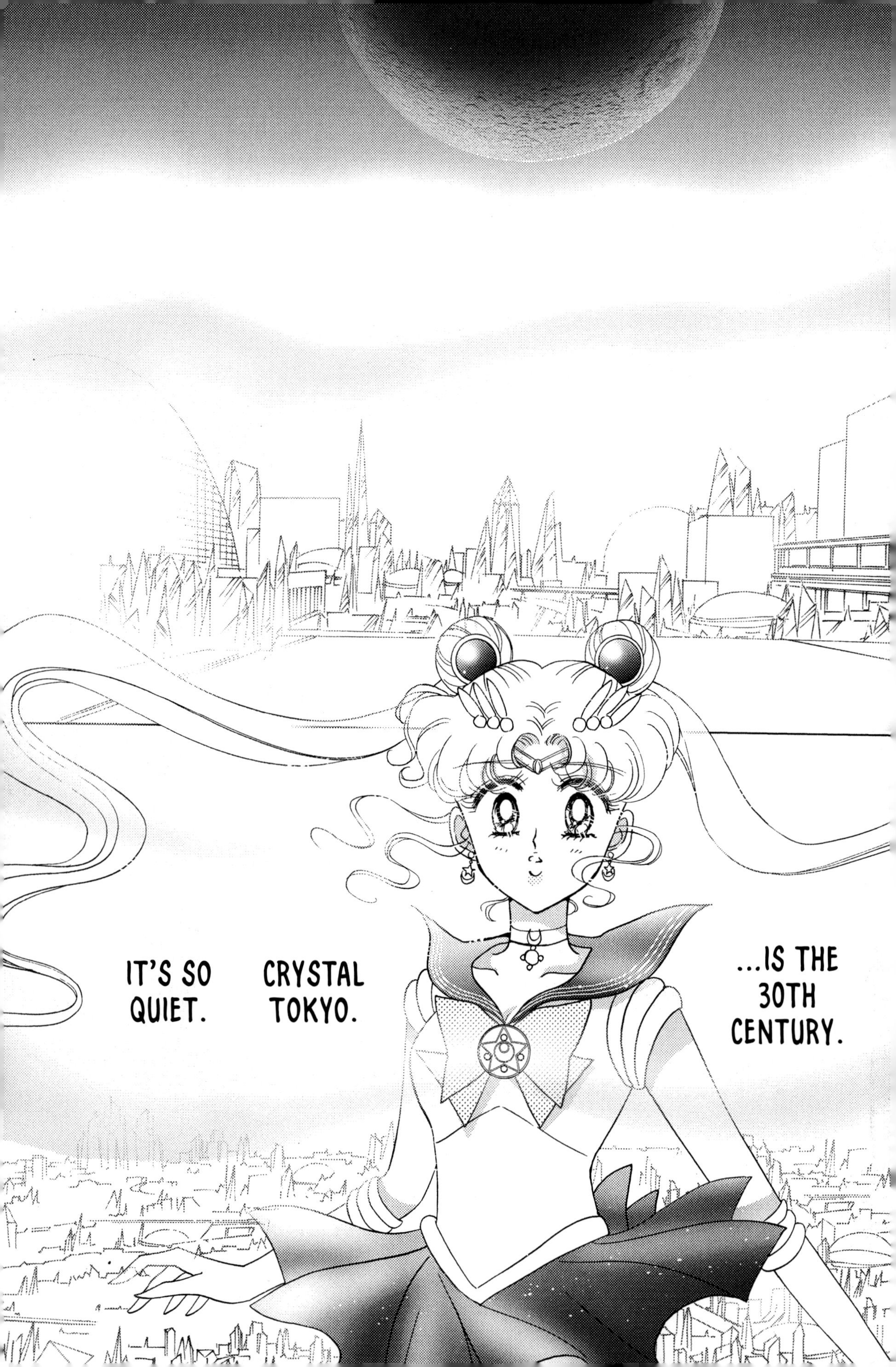
...IS THE 30TH CENTURY.
CRYSTAL TOKYO.
IT'S SO QUIET.

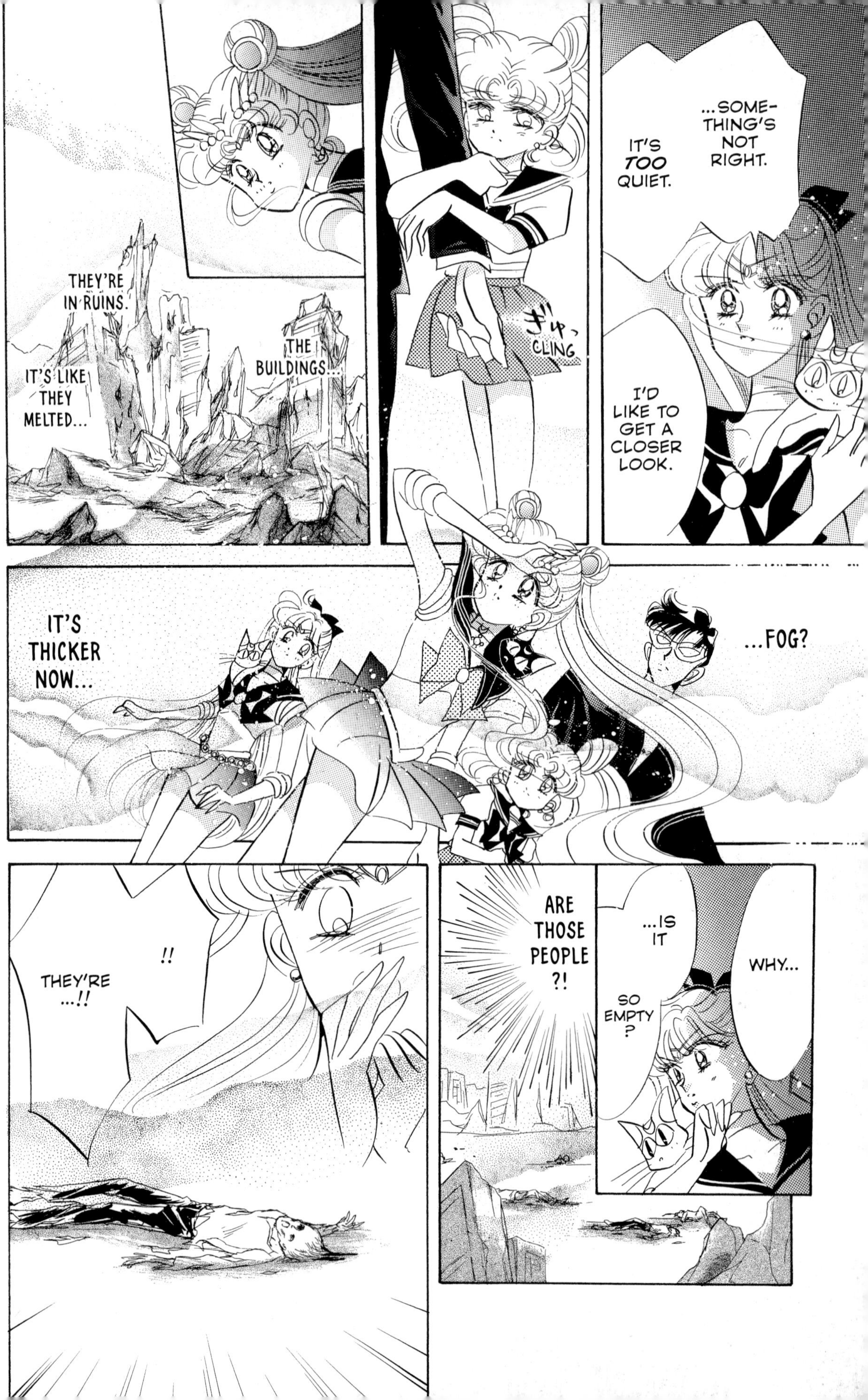
...SOME-THING'S NOT RIGHT.
IT'S TOO QUIET.
I'D LIKE TO GET A CLOSER LOOK.
ぎゅっ
CLING
THE BUILDINGS...
THEY'RE IN RUINS.
IT'S LIKE THEY MELTED...
...FOG?
IT'S THICKER NOW...
WHY...
...IS IT SO EMPTY?
ARE THOSE PEOPLE?!
!!
THEY'RE ...!!

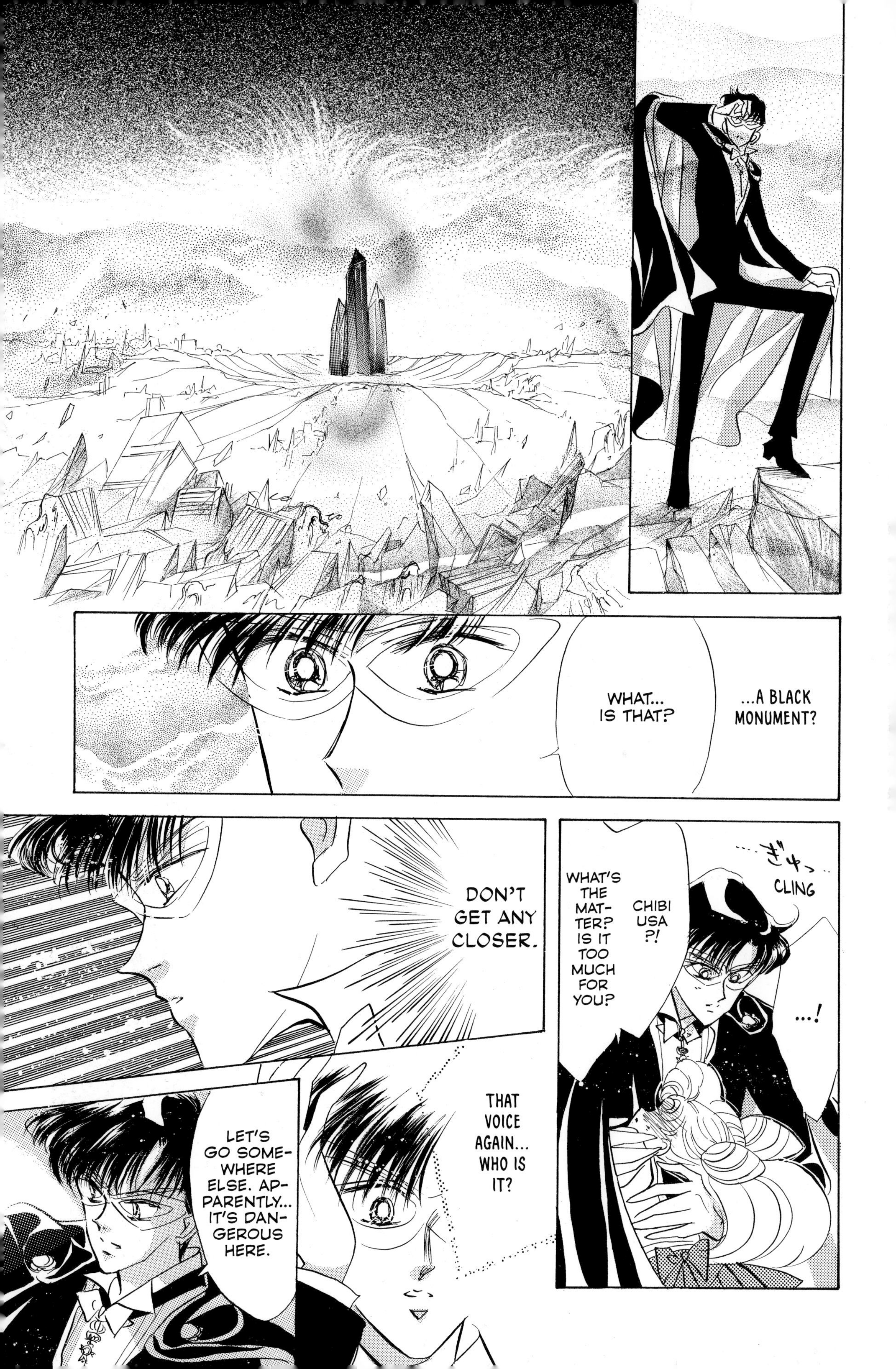
...A BLACK MONUMENT?
WHAT... IS THAT?
...ぎゅっ... CLING
...!
CHIBI USA ?!
WHAT'S THE MAT-TER? IS IT TOO MUCH FOR YOU?
DON'T GET ANY CLOSER.
THAT VOICE AGAIN... WHO IS IT?
LET'S GO SOME-WHERE ELSE. AP-PARENTLY... IT'S DAN-GEROUS HERE.

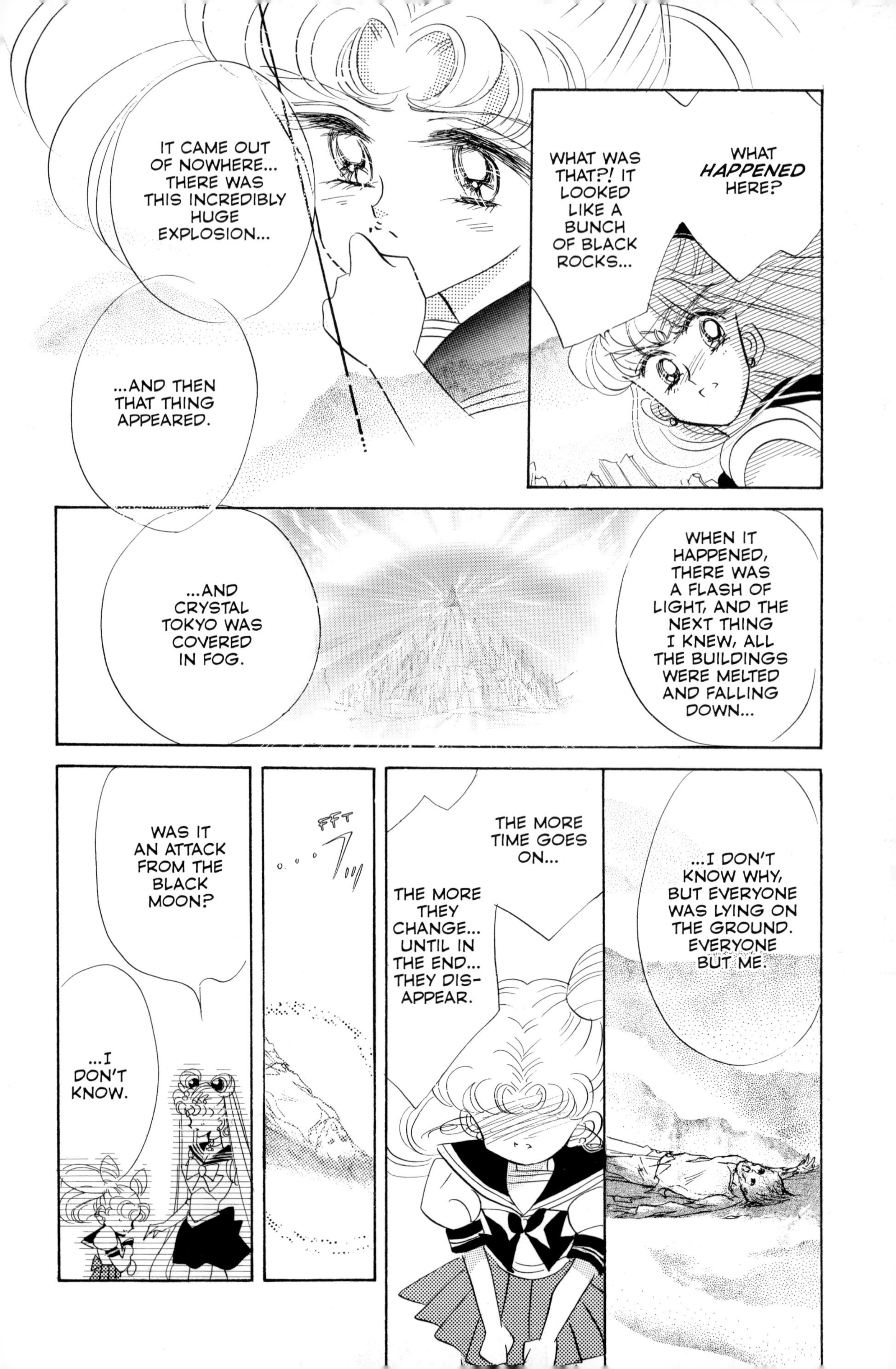
WHAT *HAPPENED* HERE?
WHAT WAS THAT?! IT LOOKED LIKE A BUNCH OF BLACK ROCKS...
IT CAME OUT OF NOWHERE... THERE WAS THIS INCREDIBLY HUGE EXPLOSION...
...AND THEN THAT THING APPEARED.
WHEN IT HAPPENED, THERE WAS A FLASH OF LIGHT, AND THE NEXT THING I KNEW, ALL THE BUILDINGS WERE MELTED AND FALLING DOWN...
...AND CRYSTAL TOKYO WAS COVERED IN FOG.
...I DON'T KNOW WHY, BUT EVERYONE WAS LYING ON THE GROUND. EVERYONE BUT ME.
THE MORE TIME GOES ON...
THE MORE THEY CHANGE... UNTIL IN THE END... THEY DIS-APPEAR.
FFT
...
WAS IT AN ATTACK FROM THE BLACK MOON?
...I DON'T KNOW.

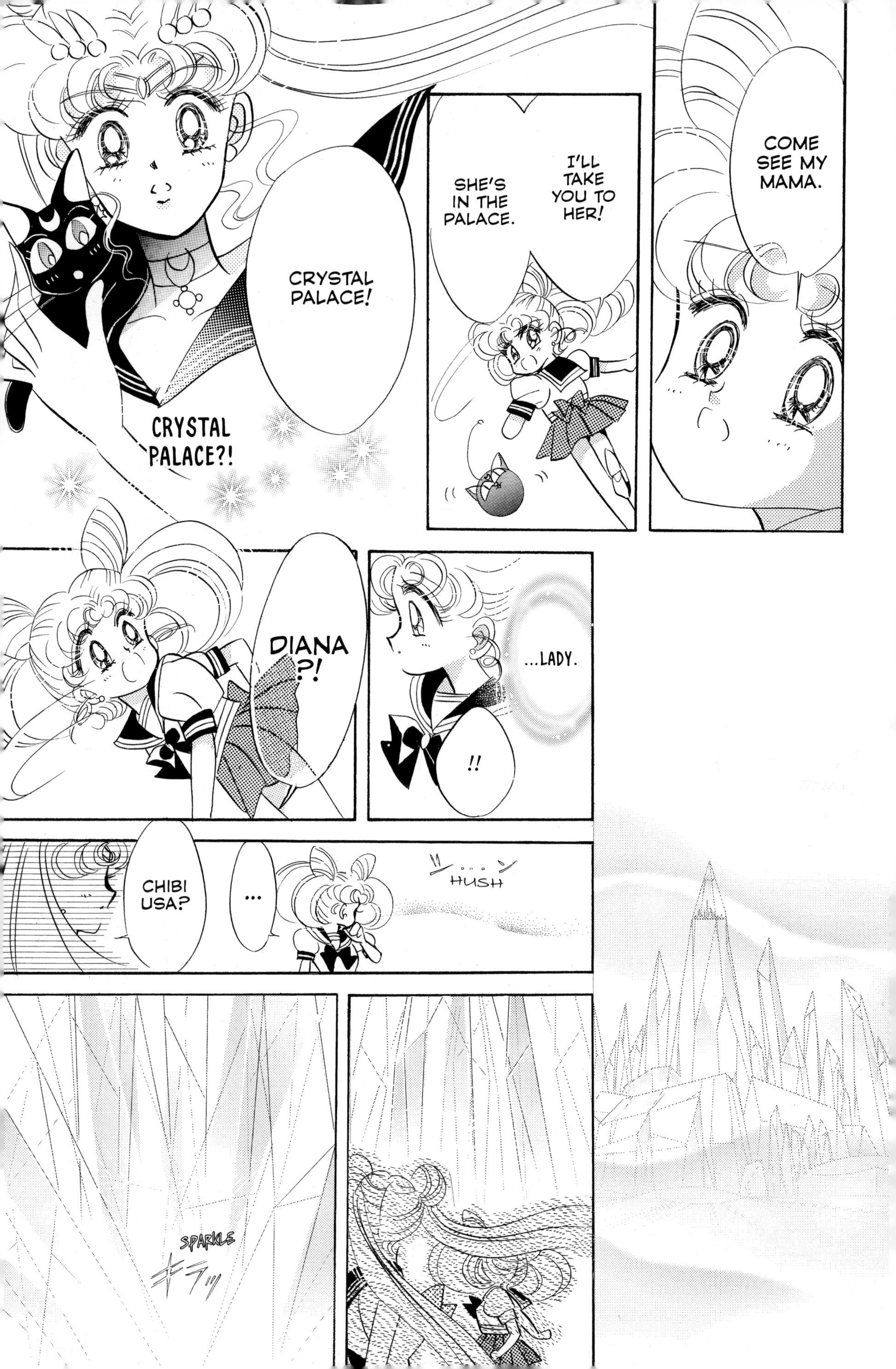
COME SEE MY MAMA.
I'LL TAKE YOU TO HER!
SHE'S IN THE PALACE.
CRYSTAL PALACE!
CRYSTAL PALACE?!
...LADY.
!!
DIANA?!
HUSH
...
CHIBI USA?
SPARKLE
キラッ

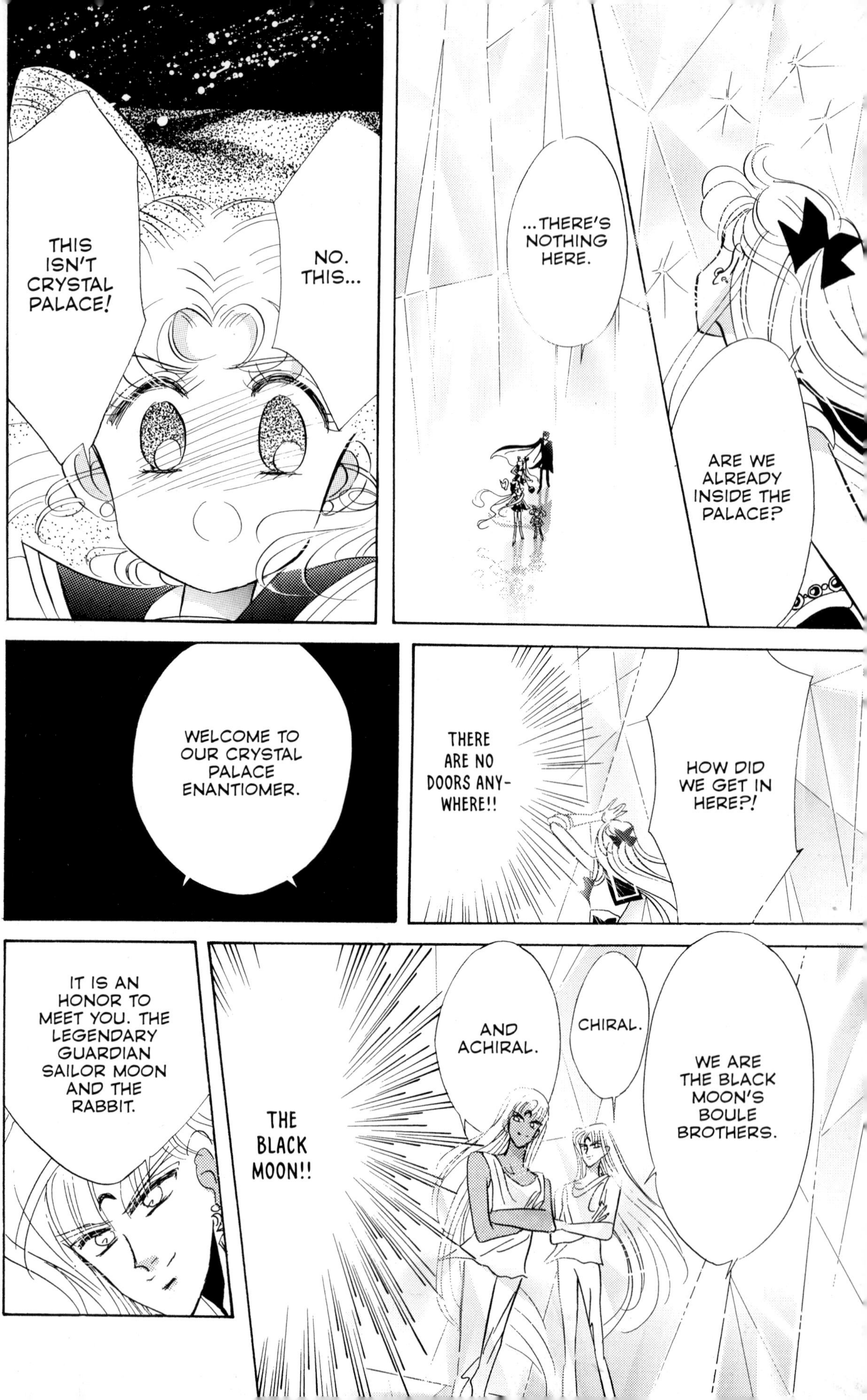
ARE WE ALREADY INSIDE THE PALACE?
...THERE'S NOTHING HERE.
NO. THIS...
THIS ISN'T CRYSTAL PALACE!
HOW DID WE GET IN HERE?!
THERE ARE NO DOORS ANY-WHERE!!
WELCOME TO OUR CRYSTAL PALACE ENANTIOMER.
WE ARE THE BLACK MOON'S BOULE BROTHERS.
CHIRAL.
AND ACHIRAL.
THE BLACK MOON!!
IT IS AN HONOR TO MEET YOU. THE LEGENDARY GUARDIAN SAILOR MOON AND THE RABBIT.

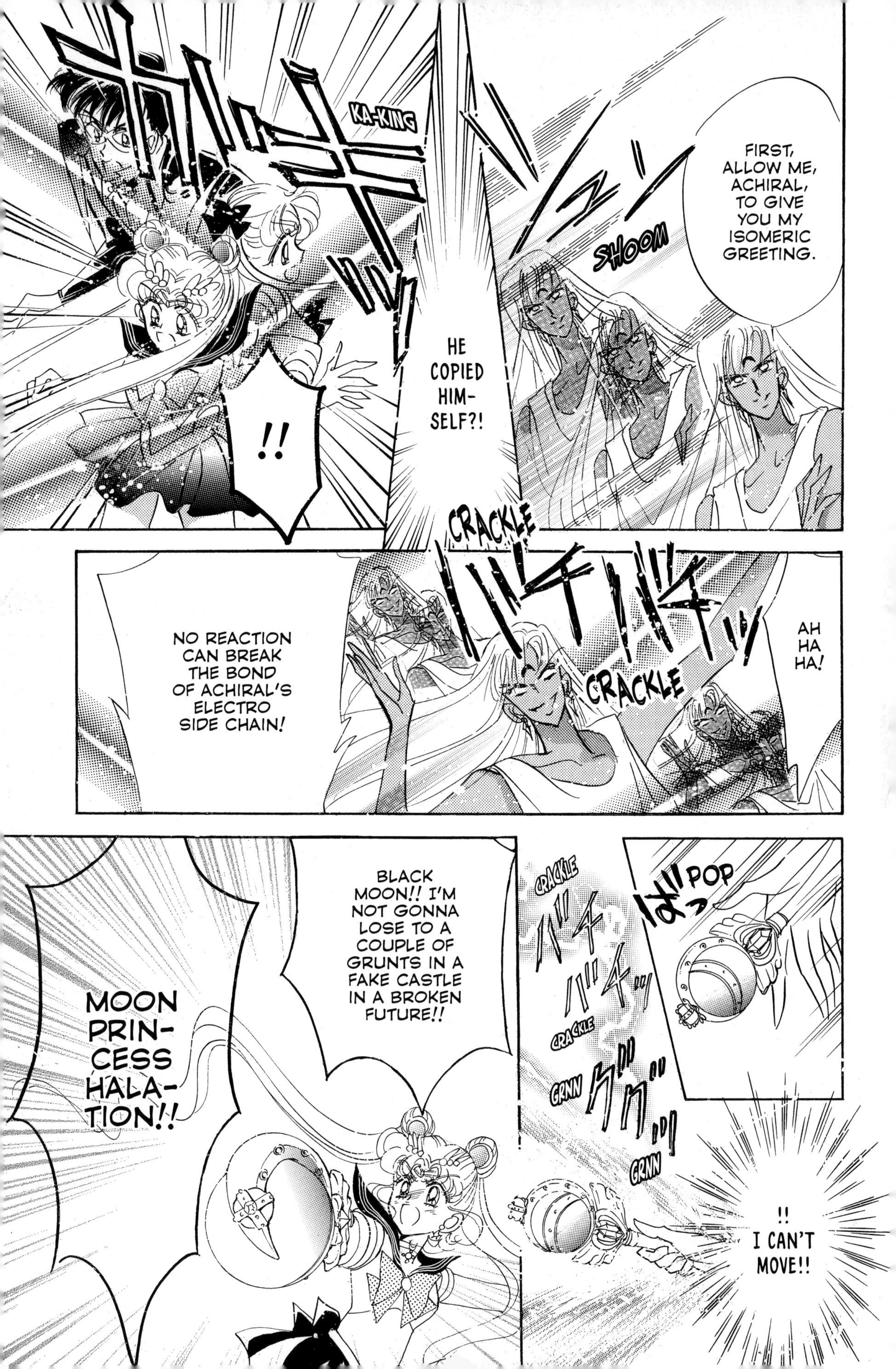
FIRST, ALLOW ME, ACHIRAL, TO GIVE YOU MY ISOMERIC GREETING.
SHOOM
HE COPIED HIMSELF?!
KA-KING
!!
AH HA HA!
CRACKLE
CRACKLE
NO REACTION CAN BREAK THE BOND OF ACHIRAL'S ELECTRO SIDE CHAIN!
POP
CRACKLE
CRACKLE
GRNN
GRNN
!! I CAN'T MOVE!!
BLACK MOON!! I'M NOT GONNA LOSE TO A COUPLE OF GRUNTS IN A FAKE CASTLE IN A BROKEN FUTURE!!
MOON PRINCESS HALATION!!

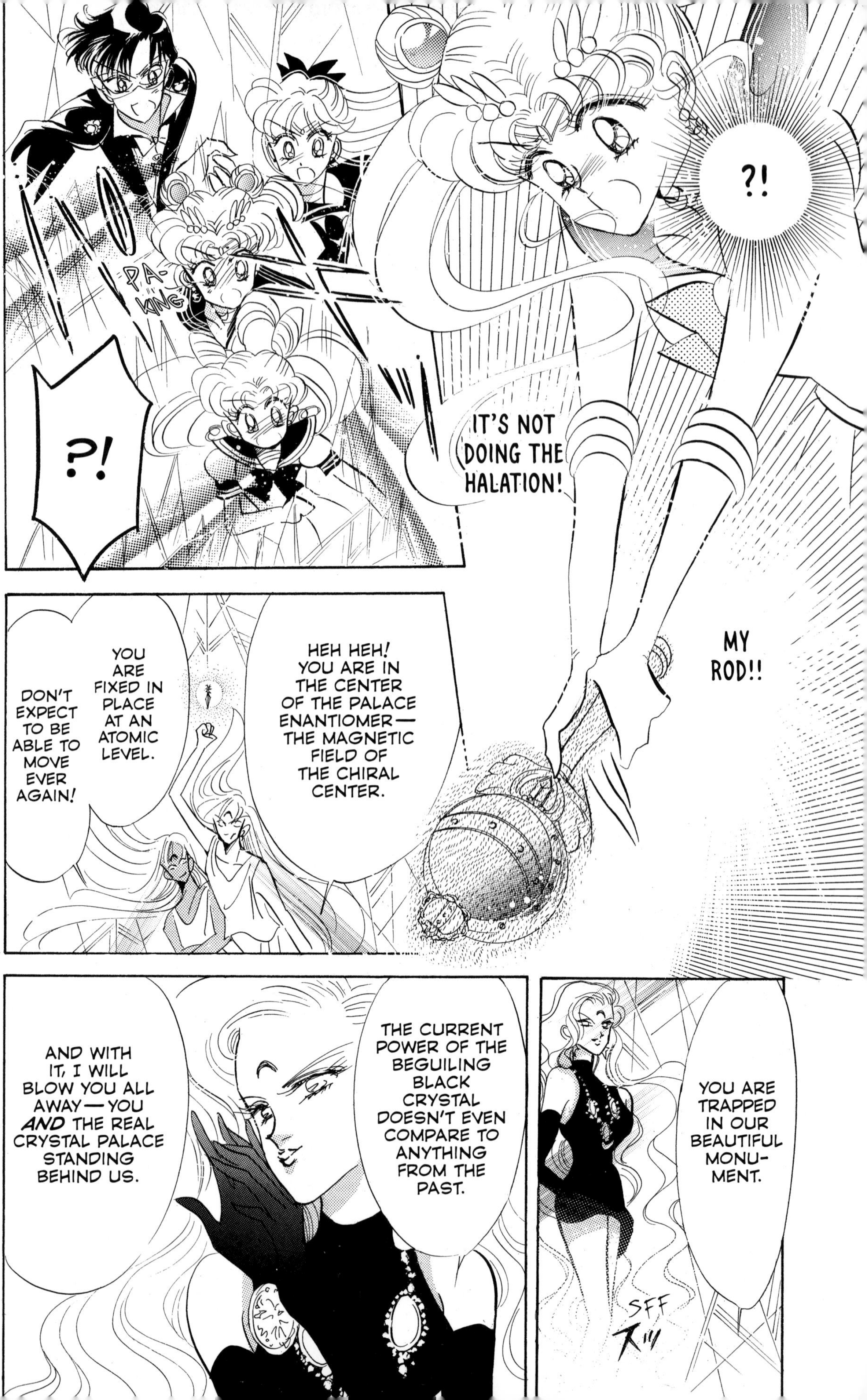
?!
IT'S NOT DOING THE HALATION!
MY ROD!!
PA-KING
?!
HEH HEH! YOU ARE IN THE CENTER OF THE PALACE ENANTIOMER— THE MAGNETIC FIELD OF THE CHIRAL CENTER.
YOU ARE FIXED IN PLACE AT AN ATOMIC LEVEL.
DON'T EXPECT TO BE ABLE TO MOVE EVER AGAIN!
YOU ARE TRAPPED IN OUR BEAUTIFUL MONU-MENT.
SFF
THE CURRENT POWER OF THE BEGUILING BLACK CRYSTAL DOESN'T EVEN COMPARE TO ANYTHING FROM THE PAST.
AND WITH IT, I WILL BLOW YOU ALL AWAY—YOU ***AND*** THE REAL CRYSTAL PALACE STANDING BEHIND US.

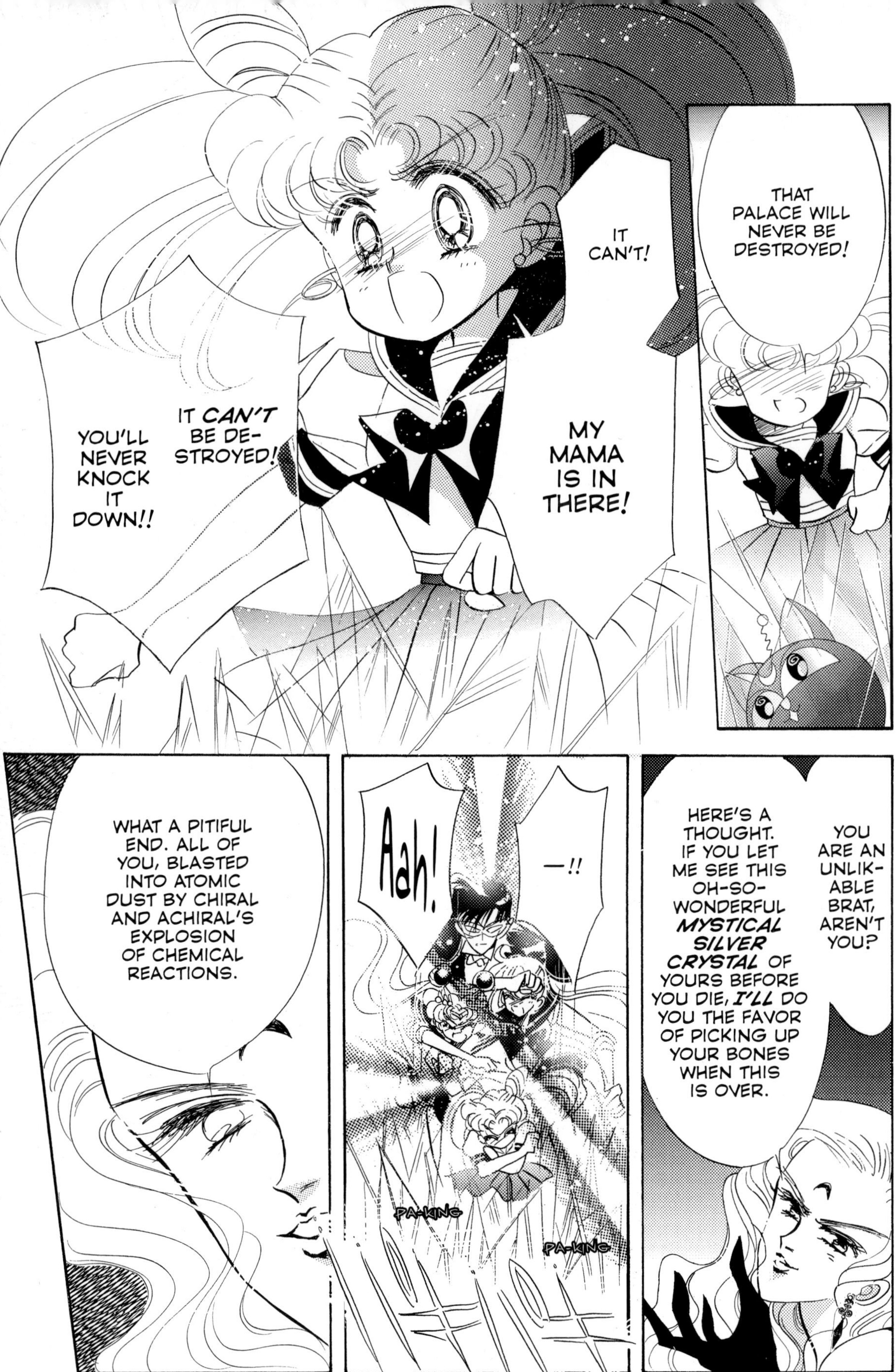
THAT PALACE WILL NEVER BE DESTROYED!
IT CAN'T!
MY MAMA IS IN THERE!
IT *CAN'T* BE DE-STROYED!
YOU'LL NEVER KNOCK IT DOWN!!
YOU ARE AN UNLIKABLE BRAT, AREN'T YOU?
HERE'S A THOUGHT. IF YOU LET ME SEE THIS OH-SO-WONDERFUL ***MYSTICAL SILVER CRYSTAL*** OF YOURS BEFORE YOU DIE, ***I'LL*** DO YOU THE FAVOR OF PICKING UP YOUR BONES WHEN THIS IS OVER.
—!!
Aah!
PA-KING
PA-KING
WHAT A PITIFUL END. ALL OF YOU, BLASTED INTO ATOMIC DUST BY CHIRAL AND ACHIRAL'S EXPLOSION OF CHEMICAL REACTIONS.

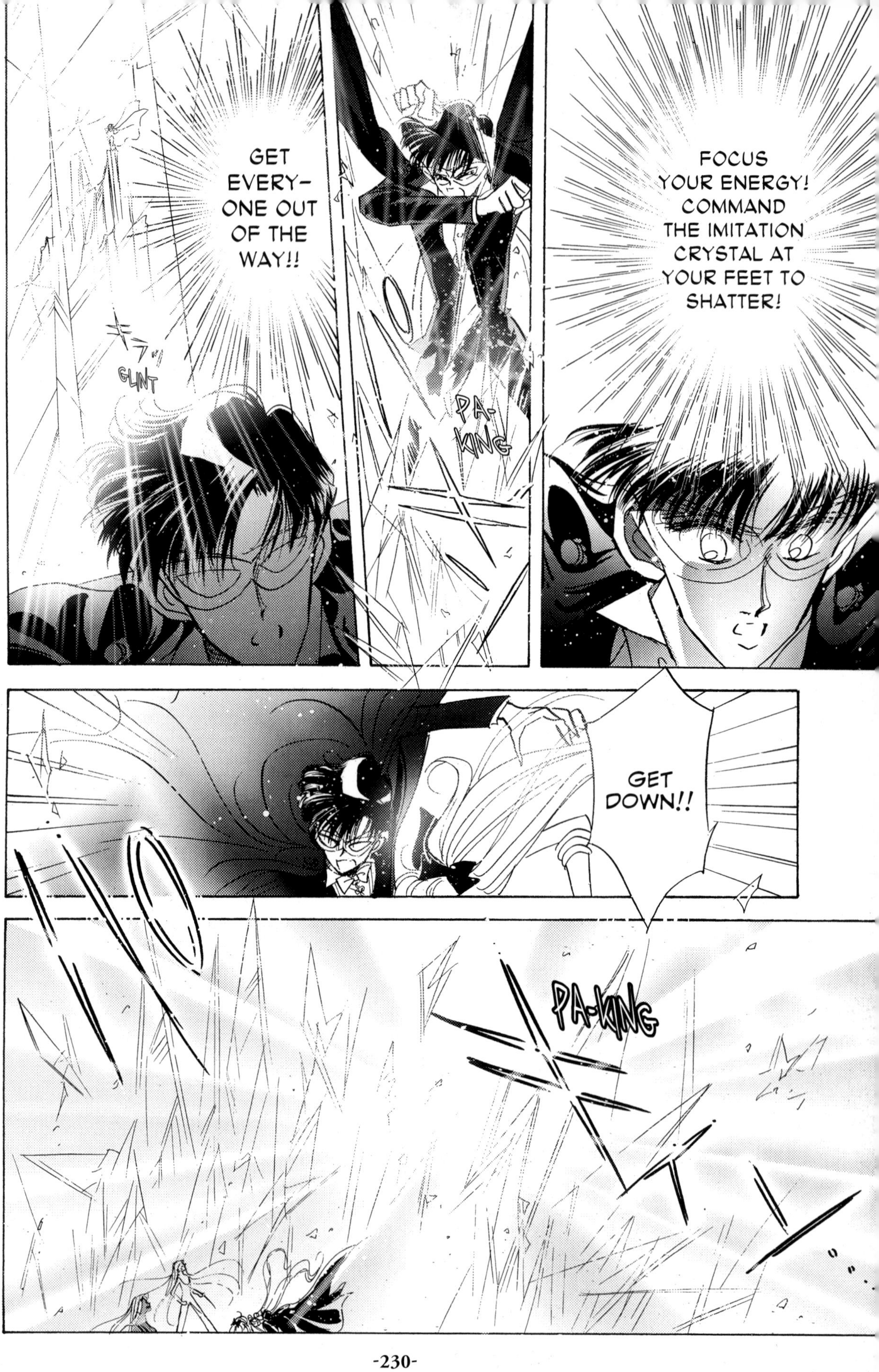
FOCUS YOUR ENERGY! COMMAND THE IMITATION CRYSTAL AT YOUR FEET TO SHATTER!
PA-KING
GET EVERY-ONE OUT OF THE WAY!!
GLINT
GET DOWN!!
PA-KING

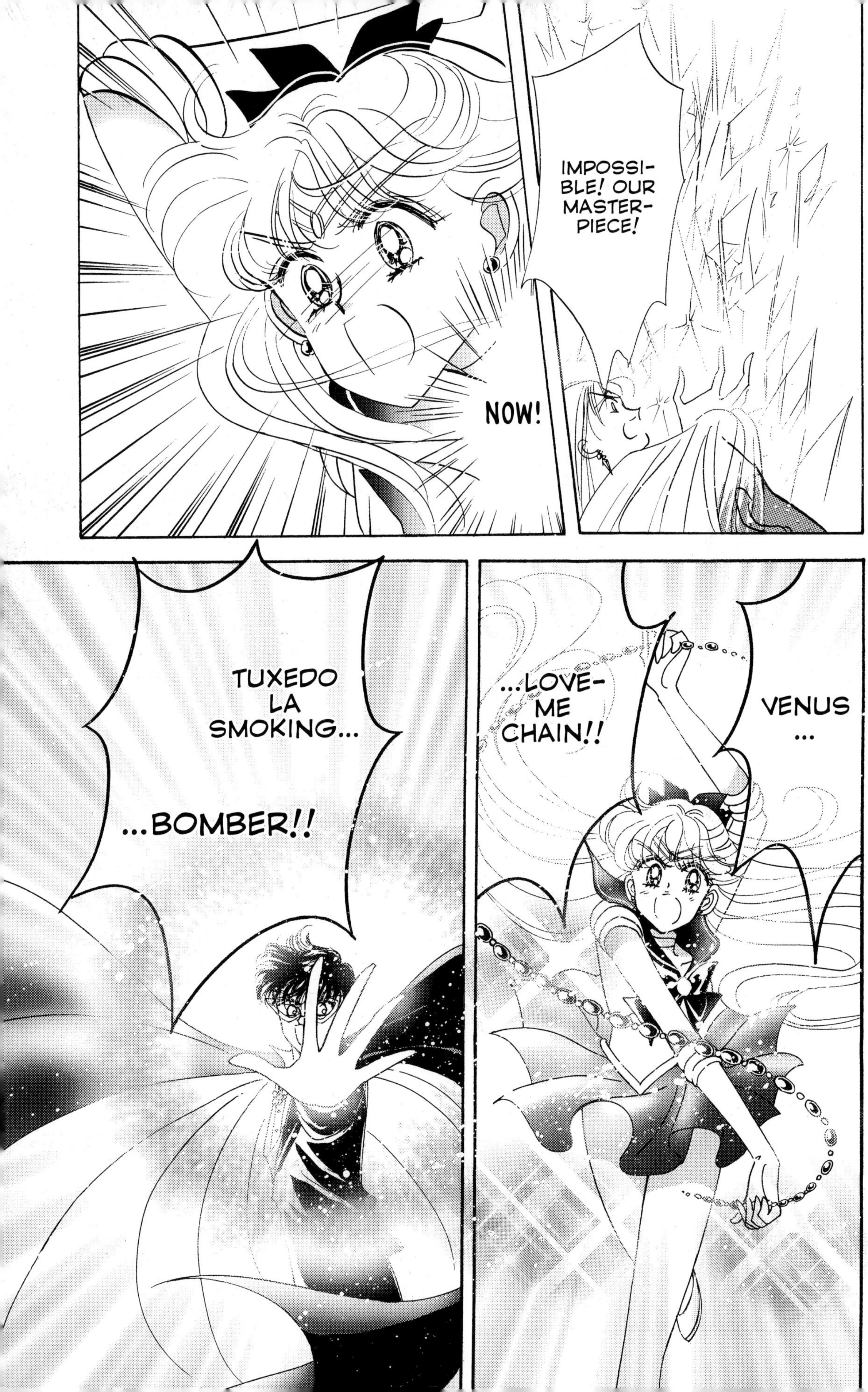
IMPOSSIBLE! OUR MASTERPIECE!
NOW!
VENUS ...
...LOVE-ME CHAIN!!
TUXEDO LA SMOKING...
...BOMBER!!

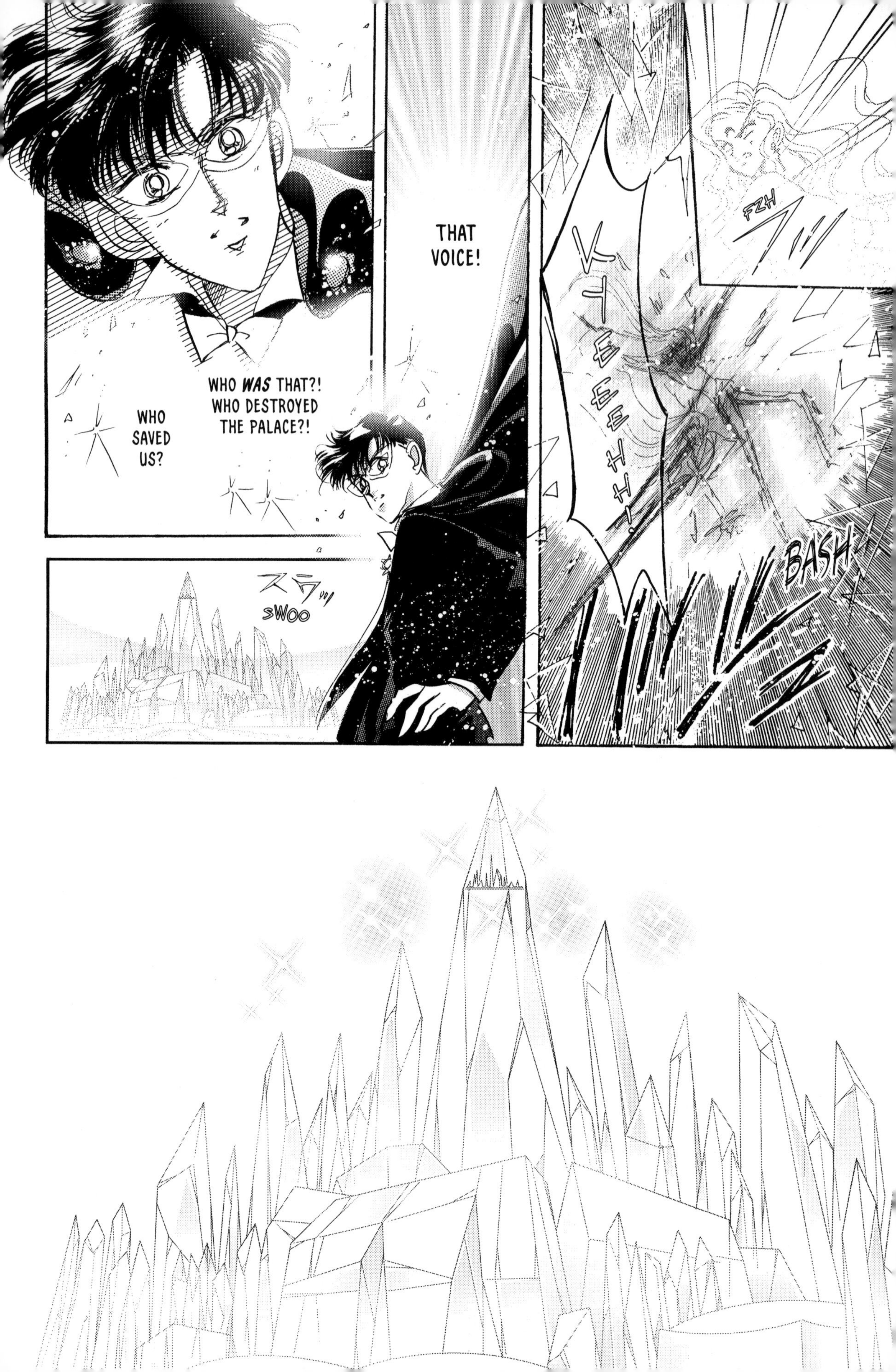
FZH
KYEEEHH!
BASH
THAT VOICE!
WHO WAS THAT?! WHO DESTROYED THE PALACE?!
WHO SAVED US?
SWOO

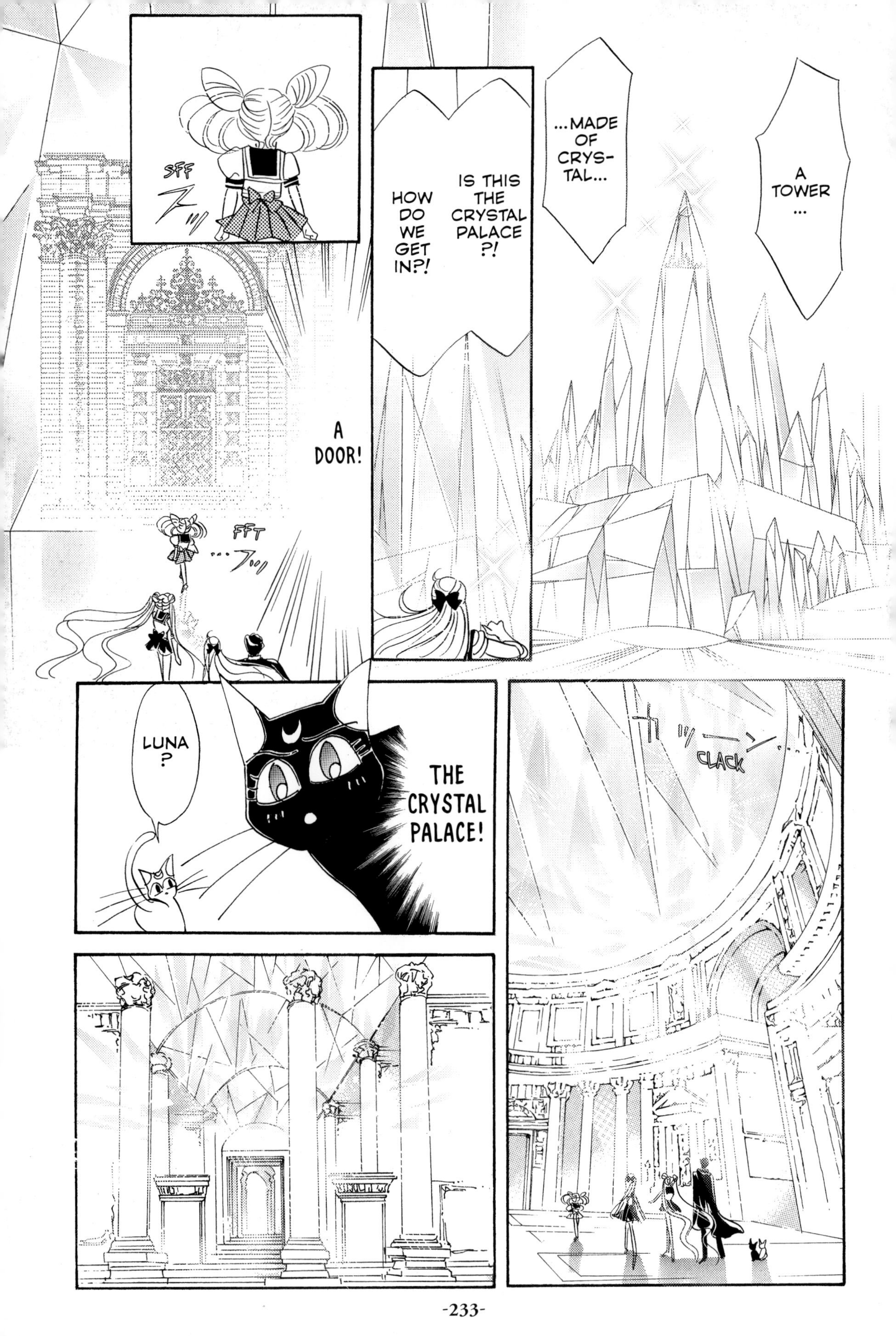

A TOWER ...
...MADE OF CRYS-TAL...
IS THIS THE CRYSTAL PALACE ?!
HOW DO WE GET IN?!
SFF
A DOOR!
FFT
CLACK
THE CRYSTAL PALACE!
LUNA ?

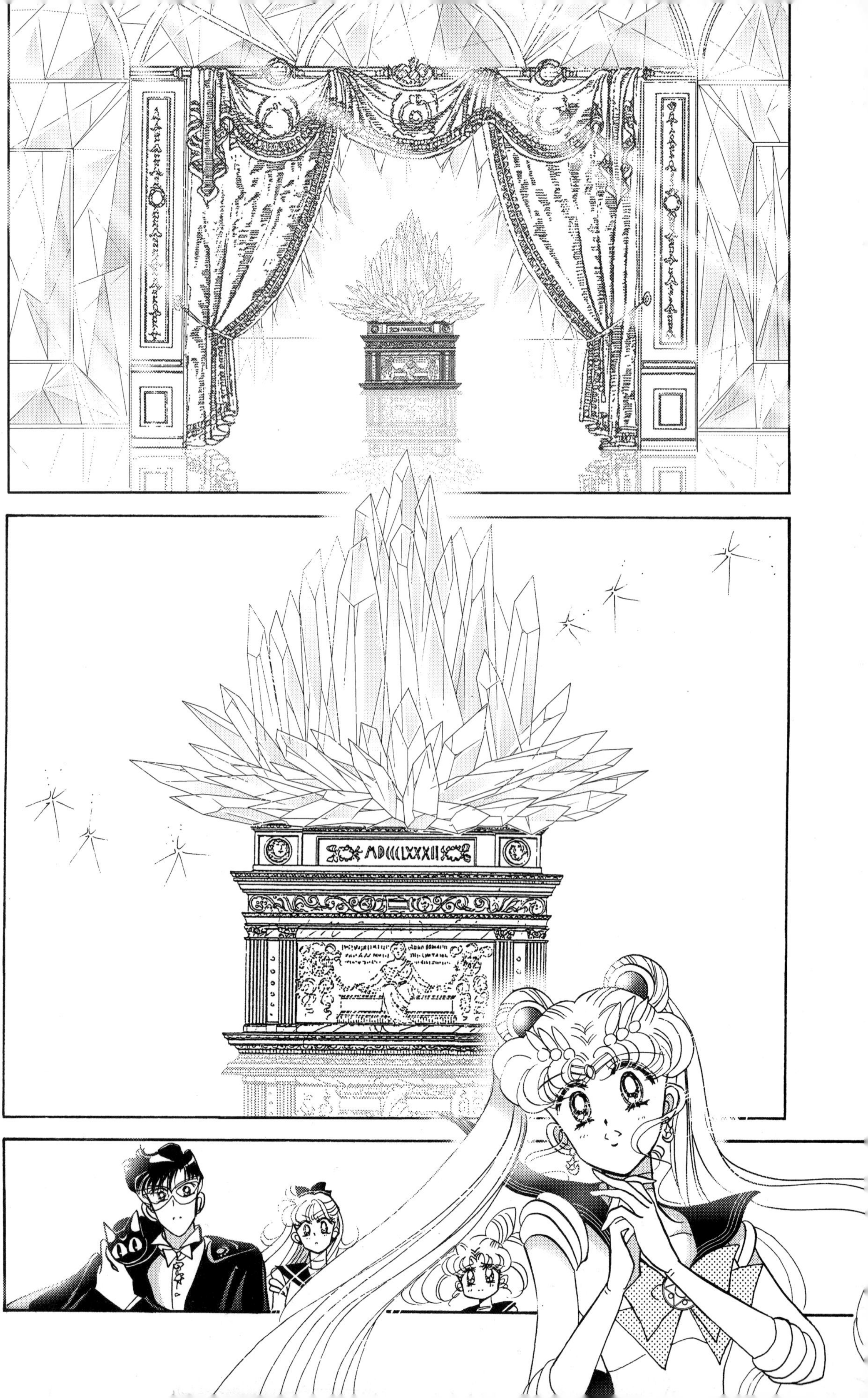
MDCCCLXXXII

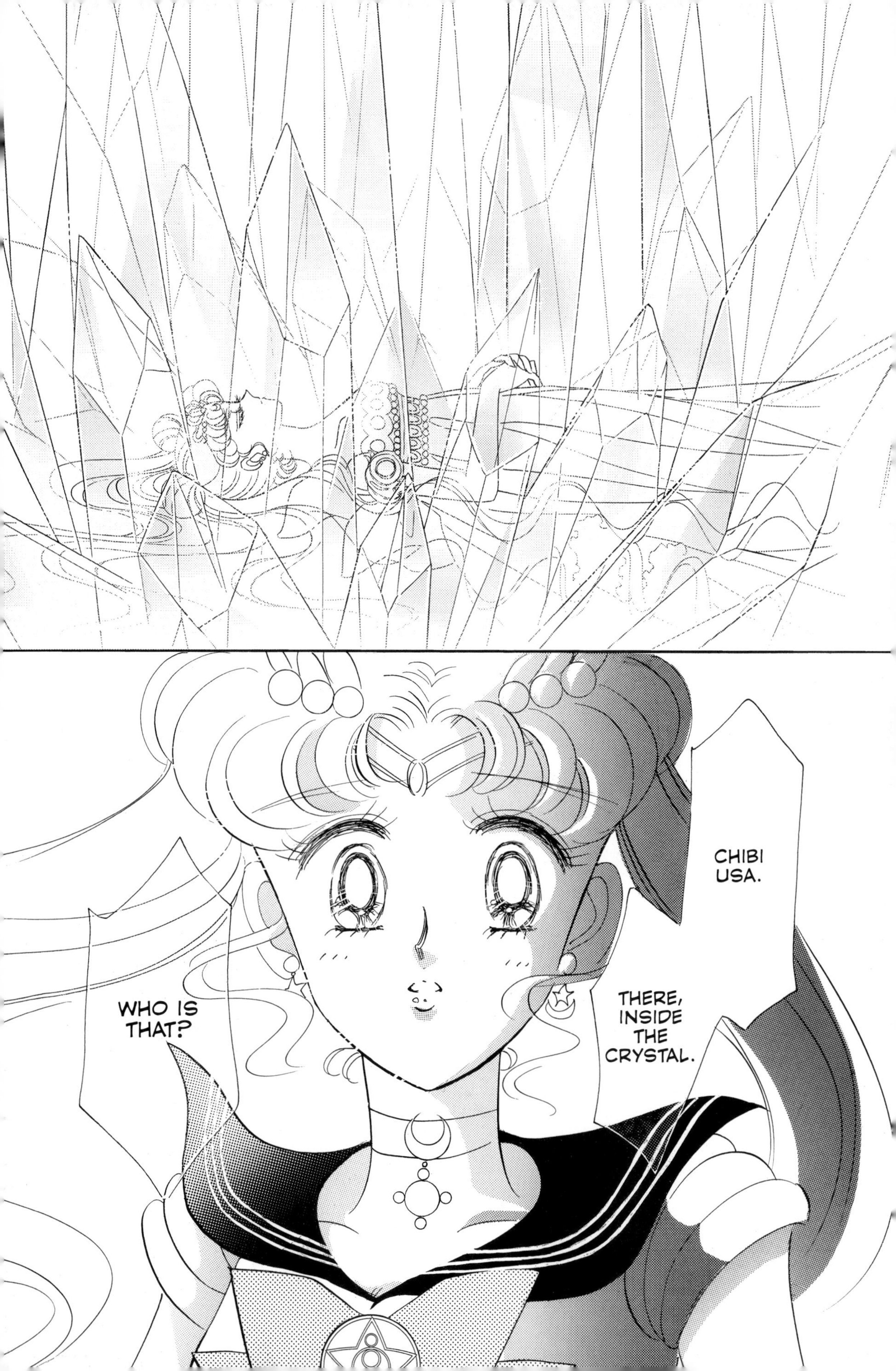
CHIBI USA.
THERE, INSIDE THE CRYSTAL.
WHO IS THAT?

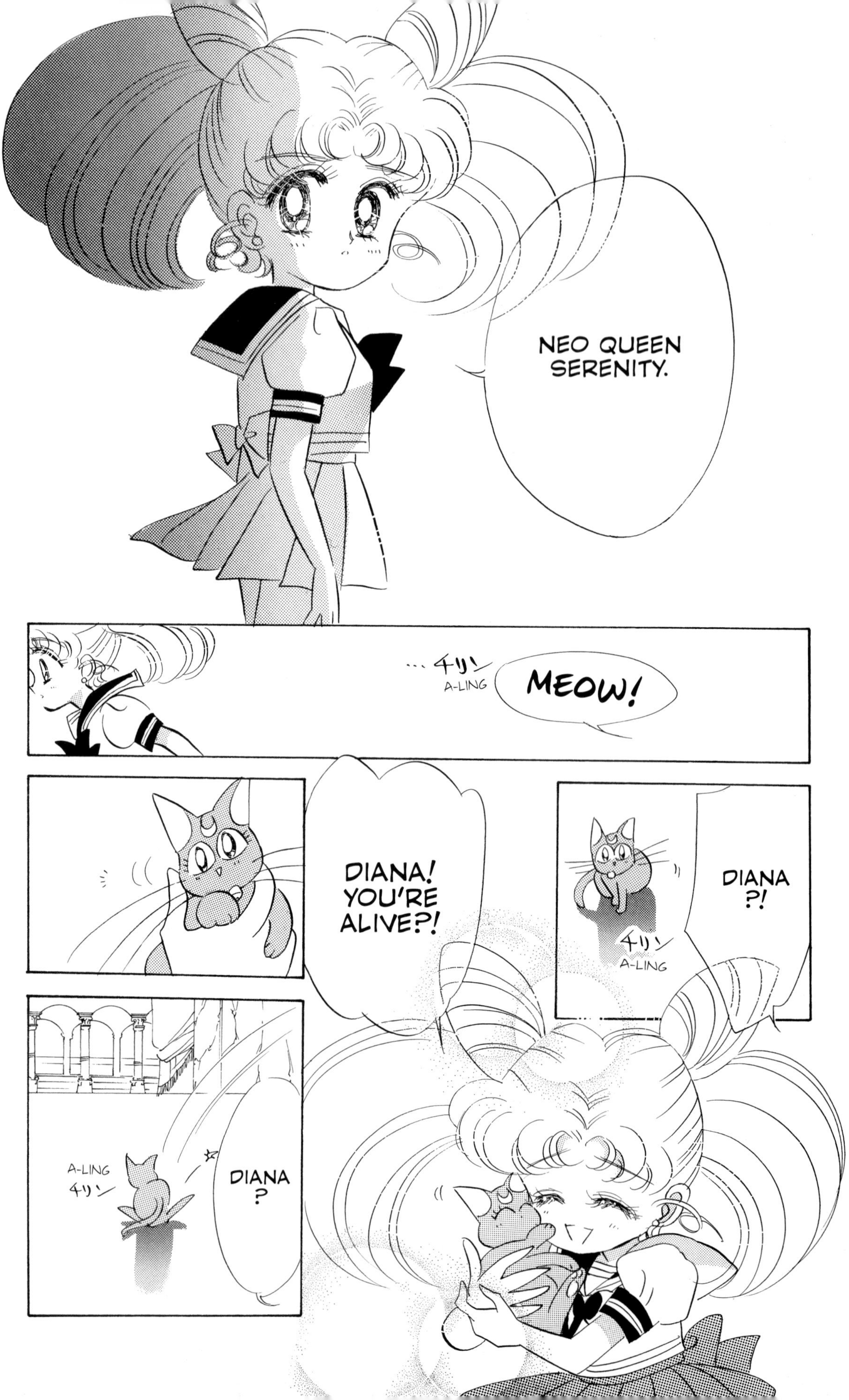
NEO QUEEN SERENITY.
MEOW!
...チリン
A-LING
DIANA ?!
チリン
A-LING
A-LING
チリン
DIANA ?
DIANA! YOU'RE ALIVE?!

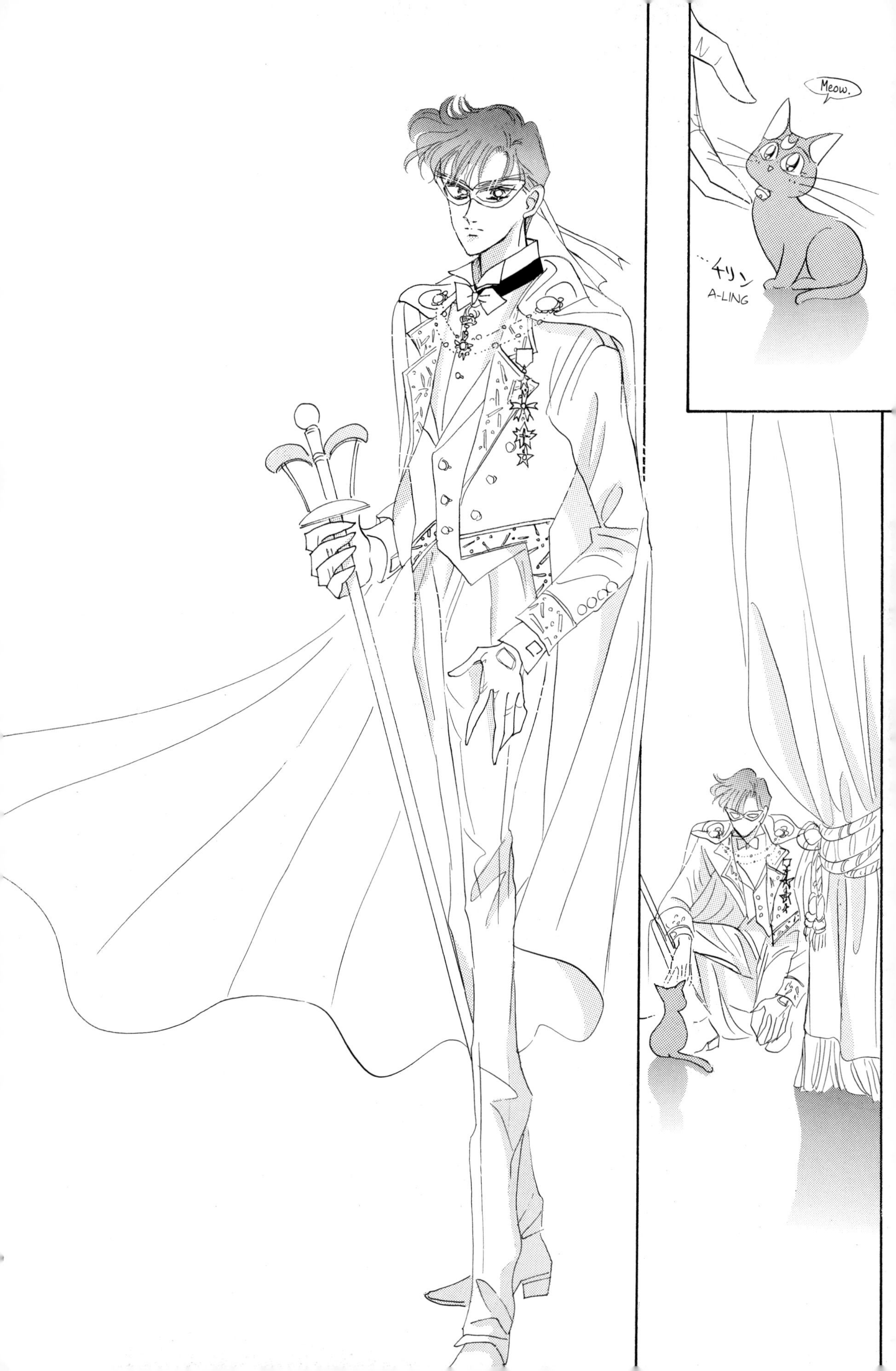
Meow.
…イリン
A-LING

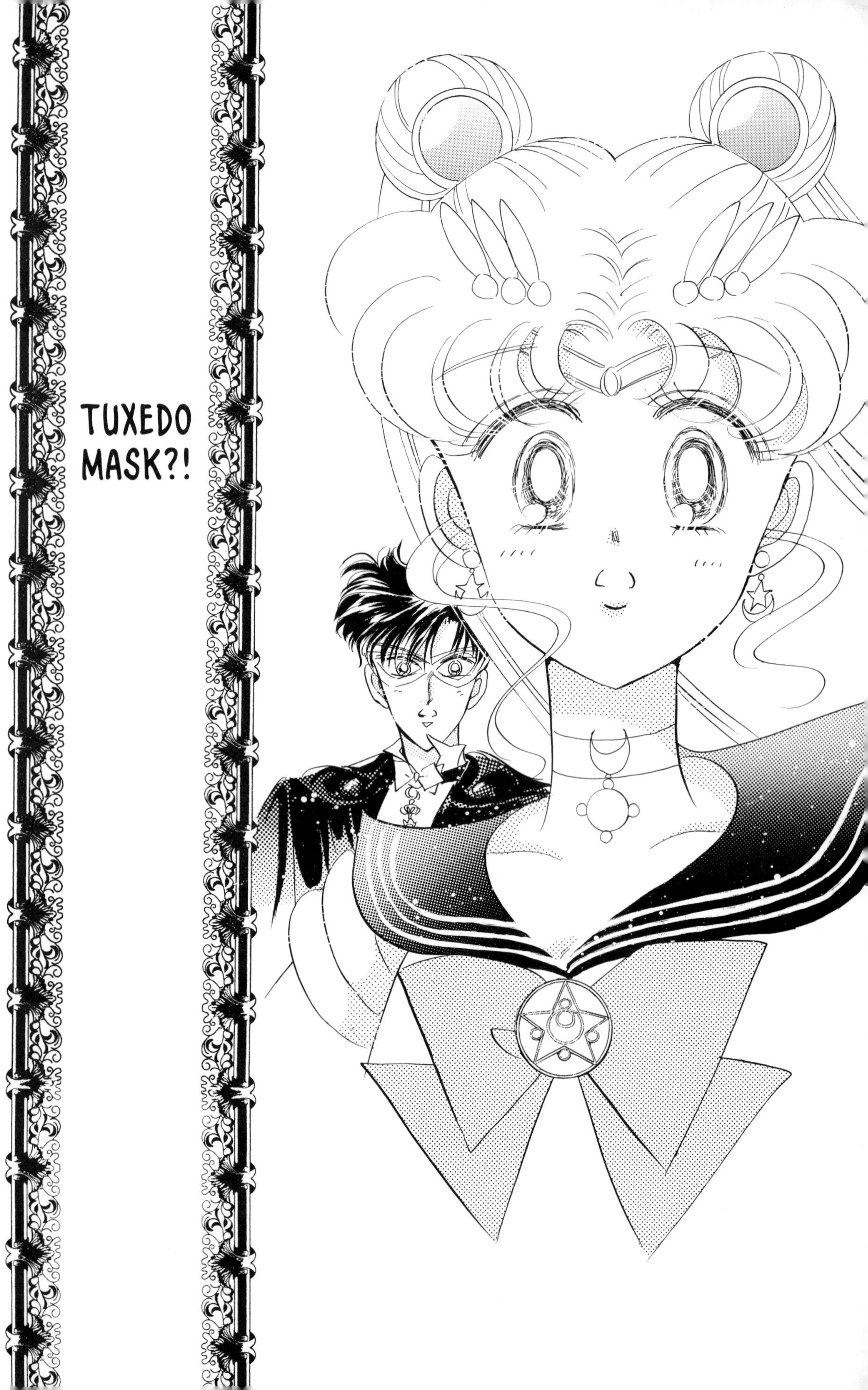
TUXEDO MASK?!

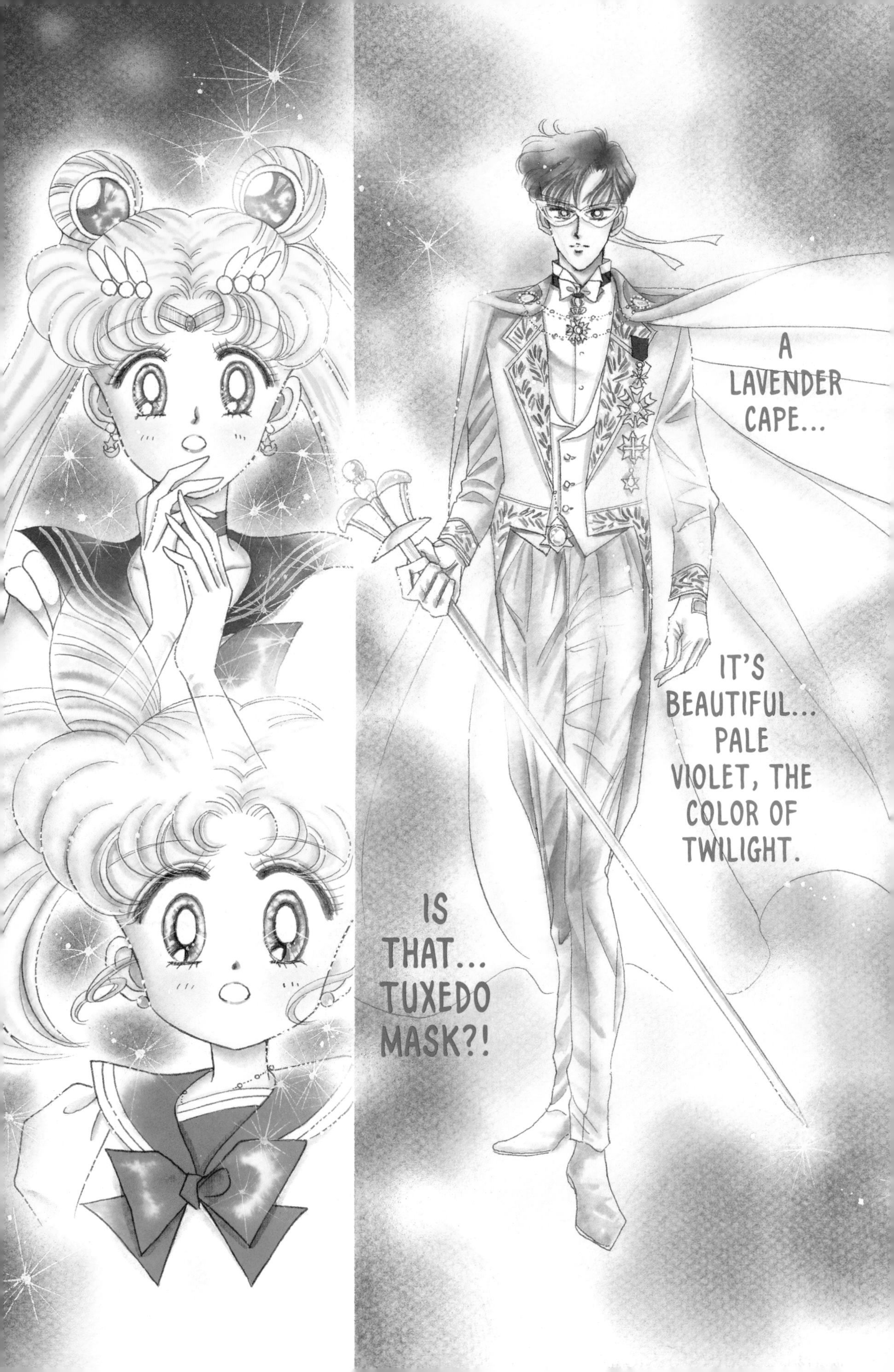
A LAVENDER CAPE...
IT'S BEAUTIFUL... PALE VIOLET, THE COLOR OF TWILIGHT.
IS THAT... TUXEDO MASK?!

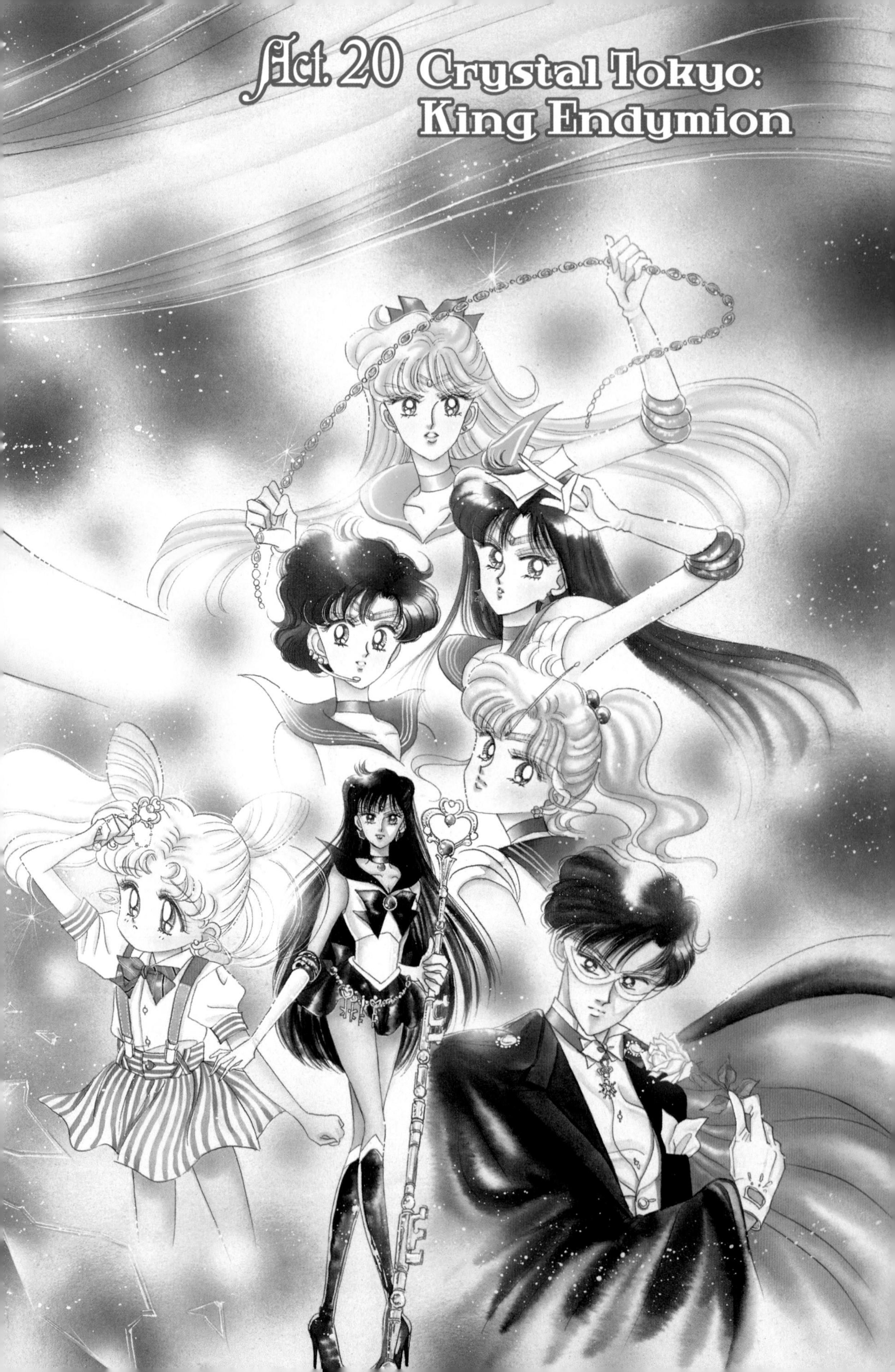
Act. 20 Crystal Tokyo:
King Endymion

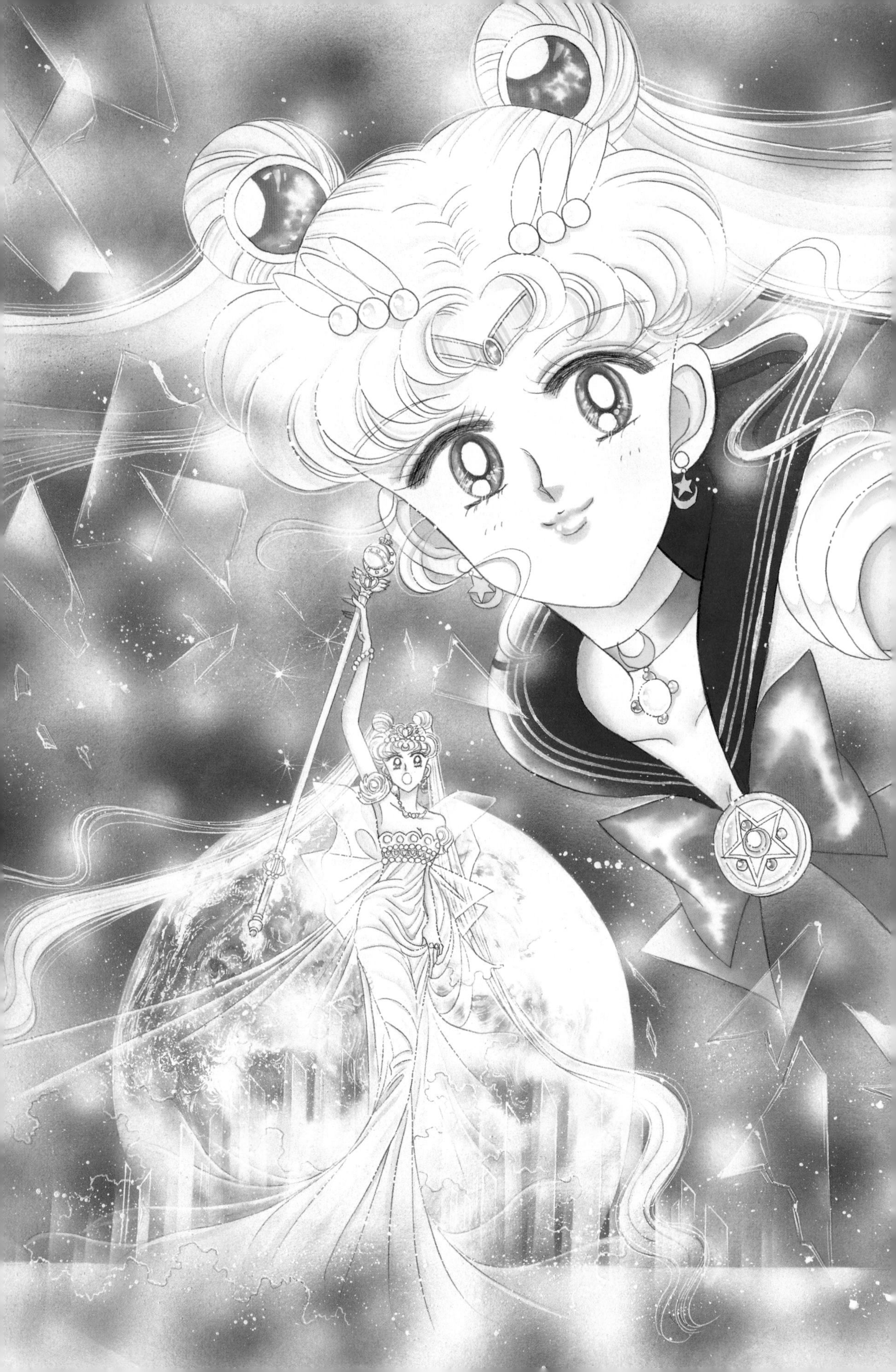

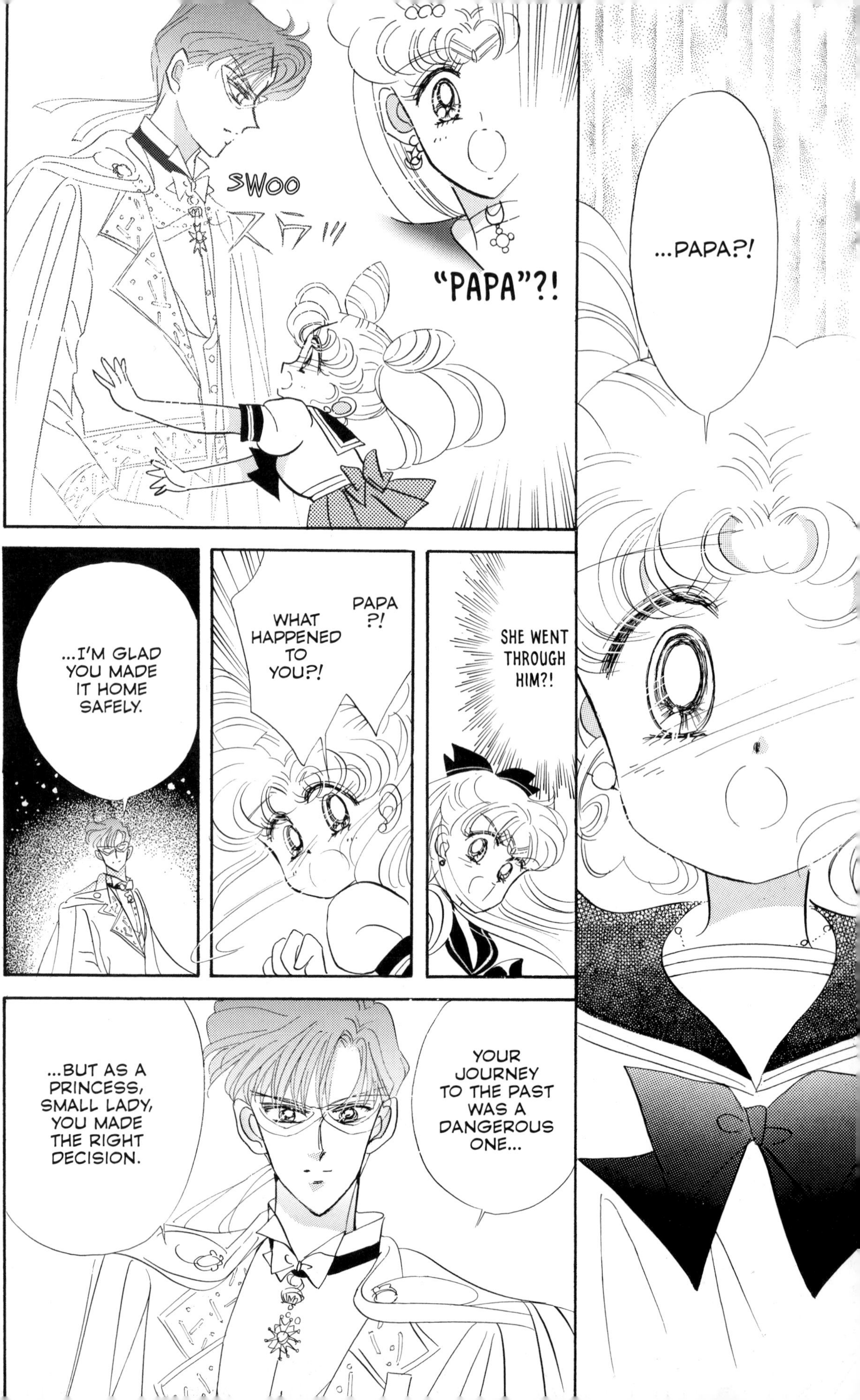
...PAPA?!
SWOO
"PAPA"?!
SHE WENT THROUGH HIM?!
PAPA?!
WHAT HAPPENED TO YOU?!
...I'M GLAD YOU MADE IT HOME SAFELY.
YOUR JOURNEY TO THE PAST WAS A DANGEROUS ONE...
...BUT AS A PRINCESS, SMALL LADY, YOU MADE THE RIGHT DECISION.

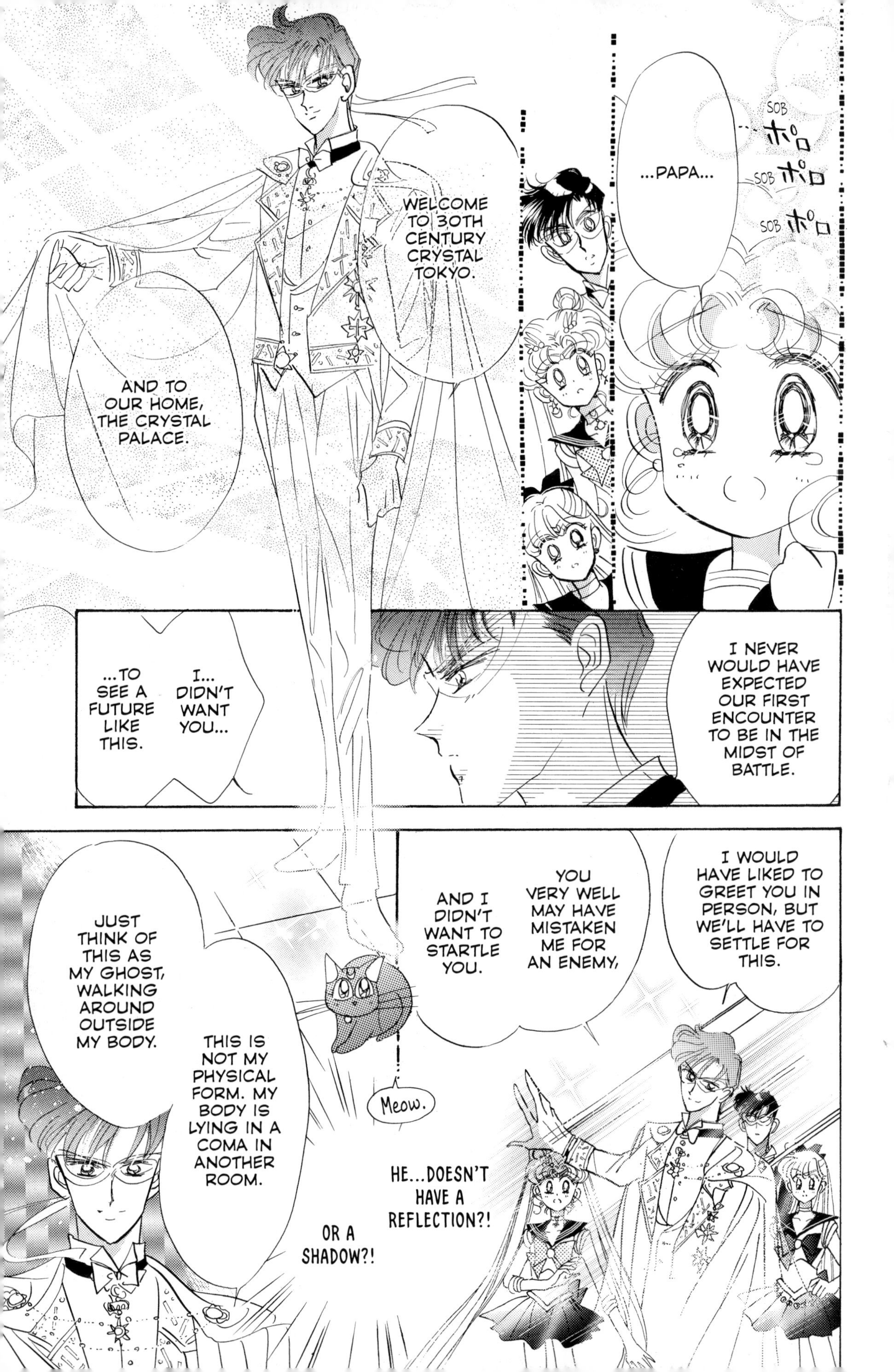
SOB ポロ
SOB ポロ
SOB ポロ
...PAPA...
WELCOME TO 30TH CENTURY CRYSTAL TOKYO.
AND TO OUR HOME, THE CRYSTAL PALACE.
I NEVER WOULD HAVE EXPECTED OUR FIRST ENCOUNTER TO BE IN THE MIDST OF BATTLE.
I... DIDN'T WANT YOU...
...TO SEE A FUTURE LIKE THIS.
I WOULD HAVE LIKED TO GREET YOU IN PERSON, BUT WE'LL HAVE TO SETTLE FOR THIS.
YOU VERY WELL MAY HAVE MISTAKEN ME FOR AN ENEMY,
AND I DIDN'T WANT TO STARTLE YOU.
Meow.
HE...DOESN'T HAVE A REFLECTION?!
OR A SHADOW?!
JUST THINK OF THIS AS MY GHOST, WALKING AROUND OUTSIDE MY BODY.
THIS IS NOT MY PHYSICAL FORM. MY BODY IS LYING IN A COMA IN ANOTHER ROOM.

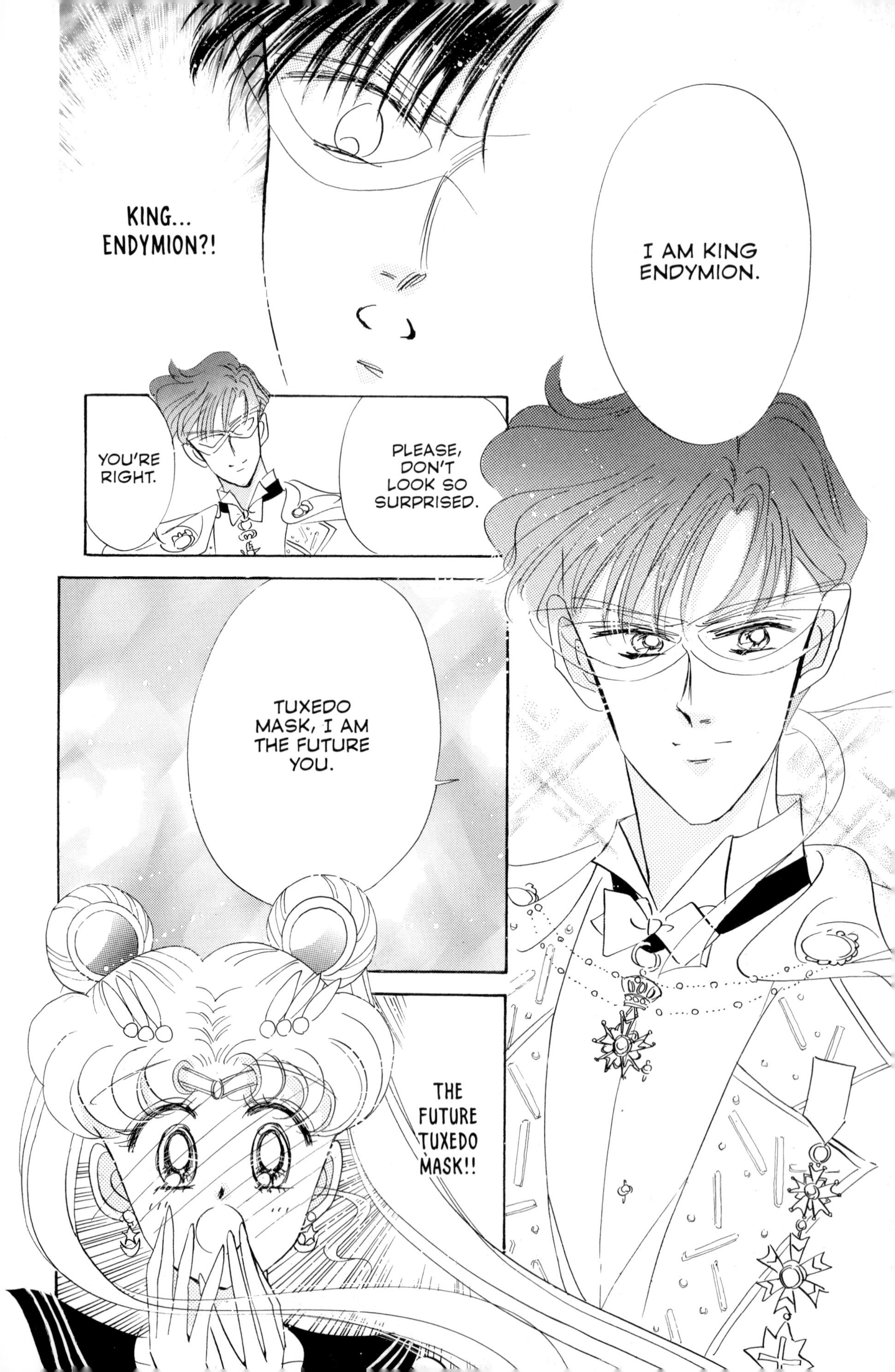
I AM KING ENDYMION.
KING... ENDYMION?!
PLEASE, DON'T LOOK SO SURPRISED.
YOU'RE RIGHT.
TUXEDO MASK, I AM THE FUTURE YOU.
THE FUTURE TUXEDO MASK!!

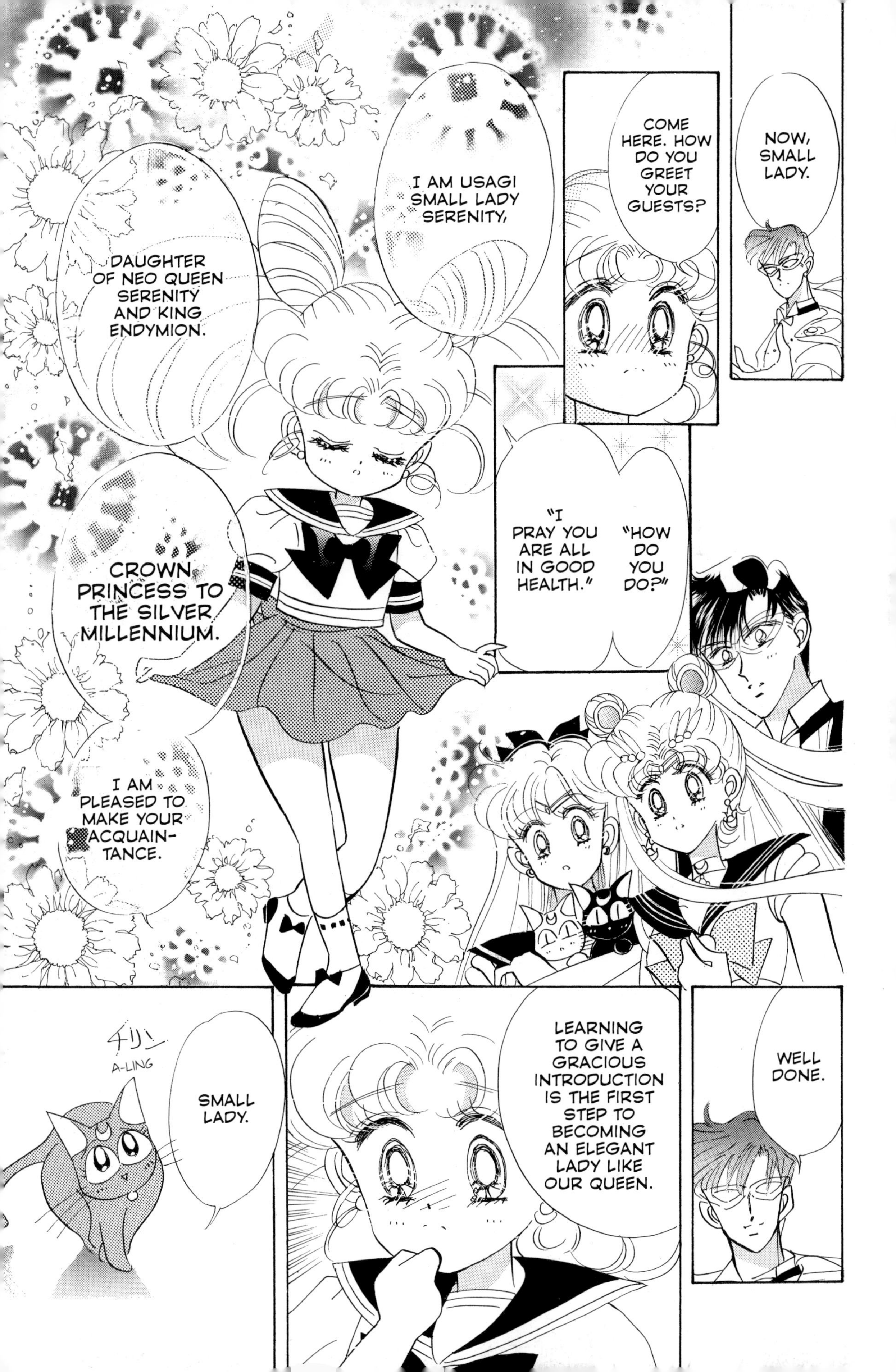
NOW, SMALL LADY.
COME HERE. HOW DO YOU GREET YOUR GUESTS?
"HOW DO YOU DO?"
"I PRAY YOU ARE ALL IN GOOD HEALTH."
I AM USAGI SMALL LADY SERENITY,
DAUGHTER OF NEO QUEEN SERENITY AND KING ENDYMION.
CROWN PRINCESS TO THE SILVER MILLENNIUM.
I AM PLEASED TO MAKE YOUR ACQUAIN-TANCE.
WELL DONE.
LEARNING TO GIVE A GRACIOUS INTRODUCTION IS THE FIRST STEP TO BECOMING AN ELEGANT LADY LIKE OUR QUEEN.
チリン
A-LING
SMALL LADY.

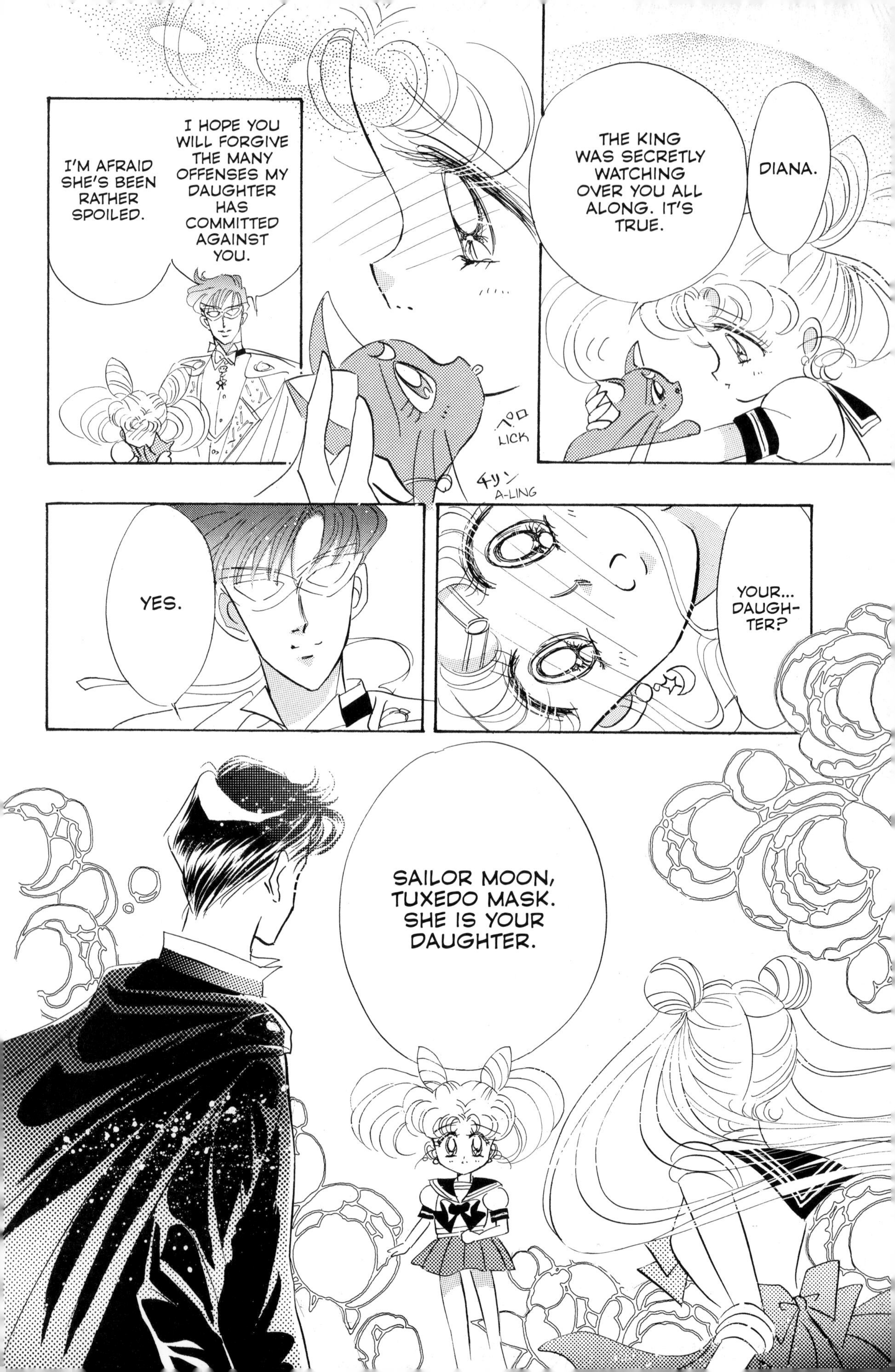
DIANA.
THE KING WAS SECRETLY WATCHING OVER YOU ALL ALONG. IT'S TRUE.
ペロ LICK
チリン A-LING
I HOPE YOU WILL FORGIVE THE MANY OFFENSES MY DAUGHTER HAS COMMITTED AGAINST YOU.
I'M AFRAID SHE'S BEEN RATHER SPOILED.
YOUR... DAUGH-TER?
YES.
SAILOR MOON, TUXEDO MASK. SHE IS YOUR DAUGHTER.

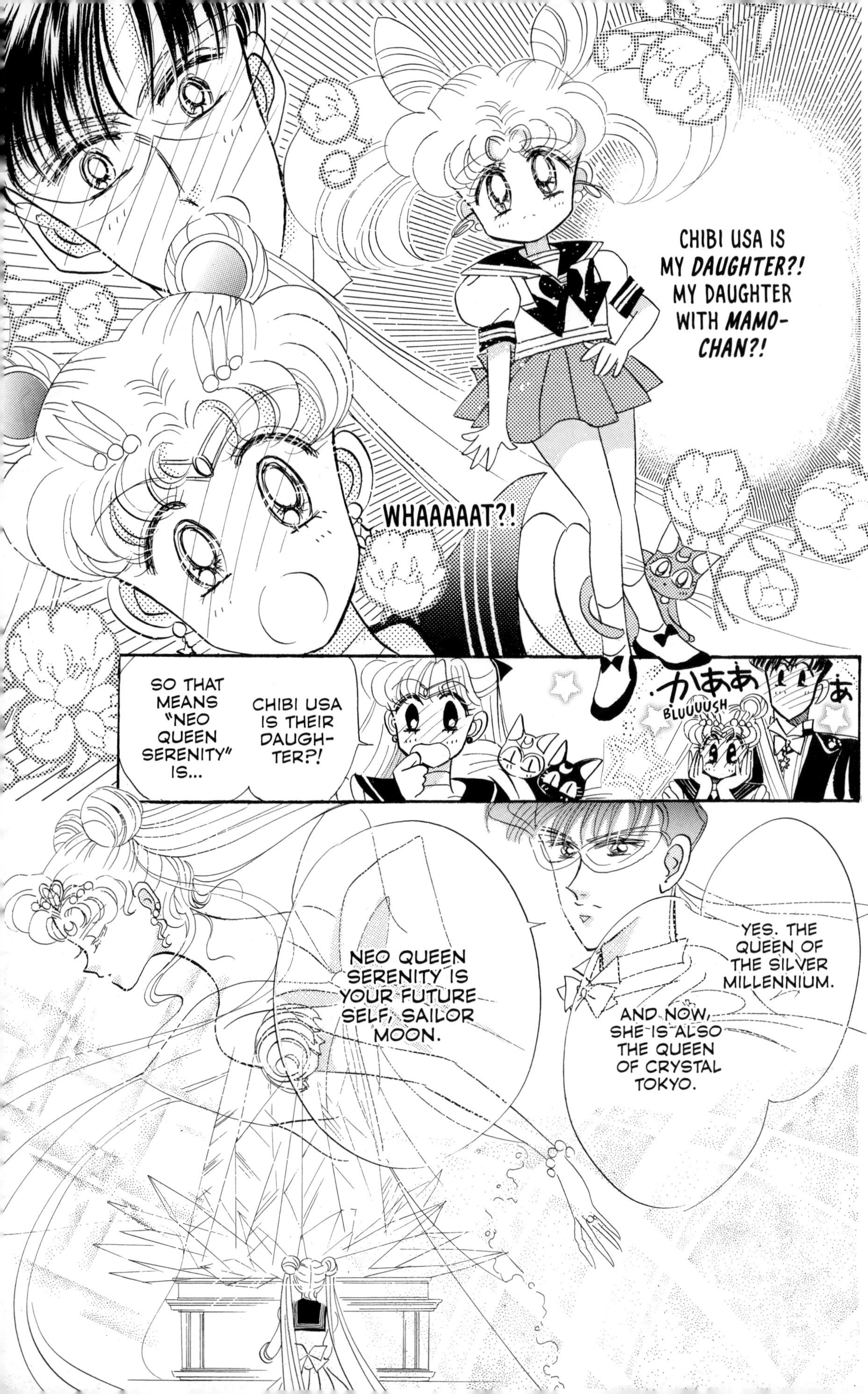
CHIBI USA IS MY DAUGHTER?! MY DAUGHTER WITH MAMO-CHAN?!
WHAAAAAT?!
かああ
BLUUUUSH
あ
CHIBI USA IS THEIR DAUGHTER?!
SO THAT MEANS "NEO QUEEN SERENITY" IS...
YES. THE QUEEN OF THE SILVER MILLENNIUM.
AND NOW, SHE IS ALSO THE QUEEN OF CRYSTAL TOKYO.
NEO QUEEN SERENITY IS YOUR FUTURE SELF, SAILOR MOON.

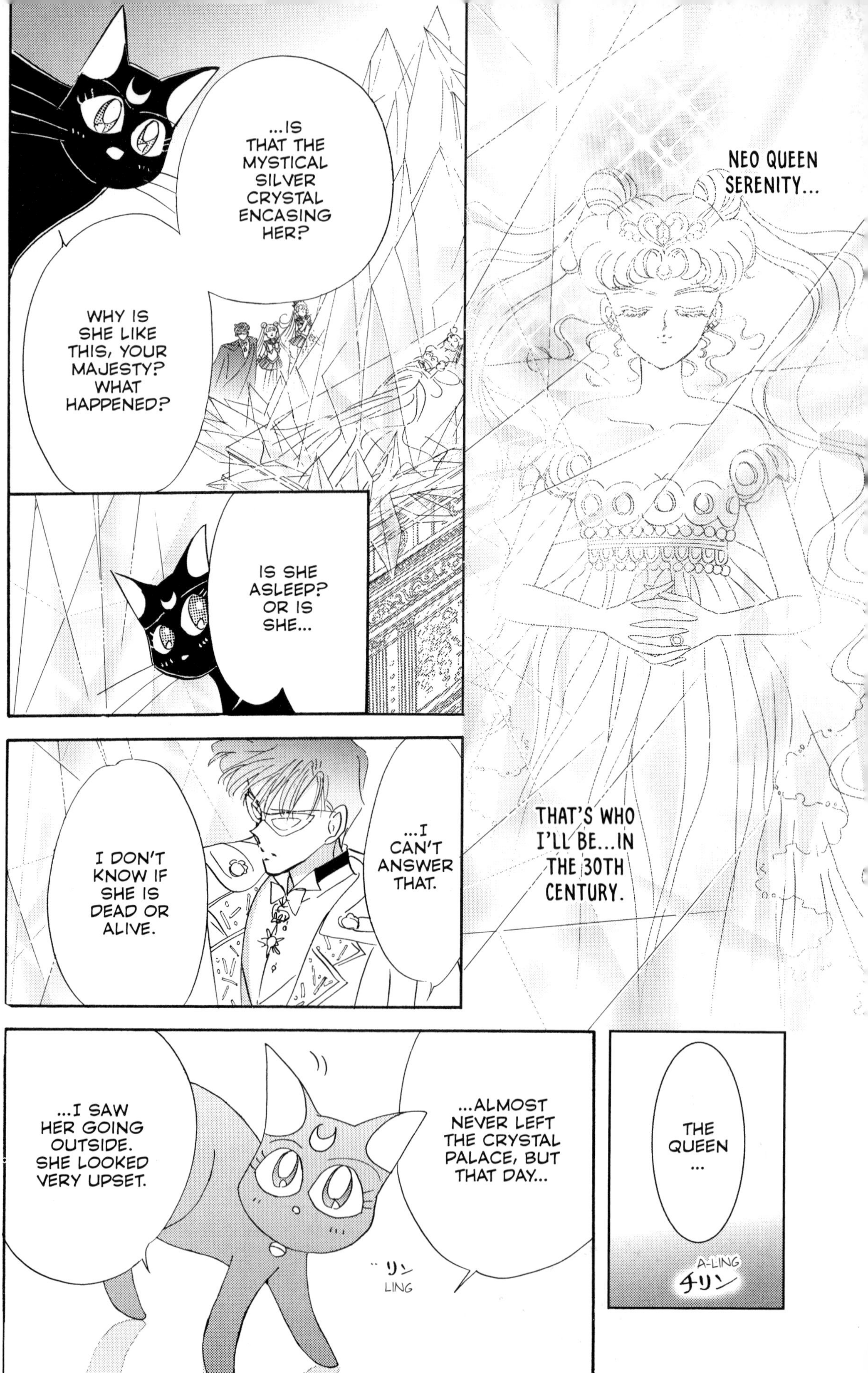
NEO QUEEN SERENITY...
THAT'S WHO I'LL BE...IN THE 30TH CENTURY.
...IS THAT THE MYSTICAL SILVER CRYSTAL ENCASING HER?
WHY IS SHE LIKE THIS, YOUR MAJESTY? WHAT HAPPENED?
IS SHE ASLEEP? OR IS SHE...
...I CAN'T ANSWER THAT.
I DON'T KNOW IF SHE IS DEAD OR ALIVE.
THE QUEEN ...
チリン
A-LING
...ALMOST NEVER LEFT THE CRYSTAL PALACE, BUT THAT DAY...
...I SAW HER GOING OUTSIDE. SHE LOOKED VERY UPSET.
リン
LING

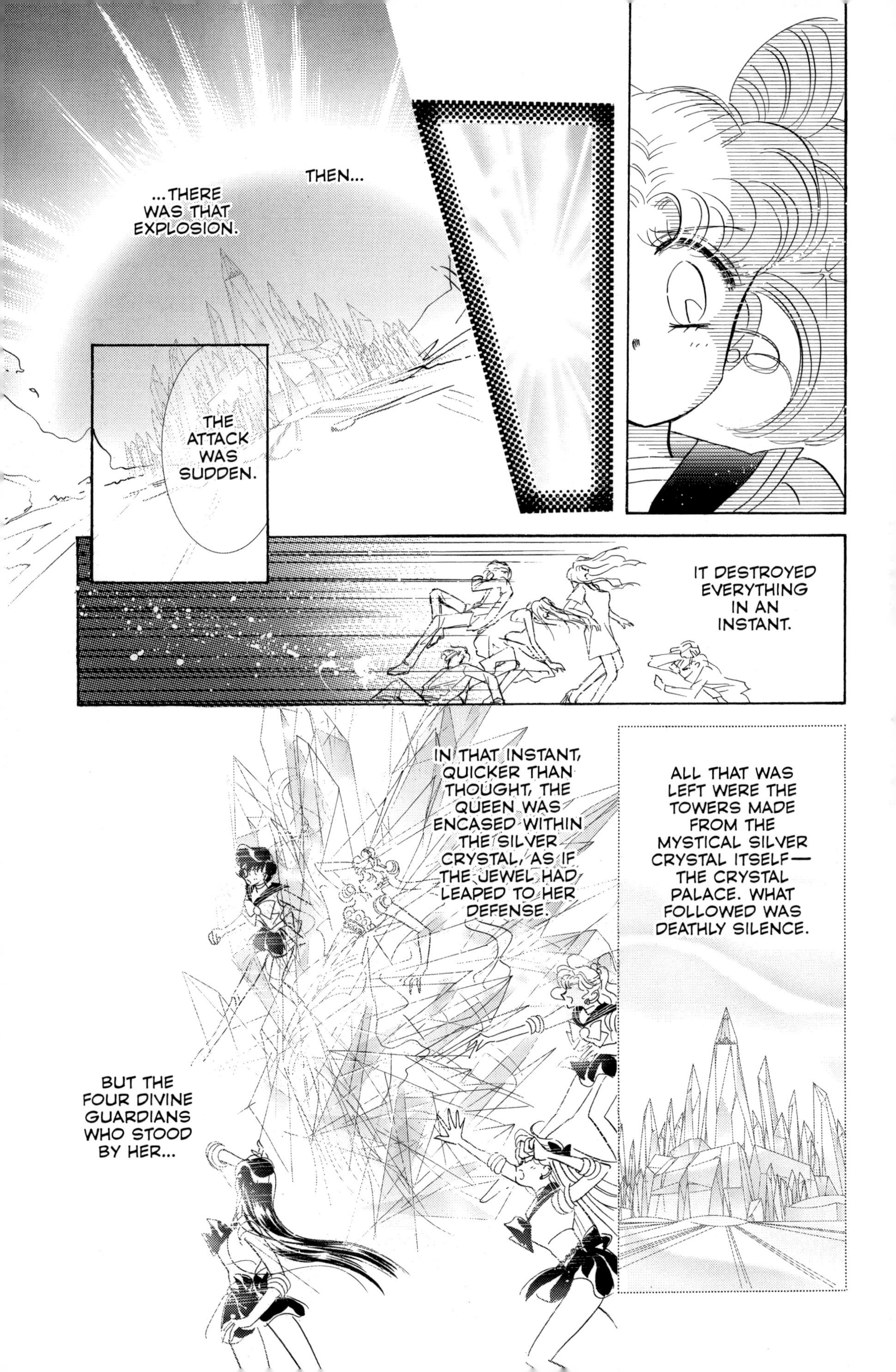
THEN...
...THERE WAS THAT EXPLOSION.
THE ATTACK WAS SUDDEN.
IT DESTROYED EVERYTHING IN AN INSTANT.
ALL THAT WAS LEFT WERE THE TOWERS MADE FROM THE MYSTICAL SILVER CRYSTAL ITSELF—THE CRYSTAL PALACE. WHAT FOLLOWED WAS DEATHLY SILENCE.
IN THAT INSTANT, QUICKER THAN THOUGHT, THE QUEEN WAS ENCASED WITHIN THE SILVER CRYSTAL, AS IF THE JEWEL HAD LEAPED TO HER DEFENSE.
BUT THE FOUR DIVINE GUARDIANS WHO STOOD BY HER...

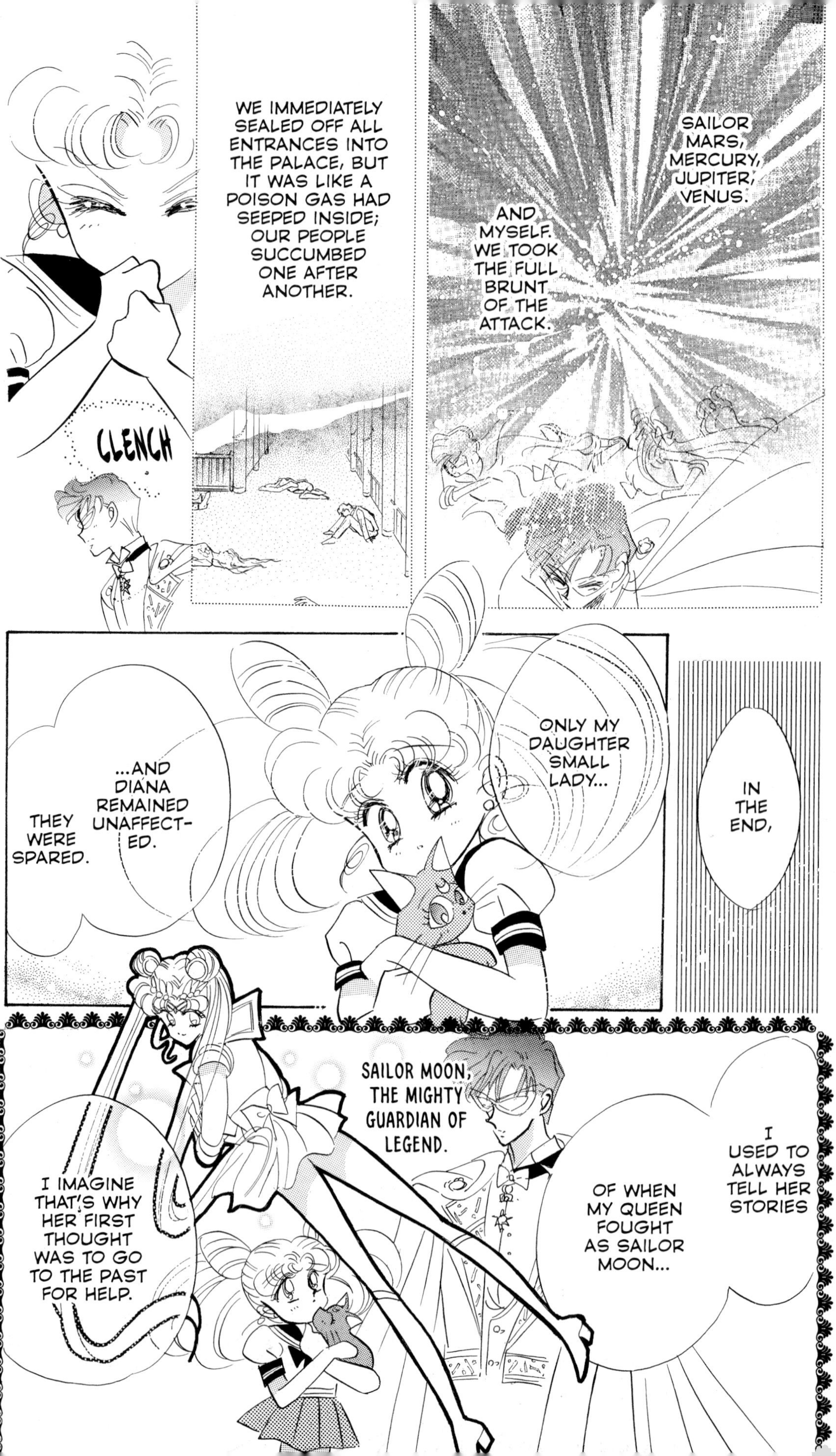
SAILOR MARS, MERCURY, JUPITER, VENUS.
AND MYSELF. WE TOOK THE FULL BRUNT OF THE ATTACK.
WE IMMEDIATELY SEALED OFF ALL ENTRANCES INTO THE PALACE, BUT IT WAS LIKE A POISON GAS HAD SEEPED INSIDE; OUR PEOPLE SUCCUMBED ONE AFTER ANOTHER.
CLENCH
IN THE END,
ONLY MY DAUGHTER SMALL LADY...
...AND DIANA REMAINED UNAFFECTED.
THEY WERE SPARED.
I USED TO ALWAYS TELL HER STORIES
OF WHEN MY QUEEN FOUGHT AS SAILOR MOON...
SAILOR MOON, THE MIGHTY GUARDIAN OF LEGEND.
I IMAGINE THAT'S WHY HER FIRST THOUGHT WAS TO GO TO THE PAST FOR HELP.

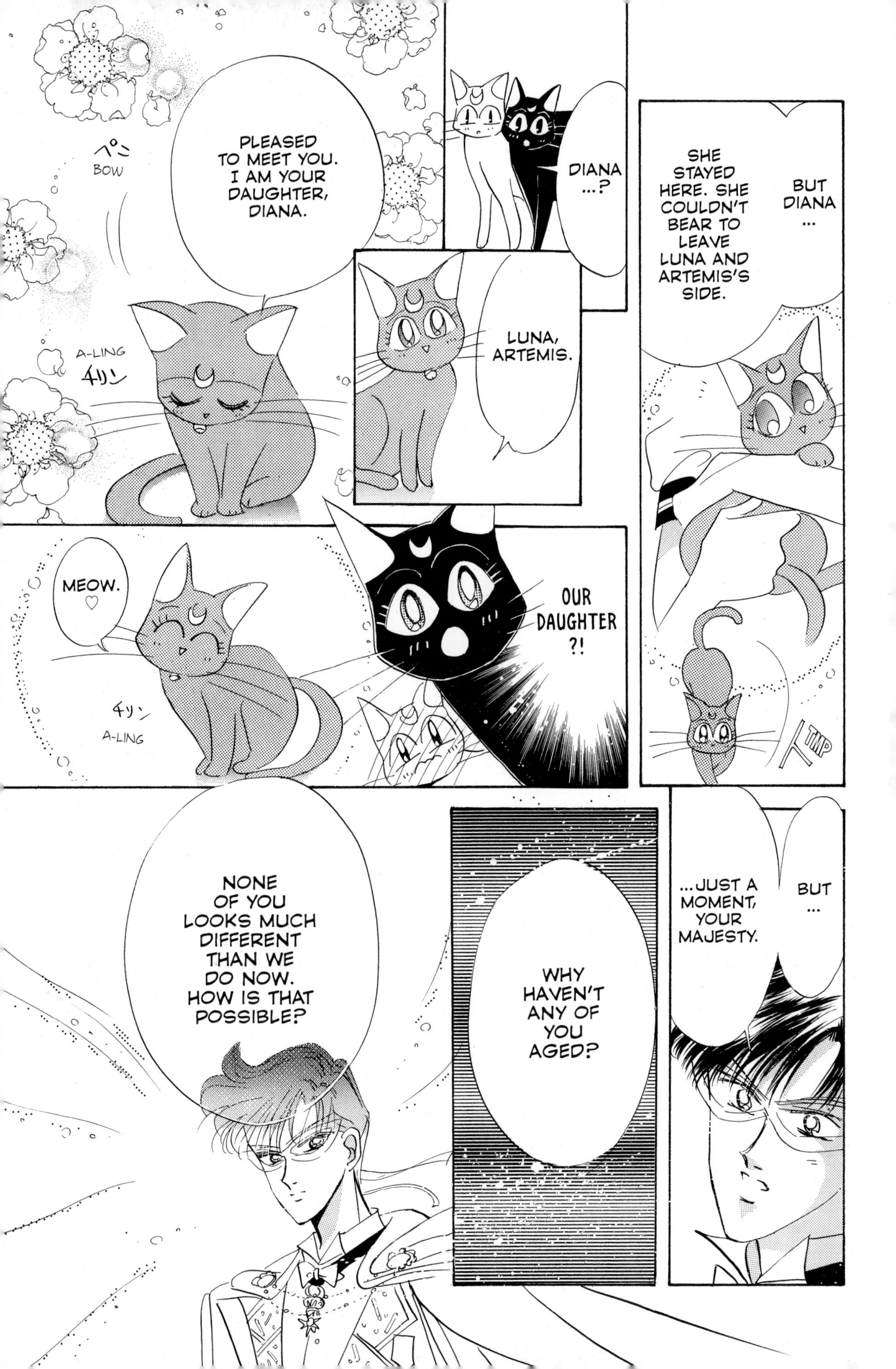
BUT DIANA ...
SHE STAYED HERE. SHE COULDN'T BEAR TO LEAVE LUNA AND ARTEMIS'S SIDE.
TMP
DIANA ...?
LUNA, ARTEMIS.
PLEASED TO MEET YOU. I AM YOUR DAUGHTER, DIANA.
ペこ
BOW
A-LING
チリン
OUR DAUGHTER ?!
MEOW. ♡
チリン
A-LING
BUT ...
...JUST A MOMENT, YOUR MAJESTY.
WHY HAVEN'T ANY OF YOU AGED?
NONE OF YOU LOOKS MUCH DIFFERENT THAN WE DO NOW. HOW IS THAT POSSIBLE?

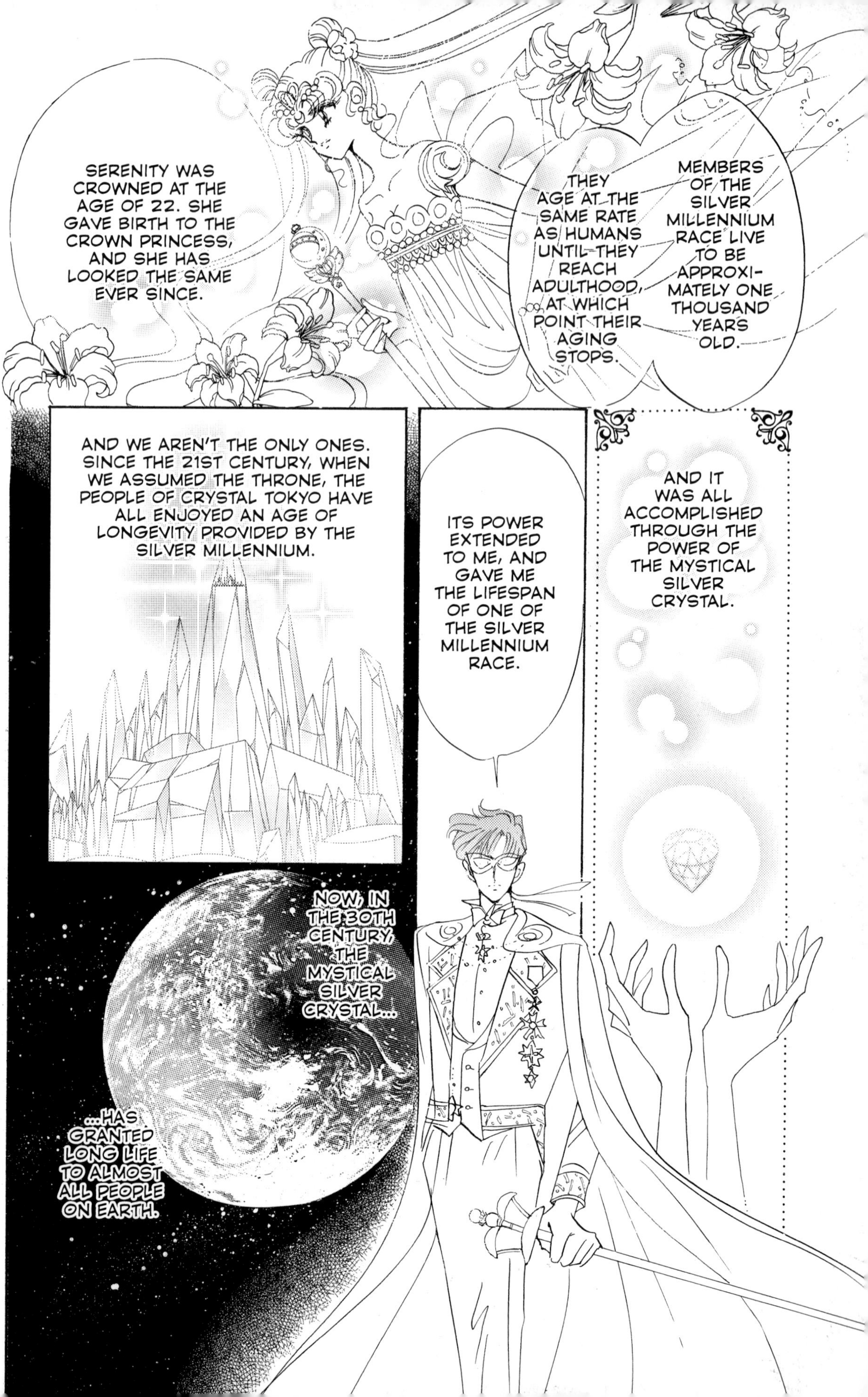
MEMBERS OF THE SILVER MILLENNIUM RACE LIVE TO BE APPROXIMATELY ONE THOUSAND YEARS OLD.
THEY AGE AT THE SAME RATE AS HUMANS UNTIL THEY REACH ADULTHOOD, AT WHICH POINT THEIR AGING STOPS.
SERENITY WAS CROWNED AT THE AGE OF 22. SHE GAVE BIRTH TO THE CROWN PRINCESS, AND SHE HAS LOOKED THE SAME EVER SINCE.
AND IT WAS ALL ACCOMPLISHED THROUGH THE POWER OF THE MYSTICAL SILVER CRYSTAL.
ITS POWER EXTENDED TO ME, AND GAVE ME THE LIFESPAN OF ONE OF THE SILVER MILLENNIUM RACE.
AND WE AREN'T THE ONLY ONES. SINCE THE 21ST CENTURY, WHEN WE ASSUMED THE THRONE, THE PEOPLE OF CRYSTAL TOKYO HAVE ALL ENJOYED AN AGE OF LONGEVITY PROVIDED BY THE SILVER MILLENNIUM.
NOW, IN THE 30TH CENTURY, THE MYSTICAL SILVER CRYSTAL...
...HAS GRANTED LONG LIFE TO ALMOST ALL PEOPLE ON EARTH.

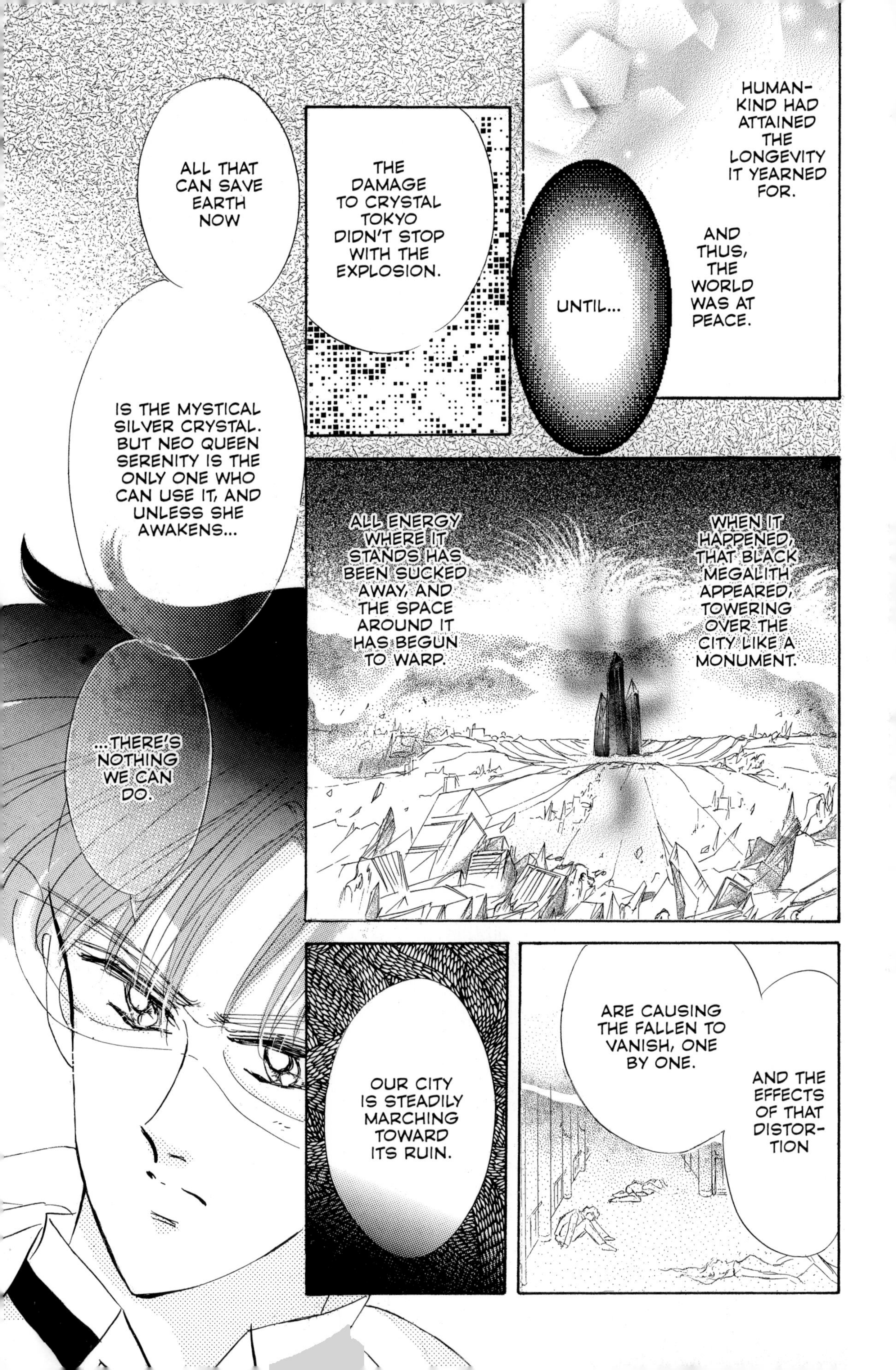
HUMAN-KIND HAD ATTAINED THE LONGEVITY IT YEARNED FOR.
AND THUS, THE WORLD WAS AT PEACE.
UNTIL...
THE DAMAGE TO CRYSTAL TOKYO DIDN'T STOP WITH THE EXPLOSION.
WHEN IT HAPPENED, THAT BLACK MEGALITH APPEARED, TOWERING OVER THE CITY LIKE A MONUMENT.
ALL ENERGY WHERE IT STANDS HAS BEEN SUCKED AWAY, AND THE SPACE AROUND IT HAS BEGUN TO WARP.
AND THE EFFECTS OF THAT DISTORTION
ARE CAUSING THE FALLEN TO VANISH, ONE BY ONE.
OUR CITY IS STEADILY MARCHING TOWARD ITS RUIN.
ALL THAT CAN SAVE EARTH NOW
IS THE MYSTICAL SILVER CRYSTAL. BUT NEO QUEEN SERENITY IS THE ONLY ONE WHO CAN USE IT, AND UNLESS SHE AWAKENS...
...THERE'S NOTHING WE CAN DO.

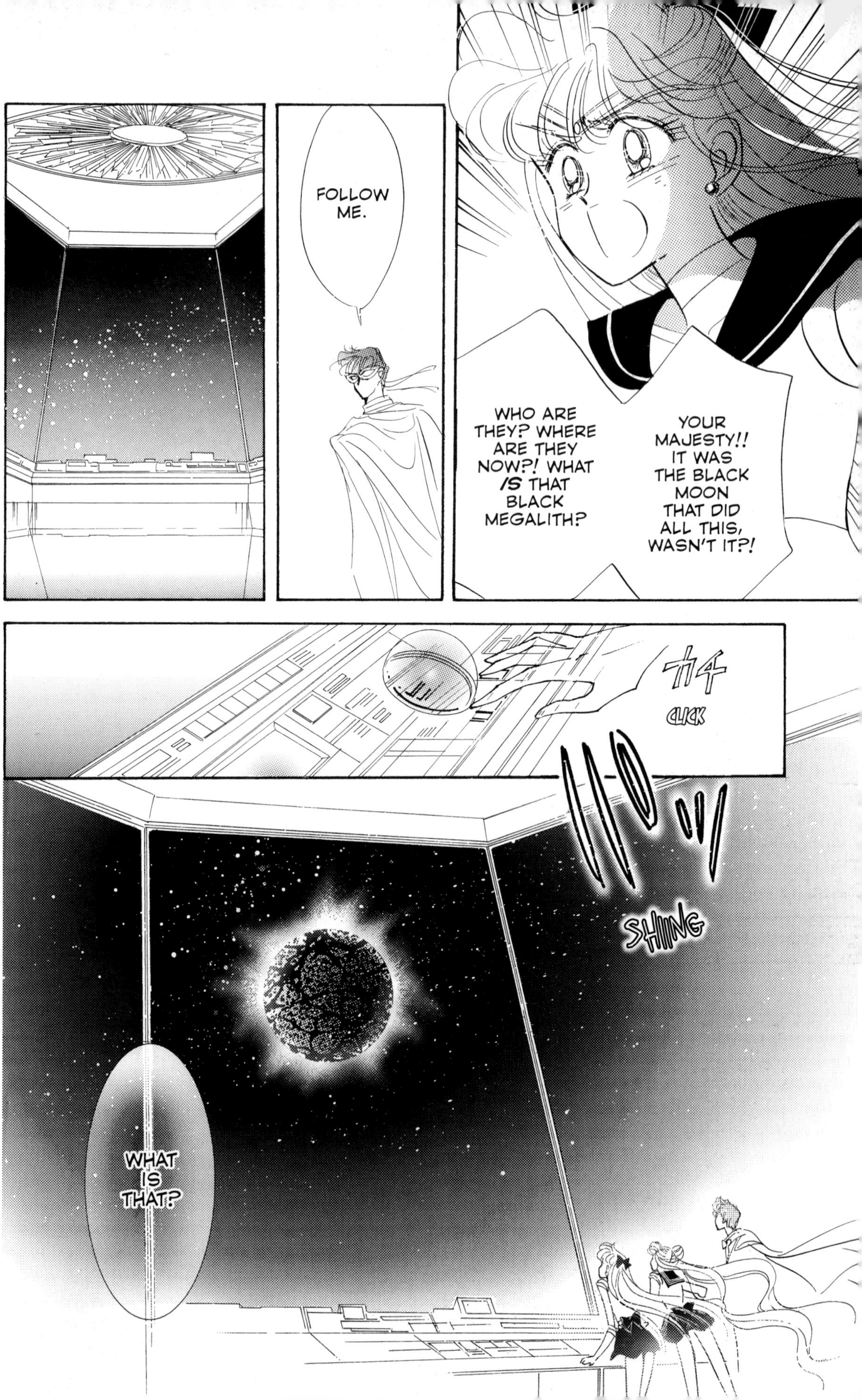
YOUR MAJESTY!! IT WAS THE BLACK MOON THAT DID ALL THIS, WASN'T IT?!
WHO ARE THEY? WHERE ARE THEY NOW?! WHAT *IS* THAT BLACK MEGALITH?
FOLLOW ME.
カチ
CLICK
SHIING
WHAT IS THAT?

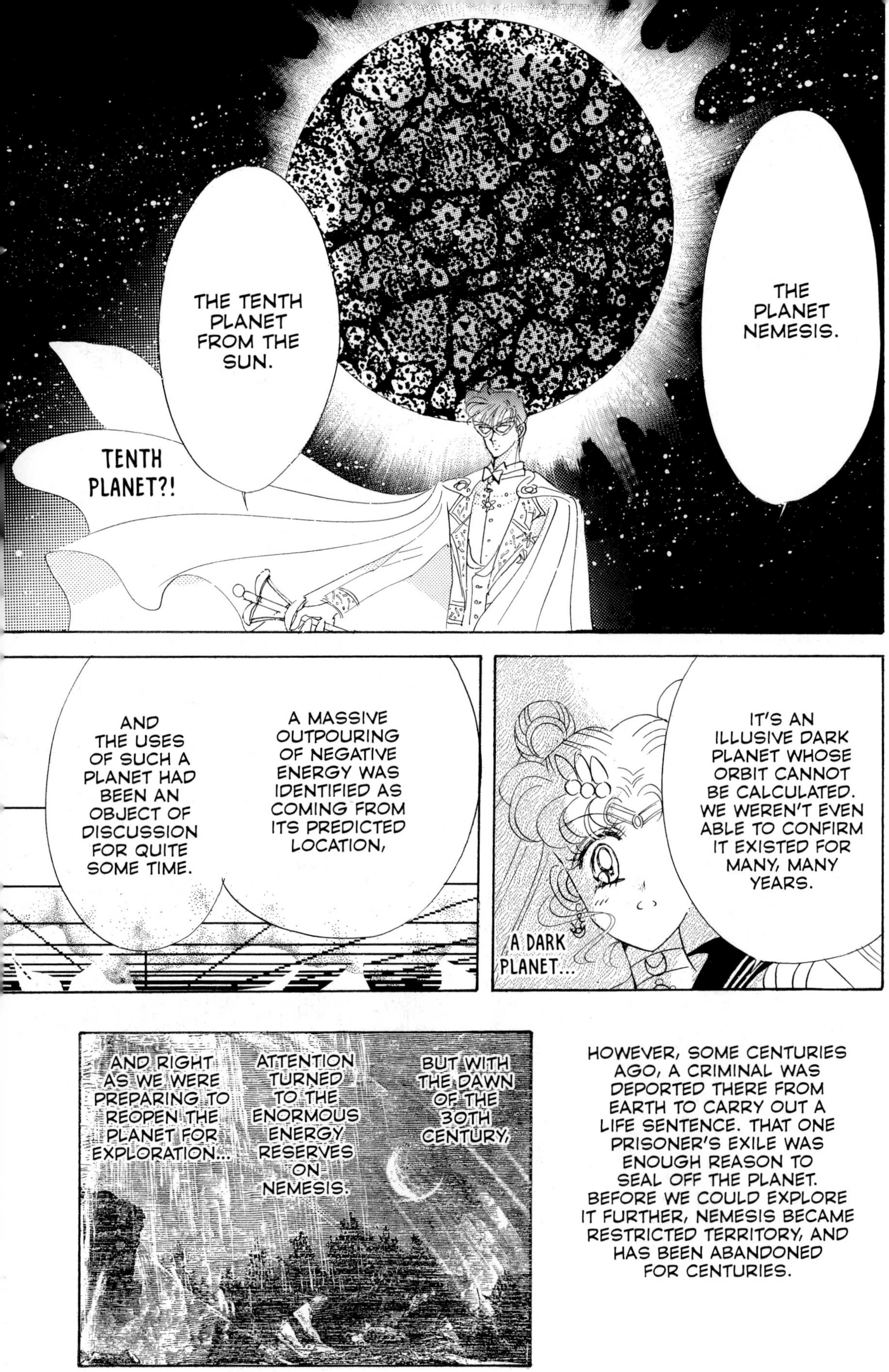
THE PLANET NEMESIS.
THE TENTH PLANET FROM THE SUN.
TENTH PLANET?!
IT'S AN ILLUSIVE DARK PLANET WHOSE ORBIT CANNOT BE CALCULATED. WE WEREN'T EVEN ABLE TO CONFIRM IT EXISTED FOR MANY, MANY YEARS.
A DARK PLANET...
A MASSIVE OUTPOURING OF NEGATIVE ENERGY WAS IDENTIFIED AS COMING FROM ITS PREDICTED LOCATION,
AND THE USES OF SUCH A PLANET HAD BEEN AN OBJECT OF DISCUSSION FOR QUITE SOME TIME.
HOWEVER, SOME CENTURIES AGO, A CRIMINAL WAS DEPORTED THERE FROM EARTH TO CARRY OUT A LIFE SENTENCE. THAT ONE PRISONER'S EXILE WAS ENOUGH REASON TO SEAL OFF THE PLANET. BEFORE WE COULD EXPLORE IT FURTHER, NEMESIS BECAME RESTRICTED TERRITORY, AND HAS BEEN ABANDONED FOR CENTURIES.
BUT WITH THE DAWN OF THE 30TH CENTURY,
ATTENTION TURNED TO THE ENORMOUS ENERGY RESERVES ON NEMESIS.
AND RIGHT AS WE WERE PREPARING TO REOPEN THE PLANET FOR EXPLORATION...

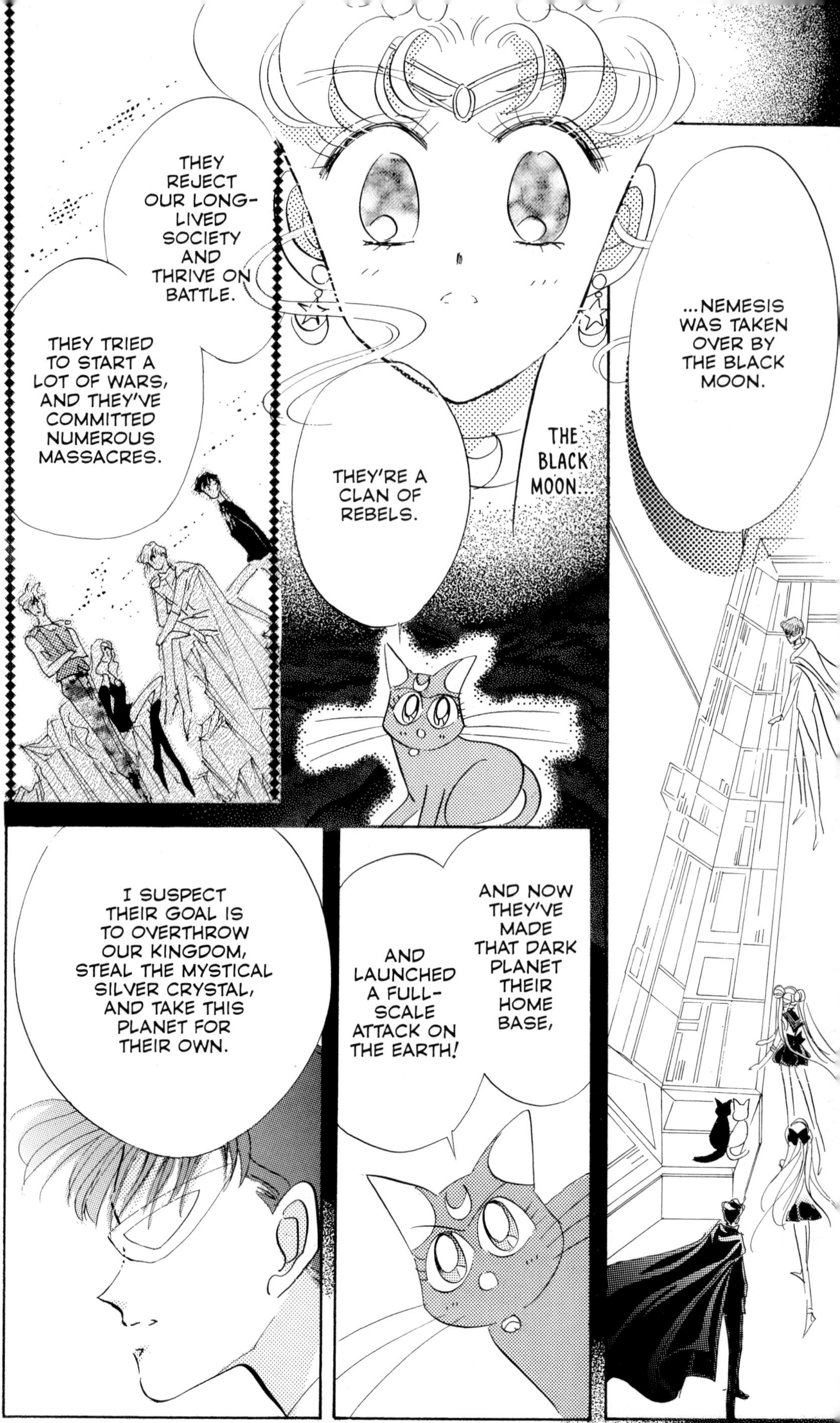
...NEMESIS WAS TAKEN OVER BY THE BLACK MOON.
THE BLACK MOON...
THEY'RE A CLAN OF REBELS.
THEY REJECT OUR LONG-LIVED SOCIETY AND THRIVE ON BATTLE.
THEY TRIED TO START A LOT OF WARS, AND THEY'VE COMMITTED NUMEROUS MASSACRES.
AND NOW THEY'VE MADE THAT DARK PLANET THEIR HOME BASE,
AND LAUNCHED A FULL-SCALE ATTACK ON THE EARTH!
I SUSPECT THEIR GOAL IS TO OVERTHROW OUR KINGDOM, STEAL THE MYSTICAL SILVER CRYSTAL, AND TAKE THIS PLANET FOR THEIR OWN.

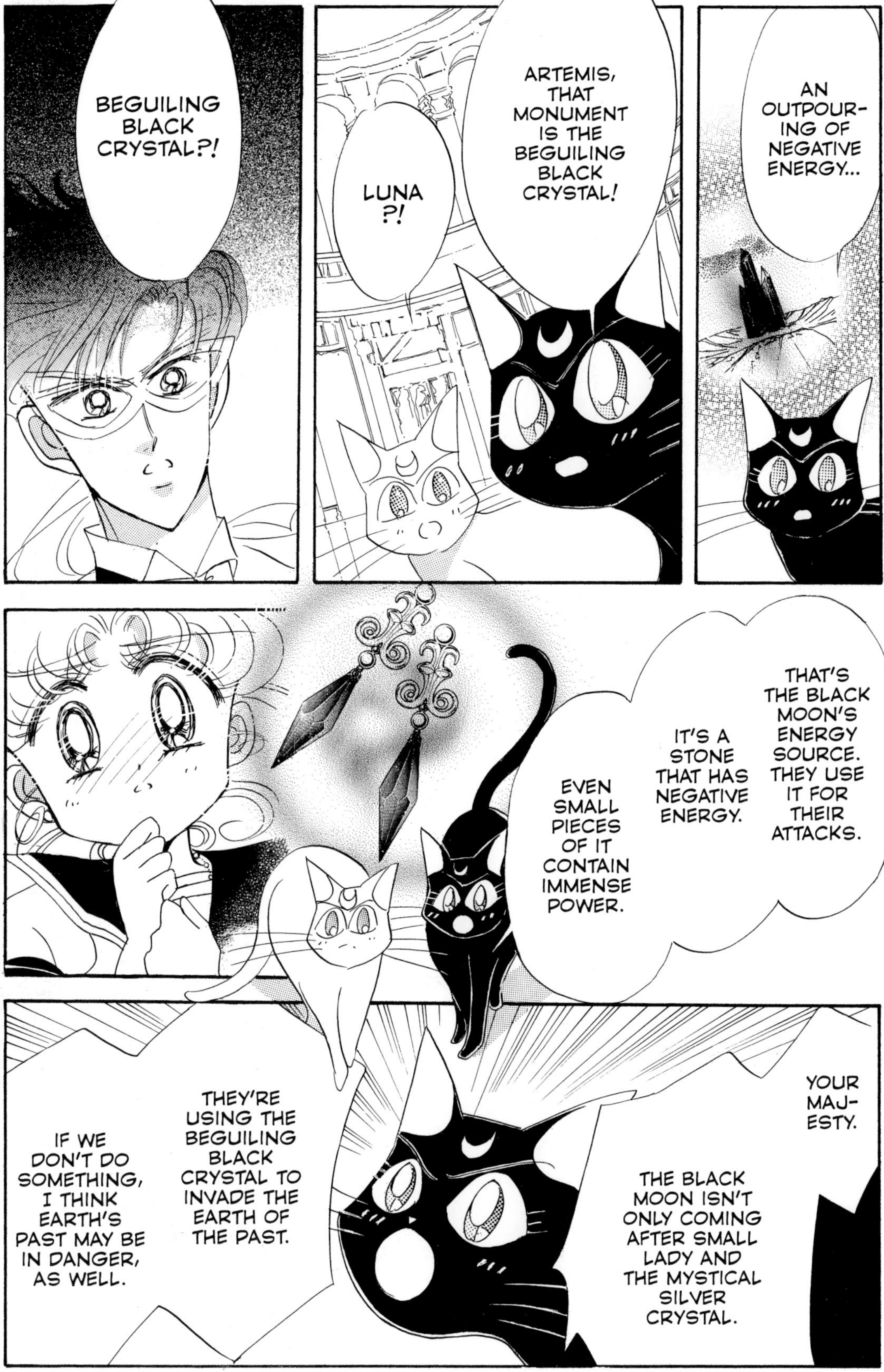
AN OUTPOUR-ING OF NEGATIVE ENERGY...
ARTEMIS, THAT MONUMENT IS THE BEGUILING BLACK CRYSTAL!
LUNA ?!
BEGUILING BLACK CRYSTAL?!
THAT'S THE BLACK MOON'S ENERGY SOURCE. THEY USE IT FOR THEIR ATTACKS.
IT'S A STONE THAT HAS NEGATIVE ENERGY.
EVEN SMALL PIECES OF IT CONTAIN IMMENSE POWER.
YOUR MAJ-ESTY.
THE BLACK MOON ISN'T ONLY COMING AFTER SMALL LADY AND THE MYSTICAL SILVER CRYSTAL.
THEY'RE USING THE BEGUILING BLACK CRYSTAL TO INVADE THE EARTH OF THE PAST.
IF WE DON'T DO SOMETHING, I THINK EARTH'S PAST MAY BE IN DANGER, AS WELL.

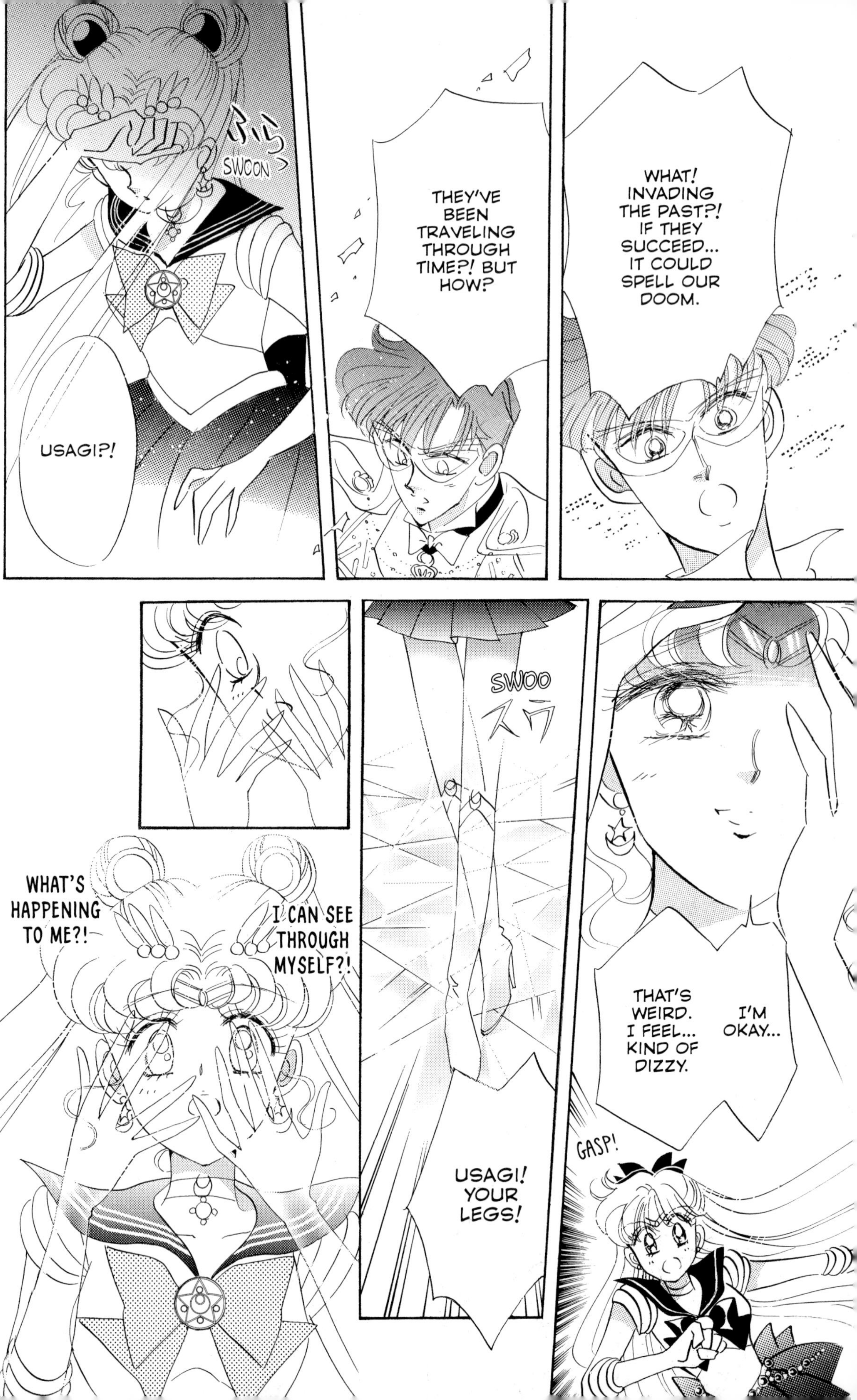
WHAT! INVADING THE PAST?! IF THEY SUCCEED... IT COULD SPELL OUR DOOM.
THEY'VE BEEN TRAVELING THROUGH TIME?! BUT HOW?
ふらっ
SWOON
USAGI?!
I'M OKAY...
THAT'S WEIRD. I FEEL... KIND OF DIZZY.
GASP!
SWOO
スゥ
USAGI! YOUR LEGS!
I CAN SEE THROUGH MYSELF?!
WHAT'S HAPPENING TO ME?!

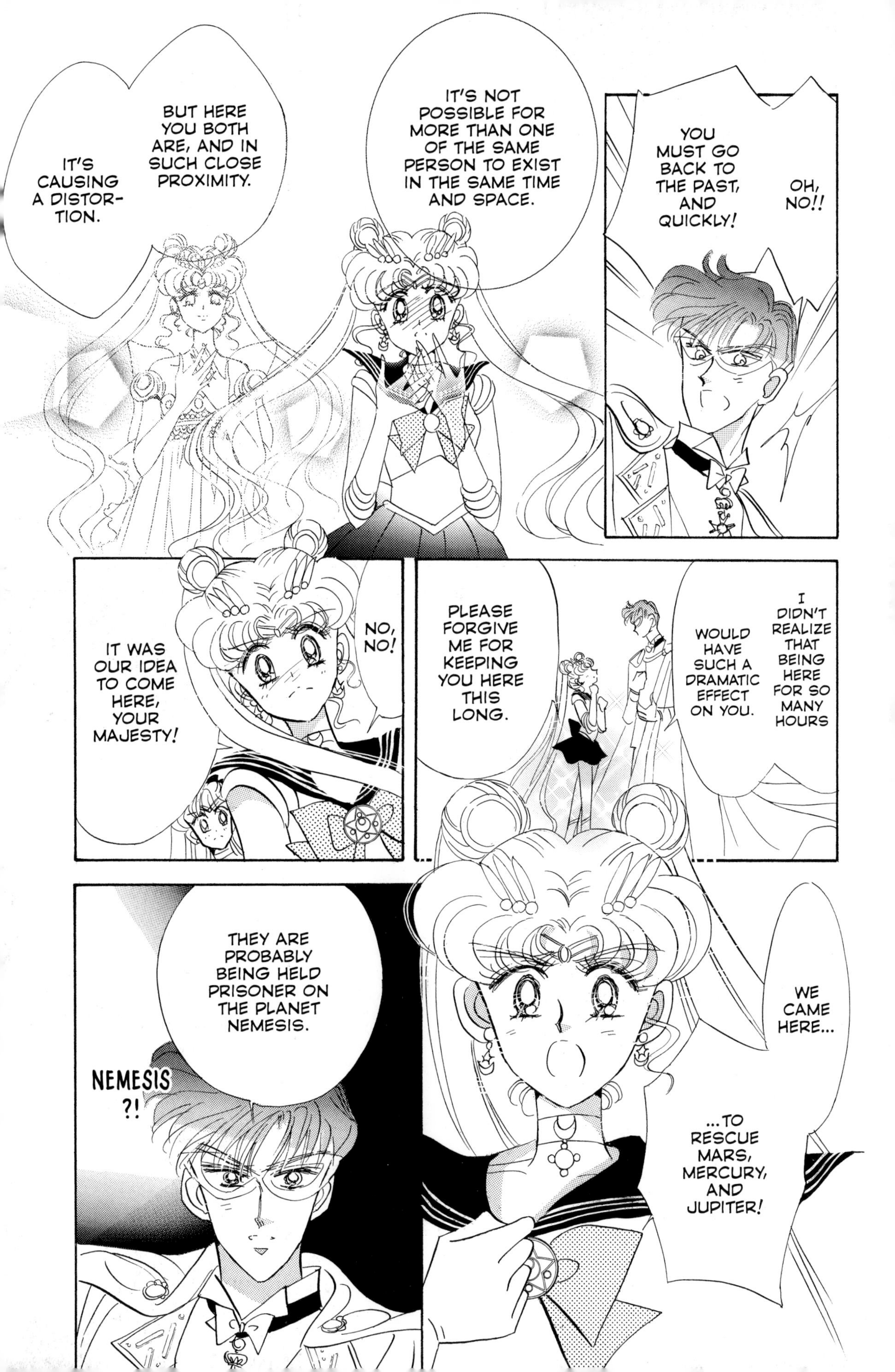
OH, NO!!
YOU MUST GO BACK TO THE PAST, AND QUICKLY!
IT'S NOT POSSIBLE FOR MORE THAN ONE OF THE SAME PERSON TO EXIST IN THE SAME TIME AND SPACE.
BUT HERE YOU BOTH ARE, AND IN SUCH CLOSE PROXIMITY.
IT'S CAUSING A DISTORTION.
I DIDN'T REALIZE THAT BEING HERE FOR SO MANY HOURS
WOULD HAVE SUCH A DRAMATIC EFFECT ON YOU.
PLEASE FORGIVE ME FOR KEEPING YOU HERE THIS LONG.
NO, NO!
IT WAS OUR IDEA TO COME HERE, YOUR MAJESTY!
WE CAME HERE...
...TO RESCUE MARS, MERCURY, AND JUPITER!
THEY ARE PROBABLY BEING HELD PRISONER ON THE PLANET NEMESIS.
NEMESIS ?!

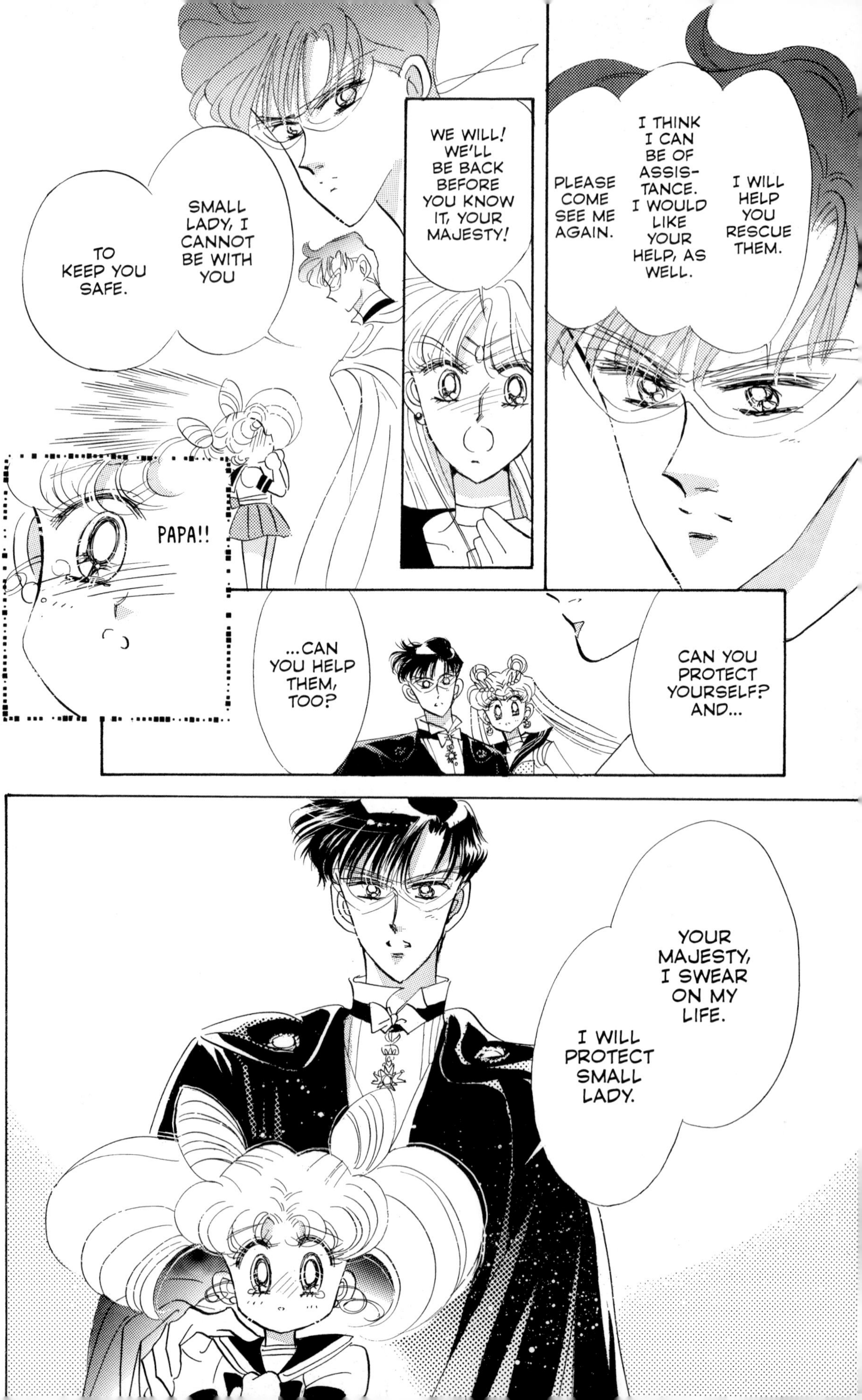
I WILL HELP YOU RESCUE THEM.
I THINK I CAN BE OF ASSIS-TANCE. I WOULD LIKE YOUR HELP, AS WELL.
PLEASE COME SEE ME AGAIN.
WE WILL! WE'LL BE BACK BEFORE YOU KNOW IT, YOUR MAJESTY!
SMALL LADY, I CANNOT BE WITH YOU
TO KEEP YOU SAFE.
PAPA!!
CAN YOU PROTECT YOURSELF? AND...
...CAN YOU HELP THEM, TOO?
YOUR MAJESTY, I SWEAR ON MY LIFE.
I WILL PROTECT SMALL LADY.

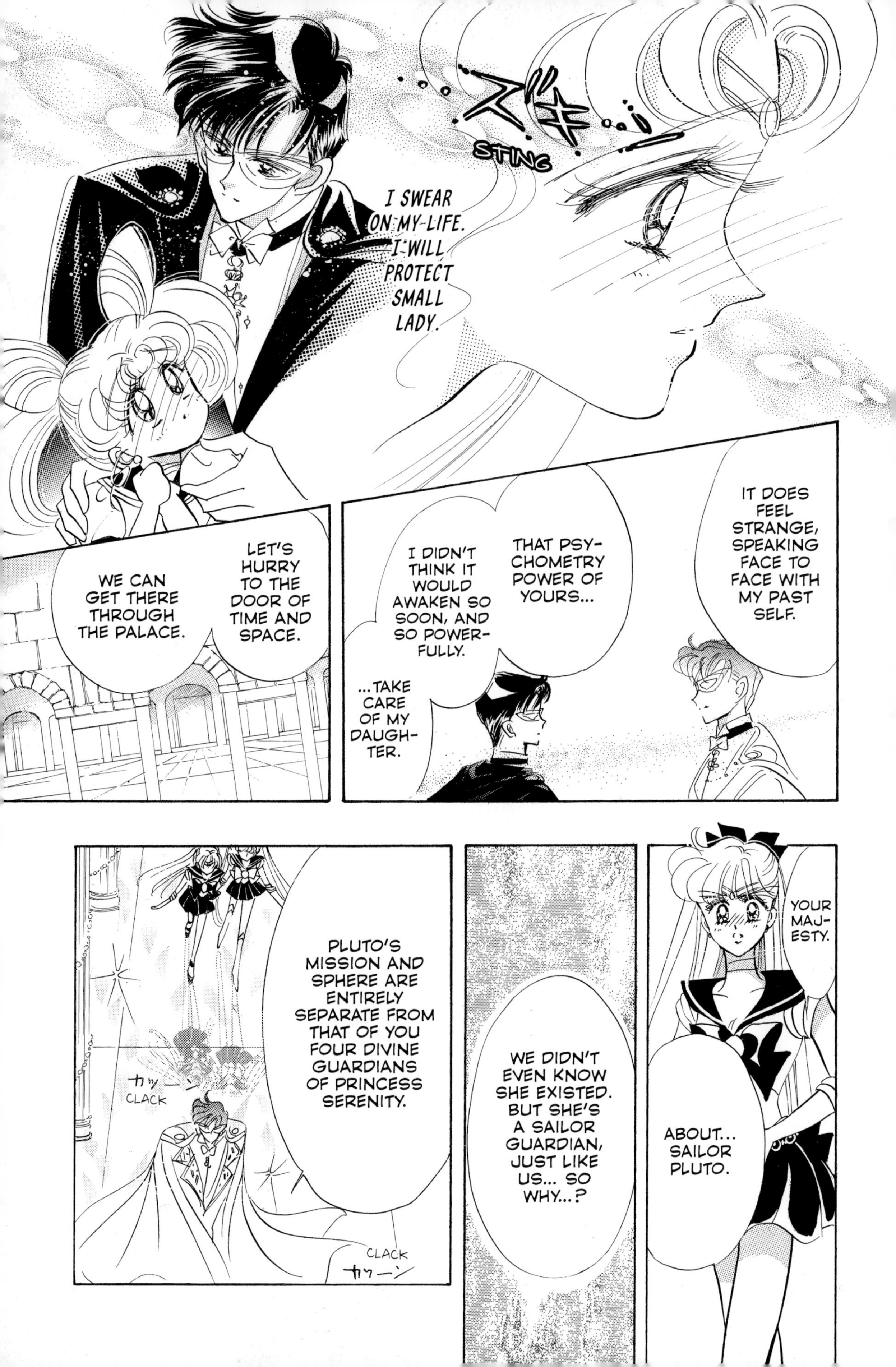
STING
I SWEAR ON MY LIFE. I WILL PROTECT SMALL LADY.
IT DOES FEEL STRANGE, SPEAKING FACE TO FACE WITH MY PAST SELF.
THAT PSY-CHOMETRY POWER OF YOURS...
I DIDN'T THINK IT WOULD AWAKEN SO SOON, AND SO POWER-FULLY.
...TAKE CARE OF MY DAUGHTER.
LET'S HURRY TO THE DOOR OF TIME AND SPACE.
WE CAN GET THERE THROUGH THE PALACE.
YOUR MAJ-ESTY.
ABOUT... SAILOR PLUTO.
WE DIDN'T EVEN KNOW SHE EXISTED. BUT SHE'S A SAILOR GUARDIAN, JUST LIKE US... SO WHY...?
PLUTO'S MISSION AND SPHERE ARE ENTIRELY SEPARATE FROM THAT OF YOU FOUR DIVINE GUARDIANS OF PRINCESS SERENITY.
CLACK
CLACK

SINCE ANCIENT TIMES, SAILOR PLUTO HAS STOOD ALONE AT THE DOOR OF TIME AND SPACE, OVERSEER OF THAT FORBIDDEN REALM.

TIME IS THE FINAL INVIOLABLE DOMAIN!

THE BLOOD OF CHRONOS, GOD OF TIME, FLOWS IN HER VEINS.

SHE IS THE BEAUTIFUL AND SOLITARY KEEPER OF THE DOOR OF THE UNDERWORLD, A LAND WHICH EXISTS IN THE RIFT BETWEEN TIMES.

KING ENDYMION?!

YES, MY KING!

GIVE ME A KEY.

PLUTO.

UNDER NORMAL CIRCUMSTANCES, THIS WOULD BE A SERIOUS CRIME, BUT IT'S AN EMERGENCY.

CLINK

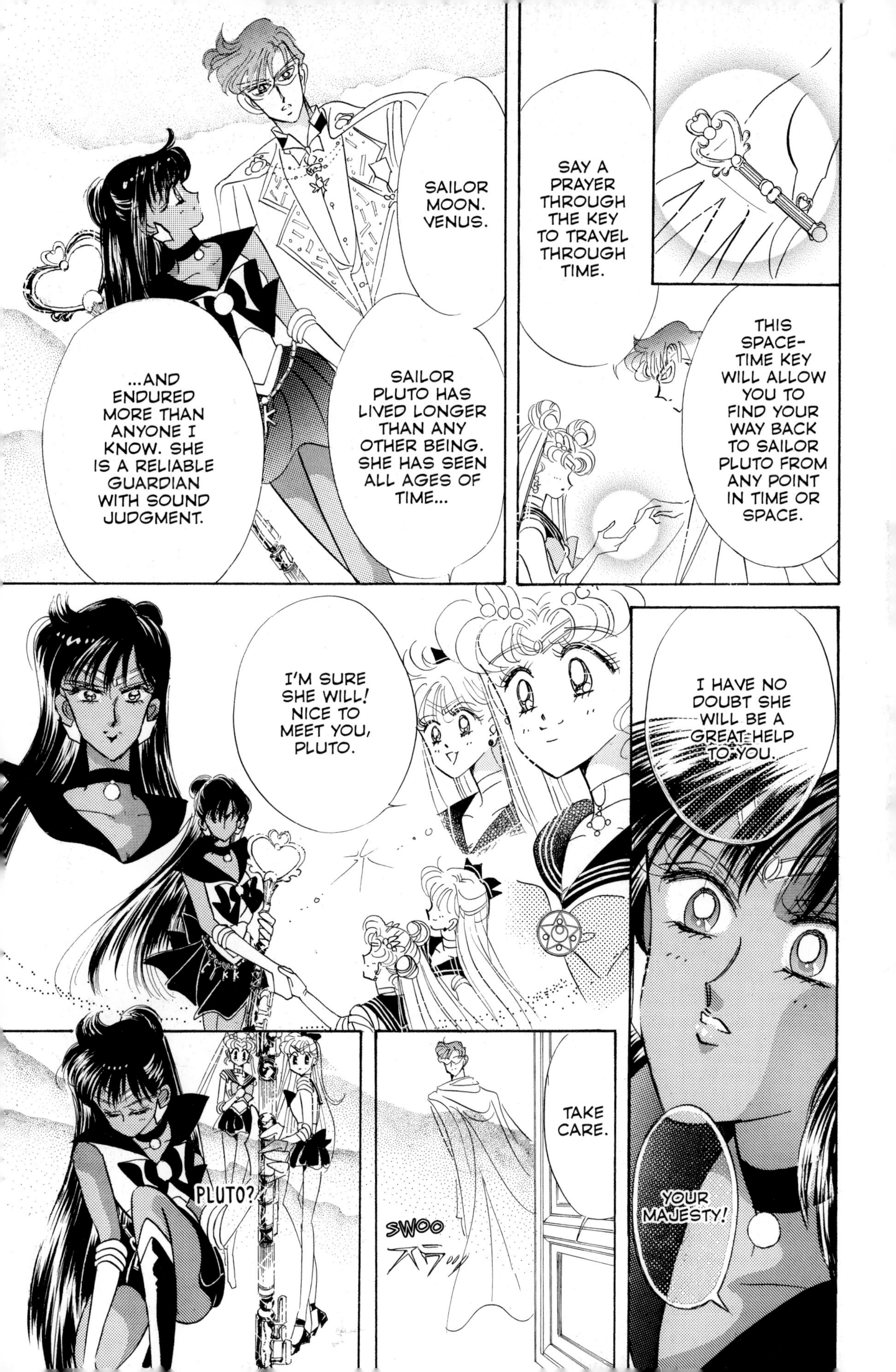
THIS SPACE-TIME KEY WILL ALLOW YOU TO FIND YOUR WAY BACK TO SAILOR PLUTO FROM ANY POINT IN TIME OR SPACE.
SAY A PRAYER THROUGH THE KEY TO TRAVEL THROUGH TIME.
SAILOR MOON. VENUS.
SAILOR PLUTO HAS LIVED LONGER THAN ANY OTHER BEING. SHE HAS SEEN ALL AGES OF TIME...
...AND ENDURED MORE THAN ANYONE I KNOW. SHE IS A RELIABLE GUARDIAN WITH SOUND JUDGMENT.
I HAVE NO DOUBT SHE WILL BE A GREAT HELP TO YOU.
YOUR MAJESTY!
I'M SURE SHE WILL! NICE TO MEET YOU, PLUTO.
TAKE CARE.
SWOO
PLUTO?

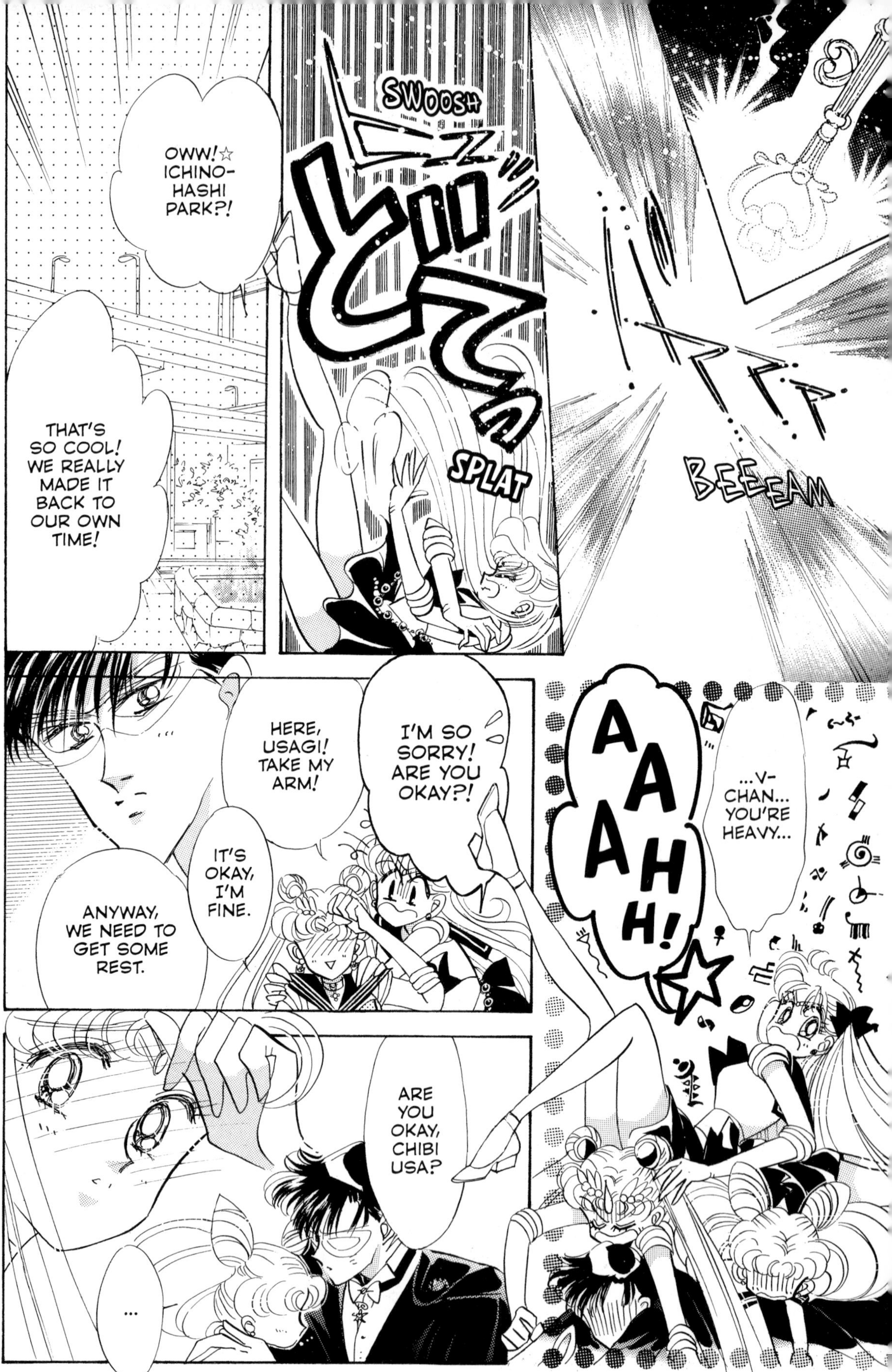
BEEEAM
SWOOSH
SPLAT
OWW!☆ ICHINO-HASHI PARK?!
THAT'S SO COOL! WE REALLY MADE IT BACK TO OUR OWN TIME!
AAAHH!
...V-CHAN... YOU'RE HEAVY...
I'M SO SORRY! ARE YOU OKAY?!
HERE, USAGI! TAKE MY ARM!
IT'S OKAY, I'M FINE.
ANYWAY, WE NEED TO GET SOME REST.
ARE YOU OKAY, CHIBI USA?
...

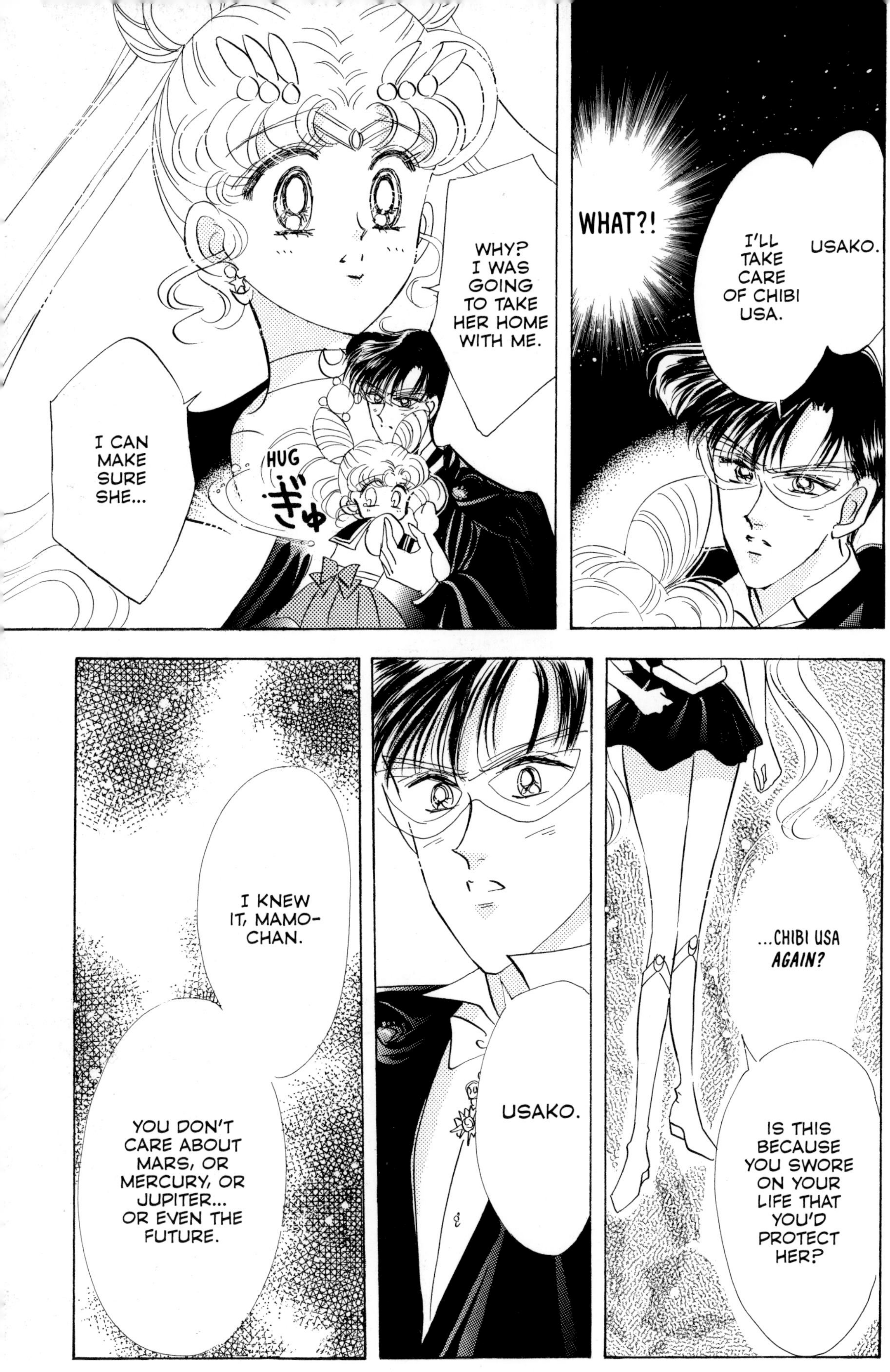
USAKO.
I'LL TAKE CARE OF CHIBI USA.
WHAT?!
WHY? I WAS GOING TO TAKE HER HOME WITH ME.
HUG
ぎゅ
I CAN MAKE SURE SHE...
...CHIBI USA AGAIN?
IS THIS BECAUSE YOU SWORE ON YOUR LIFE THAT YOU'D PROTECT HER?
USAKO.
I KNEW IT, MAMO-CHAN.
YOU DON'T CARE ABOUT MARS, OR MERCURY, OR JUPITER... OR EVEN THE FUTURE.

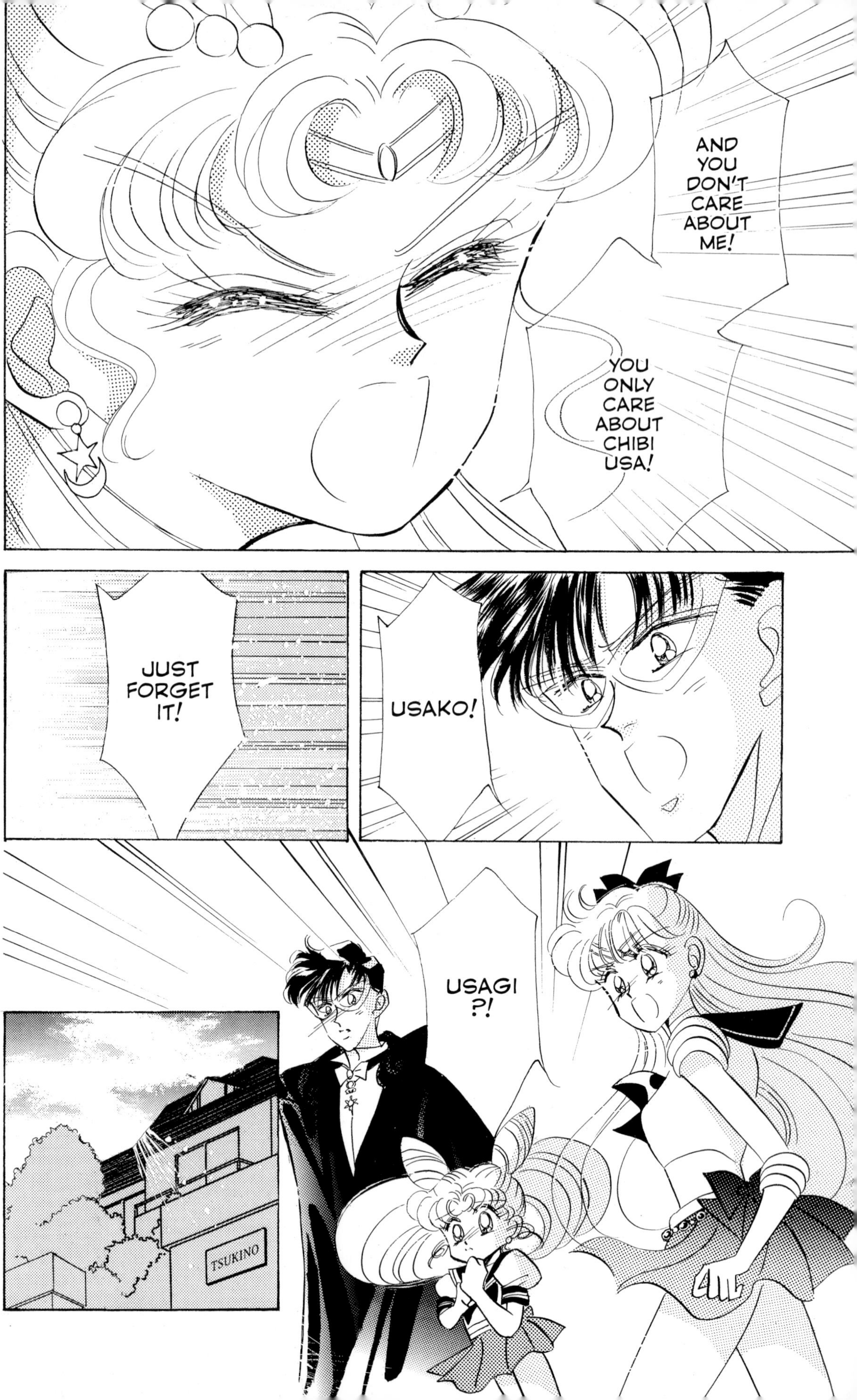
AND YOU DON'T CARE ABOUT ME!
YOU ONLY CARE ABOUT CHIBI USA!
USAKO!
JUST FORGET IT!
USAGI ?!
TSUKINO

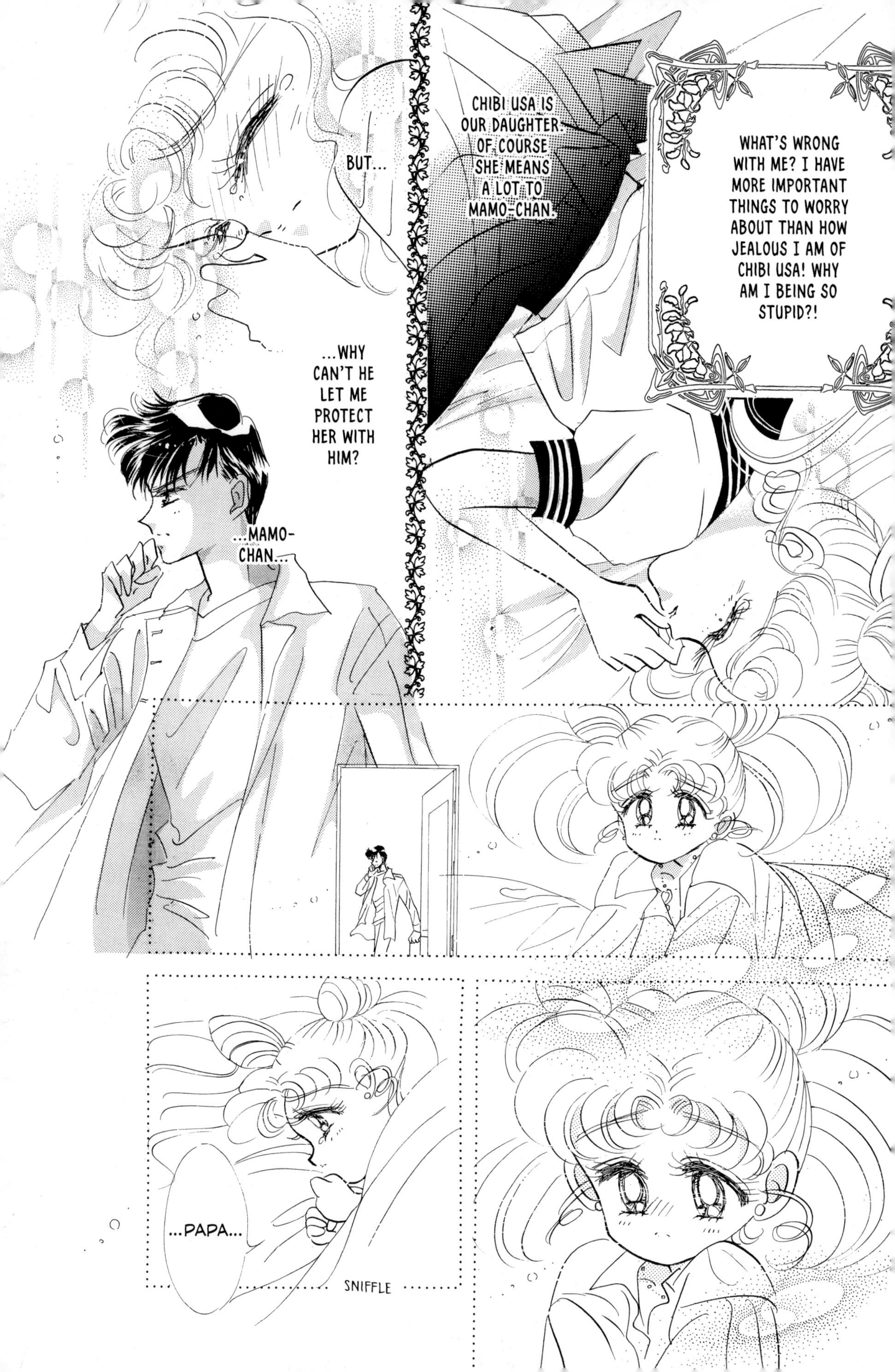
WHAT'S WRONG WITH ME? I HAVE MORE IMPORTANT THINGS TO WORRY ABOUT THAN HOW JEALOUS I AM OF CHIBI USA! WHY AM I BEING SO STUPID?!
CHIBI USA IS OUR DAUGHTER. OF COURSE SHE MEANS A LOT TO MAMO-CHAN.
BUT...
...WHY CAN'T HE LET ME PROTECT HER WITH HIM?
...MAMO-CHAN...
...PAPA...
SNIFFLE

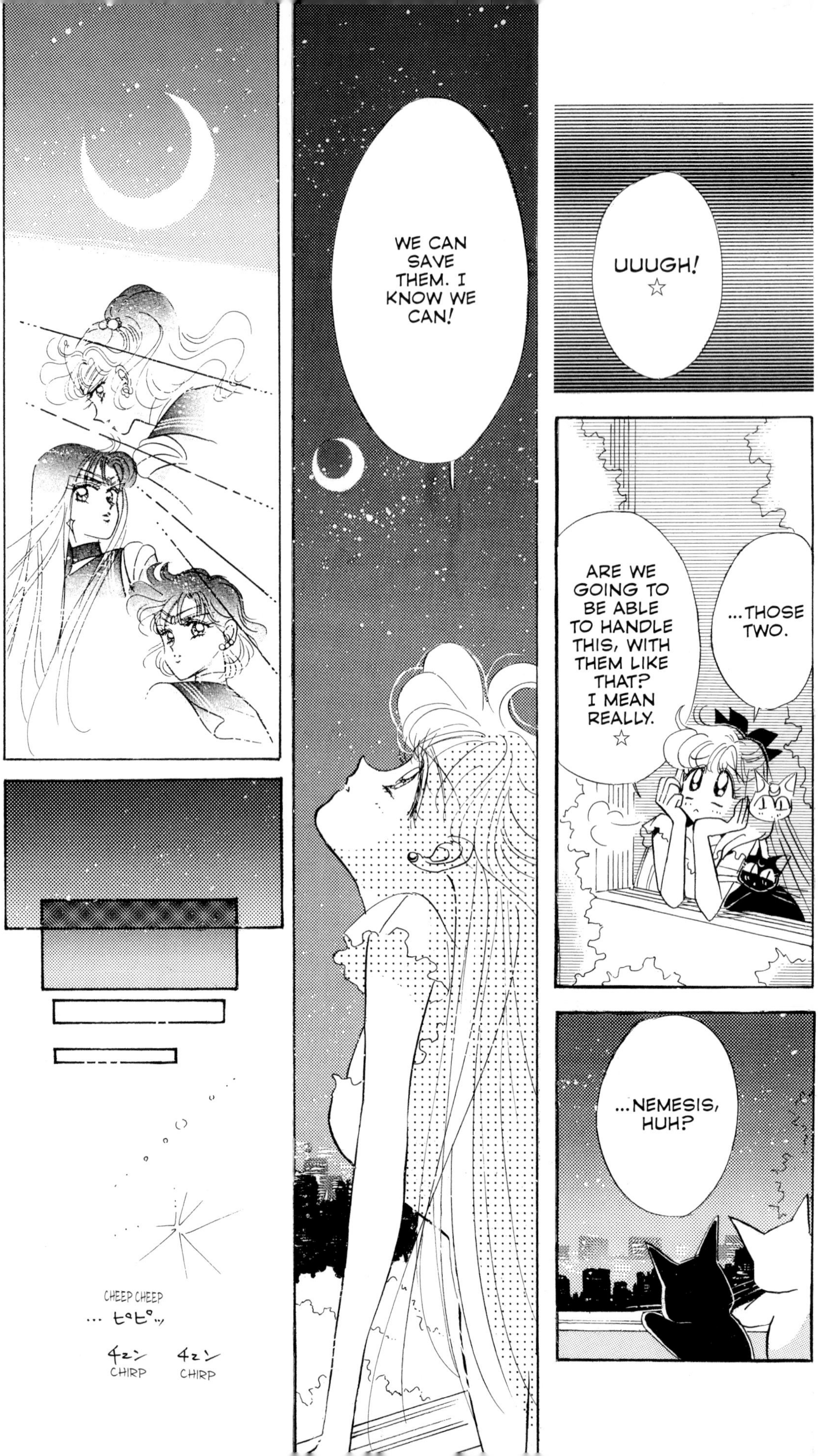
UUUGH! ☆
...THOSE TWO.
ARE WE GOING TO BE ABLE TO HANDLE THIS, WITH THEM LIKE THAT? I MEAN REALLY. ☆
...NEMESIS, HUH?
WE CAN SAVE THEM. I KNOW WE CAN!
CHEEP CHEEP
... ピピッ
チュン CHIRP
チュン CHIRP

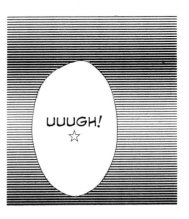

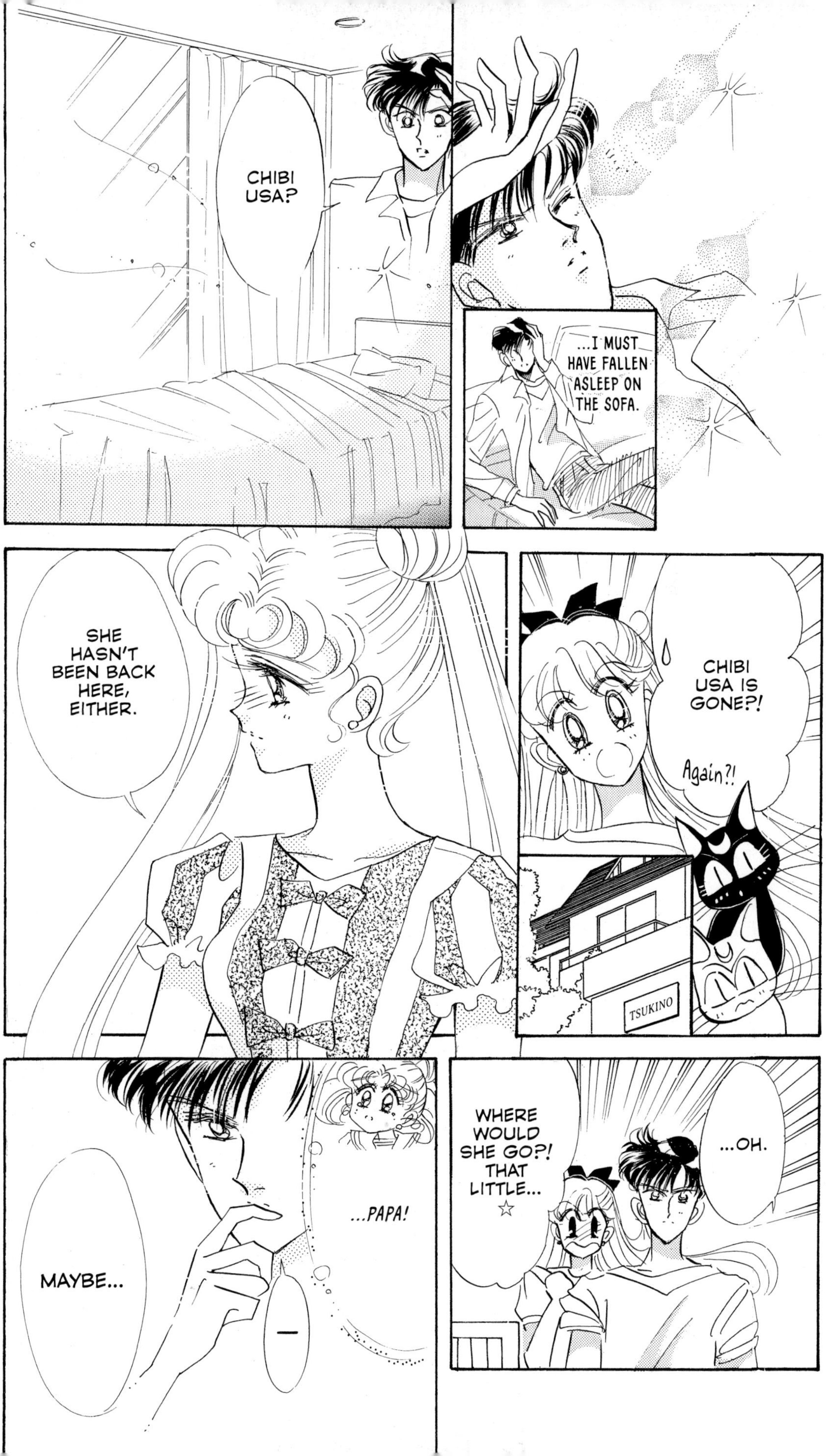
...I MUST HAVE FALLEN ASLEEP ON THE SOFA.
CHIBI USA?
CHIBI USA IS GONE?!
Again?!
TSUKINO
SHE HASN'T BEEN BACK HERE, EITHER.
...OH.
WHERE WOULD SHE GO?! THAT LITTLE... ☆
...PAPA!
—
MAYBE...

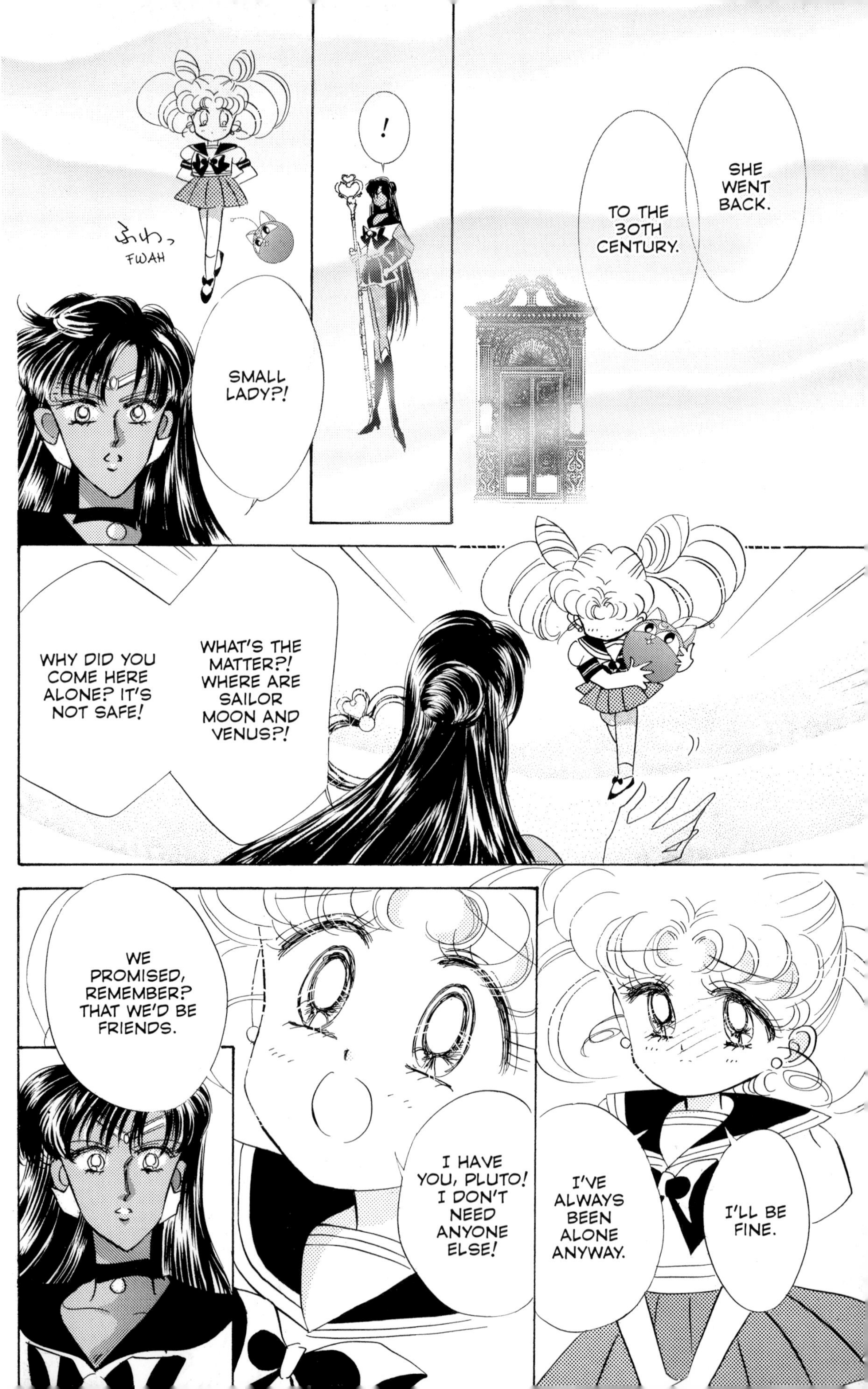
SHE WENT BACK.
TO THE 30TH CENTURY.
!
ふわっ
FWAH
SMALL LADY?!
WHAT'S THE MATTER?! WHERE ARE SAILOR MOON AND VENUS?!
WHY DID YOU COME HERE ALONE? IT'S NOT SAFE!
I'LL BE FINE.
I'VE ALWAYS BEEN ALONE ANYWAY.
I HAVE YOU, PLUTO! I DON'T NEED ANYONE ELSE!
WE PROMISED, REMEMBER? THAT WE'D BE FRIENDS.

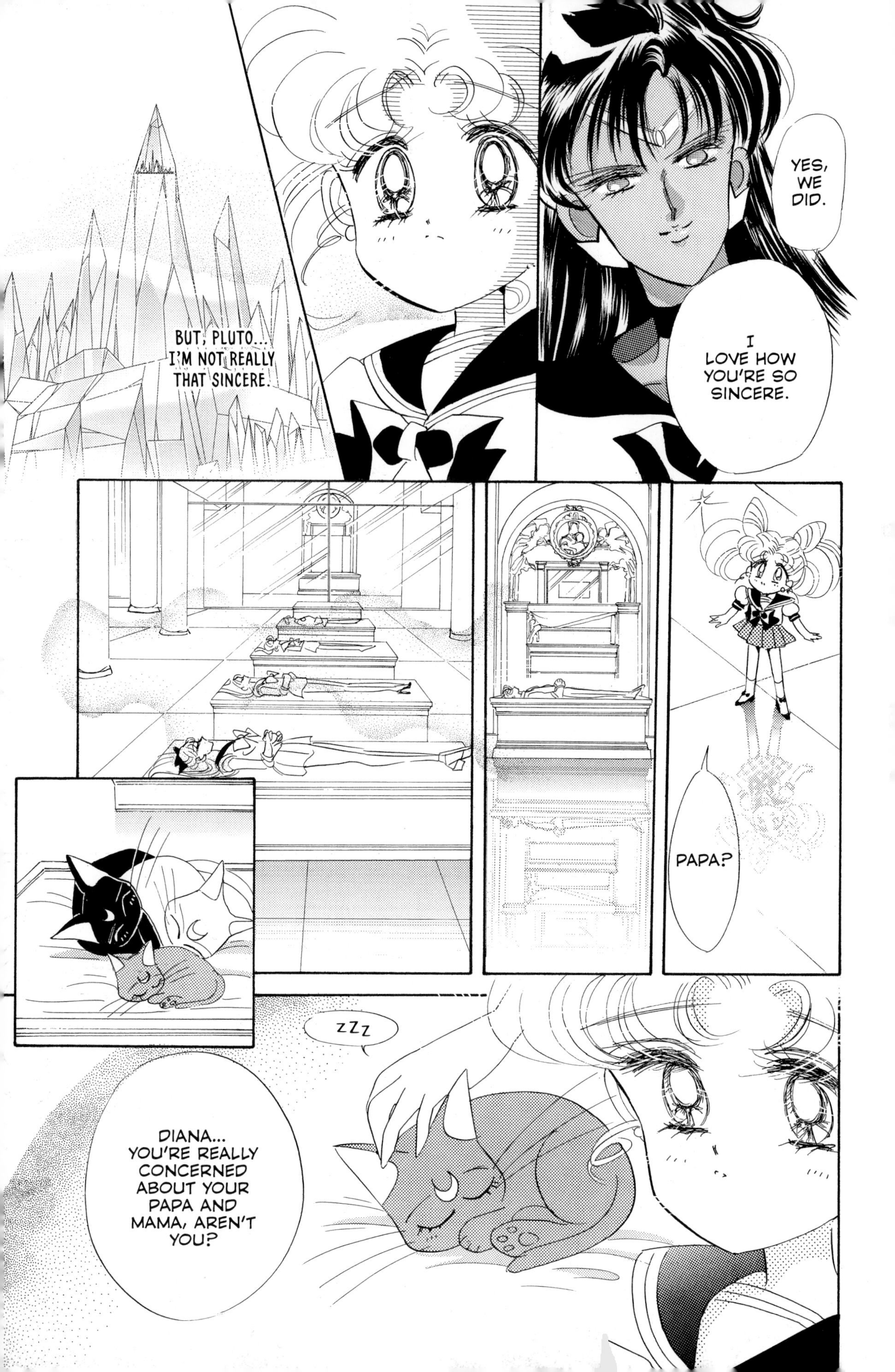
YES, WE DID.
I LOVE HOW YOU'RE SO SINCERE.
BUT, PLUTO... I'M NOT REALLY THAT SINCERE.
PAPA?
ZZZ
DIANA... YOU'RE REALLY CONCERNED ABOUT YOUR PAPA AND MAMA, AREN'T YOU?

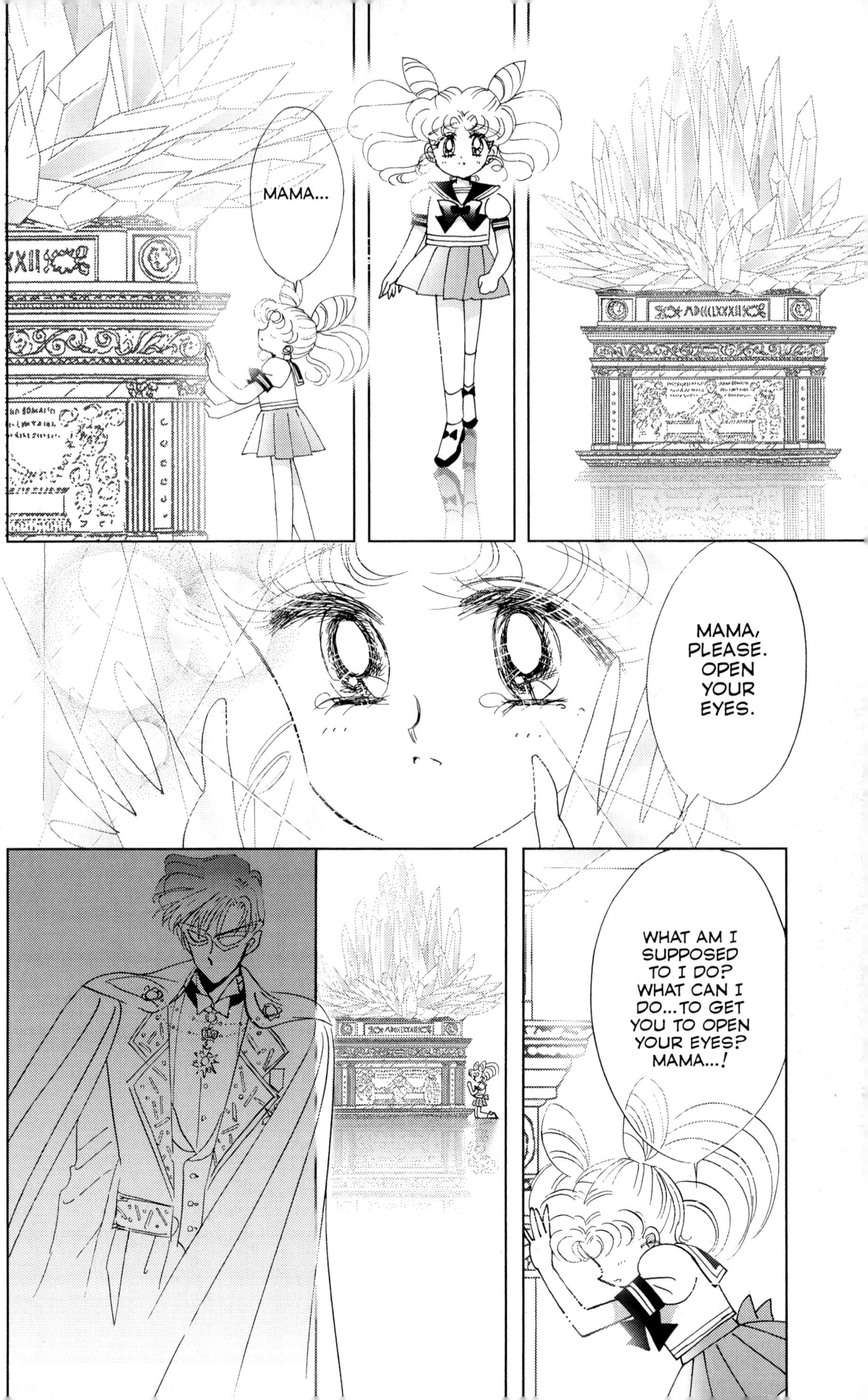
MAMA...
MAMA, PLEASE. OPEN YOUR EYES.
WHAT AM I SUPPOSED TO I DO? WHAT CAN I DO...TO GET YOU TO OPEN YOUR EYES? MAMA...!

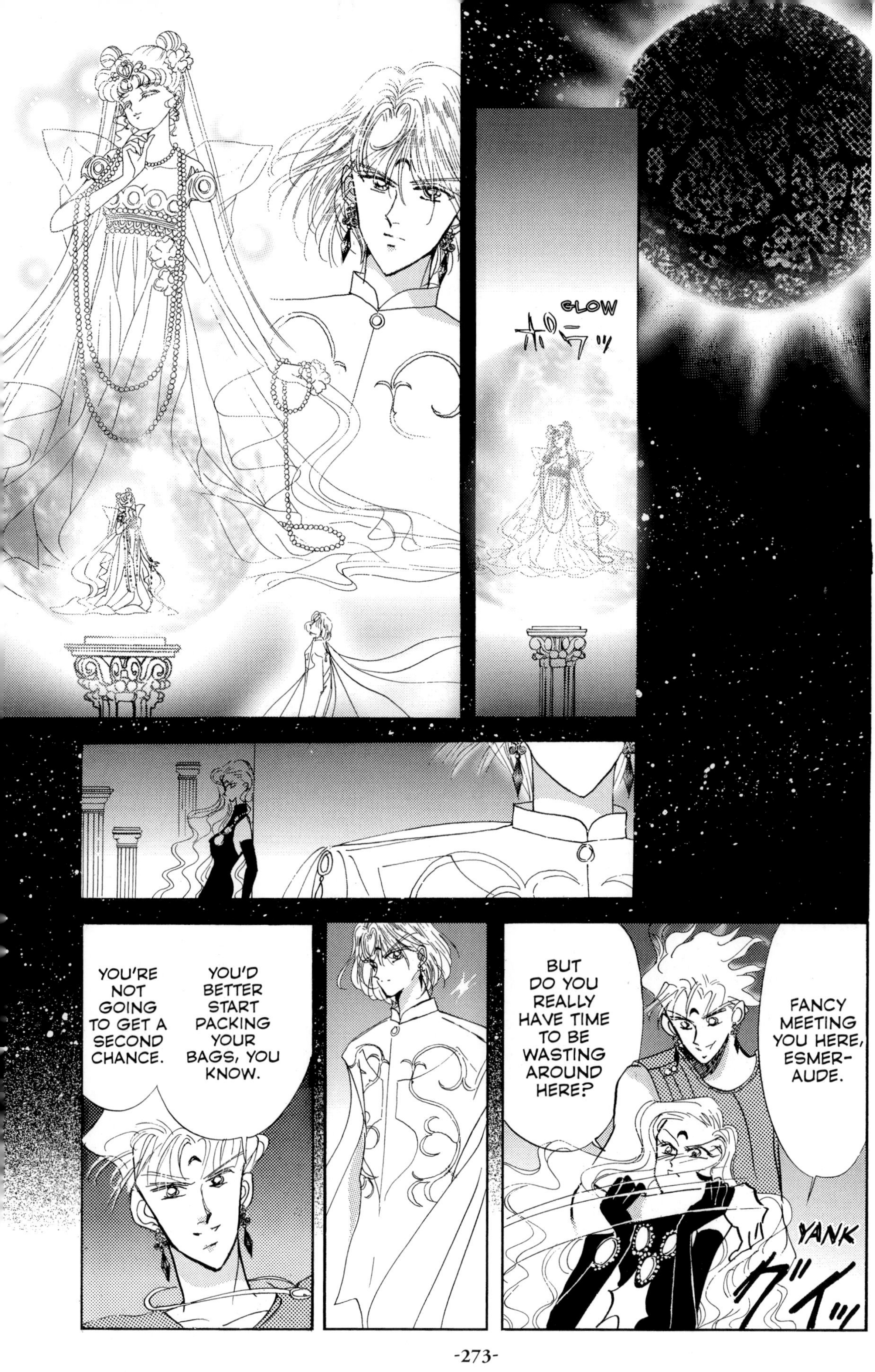
GLOW
FANCY MEETING YOU HERE, ESMERAUDE.
BUT DO YOU REALLY HAVE TIME TO BE WASTING AROUND HERE?
YANK
YOU'D BETTER START PACKING YOUR BAGS, YOU KNOW.
YOU'RE NOT GOING TO GET A SECOND CHANCE.

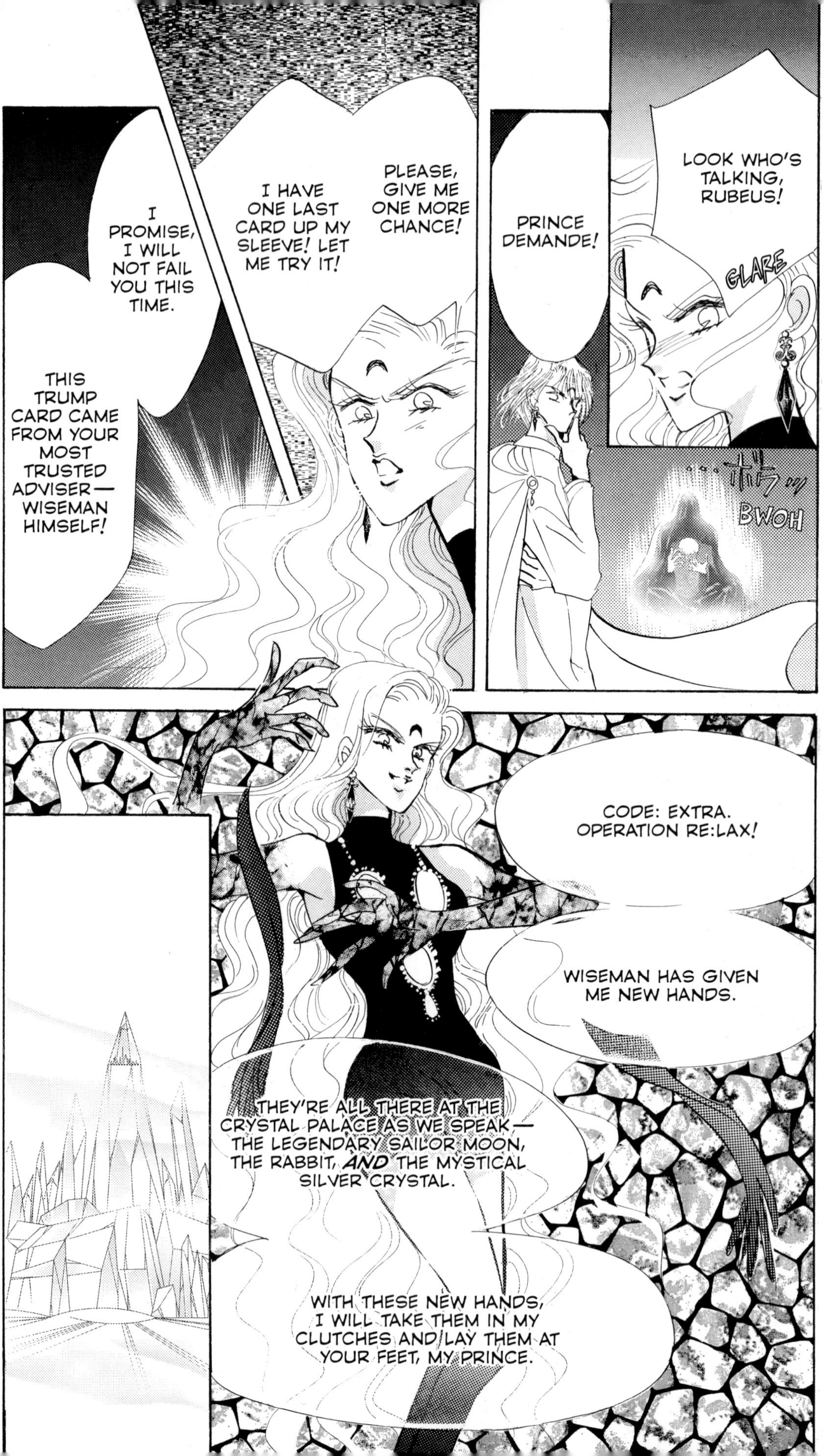
LOOK WHO'S TALKING, RUBEUS!
GLARE
PRINCE DEMANDE!
BWOH
PLEASE, GIVE ME ONE MORE CHANCE!
I HAVE ONE LAST CARD UP MY SLEEVE! LET ME TRY IT!
I PROMISE, I WILL NOT FAIL YOU THIS TIME.
THIS TRUMP CARD CAME FROM YOUR MOST TRUSTED ADVISER— WISEMAN HIMSELF!
CODE: EXTRA. OPERATION RE:LAX!
WISEMAN HAS GIVEN ME NEW HANDS.
THEY'RE ALL THERE AT THE CRYSTAL PALACE AS WE SPEAK— THE LEGENDARY SAILOR MOON, THE RABBIT, *AND* THE MYSTICAL SILVER CRYSTAL.
WITH THESE NEW HANDS, I WILL TAKE THEM IN MY CLUTCHES AND LAY THEM AT YOUR FEET, MY PRINCE.

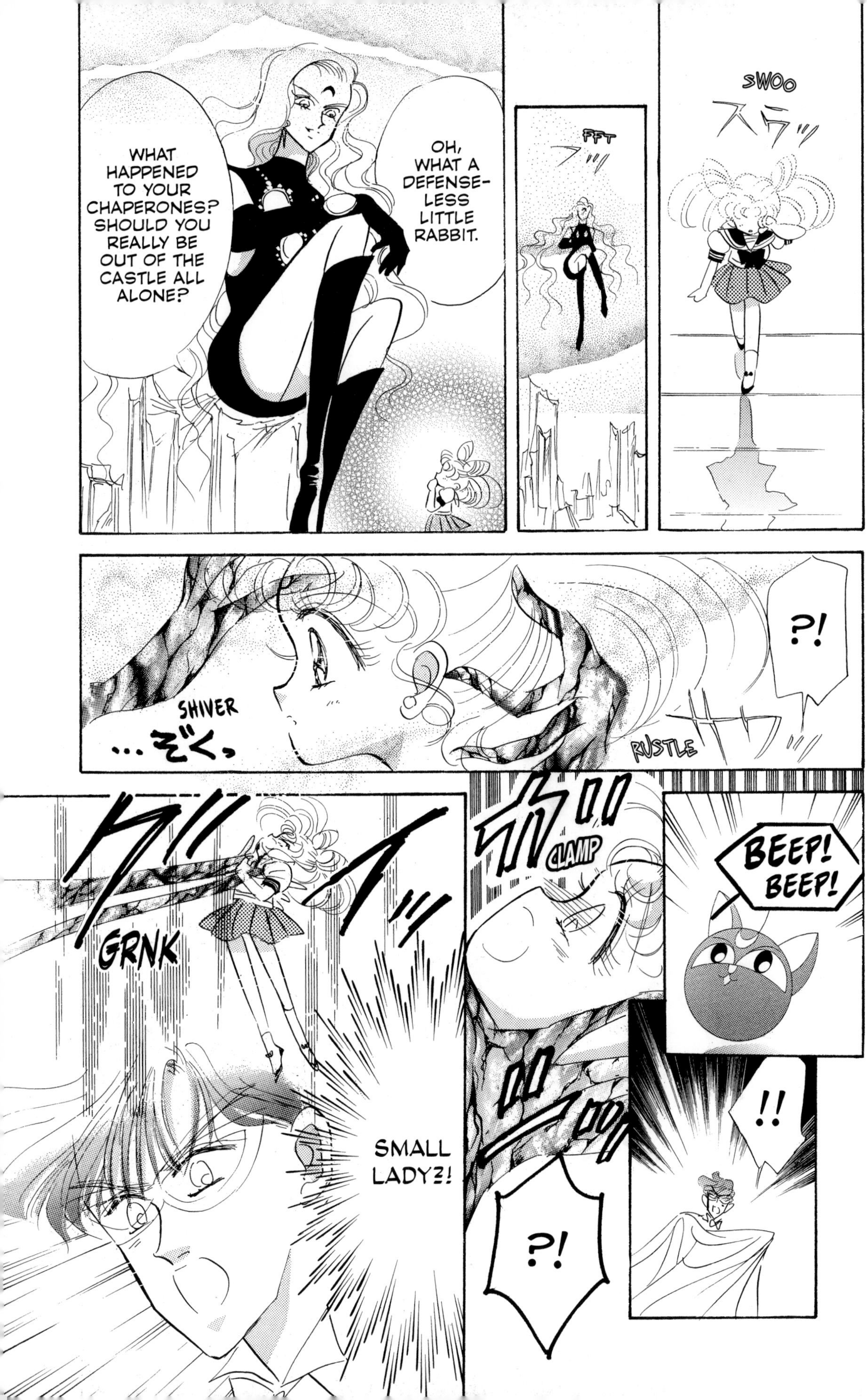
SWOO
FFT
OH, WHAT A DEFENSELESS LITTLE RABBIT.
WHAT HAPPENED TO YOUR CHAPERONES? SHOULD YOU REALLY BE OUT OF THE CASTLE ALL ALONE?
?!
RUSTLE
SHIVER
…ぞくっ
BEEP! BEEP!
!!
CLAMP
?!
GRNK
SMALL LADY?!

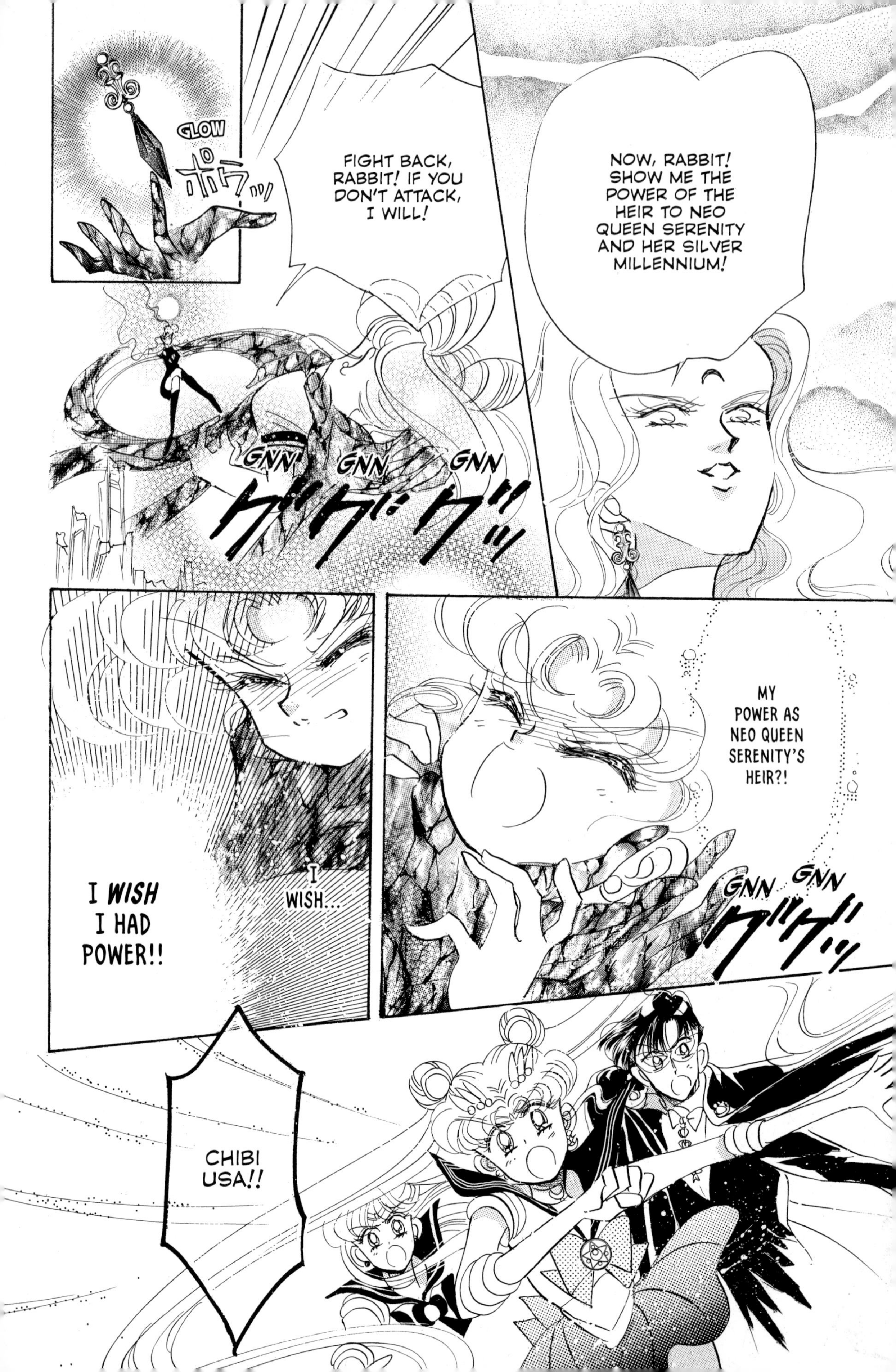
NOW, RABBIT! SHOW ME THE POWER OF THE HEIR TO NEO QUEEN SERENITY AND HER SILVER MILLENNIUM!
FIGHT BACK, RABBIT! IF YOU DON'T ATTACK, I WILL!
GNN GNN GNN
GLOW
MY POWER AS NEO QUEEN SERENITY'S HEIR?!
GNN GNN
I WISH...
I WISH I HAD POWER!!
CHIBI USA!!

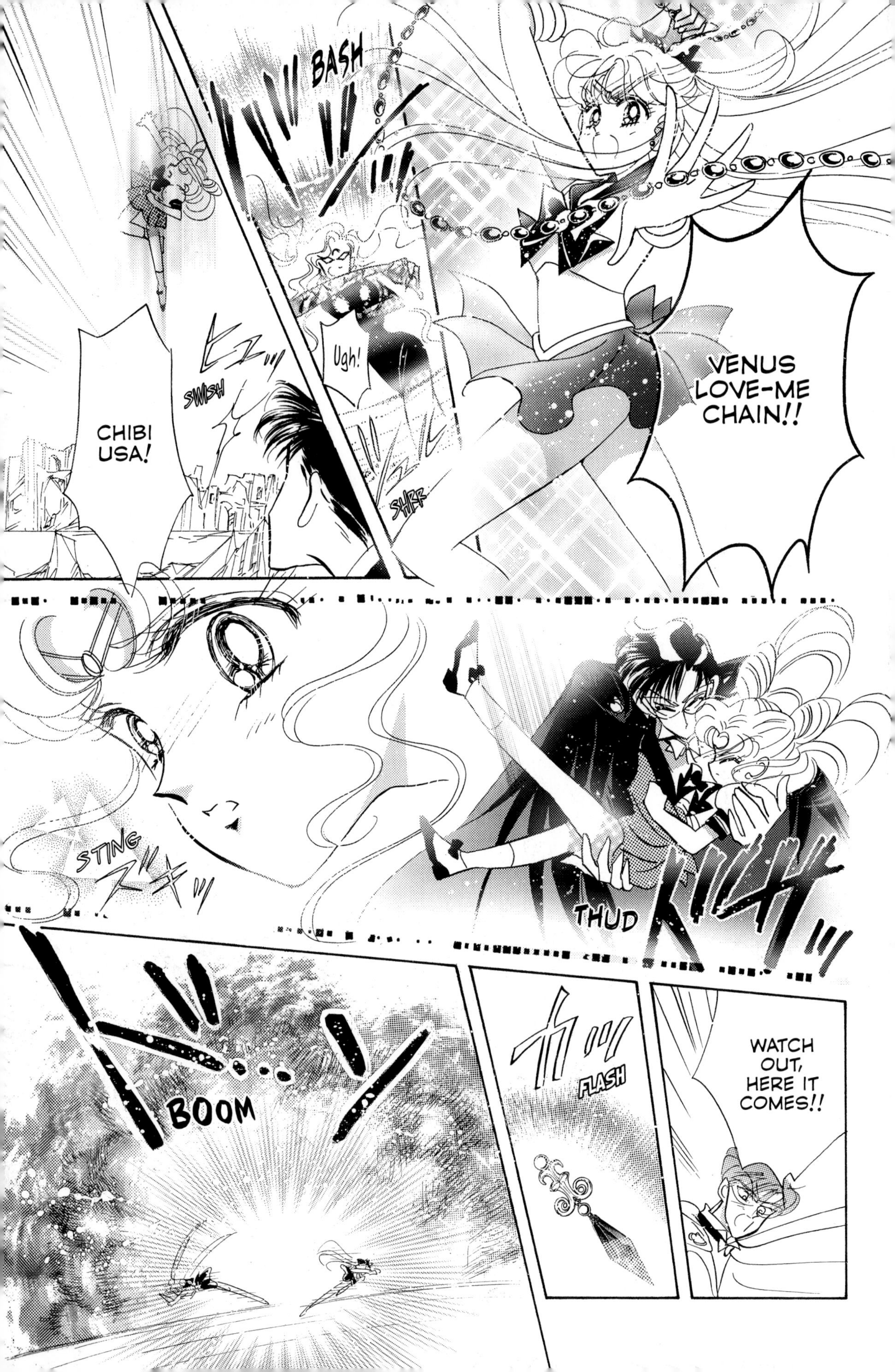
BASH
VENUS LOVE-ME CHAIN!!
Ugh!
SHRR
SWISH
CHIBI USA!
THUD
STING
WATCH OUT, HERE IT COMES!!
FLASH
BOOM

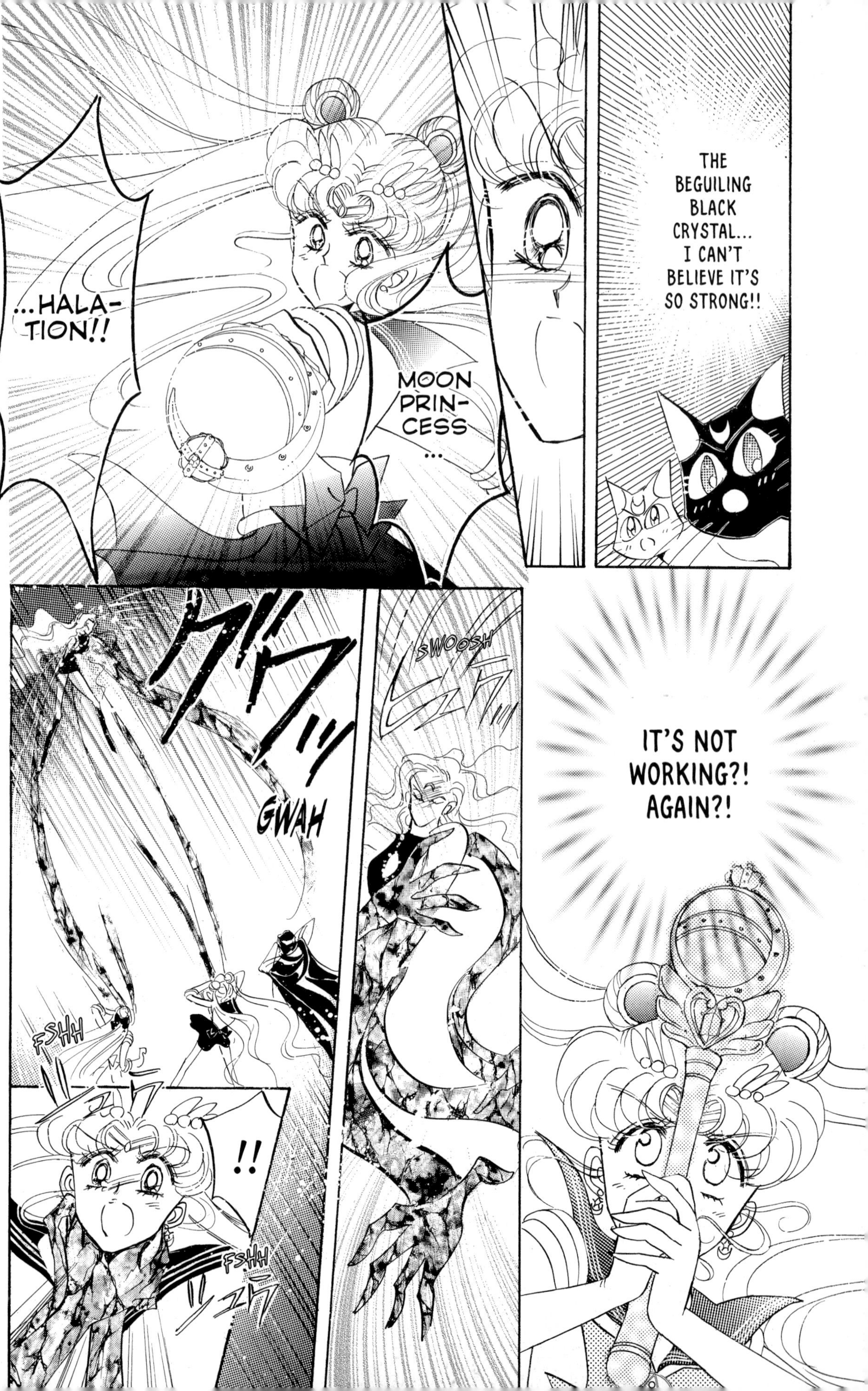
THE BEGUILING BLACK CRYSTAL... I CAN'T BELIEVE IT'S SO STRONG!!
MOON PRINCESS...
...HALATION!!
IT'S NOT WORKING?! AGAIN?!
SWOOSH
GWAH
FSHH
!!
FSHH

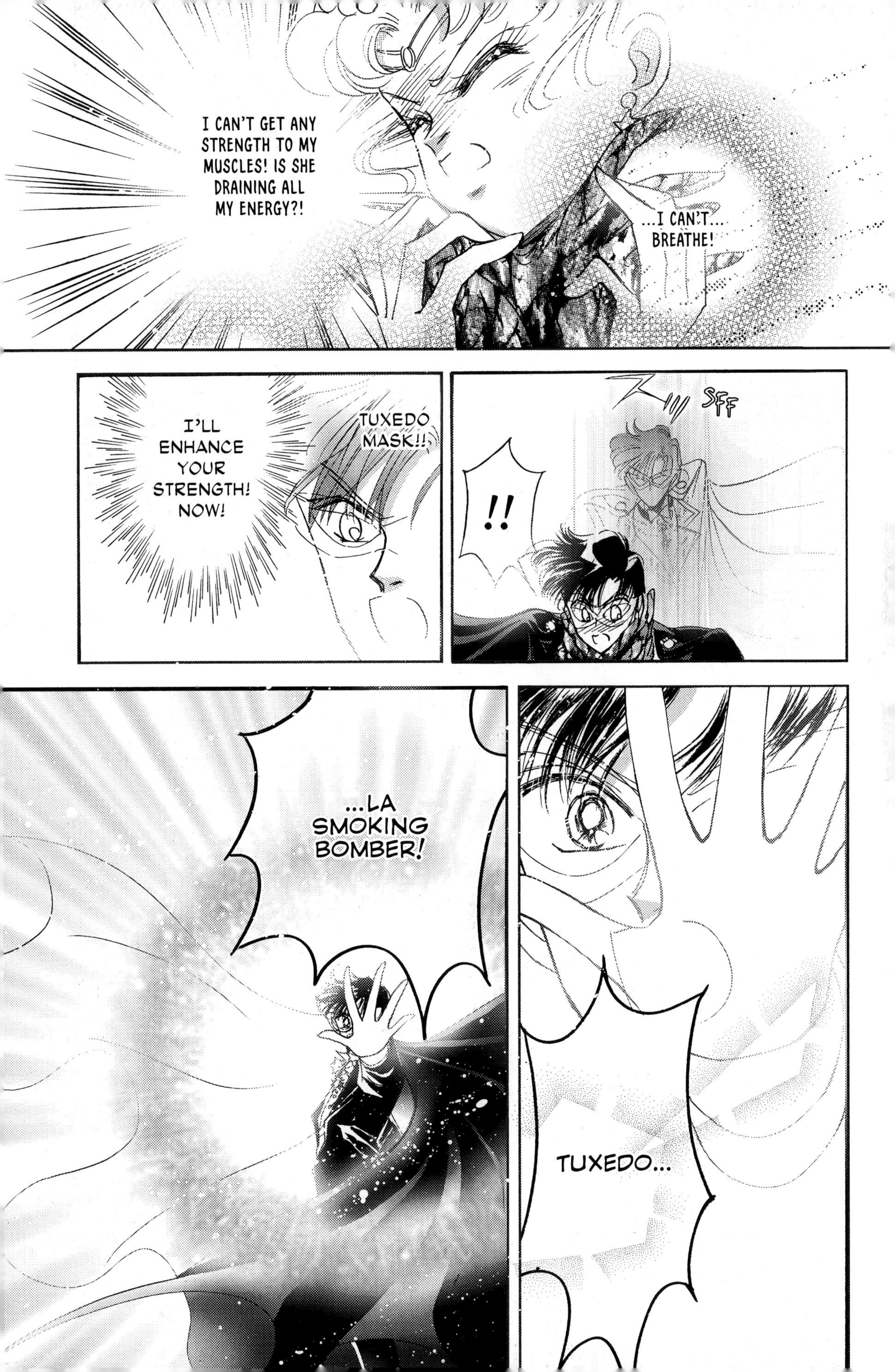
I CAN'T GET ANY STRENGTH TO MY MUSCLES! IS SHE DRAINING ALL MY ENERGY?!
...I CAN'T... BREATHE!
SFF
!!
TUXEDO MASK!!
I'LL ENHANCE YOUR STRENGTH! NOW!
TUXEDO...
...LA SMOKING BOMBER!

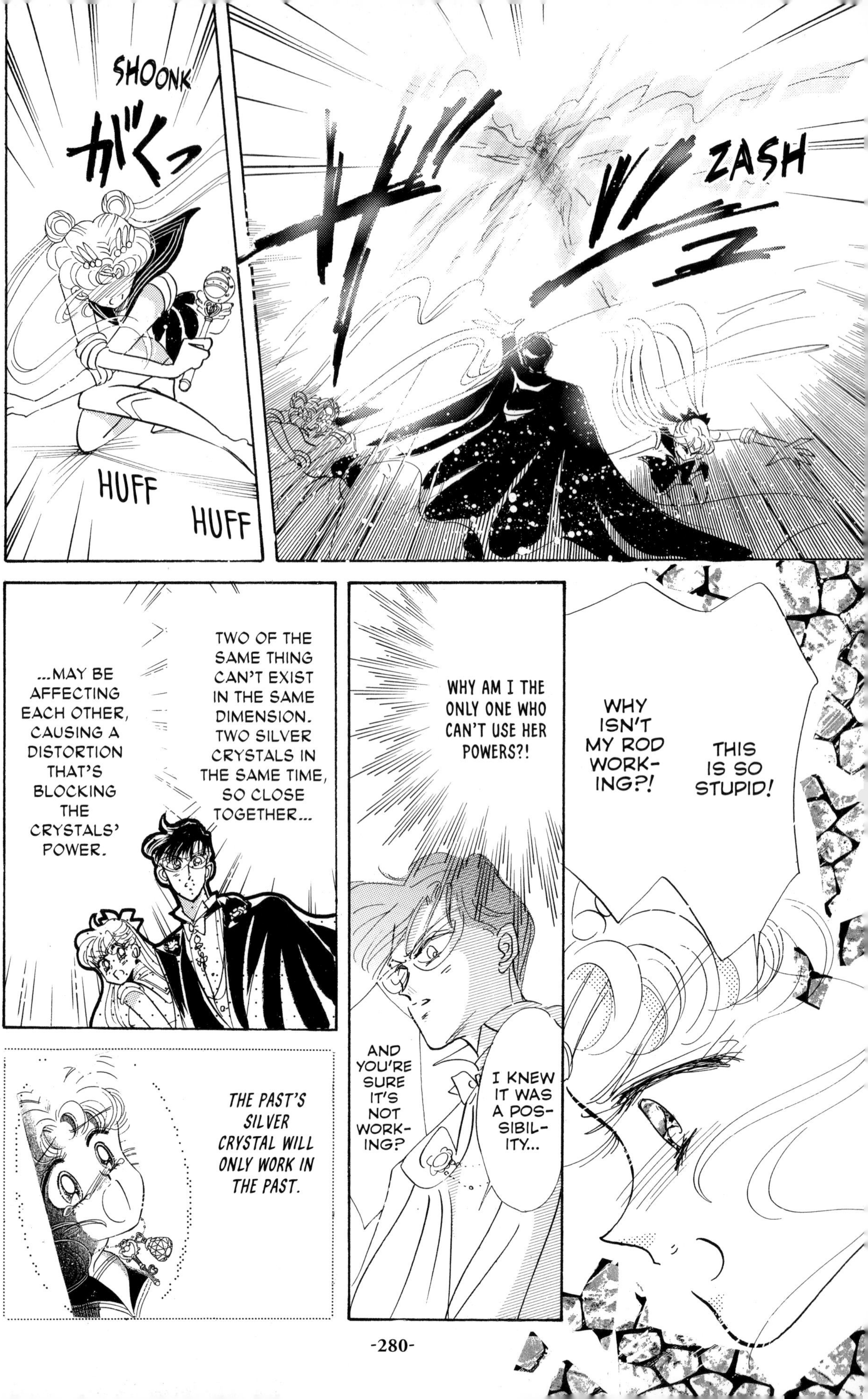
ZASH
SHOONK
がくっ
HUFF
HUFF
THIS IS SO STUPID!
WHY ISN'T MY ROD WORKING?!
WHY AM I THE ONLY ONE WHO CAN'T USE HER POWERS?!
I KNEW IT WAS A POSSIBILITY...
AND YOU'RE SURE IT'S NOT WORKING?
TWO OF THE SAME THING CAN'T EXIST IN THE SAME DIMENSION. TWO SILVER CRYSTALS IN THE SAME TIME, SO CLOSE TOGETHER...
...MAY BE AFFECTING EACH OTHER, CAUSING A DISTORTION THAT'S BLOCKING THE CRYSTALS' POWER.
THE PAST'S SILVER CRYSTAL WILL ONLY WORK IN THE PAST.

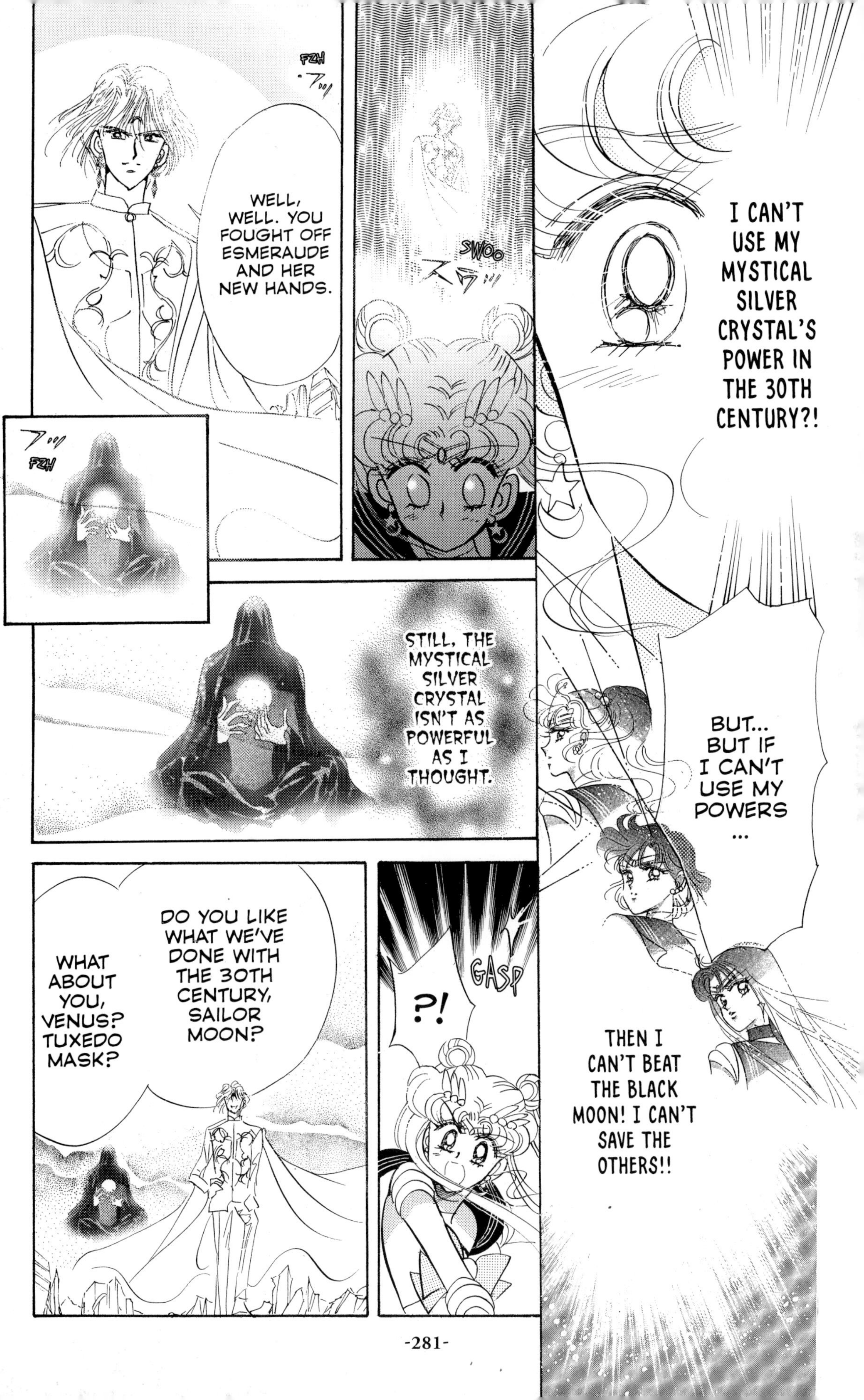
I CAN'T USE MY MYSTICAL SILVER CRYSTAL'S POWER IN THE 30TH CENTURY?!
BUT... BUT IF I CAN'T USE MY POWERS ...
THEN I CAN'T BEAT THE BLACK MOON! I CAN'T SAVE THE OTHERS!!
SWOO
FZH
WELL, WELL. YOU FOUGHT OFF ESMERAUDE AND HER NEW HANDS.
FZH
STILL, THE MYSTICAL SILVER CRYSTAL ISN'T AS POWERFUL AS I THOUGHT.
GASP
?!
DO YOU LIKE WHAT WE'VE DONE WITH THE 30TH CENTURY, SAILOR MOON?
WHAT ABOUT YOU, VENUS? TUXEDO MASK?

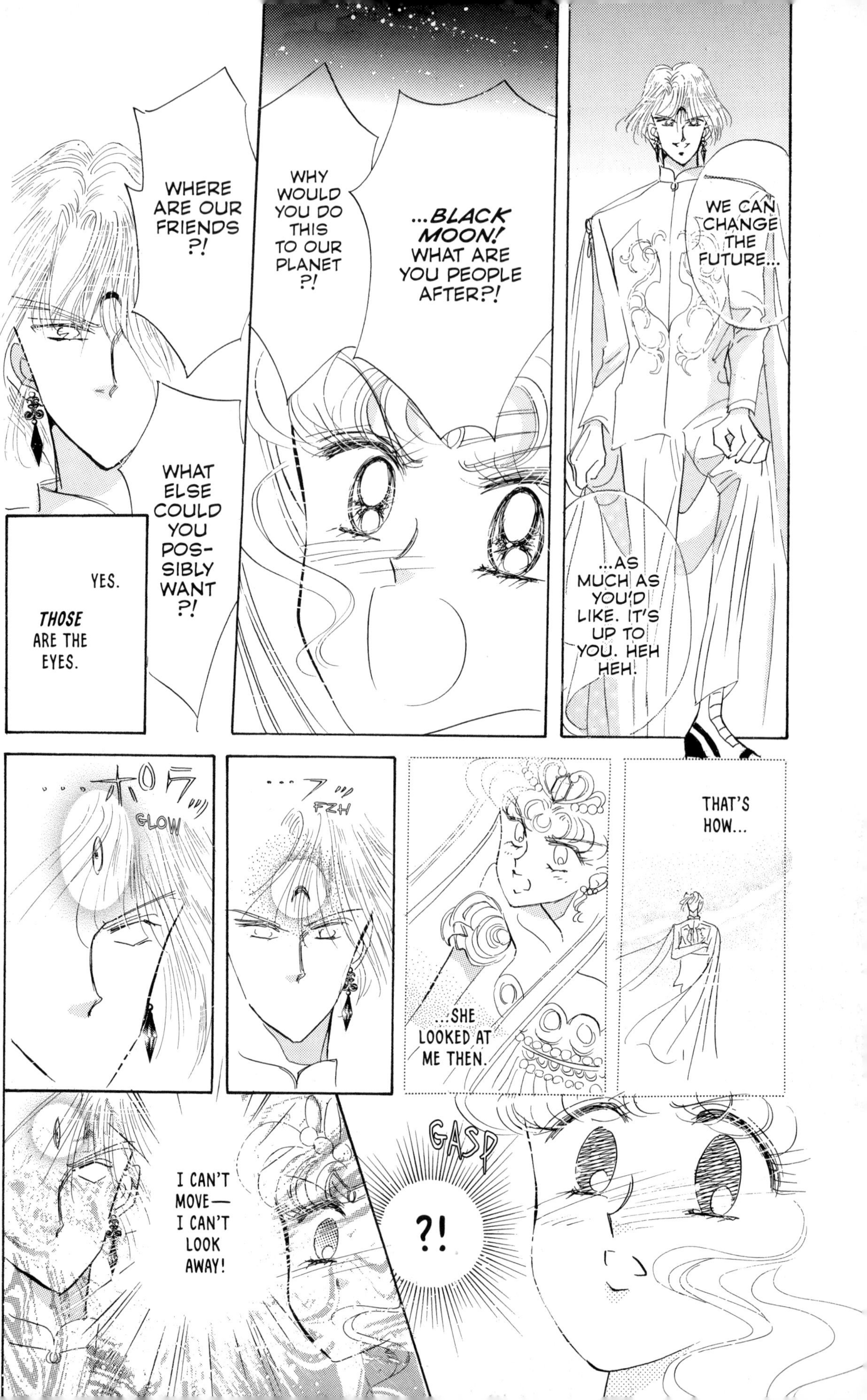
WE CAN CHANGE THE FUTURE...
...AS MUCH AS YOU'D LIKE. IT'S UP TO YOU. HEH HEH.
...*BLACK MOON!* WHAT ARE YOU PEOPLE AFTER?!
WHY WOULD YOU DO THIS TO OUR PLANET?!
WHERE ARE OUR FRIENDS?!
WHAT ELSE COULD YOU POS-SIBLY WANT?!
YES.
THOSE ARE THE EYES.
THAT'S HOW...
...SHE LOOKED AT ME THEN.
FZH
GLOW
GASP
?!
I CAN'T MOVE— I CAN'T LOOK AWAY!

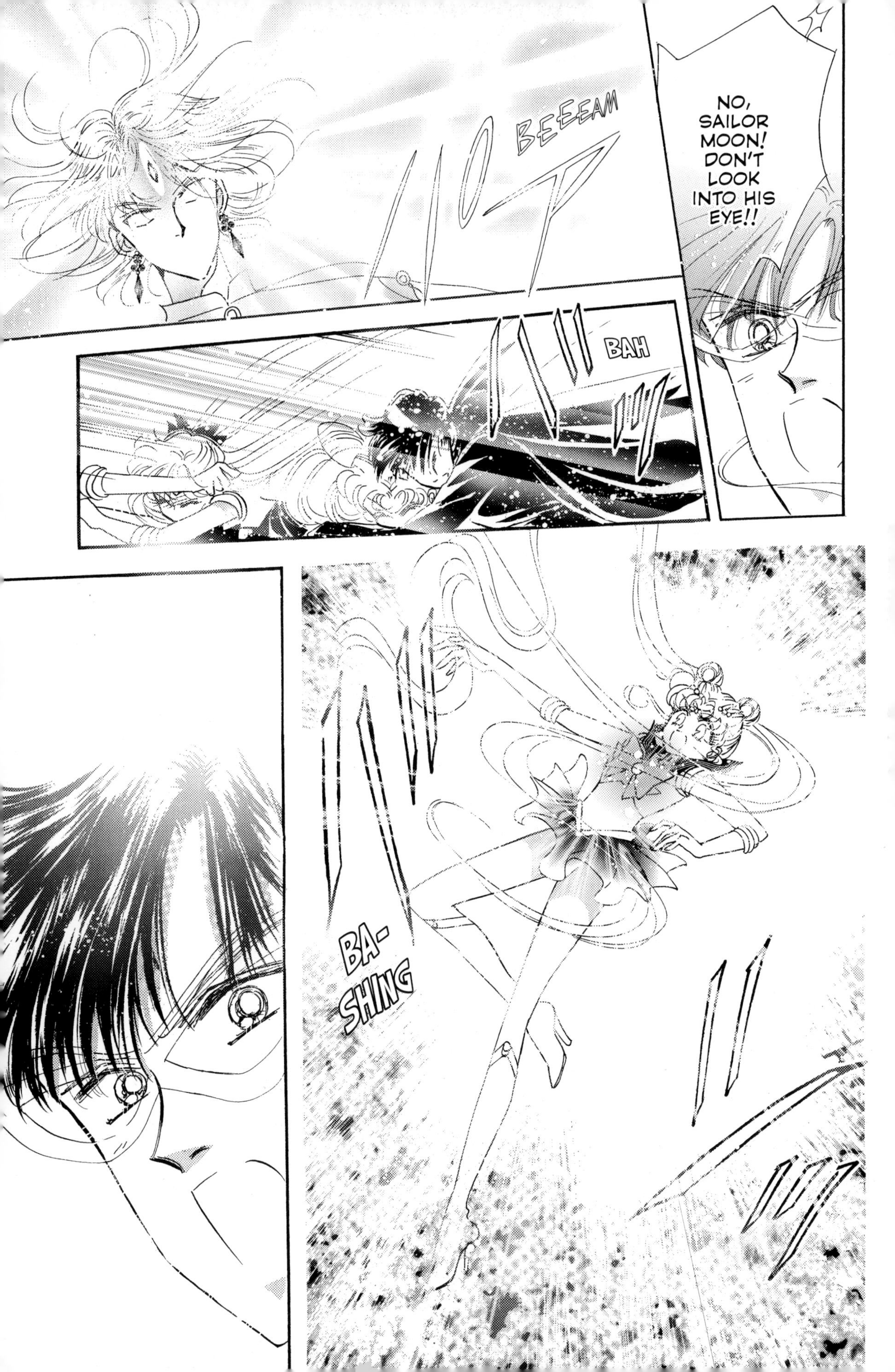
NO, SAILOR MOON! DON'T LOOK INTO HIS EYE!!
BEEEEAM
BAH
BA-SHING

Pretty Guardian

Sailor Moon

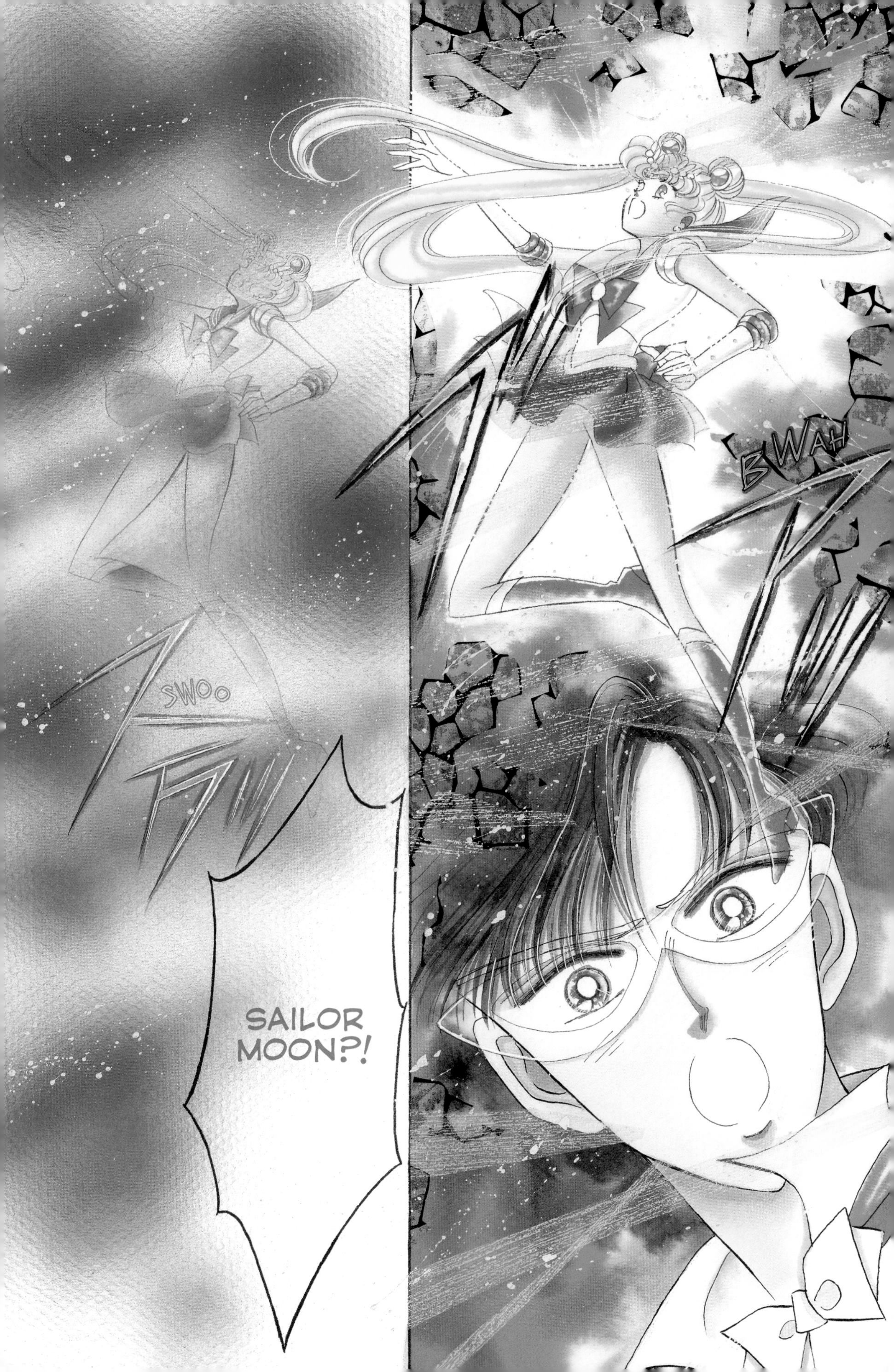
BWAH
SWOO
SAILOR MOON?!

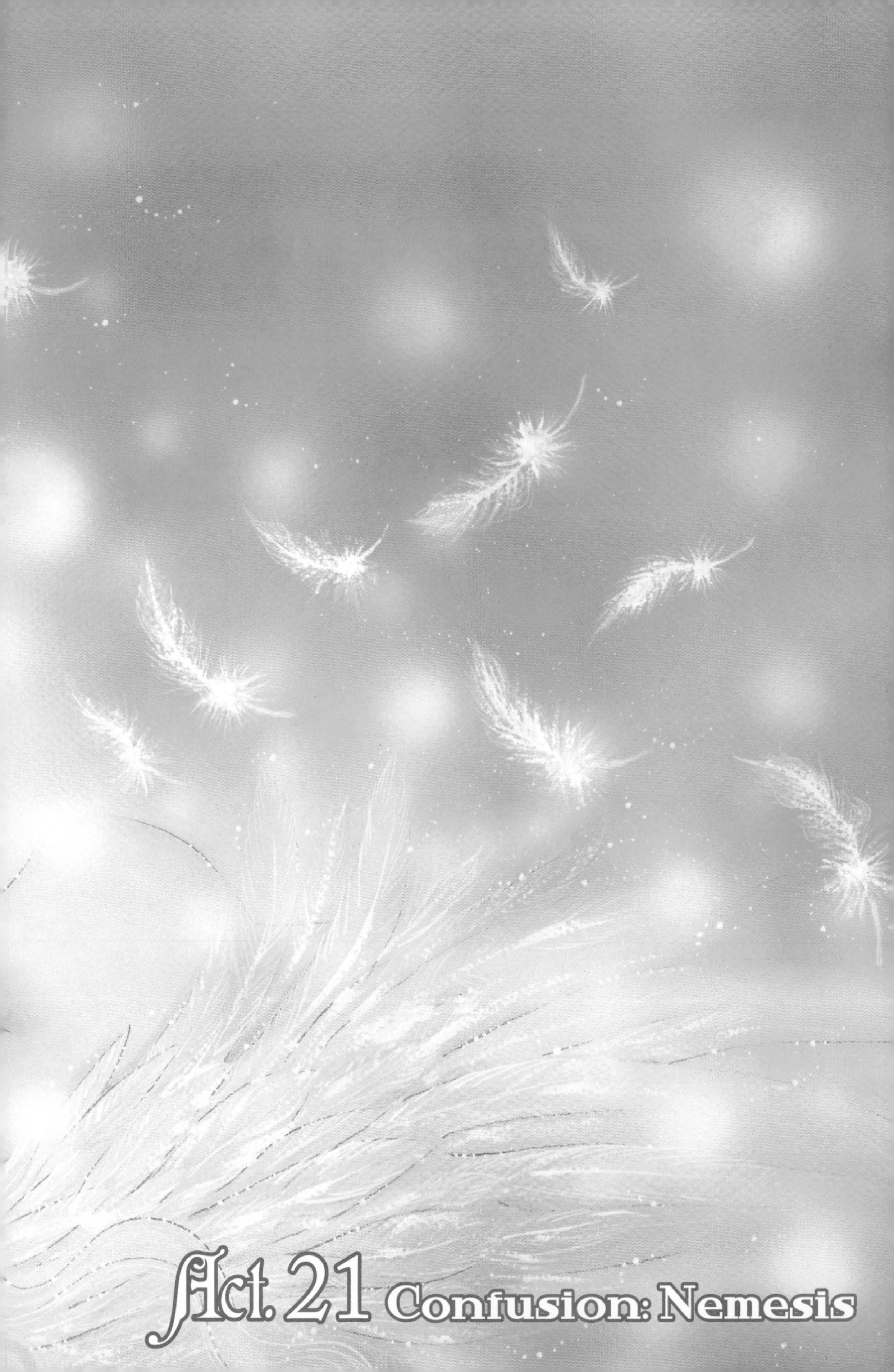

Act. 21 Confusion: Nemesis

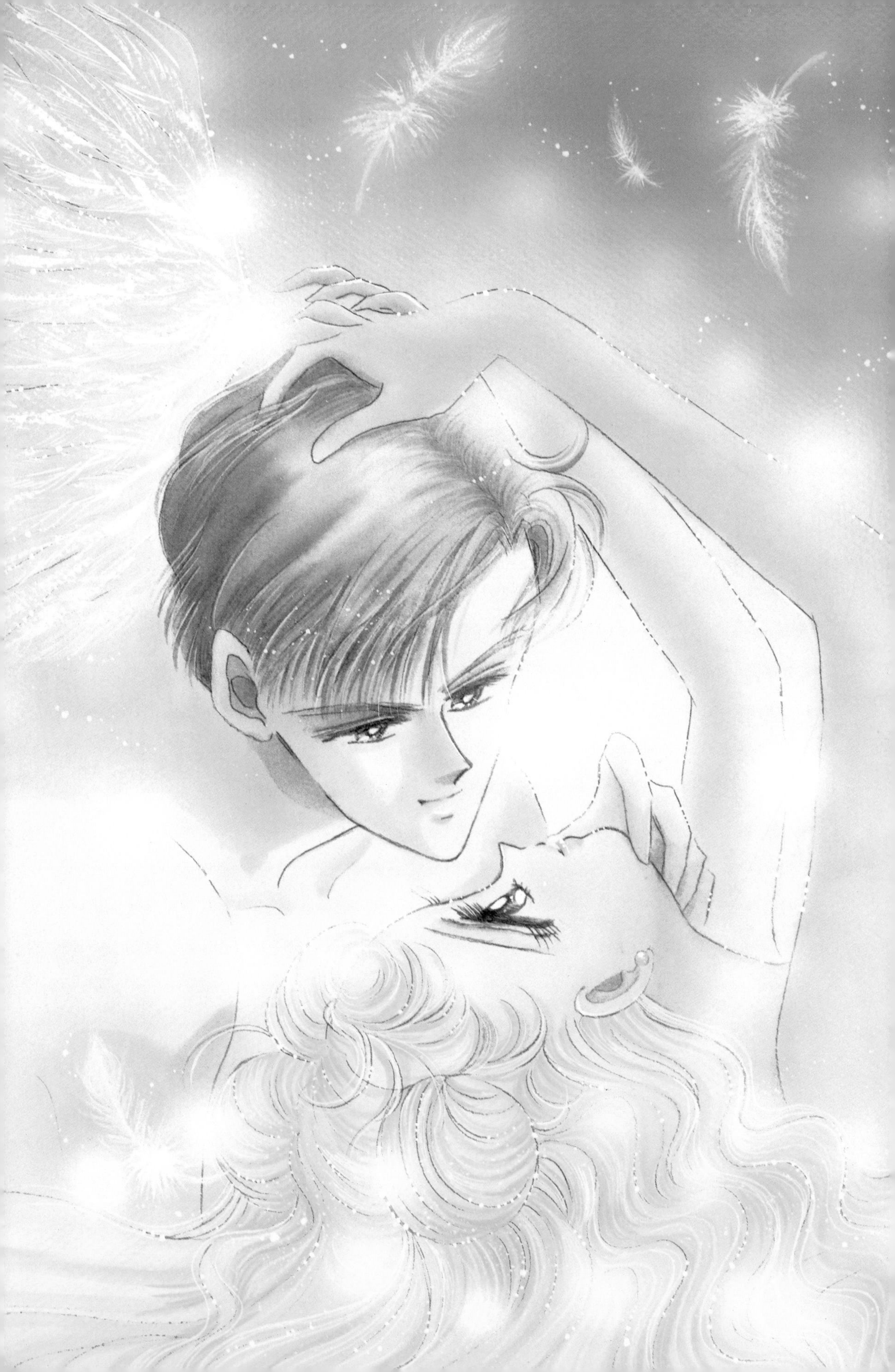

Pretty Guardian
Sailor Moon

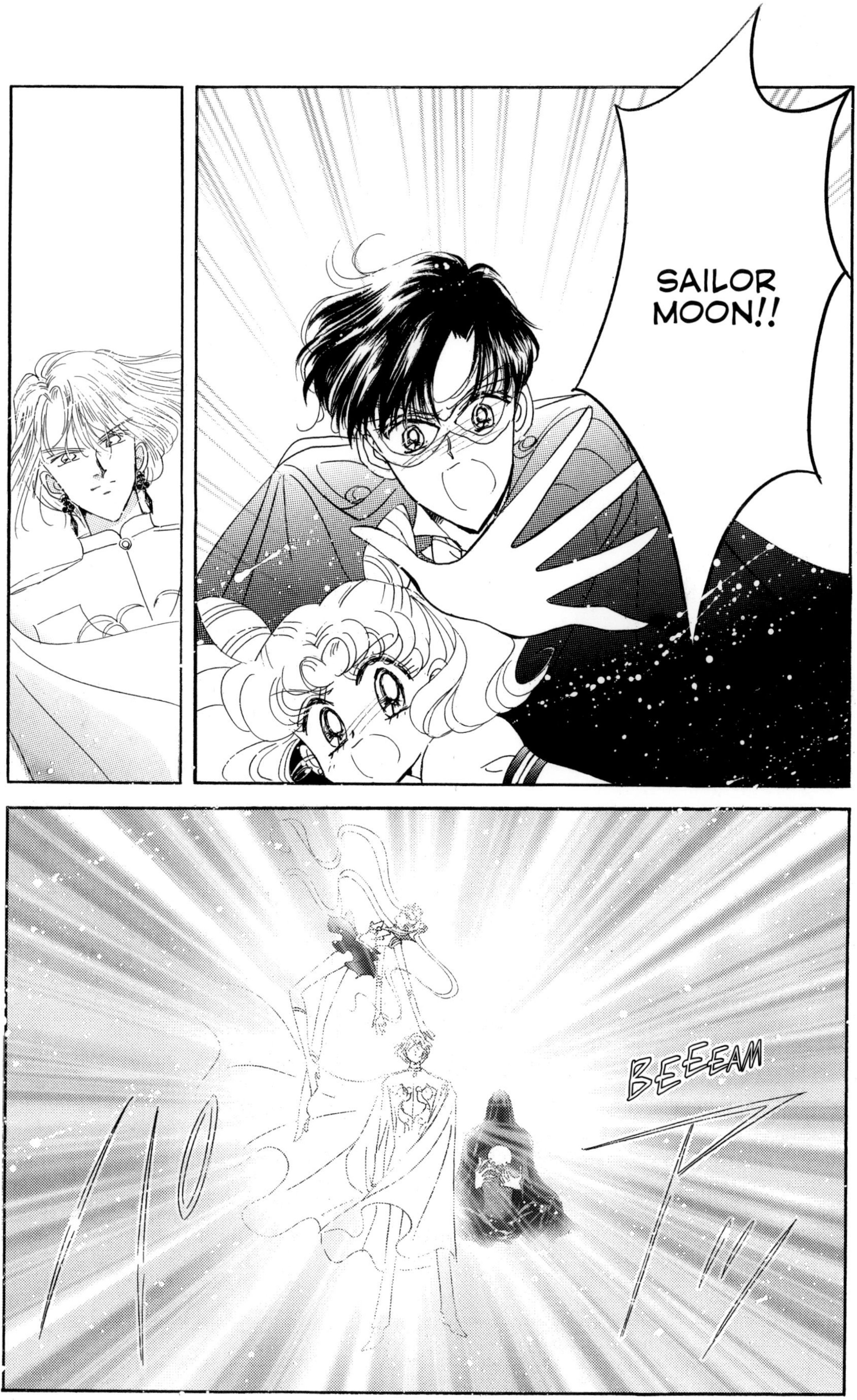
SAILOR MOON!!
BEEEAM

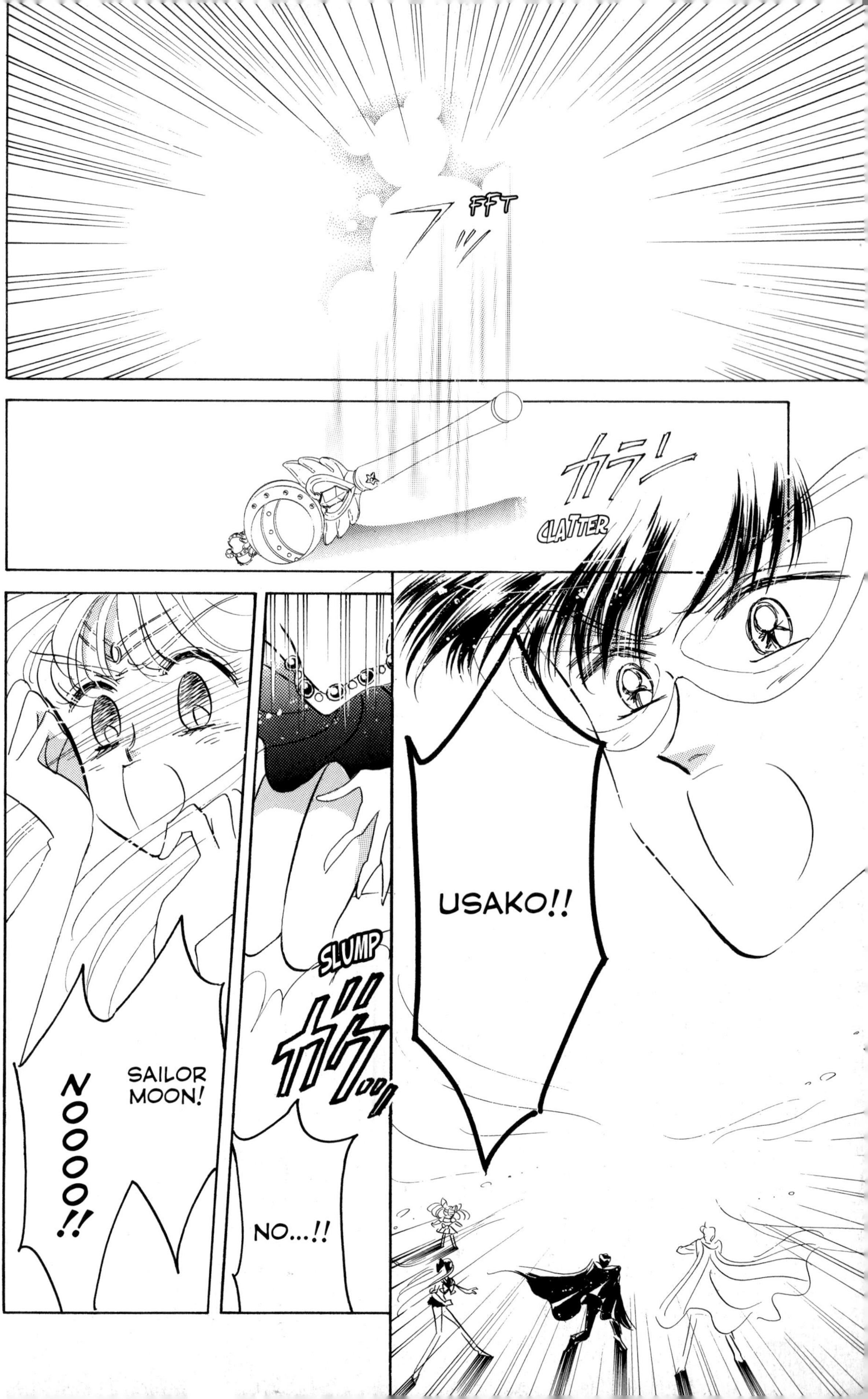
FFT
ブッ
カラン
CLATTER
USAKO!!
SLUMP
ガクッ
NO...!!
SAILOR MOON!
NOOOOO!!

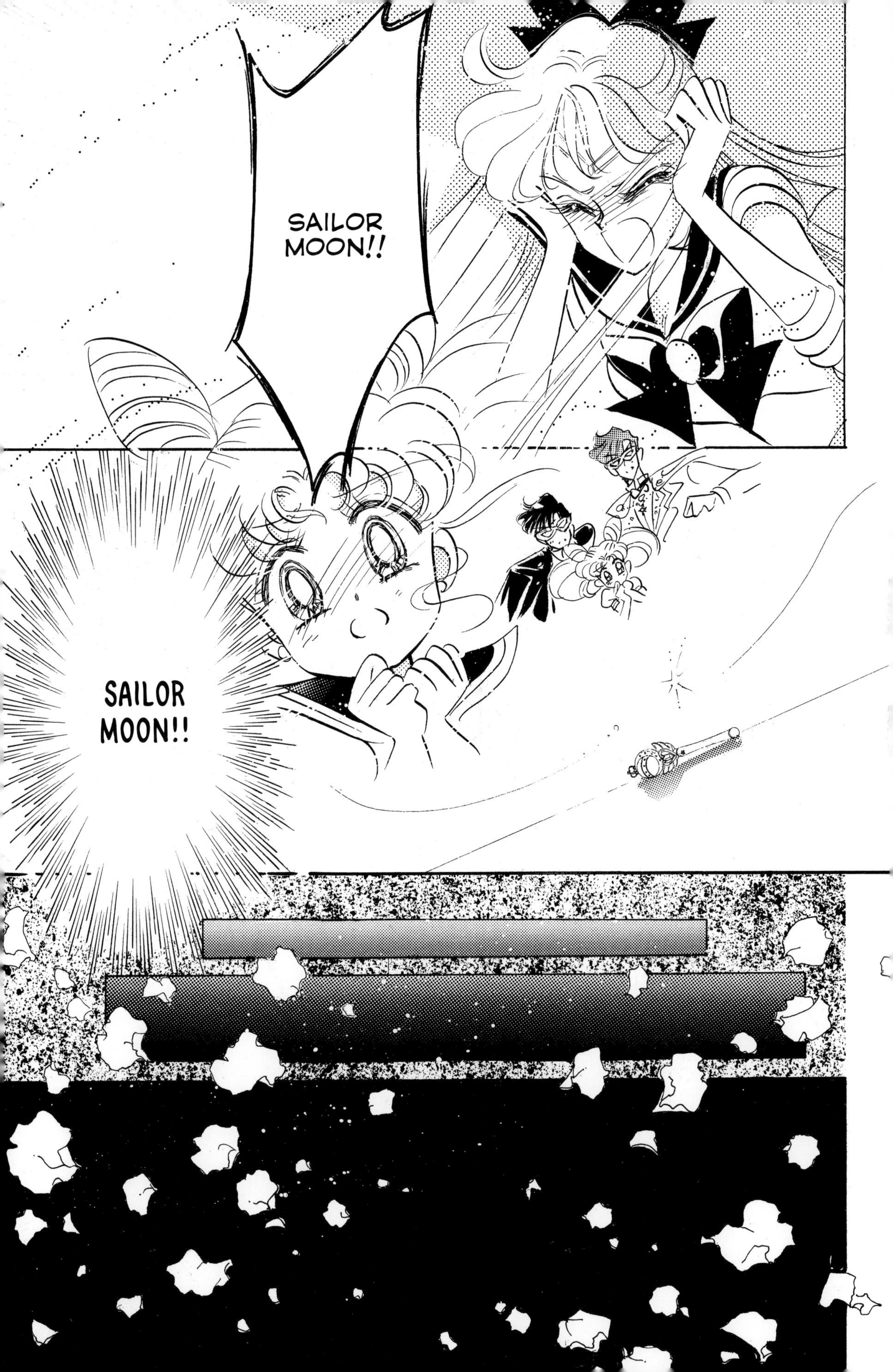
SAILOR MOON!!
SAILOR MOON!!

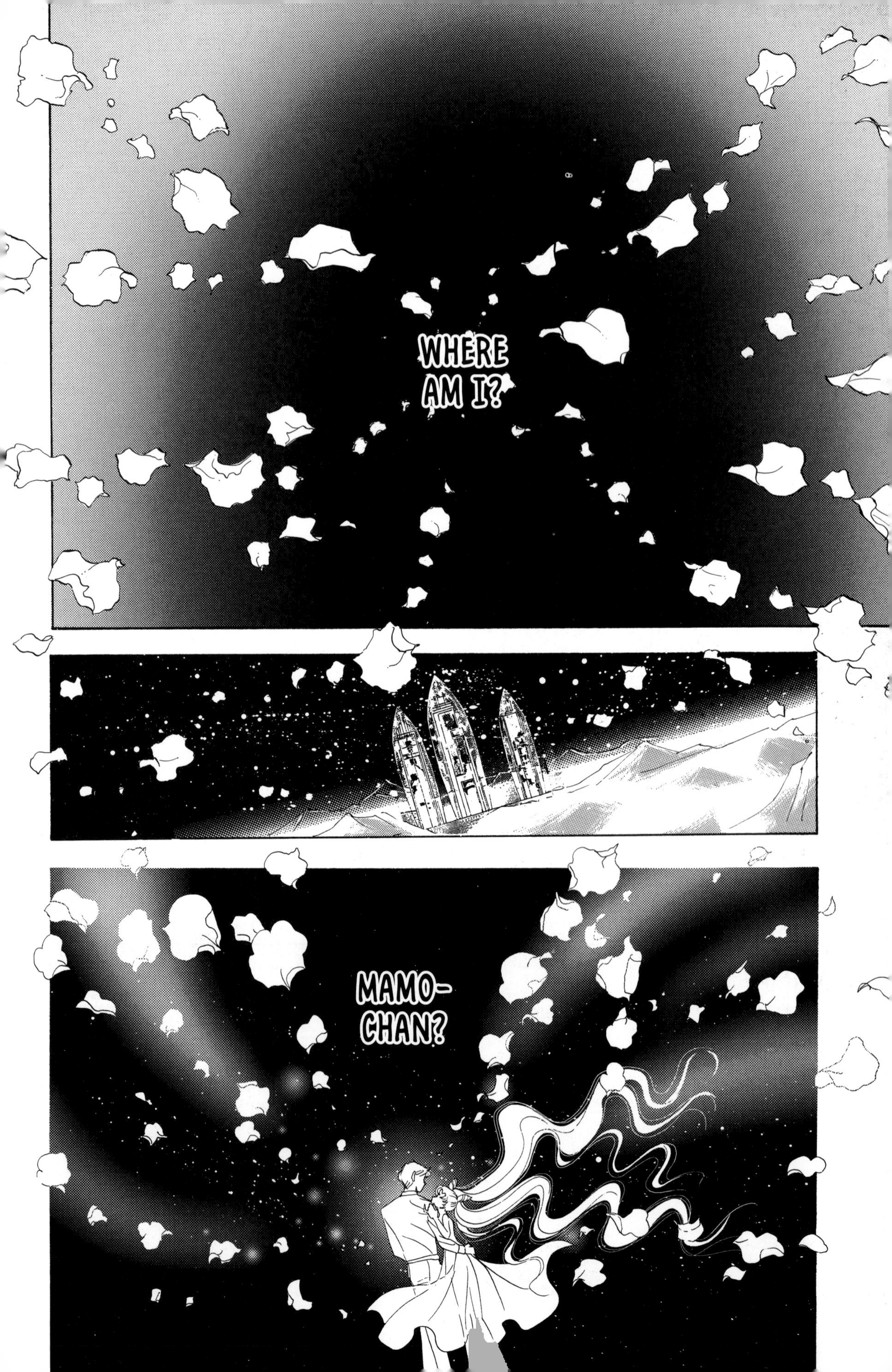
WHERE AM I?
MAMO-CHAN?

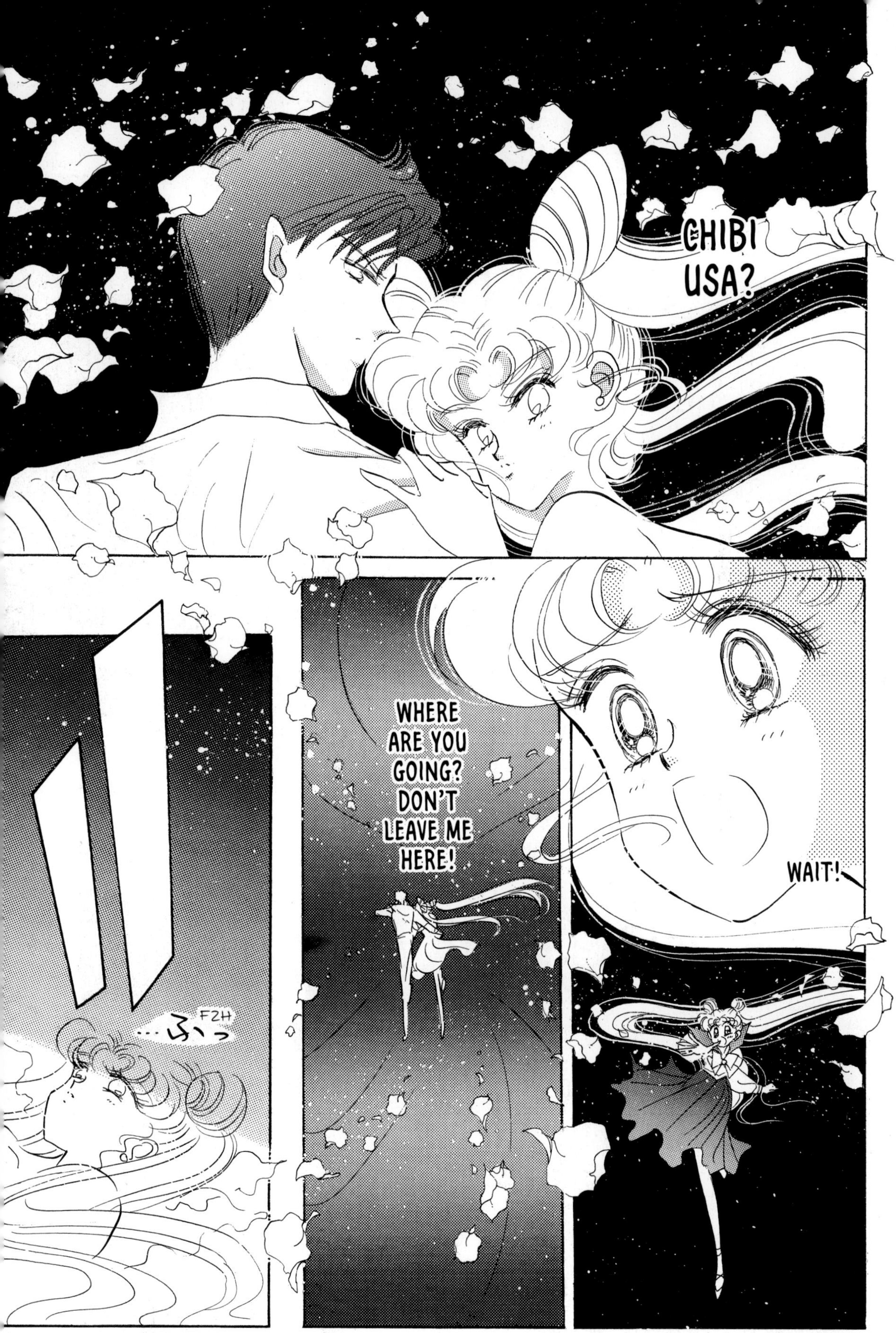
CHIBI USA?
WAIT!
WHERE ARE YOU GOING? DON'T LEAVE ME HERE!
ふっ
FZH

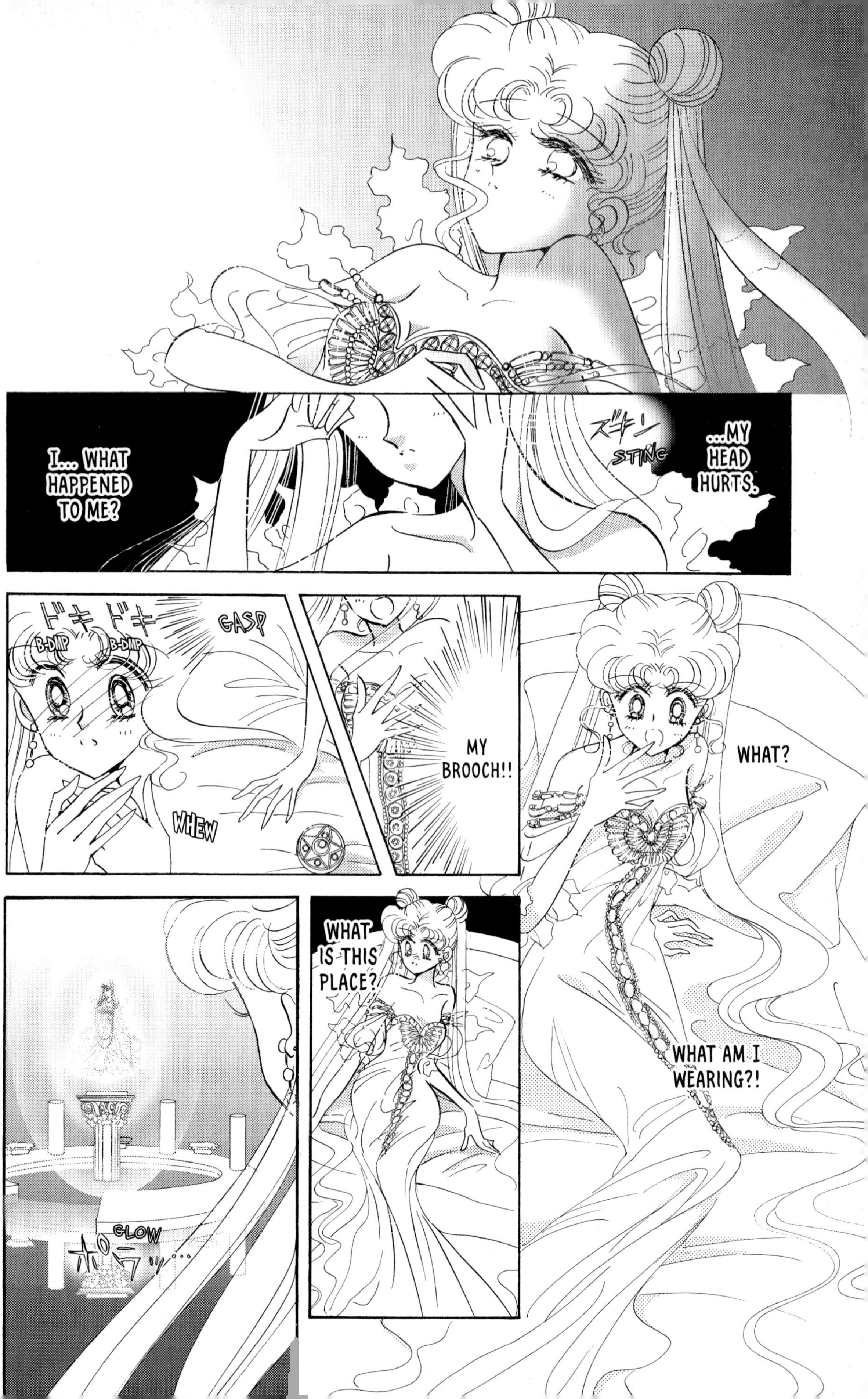
ズキン
STING
...MY HEAD HURTS.
I... WHAT HAPPENED TO ME?
WHAT?
WHAT AM I WEARING?!
MY BROOCH!!
GASP
ドキ ドキ
B-DMP B-DMP
WHEW
WHAT IS THIS PLACE?
ホワーッ...
GLOW

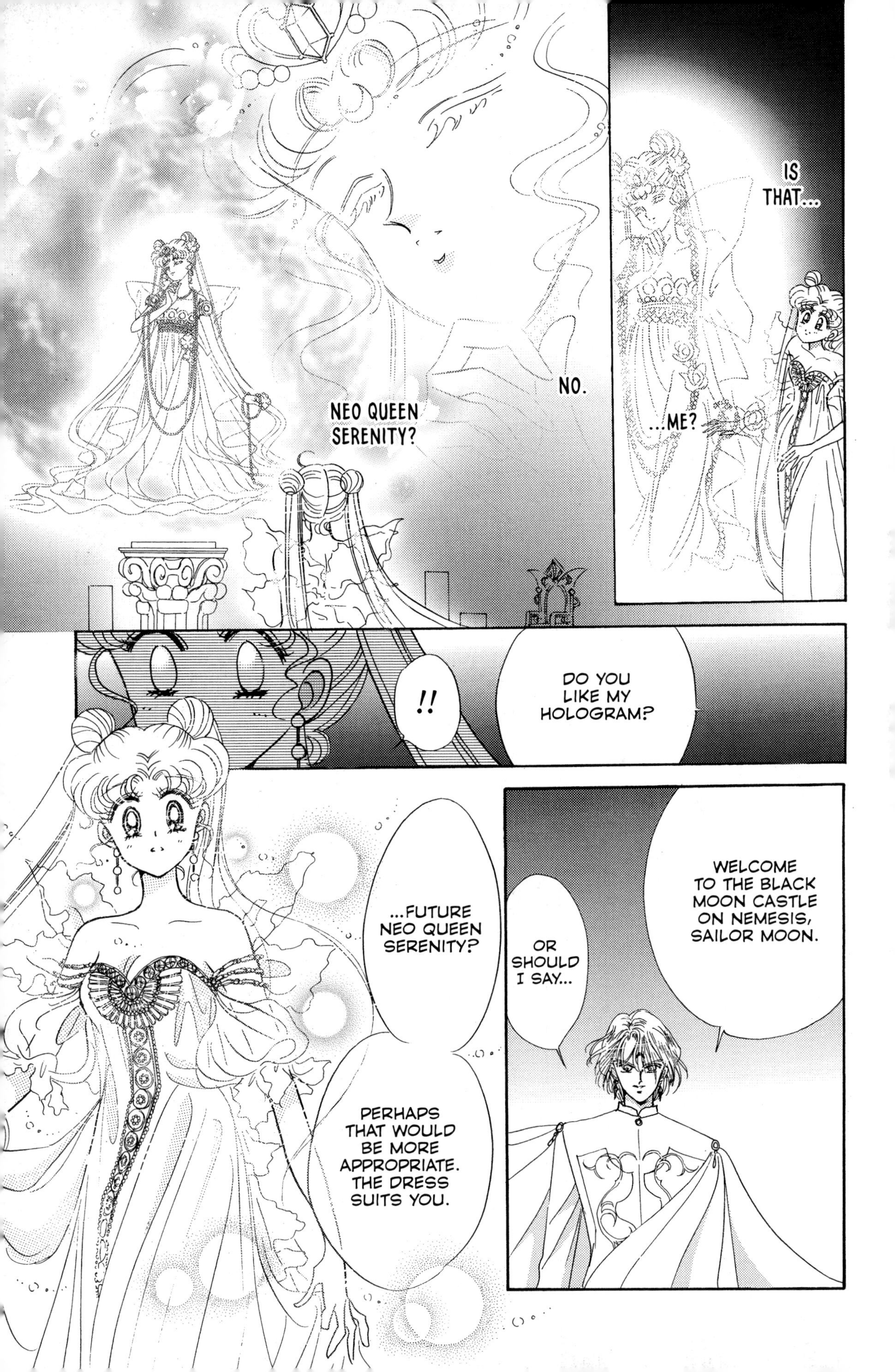
IS THAT...
...ME?
NO.
NEO QUEEN SERENITY?
DO YOU LIKE MY HOLOGRAM?
!!
WELCOME TO THE BLACK MOON CASTLE ON NEMESIS, SAILOR MOON.
OR SHOULD I SAY...
...FUTURE NEO QUEEN SERENITY?
PERHAPS THAT WOULD BE MORE APPROPRIATE. THE DRESS SUITS YOU.

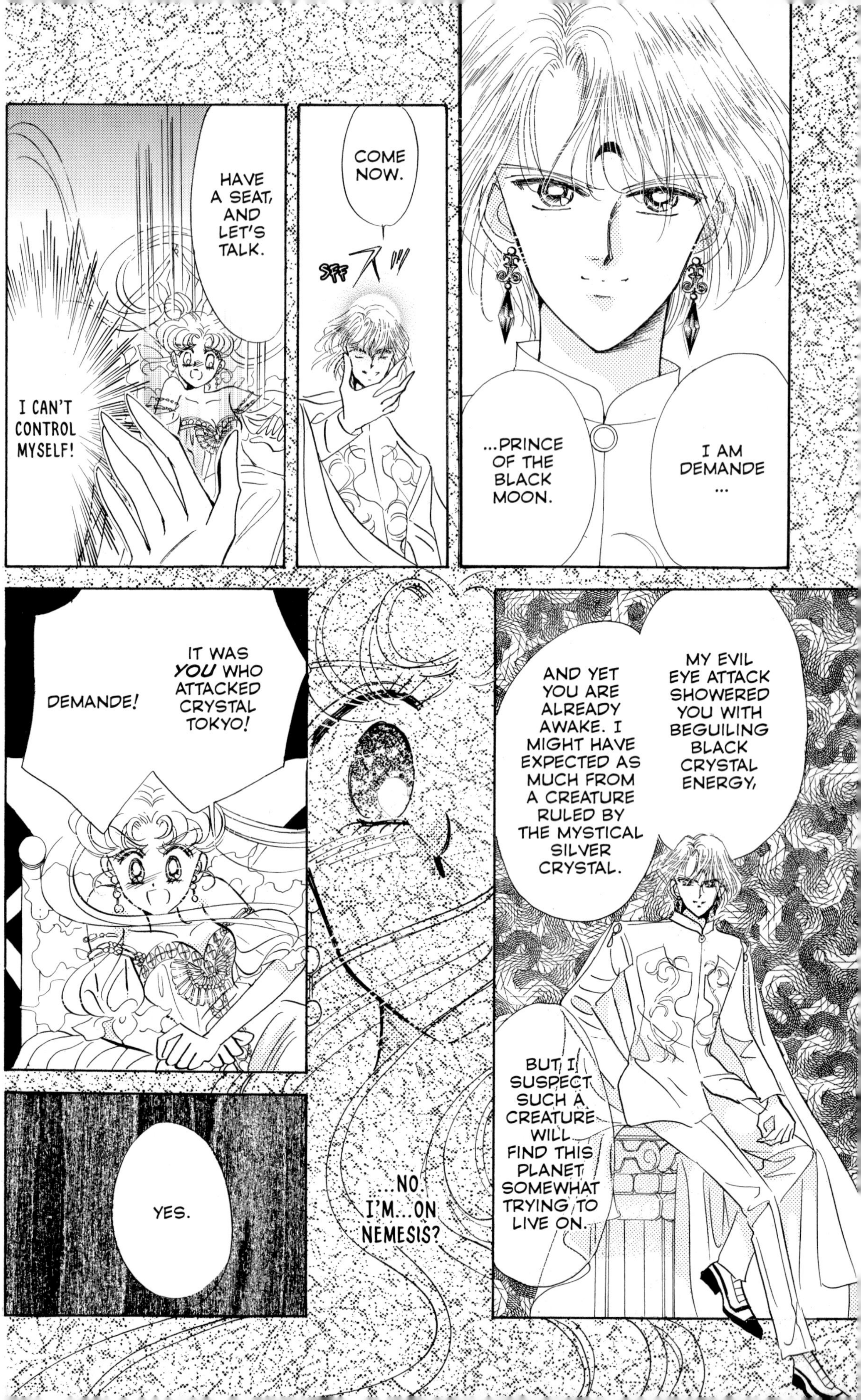
I AM DEMANDE ...
...PRINCE OF THE BLACK MOON.
COME NOW.
SFF
HAVE A SEAT, AND LET'S TALK.
I CAN'T CONTROL MYSELF!
MY EVIL EYE ATTACK SHOWERED YOU WITH BEGUILING BLACK CRYSTAL ENERGY,
AND YET YOU ARE ALREADY AWAKE. I MIGHT HAVE EXPECTED AS MUCH FROM A CREATURE RULED BY THE MYSTICAL SILVER CRYSTAL.
BUT I SUSPECT SUCH A CREATURE WILL FIND THIS PLANET SOMEWHAT TRYING TO LIVE ON.
...NO. I'M...ON NEMESIS?
DEMANDE!
IT WAS *YOU* WHO ATTACKED CRYSTAL TOKYO!
YES.

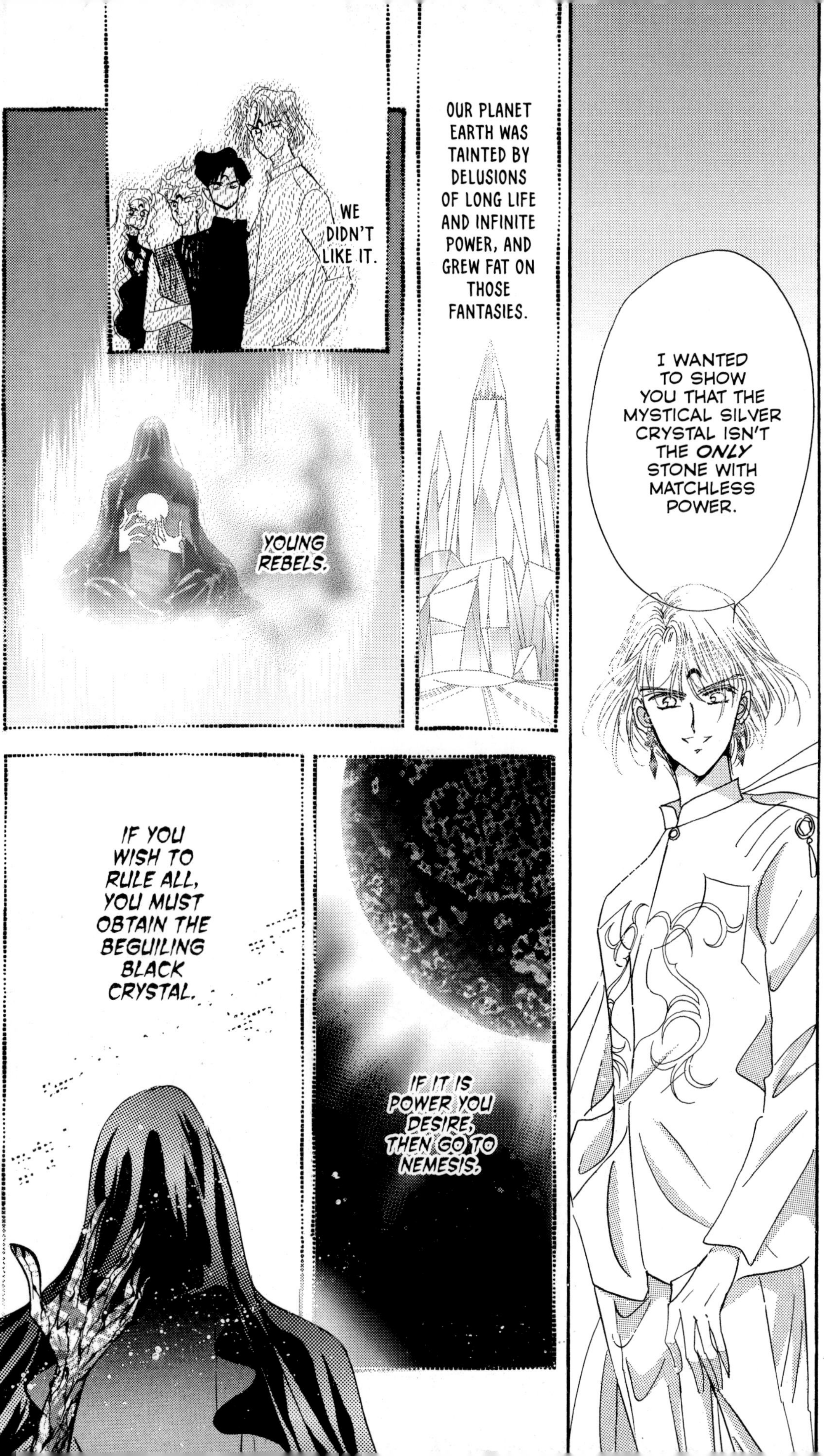
I WANTED TO SHOW YOU THAT THE MYSTICAL SILVER CRYSTAL ISN'T THE *ONLY* STONE WITH MATCHLESS POWER.
OUR PLANET EARTH WAS TAINTED BY DELUSIONS OF LONG LIFE AND INFINITE POWER, AND GREW FAT ON THOSE FANTASIES.
WE DIDN'T LIKE IT.
YOUNG REBELS.
IF IT IS POWER YOU DESIRE, THEN GO TO NEMESIS.
IF YOU WISH TO RULE ALL, YOU MUST OBTAIN THE BEGUILING BLACK CRYSTAL.

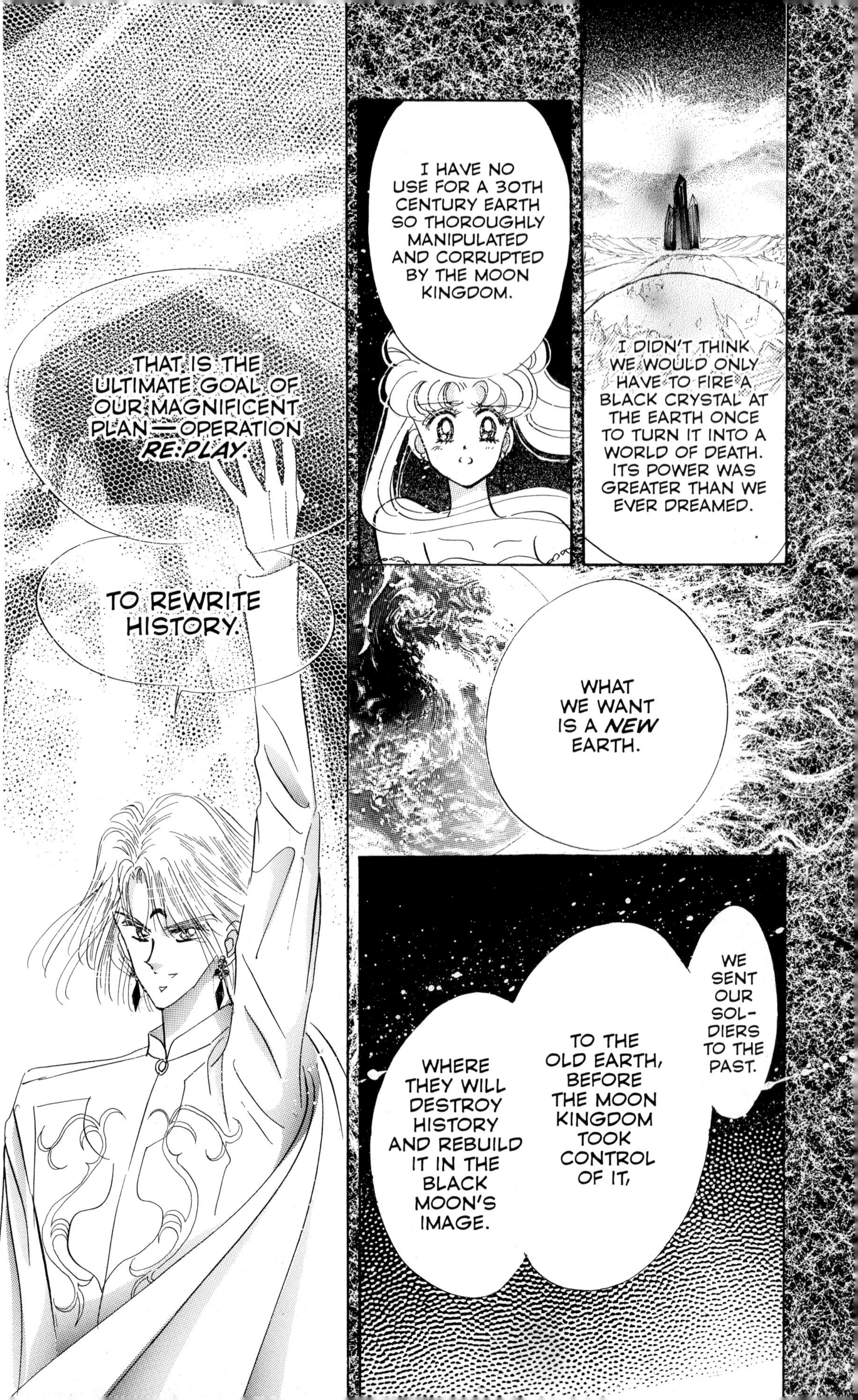
I DIDN'T THINK WE WOULD ONLY HAVE TO FIRE A BLACK CRYSTAL AT THE EARTH ONCE TO TURN IT INTO A WORLD OF DEATH. ITS POWER WAS GREATER THAN WE EVER DREAMED.
I HAVE NO USE FOR A 30TH CENTURY EARTH SO THOROUGHLY MANIPULATED AND CORRUPTED BY THE MOON KINGDOM.
WHAT WE WANT IS A *NEW* EARTH.
WE SENT OUR SOL-DIERS TO THE PAST.
TO THE OLD EARTH, BEFORE THE MOON KINGDOM TOOK CONTROL OF IT,
WHERE THEY WILL DESTROY HISTORY AND REBUILD IT IN THE BLACK MOON'S IMAGE.
THAT IS THE ULTIMATE GOAL OF OUR MAGNIFICENT PLAN—OPERATION *RE:PLAY*.
TO REWRITE HISTORY.

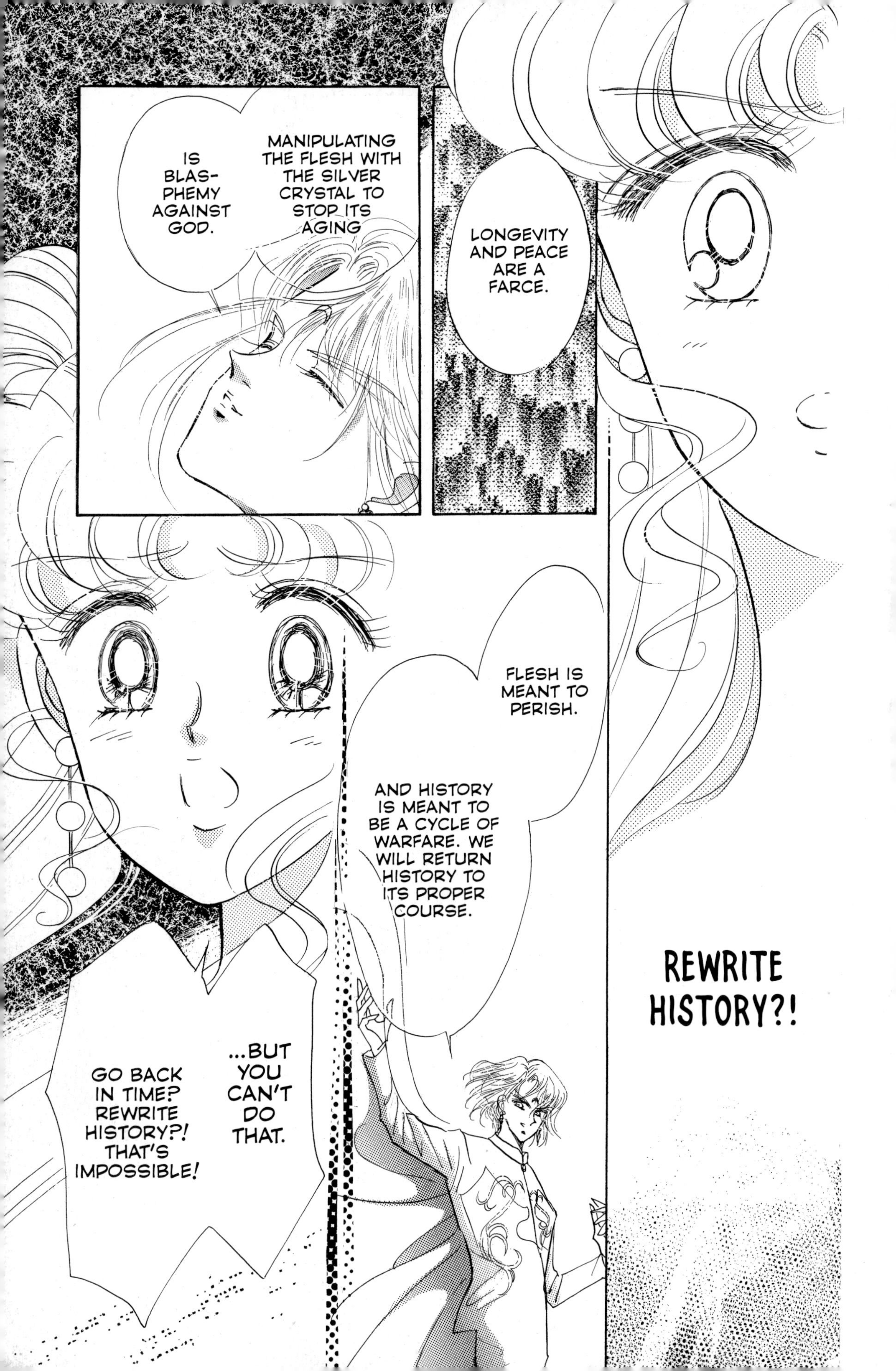
LONGEVITY AND PEACE ARE A FARCE.
MANIPULATING THE FLESH WITH THE SILVER CRYSTAL TO STOP ITS AGING
IS BLASPHEMY AGAINST GOD.
FLESH IS MEANT TO PERISH.
AND HISTORY IS MEANT TO BE A CYCLE OF WARFARE. WE WILL RETURN HISTORY TO ITS PROPER COURSE.
REWRITE HISTORY?!
...BUT YOU CAN'T DO THAT.
GO BACK IN TIME? REWRITE HISTORY?! THAT'S IMPOSSIBLE!

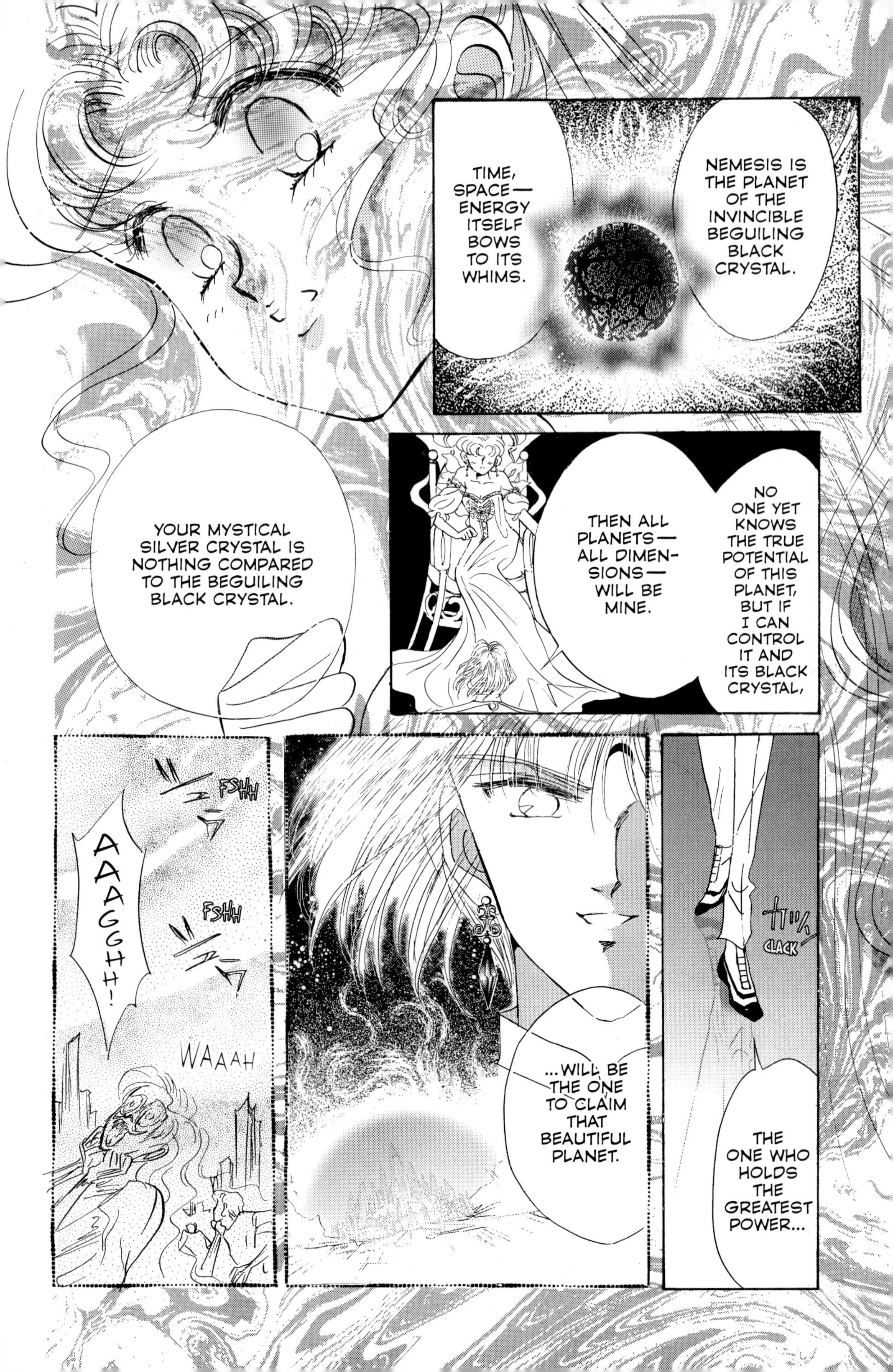

NEMESIS IS THE PLANET OF THE INVINCIBLE BEGUILING BLACK CRYSTAL.
TIME, SPACE—ENERGY ITSELF BOWS TO ITS WHIMS.
YOUR MYSTICAL SILVER CRYSTAL IS NOTHING COMPARED TO THE BEGUILING BLACK CRYSTAL.
NO ONE YET KNOWS THE TRUE POTENTIAL OF THIS PLANET, BUT IF I CAN CONTROL IT AND ITS BLACK CRYSTAL,
THEN ALL PLANETS—ALL DIMENSIONS—WILL BE MINE.
CLACK
THE ONE WHO HOLDS THE GREATEST POWER...
...WILL BE THE ONE TO CLAIM THAT BEAUTIFUL PLANET.
FSHH
AAAGGHH!
FSHH
WAAAH

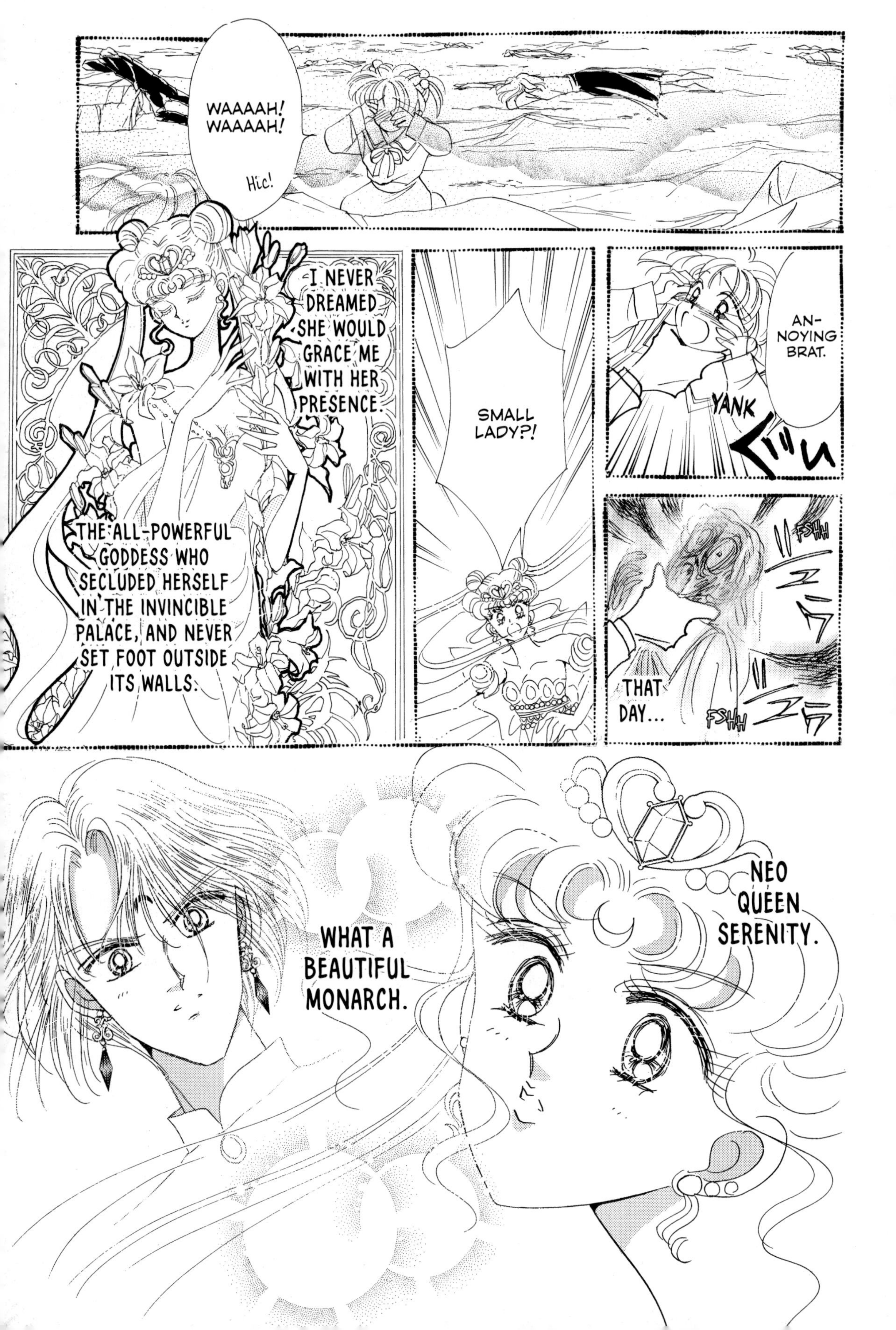
WAAAAH! WAAAAH!
Hic!
AN-NOYING BRAT.
YANK
FSHH
THAT DAY...
FSHH
SMALL LADY?!
I NEVER DREAMED SHE WOULD GRACE ME WITH HER PRESENCE.
THE ALL-POWERFUL GODDESS WHO SECLUDED HERSELF IN THE INVINCIBLE PALACE, AND NEVER SET FOOT OUTSIDE ITS WALLS.
NEO QUEEN SERENITY.
WHAT A BEAUTIFUL MONARCH.

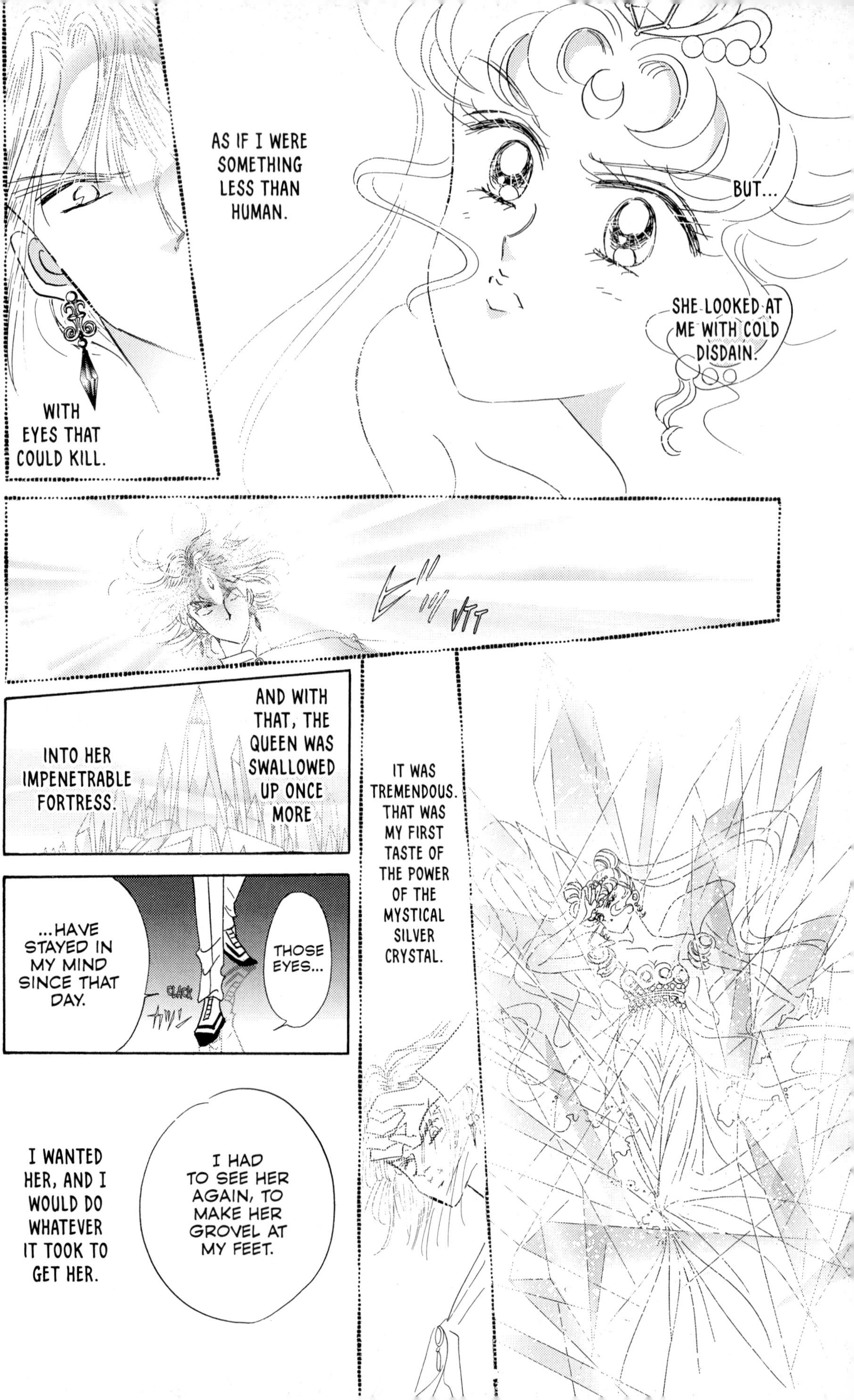
BUT...
SHE LOOKED AT ME WITH COLD DISDAIN.
AS IF I WERE SOMETHING LESS THAN HUMAN.
WITH EYES THAT COULD KILL.
ビッ VTT
IT WAS TREMENDOUS. THAT WAS MY FIRST TASTE OF THE POWER OF THE MYSTICAL SILVER CRYSTAL.
AND WITH THAT, THE QUEEN WAS SWALLOWED UP ONCE MORE
INTO HER IMPENETRABLE FORTRESS.
THOSE EYES...
...HAVE STAYED IN MY MIND SINCE THAT DAY.
CLACK
I HAD TO SEE HER AGAIN, TO MAKE HER GROVEL AT MY FEET.
I WANTED HER, AND I WOULD DO WHATEVER IT TOOK TO GET HER.

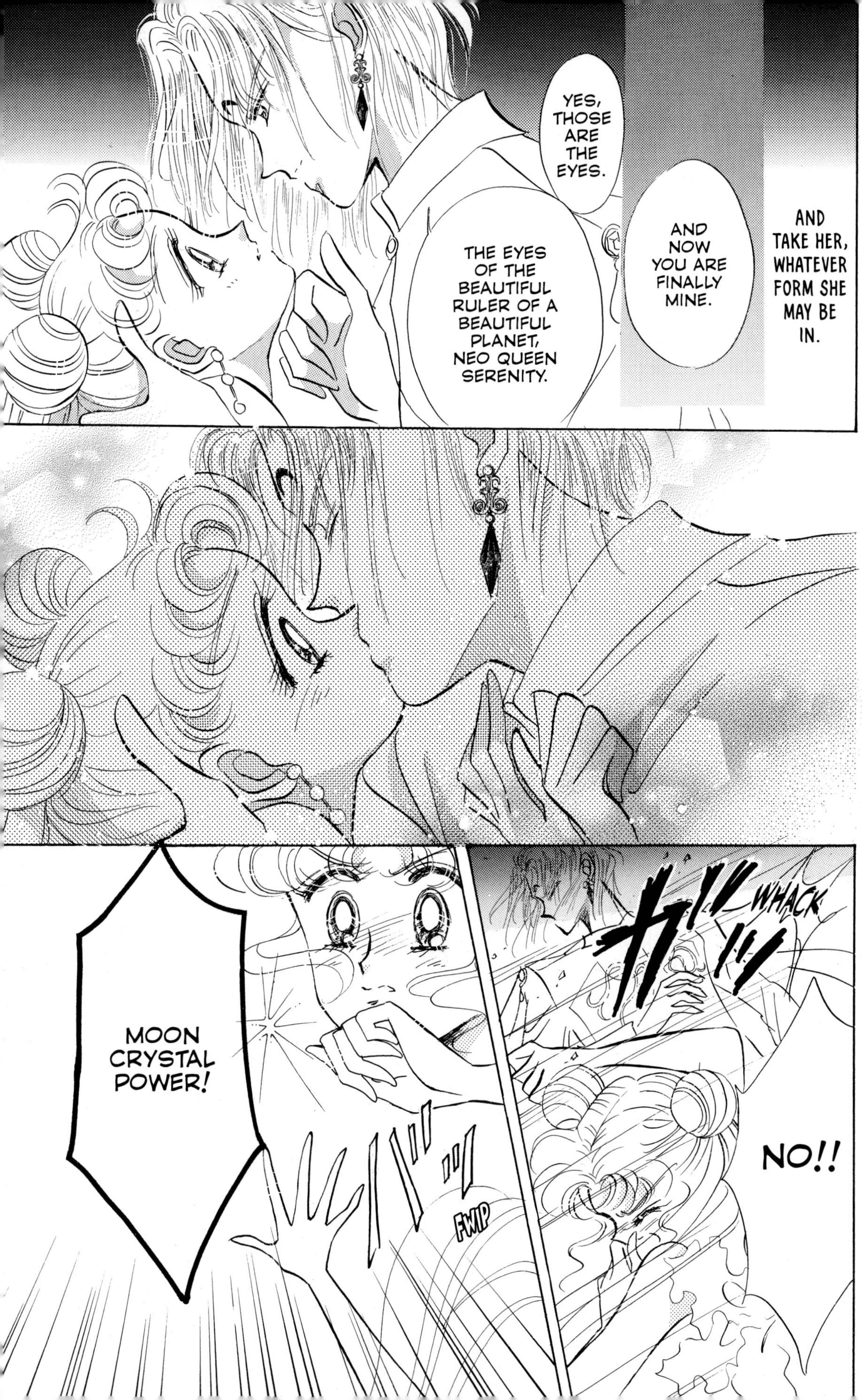
AND TAKE HER, WHATEVER FORM SHE MAY BE IN.
AND NOW YOU ARE FINALLY MINE.
YES, THOSE ARE THE EYES.
THE EYES OF THE BEAUTIFUL RULER OF A BEAUTIFUL PLANET, NEO QUEEN SERENITY.
WHACK
NO!!
MOON CRYSTAL POWER!
FWIP

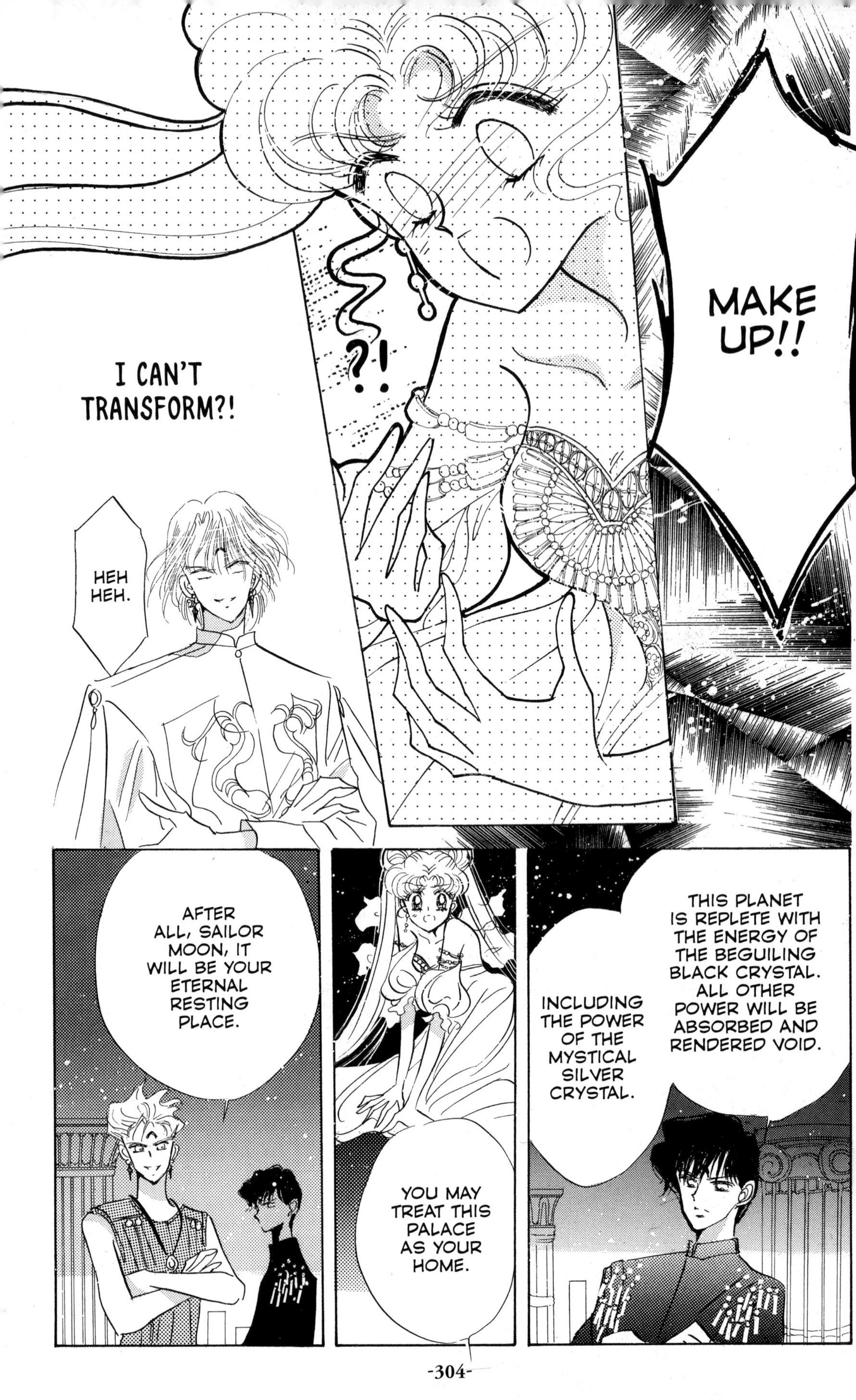
MAKE UP!!
?!
I CAN'T TRANSFORM?!
HEH HEH.
THIS PLANET IS REPLETE WITH THE ENERGY OF THE BEGUILING BLACK CRYSTAL. ALL OTHER POWER WILL BE ABSORBED AND RENDERED VOID.
INCLUDING THE POWER OF THE MYSTICAL SILVER CRYSTAL.
YOU MAY TREAT THIS PALACE AS YOUR HOME.
AFTER ALL, SAILOR MOON, IT WILL BE YOUR ETERNAL RESTING PLACE.

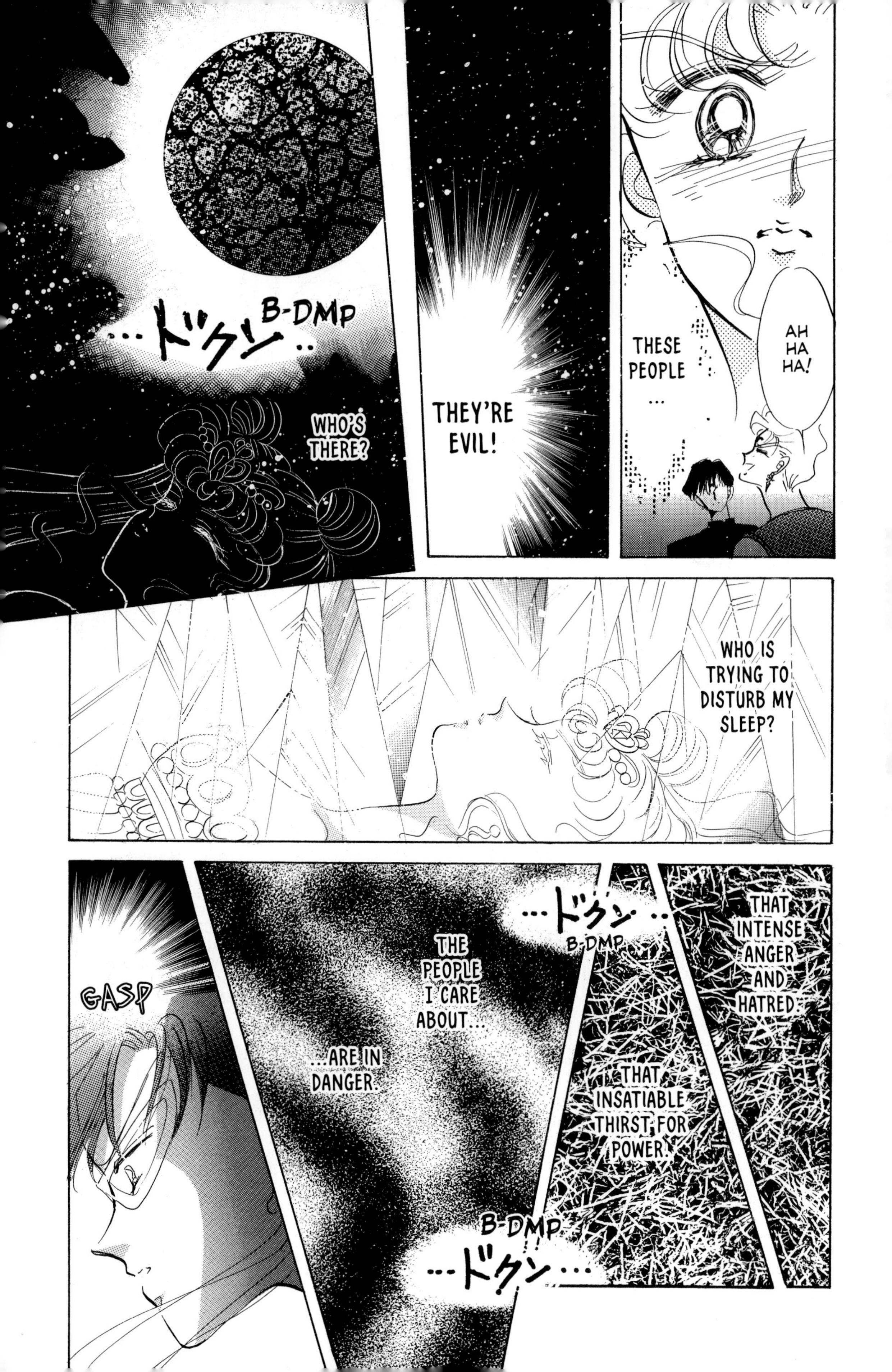
AH HA HA!
THESE PEOPLE ...
THEY'RE EVIL!
...ドクン...
B-DMP
WHO'S THERE?
WHO IS TRYING TO DISTURB MY SLEEP?
THAT INTENSE ANGER AND HATRED.
...ドクン...
B-DMP
THAT INSATIABLE THIRST FOR POWER.
THE PEOPLE I CARE ABOUT...
...ARE IN DANGER.
B-DMP
...ドクン...
GASP

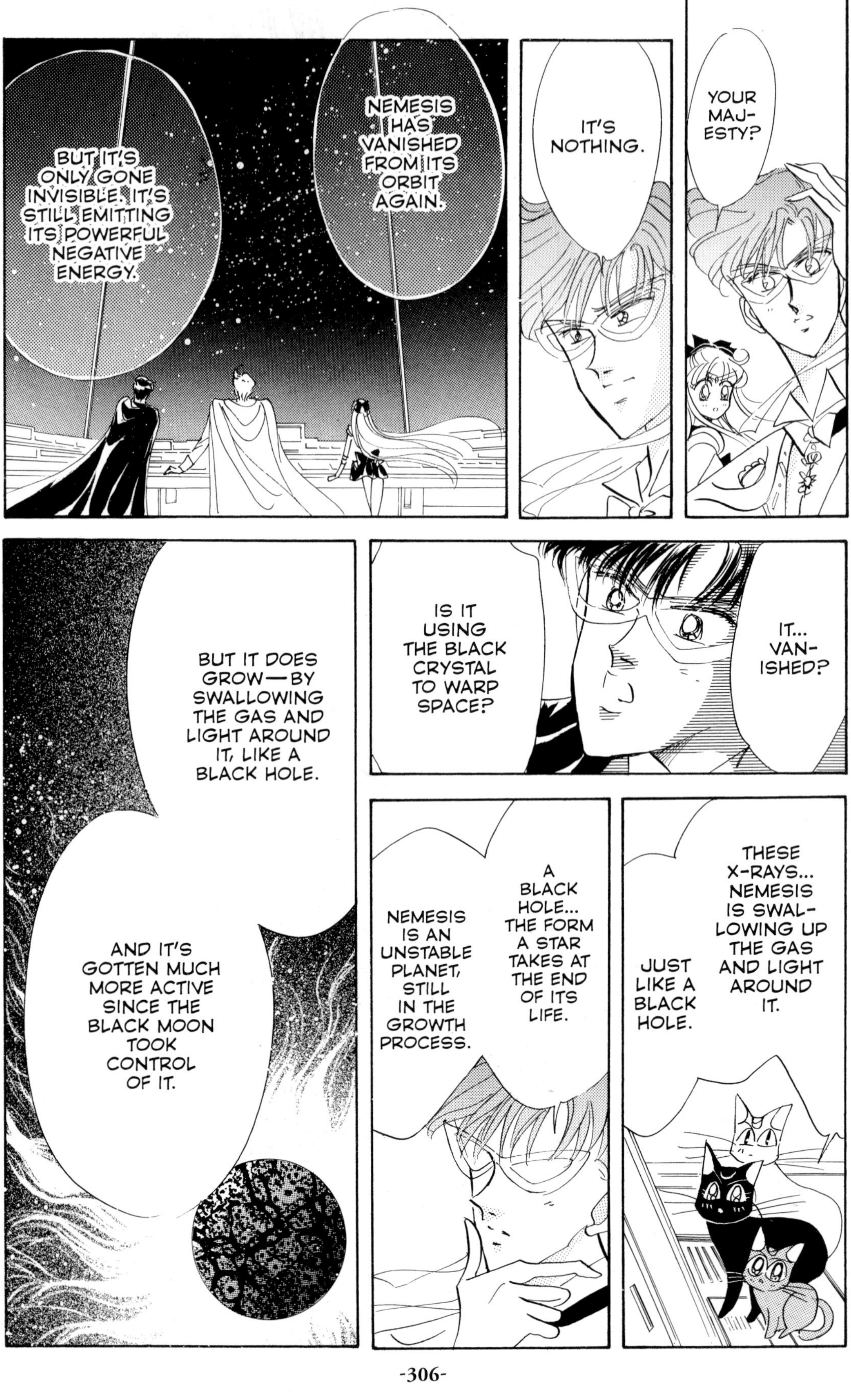

YOUR MAJESTY?
IT'S NOTHING.
NEMESIS HAS VANISHED FROM ITS ORBIT AGAIN.
BUT IT'S ONLY GONE INVISIBLE. IT'S STILL EMITTING ITS POWERFUL NEGATIVE ENERGY.
IT... VANISHED?
IS IT USING THE BLACK CRYSTAL TO WARP SPACE?
THESE X-RAYS... NEMESIS IS SWALLOWING UP THE GAS AND LIGHT AROUND IT.
JUST LIKE A BLACK HOLE.
A BLACK HOLE... THE FORM A STAR TAKES AT THE END OF ITS LIFE.
NEMESIS IS AN UNSTABLE PLANET, STILL IN THE GROWTH PROCESS.
BUT IT DOES GROW—BY SWALLOWING THE GAS AND LIGHT AROUND IT, LIKE A BLACK HOLE.
AND IT'S GOTTEN MUCH MORE ACTIVE SINCE THE BLACK MOON TOOK CONTROL OF IT.

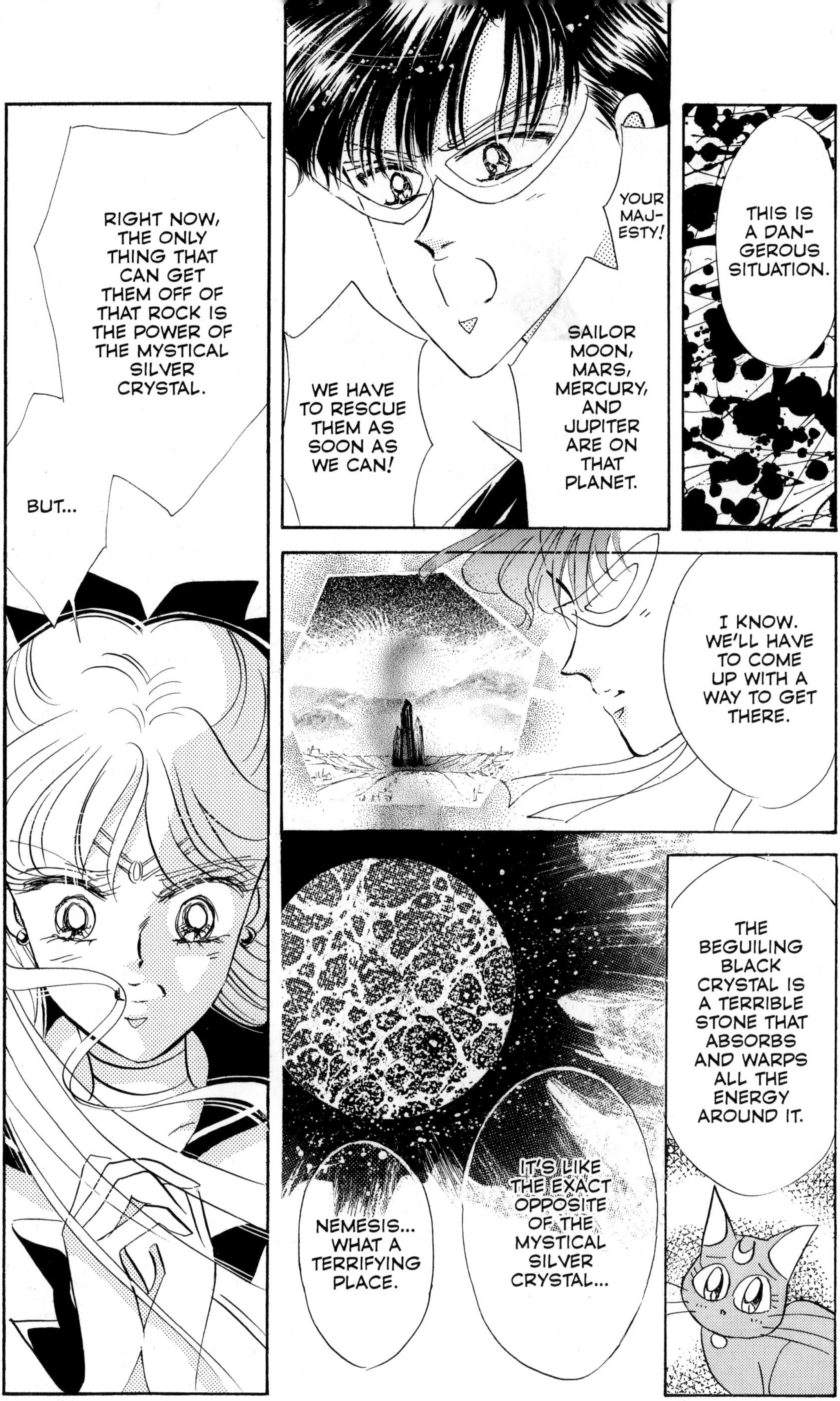
THIS IS A DANGEROUS SITUATION.
YOUR MAJESTY!
SAILOR MOON, MARS, MERCURY, AND JUPITER ARE ON THAT PLANET.
WE HAVE TO RESCUE THEM AS SOON AS WE CAN!
I KNOW. WE'LL HAVE TO COME UP WITH A WAY TO GET THERE.
THE BEGUILING BLACK CRYSTAL IS A TERRIBLE STONE THAT ABSORBS AND WARPS ALL THE ENERGY AROUND IT.
IT'S LIKE THE EXACT OPPOSITE OF THE MYSTICAL SILVER CRYSTAL...
NEMESIS... WHAT A TERRIFYING PLACE.
RIGHT NOW, THE ONLY THING THAT CAN GET THEM OFF OF THAT ROCK IS THE POWER OF THE MYSTICAL SILVER CRYSTAL.
BUT...

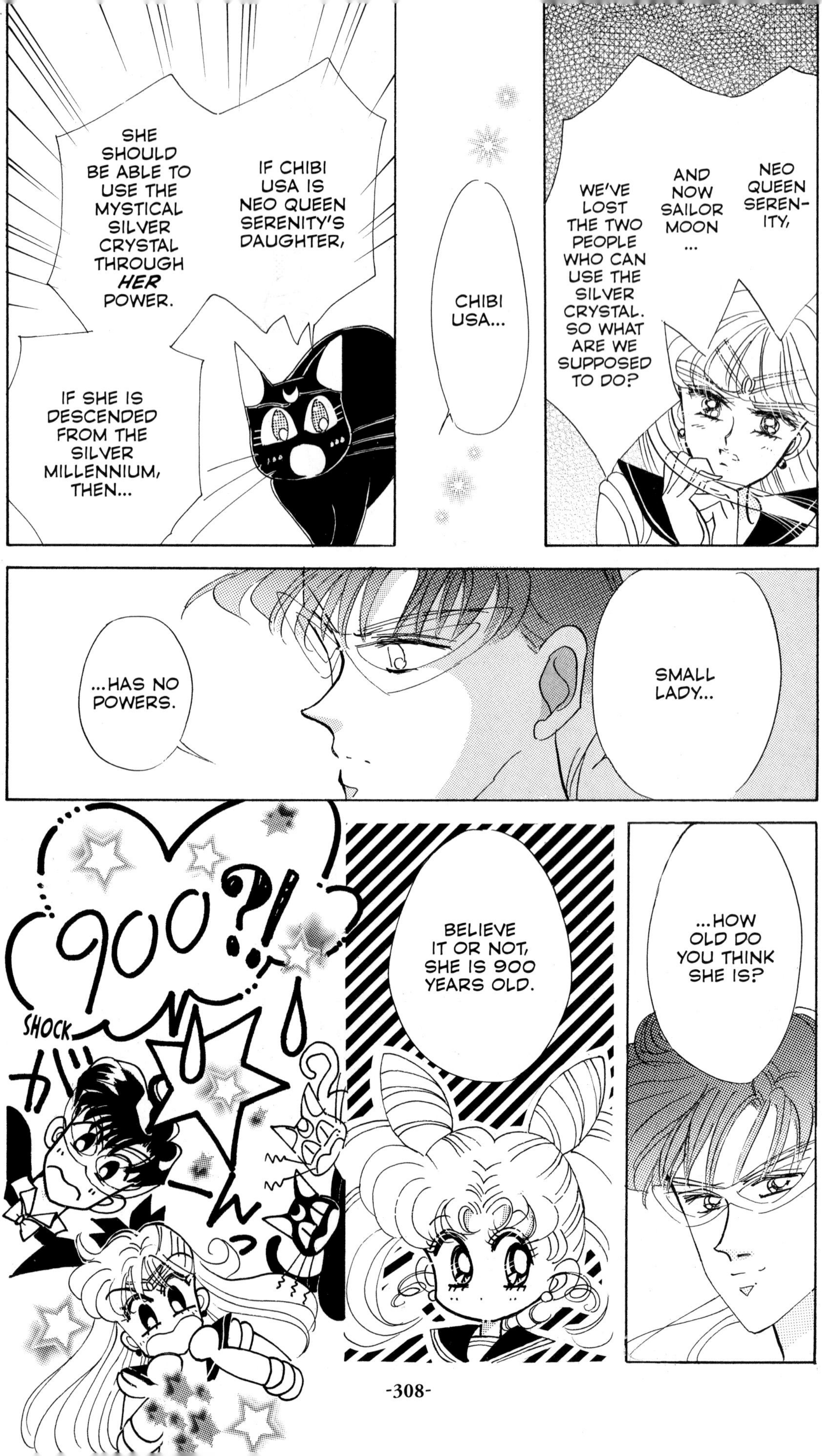

NEO QUEEN SERENITY,
AND NOW SAILOR MOON ...
WE'VE LOST THE TWO PEOPLE WHO CAN USE THE SILVER CRYSTAL. SO WHAT ARE WE SUPPOSED TO DO?
CHIBI USA...
IF CHIBI USA IS NEO QUEEN SERENITY'S DAUGHTER,
SHE SHOULD BE ABLE TO USE THE MYSTICAL SILVER CRYSTAL THROUGH *HER* POWER.
IF SHE IS DESCENDED FROM THE SILVER MILLENNIUM, THEN...
SMALL LADY...
...HAS NO POWERS.
...HOW OLD DO YOU THINK SHE IS?
BELIEVE IT OR NOT, SHE IS 900 YEARS OLD.
900?!
SHOCK

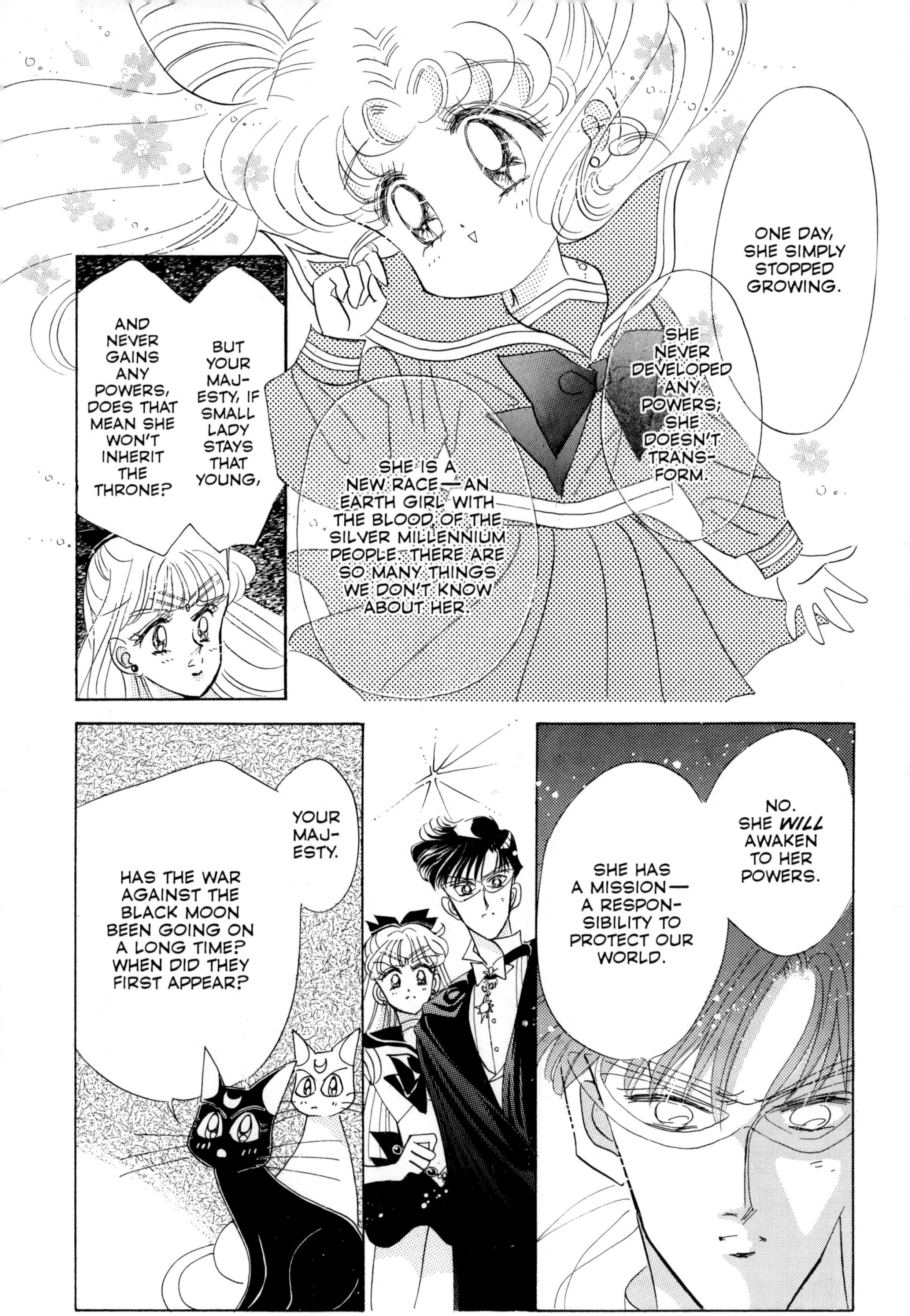
ONE DAY, SHE SIMPLY STOPPED GROWING.
SHE NEVER DEVELOPED ANY POWERS; SHE DOESN'T TRANS-FORM.
SHE IS A NEW RACE—AN EARTH GIRL WITH THE BLOOD OF THE SILVER MILLENNIUM PEOPLE. THERE ARE SO MANY THINGS WE DON'T KNOW ABOUT HER.
BUT YOUR MAJ-ESTY, IF SMALL LADY STAYS THAT YOUNG,
AND NEVER GAINS ANY POWERS, DOES THAT MEAN SHE WON'T INHERIT THE THRONE?
NO. SHE *WILL* AWAKEN TO HER POWERS.
SHE HAS A MISSION—A RESPON-SIBILITY TO PROTECT OUR WORLD.
YOUR MAJ-ESTY.
HAS THE WAR AGAINST THE BLACK MOON BEEN GOING ON A LONG TIME? WHEN DID THEY FIRST APPEAR?

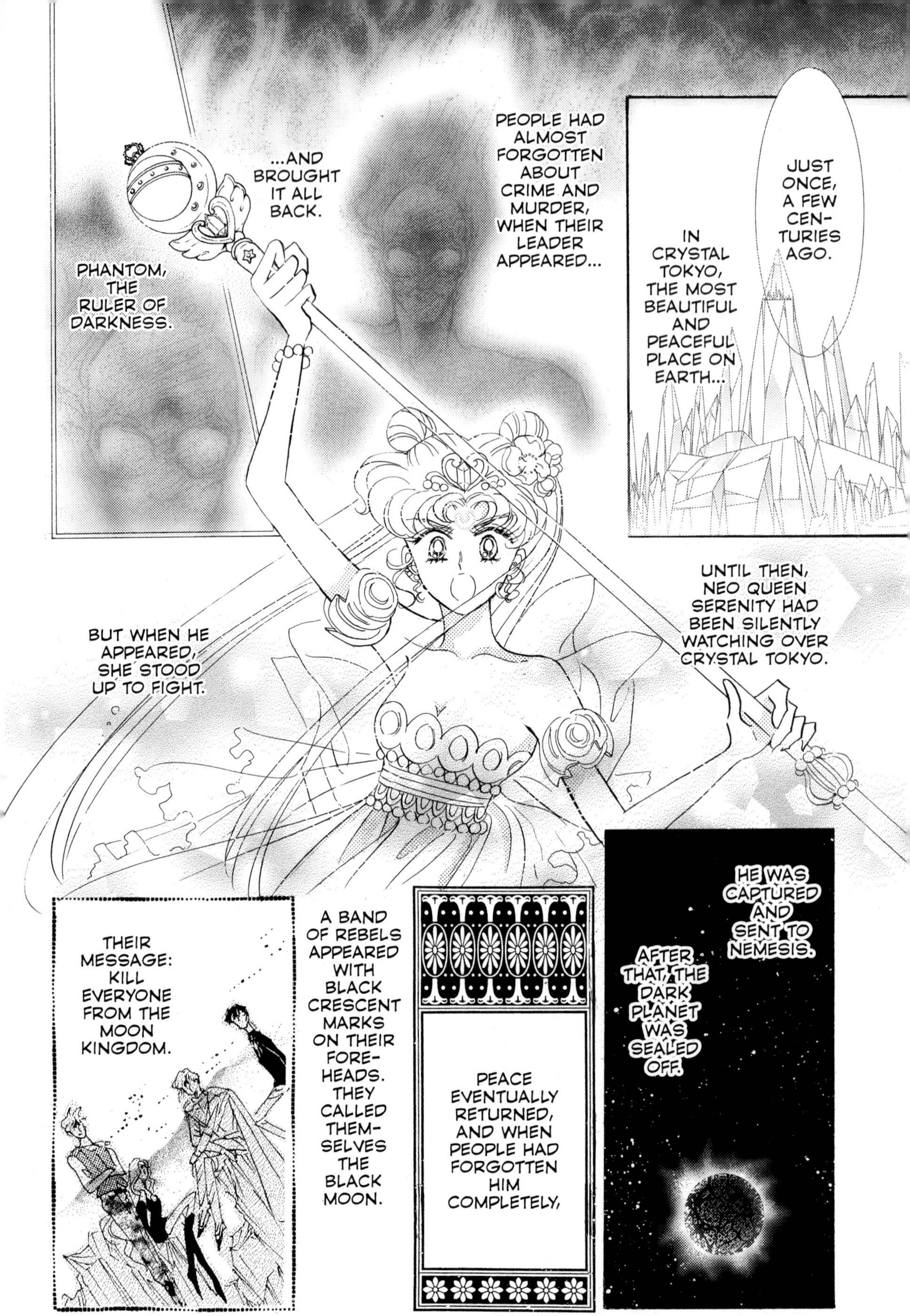
JUST ONCE, A FEW CENTURIES AGO.
IN CRYSTAL TOKYO, THE MOST BEAUTIFUL AND PEACEFUL PLACE ON EARTH...
PEOPLE HAD ALMOST FORGOTTEN ABOUT CRIME AND MURDER, WHEN THEIR LEADER APPEARED...
...AND BROUGHT IT ALL BACK.
PHANTOM, THE RULER OF DARKNESS.
UNTIL THEN, NEO QUEEN SERENITY HAD BEEN SILENTLY WATCHING OVER CRYSTAL TOKYO.
BUT WHEN HE APPEARED, SHE STOOD UP TO FIGHT.
HE WAS CAPTURED AND SENT TO NEMESIS.
AFTER THAT, THE DARK PLANET WAS SEALED OFF.
PEACE EVENTUALLY RETURNED, AND WHEN PEOPLE HAD FORGOTTEN HIM COMPLETELY,
A BAND OF REBELS APPEARED WITH BLACK CRESCENT MARKS ON THEIR FOREHEADS. THEY CALLED THEMSELVES THE BLACK MOON.
THEIR MESSAGE: KILL EVERYONE FROM THE MOON KINGDOM.

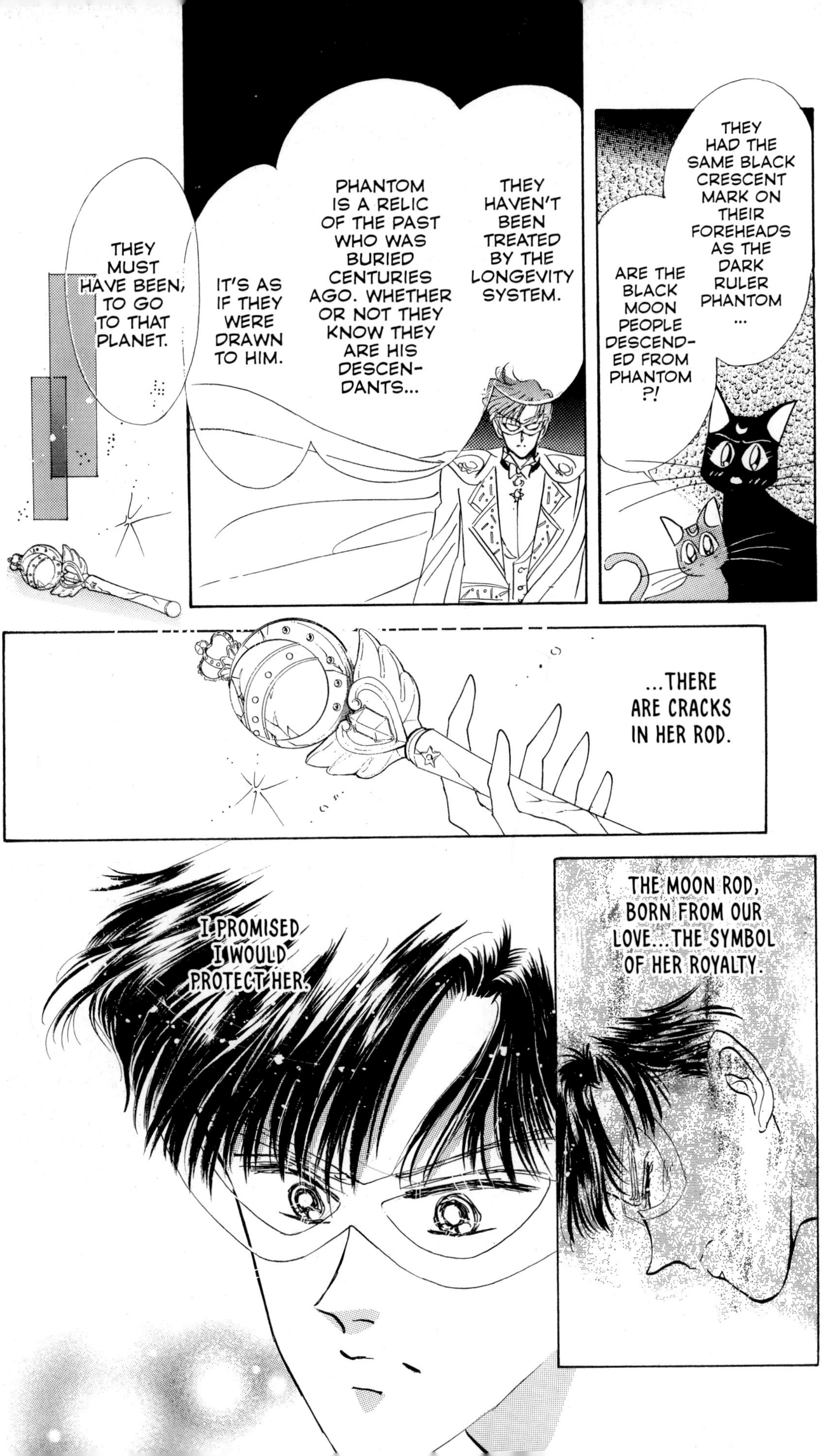
THEY HAD THE SAME BLACK CRESCENT MARK ON THEIR FOREHEADS AS THE DARK RULER PHANTOM ...
ARE THE BLACK MOON PEOPLE DESCENDED FROM PHANTOM ?!
THEY HAVEN'T BEEN TREATED BY THE LONGEVITY SYSTEM.
PHANTOM IS A RELIC OF THE PAST WHO WAS BURIED CENTURIES AGO. WHETHER OR NOT THEY KNOW THEY ARE HIS DESCENDANTS...
IT'S AS IF THEY WERE DRAWN TO HIM.
THEY MUST HAVE BEEN, TO GO TO THAT PLANET.
...THERE ARE CRACKS IN HER ROD.
THE MOON ROD, BORN FROM OUR LOVE...THE SYMBOL OF HER ROYALTY.
I PROMISED I WOULD PROTECT HER.

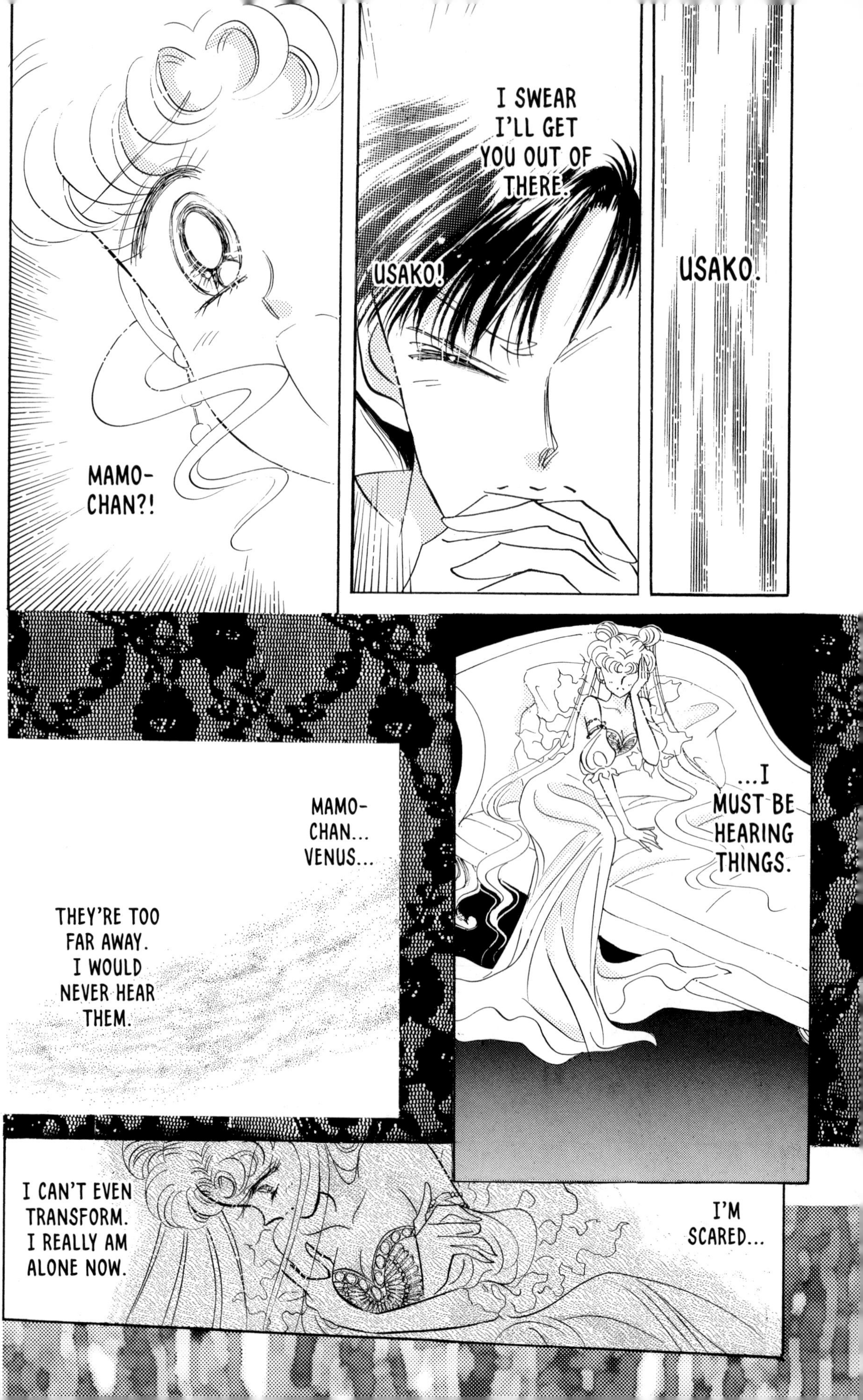
USAKO.
I SWEAR I'LL GET YOU OUT OF THERE.
USAKO!
MAMO-CHAN?!
...I MUST BE HEARING THINGS.
MAMO-CHAN... VENUS...
THEY'RE TOO FAR AWAY. I WOULD NEVER HEAR THEM.
I'M SCARED...
I CAN'T EVEN TRANSFORM. I REALLY AM ALONE NOW.

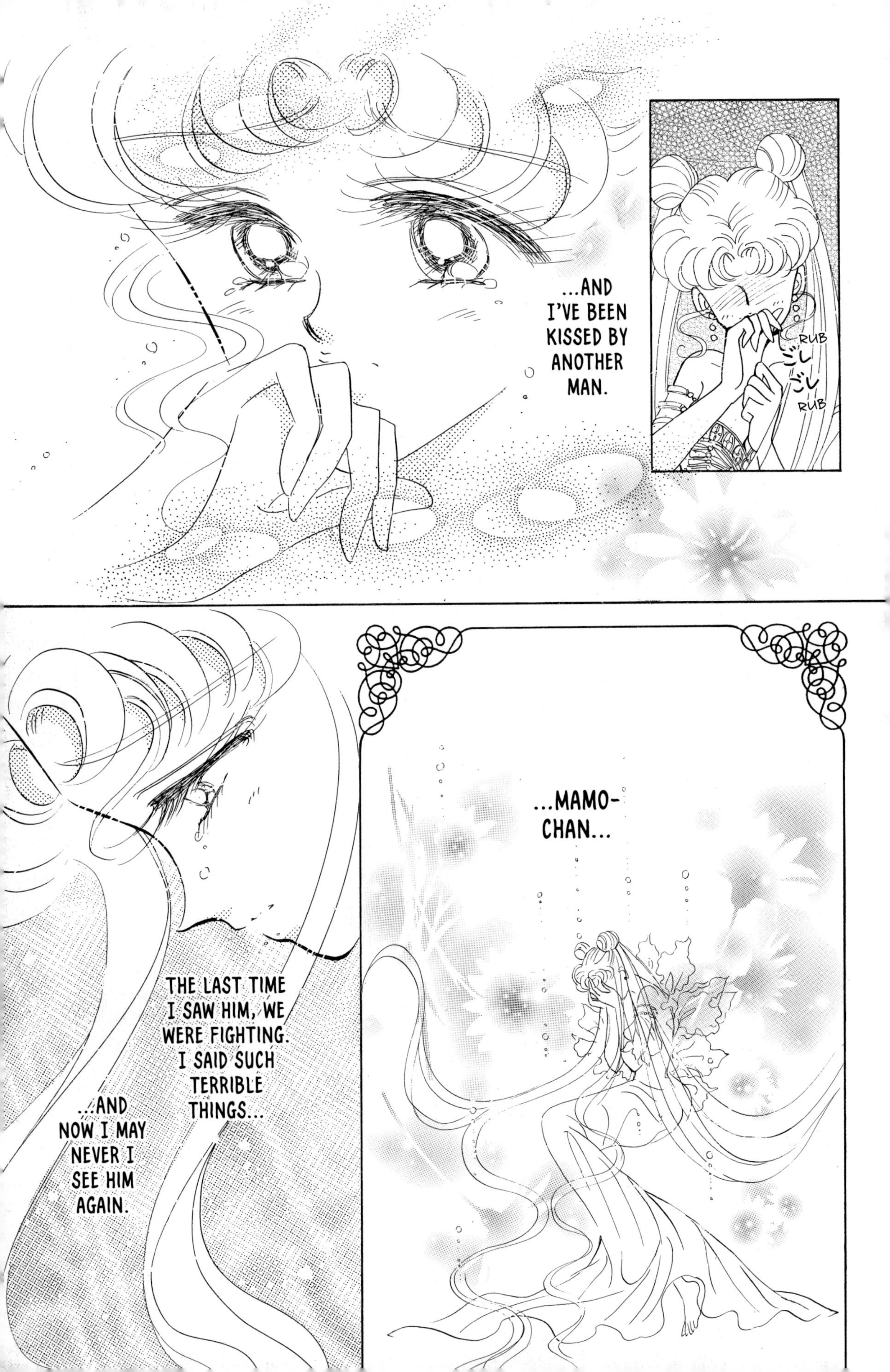
RUB
ごし
ごし
RUB
...AND I'VE BEEN KISSED BY ANOTHER MAN.
...MAMO-CHAN...
THE LAST TIME I SAW HIM, WE WERE FIGHTING. I SAID SUCH TERRIBLE THINGS...
...AND NOW I MAY NEVER I SEE HIM AGAIN.

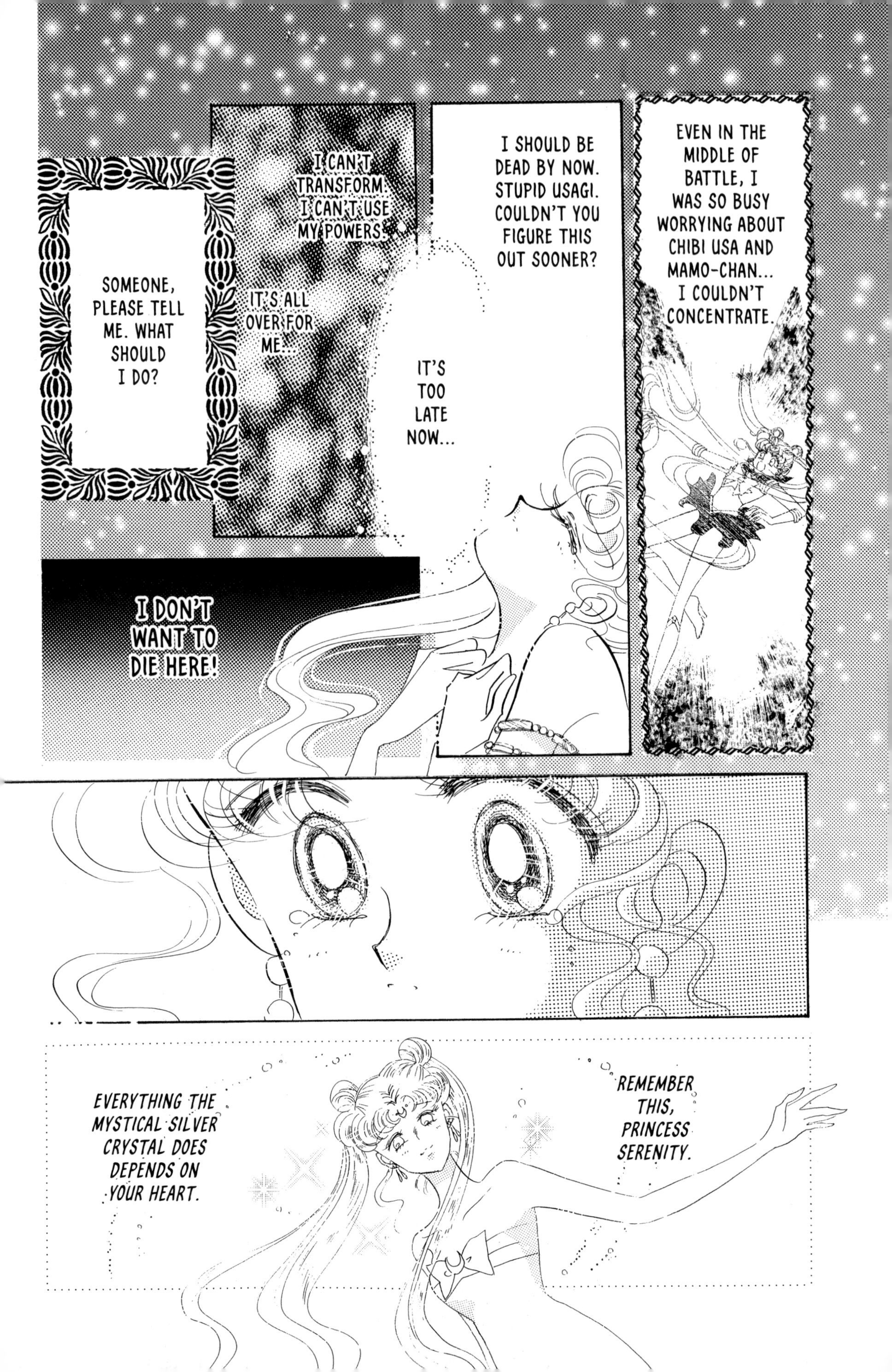
EVEN IN THE MIDDLE OF BATTLE, I WAS SO BUSY WORRYING ABOUT CHIBI USA AND MAMO-CHAN... I COULDN'T CONCENTRATE.
I SHOULD BE DEAD BY NOW. STUPID USAGI. COULDN'T YOU FIGURE THIS OUT SOONER?
IT'S TOO LATE NOW...
I CAN'T TRANSFORM. I CAN'T USE MY POWERS.
IT'S ALL OVER FOR ME...
SOMEONE, PLEASE TELL ME. WHAT SHOULD I DO?
I DON'T WANT TO DIE HERE!
REMEMBER THIS, PRINCESS SERENITY.
EVERYTHING THE MYSTICAL SILVER CRYSTAL DOES DEPENDS ON YOUR HEART.

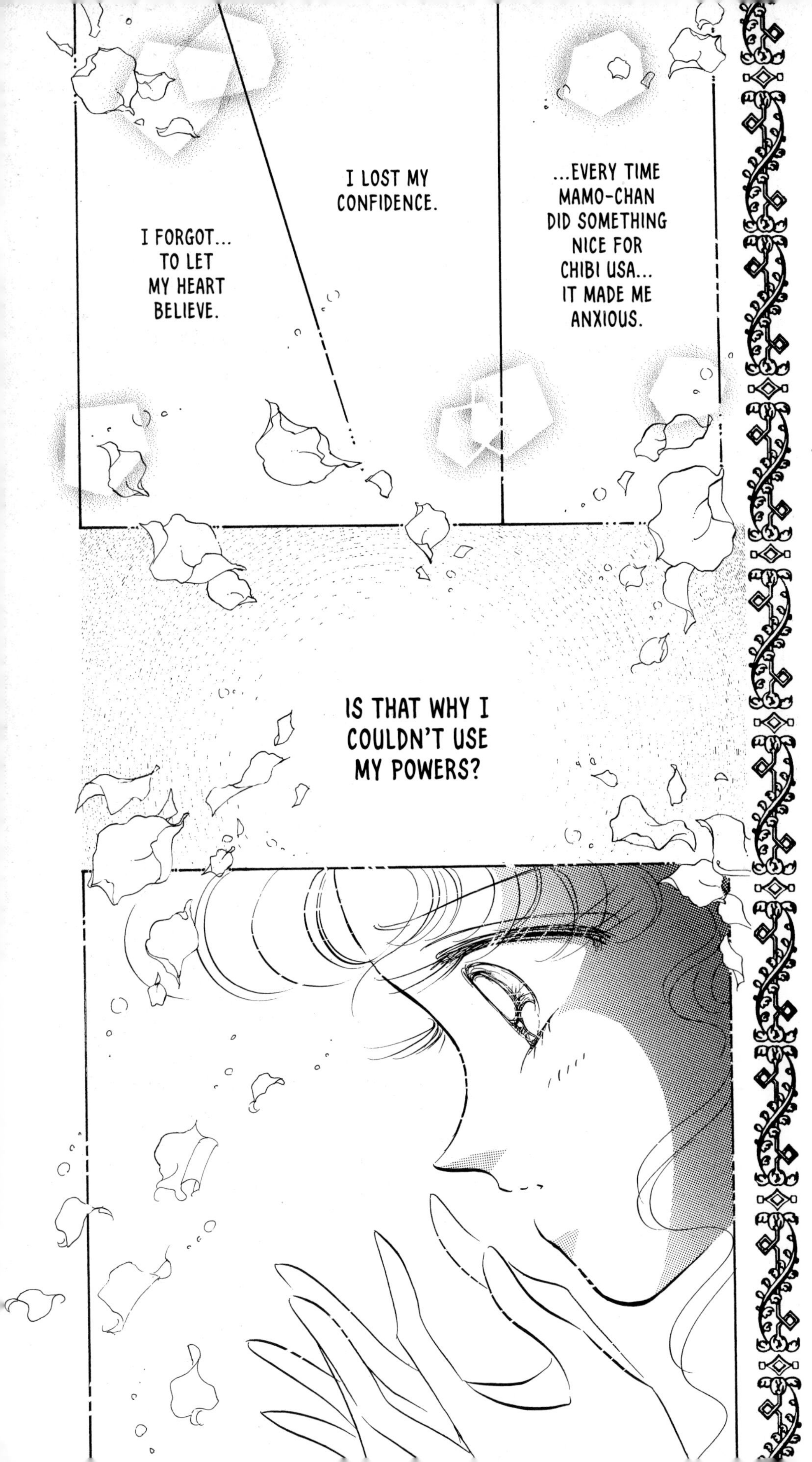
...EVERY TIME MAMO-CHAN DID SOMETHING NICE FOR CHIBI USA... IT MADE ME ANXIOUS.
I LOST MY CONFIDENCE.
I FORGOT... TO LET MY HEART BELIEVE.
IS THAT WHY I COULDN'T USE MY POWERS?

...IS THIS ALL BECAUSE MY HEART WAS FULL OF DOUBT?

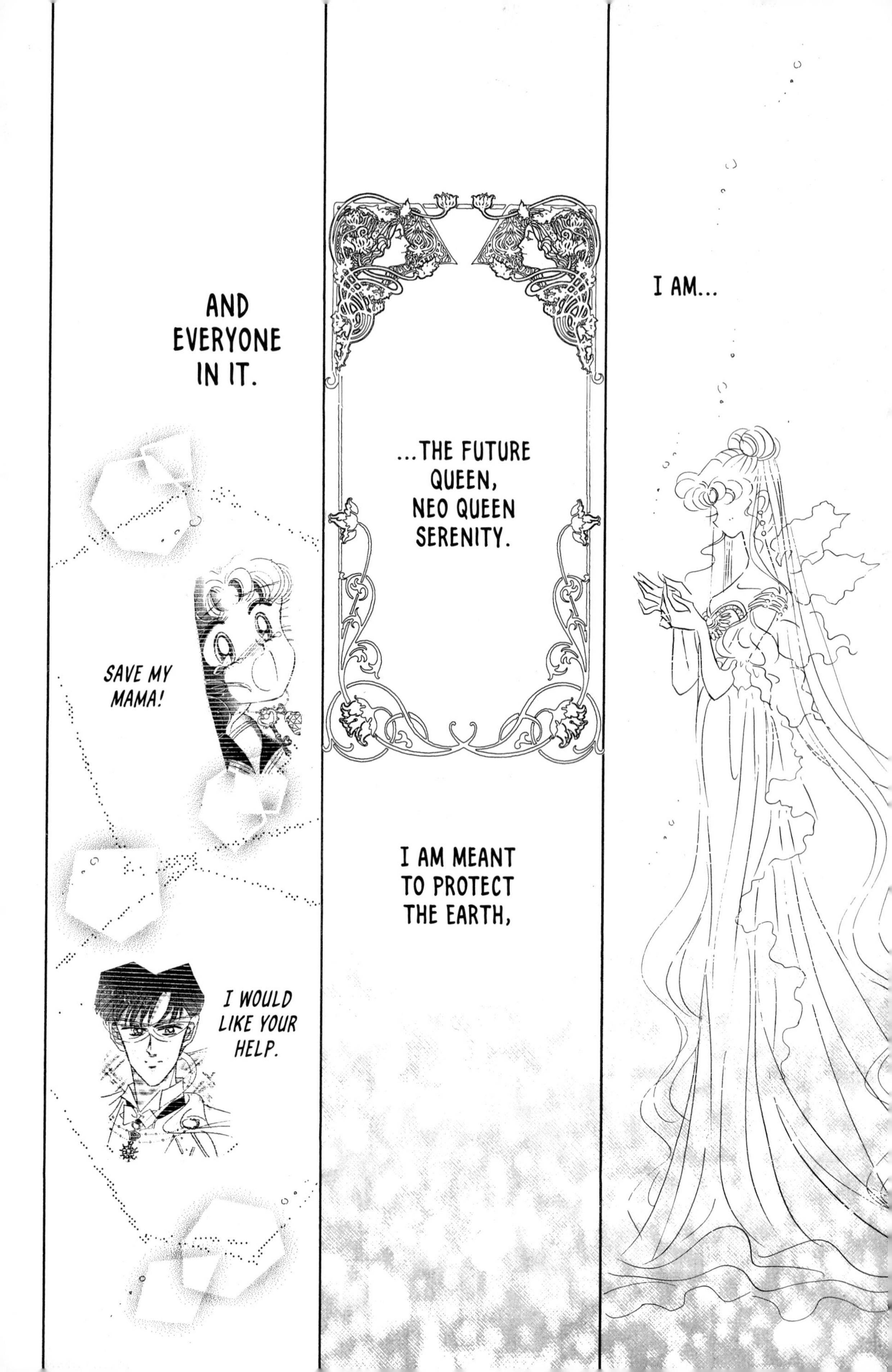
I AM...
...THE FUTURE QUEEN, NEO QUEEN SERENITY.
I AM MEANT TO PROTECT THE EARTH,
AND EVERYONE IN IT.
SAVE MY MAMA!
I WOULD LIKE YOUR HELP.

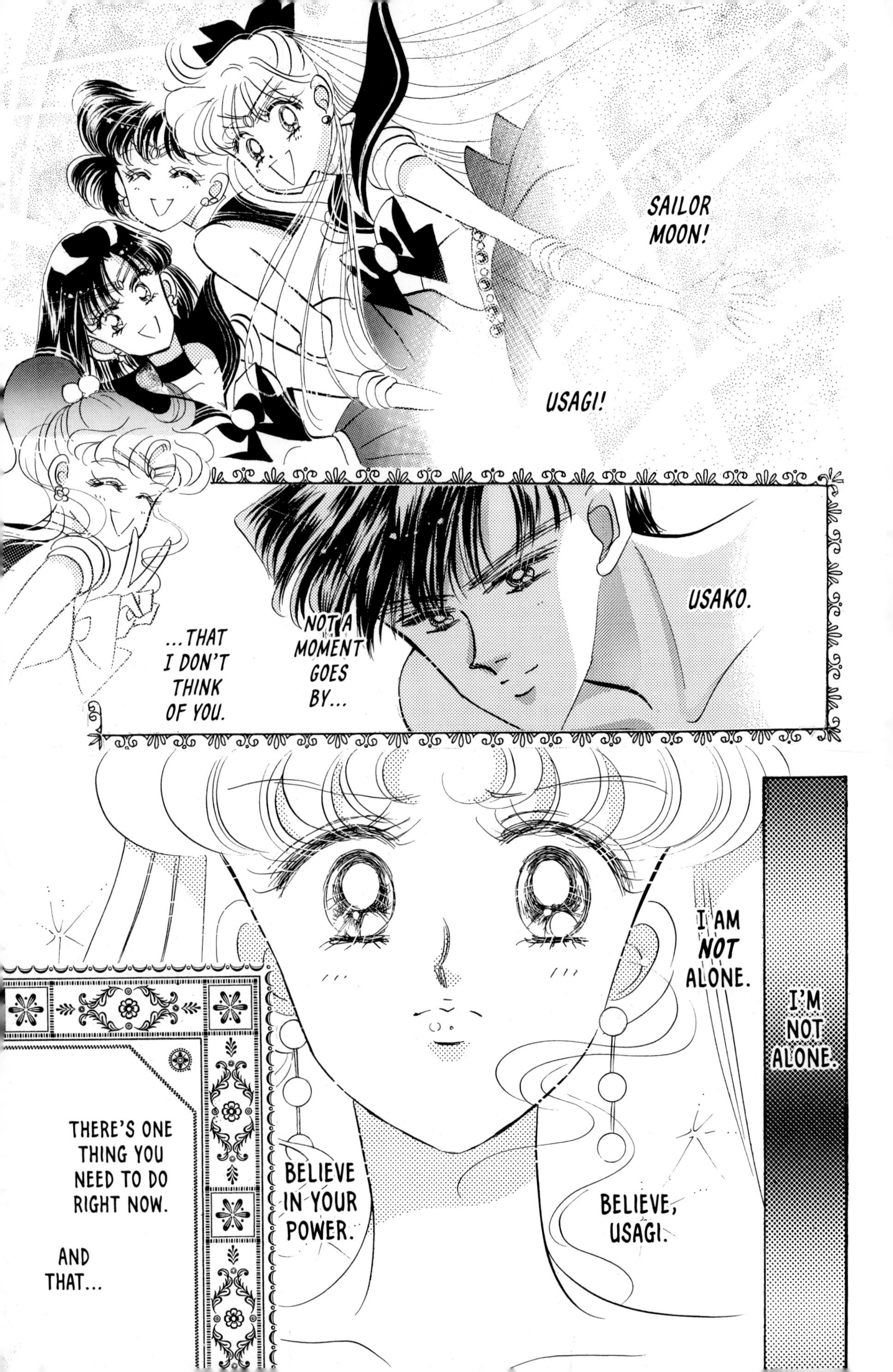
SAILOR MOON!
USAGI!
USAKO.
NOT A MOMENT GOES BY...
...THAT I DON'T THINK OF YOU.
I'M NOT ALONE.
I AM *NOT* ALONE.
BELIEVE, USAGI.
BELIEVE IN YOUR POWER.
THERE'S ONE THING YOU NEED TO DO RIGHT NOW.
AND THAT...

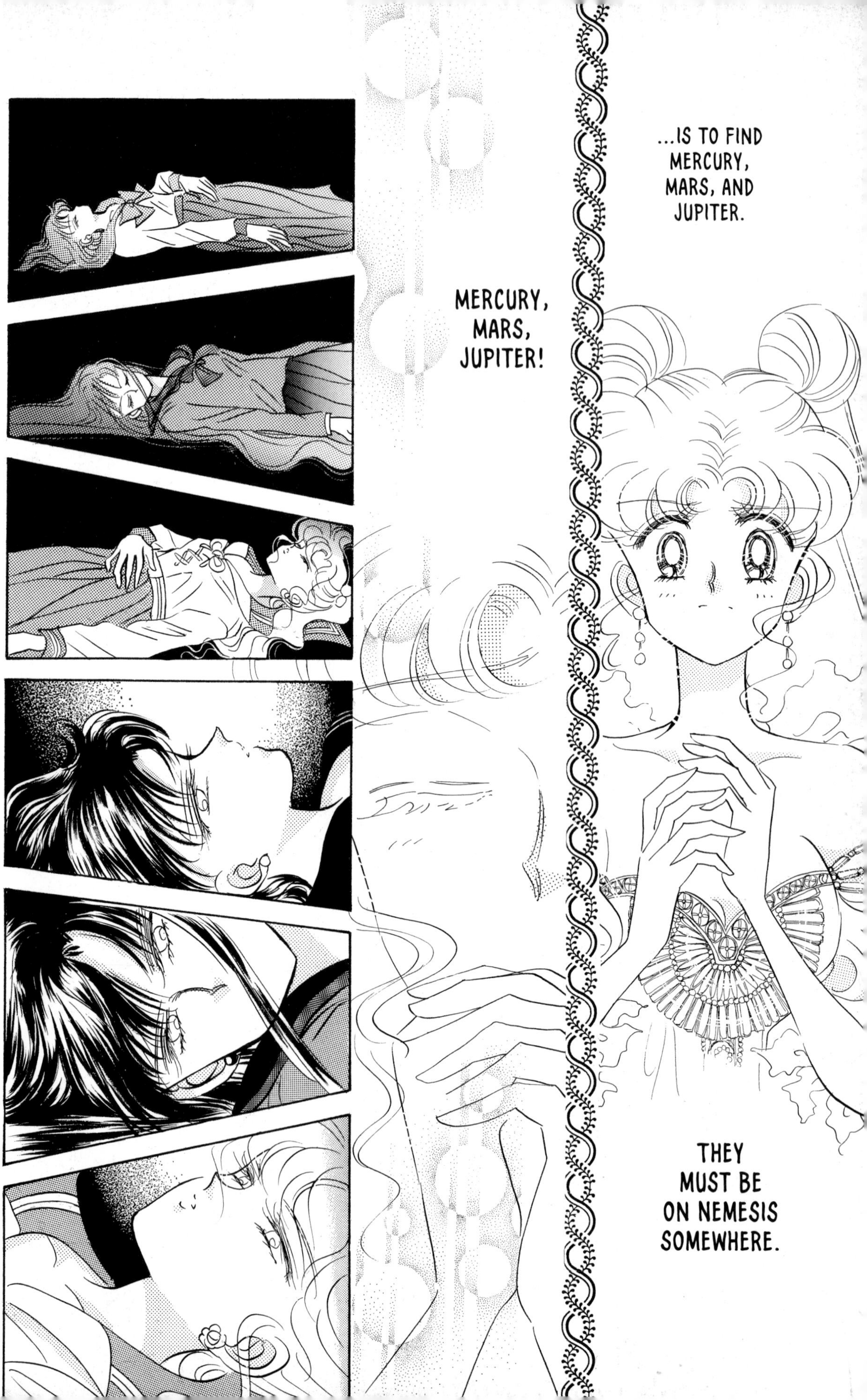
...IS TO FIND MERCURY, MARS, AND JUPITER.
THEY MUST BE ON NEMESIS SOMEWHERE.
MERCURY, MARS, JUPITER!

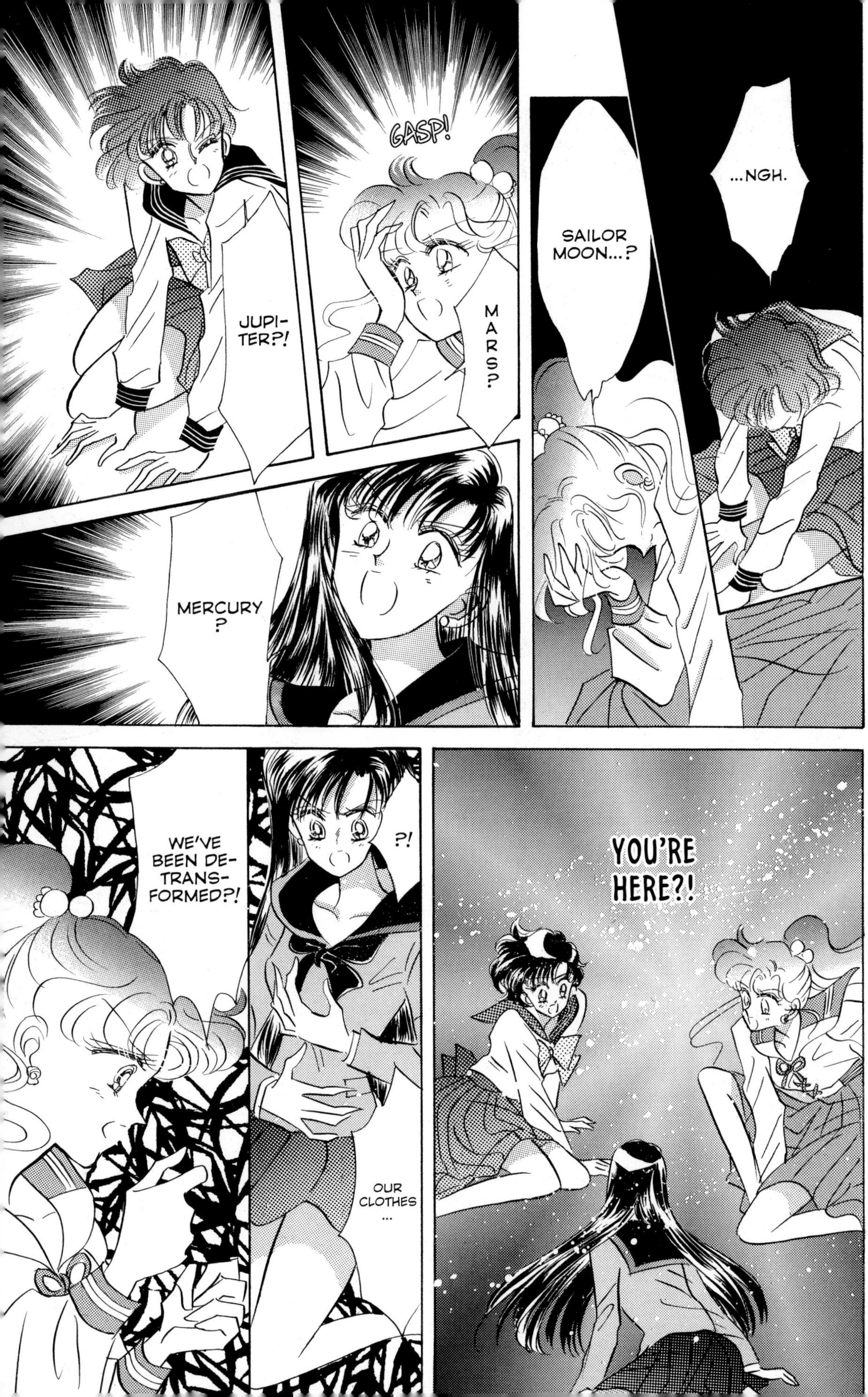
...NGH.
SAILOR MOON...?
GASP!
MARS?
JUPITER?!
MERCURY?
YOU'RE HERE?!
?!
OUR CLOTHES...
WE'VE BEEN DE-TRANSFORMED?!

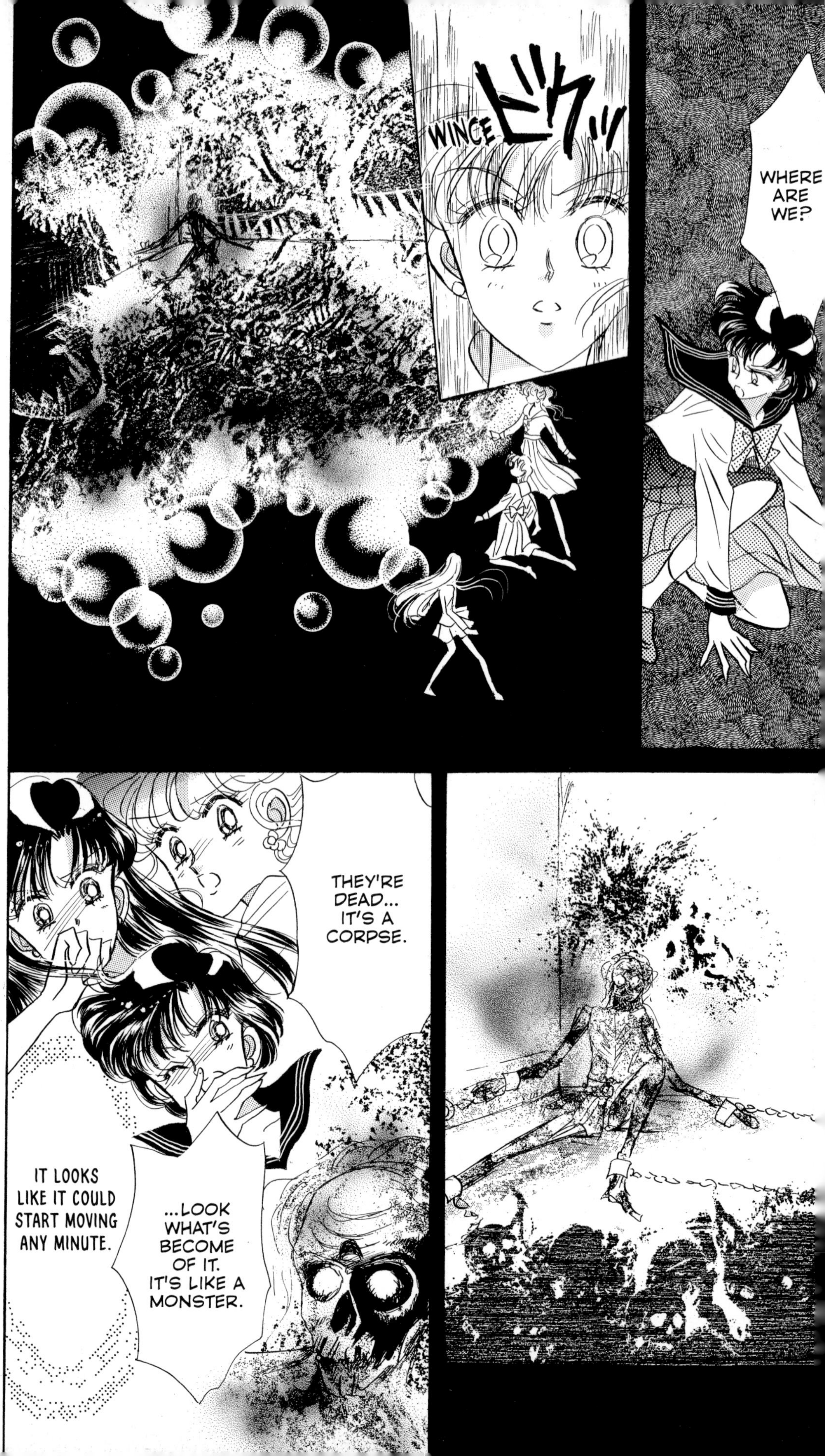
WHERE ARE WE?
WINCE
ビクッ
THEY'RE DEAD... IT'S A CORPSE.
...LOOK WHAT'S BECOME OF IT. IT'S LIKE A MONSTER.
IT LOOKS LIKE IT COULD START MOVING ANY MINUTE.

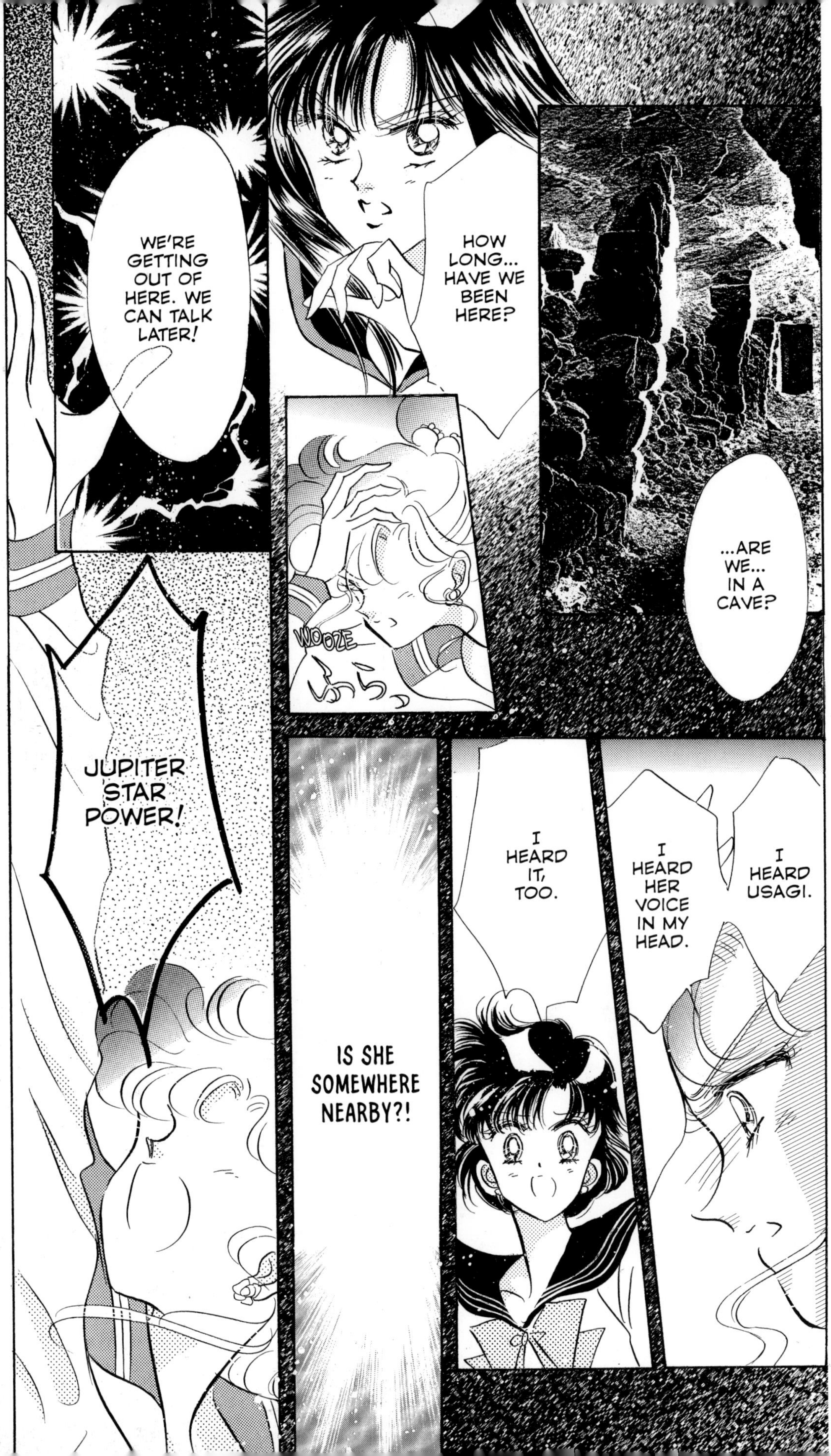
HOW LONG... HAVE WE BEEN HERE?
...ARE WE... IN A CAVE?
WOOZE
ふらっ
WE'RE GETTING OUT OF HERE. WE CAN TALK LATER!
I HEARD USAGI.
I HEARD HER VOICE IN MY HEAD.
I HEARD IT, TOO.
IS SHE SOMEWHERE NEARBY?!
JUPITER STAR POWER!

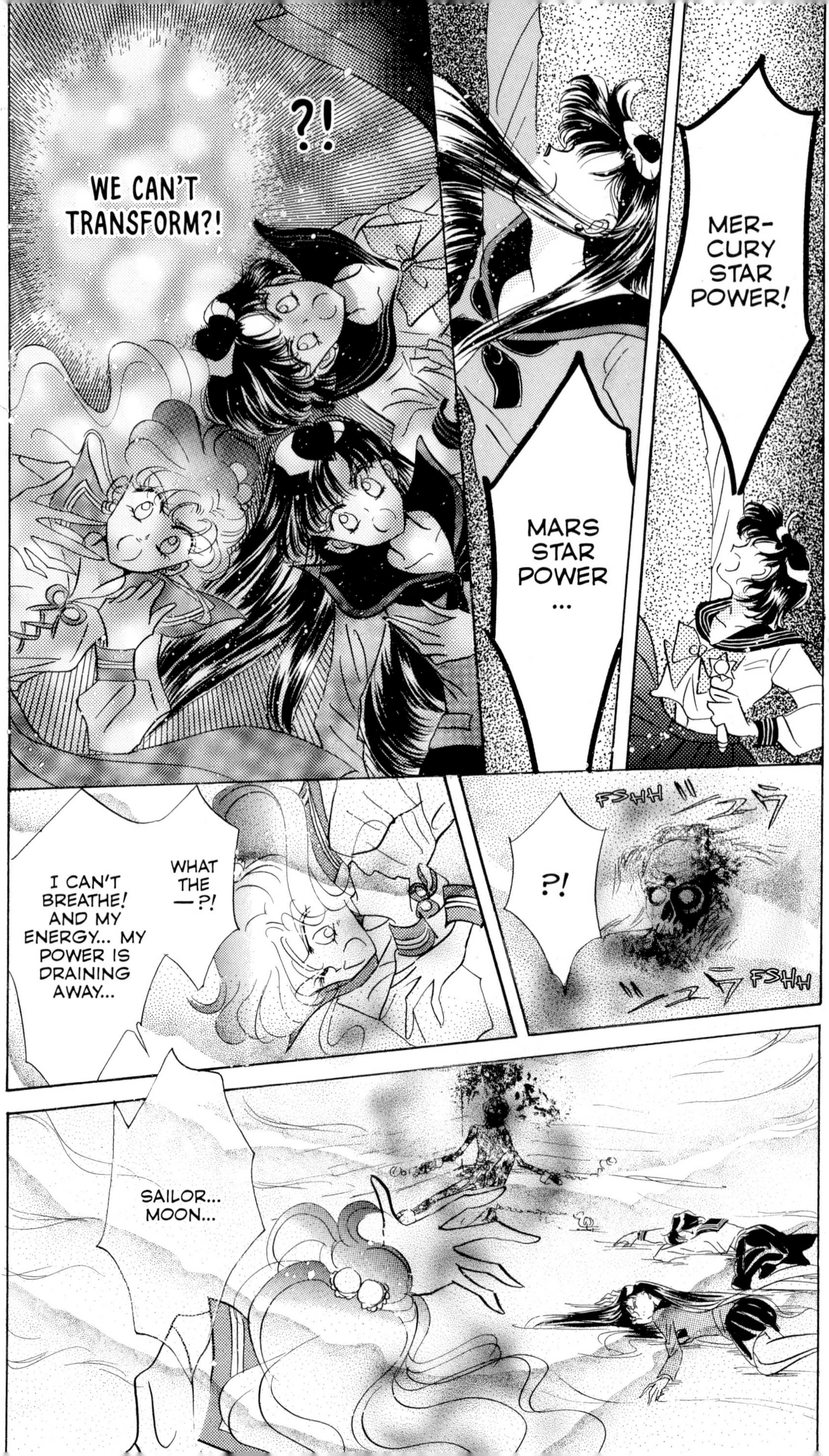
MER-CURY STAR POWER!
MARS STAR POWER ...
?!
WE CAN'T TRANSFORM?!
FSHH
?!
FSHH
WHAT THE —?!
I CAN'T BREATHE! AND MY ENERGY... MY POWER IS DRAINING AWAY...
SAILOR... MOON...

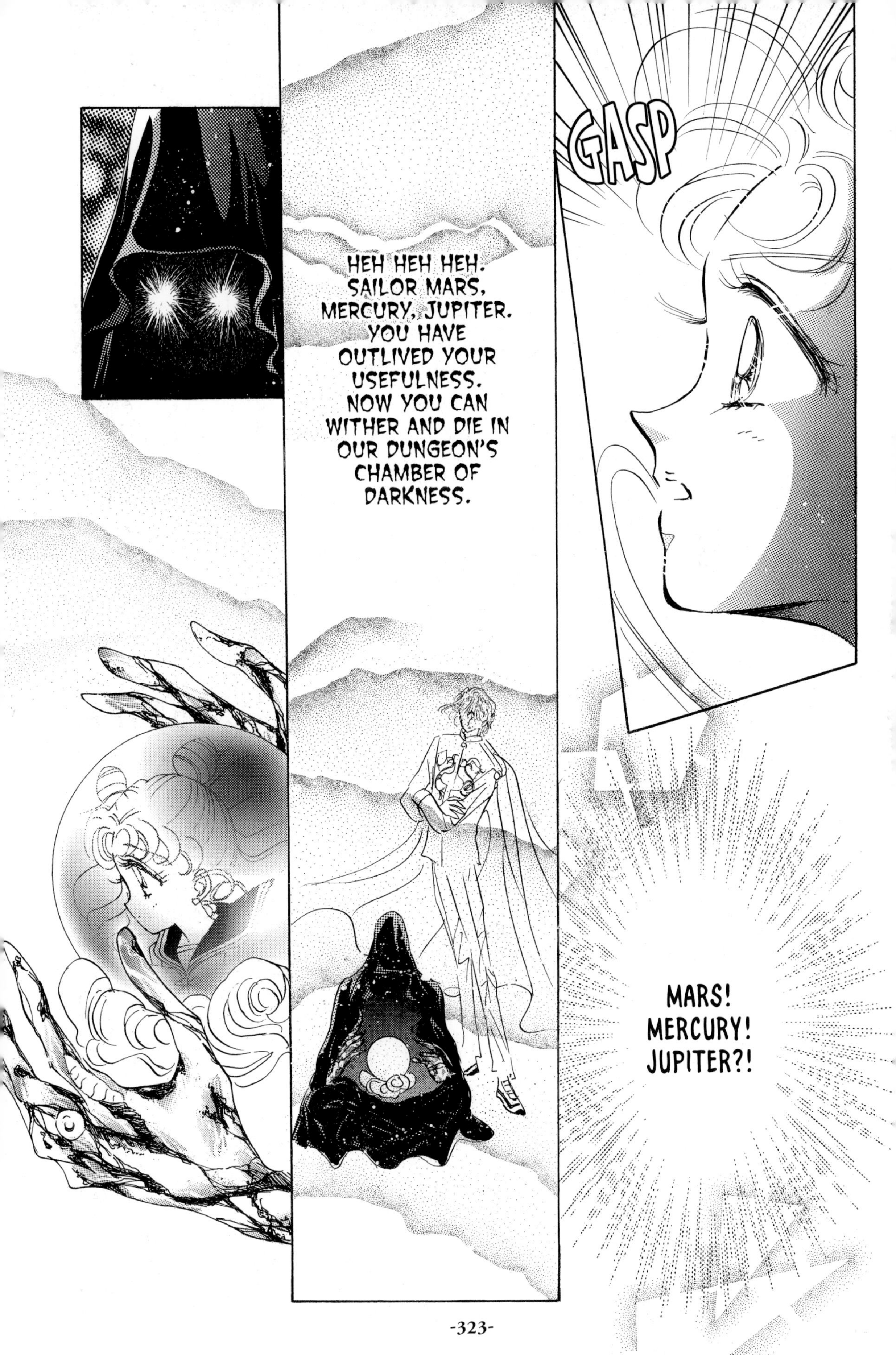
GASP
HEH HEH HEH. SAILOR MARS, MERCURY, JUPITER. YOU HAVE OUTLIVED YOUR USEFULNESS. NOW YOU CAN WITHER AND DIE IN OUR DUNGEON'S CHAMBER OF DARKNESS.
MARS! MERCURY! JUPITER?!

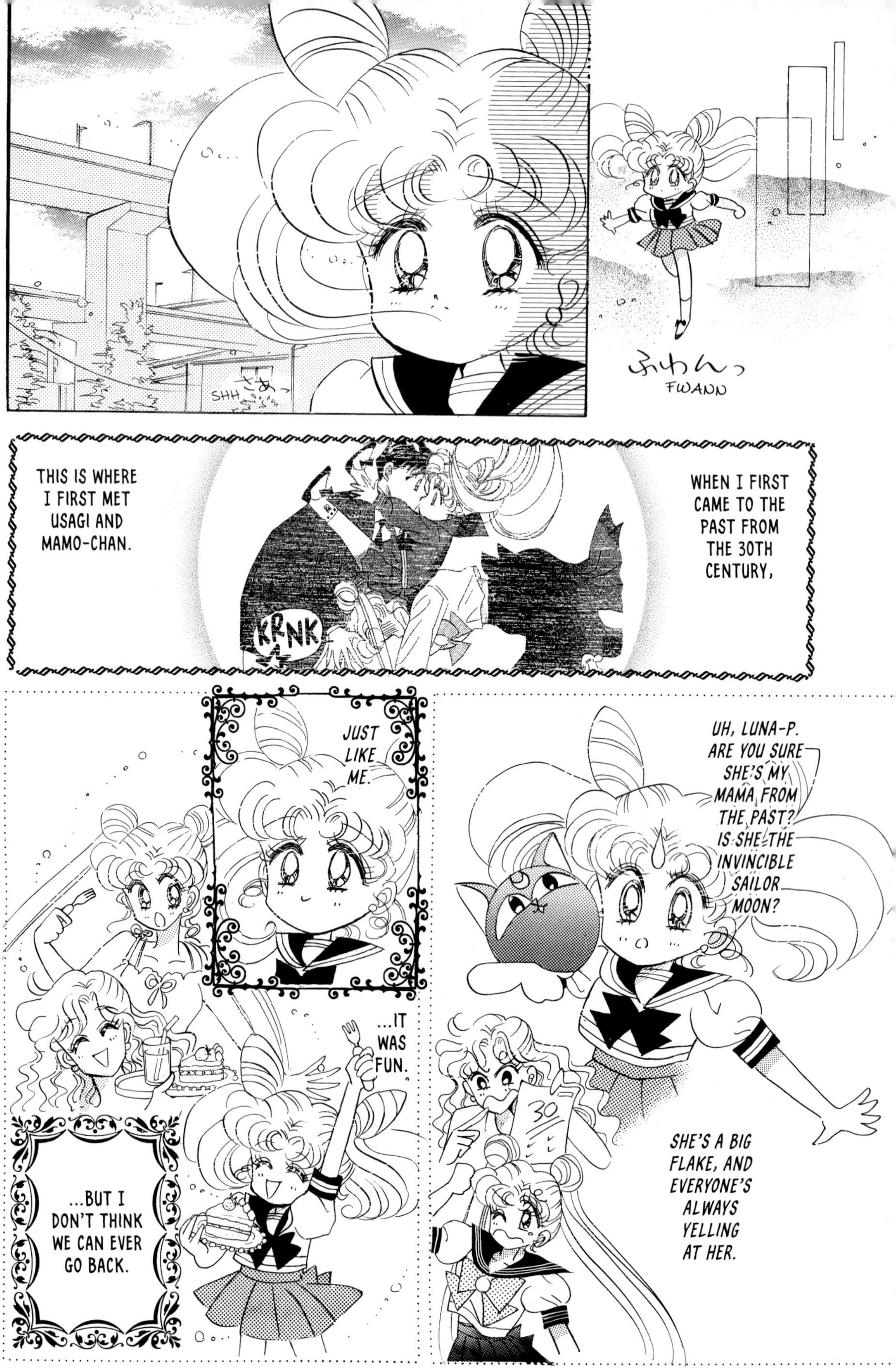
ふわんっ
FWANN
SHH さあっ
WHEN I FIRST CAME TO THE PAST FROM THE 30TH CENTURY,
THIS IS WHERE I FIRST MET USAGI AND MAMO-CHAN.
KRNK
UH, LUNA-P. ARE YOU SURE SHE'S MY MAMA FROM THE PAST? IS SHE THE INVINCIBLE SAILOR MOON?
SHE'S A BIG FLAKE, AND EVERYONE'S ALWAYS YELLING AT HER.
30
JUST LIKE ME.
...IT WAS FUN.
...BUT I DON'T THINK WE CAN EVER GO BACK.

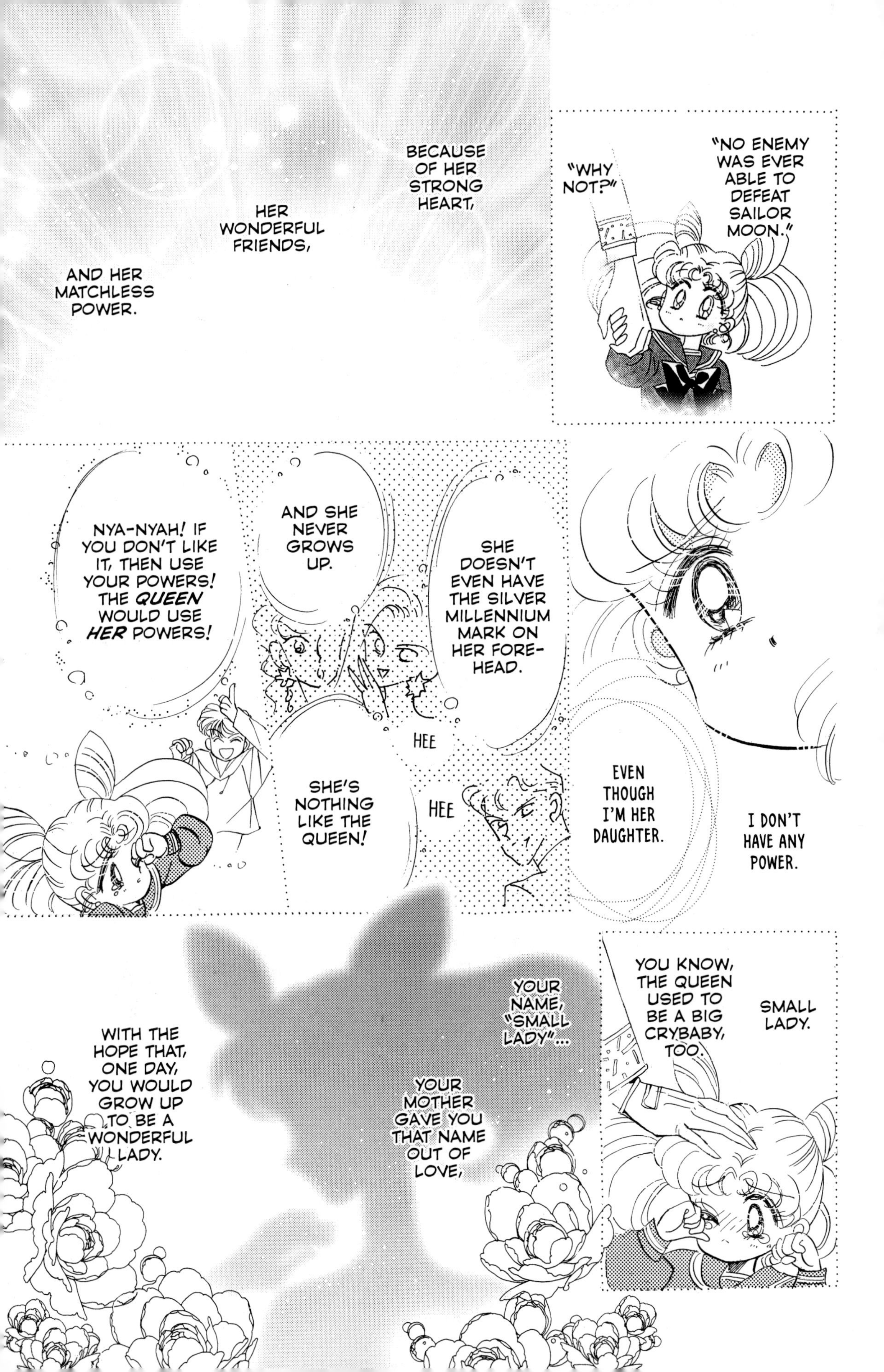
"NO ENEMY WAS EVER ABLE TO DEFEAT SAILOR MOON."
"WHY NOT?"
BECAUSE OF HER STRONG HEART,
HER WONDERFUL FRIENDS,
AND HER MATCHLESS POWER.
I DON'T HAVE ANY POWER.
EVEN THOUGH I'M HER DAUGHTER.
SHE DOESN'T EVEN HAVE THE SILVER MILLENNIUM MARK ON HER FORE-HEAD.
AND SHE NEVER GROWS UP.
HEE
HEE
SHE'S NOTHING LIKE THE QUEEN!
NYA-NYAH! IF YOU DON'T LIKE IT, THEN USE YOUR POWERS! THE *QUEEN* WOULD USE ***HER*** POWERS!
SMALL LADY.
YOU KNOW, THE QUEEN USED TO BE A BIG CRYBABY, TOO.
YOUR NAME, "SMALL LADY"...
YOUR MOTHER GAVE YOU THAT NAME OUT OF LOVE,
WITH THE HOPE THAT, ONE DAY, YOU WOULD GROW UP TO BE A WONDERFUL LADY.

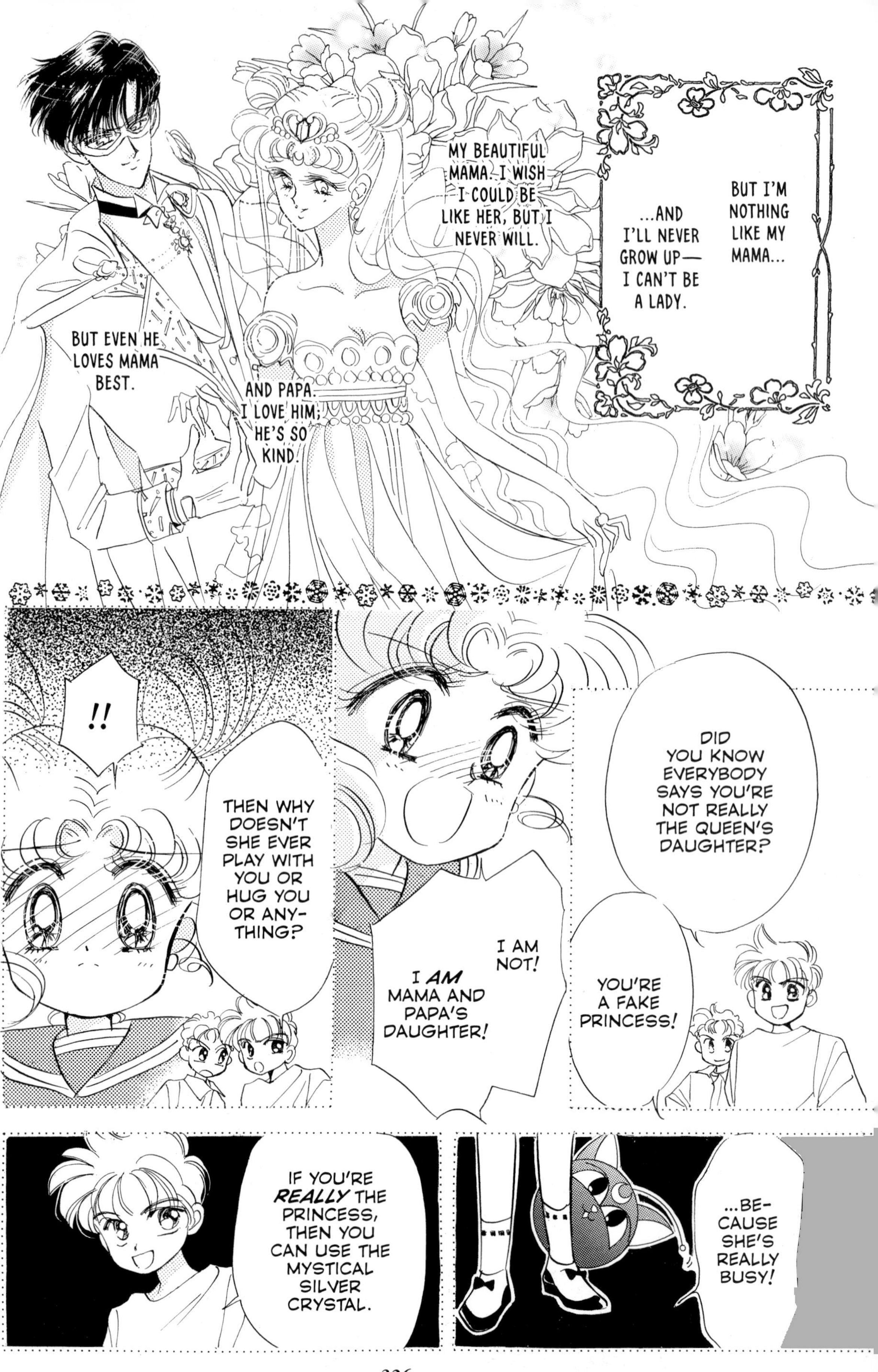
BUT I'M NOTHING LIKE MY MAMA...
...AND I'LL NEVER GROW UP— I CAN'T BE A LADY.
MY BEAUTIFUL MAMA. I WISH I COULD BE LIKE HER, BUT I NEVER WILL.
AND PAPA. I LOVE HIM; HE'S SO KIND.
BUT EVEN HE LOVES MAMA BEST.
DID YOU KNOW EVERYBODY SAYS YOU'RE NOT REALLY THE QUEEN'S DAUGHTER?
YOU'RE A FAKE PRINCESS!
I AM NOT!
I *AM* MAMA AND PAPA'S DAUGHTER!
THEN WHY DOESN'T SHE EVER PLAY WITH YOU OR HUG YOU OR ANY-THING?
!!
...BE-CAUSE SHE'S REALLY BUSY!
IF YOU'RE *REALLY* THE PRINCESS, THEN YOU CAN USE THE MYSTICAL SILVER CRYSTAL.

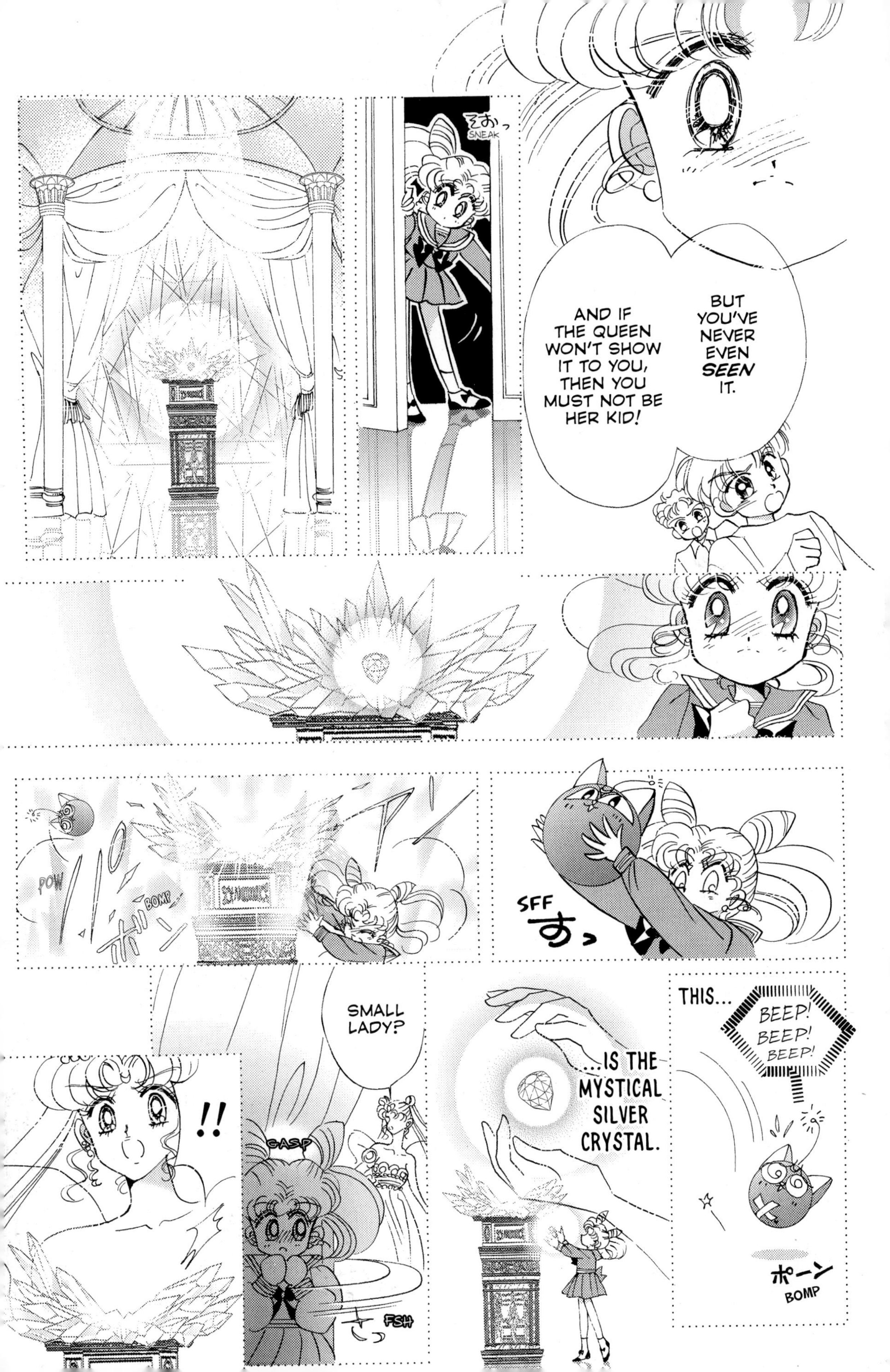
BUT YOU'VE NEVER EVEN SEEN IT.
AND IF THE QUEEN WON'T SHOW IT TO YOU, THEN YOU MUST NOT BE HER KID!
そおっ
SNEAK
SFF
すっ
POW
BOMP
ボン
THIS...
BEEP! BEEP! BEEP!
ポーン
BOMP
...IS THE MYSTICAL SILVER CRYSTAL.
SMALL LADY?
GASP
FSH
!!

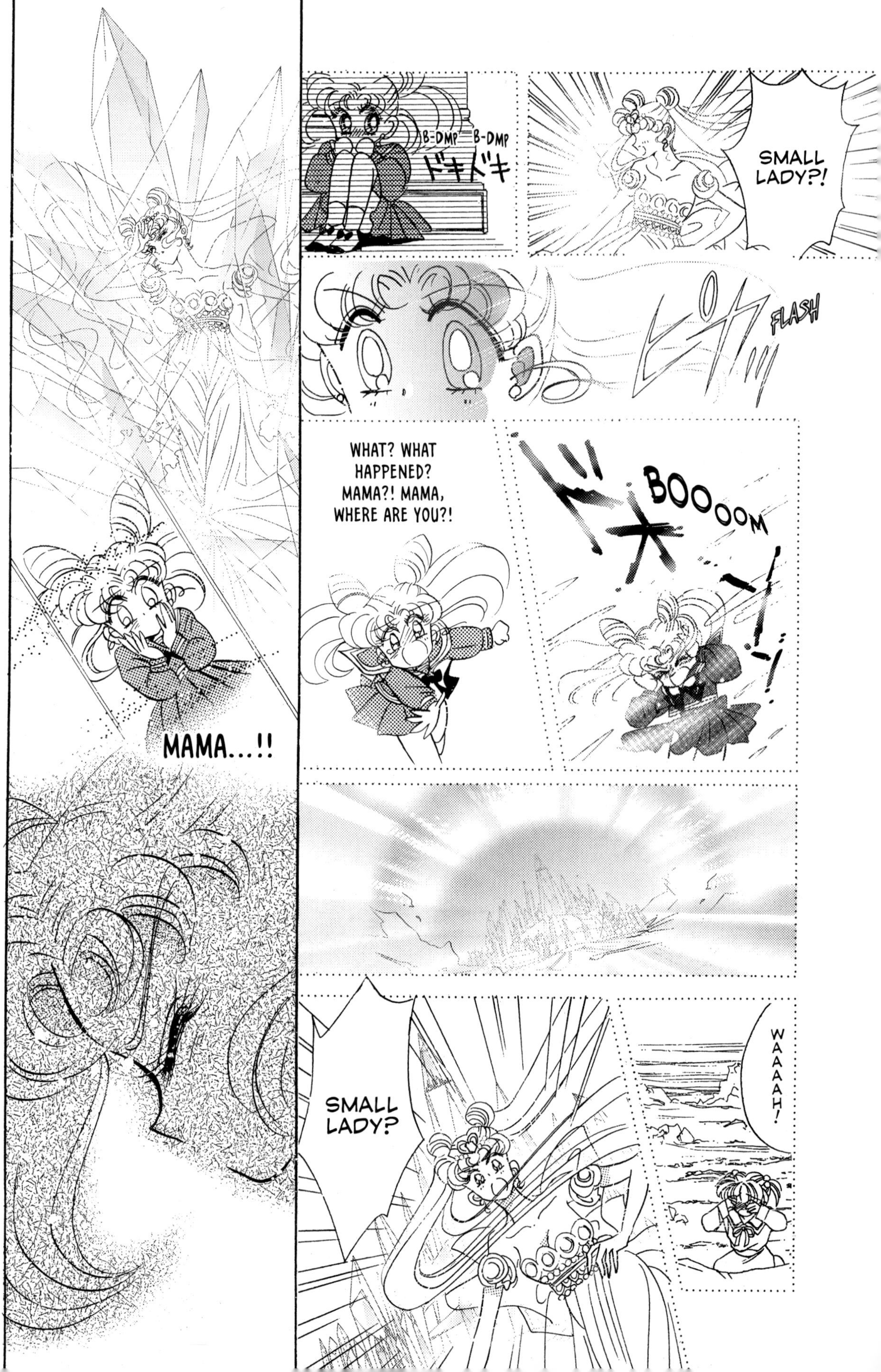
SMALL LADY?!
B-DMP B-DMP
ドキドキ
FLASH
BOOOOOM
WHAT? WHAT HAPPENED? MAMA?! MAMA, WHERE ARE YOU?!
WAAAAAH!
SMALL LADY?
MAMA...!!

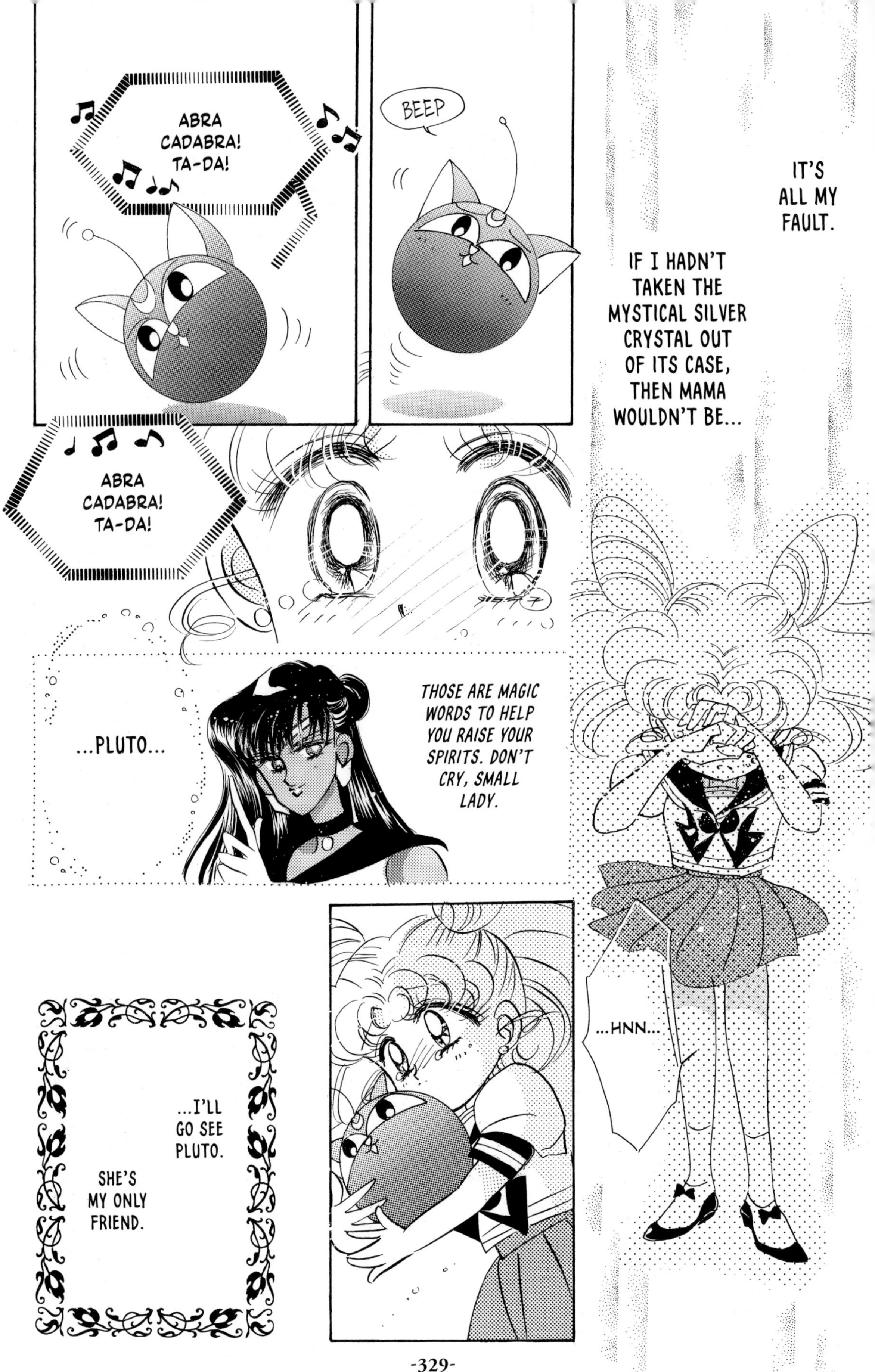
IT'S ALL MY FAULT.
IF I HADN'T TAKEN THE MYSTICAL SILVER CRYSTAL OUT OF ITS CASE, THEN MAMA WOULDN'T BE...
...HNN...
BEEP
ABRA CADABRA! TA-DA!
ABRA CADABRA! TA-DA!
THOSE ARE MAGIC WORDS TO HELP YOU RAISE YOUR SPIRITS. DON'T CRY, SMALL LADY.
...PLUTO...
...I'LL GO SEE PLUTO.
SHE'S MY ONLY FRIEND.

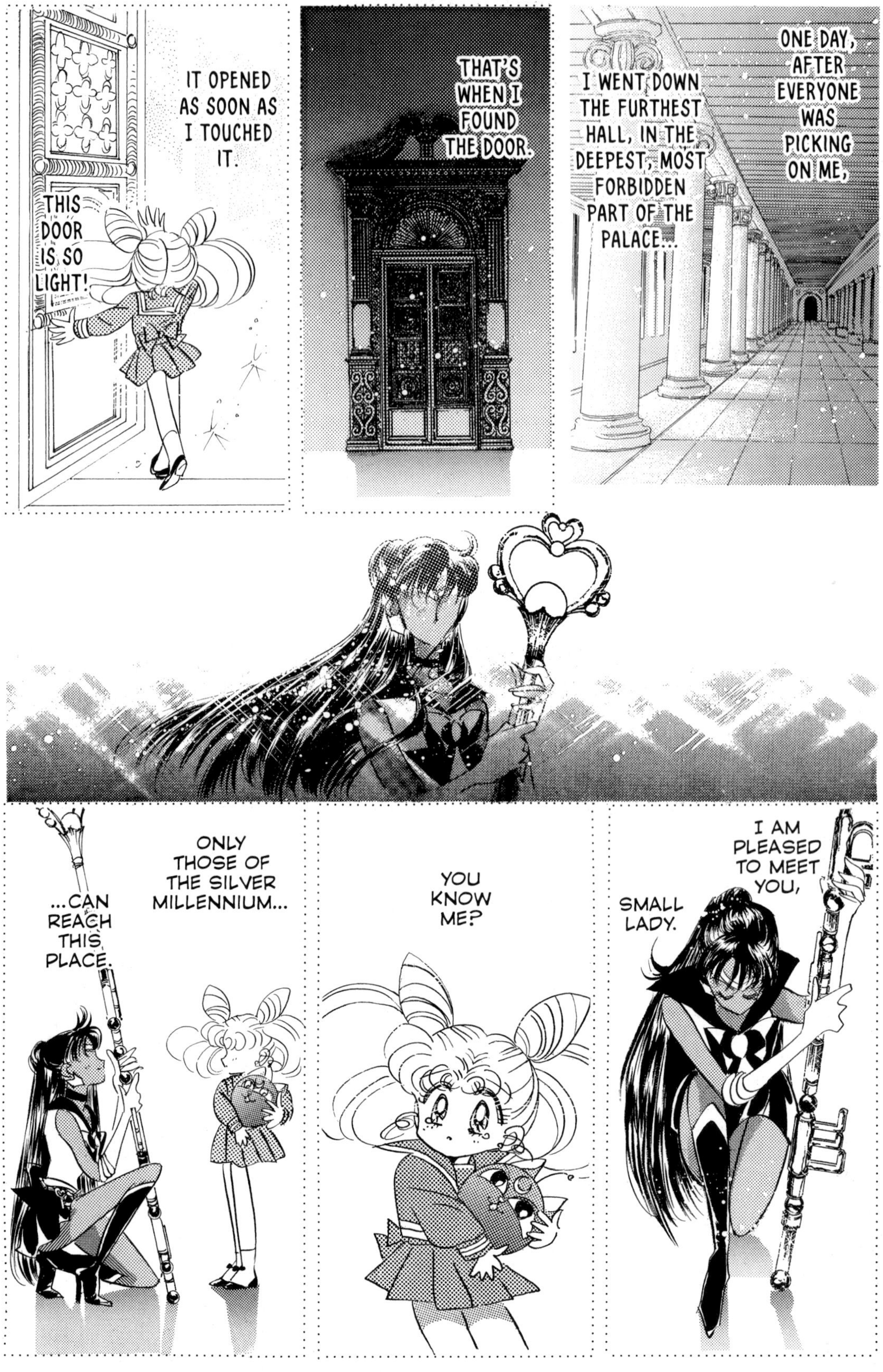
ONE DAY, AFTER EVERYONE WAS PICKING ON ME,
I WENT DOWN THE FURTHEST HALL, IN THE DEEPEST, MOST FORBIDDEN PART OF THE PALACE...
THAT'S WHEN I FOUND THE DOOR.
IT OPENED AS SOON AS I TOUCHED IT.
THIS DOOR IS SO LIGHT!
I AM PLEASED TO MEET YOU,
SMALL LADY.
YOU KNOW ME?
ONLY THOSE OF THE SILVER MILLENNIUM...
...CAN REACH THIS PLACE.

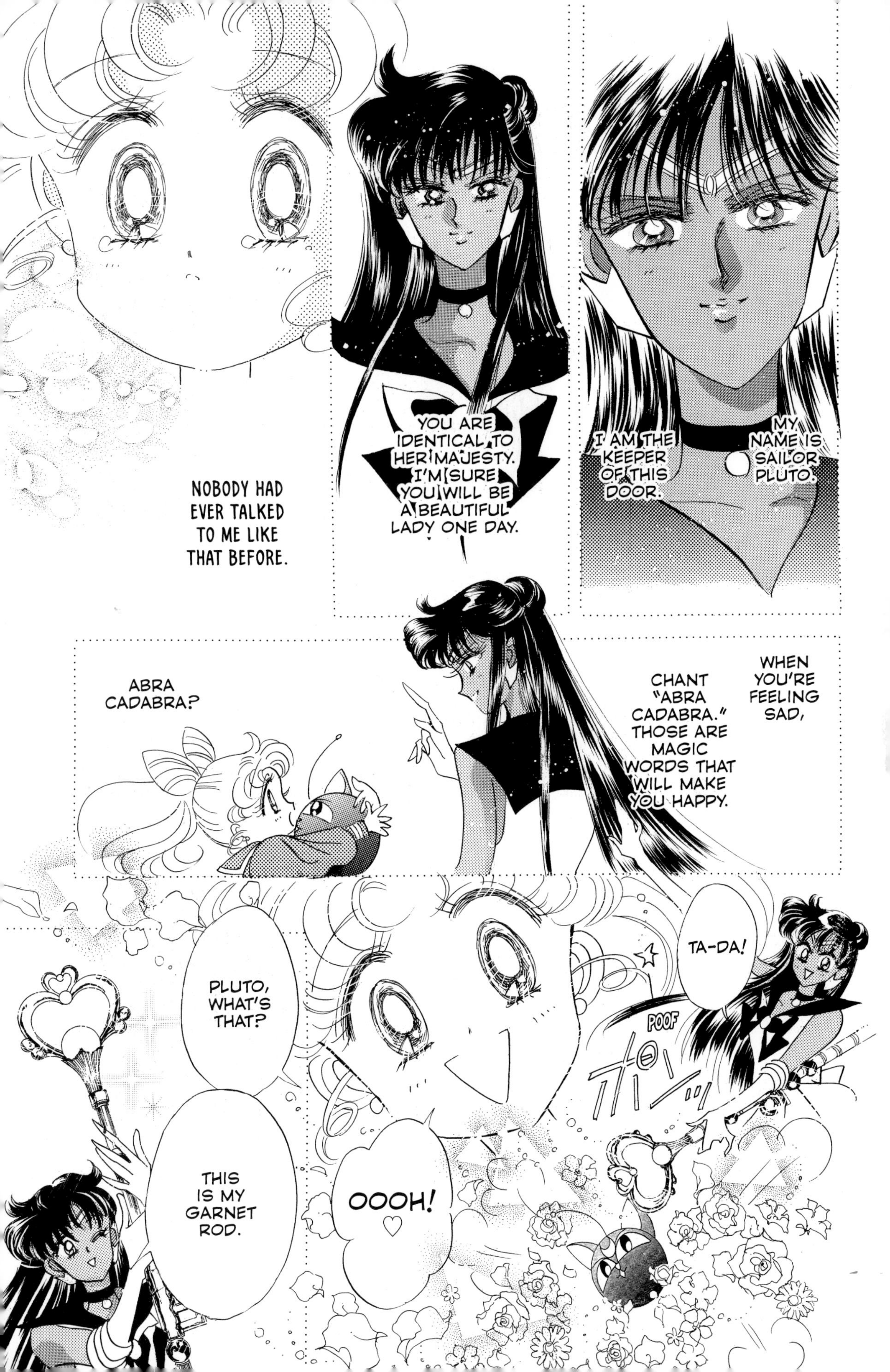
MY NAME IS SAILOR PLUTO.
I AM THE KEEPER OF THIS DOOR.
YOU ARE IDENTICAL TO HER MAJESTY. I'M SURE YOU WILL BE A BEAUTIFUL LADY ONE DAY.
NOBODY HAD EVER TALKED TO ME LIKE THAT BEFORE.
WHEN YOU'RE FEELING SAD,
CHANT "ABRA CADABRA." THOSE ARE MAGIC WORDS THAT WILL MAKE YOU HAPPY.
ABRA CADABRA?
TA-DA!
POOF
OOOH! ♡
PLUTO, WHAT'S THAT?
THIS IS MY GARNET ROD.

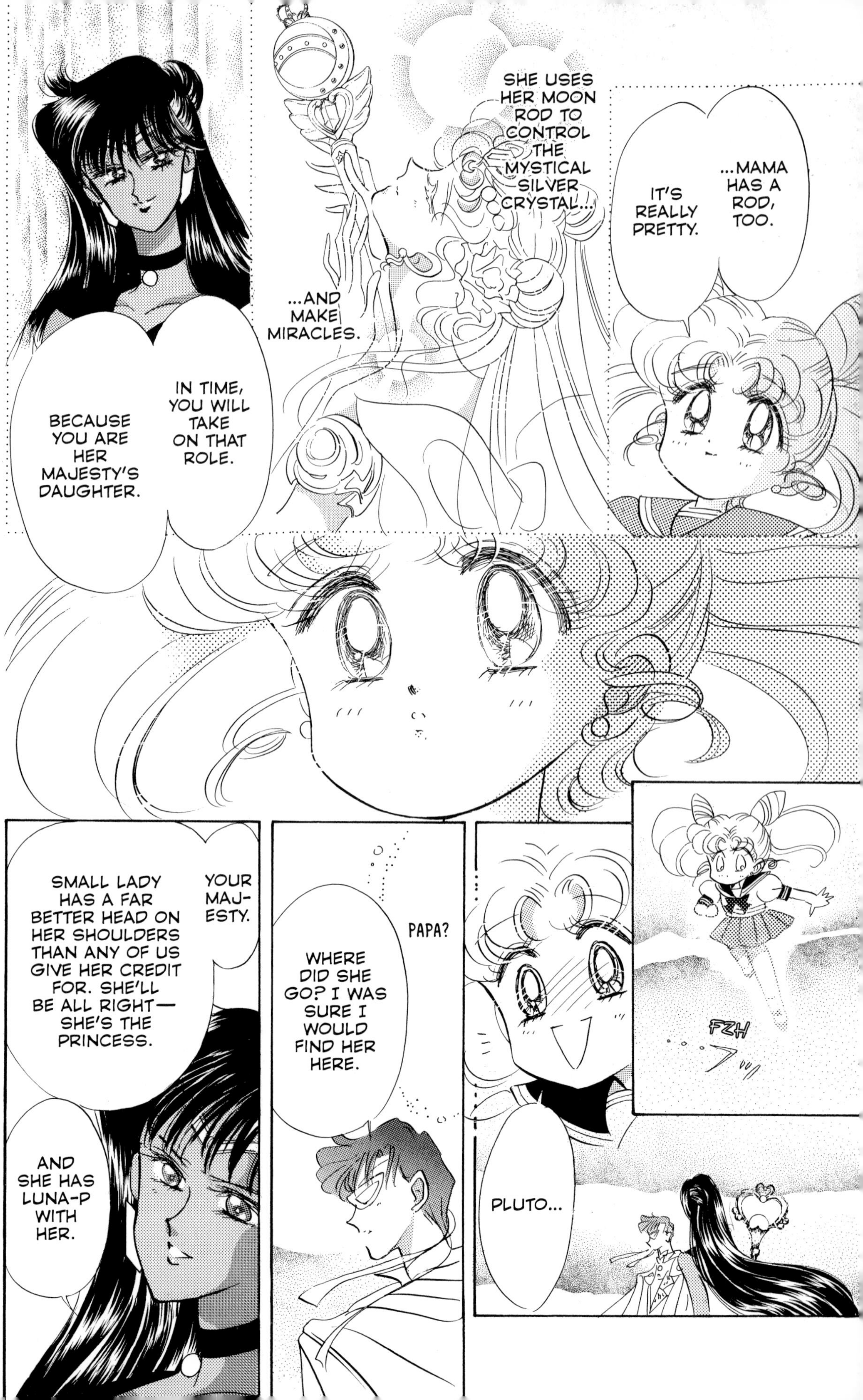
...MAMA HAS A ROD, TOO.
IT'S REALLY PRETTY.
SHE USES HER MOON ROD TO CONTROL THE MYSTICAL SILVER CRYSTAL...
...AND MAKE MIRACLES.
IN TIME, YOU WILL TAKE ON THAT ROLE.
BECAUSE YOU ARE HER MAJESTY'S DAUGHTER.
FZH
PLUTO...
PAPA?
WHERE DID SHE GO? I WAS SURE I WOULD FIND HER HERE.
YOUR MAJESTY.
SMALL LADY HAS A FAR BETTER HEAD ON HER SHOULDERS THAN ANY OF US GIVE HER CREDIT FOR. SHE'LL BE ALL RIGHT— SHE'S THE PRINCESS.
AND SHE HAS LUNA-P WITH HER.

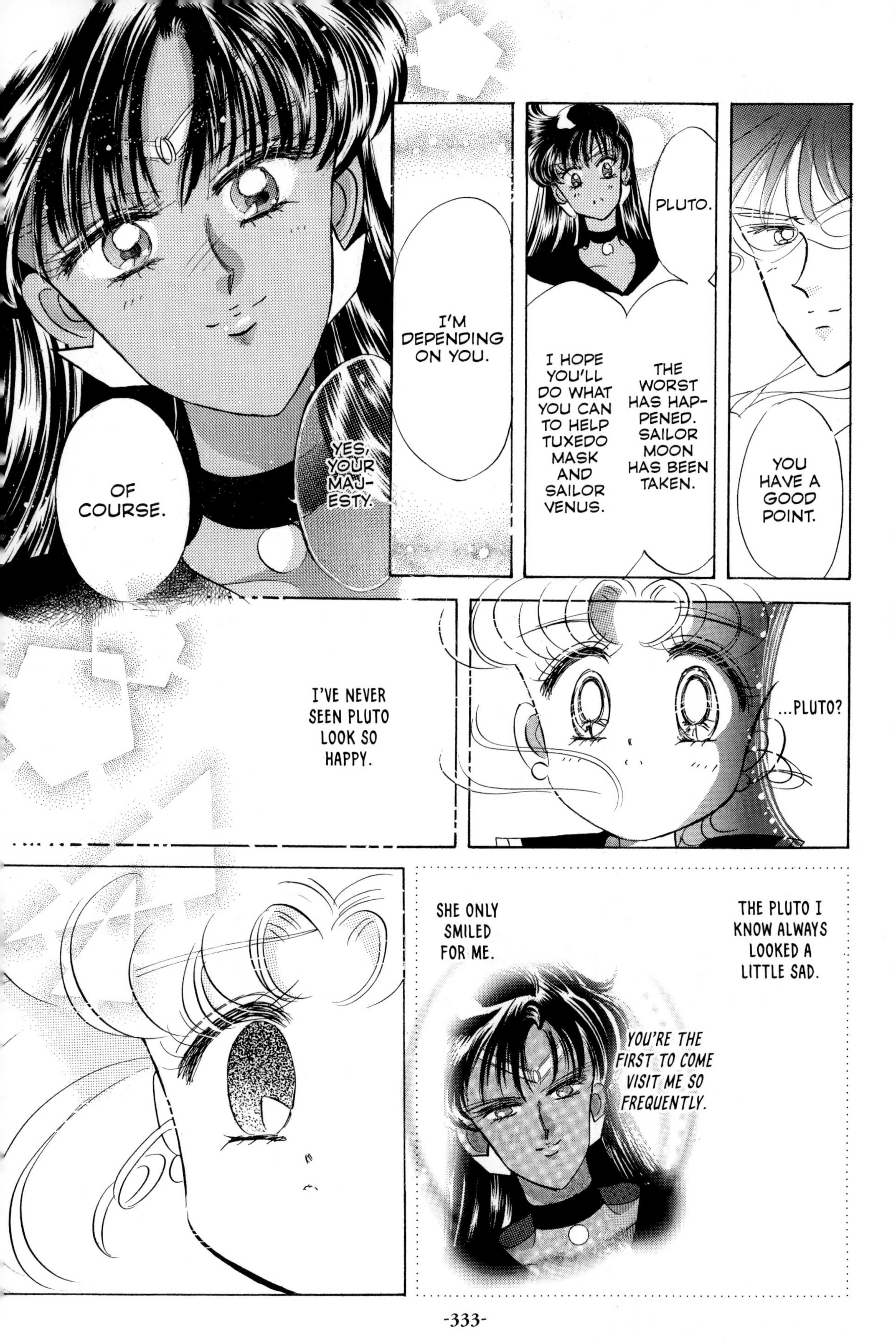
YOU HAVE A GOOD POINT.
PLUTO.
THE WORST HAS HAPPENED. SAILOR MOON HAS BEEN TAKEN.
I HOPE YOU'LL DO WHAT YOU CAN TO HELP TUXEDO MASK AND SAILOR VENUS.
I'M DEPENDING ON YOU.
YES, YOUR MAJESTY.
OF COURSE.
...PLUTO?
I'VE NEVER SEEN PLUTO LOOK SO HAPPY.
THE PLUTO I KNOW ALWAYS LOOKED A LITTLE SAD.
SHE ONLY SMILED FOR ME.
YOU'RE THE FIRST TO COME VISIT ME SO FREQUENTLY.

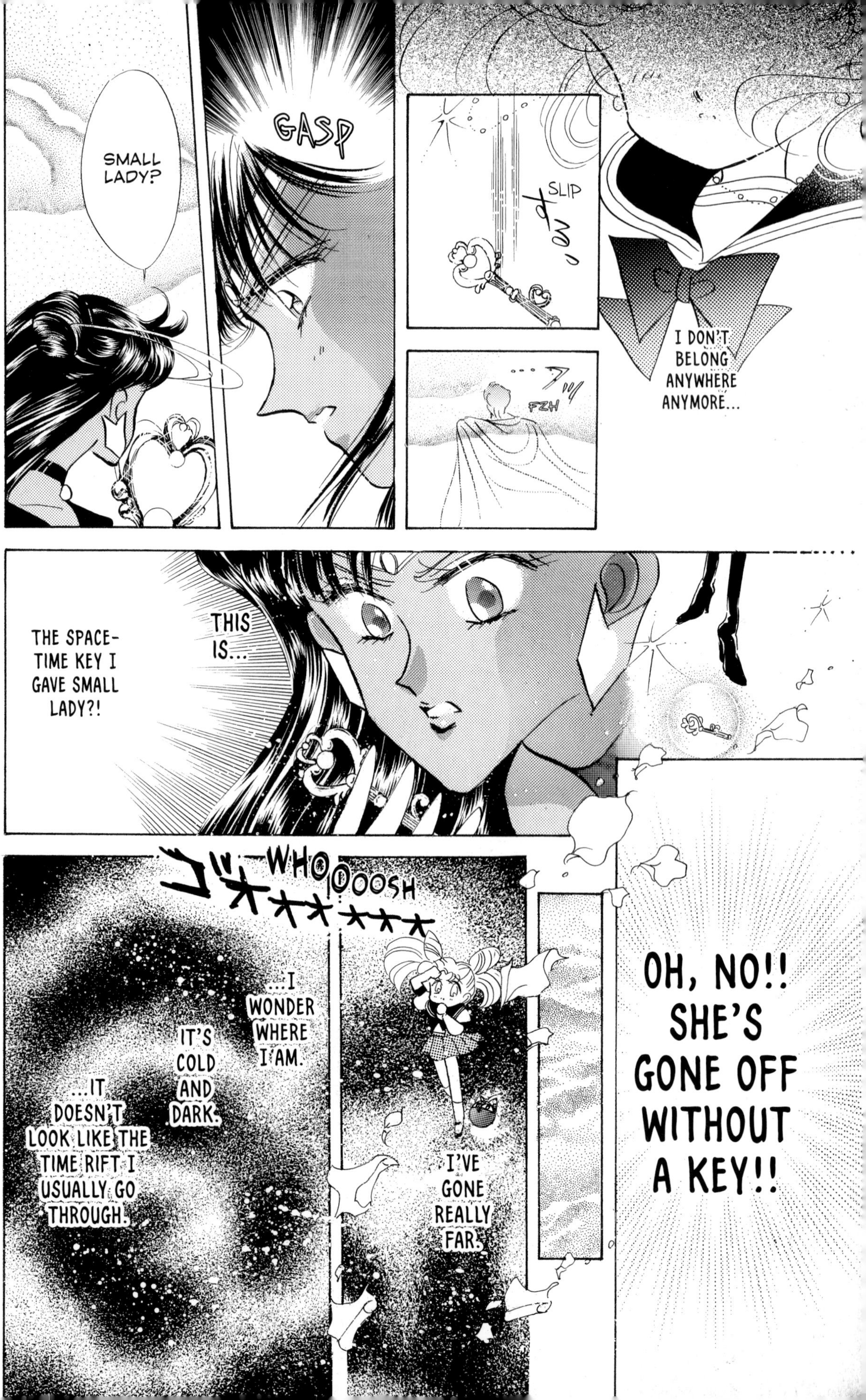
I DON'T BELONG ANYWHERE ANYMORE...
SLIP
... FZH
GASP
SMALL LADY?
THIS IS...
THE SPACE-TIME KEY I GAVE SMALL LADY?!
OH, NO!! SHE'S GONE OFF WITHOUT A KEY!!
I'VE GONE REALLY FAR.
WHOOOOSH
...I WONDER WHERE I AM.
IT'S COLD AND DARK.
...IT DOESN'T LOOK LIKE THE TIME RIFT I USUALLY GO THROUGH.

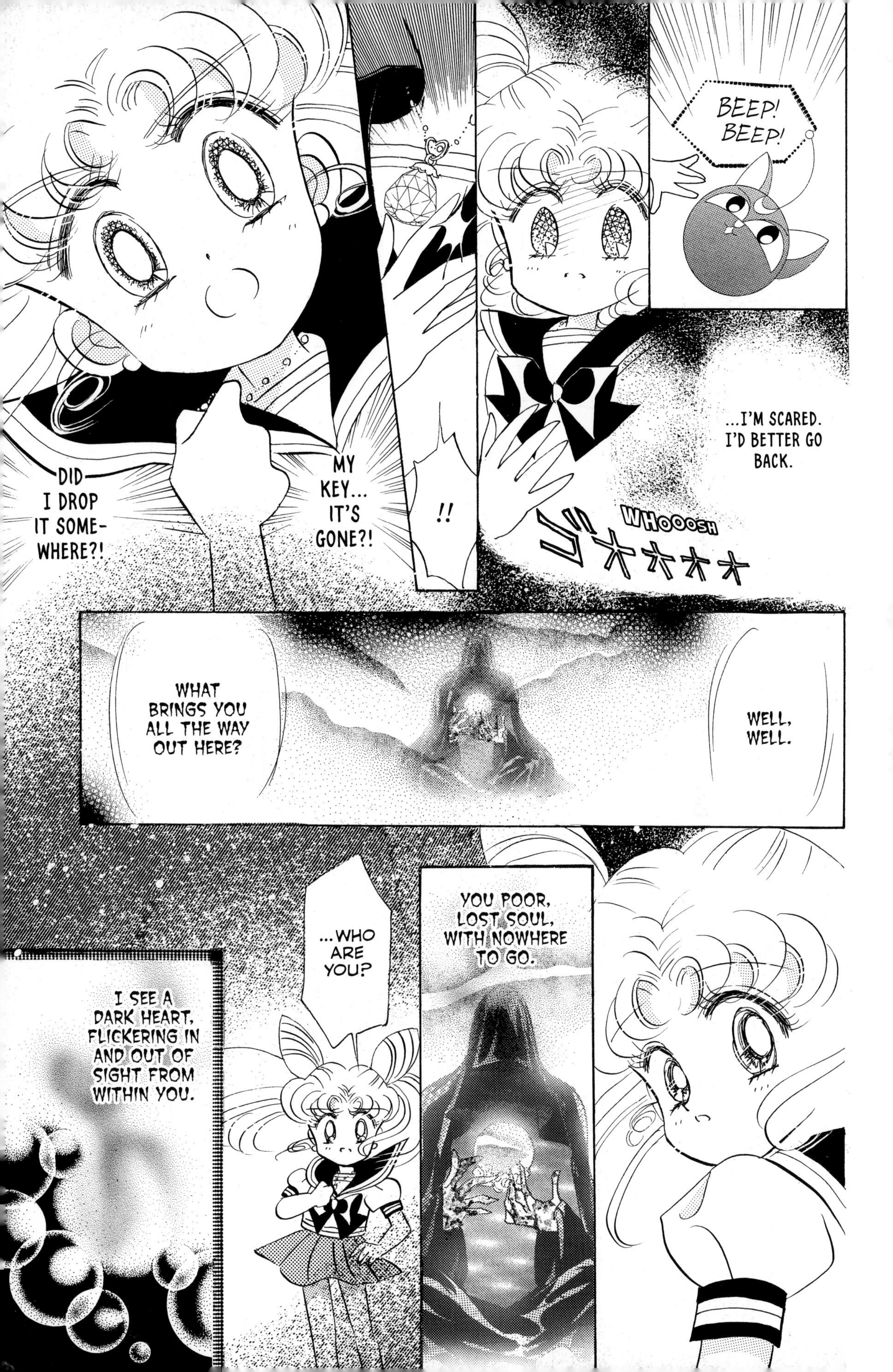
BEEP! BEEP!
...I'M SCARED. I'D BETTER GO BACK.
WHOOOSH
ゴオオオオ
!!
MY KEY... IT'S GONE?!
DID I DROP IT SOME-WHERE?!
WELL, WELL.
WHAT BRINGS YOU ALL THE WAY OUT HERE?
YOU POOR, LOST SOUL, WITH NOWHERE TO GO.
...WHO ARE YOU?
I SEE A DARK HEART, FLICKERING IN AND OUT OF SIGHT FROM WITHIN YOU.

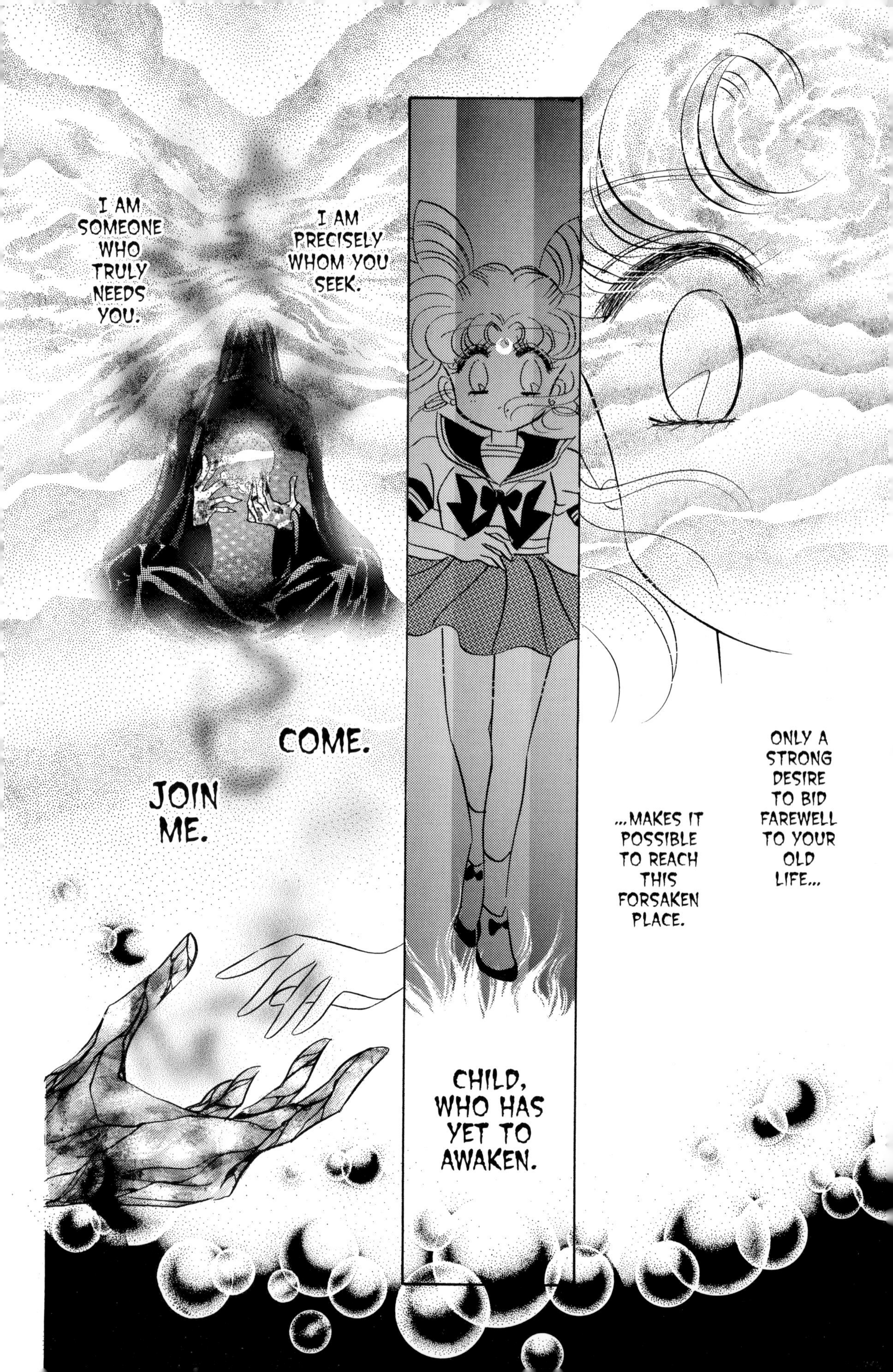
ONLY A STRONG DESIRE TO BID FAREWELL TO YOUR OLD LIFE...
...MAKES IT POSSIBLE TO REACH THIS FORSAKEN PLACE.
CHILD, WHO HAS YET TO AWAKEN.
I AM PRECISELY WHOM YOU SEEK.
I AM SOMEONE WHO TRULY NEEDS YOU.
COME.
JOIN ME.

Pretty Guardian Sailor Moon

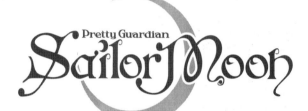

Translation Notes

Supernatural Sisters, page 11
The Japanese name for this quartet is the *Ayakashi no Yonshimai*, or *Ayakashi* Four Sisters. Specifically, an *ayakashi* is a monster that appears on the ocean's surface during a shipwreck, but in general usage, it's more of a blanket term for used to describe any supernatural phenomenon and/or creature. This makes it a fitting name for a group of sisters with supernatural powers who cause mysterious things to happen all over Tokyo.

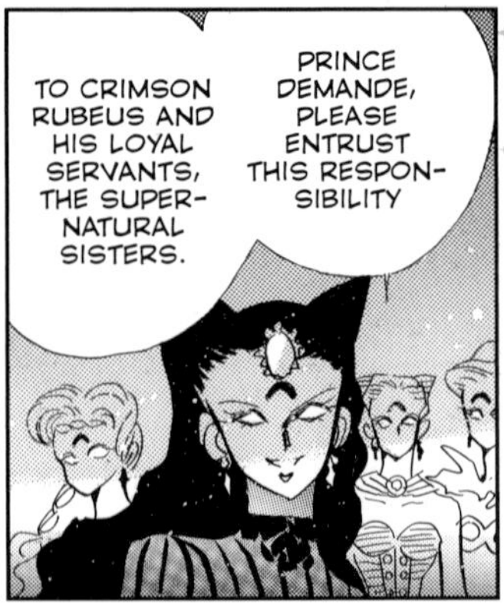
PRINCE DEMANDE, PLEASE ENTRUST THIS RESPON-SIBILITY
TO CRIMSON RUBEUS AND HIS LOYAL SERVANTS, THE SUPER-NATURAL SISTERS.

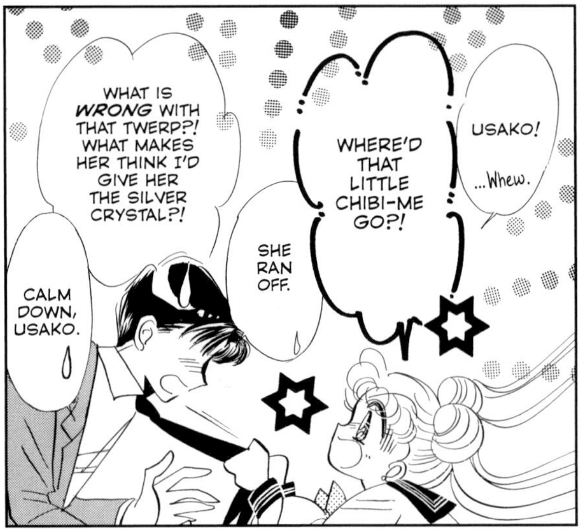
USAKO!
...Whew.
WHERE'D THAT LITTLE CHIBI-ME GO?!
WHAT IS *WRONG* WITH THAT TWERP?! WHAT MAKES HER THINK I'D GIVE HER THE SILVER CRYSTAL?!
SHE RAN OFF.
CALM DOWN, USAKO.

Chibi me, page 12
Chibi means "little" and can be used either as an insult or as a term of endearment. When Usagi uses it here, she almost certainly means it with contempt. However, when speaking of (for example) a younger sibling, it's not uncommon for family members to use it as a sort of pet name.

Senpai, page 24
The word and suffix -*senpai* literally means "companion who has gone before," and is used to refer to some-one engaged in the same endeavor as the speaker, but who started it first. In this case, Makoto started attending school before Asanuma. Normally, *senpai* would be used specifically for someone who started attending the same school as the speaker first, so it's unclear why Asanuma would be using it for Makoto. It may be that Asanuma thinks of Makoto as his *senpai* for frequenting this particular cafe, or it may have something to do with her being an associate of his idol, who is his *senpai* at the same school. The counterpart to *senpai* (as Asanuma would be in this case) is called a *kôhai*.

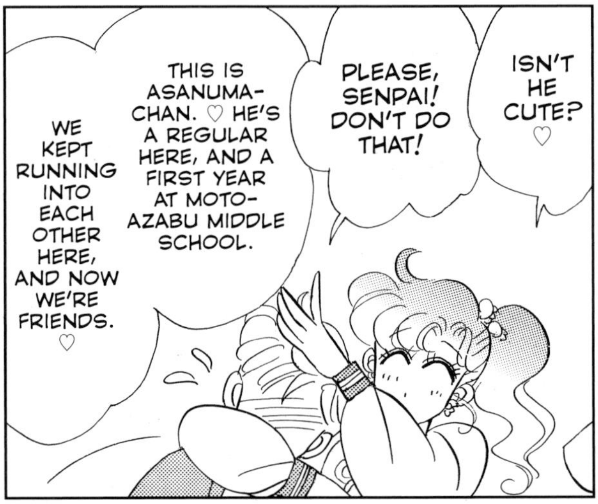
ISN'T HE CUTE? ♡
PLEASE, SENPAI! DON'T DO THAT!
THIS IS ASANUMA-CHAN. ♡ HE'S A REGULAR HERE, AND A FIRST YEAR AT MOTO-AZABU MIDDLE SCHOOL.
WE KEPT RUNNING INTO EACH OTHER HERE, AND NOW WE'RE FRIENDS. ♡

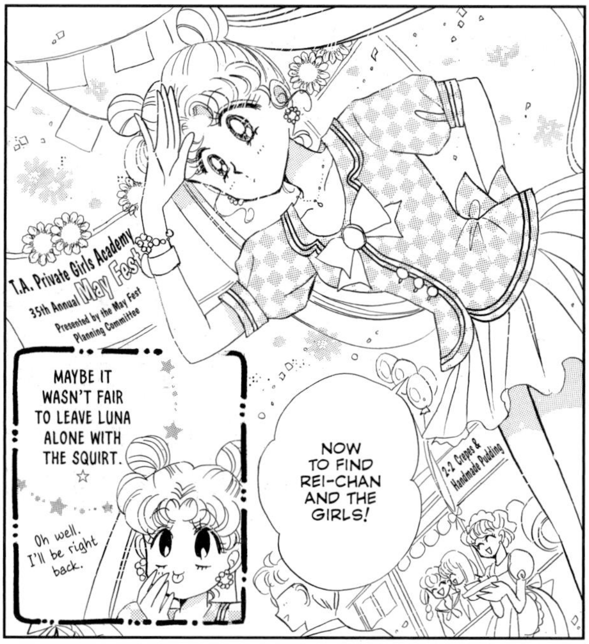
T.A. Private Girls Academy
35th Annual May Fest
Presented by the May Fest Planning Committee
MAYBE IT WASN'T FAIR TO LEAVE LUNA ALONE WITH THE SQUIRT.
Oh well. I'll be right back.
NOW TO FIND REI-CHAN AND THE GIRLS!
2-2 Crepes & Handmade Pudding

School festival, page 26
In Japan, schools will hold yearly festivals to display the students' artistic, intellectual, and business skills. These festivals are often called *bunkasai,* meaning "culture festival," to differentiate them from *taiikusai,* or "athletic festivals," in which students show off their athletic prowess. Classes and clubs will set up displays outside or in their classroom that can be anything from a restaurant to a haunted house.

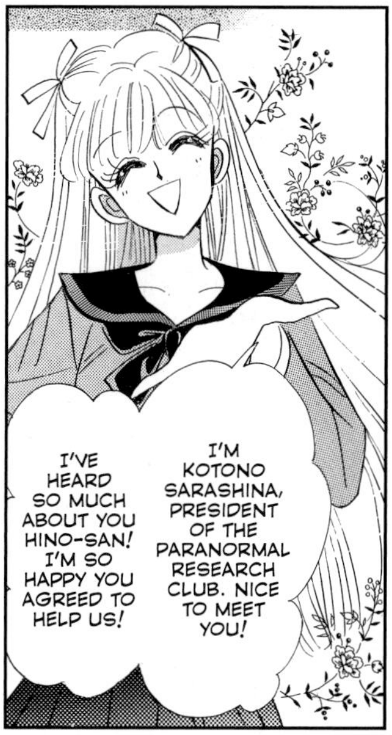
I'M KOTONO SARASHINA, PRESIDENT OF THE PARANORMAL RESEARCH CLUB. NICE TO MEET YOU!
I'VE HEARD SO MUCH ABOUT YOU HINO-SAN! I'M SO HAPPY YOU AGREED TO HELP US!

Kotono Sarashina, page 26
Fans of the *Sailor Moon* anime may recognize the name Kotono as belonging to Kotono Mitsuishi, the Japanese actress who voices Usagi. This is no accident—Naoko Takeuchi and Kotono Mitsuishi became good friends, and this character was named in Mitsuishi-san's honor.

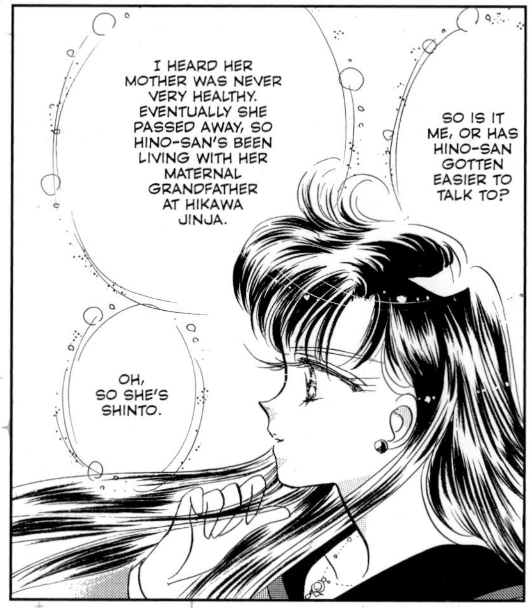
SO IS IT ME, OR HAS HINO-SAN GOTTEN EASIER TO TALK TO?
I HEARD HER MOTHER WAS NEVER VERY HEALTHY. EVENTUALLY SHE PASSED AWAY, SO HINO-SAN'S BEEN LIVING WITH HER MATERNAL GRANDFATHER AT HIKAWA JINJA.
OH, SO SHE'S SHINTO.

Oh, so she's Shinto, page 27
The girl talking about Rei here refers to her as an *ujiko-san.* It's likely that the girl is using the term to mean "someone who works and/or helps at a Shinto shrine." In that sense, one might translate this line to, "So she's a shrine maiden," which would be correct of Rei, but would not necessarily mean the same thing. The word *ujiko* refers to any Shinto believer who lives within the region protected by a god or gods at a given shrine, whether they help out at that shrine or not. In this sense, the girl may be saying, "Oh, so her religion is Shinto."

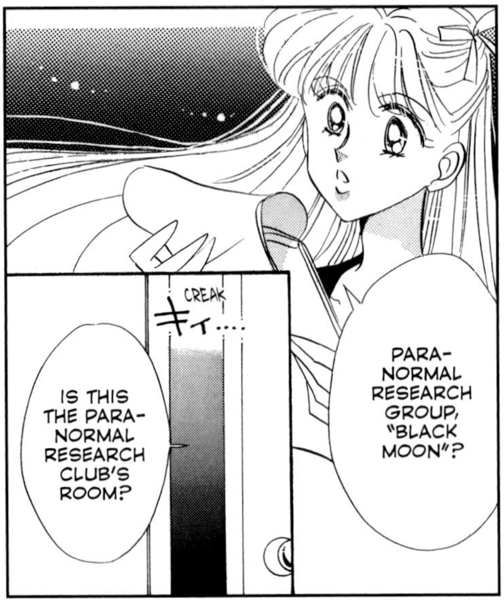
PARA-NORMAL RESEARCH GROUP, "BLACK MOON"?
CREAK
キィ…
IS THIS THE PARA-NORMAL RESEARCH CLUB'S ROOM?

Club vs. Group, page 29
Sometimes a student will want to start a new club, but will be unable to meet all the criteria to do so, such as having enough members, finding a teacher or other adult to act as adviser, etc. So instead of a club, they'll be allowed to form a *dôkôkai,* or association of like-minded people. The translators chose to use the word "group" instead of "association" because the latter sounds more official than a club, while a *dôkôkai* is not. In this case, the "group" designation likely comes from the fact that a Paranormal Research Club already exists.

Kôan Kurozuki, page 30
In keeping with the trend of naming characters after gemstones, Kôan is named for kermesite, which is *kôankô* in Japanese. Her alias surname, Kurozuki, is Japanese for "black moon."

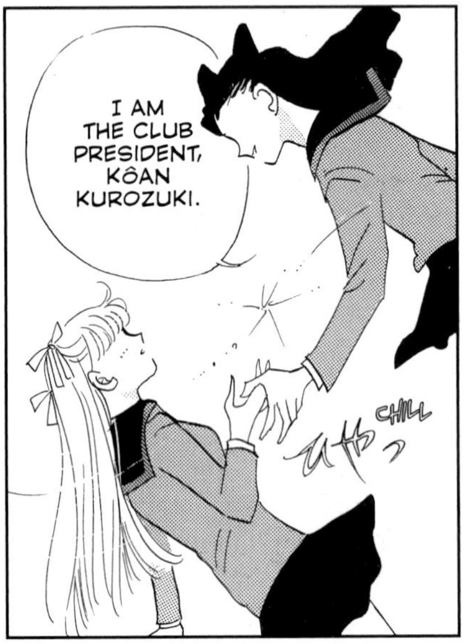
I AM THE CLUB PRESIDENT, KÔAN KUROZUKI.
CHILL

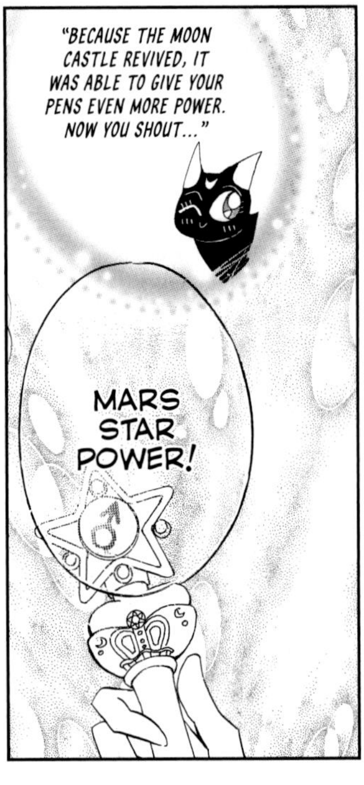
"BECAUSE THE MOON CASTLE REVIVED, IT WAS ABLE TO GIVE YOUR PENS EVEN MORE POWER. NOW YOU SHOUT..."
MARS STAR POWER!

Mars Star Power, page 38
The Japanese word for planet is *wakusei,* which means "wandering star," because the planets in our solar system, as observed from the Earth, look like stars that don't move in the same predictable paths as the others—they seem to be wandering. (In fact, the English word "planet" comes from the Greek for "wanderer.") That being the case, when discussing objects in the night sky in Japanese, it's not always necessary to differentiate between stars and planets, so both are often referred to as *hoshi.* In other words, when Sailor Mars says "Mars Star Power," it has the same meaning as "Mars Planet Power."

Beguiling Black Crystal, page 73

WHAT DOES THIS MEAN?
WHAT *IS* THIS EARRING?

This crystal has had many names throughout the various English-language versions of *Sailor Moon*—Dark Crystal, Black Poison Crystal, and Malefic Black Crystal. The Japanese name is *Jakoku Suishô,* which translates most readily to "Evil Black Crystal." The translators of this edition felt that calling it the Evil Black Crystal would be a terrible PR move on the part of the Black Moon, and hoped that the *ja* of *jakoku* perhaps had a meaning more than simply "evil." Upon further research, they determined that the Chinese character for the word is related to the one that means "snake," and one version of *ja* that uses both characters interchangeably means "to beguile." Because the word "beguile" has wicked connotations and is what the serpent did to Eve in the Garden of Eden, thus sharing the meaning of both *kanji* characters, the translators felt it was the most appropriate choice.

Furthermore, the translators believe that "Beguiling Black Crystal" may sound more like a description of the crystal's beauty, or some other poetic name for a gemstone, in the same way *Jakoku* might sound more like a shade of black than something literally evil.

YOUR DAD? WHAT DOES HE DO?
HE'S A *NIHONGA* PAINTER.

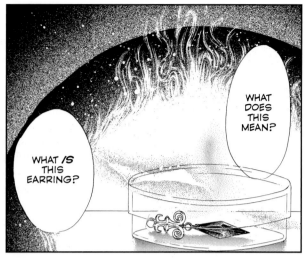

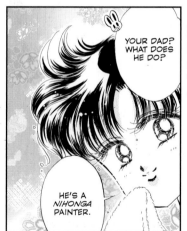

Nihonga, page 81

Meaning "Japanese picture," *Nihonga* refers to paintings done in a traditional Japanese style, as opposed to a Western-style. The paintings are generally done on silk or *washi* paper, using mineral-based paints.

USAKO AND THE OTHERS HAVE SOME THINGS TO TAKE CARE OF.
AND I HAVE TO GO TO CRAM SCHOOL.

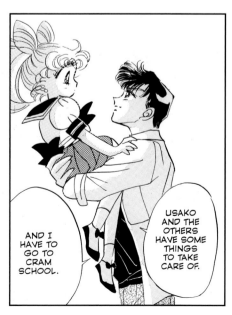

Cram school, page 107

The reader may remember that Ami attends a test-prep school to help her get into a better high school. Similarly, Mamoru, who is already in high school, is preparing to take his college entrance exams. While both types of schools have similar aims, the target demographic and teaching styles are different. Cram school is aimed at high school students and students who have not yet managed to pass an entrance exam, and the content is presented in lecture format.

I should be strong, page 130

For those readers wondering what makes Asanuma assume he should be strong, the answer is found in the original Japanese text, where he says, roughly, "I'm a man, but I can't help you at all, and that thought kills me!" Asanuma believes that any real man would help protect those he cares about, and it bothers him that all he can do is sit back and watch.

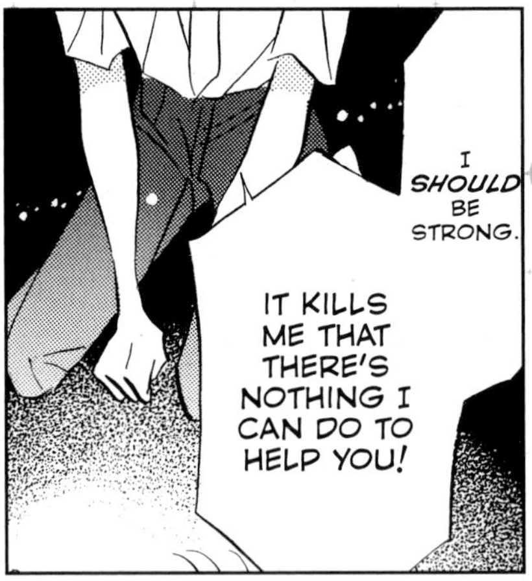

I SHOULD BE STRONG.
IT KILLS ME THAT THERE'S NOTHING I CAN DO TO HELP YOU!

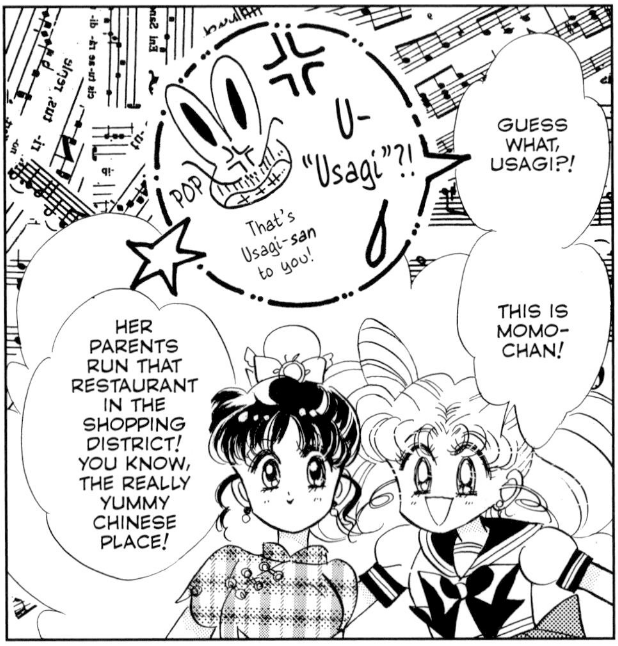

GUESS WHAT, USAGI?!
U- "Usagi"?!
POP
That's Usagi-san to you!
THIS IS MOMO-CHAN!
HER PARENTS RUN THAT RESTAURANT IN THE SHOPPING DISTRICT! YOU KNOW, THE REALLY YUMMY CHINESE PLACE!

That's Usagi-san to you, page 153

As explained in Volume 1, it can be rude to address someone without any kind of honorific. The word for that in Japanese is *yobisute*, which is what Usagi accused Chibi Usa of in the original text: "You dare to *yobisute* me?" The line was adapted to make it easier for the readers to follow, and while Usagi probably would have accepted -chan, the translators felt that in the moment, she would be annoyed enough to demand more respect.

Tuxedo la Smoking Bomber, page 184

While the reader may reasonably expect to see a lot more smoke from an attack like this one, there's more to this move's name than its ability to create cover. The tuxedo evolved from an article of clothing called a "smoking jacket," which is what wealthy men wore when relaxing with a pipe or cigar. Because of its origins, a tuxedo is still known as a "smoking" in many foreign languages. It may also be worth noting that a "bomber" is another type of jacket—the type also referred to as a "flight jacket," the kind you see stereotypically on fighter pilots.

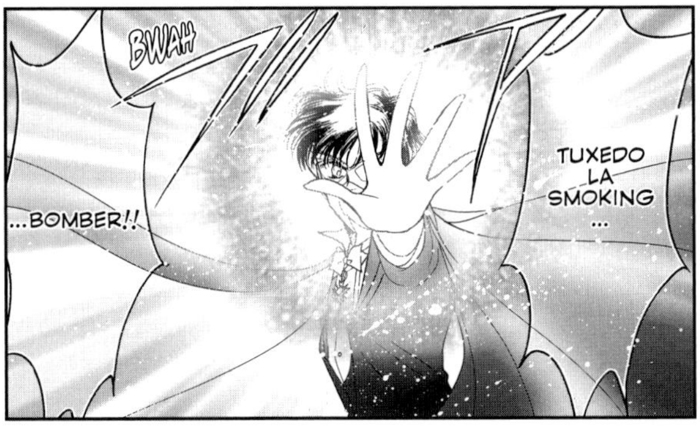

BWAH
TUXEDO LA SMOKING ...
...BOMBER!!

Chiral and Achiral, the Boule Brothers, page 209

The Boule Brothers are unique in the gemstone naming pattern, in that their name doesn't come from a natural ore. A boule is a synthetically created crystal. The names Chiral and Achiral are a reflection of their relationship as mirror-image twins. A chiral object is something cannot be superimposed on its mirror image—for example, the left and right hands are a sort of mirror image of each other, but if the reader were to place one on top of the other, with both palms facing down, the images would not line up. An achiral object is one that **can** be superimposed on its mirror image. In other words, the names are an oxymoron—either they are chiral or achiral, but they cannot be both.

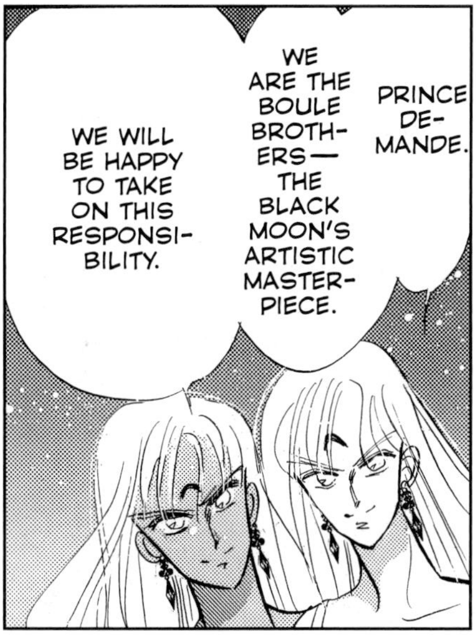
PRINCE DE-MANDE.
WE ARE THE BOULE BROTH-ERS— THE BLACK MOON'S ARTISTIC MASTER-PIECE.
WE WILL BE HAPPY TO TAKE ON THIS RESPONSI-BILITY.

Keeper of the Underworld, page 212

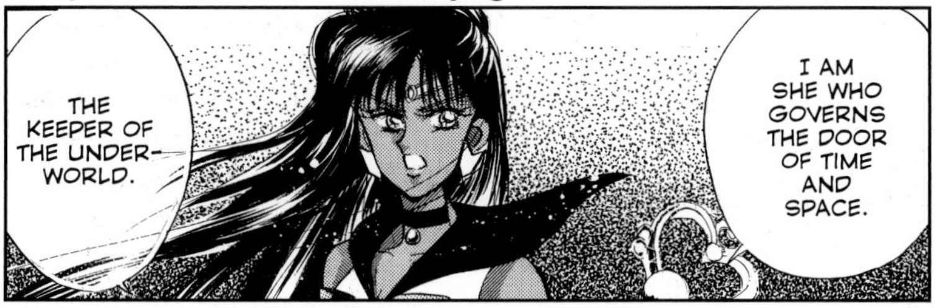
I AM SHE WHO GOVERNS THE DOOR OF TIME AND SPACE.
THE KEEPER OF THE UNDER-WORLD.

In mythology, Pluto is the ruler of the Underworld. In mythological terms, the Underworld is generally understood to be the world of the dead, but the Japanese word for it is *meikai,* which more literally means "world of darkness." As Sailor Venus pointed out earlier, there is a lot of darkness in this world the Guardians have found themselves in, so it may be that this rift between times is the Underworld that Sailor Pluto is referring to.

Crystal Palace Enantiomer, page 226

An enantiomer is a molecule that is the mirror image of another. The Boule Brothers have taken the concept to a larger scale and made a mirrored replica of the Crystal Palace.

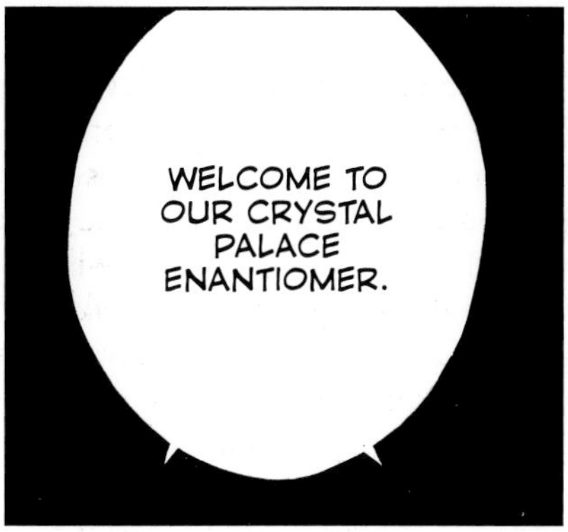
WELCOME TO OUR CRYSTAL PALACE ENANTIOMER.

Achiral's isomeric welcome, page 227
An isomer is a molecular compound that has all of the same atoms as another molecular compound, but arranged in a different way, thus giving it different chemical properties. In other words, it's made up of all the same materials, but acts differently. In this case, Achiral has created isomers of himself—they are made of the same synthetic crystal, but will behave differently (probably in a team sort of capacity). If Chiral were to make isomers of himself, the elements that create him would be rearranged around a constant chiral center that remains in place.

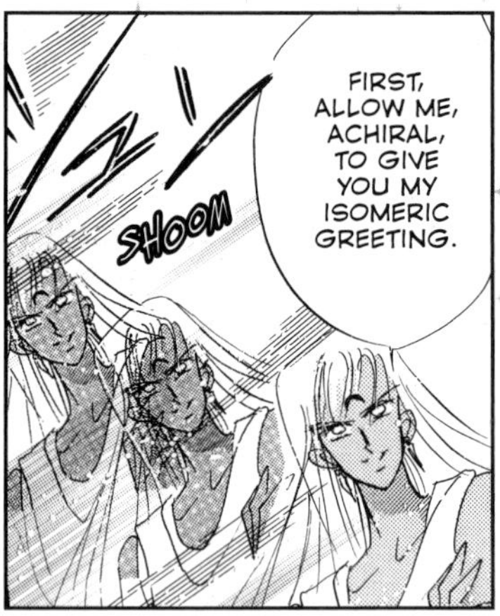
FIRST, ALLOW ME, ACHIRAL, TO GIVE YOU MY ISOMERIC GREETING.
SHOOM

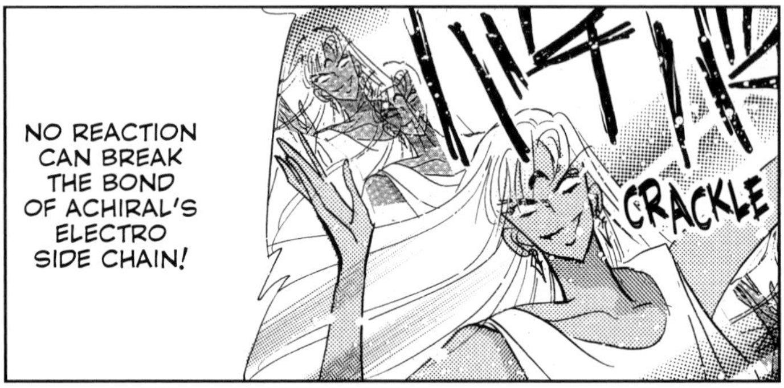
CRACKLE
NO REACTION CAN BREAK THE BOND OF ACHIRAL'S ELECTRO SIDE CHAIN!

Electro Side Chain, page 227
A "side chain" is a part of a molecule branching off of the molecule's "backbone." The backbone is the main chain of atoms forming the molecular structure, and the side chain is attached to it, affecting how the molecular interacts with other molecules, such as water. In biochemistry, side chains are most often discussed when talking about amino acids, of which there is only one of the achiral variety. This amino acid is glycine, which is a key player in causing sleep paralysis.

Nemesis, page 255
Many years ago, before the discovery of Pluto, astronomers noticed irregularities in the orbits of Uranus and Neptune, and assumed there must be a ninth planet out there causing them. Eventually, they did discover Pluto, but it was too small to be the culprit, so in the 1980s, there was much speculation about a mysterious tenth planet. In 1989, the space probe Voyager 2 gave a revised mass for the planet Neptune, which resolved the orbit irregularity issue (it was simply a miscalculation) and disproved the existence of a large tenth planet, but this did not stop scientists from searching for more objects in our solar system. Since then, several such objects have been found beyond Neptune's orbit, with Pluto being the largest and Eris, named for the Greek goddess of discord, having the most mass. If the astronomers who discovered Eris had been *Sailor Moon* fans, they may have given Eris the name Nemesis, after the Greek goddess of retribution, instead. It is also worth noting that the word "nemesis" has come to be synonymous with "enemy"—truly a fitting name for the home of "the enemy" that the Guardians are always talking about.

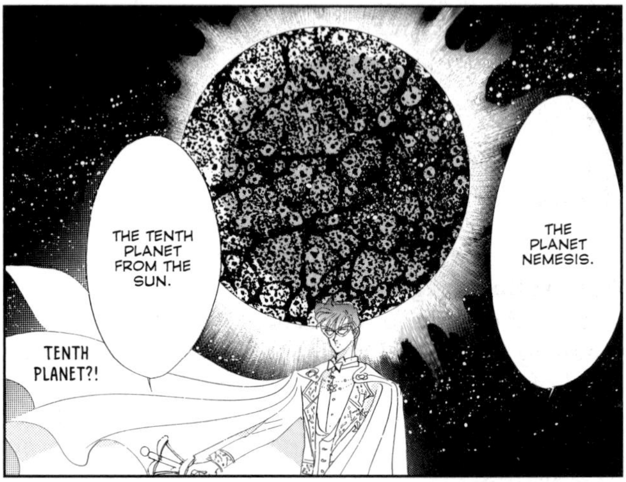
THE PLANET NEMESIS.
THE TENTH PLANET FROM THE SUN.
TENTH PLANET?!

Demande's outfit, page 297
The translators regret their oversight in failing to note this in previous volumes, and would like to express their gratitude to Prince Demande for removing his cape in this panel, thus modeling an outfit similar to that worn by the Four Heavenly Kings of the Dark Kingdom. This style is called a *gakuran,* as combination of *gakkô* (meaning school) and *ranfuku* (meaning "Dutch clothing," an old term for Western-style clothing). As such the jacket is generally worn as a boys' school uniform, usually at schools where the girls' uniforms include sailor collars.

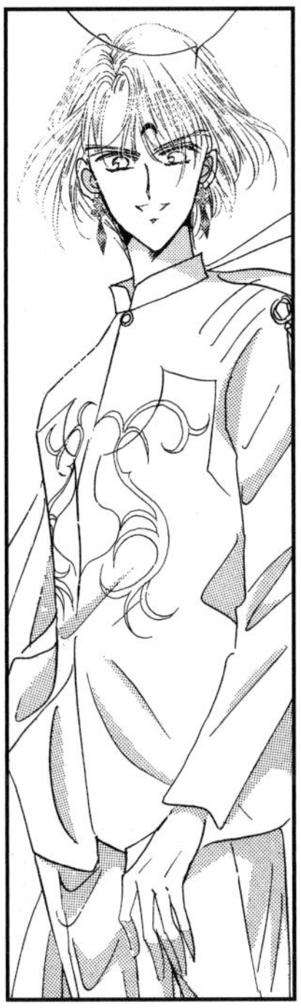

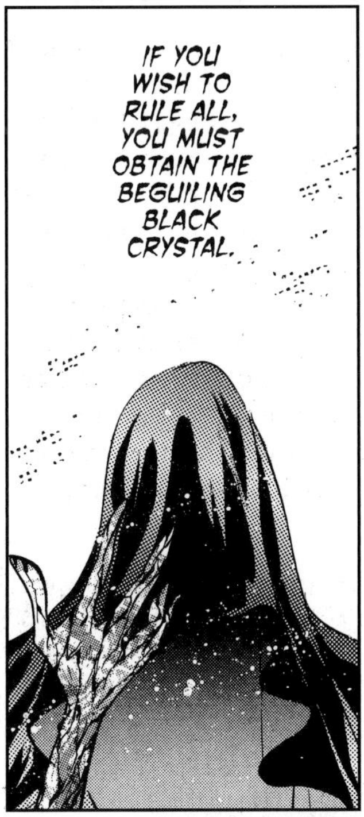
IF YOU WISH TO RULE ALL, YOU MUST OBTAIN THE BEGUILING BLACK CRYSTAL.

Wiseman and the Black Crystal, page 297
This seems like an appropriate place to point out that the English word "wiseman" is a translation of the Japanese word *kenja.* This word *kenja* can also be found associated with magical stones—specifically, the *kenja no ishi,* known in English as the Philosopher's Stone. According to legend, the Philosopher's Stone is the ultimate achievement of the alchemic arts, and, once obtained, will have the power to turn base metals into gold, as well as to create the elixir of life, thus granting immortality. It goes by many names, including Atramentum, meaning "black instrument," where *ater* is a particularly sinister, perhaps beguiling, shade of black. The translators were sorely tempted to use this name as a translation for *jakoku suishô,* but ultimately discarded the idea when they were reminded that most readers, including the translators themselves, don't know Latin.

Garnet Rod, page 331
The word garnet comes from the Latin "Garanatus," meaning "seedlike," because the stone resembles the seed of the pomegranate, and in fact the Japanese name of the stone literally means "pomegranate stone." Fans of Greek mythology will recognize the pomegranate as the fruit that Persephone, goddess of spring, ate when she was in the Underworld, thus condemning herself (by eating Underworld food) to stay in the dark world for six months of every year. The garnet has been used as a talisman to protect against evil, and is also a symbol of love and eternity.

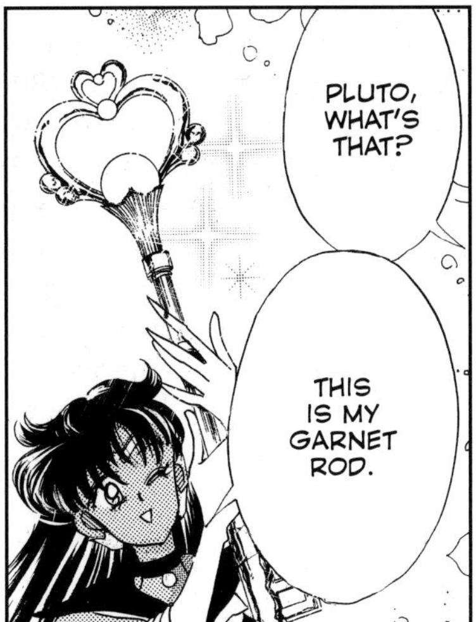
PLUTO, WHAT'S THAT?
THIS IS MY GARNET ROD.

A Kodansha Comics Trade Paperback Original
Sailor Moon Eternal Edition volume 3 copyright © 2013 Naoko Takeuchi
English translation copyright © 2019 Naoko Takeuchi
First published in Japan in 2013 by Kodansha Ltd., Tokyo.

Published in the United States by Kodansha Comics, an imprint of
Kodansha USA Publishing, LLC, New York.

Publication rights for this English edition arranged through
Kodansha Ltd, Tokyo.

ISBN 978-1-63236-154-7

Printed in Canada.

www.kodanshacomics.com

9 8 7 6 5 4 3 2 1

Translation: Alethea Nibley & Athena Nibley
Lettering: Lys Blakeslee
Editing: Lauren Scanlan
Kodansha Comics edition cover design by Phil Balsman

3/18